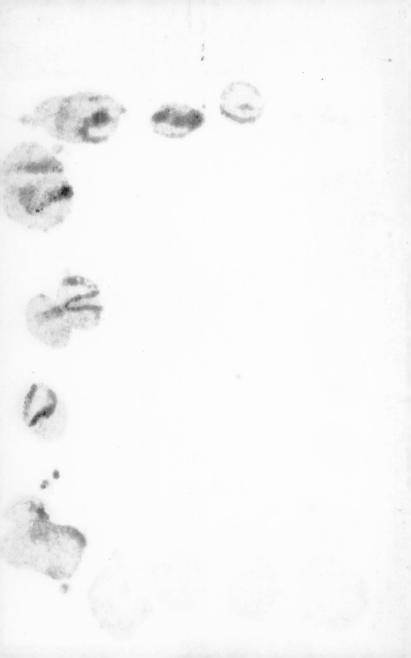

THE LIFE OF
J. M. W. TURNER, R.A.

THE LIFE

OF

J. M. W. TURNER, R.A.

FOUNDED ON LETTERS AND PAPERS FURNISHED BY

HIS FRIENDS AND FELLOW-ACADEMICIANS

BY

WALTER THORNBURY

A NEW EDITION
REVISED AND MOSTLY REWRITTEN

This edition published by

WARD LOCK REPRINTS · 1970

This revised and mostly rewritten edition was originally published by Chatto & Windus in 1877. The first edition, in two volumes, was published by Hurst . and Blackett in 1862.

Reproduced and Printed by
Redwood Press Limited
Trowbridge & London

'Nature's most secret steps
He, like her shadow, has pursued where'er
The red volcano overcanopies
Its fields of snow and pinnacles of ice
With burning smoke; or where the starry domes
Of diamond and of gold expand above
Numberless and immeasurable halls,
Frequent with crystal column and clear shrines
Of pearl, and thrones radiant with chrysolite.
Nor had that scene of ampler majesty
Than gems or gold—the varying roof of Heaven
And the green earth—lost in his heart its claims
To love and wonder.'

SHELLEY'S Alastor.

PREFACE

TO

THE SECOND EDITION.

SOON after the publication of the first edition of my 'Life of Turner,' I received a kind letter from Mr. Ruskin, dated Lucerne, December 2, 1861, which contained the following passage :—'I have just received and am reading your book with deep interest. I am much gratified by the view you have taken and give of Turner. It is quite what I hoped. What beautiful things you have discovered about him! Thank you for your courteous and far too flattering references to me.'

When my volumes made their appearance, a certain sense of irritation and disappointment diffused itself through the artist world. The younger and more passionate admirers of the painter were mortified at discovering that, after all, their demi-god was only a little, ignoble man, with sordid views and low tastes, who lived the life of a soured miser and suspicious recluse. Mr. Thomas Carlyle had long before spread the notion that genius necessarily implied both moral and intellectual perfection; and Turner's more intimate friends were indignant with me for having exposed all those small frailties which the polite biographers of fifty years ago used so discreetly to suppress. They talked of me as of a brutal undertaker, who tears the shroud with cruel indifference from the body of the dead man. They compared me to the careless embalmer who, without waiting for the spices, stuffs the corpse with bitter herbs. Several of the reviewers complained that I had set forth a most unsatisfactory and unhappy man, bare and unsoftened in the blaze of day. They said I had exposed to the strongest light, 'a figure only adapted for twilight and the shadows; an unhappy soul, whom common charity is content to accept as a great painter without special enquiry into his character, but whom the cruelty of friends forces forth into public ignominy by way of proving his right, had not circumstances forbidden, to take his place among the greatest of men.'

The marvellous combination of such a genius with such a nature it was my duty, as a man of truth, to record; and I did so very imperfectly, no diaries or journals of the painter's having been preserved ; many of his old friends refusing to furnish me with any facts that revealed the darker side of his character, and others declining to give me any assistance at all. With the aid, however, of his surviving engravers, who did not love him sufficiently to conceal the bitter truth, of the great pile of his sketch-books which Mr. Ruskin allowed me carefully to examine before they were thrown open to the world, and of some scattered letters which good fortune directed into my hands, reinforced by the assistance of a few of his intimate friends who loved truth too well to conceal either good or bad, I was enabled by degrees to piece together a memoir, of which the present is a revised and considerably enlarged edition.

I do not attempt to account for this strange combination of genius and baseness, of divine insight and contracted soul. As I look back upon him, now standing among the Alp peaks, and now watching a sunset on the Mediterranean, he seems to me like a crippled giant, who has the head of Apollo with the form of Thersites. He wanders through Italy with an eye as capable as Byron's to pierce through the beauties of Nature; he returns home to grind down his engravers, and to play shuffling tricks with the impressions of his ' Liber Studiorum.' He rakes together wealth, which he at the same time allows to crumble to dust around him. He endeavours to retrieve the selfish sins of a solitary and unhappy life by founding a charity of which his own wilfulness mars the accomplishment. Was it some grain of his mother's insanity that tainted this great genius? And might not a healthier life have directed this remarkable but distorted man to nobler ambition and higher aims? Who knows? All we have been able to do is to show him by glimpses during the several stages of his career. What he saw, and what he felt, his own works show best. His poetry in many respects resembles that of Byron, his contemporary. It was passionate, emotional, epical. Though really the founder of the Pre-Raphaelite school, he did not often, except for study and note-taking, condescend to minute and loving detail. His sight was keen and far reaching; he was fond of panoramic effects. Anxious to give the British public a vivid conception of great European scenes, he visited the Continent which war had long closed to us. He went to the Pass of St. Gothard, the Lake of Geneva, St. Peter's, the Louvre, the central points of the Rhine, Waterloo, and Mont Blanc. He did not stop for days before an oak stump or Gothic doorway. He was eager to seize the regalia of Nature, leaving others to pick up the scattered jewels. Photography had not yet come to rival the microscope, and to compel us to examine the pores and texture of everything to which it was applied. It is Byron's swift, far-reaching poetry which inspired Turner's pictures, and not Browning's. His works of pure invention, such as the ' Polyphemus,' and many studies in the ' Liber,' were inspired by the small classicism of the studios of his early days, and have nothing in common with the mediævalism of the present age. The spirit of his own time animated Turner profoundly. The omnipotency of Napoleon, and his headlong fall, are both recorded by his hand. It was places long shut to us that he was so eager to visit. He stops with regret to watch the old battleship towed to its last moorings. Like a true Englishman, he loved to show our sailors wrestling with the sea in all its moods. He was the first of our painters to invest a railway train with poetry, as he likewise was the first to invest our voyages of Arctic discovery with mystery and fascination.

Above all things, we derive one especial good from Turner. He first did for England what Sir Walter had done for Scotland. In youth, shut out by war from continental travel, he, earliest of all English landscape-painters, grasped the full beauty of English scenery, and tempted us to home exploration. It was he who first set before the eyes of rich and restless people the beauty of Yorkshire Wold and Devonshire coast. He explored England as if it was an unknown country, and proved that Dutch meadows and Venetian palaces were not indispensable to form landscapes of the highest merit.

If biography is to consist, as it too often does, of undisguised eulogy such as could only flow from the pen of an enraptured executor; if it is to be a garish picture without shadow; if it is to increase our knowledge of human nature by suppressing all that is painful, incongruous, or inconsistent; if it is to be no truer than a funeral sermon, or more reliable than one of the fulsome dedications of the last century, then can no honest man condescend to write biographies. In that event they must be left to the hireling, the parasite, and the toady to win from them what reputation may be possible.

In the present edition are incorporated sixteen previously unpublished letters of Turner to his engravers, and numerous anecdotes respecting the great artist; and the Appendix has been enlarged by the addition of the record of fourteen years' sales of his pictures. Cancelling repetitions, and reconciling apparent contradictions, I have endeavoured to tell the story of his life more simply and consecutively.

WALTER THORNBURY.

LONDON: 1876.

PREFACE

TO

THE FIRST EDITION.

SOME four years ago, when the desire to write a life of Turner first entered my mind, I determined to take no steps in such a scheme till I had ascertained whether Mr. Ruskin might not himself have some intention of one day becoming the biographer of that great painter whose genius he had done so much to illustrate. In answer to my letter of enquiry, Mr. Ruskin replied that he had no intention of writing a life of Turner, but that he should much rejoice in my doing so, and would give me all the help he could. His admonition was :—' Fix at the beginning the following main characteristics of Turner in your mind, as the keys to the secret of all he said and did:—

> *Uprightness.*
> *Generosity.*
> *Tenderness* of heart (extreme).
> *Sensuality.*
> *Obstinacy* (extreme).
> *Irritability.*
> *Infidelity.*

And be sure that he knew his own power, and felt himself utterly alone in the world from its not being understood. Don't try to mask the dark side. . . .

'Yours most truly,

'J. RUSKIN.'

Encouraged by this certainty that I was neither trespassing nor interfering with anyone, I at once set to work steadily and quietly, letting no day pass by without some search for materials, some noting down of traditions, some visit to Turner's old friends ; and resolved not to complete my book, however long it might take me, until I had collected all that patience and enthusiasm could enable me to gather together.

Through Mr. Ruskin's kind aid I became acquainted one by one with all Turner's executors; and letters of enquiry made me known to most of the English collectors of Turner pictures, water-colour drawings, etchings, engravings, and proofs. The two or three noblemen who alone of their wealthy order patronised the painter when living, readily and courteously communicated what information they could. From Turner's friends (all of whom truly loved his memory) I met with kindness and consideration. They kept nothing from me; they ransacked their memories; they searched for old letters; they established old dates; they read over to me old diaries and old note-books. Bound to me by the same sympathy, they aided me without one selfish or envious thought. Mr. Ruskin gave me a chart to steer by—all he could do; for of Turner's personal history I found he knew little.

First and foremost, I have to thank that greatest of all dead or living writers on Art, for his memoranda, more especially for his kind permission to let me examine and take notes at my leisure of the many hundred sketch-books left by Turner to the nation, and for a quiet inspection of the best of the *twenty thousand sketches* found in the trunks, chests, and portfolios of their great hoarder.

The Rev. Mr. Trimmer (eldest son of the artist's oldest executor, of Marston on Bere, Staffordshire) I also have to warmly and especially thank for a MS. volume of recollections of Turner, whom he had known for forty years. I am deeply indebted to Mr. G. Jones, R.A., another executor, for his MS. volume of Turner reminiscences, connected particularly with his friendship for Chantrey. I have also to express my gratitude to Mr. David Roberts, R.A., for several sheets of valuable anecdotes of his old friend; and to Mr. J. Griffiths, of Norwood, likewise an executor, for allowing me to study his large collection of touched proofs by Turner, and for furnishing me with a unique and most valuable index to all Turner's engraved works, an index that cost Mr. Stokes,. off and on, some twenty years' labour.

I also beg to acknowledge the kindness of Mr. H. C. Munro, of Novar, a great Turner collector, and one of the artist's few *compagnons de voyage*, in furnishing me with all he knew, and giving me full access to his matchless collection of Turner's water-colour drawings; and of Mr. F. Dillon, in enabling me to see his beautiful collection of Turner etchings; while last, not least, I may mention the great help furnished me by that celebrated engraver, Mr. John Pye, the owner of the best extant collection of the 'Liber Studiorum,' in almost every variety of condition, and a collector for the last thirty years of all matters relating to that *chef-d'œuvre* of Turner's genius. Nor must I forget to tender my warmest acknowledgments to Sir Charles Eastlake, President of the Royal Academy, Mr. E. M. Ward, R.A., Messrs. Bale and Smith, Mr. Mayall (the eminent photographer), Mr. Wilkie Collins, and the two executors, Messrs. Hardwicke and Cockerell. Further, Mr. Marks and Sir E. Landseer have indirectly furnished notes for my book.

Let me also record my obligations to all Turner's engravers—Messrs. Goodall, Cousen, Le Keux, Rawle, Wilmore, Armitage, and others ; not forgetting Mr. S. Lupton, who has from the beginning taken a special interest in the work, or Mr. J. Wykeham Archer, for a valuable page or two from Mrs. Lance.

When Mr. Ruskin first wrote to me in encouragement of my design, he admonished me that there was no time to be lost, 'for those who knew him when young are dying daily.' I do not think, however, that as yet much information has been lost in that way. Sir John Swinburne is dead, it is true; Mr. Stokes, Turner's oldest friend and enthusiastic admirer, is also gone; but the laborious catalogues and most of the stories of the latter have been handed to me by survivors. The Stokes and Hawkins collections of the 'Liber Studiorum,' certainly, have gone to pieces; but Mr. Pye's, even a richer and fuller one, still remains intact. Mr. Trimmer, Turner's preceptor in Greek and pupil in painting, also is no more; but most of his traditions have been preserved for me by his sons. Mr. Wells, too, exists not, but some of his reminiscences have been written down for me by his daughter; and the recollections of Mr. Charles Heath and Mr. Charles Turner, both of whom were well acquainted with the artist, survive in the memories of others. Mr. Lovell Reeve has preserved stories of Turner related to him by Mr. Windus, Mr. Leslie, and Mr. C. Turner; and to Mr. Wornum, of the National Gallery, I am indebted for several important items of chronology. Thus I trust that a kind Providence has allowed nothing of this great man to perish which might be useful to a future generation, either for incitement or for warning. It is only a Shakespeare who can afford to leave his works behind him as his sole monument.

A word in conclusion about my predecessors in Turner biography. Mr. Peter Cunningham once wrote a short memoir; but, if it were not for Mr. Burnett's most valuable remarks on Turner's art that accompanied it, it would be almost valueless. Little else has been printed, if we except a short memoir of Turner in an old number of 'Fraser's Magazine,' from the pen of Mr. Cyrus Redding; another by Mr. Alaric Watts, and a still shorter one in some other journal, for which Mr. Windus, of Tottenham, furnished many facts.

Mr. Ruskin's fifth volume of 'Modern Painters' contains a kind allusion to my labours. I trust my views of Turner's life may agree with those held by the great exponent of his genius. I have spared none of Turner's faults; I have tried to forget none of his excellencies. I have not striven to caricature him as a miser, because I knew that one great work of charity had been the fixed object of his whole life; while I could not ridicule him as an anchorite and a misanthrope, because I knew how tenderly he was beloved by his more intimate friends, how sensitive he was to their sufferings, and how deeply he felt their loss.

Yet I have not written this book in the unworthy spirit of a mere special pleader, but with, I hope, a stern and undeviating regard for truth. I had no motive whatever to warp me. I did not wish to write a eulogy, a fulsome funeral oration, a poem, a riddle, a rhapsody, or a mere saleable time-serving apology. I have tried to paint the man as I really believe he was; an image of gold with clay feet; a great disappointed man, whose ambition was never satisfied, and who in despair of all other pleasure sought out Nature, and in her presence felt his only real happiness.

I have sought not to put him on a higher or a lower throne than that whereon the genius of his great exponent has already placed him, but rather to gather fresh proof of his genius from the records of his personal history. In many respects I certainly do not think his mind was either so vast or so harmoniously developed as that of Michael Angelo, Raphael, or Titian; and his oil pictures, I hold, were not always equal to his water-colour drawings. But I do firmly believe that, though often defective in a sense of form, Turner was in respect of the union of copiousness, imagination, variety, quality, and originality the greatest landscape painter that the world ever has produced, or perhaps ever is likely to produce.

WALTER THORNBURY.

P.S.—I must also commemorate the kindness of Turner's old friend, Mr. F. H. Fawkes, of Farnley Hall, in Yorkshire, in sending me a catalogue of his unique collection of Turner's drawings (chiefly unpublished); of Mr. Trimmer, who supplied original reminiscences of Lawrence, Gainsborough, and others; and of Messrs. Christie and Manson, who gave me access to their valuable list of sales. I have been much indebted to Mr. Pye also, for his admirable and well verified volume on the history of English Art, which, as a treasury of dates and facts in connection especially with English engraving, cannot be equalled. Nor can I help expressing my gratitude to Mr. Ruskin for many passages in the last wonderful volumes of his on 'Modern Painters,' volumes which, in spite of minor critical differences, evidence to me a genius as versatile and profound as Turner's, and infinitely more logical, clear, and far-seeing.

I only trust that the following pages will at least show the injustice of Mr. Fairholt's assertion, 'that all reminiscences of Turner are unpleasant, and only tend to lower the man.'

CONTENTS.

CONTENTS.

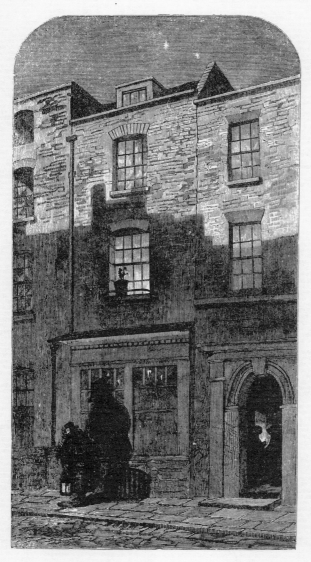

HOUSE IN MAIDEN LANE IN WHICH TURNER WAS BORN.

THE LIFE

OF

J. M. W. TURNER, R.A.

CHAPTER I.

'AND FIRST THE INFANT.'

JOSEPH MALLORD WILLIAM TURNER was born on St. George's Day (day of good omen), the 23rd of April, 1775, and was baptised on the 14th of May following in the parish church of St. Paul, Covent Garden, where the great name may still be seen in the register.

His father, William Turner (a Devonshire man by birth), was a humble hairdresser, well known in the theatrical district of the 'Garden,' who lived at the west end of Maiden Lane, on the right-hand side as you come from Southampton Street, and opposite the 'Cider Cellar' which was opened about 1730, but which at the time of the painter's birth was the studio of a society of artists.[1]   Only a side door of Turner's murky shop

---

[1] I remember the house well—I have been up and down and all over it.   The old barber's shop was on the ground floor, entered by a little dark door on the left side of Hand Court.   The window was a long, low one ; the stairs were narrow, steep, and winding ; the rooms low, dark, and small, but square and cosy, however dirty and confined they may have been.   Turner's bedroom, where he generally painted, looked into the lane, and was commanded by the opposite windows.   The house to which he afterwards removed, for more quiet and room, I suppose, is at the end of Hand Court, and is on a larger scale, with two windows in front ; but it must have been rather dark, though less noisy than his father's house.

survived when I first visited it, the rest having been absorbed
into the sticky warehouse of an ambitious grocer, and the whole
edifice was pulled down in 1861. Geographically considered,
the house consecrated by genius was No. 26 Maiden Lane,
standing at the left-hand corner of Hand Court, near the south-
west corner of Covent Garden. It was a sort of gloomy horizontal tunnel, with a low archway and prison-like iron gate of its
own, and you had to stand a good minute in the dim light of
this archway before you could see the coffin-lid door to the
left that in the days of Garrick opened into the small hairdresser's shop. The dingy front window, once grotesquely gay
with dummies in bob and cauliflower wigs, such as Hogarth loved
to stop and draw, was bare and deserted when I first knew it.

If we accept an uncertain tradition adopted by Mr. Alaric
Watts on the authority of Mr. Duroveray, the hairdresser lived
most of his time in the cellar under his shop. This is but
living in an underground kitchen, as London servants generally
do now even in grand houses; yet I am indisposed to believe
the story, because I think I see in it a sort of dramatic effort to
get contrast, elevating the son by lowering the father. It is not
improbable, however, that the Turner family cooked underground in what might be called by many people a cellar, and
spent much of their time there, keeping their upper rooms for
special holidays and festivals.

The date of Turner's birth is now beyond dispute, though
his executors inscribed it erroneously upon the painter's coffin.
The register of the Covent Garden church proves it, and the
proof is strengthened by the following fact. An extant drawing
of Westminster Abbey (an interior) has this inscription, written
by the artist himself, on a flat pavement-stone in the left-hand
foreground of the Abbey :—

WILLIAM TURNER

Natus

1775

This 'natus 1775' is ambitiously marked in the foreground of
the beautiful water-colour drawing, which was bought by Mr.
J. Dillon at the sale of Lord Harewood's pictures in 1858.
The colour of this drawing is a little blue, the figure introduced
being very graceful ; and the size of the Abbey is grandly exaggerated, after Turner's usual manner ; yet one could scarcely
wish it otherwise.

Turner, who was eminently secretive, loving to hide in a
corner and to mystify people, sometimes talked of being born
in the same year as Napoleon and the Duke of Wellington,
though he really was born six years later than either ; yet St.
George's Day surely might have been accounted quite as auspi-
cious for the birth of a great Englishman.

He used occasionally to imply that his father came from
Kent ; but there is no doubt that at least his grandfather
and grandmother spent all their lives at South Molton in
Devonshire. His father came up to London early in life,
became a hairdresser, and married a young woman of Islington
whose surname was Mallord or Marshall. An uncle of the
painter settled in Barnstaple, and became a wool merchant ;
and a descendant of his, one of the chief clerks in a Barnstaple
bank, kindly furnished me with these facts. He once called,
he told me, at the painter's house, but was refused admittance,
as he believes all Turner's relatives were if they ventured on
a visit to the gallery. Therefore Turner's assertion to Mr.
Cyrus Redding that he came from Barnstaple was a mere
generality, carelessly uttered and perhaps carelessly reported.
There is no doubt, however, that the painter was proud of
belonging to the same county as Sir Joshua Reynolds, whose
portrait he once copied. I can claim no 'blue blood' for
Turner, nor do I want to do so. All old families have sprung
originally from peasants, and every second peasant family will
one day be noble. There is no rank in souls or bodies, and
our heralds now are mere inventors of ancestry for uneasy men
who, having grown rich, are ambitious to bear arms. Pedigree
and genealogy both are vanities, and I put them behind me as
dead and gone. A family like Turner's, that produced a small
tradesman, a bank clerk, and a solicitor, must at least have

been of as good yeoman rank as Shakespeare's. It is the middle classes, indeed, that have produced England's greatest minds. As talent is said to descend on the maternal side, I will begin with some account of Turner's mother, kindly furnished to me by the rector of Heston, the eldest son of Turner's old friend and executor; Mr. Trimmer having obtained his facts from an authority no less unquestionable than Hannah Danby, Turner's old housekeeper, who personally had them from the painter's father.

Mrs. Turner, I thus learn, was a native of Islington; but at Turner's decease they had not succeeded in finding any entry of her baptism. In an unfinished portrait of her by her son, which was one of his first attempts, my informant perceived no mark of promise; and he extended the same remark to Turner's first essays at landscape. The portrait was not wanting in force or decision of touch, but the drawing was defective. There was a strong likeness to Turner about the nose and eyes; her eyes being represented as blue, of a lighter hue than her son's; her nose aquiline, and the nether lip having a slight fall. Her hair was well frizzed—for which she might have been indebted to her husband's professional skill—and it was surmounted by a cap with large flappers. Her posture therein was erect, and her aspect masculine, not to say fierce; and this impression of her character was confirmed by report, which proclaimed her to have been a person of ungovernable temper, and to have led her husband a sad life. Like her son, her stature was below the average. Towards the end of her days she became insane, and was in confinement; and from her Turner might have inherited his melancholy turn of mind. Mr. Trimmer, however, never saw her, never heard him mention her, nor ever heard of anyone who had seen her.

There is an absurd tradition to the effect that Turner's mother was of good family, and related to the Marshalls formerly of Shelford Manor House, near Nottingham, now the property of Lord Chesterfield. The vague story is that Turner in his youth paid a visit to his maternal connections, and that he was repulsed by them. Certain it is that the painter deeply resented any allusion to his mother; but this soreness may be readily explained by the unhappy circumstance of her insanity, and the son's natural anxiety not to have that generally known. We have all seen how painful an apprehension the insanity of an ancestor begets in the minds of his descendants ; and great men like Dr. Johnson, even without a deranged ancestor, have suffered all their lives from such fear. There is no doubt that Byron always remembered ' the wicked lord ' who killed Mr. Chaworth in the midnight duel, and dwelt upon that event till the fear itself touched the verge of insanity ; yet, considering there are few families in England who have not numbered a madman in their ranks, this dread is foolish and groundless. All I can positively affirm of Turner's mother is that Dr. Shand, author of ' Gallops in the Antipodes,' writes to inform me that ' Miss Marshall was first cousin to his grandmother.' In deference to minds of patrician proclivities, therefore, it may be presumed that she was not of the peasant class.

There was also a portrait of Turner senior by his son, of a date much later than that of his mother's, which Mr. Trimmer testifies was shown to his father as one of the artist's earliest efforts in that line. It was a full-face representation, most accurate as to the eyes and general expression of the subject, but less accurate as to the nose. A few years before the death of the old man, when he was decrepit, Turner the engraver executed a drawing of him, which my informant pronounces to have been a fair likeness ; but when the son heard of it he insisted upon its destruction ; and, to pacify him, the engraver, retaining the original, made a copy of it, which upon being delivered up to Turner was by him destroyed.

Mr. Trimmer's description of the painter's parent, the result of close knowledge of him, is that he was about the height of his son, spare and muscular, with a head below the average standard, small blue eyes, parrot nose, projecting chin, and a fresh complexion indicative of health, which he apparently enjoyed to the full. He was a chatty old fellow, and talked fast ; and his words acquired a peculiar transatlantic twang from his nasal enunciation. His cheerfulness was greater than that of his son, and a smile was always on his countenance.

An anecdote fortunately has been preserved which gives us

the very starting-point of the boy's Art life. It is like that dark spot in an egg which afterwards becomes the heart of the bird. It used to be related by Mr. Tomkinson, in whose father's house the determining influence was awakened. Probably it was about 1780 that the barber of Maiden Lane went to Mr. Tomkinson's to dress that gentleman's hair.

Let us imagine it to be an April morning on which, through a rainbow arch of sweet hope and promise, the barber's son, arrayed in skeleton suit and with a frill round his neck, after the type of Tommy and Harry in 'Sandford and Merton,' accompanies his father to the rich customer's house; son holding father by the hand, and father with his apron rolled up under his arm, covering powder-puff, curling-tongs, scissors, and razors. The little man is in a hurry and is bustling, while the boy snatches looks at tawny-chested Flemish brewers' horses and at prints in windows, as well as at that tearful cloud that now laughs out into sunshine. Little Billy is happy at mother's sending him out to see father curl rich Mr. Tomkinson's hair; and the boy running and looking up in his father's absorbed face is a pretty spectacle to dwell on. I watch them till they reach the great house, when the senior, looking more important than ever, pulls familiarly but modestly at the bell. The barber and his son are shown in. Some chat perhaps ensues about the Yankees and Lord North, Mr. Burke, or Dr. Samuel Johnson; and to work goes the barber. Meanwhile the boy, spoken to occasionally by the grand gentleman, sits in a corner near a table, staring with all the might of his bright blue eyes at a silver salver (emblazoned with the Tomkinson arms) which leans against the wainscot. A certain rampant lion especially astonishes him.

The decorative work proceeds; the wig is frizzed and snowily powdered till it resembles the cauliflower of our garden; the white hair is mown from the smooth blue flesh; the dressing-gown is whisked off with a vivacious dash; the silver fee is paid; and barber and boy—the latter not perhaps without cake and wine—turn their faces towards the dusky lane. The boy is silent and thoughtful all that day; he sits upstairs all apart, brooding over a sheet of paper. Mother wonders what ails him; father is consulted at tea-time; and they call for Billy, who with impetuosity produces his paper and exhibits a not unintelligible lion, twin brother to the wilder and more royal one on the salver—or table—at Mr. Tomkinson's. The gods be praised—the boy is a genius! One can fancy the reflective smile of the father and the affectionate imposition of his hand on the wavy head. Little can he estimate the child's future career—the extent of his misery, the intensity of fruitless longing that is to be his.

From that time the boy's fate is fixed; thenceforth, when old friends, looking up from under the glittering razor, mumble through obstructive lather, 'Well, Turner, have you settled yet what William is to be?' the barber will smile proudly, and, hushing the frothy torrent of his professional talk, will rest the burning, black curling-tongs between a twist of thin brown paper and reply, 'It's all settled, sir; *William is going to be a painter!*'

But who is this Mr. Tomkinson, whose house barber and child have visited? He is a rich silversmith, and is described to me as a man with a smattering taste for art, and an inclination to buy good drawings cheap and sell them dear; an inclination not unusual in our trading country. He pries about small by-shops for young men's drawings, as the boy Turner will afterwards discover; and, directly he has restlessly bought a good room-full of Sandbys and Rookers, he sets-to restlessly selling them again; so that his collection is a Penelope's web, ever weaving and never completed. He is a prosperous tradesman, not ill-natured, who is in the habit of emitting 'flatulent platitudes' about great events. For instance, when Gainsborough died of a sudden cancer, he was delivered of this profound remark: 'Good God, sir, such men should never die.'

Eventually run off the road by more progressive men, he retires to a house at the corner of Carburton Street, Portland Road, where he is in the habit of boasting, like Dogberry, that he is one who has 'had losses; go to.' He had lost, in his line, some 30,000*l.*; he had lost more money in business than anyone else had ever lost.

Mr. Tomkinson was one of those shrewd men who contrive to make money even out of their hobbies. Years afterwards he was still buying pictures of Turner; and I have no doubt he fully believed that he was one of the first men to dig up and discover a new genius, and over his wine would hint with a chuckle at his own sagacity. He bowed to beggars when he refused them a penny, for his manners were 'the portly' manners of the old school; and, when he went into the country, he would get out and creep behind his gig to get shots at crows. Through Tomkinson, perhaps, it was that Turner was afterwards introduced to Reynolds, who allowed him to copy portraits in his own studio in Leicester Square.

Turner's first ambition (and here genius helped out) was not to copy, but to go into the fields and make sketches. A son of Stothard perfectly remembered the circumstance of his father relating to him that in early life he went one day to the shop in Maiden Lane to get his hair cut, when the old man remarked to him in conversation, 'My son, sir, is going to be a painter.' About this time he fell in with Girtin the painter.

A glimpse of the artist boy a year or two later we obtain through report of a copy or imitation of Paul Sandby, the fashionable drawing-master, Richard Wilson's friend, which a gentleman purchased from the barber's window in Maiden Lane, and gave to Mr. Duroveray, who long years ago originated an edition of 'Illustrated British Classics,' which tended to elevate the character of English book illustrations generally. The same anonymous authority told Mr. Alaric Watts that at this time the Turner family lived chiefly in the underground kitchen, and that small water-colour drawings, copied from Sandby and others by Boy Turner, used to hang round the entrance door, ticketed at prices varying from one shilling to three. Between this cellar in Maiden Lane and the royal tomb in St. Paul's there were indeed many steps.

Mr. Trimmer and Turner were one day looking over some prints. 'Ah! that,' said Turner with emotion, taking up a particular one, 'made me a painter.' It was a green mezzo-tinto, a Vandervelde—an upright; a single large vessel running before the wind, and bearing up bravely against the waves. That determined his genius to marine painting'; subsequent boyish visits made him love English rivers; and later trips to Margate made him love Kent and the sea.

We have already seen his nascent genius break out at the sight of an engraved salver ; but, after all, this fine Vandervelde is the spark that lights the train. First, you see, he begins to copy Paul Sandby ; then he takes to the fields and the Thames, drawing rickety sheds and old towers and steeples; and at school we shall presently see him drawing animals with chalk on the walls. Even his relations had no doubt by this time that William was to be a painter.

'Margate Church,' executed by the artist when he was about nine years old, is one of his early drawings. Indeed, it is one of the boy's earliest works that I have yet heard of. I have not myself seen drawings of an earlier date than his eleventh or twelfth year.

Of Maiden (or Midden) Lane, the place of Turner's birth, there is little to be said. It was at that time a mere dim defile between houses clothed with the smoke of centuries ; yet, like many another such place, it had had better days. It opened from Southampton Street, so called in memory of that good Whig martyr William Lord Russell, in which Congreve and Mrs. Bracegirdle had lived, and where Garrick resided before he removed to Adelphi Terrace, some few years before Turner was born. A better place could not be imagined for a small hairdresser with a good theatrical companion, such as old Turner had. In 1633 Archbishop Sancroft, then only Dean of York, lived in the lane; and thence in 1677 honest Andrew Marvell, content to pick at his mutton bone in a poor second floor, and to spurn the bribes of a corrupt Court, addressed his constituents in Hull. Here too Voltaire lodged for three years, at the sign of the 'White Perruke,' when he came to London, rebuked Congreve, and was epigrammatised by Young of the 'Night Thoughts.' The 'Bedford Head' is mentioned by the Queen Anne poet ; and in the lane also was born Bonnell Thornton, the apothecary's son and Hogarth's acquaintance ; so that the dirty lane has contributed its quota to the mythology of our dear old London.

It was not a 'bright look-out,' as sailors say, for a child in the first scene of his life drama. Nothing elevating surrounded him ; the age, too, was poor, the religion faithless and half dead. The ebony dome, the dull roofs, the squalid life, the low ideal, were, says a certain great poet, very different from the visions of beauty that Venice revealed to the boy Titian and the stripling Giorgione.

Of a portrait of himself, painted by the artist in his early days, presented by his father to Mrs. Danby, and by her bequeathed to Mr. Ruskin, Mr. Trimmer deposes that, apparently the portrait of a youth of sixteen, it is strikingly like about the eyes and nose, but otherwise defective. The profusion of dark tresses which it faithfully represents recalls the enthusiasm with which the old man used to speak of his son's 'fine head of hair,' a point whereon his judgment may not be questioned ; and the fracture visible on the left side of the picture commemorates Turner's dissatisfaction with his work, which he expressed by knocking his fist through it. These were the traditions of Mrs. Danby, and but for them Mr. Trimmer would not be disposed to attribute the painting to Turner, for whom at that time he thinks the drawing too good ; but perhaps he was assisted by a master. According to the same authority, Turner was a day-boarder at the Brentford Free School, where he first evidenced his talent by sportively drawing with a piece of chalk figures of cocks and hens on the walls as he went to and from that seat of learning. For this anecdote Mr. Trimmer gives the authority of his father, to whom it was told by Turner himself. Between the juvenile artist of cocks and hens and the painter of the 'Téméraire,' as Mr. Trimmer observes, there is indeed a wide interval.

Reynolds, who, with all his exquisite art, seldom rose to elevation of genius as a 'creator,' was always promulgating the healthy but erroneous theory that genius is only another name for industry. Would that it were ! Being of a totally diverse opinion, and believing that genius is an innate capacity of brain, requiring opportunities and intense toil for its development, I presume that Providence knew what it was about when it made Turner the son of a theatrical barber, in a lane out of Covent Garden, in the year of our Lord 1775. As to birth, no art has been less indebted to this accident than painting. Gainsborough was the son of a small Suffolk clothier ; Caracci of a poor tailor; Flaxman of a vendor of plaster casts; Hogarth of a poor schoolmaster in Little Britain. It is not the soil but the seed which is the most important element.

In after times the little barber, who became shrunk up by long years of parsimony, which, though necessary at first, subsequently degenerated into meanness, used to boast that it was his special pride to think he had given 'William a good edycation.' He did not mean to deceive, but, after the wont of men, he had repeated the story so often that he at last came to believe it himself; for I find [1] that in 1785, when he was ten years old (eleven or twelve, Mr. Bell says; but this is obviously wrong), Turner was withdrawn from the delights of playing among the vegetable baskets in Covent Garden, from marbles and spyhei with stray apprentices and recusant errand-boys, and from London's Cimmerian gloom and crimsoning fogs, to be sent to school at Brentford, near the river's side. In consequence of a fit of illness (want of air—chief disease in London!) he was entrusted to an aunt at that place; and there he obtained the combined benefits of health and learning. It should be added here that a gentleman who was associated with Turner at Brentford in 1785 represents that Turner was first sent to a day school at New Brentford, where he boarded with an uncle on his lady mother's side—a Mr. Marshall, a butcher in that town. The site of the school, which was kept by a Mr. John White, was near the 'Three Pigeons' at Brentford Butts. It was a school, or rather an 'academy,' such as Boswell senior sneered at when he heard that his ne'er-do-weel son had foregathered with Johnson (an auld dominie, who had keept a schule, and ca'ad it an acawdemy), and numbered, when the sickly, pale lad came down to it from London, fifty boys and ten girls—all, it may be presumed, of tender age.

Thus Turner ceased drawing lions from Mr. Tomkinson's salver. He is removed by his good angel from the large-pillared church of St. Paul that Hogarth introduced into his pictures; from the railed-in burial-ground where his dear friend

[1] From a MS. book entitled *Early Recollections of Mr. E. Bell, Engraver*, kindly communicated to me by Mr. C. H. Adhurst of Edmonton.

and fellow-worker Girtin was afterwards to sleep ; from the red roofs and driving blasts of brown smoke ; from crimson fog-suns and misty slants of sunshine—to a very Land of Promise for a boy artist. To him the green fields of Paradise lay round vulgar Putney, and lonely, peaceful Twickenham ; and the birds must have been as little flying angels newly transformed. We must imagine the silent boy, dazed, confused, and tearful with memories of father and mother and home, among his companions in the academy near the ' Three Pigeons.' Pro-bably, after the manner of us all (genius or no genius), he cried bitterly the first night under the sheets, then stifled his sobs, in a day or two grew tamer and happier, and wrote home in a cheerful spirit. In a week or two he begins to get into gear and work better in the new harness ; and then comes the day when, with flaming eyes, bristling hair, cheeks pallid with rage, and clenched teeth, we fight the school bully (probably a tyrannous West Indian, who bribes crowds of small parasites with jars of tamarinds and guava jelly) who has dared to sneer at our old father the ' barber ' in Maiden Lane, and to ask his son if they baste the legs of mutton in Hand Court with bears' grease. Next come school 'scapes and bitter canings over *Propria quæ maribus*, and dreadfully difficult passages of ' Delectus' and verses of Virgil, that no earthly memory can retain.

Gradually the old instinct works through the shallow crust of Latin grammar and English history. There is much surrep-titious drawing of elm-trees and blackbirds in fly-leaves of ' Cæsar ' and ' Telemachus.' Long afterwards old school-fellows of Turner's used to say that his first attempts at art had been drawings of birds and flowers and trees from the schoolroom windows—rude attempts at the rose, the elm, and the blackbird no doubt, yet still showing the way the twig was bent. The delights of the country were undoubtedly stimu-lating the impressionable brain of the young genius. Penned in London fog, he might have become a hairdresser ; free and happy in the country, he became a landscape painter—the most true, yet the most poetic, the most marvellous, of landscape painters. Many of these early sketches, says Bell, were taken by stealth. ' Stolen waters are sweet,' says Solomon ; and his school-fellows, sympathising with his taste, often did 'his sums' for him while he pursued the bent of his compelling genius.

To these early days in the country Turner indeed owed much. As time has shown, the chestnut avenue at Bushy Park —the terraces of Hampton Palace—the green, calm meadows— the reflective cattle—the pouting, scornful swans—the fast-flowing river—the summer elms, so dense and dark and close—all touched his young heart, stirring him to poetry, and arousing his veneration, his sense of the sublime, and his passion for the beautiful. I think that no place breeds so strongly reactionary love for poetry and art as this London of ours—the vast, the negative, the miserable, the loathsome, the great, the magnificent. Indelible recollections of these early days probably led Turner in later time to fix his abode at Twickenham, near his old school ; and their influence explains the delight he took, long after, in drawing swans in all attitudes. Even the flat-roofed stone-pines of Italy did not readily efface the memory of the Bushy elms, and the Brentford meadows glowing with flowers and azure with forget-me-nots.

But before the boy William is removed from school let me, availing myself of almost contemporary accounts of schools, endeavour to communicate to the reader a mental sketch of life thereat.

They walked out two and two, and on Sundays dazzled the eyes of all beholders with stiff-skirted coats of formal cut, and of extraordinary and ever-memorable colours, such as pea-green, scarlet, sky-blue, snuff-brown, and bright claret ; some of the boys signalising the superior means of their parents by imposing smart, triangular gold-laced hats above their flowing locks of sable or flaxen. The master we may fancy to be a spare, shrivelled man in a large, bushy wig, somewhat brown from want of powder, who wore a snuffy camlet coat, with ink-stained ruffles, and coarse blue worsted stockings, and, when he walked out, swung a rather brassy-looking gilt-headed cane.

On the forms at Brentford probably it was that the cane of Mr. John White, in engraver's phrase, 'bit into' Turner the stories of the Gardens of the Hesperides, Polyphemus, the escape of Ulysses, and other classic fables, which (re-read doubtless in Lempriere) his genius afterwards selected to reframe, restore, and illuminate ; or, if he did not read them in notes to Virgil, he might at least have conned Pope's ' Odyssey,' which is generally a favourite book with schoolboys.

Presently came the father from Maiden Lane to take home little William, with his head crammed with undigested scraps of ' Delectus,' dictations, classic stories, and English history. Leaving his rough butcher uncle and his aunt on his mother's side, he has to retire again to shelter under the great shadow of St. Paul's.

Father still warming to Art, under the stimulus of artist customers discoursing of Hogarth, Paul Sandby, and Gains-borough while their heads are being shaved, the boy prattles of Brentford and the river, and exhibits his furtive hieroglyphics of birds and trees ; whereupon he is despatched, at the age of either eleven or twelve (for tradition is vague about the date), to the Soho academy. There we may picture him, serene and happy, drawing flowers and other objects, after the tambour-frame manner, for Heaven knows what indefinite commercial purpose, under a Mr. Palice, a floral drawing-master. Of the toilsome yet, it may be, not unprofitable hours so passed in the ill-omened square, haunted by the headless ghost of the brainless Duke of Monmouth, and once the scene of so many fashionable mas-querades, and dinners too, no record survives.

Let us fancy the boy gradually advancing (for he was one of the slow ripeners), trying colours, drawing houses and churches, assaying and testing everything in a patient, careful way. ' Evi-dently a genius,' is the inspiriting reflection of the father, as he runs about with the hot tongs and frizzles them clean in thin curling-paper.

At thirteen he begins to reveal a short, thick-set figure, with large features of a Jewish type, but handsome ; clear grey-blue eyes and arched eyebrows ; a boy careless of dress, but on the whole of a sturdy, determined, prudent temper, with an irresis-tible bias towards Art. Moved by I know not what reason, the father determines now to send William to his third school, kept by a Mr. Coleman, at Margate ; and thither perhaps he goes in the very hoy immortalised by Charles Lamb. It is a dreary, blundering, miserable journey, undertaken by a dense throng of seasick citizens' wives and children ; yet it is most eventful to the lad. Purely fluent, sapphire air is, in the first place, a luxury to be keenly enjoyed by one of London's smoke-oppressed inhabitants ; and to this prime source of delight we have to add the attractions of real sunlit sea-waves dashing in green sparkles over the gunwale, and of sails luminous with transverse sunbeams and other solar effects dear to the artist eye.

At Margate, which must then have seemed a wild little seaside village at a vast distance from London, and where schooling doubtless was cheap, the boy gets introduction to the pleasant family of a favourite schoolfellow. No wonder he retained to the end of his life an ardent attachment to the breezy piers and white-walled cliffs of that Kentish bathing-place ; for it was there he first saw the sea ; it was there he first learnt the physiognomy of the waves ; and there it was, moreover, that he first fell in love, powerful to effect a mighty revolution in the mind of youth. The boy painter was severely smitten with the charms of a sister of his young friend, who was of about his own age. But of this episode we shall learn more hereafter.

CHAPTER II.

THE LONDON OF TURNER'S BOYHOOD.

TINTORETTO was the son of a dyer ; Andrea del Sarto and the Caracci were the sons of tailors ; Caravaggio was the son of a mason ; Correggio of a labourer ; Guido of a musician ; Domenichino of a ropemaker ; and Albano of a silk mercer. Turner, therefore, had ample historical justification, if he needed any, for his descent from a hairdresser. It was his only chance of being original ; for had he been a great man's son in that artificial age, he might have grown up a third-rate imitator of Claude, or Berghem, or Hobbima, and have frittered away his life lounging with a spy-glass in the galleries of Rome or Florence. But the hard necessity of earning bread put steel into his blood. It made him a Titan for work, a lion for exertion, and filled him with an all-absorbing love of Nature. Let us see what the paternal shop contained. According to an old writer's description of the barbers' shops in Exeter Change, it must have been full of long spiral machines for frizzing the hair, powder-puffs, toupées, silk bags, wired cushions, braiding-pins fourteen inches long, crisping-irons, and leather rolls for forming curls. A City gentleman or an actor, about 1775, had three wigs; two being for ordinary wear, and of these one nicely powdered was brought by the barber every morning, when he came to shave the master of the family; and the third being a Sunday wig, which was taken away on the Friday and brought back on the Saturday. At spare times the barber would sit at his shop-door, surrounded by his friends, while he wove flaxen curls on a dummy. There was the eternal grinning of dummies; the scorching of wigs was ceaseless; the clack of tongs was continuous; and occasionally an artist from the studio opposite might bring in a drawing, or have a gossip about Art with the barber father.

The Wycherly and Beau Feilding wigs, 'the horror of sculptors and the antipathy of painters,' as they are characterised by Nollekens Smith, cost as much as fifty guineas each. Even in Hogarth's time old-fashioned men, like Sir James Thornhill and Jonathan Richardson, wore the cascade wig; and so in early life did Hogarth himself, before he took to the curt Busby patronised by Dr. Johnson. Nollekens Smith, writing in 1828, says : ' There are persons now living who recollected seeing the father of the late Mr. Trim of Witton wearing a flowing wig.'

As time goes by, the paternal mind begins to think it meet that the genius should turn a penny. There can be no doubt that the thrifty father, about this date, was almost inclined to make his son an architect, while at another period he half resolved that he should be a portrait painter. The boy had several times sat with a looking-glass before him in the dim bedroom in Maiden Lane, painting his own portrait; and he had also attempted that of poor Tom Girtin. Why might he not hope one day to rival the great Sir Joshua in Leicester Square, or Gainsborough in Pall Mall? The lane would then be blocked with gilded, coroneted, emblazoned carriages ; and ladies of fashion, with little Primrose Hills of powdered hair, would be painted by the son, while the father trimmed, combed, or re-arranged the pate-coverings of their lords. As for the guineas, they would pour in like flour from the hopper-spout of a wind-mill on a breezy day. All that boating about Lambeth and Battersea must now be stopped. Somehow or other, through the influence of some of his customers, perhaps with the favour of Garrick himself, familiar as he was with Reynolds, the boy will presently be allowed by the great painter to come and copy portraits in his ante-room at Leicester Square.

But, before we advance, let us note the chief features of 1775, the year of Turner's birth. We have already seen that in some respects Turner was born in an age that was adverse to his genius ; an age of artifice and conventionality, when most even of the Royal Academicians were sign painters, carriage painters, decorators, and miniature painters ; when an insolent patronage was extended to merit by a few members of the nobility, who were themselves an effete and uncultured class, devoid of all originality, who knew nought of Art but its pedantry, and who were half ashamed of the native produce. It was an irreligious, frivolous age, ignorant to the extent of barbarism of all Art save what was covered by portrait-painting and conventional landscape. It was the age when our King let Wilson and Barry starve while he pampered the cold and shallow dulness of West.

On the other hand, however, Turner had before him a stage miserably free from competitors. As yet England had had no landscape painter of eminence besides Wilson, and his struggles had cleared the way for his successors. The rage for illustrated topographical works began to give artists ample employment ; the speculations of Boydell had enlarged the circle of the print-buying public. Enabled thus to contemn the favour of a limited number of pompous patrons, a genuine artist could now appeal for support to the world at large, whose verdict seldom is un-generous. Further employment was provided for Turner by the rage that sprang up for local histories.

Of the poetic charm that enwraps London itself Turner

then, as ever, seems to have had no special appreciation. Many of his boyish days were spent on the Thames with his friend Girtin ; and of the sights thereon he kept good record. Of the yellow and madder sails ; of the dragon-fly boats, all green and vermilion ; of the shaky weather-stained piles ; of the crumbling old sheds and boat-houses of Lambeth ; of the dull brick towers ; and of the massy bridge that spanned the dull river, he took careful note. All the ripples, fitful reflections, gleams, and sparkling currents were mentally treasured. Whether under the Temple Gardens, the Savoy steps, Inigo Jones's gateway, or the Old Swan landings ; be it Strand side or Borough side, he knew them by heart. But he seems to have had no sense of the dumb grandeur of the myriads of houses over which the black dome dominates. The old gable-ends he never sketched ; the memory-haunted spots he did not care for. He could find nothing there, in what seemed to him a mere expanse of black windows and smoky streets, vaulted half the year with a sky of gloomy lead, to rouse his latent poetry or stimulate his imagination. His soul struggled, like a caged lark, to attain to clear blue ether and fresh green fields.

A glance at the period will enable us to determine whether it was really propitious or unpropitious to his genius and his art ; and thus we may more clearly discern how far Turner led and how far he followed his age. Seventeen hundred and seventy-five was a very eventful year to England—perhaps the most eventful year to our country since that in which the splendid victories of Marlborough had taken place. It was the first year of the unhappy American war. It was the year in which General Washington was appointed by Congress commander-in-chief of the American army. It was the year of the battles of Lexington, Concord, and Bunker's Hill. It was the year in which, through a series of blunders and oppression, a great colony was lost to England for ever, though much blood yet had to be spilled before the issue was determined and America could boast that she was at last free.

In the meantime, amid all the fret and angry debates of Burke and Lord North and other orators about America and ' those misguided rebels,' King George III. (now twenty-five years on his uneasy throne) passes a quiet, dull, but really well-spent summer at Kew. Good, honest, obstinate man, he rises at six, breakfasts early, and sees the five eldest children set to their tasks while the two little ones take a walk. While the Queen works the King reads to her ; then comes the children's dinner, at which the worthy old pair invariably attend as spectators ; and once a week the exemplary father accompanies them on a public promenade in Kew or Richmond Gardens, to the vast admiration of the open-mouthed rustics.

As our barber, by reason of his residence in the vicinity of Covent Garden, has numerous Thespian customers, and the lane nightly runs over with the sedan-chairs of ' the quality' who come to see Garrick personate Abel Drugger in the ' Alchemyst,' it is likely that he discusses the merit of Bannister, the witty comedian ; or, remembering his long pilgrimage up from Devonshire, he may lift up his eyes upon reading in the ' Morning Chronicle' of the horrible audacity of seven highwaymen who one night this year actually stopped the Norwich stage-coach in Epping Forest, and who, though the guard (eventually killed) shot three of them dead, persevered till the horses halted, when they robbed all the passengers. Such passengers ! The ladies wore high-heeled shoes, low looped-up gowns, long gloves, lace stomachers, small ruffles, scanty hoops, and short aprons ; with their hair piled up in front into powdered toupées, as they are in Reynolds's portraits, and with two or three large curls or each side. The gentlemen, if dandies, or ' maccaronis,' as their designation was, wore wonderfully small hats on enormous snowy mountains of toupées, short pig-tails, and striped silk knee-breeches.

In 1775 occurred the deaths of two old men, one rich, the other poor, which I must not omit to record in evidence of the close alliance of 1775 with 1675, and of the long reach to which the memory of one living eighty-six years ago could take us back.

In 1775 died a poor man named Peter Gordon at a village in the North of England, at the advanced age of a hundred and thirty-two years. He was born in Charles I.'s time. Reckoning Oliver Cromwell, he had lived under ten kings ; and remembered being sent as a boy to the forest to cut wood for spears during the Civil Wars.

The same year, following suit to this Lazarus, died Dives, in the shape of one of the old Queen Anne worthies, Earl Bathurst; he who had been the friend of Pope, Sterne, and Swift; of Congreve, Vanbrugh, and Prior; of Rowe, Addison, Arbuthnot, and Gay; a happy man who had in his time opposed Sir Robert Walpole, attacked the South Sea Bubble, and denounced lotteries.

Thus it will be seen that old Turner might possibly have talked to men who had seen Ben Jonson, and cheered Oliver Cromwell on his way to expel the factious Parliament; while, if the Earl had ever deigned to come to Maiden Lane to be shaved, the barber could have heard first-hand of the wit of Swift, the humour of Addison, and the polish of Pope. But, although the barber at that time probably was sublimely indifferent to Fame, and ignorant of the great future already dawning for his son, it becomes us to review the position of English Art at the period of the Turner *avatar*.

West and Reynolds, Wilson and Gainsborough, were the chief planets in the Art heaven of the time. Reynolds, just elected into the Florence Academy, held great levees of the poor wise, the rich foolish, the poor foolish, and the rich wise, at his house in Leicester Square. Gainsborough left Bath in 1774, and came to what was formerly the Duke of Schomberg's house in Pall Mall, where he became a formidable rival to Reynolds. Lawrence, the son of the Bristol hotel-keeper, though still a child, had already earned local fame by drawing portraits and reciting verses. As for poor Wilson, he was starving in I know not what garret, neglected by everyone but kind Paul Sandby, and a few old friends who overlooked his sour manner and his homely, honest bluntness.

West, the son of a Philadelphia Quaker, is painting a series of classical subjects for King George; and the insipid, quietly vain Court painter is Director of the Society of Artists.

Hogarth has disappeared from Leicester Square these eleven years. Turner's future exemplars and competitors were also dead; Canaletti seven summers, and Claude Lorraine, his special predecessor and enemy, a full century all but a few years,

Then as to the water-colour artists : Turner's friendly rival, Girtin, was just born ; Cozens was growing up ; Paul Sandby (born 1732) was a well-known painter and a fashionable drawing-master; while his successor, Hearne (born 1744), is in the West Indies, acting officially as draughtsman to Sir Ralph Payne. Other rivals, predecessors, and contemporaries of Turner will find mention later in this work.

Let us complete the survey by a review of the literature of the period.

There is Dr. Johnson storming about the Ossian controversy, and, like a genuine old Tory, declaring that the Americans are 'a race of convicts.' Richardson, Shenstone, Young, Churchill, Sterne, Akenside, Gray, and Smollett are all dead ; and Goldsmith has passed away a year ago. But Burke is alive, and so are Bishop Percy and Gibbon, while Sheridan has been just bringing out (rather unsuccessfully, too) his 'Rivals.' The Lake school had not yet arisen, but Thomson and Cowper had shown that simple English scenes could be treated classically and without any loss of dignity. Far away too, in an obscure part of Scotland, Burns is fast growing up to sing of love, and homely pleasures and cares, with a true inspiration that proved that there were other models for amatory and pastoral poets than Theocritus and Ovid.

And what was the London of Turner's boyhood like ?

Imagine retired citizens living in rural Islington, and hackney sedan-chairs moored in rows round Covent Garden. Imagine fields everywhere ; beyond Portland Chapel and the New Road, turnstiles, meadows, tea-gardens, and taverns ; a gallows on Kennington Common; hayricks in Osnaburg Street; Cavendish Square with a dwarf brick wall round it, and, where Harley Street now is, fields in which Whitefield preached. Behind Russell Street, on the north-west, was a farm surrounded by fields and straggling houses, where (1773 and later) lived two old maids, named Capper ; one of whom delighted to canter about in a riding-habit and man's hat, and with a pair of huge shears cut the strings of truant and trespassing boys' kites, while the other seized the clothes of bathers who violated the sanctity of the premises. Tottenham Court Road was the scene of an annual ' gooseberry fair,' where the Drury Lane actors planted their booths ; and on the western side of High Street, Marylebone, were the residences of several of the ' quality.'

Beyond Union Street was a rope-walk running north, shaded by two rows of magnificent elms under which red-nosed Wilson and Dr. Johnson's Italian friend Barretti loved to perambulate, prior to dining with Wilton, the sculptor ; and on the right-hand side of this rope-walk extended a bank with a promenade which commanded views of the distant hills and rounded eminences of Highgate, Hampstead, and Harrow.

Hoys then plied up and down the Thames ; and the great coaching inn-yards in the City were crowded with stage coaches rolling in daily (come rain or snow, sunshine or cloud) from York and Lincoln, Oxford, Salisbury, and Brighton. Ranelagh and Marylebone Gardens were then in the prime of their popularity. The Pantheon, which was built two years before Turner's birth, had been visited by Dr. Johnson and Boswell, who in one breath pronounced it inferior to Ranelagh ; and it is to exist till 1792, when Turner will visit its charred ruins and make an exquisite drawing of them. Queen Anne Street and Harley Street, to be associated with Turner's name at a later date, then were only partially built. Green fields of sooty grass, echoing to the shouts of boys in stiff-skirted coats and buckled shoes, stretched where Portland Chapel, Wimpole Street, and Devonshire Place now rear their square boxes of grim black brick ; and even Marylebone Gardens could be entered either from the High Street or at the back through fields, between which and the main road were the little binns of tea-gardens partitioned off.

But in 1775 had been effected a change in London specially interesting to us. Old Somerset House, built in 1547, was pulled down to make room for Chambers's structure. The old Savoy had not yet gone. The Royal Academy in Pall Mall adjoined Carlton House ; and between it and Dalton's print warehouse there were trees visible from the road ; while from

Leicester Square you could still get glimpses of Temple Bar, though surmounted no longer with black rebels' heads. Old Lambeth Palace, which he selected as the subject of his first drawing for the Academy, still survives to us with its smirched brick towers and the dim grey lantern chapel, unaltered as when Turner first rowed by it to make his moonlight sketch at Millbank.

Nor must we here forget another spot of old London that is especially connected with Turner's memory.

Wilton the sculptor, and his friend Cipriani, had been elected, in 1758, directors of a Statue Gallery in the Whitehall Priory Gardens, opened by the Duke of Richmond for the use of Art students. It consisted of about thirty casts from antique statues; and the liberality of the Duke was celebrated by Hayley the poet, whose friend Romney was a constant student there, while Smollett was the Duke's chaplain. In 1770, after being shut for some time, the Gallery was reopened, and placed under the direction of the Society of Artists of Great Britain, whose Academy was in Maiden Lane, and whose secretary was William Woollett. Of him Turner will write with admiration in later years.

There can be no doubt that the neighbourhood of this Academy influenced Turner's mind; and it is easy to conceive that Romney, Woollett, and others must often have come in to chat with the barber who lived over the way. Even it may be assumed that they lent drawings to the clever boy.

CHAPTER III.

THE SKY-PAINTER.

To an early period of Turner's life we may safely refer some of the many visits paid to Bristol, to a Mr. Harraway, an old friend of his father's, and a great fishmonger and glue-boiler in Broadway.[1]

[1] His niece, Miss Dart, of St. James's Square, Bristol, still has the first picture Turner ever exhibited at Somerset House. Mr. Ruskin possesses his first sketch-book.

I like to associate that dirty and venerable old legendary city with Turner. I can see him surveying the Exchange, where thin, sallow West Indian merchants are pacing, discussing the prices of sugar and rum ; in Queen Square, where the great magnates lived, facing King William's statue; at Redcliffe church, musing over the dark, sad room above the north porch where poor Chatterton wove those lies so fatal to his peace ; in the Pithay, wondering at the knightly escutcheons adorning the doors of frowsy old-clothes shops; or, most likely of all, on the river in a boat, listening to the nightingales in Leigh woods.

Many of his large drawings executed at Bristol, and given to Mr. Harraway, are still extant; and they evidence the various stages of maturity that his mind successively attained. The same family once possessed another rude drawing by him of ' Cote House, Durdham Down,' the seat of Sir Henry Lippincote, with Sir Henry, the artist himself, and old Mr. Harraway all in the foreground. Perhaps the boy had been seen at work down at the Hotwells, and was asked up, all red and smiling, to Cote House. His sketch-books of this period contain many drawings of Clifton ; and there is a view of ' Oxford,' of the same date ; to which likewise, or to a year earlier or later (either 1790 or 1791 ; not when he was eighteen, as it is wrongly inscribed), must be assigned a crude portrait of himself executed for Mr. Harraway during one of these holiday visits. The face, weakly drawn, is simple and boyish ; the long, luxuriant, curling hair streams down on his shoulders and frilled jacket ; and the nostrils and mouth are delicately traced, with a carefulness indeed that amounts to timidity. The face, which shows no promise of genius, cannot be intended for a boy much over fifteen years of age. The likeness, however, was considered good at the time. The circumstances that led to its being drawn were these : Turner (who is known to have taken his friend Girtin's portrait) had drawn likenesses of two of his friend Harraway's children, and the family pressed him to make a drawing of himself. ' How am I to do it ? ' asked the boy. ' In your bedroom, with a looking-glass,' was the suggestion ; the fruit of his acting upon which was the little coloured portrait in the black oval wood frame, now in the possession of Mr.

Ruskin. Nor was this the only essay at self-portraiture. Of several subsequent attempts one survives in the Vernon Gallery, a bold and vigorous presentment of the artist at the age of seventeen, but faulty in colour.

It has been erroneously stated in many confused versions of Turner's early life that he was entirely self-educated, owing instruction in reading to his father, and that he acquired the use of the pencil before obtaining mastery of the pen. One blunderer even goes so far as to say that he never could write with ease up to the very day of his death, while it must be allowed that he never spelt correctly. Nothing can be more untrue than these statements, which, like most scandal, arose partly from ignorance and partly from malice. Turner was reasonably well educated. As we have seen, he went to school at Brentford, at Margate, and in Soho ; and, further, he is known to have attended a drawing-school in St. Martin's Lane, where the fashionable Paul Sandby, then an Academician, taught drawing. Fired by Sandby's drawings, and having gathered somewhat from the days gone to wreck at Brentford and Bristol among the boats and the ships, the clever boy busies himself at home down in the cellar and up in the bedroom, colouring prints for a printseller in the same street, for whom another clever boy of the same age, named Girtin, a friend of his, also works. Thus he probably gets a shilling or two for flat washes of pink, and brown, and green, such as you see on coloured Gillrays still extant. The process, though not one peculiarly grateful to the imaginative mind, yet requires care and neatness, with some evenness and purity of colour; and it has an educational value for the nascent artist. His employer, John Raphael Smith, a miniature painter, just then known as an excellent mezzotinto engraver, was acquainted with Cozens, one of the most poetical of our early water-colour painters, and an early model of Turner's, and with Dr. Munro, one of his early patrons.

The barber's window meanwhile has ticketed at three shillings apiece copies of Paul Sandby, and neat pale green imitations of Dayes, the landscape draughtsman and geographic artist, Girtin's master, which Mr. Crowle and Mr. Tomkinson eagerly purchase and chuckle over. The propinquity of Hand Court to Smith's shop has the additional advantage of serving for the entrapment of passing amateurs. But Turner at this period, immediately subsequent to quitting school at Margate, had other occupations besides copying Sandby, Nicholson (of whom he used to avow himself a copyist), Dayes, and Hearne, the successful water-colour men of the day. When not visiting his Margate friends or his butcher uncle at Brentford, or the Bristol glue-boiler, he is employed in touching up amateurs' drawings, and adding skies and backgrounds to architects' designs ; rolls of white clouds and blue wastes of summer sky.

It must have been before Turner went to Margate—it could scarcely have been after, for I am assured he was at school at Margate at thirteen, and he was certainly admitted a student of the Royal Academy at fourteen (1789)—that he was sent by his cautious and anxious father to Mr. Thomas Malton (Tom Malton, as he was usually styled in that familiar age), a perspective draughtsman who kept a school at his lodging in Long Acre ; the great coach-building street, historically ennobled by the birth therein in after time of Stothard, and memorable as being that in which poor, half-starved Wilson's noble landscapes were exposed in a shoemaker's window for sale. This Tom Malton was the son of the author of a good practical book on 'Geometry and Perspective' (of which the second edition is dated 1793), which commences with a bold and honest preface denouncing the degrading flattery and servility of the current practice of dedications. If the son was anything like the paternal schoolmaster, whose volume was a worthy successor to that written by Kirby, Hogarth's friend, I should take him to have been a clever, irascible, bluntly honest man. In after years Turner was accustomed to speak of him with hearty commendation.

By this time the boy had begun to make somewhat from his embellishment of architectural drawings. The late Mr. Duroveray, whose illustrated edition of the popular British classics contributed so largely to advance the public taste of his day, had, as I have already said, a drawing after the manner of Paul Sandby, signed

'W. TURNER,'

which he purchased from the window in Maiden Lane ; and some of the pale water-colour imitations of the same artist, exhibited in the same place, were purchased by the late Mr. Crowle, and now adorn that splendid illustrated copy of Pennant's ' London,' in seventeen volumes, which was bequeathed to the British Museum, and at present lies entombed in the Print Room, where it may be said to be as good as lost to the world.

But to return to Tom Malton's room in Long Acre. The thrifty barber finds himself profiting by the son whom he had himself taught to read (to save the dame's school, I suppose), and who could draw before he could write. The boy must be an architect, insists John Raphael Smith ; and his recommendation is supported by lucky Mr. Tomkinson, one of his best patrons. He must learn the science of perspective, even as Girtin at the same time was learning it with Dayes.

From the great resemblance between his early works and those of Tom Malton,[1] we must suppose that Turner profited by his master. Indeed, he used to say in after life, when reference was made to a school where Sandby taught, ' But my real master, you know, was Tom Malton of Long Acre.' Under Malton, then, Turner acquired his knowledge of perspective while Girtin was under Dayes ; but the two pupils must have interchanged their styles when they afterwards worked at Dr. Munro's in the Adelphi, for Girtin takes more to Malton's manner and Turner to that of Dayes.

Among others who employed him at this time was Porden, an almost unknown architect, who built part of the absurd Brighton Pavilion for the Prince Regent. Turner swept in gravel walks winding up to Porden's Grecian porches, floated blue skies over his composite pediments, and pencilled in grass-tufts and patches of dock as the foregrounds to his Corinthian mansions. Porden was delighted with the lad's facility and quickness; the designs gained much by the setting. Perhaps dilettanti praised the style, and thought it prudent Porden's, for such suppressions of authorship are not unknown. One day accordingly comes Porden in full dress to Hand Court,

---

[1] The Malton family still retain many of their ancestor's designs. They are painted in the Turner manner ; perhaps Turner worked on some of them.

with a bland proposal to take young Turner as an apprentice
without a premium. Oily Mr. Porden! Without a premium,
indeed! Why, in seven years young Turner would have
painted you drawings worth three times your premium. Go
to! Crafty old Turner, however, who has been awakening to
a sense of the numerous shillings rolling in from his son's
drawings and print-colourings, refuses the gracious offer; so
the boy still continues washing in blue skies for Grecian
temples and country-houses, and warming the foregrounds of
Corinthian mansions with semicircular orange gravel-walks.
That these tinters of backgrounds still survive may be seen
from the subjoined advertisement recently taken from a professional paper :—

TO ARCHITECTS.—COMPETITION AND OTHER DRAWINGS.

MR. COBALT BLUE, Member of the New Society of
Painters in Water Colours, &c., and so long favourably
known to architects of the first eminence, again offers his services
in tinting Backgrounds, Landscapes, and Perspectives. From the
many years' experience he has had on such subjects, he is fully
aware of the points essentially necessary to be attended to.

Address—Mr. C. B., Albany Street, De Beauvoir Town.

And now occurred one of the strangest episodes in Turner's
Art life.

His fellow-pupils at Malton's are budding architects and
engineers; and the stripling finds the world of circles and
triangles a mere wiry cobweb of a world, after the green lawns
of Brentford and the swans and osiers of Twickenham Ait.
He is no genius, they all whisper; he can do nothing. Days
and days are spent in trying to teach him a proposition of
Euclid. The Pons Asinorum requires a toll he cannot pay,
and back he goes, to cross the river some other way. His
master cannot teach him even the elementary lines of geo-
metrical drawing; he can make nothing of the boy. Old
architects now alive still remember the sad day when Malton,
in sheer desperation, shut up the books, and, rolling up the
blotted diagrams, took the crestfallen boy back to Maiden Lane.
Black enough must the arch of Hand Court have then looked

to the unpromising pupil. 'Mr. Turner,' he exclaimed, 'it is no use ; the boy will never do anything ; he is impenetrably dull, sir; it is throwing your money away ; better make him a tinker, sir, or a cobbler, than a perspective artist !' A dismal night must that have been for the old man when William was thus returned, to the utter dissipation of all the paternal anticipations. But the father entreats Malton to give the poor boy one more trial. The boy accordingly does try again ; he applies himself to his occupation with genuine industry ; but he has got in the wrong track, and his anxiety will not allow of his brain working calmly or with full power. Concentric circles fairly overcome him : this time he palpably breaks down, and is returned once more. Faint-hearted strugglers in life's race—especially young artists—remember that Newton was whipped for blundering over a sum in addition ; Watt was caned for letting a kettle boil over ; and Turner was plucked in elementary geometry, he who afterwards became Professor of Perspective at the Royal Academy, and the greatest landscape artist the world has ever known. Verily time 'brings its revenges.'

As Turner never went back to Malton, he must have acquired his elementary knowledge of perspective from Dayes, through his friend Girtin ; but it is to a certain picture accidentally seen in a window in Long Acre, and to a Vandervelde, as we have before said, that Turner is said to have owed his awakening and that 'election' which, though with some temperaments it is the slow work of years, in others bursts out in a moment, as if suddenly the great golden doors of heaven had been flung open to the votary's eyes.

The attention of Dr. Munro, George III.'s mad doctor, has just been attracted by the clever drawings in the barber's window in Maiden Lane ; Porden, the architect, employs him for skies and backgrounds ; and Raphael Smith—first in Maiden Lane, then in King Street, Covent Garden—to colour prints. With the aid of Tom Girtin, the clever apprentice of Dayes, who is patronised by the Duke of York, the boy advances.

Turner told Mr. Trimmer that he got his first lessons in

painting from a person who taught him to place a small piece of carmine in the centre of the cheek, and to lose it by degrees. This might have been the itinerant painter who painted his father's blocks, and who is actually said to have instructed him.

'I have been told,' says Mr. Trimmer, 'that old Turner was left by a relation 200*l.*, with which sum he placed out his son with an architectural draughtsman, who, seeing some of his productions subsequently, said, "He is not indebted to me for this."'

It was when Turner was probably about fourteen that his father resolved on this important step.

The several architects who employed his son to wash in blue seas of sky had gradually impressed the old man's narrow, scraping mind with a sense of the importance of the Vitruvian profession. Accordingly, not venturing to try plausible Porden again, he arranges with Mr. Hardwick, the architect, who probably has employed his boy before now ; and to that gentleman's office the boy goes, and there he continues for some time. Much of the work he then executed survives in the house of the present Mr. Hardwick, the designer of St. Katherine Docks ; and I was looking at the sketches only the other day. They show wonderful skill for a boy of fourteen, being robust and firm in execution, though prosaic and dry in style, and are careful and full of thought. The most interesting of them is one of Wanstead New Church, built by his master—a rectangular, plain structure, rather in the meeting-house manner. The sky in this is finely treated, and the dull length of the receding side-wall cleverly varied by a gleam of reflected light. Besides these there are several very early water-colour drawings of the pupil's ; perhaps as early as any of the genuine survivors of the time. One of them is a very harsh, rude sketch of Wanstead Old Church—taken before its demolition, I suppose, by way of preserving some memory of the hideous, pagan-looking stuccoed edifice, with the bricks showing here and there through the rents and doors ; and in the front a sexton digging a grave. The execution betrays a very childish hand. It looks like a first effort in sketching in colours from Nature.

The same collection, probably dating from nearly the same

time, shows Turner at Isleworth sketching the river and boats with the conventional Indian ink and umbery sails; and also at Lambeth, in a street behind the Palace, drawing a suburban inn, and some curious old houses, with a tall, gaunt, ill-shaped man leaning in a doorway. These two sketches are, however, great advances on that of Wanstead Old Church.

When Mr. Hardwick, years after, showed the artist these drawings of his youth, Turner remembered them, and, pointing to the Lambeth public-house, said, ' Ha ! yes; up against that inn there was a board stuck up, on which was written—

"BE SOBER, BE VIGILANT;"

and close by were the parish stocks, I remember.' On looking closely into the drawing, which is neat, low-toned, and careful, may be discerned a board on the wall; which probably represents the one on which the warning to topers was written, perhaps by some ecclesiastic connected with the Palace.

It is difficult to fix the exact date of Turner's going to Mr. Hardwick's, but his drawing of Wanstead Old Church proves it to have been about 1789 or 1790, when he was fourteen or fifteen years old. As the church was rebuilt in the latter year, Turner must have visited it in the former, since his drawing was anterior to the erection of the scaffold or other preliminary to rebuilding. The ugly brick tower, with its plaster half peeled off, is as crudely sketched as the trees in the foreground, where the sexton plies his vocation. Evidently it is one of the boy's earliest essays in water-colours, and it is not in monochrome. The architectural drawing of the new church, with its Portland stone porches, Doric portico, cupola at the west end, and Doric pillars, evidences an advance in art, simple as the colour is, for again the dull line of the side wall is cleverly and truthfully illumined by a white reflection from the ground; and the sky also is solid. Quite a year's difference is visible in the work of the two drawings.

In 1789, or soon after, under Mr. Hardwick's advice, Turner must have become a student of the Royal Academy. Here he drew the ' Genius of the Vatican ' and other subjects, studied hard, and pursued his work till fuller employment on topographical themes sent him wandering in Kent, Wiltshire, Yorkshire, and Oxfordshire; a pilgrimage as long as it was fruitful. On the banks of the Thames—our dear, dirty old river—Turner began his art; and on the banks of the Thames he lay down to die.

How long Turner remained in this architect's office cannot be discovered; probably the period did not extend over many months. He was but making trial of the profession, and never set his thumb on the red seal of an indenture. His ambition for copying was fast getting fainter, while his passion for sketching in the open air was increasing in intensity. His imagination was beginning to bud. Palladio, Vignola, and Vitruvius could not compete with Nature. The brush he found to be better than the compass; the pencil than the T-square. Mr. Hardwick, more generous than Porden, not desiring to enslave the boy for seven years—to his own misery, but to his master's infinite profit—went to Hand Court, and informed the barber—whom one can mentally picture listening to him, tongs and wig in hand—that the boy was too clever and too imaginative to be tied down to severe science. He recommended him to be sent as a student to the Royal Academy, for the purpose of qualifying himself for the profession of an artist.

This generous advice being accepted by the father, Turner is sent to the Academy, where he goes through the usual forms and ceremonies. As a proof of fitness, in two months' time he submits a drawing of a Greek statue, a foot long, and carefully shaded and stippled; and at the next council held by the Academicians he is admitted as probationary student. But, ere he can claim the privilege of gratuitous instruction, he has to attest his progressive fitness. A second Greek statue has to be drawn, equally accurate with its predecessor in respect of anatomical details and of light, shade, and outline; and this is to be attended by a ghastly companion—the correct outline of a human skeleton. These accepted by his judges, he will obtain the 'bone,' or ticket of admission, good for so many years; and thus he will at length attain the position of a full-plumed Royal Academy student, entitled to compete for admission into the 'Life School.'

Like most other students, Turner, I dare say, flung bread about and cut jokes on the keeper, fits of idleness alternating with fits of application. What we do know for certain is that, when he was about the age of fourteen, he was at work in the Academy school, a recognised student. At the same time he was colouring prints ; and one of his early drawings from the cast, which I have seen, is in the possession of Mr. Hardwick of Cavendish Square. It is a timid but correct representation of a statue, rudely shaded in pencil; the shadows being neither flat nor well defined. It is far from being a vigorous performance ; indeed, rubbed as it is (and it is now an antique itself), it gives no high promise of the juvenile artist. Since, however, it was used only as the mount to a water-colour drawing, possibly it might have been executed before his admission as a student to the Academy.

That Turner at a later period could draw the figure powerfully and nobly, is evident not only from the admirable picture of 'Venus and Adonis' (in the collection of Mr. Munro of Hamilton Place), which is an imitation of Titian, but from a life study (in the same collection) which I am unable to assign to any special period, but which is worthy of Etty for power, and of Mulready for correctness. The smaller figures in some of his great pictures, though mere dots, are matchless for their subtle implication. The drawing to which I now refer is a black chalk representation of a male model with one hand fastened up, the body semi-recumbent, and the abdomen and thigh in most difficult foreshortening.

With the eye of imagination we must pierce as well as we can the darkness enveloping his Academic studies to discover him seated, like his fellows, on a small, square, sharp-edged box, the slave and worshipper of some Apollo or Antinous ; in adoration before whom he scrapes his chalk, his hard black and his soft white, and kneads his bread, as now he sweeps in lines or dots, and now he stipples the shadows with anxious care. Hope and fear cast on the bending boy alternate sunshine and cloud through the Strand windows of the Somerset House Academy, in the year of grace 1789.

Mr. Ruskin in the following remarks is very justly severe on the early days of the Academy :

'It taught Turner nothing, not even the one thing it might have done—the mechanical process of safe oil-painting, sure vehicles, and permanent colours. Turner, from the beginning, was led into constrained and unnatural error. Diligently debarred from every ordinary help to success, the one thing which the Academy ought to have taught him (barring the simple and safe use of oil colour) it never taught him ; but it carefully repressed his perceptions of truth, his capacities of invention, and his tendencies of choice. For him it was impossible to do right but in a spirit of defiance ; and the first condition of his progress in learning was the power to forget.

'One most important distinction in the feelings of Scott and Turner throughout life was necessitated by this difference in early training. Scott gathered what little knowledge of architecture he possessed in wandering among the rocky walls of Crichton, Lochleven, and Linlithgow, and among the delicate pillars of Holyrood, Roslin, and Melrose. Turner acquired his knowledge of architecture at the desk, from academical elevation of the Parthenon and St. Paul's ; and spent a large portion of his early years in taking views of gentlemen's seats, temples of the Muses, and other productions of modern taste and imagination ; being at the same time directed exclusively to classical sources for all information as to the proper subjects of Art. Hence, while Scott was at once directed to the history of his native land, and to the Gothic fields of imagination, and his mind was fed in a consistent, natural, and felicitous way from his youth up, a certain good arose even out of this warped education—namely, his power of more completely expressing all the tendencies of his epoch, and sympathising with many feelings and many scenes which must otherwise have been entirely profitless to him. Scott's mind was just as large and full of sympathy as Turner's ; but having been permitted always to take his own choice among sources of enjoyment, Scott was entirely incapable of entering into the spirit of any classical scene. He was strictly a Goth and a Scot, and his sphere of sensation may be almost exactly limited to the growth of heather.

But Turner had been forced to pay early attention to whatever of good and right there was in things naturally distasteful to him. The charm of early association had been cast around much that to other men would have been tame ; while making drawings of flower gardens and Palladian mansions, he had been taught sympathy with whatever grace or refinement the garden or mansion could display, and to the close of life could enjoy the delicacy of trellis and parterre, as well as the wildness of the wood and the moorland ; and watch the staying of the silver fountain at its appointed height in the sky, with an interest as earnest, if not as intense, as that with which he followed the crash of the Alpine cataract into its clouds of wayward rage.

'The distinct losses to be weighed against this gain are, first, the waste of time during youth in painting subjects of no interest whatever ; parks, villas, and ugly architecture in general ; secondly, the devotion of his utmost strength in later years to meaningless classical compositions, such as the fall and rise of Carthage, Bay of Baiæ, Daphne, and Leucippus, and such others, which, with infinite accumulation of material, are yet utterly heartless and emotionless, dead to the very root of thought, and incapable of producing wholesome or useful effect on any human mind, except only as exhibitions of technical skill and graceful arrangement ; and, lastly, his incapacity, to the close of life, of entering heartily into the spirit of any elevated architecture ; for those Palladian and classical buildings which he had been taught to admire being wholly devoid of interest, and in their own formality and barrenness quite unmanageable, he was obliged to make them manageable in his pictures by disguising them, and to use all kinds of playing shadows and glittering lights to obscure their ugly details ; and as in their best state such buildings are white and colourless, he associated the idea of whiteness with perfect architecture generally, and was confused and puzzled when he found it grey. Hence he never got thoroughly into the feeling of Gothic ; its darkness and complexity embarrassed him. He was very apt to whiten by way of idealising it, and to cast aside its details in order to get breadth of delicate light. In Venice, and the towns of Italy generally, he fastened on the balcony buildings, and used those which he chose merely as a kind of white clouds to set off his brilliant group of boats, or burning spaces of lagoon.'

In various other minor ways we shall trace hereafter the evils of this false early training.

Turner is now growing up. He had been allowed to copy two of Reynolds's wonderful portraits ; and it is impossible to say what might have been the effect on his future life of this contact with a great painter's mature mind ; but it was of short duration, for Sir Joshua one day, engaged upon Lady Beauchamp's portrait, finds his eyes beginning to fail, and with a sigh resigns his brush all but for ever. On that sad July day when the sunshine seems to him suddenly to change to blackness, Turner might have been moved to tears upon hearing the exclamation of Reynolds : 'I know that all things on earth must come to an end, and now I am come to mine.' Blind and dejected, Sir Joshua is next seen groping about Leicester Square in search of an errant pet canary ; and soon thereafter his remains are laid in state in Somerset House ; with the young Art aspirant most likely in the crowd, and Burke and Barry, Boswell and Langton, John Kemble and John Hunter, Townley and Angerstein, looking on in the room draped with black cloth. With the death of Reynolds Turner apparently ceased to think much of portraits. Yet his picture of himself at the age of seventeen, now in the Vernon Gallery, shows that he had attained no mean skill in that branch of Art. Destitute though he may be of the grave, wise firmness of Reynolds, and unequal to the production of mellow reds, pearly greys, and sunny browns, still he must have learnt many secrets of execution from this description of copying.

It was towards the close of the great portrait painter's career that Turner had access to Reynolds's house for the purpose of copying those exquisite women and dignified men. The octagonal, snuff-strewn painting-room with the high northern window doubtless is a source of attraction to him ; but he paints in the inner room, containing the casts and the rejected portraits, and where the Velasquez and Claudes are. We can fancy Sir

Joshua, with the shrewd face and scarred lip, the white wig, the beaming spectacles, and the ear-trumpet, regarding him approvingly, and patting him on the head as he enters with his square boxwood palette and long mahogany brushes. He must often have heard Sir Joshua's oracular dicta about Michael Angelo, to which neither master nor pupil attended in practice.

Turner might even have been working hard in Leicester Square on that same sad July day (1789) when Sir Joshua rose from before Lady Beauchamp's portrait with the consciousness of failing sight; certainly not in the sanctum, the octagonal room where the red cloth platform on castors is, where the diary of visitors' names is kept, and the palette and the long cloth-yard brushes; but in the inner room, in which are a few old masters that have been frayed and otherwise subjected to scrutiny—the room where sour, handsome Northcote sits, where Zoffany chats, where Humphrey copies, and where Jones, and Gill the Bath pastrycook's son, finish drapery for Sir Joshua in the broad, generalising, historical way.

Perhaps the Duchess of Devonshire is on the easel when Turner is there; or it may be leering Laurence Sterne, or nervous Dr. Beattie, or tender-hearted Goldsmith, or that tremendous Marquis of Granby, the Mars Ultor of inn signs. We know for a certainty that the long-haired youth was present as an ardent student on that eventful day when, as Sir Joshua was lecturing in the great room at Somerset House, the floor suddenly gave way. A dreadful panic ensued among the lords and wits and artists then congregated; but Sir Joshua sat calm as Jove, and, when he was asked afterwards what his thoughts had been at that critical moment, his reply was, 'I was thinking that, if we all had perished, the art in England would have been thrown back five hundred years.' But I suppose, after the first alarm, Sir Joshua also retreated with the calmest of those who still remained unmoved, for my story has it that in escaping Turner and Sir Joshua were close companions. Little thought he then that the long-haired student, the observant lad who came to his studio to copy, and who on that occasion

moved calmly by his side, was a great genius destined to advance painting beyond the furthest triumph it had at that
period achieved.

The catalogue of pictures exhibited by Turner at the Royal
Academy, which was published by Messrs. Boone in 1857,
opens with ' Dover Castle,' assigned to 1787, when Turner was
twelve ; and the record includes 'Wanstead House, the Seat of
Sir James Tilney Long,' to which is appended ' W. Turner, at
Mr. G. Turner's, Walthamstow ;' but this picture is not by our
J. M. W. Turner, but by some one of the same name. It is
curious, however, that one of the great painter's earliest sketches
was at Wanstead, and one of his earliest copies a view of
Dover.

To most of the early Bristol drawings the family ascribe
the same date as that of his first picture, which would make
Turner fifteen at the time, 1790 being the year after he entered
the Academy, and that in which was exhibited 'Lambeth
Palace.' The Turner family also have in their possession a
drawing of Redcliffe Church, simple and careful, painted when
he was eighteen. That of the Palace is inscribed 'Done by
J. M. W. Turner, when a lad about sixteen or seventeen years
old ;' but this is evidently a mistake, as the fact of its exhibition in 1790 is well known and undisputed.

Among the boy's earlier works is a rude drawing of ' The
Clifton Hotwell House,' long since pulled down. It is entirely
deficient in atmosphere, and the objects all crowd on the eye
after the manner of a Chinese landscape. A vessel in full sail
is coming up the river, and there is a boat on shore on the
stem of which is lettered ' William Turner.'

All this time Turner was colouring prints and washing in
skies for architects. When artist friends in after life used to
express their wonder to him at his having ever worked, as
a boy, at half a crown a night putting Indian-ink skies to
amateurs' sketches, he used to say defensively, ' Well ! And
what could be better practice?' And he was right, for he
acquired facility from those sketches, and he learnt the value
of gradation from the habit of using only one colour. It prepared him to work for the engraver, who has but one colour,

and has to make the most of it. A great man indeed can do nothing, see nothing, from which he does not gain instruction. We have already observed that the existing Indian-ink drawings of Malton have much of his pupil's simplicity and breadth, with a certain stolidity and dulness superadded. Malton's school in Long Acre taught Turner how to put backgrounds to architects' drawings—one of the sources of income to the struggling artist of Turner's age. Profits were small then, and employment was scanty. The pictures of English artists, unless portrait painters, were little cared for. ' I knew him,' says an old architect still living, ' when a boy, and have often paid him a guinea for putting backgrounds to my architectural drawings, calling upon him for this purpose at his father's shop in Maiden Lane, Covent Garden. He never would suffer me to see him draw, but concealed, as I understood, all that he did in his bed-room.'

Turner at this time, says Mr. Lovell Reeve, was a short, sturdy, sailor-like youth, endowed with a vigorous constitution, and inured to hard beds and simple fare. There could not be better qualifications for the pedestrian sketching tours that he now commenced. He often walked from twenty to twenty-five miles a day, with his baggage tied up in a handkerchief swinging on the end of his stick; rapidly sketching all the good pieces of composition he met ; making quick pencil-notes in his pocket-book, and photographing into his mind legions of transitory effects of cloud and sky with the aid of a stupendously retentive and minute memory.

One of his earliest tours was to Oxford for the purpose of executing some commissions for his kind patron Mr. Henderson. The tour was made on foot, in the company of a poor artist named Cook, who afterwards turned stone-mason. Cook's feet got sore, and I believe he was soon left behind by the indefatigable Turner. As for sleeping, the thrifty lad, careful never to affect prematurely the style of the fine gentleman, rested in any humble village public-house whereat he could obtain shelter.

Mr. Ruskin devotes a very noble but mistaken chapter to a contrast between the Venice of Giorgione's boyhood and the

London of Turner's. The golden city paved with emerald (dreadful bilge-water smell, by the way, always in Venice), where the deep-hearted, majestic men moved in sway of power and war (terrible Tartars, with pozzi and thumbscrews), he compares with dirty, foggy, low-spirited, peddling, cramped-up, dear old London. And yet I really think (in all humility) that Turner had not so much, after all, to lament. If he had not men with sea-rust on their armour, he had at least freedom; he had none of those horrid burning prisons under the leads. If he had not the ships of Lepanto, he had Nelson's men-of-war. If he had not Venetian discoverers, he had Cook and Anson; and I verily believe he was not so badly off with poor Old England and her great glory as his birthright, after all.

Speaking of Maiden Lane, Mr. Ruskin says Turner all his life loved to draw and paint anything resembling Maiden Lane or the Thames shore; wherefore he liked 'dead brick walls,' blank square windows, old clothes, market-women, anything fishy and muddy recalling Billingsgate or Hungerford Market, black barges, patched sails, and every possible condition of fog, dinginess, smoke and soot, dirty sides of boats, weeds, dung-hills, straw-yards, and 'all the soilings and stains of every common labour.' He liked litter, too, 'like Covent Garden wreck after market.' 'The last words,' says his critic, 'he ever spoke to me were in gentle exultation about his "St. Gothard" —"that *litter* of stones which I endeavoured to represent."'

Turner soon began to teach water-colour drawing at schools, obtaining first five shillings a lesson, then ten shillings, and subsequently a guinea; and, his talent becoming known, he was employed at even more advanced prices to make drawings for Mr. Harrison, a publisher of Paternoster Row. He was also engaged to make views for the Oxford Almanac. Thus he acquired a reputation which caused his drawings to be sought after, and procured for him introduction to several noblemen and gentlemen. We are now arrived at the period of Turner's life when he had become fairly established in his profession.

CHAPTER IV.

LOVE AND AMBITION.

To this period of the painter's life perhaps it is that we must assign an event that undoubtedly affected his mind for ever. When he was at Margate, as we have before said, Turner had formed an acquaintance with the family of one of his school-fellows; and to his school comrade's sister he soon became attached. She has long been dead now; but, whether she was beautiful or not, Turner was one of those who could have seen 'Helen's beauty in a brow of Egypt.' That he loved her there can be no doubt. The misery of his whole scathed life, and the constant dwelling on those sad words 'THE FALLACIES OF HOPE,' are fully sufficient to prove that; and love must have transformed the dull houses of Margate, which he afterwards was so fond of visiting, to golden palaces.

Turner at this time was not, let us remember, the red-faced, blue-eyed, slovenly dressed old painter he afterwards became. He was a bright-eyed young genius, always old-looking, as tradition says, but still winning and agreeable. He did not grunt out his dry monosyllables then; the love of money had not yet corroded into him; he was not silent, suspicious, and mistrustful, though already reserved about his art and anxious about his profits.

He caught the old ailment we all have suffered from: he sighed, wrote verses, blushed, and, doubting certainties, was certain about love tokens that to any sane person were more than doubtful. He wished himself dead; he trembled; his heart was now a lump of lead, and now it seemed to sing for joy. He grew hot; he grew cold; he turned pale; he turned red; he talked nonsense at twilight; he walked, swam, rode, and drove, thinking but of her; seeing her name written on the sands and radiant in the clouds, hearing it whispered by the trees and warbled by the birds above the hop-fields of Kent.

One eventful hour in the summer dusk he dares to ask the question; and, when the bashful 'Yes' is returned, his soul

soars up again to the seventh heaven, and there joy crowns it.
Now he cares not if pictures fail or not; if work comes not, or
comes; if rivals triumph, or if patrons grind. But here a
blunder creeps into the tradition, for it goes on to say that the
courtship proceeded until Turner, at the age of nineteen, went
abroad in order to study his art, and that, before leaving, vows
of fidelity were exchanged between the two lovers. Now,
Turner did not make his first tour till he was twenty-seven; yet
the story comes to me from one who heard it from relations of
Miss ——, to whom she herself told it.

Perhaps the date of the lovers' separation was not Turner's
first Continental tour, but that of his first setting out on his
home tours in Wales or Yorkshire, betokening the increase of
business and employment—that greatest foe to love. In
default of better dates, therefore, let us take it as some tearful
day in 1796, when he was twenty-one, on which the lovers
parted, heedless of the omens of evil that issued from the
moaning sea. The young painter promises that he will write
frequently, and that their marriage is soon to take place. He
leaves her—as a pledge—his portrait, painted by his own hand.
I wish I could think that it was the one preserved now in the
Vernon Gallery—the dark, pale face. Month follows month,
and no letters come from him; but Hope, at first chilled and
sad, still guards the dear memory. The forsaken girl, however,
begins to find home miserable, for a step-mother rules there,
and treats her as step-mothers do so often treat their adopted
children. Still no line from her lover—no token that she is
remembered. If she hears of him it is only at a distance,
through some newspaper recording his excellent contributions
to a London exhibition; and this intelligence serves but to bring
the tears into her eyes, and to inflict a fresh pang of disappointment and grief. Unhappy at home, and persuaded fully that
the young artist must either have forgotten her or have transferred his love to some one else, the poor girl, with no one to
confide in, anxious to escape from her step-mother, and
feeling forsaken by one she really loved, began to listen to
another lover, who in the meantime had been pressing his
suit.

After the lapse of two years, when she believed herself to be free, Miss ——, unable any longer to resist the chance of disengaging herself from her step-mother's persecution, yielded to her suitor's importunities, and gave him her hand. The day for the marriage was fixed ; the dresses were prepared. Within a week of the appointed day Turner suddenly arrived from a distant tour. He immediately went to visit his accepted bride ; and he was frantic at hearing of what had occurred. He had written constantly ; and, notwithstanding he had received no replies, his faith in Miss —— had remained unshaken. He still loved her with all fervour and all truth ; and he urged her in the most passionate terms to break off the alliance she was about to form. But the lady, reckoning her honour involved, pronounced mournfully that it was then too late, and that she felt she had no resource left but to take the step that was imminent. Entreaties and adjurations were unavailing ; all a lover's arguments were employed in vain ; and Turner left her in bitter grief, declaring that he would never marry, and that his life henceforth was hopeless and blighted.

The marriage, which took place within a few days of this singular interruption of the course of domestic events, proved to be most unhappy ; Turner's curse was upon it, a superstitious person might have said ; and not till after it was it discovered that the cruel step-mother had intercepted all his letters. Thus the machinations of one bad woman availed to wreck the happiness of two lovers and to spoil two lives. Incalculable was the harm this early and sore disappointment wrought upon Turner's nature. He gradually began to change—not into the misanthrope, for that he never was—but into the self-concentrated, reserved money-maker. It contributed towards souring the natural generosity of his character ; yet it had the effect of intensifying his passionate devotion to Art, for his love of it for its own sake was stimulated and enforced by his love of it for the money's sake. Let us not forget that habits of thrift and accumulation had been early instilled into his mind by the scraping old barber. 'How can you wonder?' Turner used to say sometimes to his old friends. 'Dad never praised me for anything but saving a halfpenny !'

Saving was in the Turner blood ; and the thriftiness which had once been a virtue had by degrees degenerated into something almost like a vice, for the repression of which marriage and its unselfish cares alone would have availed.

About this time Mr. Bell, an engraver associated in business with Groyer, was introduced to the celebrated water-colour painter residing with his father in Maiden Lane. From his MS. notes (communicated to me by Mr. Adhurst) I find that this introduction took place in 1795, and that Mr. Bell stood by in the little room of Maiden Lane while Turner made his first attempt in oil, from a sketch in crayon, of a sunset on the Thames, near the Red House, Battersea. The sketch had been taken on the previous day, when the boat in which were Bell and Turner having, by the action of the tide, nearly got stuck fast in the mud at some distance from the shore, it was with great difficulty that they eventually got afloat, so heedless had the enthusiasts been of either tide or time. The same valuable record mentions also that Turner's first oil picture of any size or consequence was a view of flustered and scurrying fishing-boats in a gale of wind off the Needles, which General Stewart bought for 10*l.*

Mr. Bell had previously accompanied Turner on his first tour, which extended to six weeks, to Margate, Canterbury, and elsewhere. 'On our return to London,' says the writer, 'we often went on the river Thames sketching.' This brief note we are able to verify from another source ; for we find that in 1793 a Mr. Walker planned a topographical work, which was to eclipse all its predecessors, and, like the last rocket, to rise higher and shine brighter than all the rest. Girtin, growing rich and famous, and always careless and independent, at first refused his aid, but finally joined the company, while Turner, always saving and cautious, lost no time in associating himself.

In the summer of 1793, at the age of eighteen, full of hope and life, Turner started on the very six weeks' tour mentioned by Mr. Bell, his companion. Past hop-fields and green meadows speckled with golden blossoms, past old castles, manor-houses, and dockyards, the young artist must have tramped on towards the white chalk cliffs buffeted by the trampling waves. During this tour it was that Turner visited Rochester, and made a drawing, which was engraved. He had frequently visited the town before, and indeed was so fond of the river Medway that in after years he loved to throw out those dark hints that made many curious people believe he was a Kentish man. He had been to school at Margate, so dear to him in memory ; and there he first studied the green water of the incoming wave that turns the chalk rock it covers, for a moment, to an emerald wall. With the fishermen's houses at Dover and the pig-tailed sailors he was quite familiar, for he had copied and coloured them in his juvenile days from his patron Mr. Henderson's sketches. In Kent, in fact, he had received several topographical commissions. The zest of Walker's money, and the pleasures of those long country rambles, sank deep into Turner's memory ; and with the tour is connected the tradition of another oil picture by him that claims to be as early as that of the Battersea sunset.

A gentleman at Rochester, who had adopted the notion of the Sandbys that water-colour painting was but a secondary branch of the profession, now easily inflamed the lad's ambition, absolutely bringing him the colours with which to make his first effort.

It was in the parsonage at Foot's Cray, the residence of the father of Dr. Nixon, the Bishop of Tasmania, that what was Turner's first oil picture (according to this tradition) was finished ; a view of Rochester Castle, with fishermen drawing their boats ashore in a gale of wind. One who has seen it pronounces that it bears a strong resemblance to De Loutherbourg, and is well drawn ; being carefully and thinly painted, with thin scumbles of semi-opaque colour used in so fluid a state as still to show where it had run down the picture from his brush. It reveals the experienced water-colour painter at first using a new and denser material timidly, and with a hesitating hand that was soon to grow more daring.

On one of these tours Turner is reported to have subsisted for four or five days on a guinea. He once told a friend that in some of his early sketching rambles the price of the drawing— thirty pounds—did not pay his expenses ; whereupon he took

to a broader, quicker style.   While travelling for Mr. Cadell it
is remembered that he declined to saddle the publisher with
the expense of a post chaise, but took the ordinary mail coach,
for Turner was always thrifty.

CHAPTER V.

TURNER'S PREDECESSORS IN WATER AND OIL.

IT behoves me here to give a short account of the more eminent
water-colour painters who had already risen to eminence when
Turner appeared upon the stage; particularly Paul Sandby,
whom he learned to pencil from; Hearne, whose quiet purity
and simplicity he imitated; and Cozens, one of the earliest
painters who attempted to convey a sense of vastness and
multitude in sunsets and Alpine effects; a great model for
Turner at the outset of his career.   Paul Sandby, the generous
friend of Wilson and Barry, and a fashionable drawing-master
and celebrity, was born at Nottingham in 1732.   He therefore
was considerably Turner's senior.   As a boy of fourteen, he
came to London, and was admitted a student in the drawing-
room at the Tower, where he made great progress and evinced
much talent.   In 1748—that is, three years after the great rebellion in Scotland—Sandby was appointed draughtsman to General
Watson, and travelled with him through the Highlands.   On
his return to Edinburgh he made etchings of the sketches he
had taken, which on his return to London he published in a
folio; thus first attracting the world to the hitherto unknown
wild and beautiful scenery of Scotland.   In 1752 he went to visit
at Windsor, where Sir Joseph Banks purchased seventy drawings
of his scenes in the neighbourhood, that were then considered
wonderful for accuracy, taste, and spirit.

Next he accompanied Sir Joseph to Wales, where, under the
patronage of Sir Watkin Williams Wynne, he filled his portfolio
with sketches of North Wales, which soon after were published
in aqua-tinta, in imitation of bistre or Indian-ink drawings; a pro-

cess said to have been taught him by Mr. Charles Greville, an eminent dilettante.

In 1753 Sandby exerted himself vigorously to extend the usefulness of the St. Martin's Lane Academy, which Hogarth vigorously opposed, declaring that gratuitous education would fill the studios with lazy fellows whose parents wished to save the cost of schooling. This led to much bitterness of controversy and feeling ; and Sandby, himself a humorist, was daring enough, when Hogarth published his ' Analysis of Beauty,' to produce six or eight prints in ridicule of the theory of the undulating line, which Hogarth never openly resented. The good-hearted man, however, had the still greater mental fortitude to express his regret for their issue.

In 1768, when the Royal Academy was founded, Sandby became one of its members, and in the same year he was appointed to the post of chief drawing-master at the Military Academy at Woolwich, which he held down to the date of his death, which occurred on November 7, 1808.

At a time when Gainsborough's house in Pall Mall was crowded with unsold Suffolk landscapes, and when poor Wilson was hawking his Italian scenes in the smoky window of a boot-maker in Long Acre, Sandby was helping to make the landscape of our own land fashionable. In colour he was truthful and transparent, yet low-toned, timid, and conventional ; and he may fairly be considered as one of the special precursors of the style of Turner.

In 1807 Hearne published his ' Antiquities of Great Britain ' in two volumes, illustrated by views of monasteries, castles, and churches, and Turner's name appears in the list of subscribers. They were engraved by Byrne, F.S.A., in a sound but rather monotonous manner ; and the sketches for many of them seem to have been taken as early as 1778, three years after Turner's birth. Wherever there is stone it is indicated by parallel wavy lines ; the ground is nearly always filled up with dotted diamonds; and the skies are thin, flat, hard-edged, yet effective. The Gothic work is seldom given with any detail ; and, in nearly all the sketches of abbeys and ecclesiastical ruins, pigs, horses, or donkeys are introduced, by way of conveying, it is to be presumed, a

sense of desolation. The gentleman travellers, or sight-seers, wear
cocked hats and pig-tails ; and the ladies little cockle-shell hats,
poised on small mountains of hair. The letter-press is of the
baldest and most unfeeling kind ; dwelling on dates, tenures,
and the heraldry of country gentlemen who were his subscribers.
Distance and luminousness are little aimed at, and his trees are
conventionalised ; still he often gives us a sense of peculiar
calm and repose. Sometimes, as in the view of Hereford
Cathedral, he preserves the record of a memorable event. For
instance, he shows us the state of the cathedral after the fall of
the west tower in 1786.

Thomas Hearne, the designer of these engravings, and one
of the patriarchs of English water-colour art, was born at Brink-
worth in Wiltshire in 1744. He came up to London at a tender
age, designed for commercial life ; but, upon revealing a taste
for Art, he was articled to Woollett, the famous engraver of
Wilson's ' Niobe,' with whom he continued for six years. Soon,
however, he relinquished engraving ; and engaging as draughtsman to the first Lord Lavington (then Sir Ralph Payne), who
had been appointed Governor of the Leeward Islands, he accompanied him to the West Indies, where he continued to burn and
yellow for nearly five years. On his return to England in 1776
(a year after Turner's birth), his fondness for antiquities led him
to study landscape and Gothic architecture, and to the taste he
thus fostered we owe much of Turner's subsequent loitering
among ruins. In 1778 he associated himself with Byrne, and
executed the whole of the afore-mentioned drawings for the
' Antiquities of Great Britain,' which proclaimed the first dawn
of the modern Gothic and Romantic revival.

Hearne's manner was small and careful, and his colour pale
and neutral, with a uniformity of buff stone, cold green trees, and
pale, sketchy sky. As a man, he was distinguished by a good
judgment and a correct, retentive memory. His manners (his
biographer says) were ' agreeable, gentlemanly, and modest.' He
died in Macclesfield Street, Soho, April 13, 1817.

Our third patriarch is Michael Rooker, the son of an engraver
of architectural subjects, born in 1743 ; also, therefore, Turner's
senior. He was a pupil of Sandby, and in 1772 exhibited a view

of Temple Bar, which was considered meritorious. Loutherbourg at that time scene-painting for Garrick at Drury Lane,
Rooker became scene-painter for the then little theatre in the
Haymarket ; in the summer often breaking loose from the din
and smoke of London into the quiet and sunny clearness of the
country, where he took sketches for drawings to be afterwards
completed. Anticipating Turner in that respect, he made accurate drawings for the headpieces of the Oxford almanacs, which
he also engraved himself, receiving for each what was in those
days the very liberal remuneration of fifty pounds. This engagement he relinquished some years before his death, from dislike to the toil of engraving. He died March 3, 1801, and was
buried in the cemetery of St. Giles's-in-the-Fields. His drawings
(during a sale of four days) produced the sum of 1,240*l*. Rooker
was one of the first elected Associates of the Royal Academy.

Our next water-colour pre-Adamite is Alexander Cozens, a
Russian (according to a foolish tradition, an illegitimate son of
Peter the Great) who settled in London as a drawing-master.
He was a dashing, reckless painter, who, though he never
troubled Nature much, yet had considerable poetry of imagination. One of his fancies was to follow the example of Leonardo
da Vinci, who used to derive suggestions for landscapes from
the stains on old plastered walls. While Hogarth was painting
from wax figures, and Gainsborough from pieces of moss and
stones, Cozens covered his paper or china plate with blots and
flourishes of paint, from which he afterwards, with absurd
industry, culled his landscape outlines, in disdain of Nature,
who in vain spread her countless changing pictures around him.
Sometimes by chance, naïvely says Pilkington, ' he elicited
grand objects; but they were in general indefinite in their execution and unpleasing in colour.' This idealist published a tract
upon the subject of his process, and another on the ' Principles
of Beauty relative to the Human Head,' with plates by Bartolozzi,
the great coadjutor of Cipriani. He also wrote an eccentric
work on ' The Various Species of Composition in Nature.' Like
Paul Sandby, he was for some time a fashionable drawing-master.
He taught at Eton, and gave some lessons to George IV. when
Prince of Wales. He died in 1786.

His father's position must have given a fair start in life to his son, John Cozens, who, abandoning the paternal dreams and theories, went straight to the only true instructress—Nature. His colour was pale; his trees were generally of a tender willowy green, and his distances of an evanescent pallid blue: but he was, nevertheless, a true artist, and carried his art many degrees further than his predecessors. Always careful and minute, he attempted atmospheric effects undreamt of by Hearne and Sandby. He soon became a fashionable drawing-master, and the Cozens manner was long the rage with the ladies of Queen Charlotte's dull Court. His greatest triumphs in Art were obtained when making a tour with Beckford, the Wilts millionaire, a young man of the most refined taste and of the most doubtful morals, who had been brought up with Pitt, had gathered political wisdom from the Earl of Chatham, and had learnt music from Mozart and architecture from Sir William Chambers; a man who, at his majority (for the father, the democratic Lord Mayor, had died when the son was a child), came into a million of ready money and one hundred thousand a year.

Guided by and at the same time guiding the taste of the plutocrat, Cozens rambled, sketching, over Switzerland and Italy; his style soon becoming more ambitious, and soon withal more chaste, tender, and reflective. The view of a Glacier Valley,[1] executed at this period, is worthy of all praise for its multitudinousness, breadth, and grand, harmonious simplicity, as well as for the dazzling purity of its colour. In other works of his[2] I find the most admirable taste, particularly in some curious Sicilian scenes; in a pale, rosy sunset outside Rome, with St. Peter's a mere opaque mound of shadow, and quiet deer feeding dozily under the stone-pines of the Medici Gardens; and notably in a minutely finished drawing of an English country seat, with a beautiful distance of bosky, receding hills.

Dr. Munro had many Cozens's, which Turner must have

---

[1] Now in the admirable collection of that refined *virtuoso* Mr. Bale of Cambridge Terrace.

[2] In Mr. Munro's and Mr. Girtin's col ections; the first unsurpassed n Great Britain.

studied and thought over much. Some of these Girtin, I know, copied at the Doctor's request. Among them were ten sketches of 'Swiss and Italian Views,' 'View on the Coast near Naples,' the 'Bay of Salerno and Lake Nemi,' the 'Tomb of Virgil and Villa Sanazzaro,' and 'Scenes on the Neapolitan Coast.' These probably had all the artist's merits and defects.[1] Among the former we find lumpy and shapeless trees, feebly defined; water too pale; timid and rather green skies, and generally a rather feminine and small touch; while among the latter are miles of receding air, and a sublime sense of infinity, distance, and multitude, to which up to that period landscape art in any country had been a total stranger.

From this artist Turner learnt much; indeed, the poetry of his art descended from Cozens in a direct line. Dayes had made him minute and careful. From Nicholson (as he himself owned[2]), Sandby, Hearne, and Girtin he learnt much, as he did also from Wilson, Gainsborough, and Loutherbourg; but from Cozens he acquired his earliest relish for the higher poetry of landscape, and for the special qualities of infinity, distance, and aërial perspective, which subsequently became his own.

Poor Cozens became a lunatic in 1799. Whether the affliction took the form of melancholy or of ambitious madness I do not know. Mr. Henderson, of Montague Street, possesses his last work, an Italian scene executed for his father; a feeble performance, showing painful symptoms of a relaxing hand and a weakened brain. The water is rippled in a hesitating way, that only too clearly implies the extreme doubt with which it was executed; yet even this last effort has the tender air of poetry which characterises all he did. Cozens died in a madhouse under the care of the same Dr. Munro who was the patron of Turner and his young friend Girtin. Art has not sent many of its votaries to that dreadful Valley of the Shadow of Death; but Cozens, Newton, and Dadd, alas! were of the limited number.

[1] 'Cozens saw with an enchanted eye, and drew with an enchanted hand,' was the judgment of Fuseli.

[2] To his friend Mr. Munro of Hamilton Place.

Cozens washed in his effects on the spot. His cloud and distant mountain tints he compounded of Indian red, a small portion of lake, indigo, and yellow ochre ; in the middle dis-tance he used diluted black ; and his foregrounds were chiefly of black and burnt umber. His distant trees he toned down with the warm washes used in his skies, and those nearer still with yellow ochre, indigo, and sometimes burnt sienna ; the same tint, darker and stronger, being used for the foreground. The pale greenish tints of Cozens's distance are clearly visible in Turner's early works ; and Girtin also copied him in many points of manner, though he was incapable of his tender deli-cacy and poetry.

This is a fitting place to briefly particularise a few of the English landscape oil-painters who preceded Turner. Barrett, Wilson's successful rival, passed away when Turner was still young, for he died and was buried at Paddington in 1787, when Turner was twelve years old.   He was a Dublin man, and came to England about 1763. His scenes were mostly from the English Lakes, and he was famous for aërial perspective and flat distances. The dark pictures were thought the best, the warmer ones being too powerful in colour for the age ; and his blacklead studies of trees (particularly the ash and willow) were lauded as most light, firm, and spirited. His pictures were unequal, because Barrett was loaded with commissions and employed hosts of subordinates. While Wilson was all but starving, he was making two thousand a year, and carrying off Art prizes for landscapes. Eventually he failed, and caused great misery to his family by his extravagance.

Then there was Loutherbourg's pupil, Sir Francis Bourgeois, who was knighted for painting a portrait of a son of the King of Poland. He never studied from Nature, so that he soon became a mere mannerist ; his light and shade being spotty, his colouring chalky, and his figures and animals often being outrageously ill drawn.

Brooking, who was a marine painter of great promise, after having being, during his career, an obscure slave of the dealers, died at an early age. He certainly understood ships. His colouring is bright and clear, and his water transparent. His contemporary, Dayes, accorded to him the credit of having ' a firm, broad, spirited touch.'

Thomas Daniel, born at Kingston-on-Thames, was an unsuccessful painter who, on his return from a trip to the East Indies, published a fine series of aquatints. Dayes characterised his colouring as sweet, though not always solid, and his touch as firm, particularly in his buildings. Such of his sketches as I have seen seemed to me too dark and cold to represent accurately Indian atmosphere.

Joseph Farrington, R.A., like Sir George Beaumont, was a pupil of Wilson. Critics pronounced his colour transparent and brilliant ; but his composition was poor, and his pencilling often hard.

William Hodges also was a pupil of Wilson, known for his East Indian aquatint views and his illustrations to Cook's last voyage. Competent judges held that his colour was monotonous, and often abrupt and heavy. His best ideal work was a forest landscape from ' As You Like It,' well engraved by Middiman. Having realised a fortune, Hodges took to banking whereat he failed ; and at his death in 1797 he left his wife and children in great distress.

Julian Ibbetson was originally a ship painter at Scarborough, but he turned artist, and accompanied Lord Cathcart on his mission. In poverty he took to copying Berghem, in a clear, firm, rather hard manner, with clayey tones. His cattle pieces were most esteemed.

James Marlow, a landscape painter of this date, was famous for buildings. Though his distances were low and his trees ill-formed, he was admired for a rich ambery tone he knew how to impart. His master was Scott, one of the earliest of modern men to attempt to assimilate the strength of water-colour drawings to that of paintings. His ' Bridge and Castle of St. Angelo by Moonlight' is much praised by Dayes.

Abraham Pether is styled by Dayes an ingenious little man, who was not merely a painter, but also an excellent musician and mechanic. He was famous for ' sweet distances,' clear and brilliant colours, and great power of handling ; but he had only a limited knowledge of clair-obscure, and repeated himself through the infrequency of his visits to Nature.   His cousin William was a portrait and miniature painter. He also engraved in mezzotinto from Rembrandt and Wright of Derby, and executed some tolerable landscapes in oil.

Though last not least comes Wilson, whose genius, great as it was, owed so much to the even greater mind of his engraver, Woollett.   Poor Wilson, classical as he was with his Tivolis, Niobes, and solemn Italian compositions, was never appreciated in his own day; even the pawnbrokers being impatient of his fine works, and the King disregarding him, to pamper the mediocrity of West.   After a miserable life of poverty and pining the unfortunate man, who drank hard, expired in Wales, whither he had retired to end his days in peace, in a condition of extreme distress both physical and mental.

Gainsborough's graceful and poetical (but somewhat flimsy) landscapes, though little appreciated in their day, also conspired with Morland's to have an effect on the mind of Turner, than whom no man was more ready to admire and profit by the talent of another.

CHAPTER VI.

TURNER AND GIRTIN AT DR. MUNRO'S.

It is generally supposed that Turner's early patron, Dr. Munro of Adelphi Terrace, was first attracted to his works, about 1793, by seeing some of his rural sketches suspended at the dingy door in Maiden Lane.   It is not improbable, however, that he may have heard of the juvenile artist through his friend Ralph Smith, the engraver, Morland's friend, who was at this time employing a clever lad named Girtin, with Turner, to colour prints; and who was intimate also with Cozens, the celebrated landscape painter who had accompanied Beckford, the young millionaire of Wiltshire, to Italy.   If indeed the acquaintance arose as late as 1790, when Turner began to exhibit, the lad's own productions at Somerset House would have been quite enough to attract an exhibition-haunting amateur.

His other great patron in Adelphi Terrace, Mr. Henderson, probably heard of Turner through Dr. Munro. Dr. Munro, one (but not the most famous) of George III.'s mad doctors, lived at No. 4 or 6, I am not sure which ; and Mr. Henderson at No. 3 or 4 ; while Garrick, who died in 1779, had inhabited No. 5, the centre house. Topham Beauclerk—Dr. Johnson's great friend, so often mentioned by Boswell—had lived in the same row, built by the two Scotch brothers, whom the Earl of Bute patronised, on the site of one of the old Strand palaces.

On winter evenings (for in summer the lads were out at work on the Thames or in the country) Turner and Girtin repaired to the Doctor's costly furnished house, where they spent an hour or two in sketching and in colouring. The 'good Doctor,' as Turner was wont to call him in after life, was in the habit of giving them half a crown each for their night's drawing, and a supper into the bargain. Nor was Turner forgetful of the Doctor's kindness, says Mr. Alaric Watts, for a reference to that period of his career, in the course of a conversation with David Roberts, elicited the remark, ' There !' pointing to Harrow, ' Girtin and I have often walked to Bushy and back to make drawings for good Dr. Munro at half a crown a piece and a supper.' Girtin, it is noted, had enjoyed the benefit of a more regular education than had fallen to the lot of Turner, through having been a pupil of Dayes, and a student of the Royal Academy for nearly three years ; and he had also the advantage of having accompanied one of his early patrons on repeated tours amid the most picturesque scenery in England, Scotland, and Wales, at a time when his friend's means afforded him no opportunity of sketching from Nature beyond the outskirts of the metropolis.

The cheery fire, on those pleasant winter evenings, shone especially on a wild landscape by Salvator Rosa, the ' Search for Orlando ;' ' A View of the Ponte Sesto,' by Van Lint; an Italian landscape, by Zuccarelli ; ' A Boy Picking Fruit,' by Snuyders ; the ' Condemnation of Haman,' by Rembrandt— Esther, in sheeny white satin, miraculously mellow and dimpled with light, not to be forgotten ; and a fascinating Gainsborough landscape, brown and transparent ; an Italian villa, with a man leading horses, full of the Suffolk man's witchery and ease. On this last Turner no doubt often fixed his keen eyes.

The Doctor's portfolios—swollen with wealth—must also have furnished copious matter for thought. Both lads, with the plastic minds of their age, must have derived deep impressions from these sketching and copying evenings. Here Girtin saw the Canaletti drawings of London and Venice that he so much loved to imitate. Here Turner saw the Loutherbourgs, the Hearnes, the Sandbys, and the Cozens's from which he learnt so much, and which we shall presently find him first copying, then rivalling, and lastly excelling. Here, too, he saw many of those neat, careful, dry architectural studies by Dayes, Girtin's master; and here he pondered over Wilson's and Gainsborough's studies, learning grace from the former, and dignity, harmony, and breadth from the latter.

Fortunately we are enabled, by means of a catalogue of Dr. Munro's pictures kindly supplied to me by Mr. G. Christie, to learn what were the sketches the two lads executed under Dr. Munro's eye.

It is easy for us to imagine them looking round the walls and over the portfolios. They would both of them admire the playful grace of Gainsborough's sketchy landscapes; his airy pencillings, his 'Figures at a Cottage Door,' his 'Cart on a Road,' his 'Figures Dancing,' and his 'Cows Crossing a Brook.' Turner would chuckle, too, over the Suffolk man's humorous 'landscapes on blotting-paper;' and his blue paper would suggest the atmosphere that might be obtained by using such material, while Dr. Munro, contemplating some day living at Harrow, would point out Gainsborough's view of its pleasant hill on blue paper. Here Turner had access to other Gainsboroughs—a 'Gentleman's Seat;' 'Horses and Cattle at a Shed;' 'Landscape, with Pigs;' 'Road Scenes, with Sheep;' 'Trees and Pool of Water;' 'Landscape, with Tower;' 'River Scene, with Sloop and Figures;' 'Road Scene, with Mounted Figures;' and 'Rocky Landscape, with Waterfall'—all misty, sketchy, graceful fragments of an unsuccessful landscape painter's poetry.

Then, if the patron is in a very good humour, perhaps he shows them the camera obscura, with ten subjects of landscapes, sea-pieces, and moonlights, beautifully painted by Gainsborough; or takes down the spirited and clever sketch in oil, by the same artist, for them to look at—' A Landscape with an Italian villa and trees, near a wood, in which is a man leading a horse.' Of this delightful painter indeed the Doctor is proud, for he has many copies from him, and sketch-books besides, from which valuable hints are to be got.

The Doctor is also rich in Cozens's, which Girtin copies, and which Turner studies closely; landscapes and pen sketches, Swiss views and Italian views, particularly on the Neapolitan coast and from the Bay of Salerno and the Tomb of Virgil, from which the lads may learn aërial perspective and poetry combined. So also of Dayes, with his neat small figures and his slight dry manner, there are many specimens, comprising coloured sketches of antiquities, and views in Wales and on the Lakes; Kentish scenes, castles and cathedrals, in blue and Indian ink, and the Thames from Greenwich Park; just as Turner was afterwards to sketch them.

Nor did the big portfolios lack Hearne's views of the very scenes that Turner either had already visited, or would soon visit and gather laurels at; views at Bristol, and on the Border; lonely castles and Scotch ruins; Wiltshire Druidical temples; and Edinburgh and Kenilworth, so soon to be irradiated by Scott's genius.

Then there was plenty by the dull tribe; Barrett, with his commonplace parks and waterfalls; and Smith of Chichester, with his broad but slight ' Italian buildings in black chalk,' and his ' Italian views and hills on blue paper.' Of great Wilson there are ' Lambeth and Westminster from the River, on coloured paper heightened with white; ' ' Cottage from the River, on blue paper heightened by white; ' and ' View on the Thames at Twickenham, on drab paper heightened with white; ' while Sandby, Wilson's tender friend, was represented by a box of architectural designs, besides views of Conway, Dartmouth, Windsor, Salisbury Cathedral, Glasgow, and Richmond Castle. These sketches must at least have tended to direct Turner's mind to the subjects he should like best to paint in England. Finally, of Loutherbourg, whose neighbour Turner subsequently

became and whose art he so much admired, there were a few
'washed views in Switzerland;' pen-and-ink sketches on card,
made in Wales; Indian-ink notes of English scenery; studies
of shipping and costume; and one special view in the neighbourhood of Schaffhausen.

For Girtin there were Canaletti drawings to copy; and for
both, pen-washed, bistre, and Indian-ink drawings by Rembrandt, Ostade, Paul Potter, Vandervelde; above all, a robust
landscape in pen and ink by Titian, and Italian buildings by
Claude, revealing the very skeleton and framework of their art;
besides flighty sketches by Kobel, Momperts, Boucher, and
hosts of smaller men—all showing what to seek and what to
avoid.

As Dr. Munro in after years bought whole bound volumes
of Turner's sketches in Italy and Switzerland, as well as books
of sketches in Wales, round Dover, or on the Lakes, it is difficult
to determine accurately from the catalogue which were the early
sketches made in Adelphi Terrace under the system of half a
crown a night and a supper, which was continued even after the
removal of the patron to Harrow. One may feel pretty sure,
however, that the earliest were those of London and home subjects, and those that went at low prices from being in the timid
and imitative manner characteristic of youthful efforts.

Among those drawn for Dr. Munro we may specify (Views
and Ruins in colours on cards) 'View in North Wales;' a 'View
of London from the Temple Gardens, in blue and Indian ink;'
'Hadley Church, Wilsden and Waltham;' Norbury Park; Shipping in Dover Harbour; 'Imitations of Loutherbourg;' 'Views
on the Thames;' Boxhill, Mickleham, and Dorking Churches;
the 'Ruins of the Savoy Palace;' and 'a Street in Dartford'—
the same, probably, that Girtin copied from Mr. Henderson's
sketch. Now, if these were the drawings obtained for half a
crown each, the patron's kindness obtained a better reward than
such truly disinterested kindness generally does, for we find, at
the sale of his effects in 1833, the 'View of London from the
Temple Gardens' fetching four guineas, and the 'Ruins of the
Savoy Palace' three. By this time they are probably worth
twice as much, and they will go on advancing in price.

Of Girtin's drawings the Doctor does not seem to have possessed many. What he had, however, show us pretty well what sort of work Girtin did in those pleasant river-side rooms—views after Cozens, Hearne, and Barrett; pencil sketches of York; and views in Surrey (Boxhill and Norbury Park amongst them, probably sketched in company with Turner). 'Monmouth Bridge' is the furthest afield he seems to have gone, though his 'Foreign Views' may be either copies, or some of the results of his last tour in France.

At the residence of that great Art amateur Mr. Henderson, in Adelphi Terrace, Girtin and Turner also met to draw and copy, even as they did at their other patrons'. Here Girtin copied Canaletti's works especially, and studied Piranesi's prints. Mr. Henderson possessed many of Malton's engraved London views, with Girtin's copies of them; among these were the present site of the Bank, and St. George's, Hanover Square, with a sedan-chair passing. In every case the copy is better than the original, for it is rather a paraphrase than a copy, and invariably is more thoughtful and judicious. For instance, Malton has a view of the Mansion House, with the Mansion House, the special object of the engraving, thrown into shadow. Girtin in his copy has irradiated it with light, and thus it becomes the proper centre of the picture. Malton's work, though very dull and unfeeling, has a breadth which perhaps Girtin admired; and it is never small and dry, or 'cut up.' Girtin's copies of Canaletti (notably one, done with the reed pen, of the Rialto) are specially admirable, the little dotted touches being very free and decisive; and in some of those of the Venetian pictures the figures seem boldly put in at once with the brush, without pencil outline.

The same collection embraced pencil sketches of scenes at and near Dover, with pig-tailed boatmen and old, shaky seaside houses, drawn by Mr. Henderson's father, who was himself an admirable amateur artist. There is, for instance, a view of the chief street at Dartford (1794), copied by Girtin after an existing sketch by Mr. Henderson; executed, I suppose, as a sort of drawing-lesson. There are also several scenes after Hearne, one very admirable one of Tintern; and many on the river Thames, varied from sketches by Mr. Henderson of the shot-tower and buildings opposite his Adelphi balcony.

There were two water-colour drawings that specially interested me ; two rival views of Dover Castle by Turner and Girtin after a sketch by Mr. Henderson. Both are weak and timid, for neither yet had probably seen chalk cliffs or sea. In the former the cliff is grand out of all proportion ; in the latter the black roll of coast is daring, but altogether superfluous and untrue. In both, however, the boats (which they had already drawn on the Thames) are well executed. There was also a copy by Girtin of Morland's vulgar picture ' Dogs Hesitating about the Pluck,' ' Dogs Preparing to Fight over their Food ;' but there can be no doubt that the Canalettis to which he had access at both Dr. Munro's and Mr. Henderson's were what eventually formed Girtin's manner, and gave him that crisp, staccato touch which imparted such breadth to all his architecture. At first he was little more than a monochromist, his local colour being far more sombre than that of Nature ; but latterly he threw a golden tone over his work that was Turner's special delight. When a friend wished to please the latter in his old age, he had but to extract from his portfolio some of ' poor Tom's yellow drawings,' and Turner's satisfaction was complete.

Dr. Munro died in 1833 ; and at his sale Turner, I believe, bought up many of his own drawings. A portion of this catalogue, as connected with our theme, will be found in the Appendix. The Doctor is represented to have at some later date given Turner a commission for one hundred drawings ; but Turner was then rising, and abstained from executing it.

And now I must devote a short chapter specifically to that ill-fated young genius Girtin ; a painter who not only is far too little appreciated, but deserves to take the highest rank among English artists as an imitator of his friend Turner's talent.

CHAPTER VII.

TURNER'S FRIENDLY RIVAL, GIRTIN.

GIRTIN was born in February 1775 ; so that he was only two months older than his companion and neighbour. It was to Chambers Hall that Turner once said of one of Girtin's yellow drawings, now in the British Museum, ' I never in my whole life could make a drawing like that ; I would at any time have given one of my little fingers to have made such a one.' Girtin's father, who was, I believe, a rope manufacturer, was killed out hunting ; and his widow, with her two boys, the future painter and the future engraver, took rooms over a shop in St. Martin's-le-Grand. She subsequently married Mr. Vaughan, an eminent pattern-drawer ; but this was not till near her son's last illness, or after his death. Chambers Hall purchased Vaughan's fine collection of thirty-six Girtin drawings (which he afterwards left to the British Museum, where they now lie buried) from Jackson, the father-in-law of Girtin's half-brother, an eminent builder who contributed to the extension of Pimlico ; Jackson himself having bought them of Girtin's brother, who laid claim to all he could find at the painter's house in compensation for money lent. Girtin died at his brother's residence, from which he was too ill to be removed.

Girtin married the only daughter of Mr. Borritt, a rich liveryman of the Goldsmiths' Company, who was fond of Art, and had all but adopted the young artist. He regarded his son-in-law with great affection, insomuch that for years after his death he could scarcely speak of him without tears. Lord Essex, Lord Harewood, Lord Mulgrave, and Sir George Beaumont were all patrons of Girtin. A malicious notice of him by Edwards contains the reflection that ' intemperance and irregularity have no claim to longevity.' In opposition to this we have the testimony of Girtin's son, a surgeon still living at Islington, and the author of the capital book ' The House We Live In,' who says, ' My father was almost ascetically temperate, and his taste always inclined to the refined and elegant.'

In early life, as we have before seen, Girtin was apprenticed to an architectural draughtsman, who had no sympathy for his genius, and treated him as a mere means of making money.   Dayes was a conceited, jealous man, who eventually got embarrassed and committed suicide, partly, it was thought, from envy of the progress of his contemporaries—Turner and his old pupil.   His works ('Tour in Yorkshire' and 'Art Biographies') were published after his death for the benefit of his widow.   Girtin, naturally bold and reckless, soon began to find that he was more than paying back by work the premium paid for his apprenticeship.   Accordingly he refused to wash in any more skies for his master, and demanded in justice the cancelling of his indentures.   Dayes refusing to consent to it, Girtin became obdurate ; wherefore he was had up before the City Chamberlain and committed to Bridewell as a contumacious apprentice.   Here Girtin amused himself by covering the walls of his cell with chalk landscapes.   The turnkey, who was at once delighted and astonished at these works of the imprisoned genius, informed his friends of them, and brought many of them to inspect the frescoed cell.   Among others who thus heard of the singular achievement was the Earl of Essex, who hastened to the scene, and was so impressed by what he saw that he forthwith went to Dayes and bought up the apprentice's indenture, which being burnt before Girtin's eyes secured his liberty.   The Earl then took him down to the almost regal luxury of Cashiobury, where Girtin, free and happy, produced some of his greatest works.   Even as Fra Lippo Lippi's liberation from slavery was owing to a portrait he took of the Moor his master, our contumacious apprentice's release from Bridewell was effected by his decorating the white walls of his cell with chalk landscapes.

At Raphael Smith's—the pupil of Pether, the mezzotinto engraver—Turner and Girtin were associated in colouring etchings; and they subsequently worked together, putting in skies and flat tints for the architects, and touching up sketches and topographical views for amateurs.

That Dayes never forgave his contumacious apprentice is, I think, quite clear from the fact that, when years after Girtin's death he himself committed suicide under the pressure of debt, a depreciatory account of Girtin was found among his papers, and published by his executors among other fairer biographies of those contemporaries who had outstripped him in the race, and jealousy of whose success is said to have been one of the accelerating causes of his dreadful death. It runs thus :—

'This artist died November 9, 1802, after a long illness, in the twenty-eighth year of his age. Biography is useful to stimulate to acts of industry and virtue ; or, by exhibiting the contrary, to show the fatal consequences of vice. While our heart bleeds at the premature death of the subject of this paper, it becomes equally an act of justice to warn young persons against the fatal effects of suffering their passions to overpower their reason, and to hurry them into acts of excess that may in the end render life a burden, destroy existence, or bring on a premature old age. Though his drawings are generally too slight, yet they must ever be admired as the offspring of a strong imagination. Had he not trifled away a vigorous constitution, he might have arrived at a very high degree of excellence as a landscape painter.'

Of Turner, in 1804, Dayes writes—

'Highly to the credit of this artist, he is indebted principally to his own exertions for the abilities which he possesses as a painter, and for the respectable situation he holds in society. He may be considered a striking instance of how much may be gained by industry (if accompanied by temperance), even without the assistance of a master. The way he acquired his professional powers was by borrowing, where he could, a drawing or picture to copy from, or by making a sketch of any one in the Exhibition early in the morning, and finishing it at home. By such practices, and by a patient perseverance, he has overcome all the difficulties of the art ; so that the fine taste and colour which his drawings possess are scarcely to be found in any other, and are accompanied with a broad, firm chiaroscuro and a light and elegant touch. This man must be loved for his works, for his person is not striking, nor his conversation brilliant. He was born in Maiden Lane, where his father conducted a decent trade. Though his pictures possess great breadth of light and shade, accompanied with a fine tone of colour, his handling is sometimes infirm and the objects are too indefinite ; he appears, indeed, to have but a superficial notion of form.'

Girtin, who had studied under a pupil of Pether, and had acquired Malton's traditions—whatever they might be worth—from Turner, gained facility from print-colouring for Raphael Smith. From the redrawing and touching up of amateur sketches, and the washing in of skies for architects, he no doubt derived his breadth of tone and ease of composition.

At Mr. Henderson's and Dr. Munro's he copied Piranesi and Canaletti, as well as Hearne, and many of the other topographical artists of the day. Like Turner, he also studied Cozens for gradations of tone and aërial effect ; you always feel you can breathe in one of the Cozens's landscapes. By slow degrees he launched out strongly into the beautiful world of colour (his earliest works were mere monochromes in sepia)—here a red slab of tile, there a blue tinge of slate ; here a patch of yellow moss, there a grey paling. Surely, yet timidly, colour began to rise over his works, and tinge them with lustre and beauty.

From Piranesi he acquired vigour, and from Canaletti his firm staccato touch; but his sense of Art soon began to lessen his desire for truth, while with Turner, on the contrary, it only served to increase it. His boldness is often recklessness; his vigour but carelessness and disregard of form; and his breadth, always admirable, is sometimes conventional, and obtained by the sacrifice of truth. Girtin, in short, was a great artist ; but he was not a great poet, as Turner was.

Girtin and Turner's first sketching trips were short flights up the Thames, to the rickety boat-sheds and fishermen's houses at Westminster and Lambeth; old crippled buildings with overhanging gables, rusty planks crutched up with posts and logs and broken pillars ; but places where once cavaliers took wine and merchants dwelt. They delighted in these, finding in them the poetry of the ruins they had heard of as existing elsewhere, but had not yet seen. Sandby had already drawn their attention to them. In fact, it was a drawing of the Savoy to which Girtin attributed his rise in the world, even as Turner traced his success to 'Norham Castle.' The Savoy that Girtin sketched was a water-side fragment of the old palace of John of Gaunt, partly rebuilt after Wat Tyler's rebellion, and becoming, by various transmutations of time, a rogue's sanctuary, a deserter's prison, a printing-office, a beggar's haunt, and a parish church.

About the time that Turner was beginning his country tours, Girtin also was on the move. Mr. James Moore, an amateur artist and Fellow of the Society of Antiquaries, following the example of Hearne's and Sandby's patrons, took the clever dark-eyed lad to Scotland with him to make drawings and help him in sketching, altering, and putting in effects. Several of these views were subsequently published, somewhat unfairly, with only Moore's name appended to them. Turner meanwhile was busy at Oxford and Lincoln, in rivalry of numerous illustrated topographical works. For Miller's 'Picturesque Views' Girtin eventually made drawings of Windsor, Totnes, Kingsweare, Pembroke, Marlow, Newcastle, Bamborough, Warkworth, the Marine Barracks at Davenport, Appleby, Newcastle-upon-Tyne, Christchurch, Abernethy and Tarnaway Castles, and lastly Woolwich.

Girtin and Turner profited by their separation, one being in Kent and the other in Scotland. They individually became more original. The one increased in breadth and harmony of colour, while the other grew more delicate, accurate, and atmospheric ; but neither forgot the lessons he had learnt from the vast fragments of mutilated masonry at the Savoy, or from the brick towers of Lambeth Palace. They remembered the white, billowing clouds at which they had wondered as they floated through the arches of the London bridges; nor did they forget the red, brazen ruins viewed through crimson fogs, or the molten gold of London sunsets.

Girtin was too frank and careless not to have numerous amateur followers. His imitators were jealous of him. If he saw a man had no talent, he told him so, for he had none of the oleaginous insincerity of the courtier about him. One of his great cronies was 'Jack Harris,' a picture-frame maker in Gerrard Street, Soho, who, moreover, was a dealer in drawings;

and through his agency both Girtin and that wild reprobate Morland, who equally disliked collectors, disposed of many of their works. Girtin was a humorist, and that mental quality made him indifferent to high life, where fashionable indifferent-ism, reserve, and forced equality destroy all individuality. The foolish chatter of dilettanti was his aversion likewise; yet he had moments, after his visits to Cashiobury, when he would lament to his wife that, after association with great people, the manners of the women of his own rank in life became ungrate-ful to him. But, when once engaged in familiar chat about Art at Jack Harris's tavern club, he soon forgot Cashiobury and all its attractions.

Girtin now established a sketching class, which was open to patrons and amateurs as well as to artists; and for three years this little society of enthusiasts met on winter evenings for mutual improvement. 'No little coterie could be more re-spectable,' says a frequent visitor. How often the talent of the hairdresser's son must have been discussed in that circle! This society was the model, no doubt, for the celebrated one at whose meetings Chalons, Leslie, and Landseer, long after, spent so many happy hours. They met alternately at each other's houses. The subject was generally taken from an English poet, and was treated by each in his own way. The member at whose house they met supplied stained paper, colours, and pencils, and all the sketches of the evening became his property. The society consisted of ten members—T. Girtin (the founder), Sir Robert Ker Porter, Sir Augustus Callcott, J. R. Underwood, G. Samuel, P. S. Murray, J. T. Colman, L. Francia (pupil of Girtin's), W. H. Worthington, and J. C. Denham.

They met at six o'clock (hours were earlier then), and had tea or coffee, reading over their harmless cups the verses re-lating to the subject, and discussing its treatment and the several results to which it would naturally give rise. After this, with heads down and bated breath, they worked hard till ten, when came in cold meat, bread and cheese, or other such humble, solid fare; and at twelve, as the day expired, they separated with hearty greetings. Beautiful works of art were often produced in this impromptu way, and the first ideas of great pictures were often suggested in dreamy hints that sometimes possessed a charm almost exceeding that revealed by their completion. Turner, however, would never join this club. Already he had his secret, and preferred working in solitude; and he could not at this time afford to sell a ten-pound sketch for a cup of tea and a slice of bread and cheese. Perhaps, too, he was at this time slow in execution, and found two hours insufficient to elaborate any thought worth painting.

About this time Girtin had married the daughter of the rich City goldsmith, and begun to assume a position in the Art world more worthy of his vigorous genius.

He has been most unfairly set down as a careless, dissolute artist, fond of low society. Nothing can be more untrue. The fact is that he was of humble origin, and by nature rather shy. Early associations, a love of character, and a free, kindly disposition made him a favourite with all ranks, from Jack Harris, the picture-frame maker, up to Lord Elgin and the Earl of Essex. The very vicissitudes of his wandering profession led him among poor wayfarers, whom he wisely sought to please, and from whom he tried to extract amusement in turn. He was eminently a sociable man; and he liked to have friends round him as he worked, which Turner (I think wisely) did not. As a shy man Girtin perhaps felt more at ease with the poor than with the rich, amongst whom his monetary dependence compelled him to move as a tolerated inferior; a position degrading to honest pride. He began life not knowing but that he might have to go through it as a poor man; he therefore studied the poor, whom he might have to make his companions.

Far be it from me to sneer at Girtin's relish for humour and adventure, or at his going to Northumberland in a dirty collier, eating salt beef, smoking black pipes, and bandying North Country jokes. A young prig of a dandy would have maintained a dogged silence, except now and then to express his nausea and disgust at the general filthiness of the vessel and the boorishness of the 'crew.' The one would have been dubbed 'a cursed jackanapes;' the other would have been cheered at parting as 'a right-good-hearted fellow as ever trod shoe-leather.'

In the inland counties Girtin resorted to the inn kitchens, just as Hogarth did when he visited Salisbury or Rochester. There he would quaff his ale and sketch the waggoners and post-boys, as Morland sketched smugglers and fishermen in the Isle of Wight cabins, or Salvator Rosa the robbers of the Abruzzi. There he was independent, free, and happy, whereas at Cashiobury every word and look had to be planned according to the rules of polite slavery.

Had Girtin stooped to flattery, there is no knowing what social eminence he might not have gained. The inn kitchen was his not from any necessity, but from choice. Lord Elgin wished to take him to Greece with him, even as previous noblemen had taken Hearne and Sandby, and as Beckford took Cozens to swell his suite. Gentlemen of high birth were among the members of his sketching club; at which I must not forget to add that Miss Jane Porter, the novelist, was a frequent attendant, even selecting themes for the evenings. Girtin was a visitor at Lord Hardwicke's; the Earl of Essex was his great patron; and the Hon. Spencer Cowper had the finest collection of his drawings possessed by anyone of that day. Lord Mulgrave also admired his frank spirit and his genius, and after his death offered princely aid to the widow to educate her only son, which she refused with an independence worthy of the brave spirit of her husband.

Undoubtedly he never manifested the prudence and progressive ambition of his friend and rival Turner. He did not exhibit at all till 1794, when Turner had been four years an exhibitor; and he did not attempt oil-painting (his only chance of becoming an R.A.) till 1801, when Turner had essayed oil-painting for many years. The next year he went to France for his health; and in the autumn thereof he died. In the same year Turner set out on his first foreign tour. Thus it was only in his compulsory visit to the Continent that Girtin anticipated his younger rival.

An epitomist of his career says—

'Girtin exhibited his first drawing in 1794, at which time

he resided with his mother at No. 2 St. Martin's-le-Grand. It was a view of Ely Cathedral. In the following year he exhibited three drawings. These were views of Warwick Castle, and Peterborough and Lichfield Cathedrals. In 1797 he had removed to No. 35 Drury Lane, and in that year he exhibited ten drawings—an Interior of St. Alban's Church, two views of Jedburgh, two of St. Cuthbert's, Holy Island, four views of York, and one of Ouse Bridge in the same city. His next residence, in 1798, was at 25 Henrietta Street, Covent Garden, in which year he exhibited nine drawings—" Coast of Dorset," " Berry Pomeroy Castle," two drawings of Rivaulx Abbey, Interiors of Exeter and Chester Cathedrals, " Cottage from Nature," a view of a Mill in Derbyshire, and St. Nicholas's Church, Newcastle. In 1799 he had again removed, and we find him, while residing at No. 6 Long Acre, exhibiting a " Mill in Essex," two views of Bethgellert, " Warkworth Hermitage," a " Study from Nature," and " Tatershall Castle." Girtin next resided with his wife's father, Mr. Phineas Borrit, at No. 11 Scott's Place, Islington, and in 1800 exhibited—" Bristol Hot Well," " York," and " Jedburgh." This year Turner had been elected an A.R.A., and it is possible that Girtin may have aspired to the same honour, which, while he continued to exhibit water-colour drawings only, he could not obtain. We therefore find him, in 1801, sending to Somerset House for the first time a picture in oil. This was ' Bolton Bridge,' and the last time he appeared on the walls of the Royal Academy, for in the spring of the following year he went to France, and in the autumn of the same year he died.

' Amid his numerous works Girtin completed a panorama of London, said to have been one of the finest views of a city ever painted. It was amongst the first of those topographical representations which have since his day become so popular, and represented a view of St. Paul's, with the buildings running east and west. It was taken from the lofty roof of the Albion Mills, which were then standing at the foot of the south side of Blackfriars Bridge, and was universally admired when exhibited in Castle Street, Leicester Square, and in the Great Room, Spring Gardens. For several years after his death it

was rolled up and in the possession of an architect named
Howitt, in St. Martin's Lane, who, about the year 1825, sold it
to a Russian nobleman, and by him it is said to have been
taken to St. Petersburg.

'In Paris he made a beautiful series of drawings, which
were purchased by the Earl of Essex, but are now in the collection of the Duke of Bedford; which he etched and published in a style of engraving then recently introduced, but
now almost obsolete, called "aquatinta." The first of these
etchings he has dated June 16, 1802, and the last October 4
of the same year, or but little more than a month before he
died. We may almost trace the decline of the master hand in
the appended dates, and by the longer intervals that intervened
between the production of each plate: they also prove that
he "died in harness," working to the last.

June	July	Aug.	Sept.	Oct.
16	6	4	2	4 !!!
18	12	9	29	
25	16	17		the last.
28	19			

'They were published by his brother, John Girtin, a writing
engraver, who lived in Castle Street, Leicester Square, until his
house and stock were destroyed by fire a few years after his
brother's death. His wife, who was ill at the time, died in his
arms as he was carrying her out through the surrounding flames.
This fire destroyed many of Girtin's best works.'

The drawings Girtin made in Paris during the lull of the
Peace of Amiens were executed under circumstances of great
difficulty. Forbidden to sketch, he drew them from the window of a *fiacre*. They are very elaborate, and fuller of colour
than his previous works; yet they are broad and free, with
something in the village scenes of the dotty Edridge manner
that Prout afterwards imitated so successfully. The figures,
even in masses, are painted with great truth and beauty.

Meanwhile the bony hand came gradually nearer and
nearer, pushing him onward towards the clean, square-cut
grave. Girtin, who had never been strong, had dangerously

indulged in late hours. Careless liver though he might be, intemperate he never was. Brain work all day, and bodily exhaustion resulting from the social strain of sitting up through the night, brought on pulmonary disease. The spring-time of 1802, spent in the milder and more equable climate of France, was not equal to saving the invalid, especially when he persisted in spending half his day at work.

Poor Girtin died at Rome in the same autumn in which Turner went to Macon to see the vintage, and was buried in St. Paul's, Covent Garden. Turner, who always loved to speak of 'poor Tom,' must have pondered much on this death, and have set to work with greater vigour than ever to develope his own genius, lest that also should be quenched in the cold earth with similar rapidity. His generous heart could never have felt envy of his friend's talent, whatever foolish friends and small, malignant enemies may have done to rouse his jealousy, for he was incapable of such a base passion. Girtin, it should be recorded, received his first instruction from Fisher, a drawing-master in Aldersgate Street. At a later period he was under Dayes, who ridiculed the low, dirty colour of his imitators.

Turner painted his friend's portrait in oil. It is, I believe, still extant, but I have never seen it. I am familiar, however, with the admirable, stalwart likeness Cornish Opie took of him.[1] It reveals the frank, generous nature of the hearty, kindly fellow whom Turner and everyone would love; the strong black brow, the crisp dark hair curling down over it, the keen, far-seeing eyes, the bold chin, and the pronounced features. And, as I look at it, Turner's statement, 'Had Tom Girtin lived, I should have starved,' rises to the memory as testifying his great and genuine admiration of the deceased. At the time of Girtin's death, indeed, there were many who regarded him as a greater artist than Turner; and even now there are not a few who hold that, had Girtin lived, he would have surpassed Turner.

Certainly I am not of that opinion. It is true that Girtin's prodigious dash, vigour, and breadth had become the rage to

[1] Now at the house of Mr. Girtin, Canonbury Square.

such a degree that foolish admirers even imitated his low tone by washes of dirty colour, and with hues never seen either in the heavens above or on the earth beneath. They smeared immense sheets of atlas with brown and indigo, and thought they had succeeded in catching their master's gem-like depth and grand simplicity. But Girtin, though sometimes rapid, was strikingly patient. He was as bold as Wilson, and equally careful. His vigour and richness he obtained not by slavish copying of Canaletti, but by looking at Nature with his own eyes. Beginning with mere neutral greys and greens, he soon advanced to laying the chiaroscuro with the three primitive colours, producing warm and cool russets by their combination, and afterwards glazing. Subsequently, however, like Turner, he laid in at once the local colour that he saw in an object.

That Girtin had an imaginative mind I do not think. He had a fine, dashing, broad manner, frank, pure, and honest as his own nature; but he could never have designed the ' Dragon of the Hesperides,' nor could he have thrown such an atmosphere of poetry round the old ' Téméraire ' as Turner did. His mind was not so far-reaching, so insatiably active, so comprehensive. He was a social man, and he did not live for his art alone. He was not the enthusiast, all compact, like Turner; and yet I have seen (thanks to Mr. Wilkie Collins) an evening view at Battersea by him so full of tranquil poetry that I have for the moment been inclined to rank him almost above Turner. Even Cuyp himself scarcely ever produced a harmony more perfect, more full of inner yet half-dimmed light. It has something of De Wint's low-toned colour, but is instinct with a higher genius.

' Just before Girtin's death,' says one of his contemporaries, 'Dayes happened to call on a collector of drawings—an old drivelling dilettante—who patronised every dashing style, when he saw a smart portfolio inscribed in gilt letters with the name of one of Girtin's closest imitators. "What have we here?" said Dayes. " They are the works of a pupil of your old disciple," replied the collector. " Pray, Mr. Dayes, look at them, and favour me with your opinion." Dayes untied the portfolio, and on beholding the first subject, a large drawing of a mountainous scene among the lakes in Cumberland, he exclaimed, in his emphatic manner, "Oh, ye gods, the blue-bag! the blue-bag!" Dayes was a man of quick discernment, and very pointed in his remarks, and nothing could be more characteristic of the whole collection than his exclamation; and so he kept on, as he turned over every drawing, still making the burthen of his song, "Oh, the blue-bag! the blue-bag!" "So," said he, "because Master Tom [Girtin] chooses to wash in dirty water, *ergo* this puppy, this ass, this driveller, and the rest of this herd forsooth must wash in dirty water too! Yes, by the Lord! and with the very puddle-water which he has made more dirty!" Then laughing aloud, he exclaimed, "Dietreci begat Cassanova! Cassanova begat De Loutherbourg! Loutherbourg begat Frankey Bourgeois [the founder of the Dulwich Gallery]; and he, the dirty dog, quarrelled with Nature and bedaubed her works."'

A contemporary writer pronounces—

'It was a great treat to see Girtin at his studies. Unlike Turner, he was always accessible. When he had accomplished the laying in of his sky, he would proceed with great facility in the general arrangement of his tints on the buildings, trees, water, and other objects. Every colour appeared to be placed with a most judicious perception towards effecting a general union or harmony. His light stone tints were put in with thin washes of Roman ochre, or the same mixed with light red, and certain spaces, free from the warm tints, were touched with grey, composed of light red and indigo, or, brighter still, with ultramarine and light red. The brick buildings with Roman ochre, light red, and lake, and a mixture of Roman ochre, lake, and indigo, or Roman ochre, madder brown, and indigo; also with burnt sienna and Roman ochre, and these colours in all their combinations. For finishing the buildings which came the nearest to the foreground, where the local colour and form were intended to be represented with particular force and effect, Vandyke brown and Cologne earth were combined with these tints, which gave depth and richness of tone, that raised the scale of effect without the least diminution of harmony : on the contrary, the richness of effect was increased from their glowing warmth, by eutralising the previous tones, and by throwing them into their respective distances, in proper keeping. The trees which he frequently introduced in his views, exhibiting all the varieties of autumnal hues, he coloured with corresponding harmony to the scale of richness exhibited on his buildings. The greens for these operations were composed of gamboge, indigo, and burnt sienna, occasionally heightened with yellow lake, brown pink, and gamboge; these mixed, sometimes, with Prussian blue. The shadows for the trees were of indigo, burnt sienna, and a most beautiful shadow-tint, composed of grey and madder brown, which, perhaps, is nearer to the general tone of the shadow of trees than any other combinations that can be formed with water colours. He so mixed his greys that, by using them judiciously, they served to represent the basis for every species of subject and effect, as viewed in the middle grounds under the influence of Girtin's atmosphere, when he pictured the autumnal season in our humid climate, which constantly exhibits to the picturesque eye the charms of rich effects in a greater variety than any country in Europe.'

Another version of his favourite tints has it that for blue clear skies he used washes of indigo and lake, and for cloud shadows, Indian red and indigo, with an occasional addition of lake; while his favourite greys were Venetian red and indigo, or Indian red and indigo; Roman ochre, indigo, and lake being employed for a warm, and cold, and harmonious one.

Chambers Hall had a drawing said to be by Girtin, but bearing evidence of Turner's hand, in which the former—as if by an after-thought—has introduced a boat, with a figure pushing it along by means of a boat-hook. On the hill by a cathedral are some houses, and here also are notable the same handling and colour, as if, while working upon it, Turner had observed the drawing to be weak or defective in that particular part, and retouched it. Mr. Henderson has a copy of the same drawing, but by whom done, unless by his father, it is impossible to say. This also has the boat and figure above mentioned.

Like Turner, Girtin was beyond his age. His mind was an original one. Paul Sandby, Michael Angelo Booker's master, was truthful and picturesque; Hearne was chaste in manner; Cozens was better than either, for he was original and poetic, and had a great power of representing vastness of space, but still his colour was scarcely more than tinted chiaroscuro. Before that we had little but pasticcios of Pillemant and Chatelain, touched in black chalk and tinted, or drawings with penned outlines, shaded with Indian ink, and washed with thin colour. Girtin and Turner, in fact, invented modern water colours; and the former was one of the first to give the correct local colour of each object. He neglected form and detail, however, and was careless in execution. No longer using one shadow-colour for every object, he aimed at low chiaroscuro; splendid tone and magical effect of colour. His mountains were grand; his hazy vapours of receding darkness admirable; his valleys blue and fresh; and his light was exquisitely carried through. His masses were low, broad, and abrupt; his harmony was low-toned, but perfect. His clouds were generally in large groups, but sometimes quiet, serene, and simple.

'He laid on his skies first,' says a contemporary; 'and they were always remarkably luminous. Sometimes he used warm tinted paper and left it for the light; his moonlight was brilliant, his variety of light and shade captivating; but his style was not light and elegant enough for pastoral and classical landscapes, like Turner's. Girtin was a poet in a masculine way, but not an idealist.'

Girtin's imitators exaggerated all his faults. They rudely opposed cold and warm colour; they introduced shapeless architecture and nondescript trees; they left blank spaces; their animals and figures were incoherent; their darks were dotted and splashed.

It is said that Girtin was one of the first to attempt an evening effect in water colours. He had gone to an old town and made an outline sketch of it in the daytime. The same evening he passed it again, and the dark arches, the reflections, and a gleam of pale horizon determined him to attempt a twilight effect. He did so, and succeeded.

Gainsborough's cork models and careless blue paper drawings had been as mischievous to Art as the elder Cozens's mode of studying compositions from the chance figures formed by paint splashed into a china plate. So had been Sandby and

Hearne's efforts to throw back the distance by darkening the foreground and making it blacker towards the lower edge, or perpetually introducing banks and hollow trees for deep shadows, in their right or left hand corner.

But, tardy though its arrival was, improvement had come. J. Varley, who taught drawing, had introduced a classic air and poetical effect. W. Havell, who had a great love for Cumberland scenery, was broad, bold, and highly finished in style, taking out his high lights for future glazing with bread, handkerchief, and clean brush. Heaphy, whom Reynolds praised, delighted in night-cellar, fish-market, and low scenes; and Cristall, whose execution was broad, bold, and slight, drew classic figures, Virgilian peasants, and cottage groups in a large manner. But Girtin surpassed them all in depth, breadth, and harmony.

Canaletti for touch, and Rubens for colour, were his chief models. He first introduced the system of drawing upon rough-lined double cartridge-paper (purchased at a shop at Charing Cross); by which means he got force and freedom, and avoided 'the spotty, glittering glare' of the ordinary white paper. This paper became so fashionable that collectors even liked to see on their property the mark of where it had been hung across a string to dry. At first he drew in his work with a reed pen, but latterly, to avoid hardness and edginess, he blotted in the general form with Indian ink. His enemies said he used the architect's rule too much, as in his copies of Canaletti, and that his effects were tricks; but the criticism is absurd, for he really owed his success to his free hand and sure eye. He used, too, a richer palette than any of his contemporaries, with the exception of Turner, and gave water-colour painting rather the appearance of oil.

'Whoever inspected his palette,' says an Art critic, 'would find it covered with a greater variety of tints than almost any of his contemporaries employed.' He accompanied his first patron, Mr. Moore, to Peterborough, Lichfield, Lincoln, and many other places remarkable for their rich scenery, either in nature or architecture. That gentleman had a drawing by Girtin of Exeter Cathedral, which was principally coloured on

the spot where it was drawn, for he was so uncommonly indefatigable that, when he made a sketch of any place, he was
loth to quit it until he had given it all the proper tints.

The artist's best pictures now in the possession of his son
at Islington are 'Stoke Pogis Church,' 'A Mill in Essex'
(splendid in tone and breadth, occasionally degenerating into
carelessness), 'Kirkstall,' 'Rivaulx,' and 'Ouse Bridge, York.'
Chambers Hall, who once went to try and purchase some
Girtins of Jackson, overheard him in the next room rating Lord
Essex for his insolence in treating him with aristocratic pride, as
if he were a mere vendor of pictures. Of course Hall despaired
of ever prevailing on him to part with any of the pictures ; but,
to his astonishment, Jackson presented him with them all.

The artist of Turner's admiration, next to Girtin, was Reynolds. He drew his purse to buy Sir Joshua's palette to present
to Shee. 'His admiration for Girtin took a less tangible form,'
says Peter Cunningham. 'In a fit of generosity he talked of
erecting a monument to mark the grave of his friend and rival
in Covent Garden churchyard ; but when the amount was
named—a few shillings over ten pounds—he shrugged his
shoulders, and rested satisfied with the bare intention. The
grave, we are sorry to say, is still unmarked. A headstone to
Girtin would be a graceful tribute from either the Old or the
New Water-Colour Society.' Now, all this is just an example
of the way in which men write when they are determined to
blame. A tombstone *was* put up to Girtin ; but whether by
Turner or not, I do not know. A friend of mine saw it, made a
sketch of it, and warned the sexton of its precarious state.
It has since been removed.

CHAPTER VIII.

TURNER THE DRAWING-MASTER.

THERE are old people still living who remember Turner in
1795 or 1796—that is to say, when he was twenty or twenty-
one, and taught drawing in London, at Hadley (Herts), and at
other places. One of them, in a letter to myself, describes him

as ' eccentric, but kind and amusing.'   He was too reserved
and too tongue-tied to be able to teach what he knew, even if
he had cared to disclose his hard-earned secrets.   He would
hate the work, though it did bring some ten shillings a lesson.
His ambition would render him impatient of amateurs ; and
he would not flatter like the ordinary time-serving teacher.   He
would be silent and rough, and leave the puzzled pupils pretty
well alone while he thought over some sketch of his own.
Indeed, Turner always held that those who could not understand a hint would not understand a volume of advice.   Blake,
who was one of his pupils, complained of being left quite alone,
and one day, indignant at his master's heedlessness of some
commissions for drawings he had obtained for him, went and
rubbed out the addresses he had already given, and so cancelled
the orders.   I have no doubt Turner's disregard of the commissions meant something, and that he took the cancelling
quietly and as matter of course.

But, now that we are discussing Turner's life as a teacher
and a water-colour painter, let us consider the nature of the art
he taught, and the various improvements he introduced into it.

On the interesting question of Turner's method of water-
colour painting, our greatest authority, Mr. Ruskin, writes :
' The large early drawings of Turner were sponged without
friction, or were finished piece by piece on white paper ; as he
advanced he laid the chief masses first in broad tints, never
effacing anything, but working the details over these broad tints.
While still wet, he brought out the soft lights with the point of
a brush, the brighter ones with the end of a stick ; often, too,
driving the wet colour in a darker line to the edge of the light,
in order to represent the outlines of hills.   His touches were
all clear, firm, unalterable, one over the other : friction he used
only now and then, to represent the grit of stone or the fretted
pile of moss ; the finer lights he often left from the first, even
the minutest light, working round and up to them, not taking
them out as weaker men would have done.   He would draw
the dark outlines by putting more water to wet brushes, and
driving the colour to the edge to dry there, firm and dark.   He
would draw the broken edges of clouds with a quiver o   the

brush, then round the vapour by laying on a little more colour into parts not wet, and lastly dash in warm touches of light when dry on the outside edges.

' In his advanced stage, and in finished drawings, he no doubt damped and soaked and pumped on his paper, so as to be able to work with a wooden point. The superfluous colour he would remove, but he never stifled or muddled one tint with another ; nor would he use friction so as to destroy the edge and purity of a colour. His finer vignettes (as for his Milton) are on smooth cardboard, his coarser ones on sheets of thin drawing-paper; and in some of his sketches he would colour on both sides, so that the paper could never have been soaked. There is no doubt, too, that besides his work on wet paper with wooden point, and his wonderful method of taking out high lights with bread, he had many secrets of manipulation, as, for instance, in imitating the dark broken edges of waves. In an Italian drawing that Mr. Allnutt now possesses there is an evident intentional graining given to a large block of stone in the right foreground by the pressure of a thumb in half-wet colour. You can still see the impression of the pores of the painter's skin.

' The painting exhibited by Turner in 1805, " The Battle of Fort Rock in Val d'Aosta," combines all the painter's peculiarities. There are lights bluntly wiped out of the local colour of the sky, and sharply and decisively on the foreground trees ; others scraped out with a blunt instrument while the colour was wet, as in the moss on the wall, and part of the fir trees on the right-hand bank ; lights scratched out, as in one of the waterfalls; others cut sharp and clear with a knife from the wet paper, as in the housings of the mules on the mountain road ; and then for texture and air there has been much general surface-washing.

' In the " Hornby Castle " (South Kensington), painted in his best time, all his expedients to secure effect are employed. He has washed down broken tints to obtain variety and gradations in the distance by (I quote again Mr. Redgrave) abrasion of the paper, thinning the surface for sharp and sunny glitters of light, and removing lights by wiping out.'

In one drawing I find what appear to be touches of yellow chalk over a scratched surface. In fact, as Reynolds is said to have worked snuff and cinders into his pictures, so Turner seems to have rejected the aid of no accident.

Touching the gradual introduction of colour into Turner's work, Mr. Ruskin says—

' The " Crossing the Brook," and such other elaborate and large compositions, are actually painted in nothing but grey, brown, and blue, with a point or two of severe local colour in the figures ; but in the minor drawings tender passages of complicated colour occur not unfrequently in easy places ; and even before the year 1800 he begins to introduce it with evident joyfulness and longing in his rude and simple studies, just as a child, if it could be supposed to govern itself by a fully developed intellect, would cautiously, but with infinite pleasure, add now and then a tiny dish of fruit or other dangerous luxury to the simple order of its daily fare. Thus in the foregrounds of his most severe drawings, we not unfrequently find him indulging in the luxury of a peacock ; and it is impossible to express the joyfulness with which he seems to design its graceful form, and deepen with soft pencilling the bloom of its blue after he has worked through the stern detail of his almost colourless drawing. A rainbow is another of his most frequently permitted indulgences ; and we find him very early allowing the edges of his evening clouds to be touched with soft rose-colour or gold ; while whenever the hues of nature in any wise fall into his system, and can be caught without a dangerous departure from it, he instantly throws his whole soul into the faithful rendering of them. Thus the usual brown tones of his foreground become warmed with sudden vigour, and are varied and enhanced with indescribable delight, when he finds himself by the shore of a moorland stream where they truly express the stain of its golden rocks, and the darkness of its clear, Cairngorm-like pools, and the usual serenity of his aërial blue is enriched into the softness and depth of the sapphire, when it can deepen the distant slumber of some Highland lake, or temper the gloomy shadows of the evening upon its hills.'

Bearing witness to Turner's versatility, the same eloquent writer says—

' There is architecture, including a large number of formal "gentlemen's seats"—I suppose drawings commissioned by the owners; then lowland pastoral scenery of every kind; including nearly all farming operations—ploughing, harrowing, hedging and ditching, felling trees, sheep-washing, and I know not what else; then all kinds of town life— courtyards of inns, starting of mail coaches, interiors of shops, house-buildings, fairs, and elections; then all kinds of inner domestic life—interiors of rooms, studies of costumes, of still life and heraldry, including multitudes of symbolical vignettes; then marine scenery of every kind, full of local incident; every kind of boat and method of fishing for particular fish being specifically drawn, round the whole coast of England; pilchard-fishing at St. Ives, whiting-fishing at Margate, herring at Loch Fyne; and all kinds of shipping, including studies of every separate part of the vessels, and many marine battle pieces—two, in particular, of Trafalgar, both of high importance—one of the " Victory " after the battle, now in Greenwich Hospital; another of the death of Nelson, in his own gallery : then all kinds of mountain scenery, some idealised into compositions, others of definite localities ; together with classical compositions—Romes and Carthages, and such others by the myriad, with mythological, historical, or allegorical figures—nymphs, monsters, and spectres, heroes and divinities. What general feeling, it may be asked incredulously can possibly pervade all this ? This, the greatest of all feelings —an utter forgetfulness of self. Throughout the whole period with which we are at present concerned, Turner appears as a man of sympathy absolutely infinite—a sympathy so all-embracing that I know nothing but that of Shakespeare comparable, with it. A soldier's wife resting by the roadside is not beneath it; Rizpah, the daughter of Aiah, watching the dead bodies of her sons, not above it. Nothing can possibly be so mean as that it will not interest his whole mind and carry away his whole heart; nothing so great or solemn but that he can raise himself into harmony with it; and it is impossible to prophesy of him at any moment whether the next he will be in laughter or in tears.'

Of Turner's extraordinary rapidity Mr. Ruskin tells the following interesting story:—

'There is a drawing in Mr. Fawkes's collection of a man-of-war taking in stores; it is of the usual size of those of the England series, about sixteen inches by eleven. It does not appear one of the most highly finished, but is still further removed from slightness. The hull of a first-rate occupies nearly one-half of the picture on the right, her bows towards the spectator, seen in sharp perspective from stem to stern, with all her portholes, guns, anchors, and lower rigging elaborately detailed. There are two ships of the Line in the middle distance drawn with equal precision, a noble breezy sea dancing against their broad bows, full of delicate drawing in its waves; a store-ship beneath the hull of the larger vessel, and several other boats, and a complicated cloudy sky. It might appear no small exertion of mind to draw the detail of all this shipping, down to the smallest ropes, from memory, in the drawing-room of a mansion in the middle of Yorkshire, even if considerable time had been given for the effort. But Mr. Fawkes sat beside the painter from the first stroke to the last. Turner took a piece of blank paper one morning after breakfast, outlined his ships, finished the drawing in three hours, and went out to shoot.'

To the surprising knowledge of Nature displayed by Turner in some of his early water-colour drawings Mr. Ruskin bears full testimony in the ensuing admirable analysis. Of the ' Nottingham ' he writes—

' Now one instance will be sufficient to shew the exquisite care of Turner in this respect. On the left-hand side of his Nottingham ' the water (a smooth canal) is terminated by a bank fenced up with wood, on which, just at the edge of the water, stands a white sign-post. A quarter of a mile back, the hill on which Nottingham Castle stands rises steeply nearly to the top of the picture. The upper part of this hill is in bright golden light, and the lower in very deep grey shadow, against which the white board of the sign-post is seen entirely in light relief, though, being turned from the light, it is itself in delicate middle tint, illumined only on the edge. But the image of all this in the canal is very different.   First, we have the reflection of the piles of the bank sharp and clear, but under this we have, not what we see above it, the dark *base* of the hill (for this being a quarter of a mile back, we could not see it over the fence if we were looking from below), but the golden summit of the hill, the shadow of the under part having no record nor place in the reflection.   Now this summit, being very distant, cannot be seen clearly by the eye while its focus is adapted to the surface of the water, and accordingly its reflection is entirely vague and confused ; you cannot tell what it is meant for—it is mere playing golden light—but the sign-post, being on the bank close to us, will be reflected clearly, and accordingly its distinct image is seen in the midst of this confusion, relieved, however, not now against the dark base, but against the illumined summit of the hill, and appearing therefore, instead of a white space thrown out from blue shade, a dark grey space thrown out from golden light.   I do not know that any more magnificent example could be given of concentrated knowledge, or of the daring statement of most difficult truth.   And if we have a further instance in this passage of the close study which is re-quired to enjoy the works of Turner—for another artist might have altered the reflection and confused it, but he would not have reasoned upon it so as to find out *what the exact alteration must be*—and if we had tried to account for the reflection, we should have found it false or inaccurate.   But the master mind of Turner, without effort, showers its knowledge into every touch, and we have only to trace out even his slightest passages, part by part, to find in them the universal working of the deepest thought, that consistency of every minor truth which admits of and invites the same ceaseless study as the work of Nature herself.   There is, however, yet another peculiarity in Turner's painting of smooth water, which, though less deserving of admiration as being merely a mechanical excellence, is not less wonderful than its other qualities, nor less unique—a pecu-liar texture, namely, given to the most delicate tints of the surface, when there is little reflection from anything except sky or atmosphere.'

Describing the conventionalism of Turner's young days, and the daring and originality he must have possessed to have been able to escape from its paralysing atmosphere, Mr. Ruskin writes :—

'Turner's drawing is even better than a model of the ground, because it gives the aërial perspective, and is better than a photograph of the ground, because it exaggerates no shadow, while it unites the veracities both of model and photograph. Nor let it be thought that it was an easy or creditable thing to treat mountain ground with this faithfulness in the days when Turner executed these drawings. In the " Encyclopædia Britannica " (1797), under article " Drawing," the following are the directions given for the production of a landscape :—

'If he is to draw a landscape from Nature, let him take his station on a rising ground, when he will have a large horizon, and mark his tablet into three divisions downwards from the top to the bottom, and divide in his own mind the landscape he is to take into three divisions also. Then let him turn his face directly opposite to the midst of the horizon, keeping his body fixed, and draw what is directly before his eyes upon the middle division of the tablet ; then *turn his head, but not his body* [What a comfortable as well as intelligent operation sketching from Nature must have been in those days !], to the left hand, and delineate what he views there, joining it properly to what he had done before ; and, lastly, do the same by what is to be seen upon his right hand, laying down everything exactly, both with respect to distance and proportion.

'The best artists of late, in drawing their landscapes, make them shoot away, one part lower than another. Those who make their landscapes mount up higher and higher, as if they stood at the bottom of a hill to take the prospect, commit a great error ; the best way is to get upon a rising ground, make the nearest objects in the piece the highest, and those that are farther off to shoot away lower and lower, till they come almost level with the line of horizon, lessening everything proportionably with its distance, and observing also to make the objects fainter and less distinct the farther they are removed from the eye. He must make all his lights and shades fall one way, and let everything have its proper motion ; as trees shaken by the wind, the small boughs bending more, the larger ones less ; water agitated by the wind, and dashing against ships or boats, or falling from a precipice upon rocks and stones, and spirting up again into the air and sprinkling all about ; clouds also in the air, now gathered with the winds, now violently condensed into hail, rain, and the like ; always remembering that whatever motions are caused by the wind must be made to move all the same way, because the wind can blow but one way at once.'

'Such was the state of the public mind and of public instruction at the time when Claude, Poussin, and Salvator were in the zenith of their reputation ; such were the precepts which, even to the close of the century, it was necessary for a young painter to comply with during the best part of the years he gave to study. Take up one of Turner's views of our Yorkshire dells, seen from about a bank's height of expanse above the sweep of its river, and with it in your hand, side by side read the old " Encyclopædia " paragraph.'

The following quizzical note, which appeared about 1789, conveys an idea of the ordinary process of washing in skies to water-colour drawings :—

' " What a fine, clear morning ! I will do my sky. Betty ! tell your mistress, if anyone calls, I can't be seen—I'm skying. Betty ! Betty ! bring me up a pan of water, and wash that sponge : it really is so hot, I cannot lay my colour smooth. Where's the flat brush ? Oh dear ! that Prussian blue is all curdled." " Please, pa, ma says, will you take any refreshment ? " " Get away ! get away ! how ever can your ma think about refreshment, when she knows I'm doing my sky ? There, you've knocked down my swan's quill, and how am I to soften this colour ? It will all be dry before you wash out the dirt. Give me that brush. Oh, it is full of indigo ! there is the horizon spoilt ! Quick ! quick ! some water ! Oh, that's gall ! And the sky is flying away ! Why did your mother send you here ? She might have known that I was skying." '

At a late exhibition of early water-colour paintings at the Society of Arts, I made the following notes upon Turner and some of his youthful contemporaries :—

J. A. Gresse is remarkable for simple breadth. John Cozens ('Elba and Chigi Palace at Albano') is clear and pure

in tone ; in the latter, gleams of light and shade bar the height
on which the palace stands ; quite an early Turner effect.   A.
Davis's 'Landscape' is simple and pleasing.   Loutherbourg's
'Storm' is excellent for spirit, effect, and sympathy.   Edridge's
'Le Pont Neuf' is vigorous.   'Chinese Drawing' by Alexander
is neat, delicate, well drawn, and with some atmosphere.   J. T.
Serres's 'Waterford, 1785' is pleasing.   J. A. Carne's 'Wood
Scene' shews elegance in composition of trees.   M. A. Rooker's
'St. Botolph's Priory' is full of light.   Glover's 'Views of
Tivoli' are marked by good distance.   Dayes's 'Hyde Park,
with Ranger's Cottage' discloses breadth of light and true distance.   J. Webber's 'Near Bala' is full of light.   Girtin's
'Jedburgh Abbey' is monochrome almost ; but parts of it are
fine, and the general effect is broad and powerful ; while his
'St. Asaph's Cathedral' is elegant in arrangement of lines and
treatment of subordinate parts.   J. Varley's 'Beddgelert Bridge'
is admirable, with light coming suddenly through mist.   Nicholson's 'View on the Hill near Ripon' is poetical in tone, and
tranquil ; and in Howell's 'Kilgaran Castle' the forms are fine
and the colour is good.

Turner's 'St. Alban's Abbey' struck me as remarkable for
good daylight effect, still more for poetry and power ; the
'Waterfall,' for its ponderous motion, though the objects round
it are entirely artificial in colour.   In his 'Easby Abbey, Yorkshire,' the colour is nearly a deep cold green ; the warm light
on the ruined wall to the right being rather sudden and limited,
but of a delicious mellow sunset tone.

At a recent Turner exhibition at Manchester, that manly
and honest writer on Art, Mr. Tom Taylor, singled out for
praise first his outline drawings in pen or pencil, slightly washed
in Indian ink or Prussian blue, and next the noble works of his
early manhood—'The Falls of Clyde,' and 'The Loudon,'
wrought out in a narrow scale of colours, but still masterly in
composition, atmosphere, light, and shade, and subordination of
parts to the whole.   For poetry he particularised the magnificent 'Land's End' and the little vignette 'The Bridge of Sighs.'

Turner did not abandon teaching ; but teaching about this
time probably abandoned Turner.   He was too rough and odd

for fashionable people. As he was not disposed to reveal guinea secrets for five shillings, he let his pupils paint on as they liked.

CHAPTER IX.

RISE AND PROGRESS OF WATER-COLOUR PAINTING IN ENGLAND.

I WILL here devote a chapter to the origin of the art of water-colour painting in England.

That accomplished writer on antiquarian art Mr. Scharf says that the earliest Saxon and Old English MSS. have passages of transparent colour, either upon white grounds, or introduced to enrich tempera pictures—that is, pictures painted in opaque colours. Queen Mary's Psalter, for instance, in the British Museum, has its tender and delicate outlines on vellum enriched with transparent tints.[1]

The old Italian masters (as we see by the beautiful drawings in the Louvre and elsewhere) were in the habit of tingeing the glorious creatures they had built up and vivified with green and brown tints, by way of accentuating the shadows already expressed with the chalk point or the reed pen.

Raphael's angelic drawings are pure water-colours, heightened with washes of sepia and bistre.[2] The Flemings also painted tapestry on cloth or linen dipped in gum-water, and then strained on frames. The same principle is seen in the illuminated books and paintings of King René of Anjou; the weak dilettante monarch whom Scott brings so clearly before us in 'Anne of Geierstein.' His landscape and drapery painting was all the result of water-colour painting, probably derived from Flanders.

To return to the Italians: Raphael's grand portrait of

[1] The MS. Life of King Edward the Confessor, in the library of Trinity College, Cambridge, exhibits the same technical peculiarities and glazings.

[2] Sir Charles Eastlake quotes a MS. of Alcherius, of the date of 1410, mentioning the fact that London artists painted in *transparent* water-colours tempered with gum arabic.

Timoteo della Vite, now in the British Museum, shews the effect of transparent washes of colour; but Jordaens really was one of the first artists to attempt varieties and intensities of colour. Ostade and Rembrandt continued the process with great success; and pen-washed drawings of Rembrandt are also frequently found. In these Dutch drawings the high lights are not marked with opaque white, but are left on the light paper.

In England water-colour drawings were from the first found to be the quickest and best way of taking topographical views, as the originals then served as copies for the print-colourer. The opinions entertained by Mr. Redgrave, an excellent authority upon the subject of the origin of English water-colour art, are most true and valuable. He says that for water-colour miniatures the English were always celebrated from the earliest times, even on the Continent. Hillyard, the two Olivers, Hoskins, and Cooper were the best masters of this art; they used opaque pigments, but inclined chiefly to transparent colours, in which respect they resembled the missal painters. Water-colour art declined in Charles II.'s time.

Opaque pigments tempered with water were used by Lambert, the scene painter, and Taverner, whom Walpole foolishly compared to Poussin. Paul Sandby also painted sometimes in solid opaque colour; but from what was called stained drawing modern water-colour art really emerged. By this method topographic drawings were carefully wrought up in Indian ink, and a few tints of pale local colour added timidly as a finish. The South Kensington collection shows specimens by Rooker, executed in 1795; Hearne, in 1796; and Payne, about the same date. Of about the same period there are examples of Ibbetson, 1795; Pococke, 1790; Weber, circa 1790-1; and Alexander, 1796. To this style of art Hearne and Rooker (like Prout and Nash afterwards) added pen outlines drawn in before the colour was applied. This pen-drawing (perhaps in Edridge's manner) was frequently adopted by Girtin; but latterly he took to drawing with his brush only.

Cozens was one of the first men to break away from this coloured print practice to a blue and grey monochrome, feeble, yet exquisitely delicate and poetically beautiful. Turner and Girtin, however, were the real founders of the art. Turner's earliest works (executed when he was sixteen) shew negative tints and pale colour of the stained drawing kind. The 'Malmesbury Abbey,' dated 1791, and a view of Cook's Folly, on the River Avon, have the local colours added. The latter work, though probably of the same date, evidences a rising genius for colour.

About 1795 the mode of working water colours began to change. Monochrome being abandoned, the local colour was laid on at once on its proper spot, and shadowed and tinted with graduated tones varied by reflections. The old practice was reversed: the local tints were first laid in, and the shadows added after. Paintings by Girtin, before 1802, attest the change, as does Turner's magnificent 'Edinburgh,' painted in 1804.

'The grey ground is no longer used in its entirety as a preparatory method, but is judiciously confined to the large and broad masses of shadow, as on the castle in the distance, the bridge and buildings in the middle ground, and the mass of the rock on the left of the picture; in the lights local colours are laid on primarily, and advanced by their own neutralised tints or shadows.

'But even in this fine work it may be presumed that the flat masses of grey tint were judiciously retained to supply the broad cool masses of sun-setting shadow, since we find in a picture by F. Stevens, if the date (1806) is correct, how completely the art had thrown off the trammels of the old manner. The transition period was a short one; and a painting by John Smith, dated 1803, and the works by Prout, may be studied to illustrate it. Power, brilliancy, and truth were so evidently the result of the new manner that it soon superseded the old one; and such works could no longer be classed, as heretofore, as *drawings*, but began to take rank as water-colour paintings. Water colour, as thus practised, has an innate brilliancy arising from the transparency of the colours and the pure white ground of paper beneath them. This constitutes much of its peculiar excellence, subjoined to delicacy and refinement,'

Writers on Art differ widely about many things, but about none more than the true origin of water-colour drawing. The missal painters, it is true, employed water colours; but it is to Holland and the Bloemarts, Everdingen, and others that we really owe the chief improvement and the extension of the process for modern uses. Van Huyssen painted landscapes in water colours. Towards 1800 the new art broke away from mere topographic record, and culminated (but not suddenly) in Turner. Cozens used transparent colour timidly yet beautifully, washing it over drawings already made out in neutral blue tints. Poetry, delicacy of colour, and repose are his great characteristics. Nicolson, whom Turner imitated before he established his own individual style, was famous for coasts with stormy seas; and in his later works, as in the 'Waterfall of Rhaider Mawr,' he resorted to the new method of rubbing and cutting out. Cristall, about 1814, and Turner as early as 1808, wiped and picked out freely, with no hesitation. John Varley was famous for the firmness of his broad washes, the quietness of their unbroken surfaces, and the transparency and tenderness of his skies. He was among the first to practise the art of obtaining deep tone by keeping the paper he worked on constantly moist. Of Turner's best works at South Kensington, 'Eastby Abbey,' of which the tone is subdued, shews him distancing his contemporaries; and 'Hornby Castle, Lincolnshire,' reveals nearly his highest powers; while 'Edinburgh' and the 'Mist in the Valley' are fine examples of a later period.

In 1805, when Turner was in his thirtieth year, the water-colour painters had grown strong enough to brave the Academy and open an exhibition of their own. They complained that their small transparent pictures were crowded out into corners by the large, pretentious oil pictures, which made their simple works appear poor, thin, and flimsy. Resolved to do justice to themselves, they held their first meeting to consult on the matter at the rooms of a well-known miniature painter named Shelley, a protégé of Sir Joshua, and, subsequently obtaining the adhesion of the other members of their profession, arranged to open an exhibition, limited to water-colour paintings executed by the members of the new society only. Accordingly the first exhibition of the Society of Painters in Water Colours was opened to the public on April 22, 1805, at the rooms built by Vandergucht, the engraver, afterwards a picture seller, in Lower Brook Street, Grosvenor Square. After a time their exhibitions were removed to Bond Street, and next to Spring Gardens; and finally, on the changes made in that neighbourhood under the direction of Nash, the architect, to the rooms in Pall Mall East, where the annual exhibition continues still to be held. The original members were G. Barrett, J. Cristall, W. J. Gilpin, J. Glover, W. Havell, R. Hills, J. Holworthy, J. C. Nattes, F. Nicholson, W. H. Pyne, S. Rigaud, S. Shelley, J. Varley, and C. Varley, W. F. Wells.

Girtin had died three years before; the very year, in fact, in which Turner became a Royal Academician. Turner now was all intent on earning fame by oil painting, and he was, moreover, obliged to exhibit at the Academy, to which he remained always loyal.

Not having to depend entirely on topographic works, and with the aid of patrons, water-colour artists now rapidly advanced the new art. Many improvements in execution were effected, and several ingenious artifices originated. Of these the most important, Mr. Redgrave says, were due to the genius of Turner. Girtin had introduced coarse paper; Varley had attained deeper tones; and Cozens had secured matchless simplicity and purity: but Turner, versatile, thoughtful, and inventive, discovered a hundred different means of obtaining new effects. Scratching and scraping he invented for himself, besides improving the inventions of others. He was the first to take out lights from masses of colour by means of bread, which startled and delighted his rivals and friends when he exhibited works so treated; he used repeated washings, as Robson and others did later, to obtain a granulated surface; he stippled, as the cattle painter Hills afterwards did to excess.

Turner seldom, if ever, cared to sacrifice the purity and transparency of his beautiful material by loading with opaque colour in hopes of obtaining crispness and solidity. He never tried to rival oil; he never used gum or body colour, or but rarely ; and he never forgot that oil and water have each their own individual beauties, excellences, and drawbacks.

With the extension of water-colour painting, and the increase of professors of the art, arose the necessity for a special exhibition ; and, accordingly, in the year 1832 was formed a society called the New Society of Painters in Water Colours. They adopted the same principles as the older society of exhibiting only the works of members.

When Turner was only thirteen he employed himself in copying pictures by Morland in oil; but 'Moonlight at Mill-bank,' exhibited in 1797, when he was twenty-two, was his first oil-picture introduced to the public, as 'Lambeth Palace' was his first water-colour drawing similarly submitted. Another production pertaining to the same year was suspended in the ante-room in the company of his four architectural drawings. 'Morning among the Coniston Fells,' which was his effort the next year, revealed his powers as a painter; whereas, in the anxiety to avoid over-transparency and slightness of manner, his first essays in oil were dark and heavy.

In 1844 he also exhibited 'Van Tromp's Shallop at the Entrance of the Scheldt,' and 'Rain, Steam, and Speed : the Great Western Railway.' The latter is a fine effect of a train visible in a mist, with a hare running before the engine ; the velocity of the train being expressed by the large intervals between the puffs of smoke. With the lapse of time, unfortunately, the beautiful sky has become sadly discoloured.

CHAPTER X.

TURNER IN YORKSHIRE.

TURNER liked Kent, but there was no county in England to which he was so deeply attached as he was to Yorkshire. There his first great successes had been gained, and there he had found his kindest patrons. Moreover, it was on the wolds and beside the banks of the Wharfe that he first (after Wales) saw really wild scenery.

His first visit to Yorkshire cannot, I think, be placed earlier

than 1797, when he was twenty-two ; and in 1798 he exhibited
' Autumnal Morning, Winesdale, Yorkshire ; ' ' Refectory of
Kirkstall Abbey ; ' and ' Dormitory, Fountains Abbey.' In
1798 he contributed drawings of Sheffield and Wakefield to
Walker's ' Itinerant ; ' and in 1800 Whitaker's ' Parish of
Whalley ' had several by him, among which was one of Farnley.
The early Yorkshire efforts that I have seen are very fine, and
chiefly in the Girtin manner ; the hot and cold colour strongly
opposed, but both hot and cold melted into one fine and
solemn harmony of tone.

One of his oldest and dearest friends was Mr. Fawkes, of
Farnley Hall, near Otley, in Yorkshire. With this kind and
hospitable squire he became acquainted about 1802, in the
course of one of his early topographical tours in the country,
made for the purpose either of visiting Richmond for Whittaker,
or of sketching for Lord Harewood, who lived not far from
Fawkes.

Some ten thousand pounds' worth of his water-colour drawings and oil pictures still adorn the walls of Farnley.

The early oil pictures founded on Yorkshire sketches are, as
Mr. Ruskin describes them, solemn and simple in subject,
gloomy in chiaroscuro, and brown in tone. The drawing is
manly, but careful ; the minutiæ often are exquisitely delicate.
The best of these pictures are generally mere views, or unam-
bitious, quiet, detached thoughts, such as the ' Calder Bridge,' the
property of Mr. Bicknell. He had not yet founded his system
of colour ; he was feeling his way by a series of experiments.

Turner never sketched much in oil ; he always got the
colour too brown, as he once told his travelling companion Mr.
Munro. When the executors were examining his boxes after
his death, they suddenly came upon several oil sketches. ' Now,'
said Sir Charles Eastlake, ' we shall find many more of these,
for I remember being with Turner once in Devonshire, when
he made sketches in oil.' But no more were found. He generally preferred the pencil-point, writing in here and there the
colours and effects.

' In this respect he had,' writes Mr. Ruskin, ' some peculiar
views induced by early associations. His first conceptions of

mountain scenery seem to have been taken from Yorkshire; and its rounded hills, far-winding rivers, and broken limestone scars to have formed a type in his mind to which he sought, as far as might be obtained, some correspondent imagery in all other landscapes. Hence he almost always preferred to have a precipice *low down* on the hill-side, rather than near the top; liked an extent of rounded slope above, and the vertical cliff to water or valley, better than the slope at the bottom and wall at the top; and had his attention early directed to those horizontal, or comparatively horizontal, beds of rock which usually form the faces of precipices in the Yorkshire dales; not, as in the Matterhorn, merely indicated by veined colouring on the surface of the smooth cliff, but projecting, or mouldering away, in definite succession of ledges, cornices, or steps.

'This decided love of the slope or bank above the wall, rather than below it, is one of Turner's most marked idiosyncrasies, and gives a character to his composition as distinguished from that of other men; perhaps more marked than any which are traceable in other features of it (except, perhaps, in his pear-shaped ideal of trees, of which more hereafter). For when mountains are striking to the general eye, they almost always have the high crest or wall of cliff on the *top* of their slopes, rising from the plains first in mounds of meadow-land, and bosses of rock, and studded softenings of forest; the brown cottages peeping through grove after grove, until, just where the deep shade of the pines becomes blue or purple in the haze of height, a red wall of upper precipice rises from the pasture land, and greets the sky with glowing serration. . . .

'Now, although in many of his drawings Turner acknowledges this structure, it seems always to be with some degree of reluctance; whereas he seizes with instant eagerness, and every appearance of contentment, on forms of mountain which are rounded into banks above, and cut into precipices below, as is the case in most elevated tablelands, in the chalk *coteaux* of the Seine, the basalt borders of the Rhine, and the lower gorges of the Alps;' so that Turner literally humbled the grander Swiss mountains to make them resemble the Yorkshire scaurs. 'The simpler a line is, so that it be cunningly buried within its simplicities, the grander it is; and Turner likes to enclose all his broken crags by such a line.' This was one of the great man's mannerisms, as also were his elongated figures and oval elms, and his flat-topped pines.

'Nevertheless, I cannot but attribute his somewhat wilful and marked rejection of what sublimity there is in the other form to the influence of early affections; and sincerely regret that the fascination exercised over him by memory should have led him to pass so much of his life in putting a sublimity not properly belonging to them into the *coteaux* of Clairmont and Meauves, and the vine terraces of Bingen and Oberwesel, leaving almost unrecorded the natural sublimity, which he could never have exaggerated, of the pine-fringed mountains of the Isère and the cloudy diadem of the Mont Vergi.

'In all cases of this kind it is difficult to say how far harm and how far good have resulted from what unquestionably has in it something of both. It is to be regretted that Turner's studies should have been warped by early affection from the Alps to the Rhine; but the fact of his *feeling* this early affection, and being thus strongly influenced by it through his life, is indicative of that sensibility which was at the root of all his greatness. Other artists are led away by foreign sublimities and distant interests, delighting always in that which is most markedly strange and quaintly contrary to the scenery of their homes. But Turner evidently felt that the claims upon his regard possessed by those places which first had opened to him the joy and the labour of his life could never be superseded. No Alpine cloud could efface, no Italian sunshine outshine, the memory of the pleasant dales and days of Rokeby and Bolton; and many a simple promontory dim with southern olive, many a lone cliff that stooped unnoticed over some alien wave, was recorded by him with a love and delicate care that were the shadows of old thoughts and long-lost delights, whose charm yet hung like morning mist about the chanting waves of Wharfe and Greta.

'The first instance, therefore, of Turner's mountain drawing was from those shores of Wharfe, which, I believe, he never could revisit without tears; nay, which, for all the latter part of his life, he never could speak of but his voice faltered. We will now examine this instance with greater care.

'It is first to be remembered that, in every one of his English or French drawings, Turner's mind was, in two great instincts, at variance with itself. The affections of it clung, as we have just seen, to humble scenery and gentle mildness of pastoral life. But the admiration of it was, more than any other artist's whatsoever, fostered on largeness of scale. With all his heart he was attached to the narrow meadows and rounded knolls of England; by all his imagination he was urged to the reverence of endless vales and measureless hills; nor could any scene be too contracted for his love, or too vast for his ambition. Hence, when he returned to English scenery after his first studies in Savoy and Dauphiné, he was continually endeavouring to reconcile old fondnesses with new sublimities.'

The attachment of Turner to place, the debt of gratitude he felt for special localities, was a very marked feature of his character. Kent he loved, because at Dover and Margate he had made his earliest drawings, and at Rochester his earliest, or one of his earliest, efforts in oil. Devonshire he loved, because his race came from there, and because he had there collected the materials for his grand picture of 'Crossing the Brook.' But he loved Yorkshire, because from its ruined abbeys he had gathered the chief treasures of his 'Liber,' and because there among pleasant friends he had found the past and present times in the most striking juxtaposition. Long years afterwards he delighted to reproduce Scarborough and Whitby; and our only regret is that he died without illustrating Wordsworth's beautiful poem of the 'White Doe of Rylstone' with a complete panorama of the lovely Wharfe scenery. On this subject we cannot quote a higher authority than Mr. Ruskin:—

'The scenery whose influence I can trace most definitely throughout his works, varied as they are, is that of Yorkshire; of all his drawings, I think those of the Yorkshire series have the most heart in them, the most affectionate, simple, unwearied, serious finishing of truth. There is in them little seeking after effect, but a strong love of place; little exhibition of the artist's own powers or peculiarities, but intense appreciation of the smallest local minutiæ. These drawings have unfortunately changed hands frequently, and have been abused and ill-treated by picture dealers and cleaners : the greater number of them are now mere wrecks. I name them not as instances, but as proofs of the artist's study in this district ; for the affection to which they owe their excellence must have been grounded long years before. It is, I believe, to those broad wooded steeps and swells of the Yorkshire downs that we in part owe the singular massiveness that prevails in Turner's mountain drawing, and gives it one of its chief elements of grandeur. I am in the habit of looking to the Yorkshire drawings as indicating one of the culminating points in Turner's career. In these he attained the highest degree of what he had up to that time attempted— namely, finish and quantity of form united with expression of atmosphere, and light without colour. His early drawings are singularly instructive in this definiteness and simplicity of aim.'

Of Turner's early love for Yorkshire Mr. Ruskin in another place writes beautifully:—

' At last, Fortune wills that the lad's true life shall begin, and one summer's evening, after Turner's wonderful stage-coach experiences on the north road, which gave him a love of stage coaches ever after, he finds himself sitting alone among the Yorkshire hills. For the first time the silence of Nature around him, her freedom sealed to him, her glory opened to him. Peace at last, and freedom at last, and loveliness at last : it is here, then, among the deserted vales—not among men ; those pale, poverty-struck, or cruel faces—that multitudinous marred humanity—are not the only things which God has made.'

Here is something He has made which no one has marred :—

' He must be a painter of the strength of Nature ; there was no beauty elsewhere than in that ; he must paint also the labour, sorrow, and passing away of men—their labour, sorrow, and death.'

Turner's early Yorkshire drawings, such as ' Ingleborough,' are of great purity of colour and of infinite beauty. The colour has a slightly greenish-blue tinge, which, despite its mannerism, is not unpleasing. The sense of space is great without being exaggerated, and the detail is wonderfully treated. About many of the larger ones, such as 'Eastby Abbey,' there is a deep sense of profound tranquillity and peace.

CHAPTER XI.

TURNER'S FIRST CONTINENTAL TOURS.

AFTER labouring, writes Mr. Alaric Watts, for five years as a patient Academy student at his father's humble abode in Maiden Lane, Turner, in 1796, took a house in Hand Court. During that brief period he exhibited no fewer than fifty-nine pictures. In 1800, when he was twenty-five years of age, he removed to No. 64 Harley Street—a step which may be regarded as indicating improved resources; and in the same year he was elected an Associate of the Royal Academy, at which he had been an annual exhibitor for ten years. In 1802, the year of his first foreign tour (the French war having previously debarred him from travel), he attained the distinction of Royal Academician. This dignity seems to have aroused his ambition to the full, for in the same year he exhibited his first oil pictures— 'Ships Bearing up for Anchorage,' 'Fishermen upon a Stormy Lee Shore,' and 'Kilchern Castle, with the Cruchan-Ben Mountains.' His power over his new materials was at once acknowledged.

Bright the artist and Turner once either travelled together or met on the Continent. They even became intimate, and Turner is said to have bought pictures of his companion. It were curious to speculate as to what became of these. Certainly no tradition exists, known to me, of the purchase by Turner of any pictures, except Bright's and Girtin's. Mr. Newby Lowson, of Witton-le-Wear, in Durham, also travelled with Turner, I believe, in Italy. He had the reputation, confirmed to me in various quarters, of being a gentleman of great taste, and of no mean skill as an amateur; and the presentation to him of a picture in water colours may perhaps be accounted for, independently of these qualifications, by the circumstance that he acted as paymaster during the tour.

When I think of Turner abroad, I seem to see him wherever I have myself been. I find him on the Cypressed Hill, looking down from San Miniato on the red-tiled dome of Florence, on the Arno, and among the sapling trees of the Cascini. I see him at Naples, where, in the calm sunshine, Vesuvius feathers up its quiet plume of pure white smoke. I meet him at Rome under the shadow of the massy double arches of the Coliseum. I spy him on the Montanvert, watching the keen, icy Aiguille pierce the sunset. I recognise him on the blue Moselle, and, as the vessel floats on, dreaming of a still fairer river and of still more radiant skies. I observe him at Paris, in Père la Chaise, looking down upon the little dome of the Invalides, blue in the distance. Where Schaffhausen thunders, and where St. Gothard glooms, Turner presents himself to me.

The Rev. Mr. Judkin once met him suddenly at Boulogne, when he did not relish the blunt 'Why, who expected to see you here?' Mr. Judkin saw no more of him till just as he was leaving, when he caught a glimpse of him in a boat bobbing off the shore, drawing in an anxious, absorbed way, and heedless of all else. He also met him once on a Margate coach; and he found they had been travelling together for some time without any approach on Turner's part. When reproved for his shyness, Turner jocularly exclaimed, 'Why, how could I venture to speak to a great divine?'

Mr. Wornum, a great authority, assigns the date of 1801 to Turner's first Continental tour; and, according to him, Mr. Newby Lowson accompanied the painter either on this or on a subsequent journey; the condition imposed on the association being that he never sketched any view of his own selection. Turner, it is added, did not show his companion a single sketch.

He told one fellow-traveller that to mix oil with water colours was dangerous, and expressed his dislike of drawing with pens because they were apt to splutter. He used to stick wafers on a picture to show the faults. 'He preferred to spit in his powder colours,' is the vigorous phrase of an eye-witness.

Among Turner's later coloured sketches, says Mr. Ruskin, 'there was one magnificent series of sketches made on or near that east and west reach of the Rhine between Constance and Basle. Most of these were of Rheinfelden, Seckingen, Lauffenbourg, Schaffhausen, and the twin Baden.'

We so seldom succeed in obtaining glimpses of Turner on his tours that I gladly insert here two letters which show him, in October and November 1828, hard at work in quiet lodgings, at No. 12 the Piazza Mignanelli, Rome.

The letter to his old 'fat' friend Chantrey seems to me full of kindly fun and outspoken common sense. How whimsically he criticises Gibson's superfluous Cupid, and *Thorwaldsten's* (spelt wrong, of course) love of animals !

To Francis Chantrey, R.A.

No. 12 Piazza Mignanelli, Rome:
Nov. 6, 1828.

MY DEAR CHANTREY,—I intended long before this (but you will say, Fudge) to have written : but even now very little information have I to give you in matters of Art, for I have confined myself to the painting department at Corso ; and having finished *one*, am about the second, and getting on with Lord E.'s, which I began the very first touch at Rome ; but as the folk here talked that I would show them *not*, I finished a small three feet four to stop their gabbling : so now to business.

Sculpture, of course, first, for it carries away all the patronage, so it is said in Rome ; but all seem to share in the goodwill of the patrons of the day. Gott's Studio is full. Wyatt and Rennie, Ewing, Buxton, all employed. Gibson has two groups in hand, 'Venus and Cupid ;' and 'The Rape of Hylas,' three figures, very forward, though I doubt much if it will be in time (taking the long voyage into the scale) for the Exhibition, though it is for England. Its style is something like 'The Psyche,' being two standing figures of nymphs leaning, enamoured, over the youthful Hylas, with his pitcher. The Venus is a sitting figure, with the Cupid in attendance ; and if it had wings like a dove, to flee away and be at rest, the rest would not be the worse for the change. Thorwaldsten is

closely engaged on the late Pope's (Pius VII.) monument.
Portraits of the superior animal, man, is to be found in all. In
some the inferior—viz. greyhounds and poodles, cats and
monkeys, &c. &c. . . .

Pray give my remembrances to Jones and Stokes, and
tell *him* I have not seen a bit of coal stratum for months.
My love to Mrs. Chantrey, and take the same and good
wishes of,

Yours most truly,
J. M. W. TURNER.

The letter to Mr. Jones is still more frank and characteristic.
How capital his pretended fit of the spleen at seeing the white
mountains out of which Chantrey had scooped so many thousands! How considerate his anxiety that his 'people' at
Queen Anne Street should not be alarmed by exaggerated
reports of his illness !

To George Jones, R.A.

Rome: Oct. 13, 1828.

DEAR JONES,—Two months nearly in getting to this Terra
Pictura, *and at work*; but the length of time is my own fault.
I must see the South of France, which almost knocked me up,
the heat was so intense, particularly at Nismes and Avignon ;
and until I got a plunge into the sea at Marseilles, I felt so
weak that nothing but the change of scene kept me onwards
to my distant point.

Genoa, and all the sea-coast from Nice to Spezzia, is remarkably rugged and fine ; so is Massa. Tell that fat fellow
Chantrey that I did think of him, *then* (but not the first or the
last time) of the thousands he had made out of those marble
craigs which only afforded me a sour bottle of wine and a sketch ;
but he deserves everything which is good, though he did give
me a fit of the spleen at Carrara.

Sorry to hear your friend Sir Henry Bunbury has lost his
lady. How did you know this ? You will answer, of Captain
Napier, at *Siena*. The letter announcing the sad event arrived
the next day after I got there. They were on the wing—Mrs.
W. Light to Leghorn, to meet Colonel Light, and Captain and

Mrs. Napier for Naples ; so, all things considered, I determined to quit instanter, instead of adding to the trouble.

Hope that you have been better than usual, and that the pictures go on well. If you should be passing Queen Anne Street, just say I am well and in Rome, for I fear young Hakewell has written to his father of my being unwell ; and may I trouble you to drop a line into the twopenny post to Mr. C. Heath, 6 Seymour Place, New Pancras Church, or send my people to tell him that, if he has anything to send me, to put it up in a letter (it is the most sure way of its reaching me), directed for me, No. 12 Piazza Mignanelli, Rome, and to which place I hope you will send me a line? Excuse my troubling you with my requests of business. Remember me to all friends. So God bless you. Adieu.

J. M. W. TURNER.

Mr. Rippingille, who instituted enquiries in Rome as to the appreciation of Turner, writes—

' No other country appears to have felt his kind of merit as it was felt at home, and in this we see the clue to Turner's great success and popularity. I do not find that in foreign countries Turner was at all esteemed. In a subsequent portion of his life Turner was in Rome, and there exhibited pictures which (no disgrace, I must say) won him no credit. At the time he was in the Eternal City, an English tradesman was living there who made a great to do, and sold English mustard ; and, when his namesake came and exposed his wares, the Romans, who are a peculiar class of jokers, proclaimed that one sold mustard and the other painted it. Some intelligent Romans, with whom I talked, wondered that the English could be so devoid of taste as to admire and tolerate such extravagant productions.'

There is a story told of Turner meeting a well-known water-colour painter on the Moselle, and fraternising with him. He even went so far as to invite him to rather a handsome dinner, whereat the wine passed freely as the comrades discussed the scenery with enthusiasm. At last it was time to separate, and Turner and his guest exchanged friendly farewells. The next

morning the weaker vessel arose late. His first enquiry was if
Monsieur Turner had gone out sketching yet. 'Left for good at
five o'clock this morning, and said you would settle both bills,'
was the petrifying answer.

Home of course returned the artist to give in the last bulletin
of Turner's meanness; not seeing that the whole thing was a
rough practical joke, which no one would have enjoyed more
than the perpetrator himself, had he been the victim.

Mr. John Murray, Byron's eminent publisher, met Turner
twice; once at Dijon and once in the Tyrol. At the latter
place he had much court paid to him by a small official of the
neighbourhood who had a taste for painting. A carriage was
obtained; and away went Turner and his cicerone to visit every
rock worth seeing as a point of view in the valley of the Inn:
but Turner was very careful to let the over-zealous and probably interested official pay for the carriage. One night he
took up his candle, and wished Mr. Murray good night. The
next morning he was off at daybreak, without a word of salutation.
It was eccentric, this abruptness; but, unless he had loaded
Mr. Murray with professions of friendship, we can see no insincerity in it.

One day Mr. G. Jones, having discussed the merits of the
'Bay of Baiæ' with a traveller who had recently been there,
was surprised to find that half the scene was sheer invention;
upon which Mr. Jones playfully wrote on the frame, 'SPLEN-
DIDE MENDAX.' When the inscription caught his eye, Turner
only laughed; and when his friend protested that, where he had
planted some hills with vineyards, there was nothing in reality
but a few dry sticks, he observed with a smile that it was all
there, and that all poets were liars. The inscription remained on
the frame of the picture for years; Turner never removed it.

Of all his tours, the amplest records pertain to the one
he took with Mr. Munro in 1836; and this one of itself
attests the painter's almost womanly tenderness for those he
really received into friendship. A serious depression of spirits
having fallen on Mr. Munro, which gradually became a burden
he could not shake off, Turner proposed to divert his mind

into fresh channels by the expedient of travel. Starting from a part of France which Turner desired to inspect, and after visiting Chamouni and Mont Blanc, which he ardently longed to behold, they went by the Valley of Aosta into Italy, re-tracing their steps by way of Turin.

Mr. Munro found, as he told me himself, that Turner enjoyed himself in his way—which was a sort of honest Diogenes way—but he disliked teasing questions as to how he got this or that colour. On one occasion, in the Aosta Valley, he was dis-satisfied with a sketch, which he altered and sponged till the drawing got a sort of white greenness about it which was not pleasant. He became quite fretful thereat, and his abuse of colour-sketching wound up with the remark, 'I could have done twice as much with the pencil.' His first enquiry in the morning, when they started to sketch, was always, 'Have you got the sponge?' It was with the sponge that he obtained many of his misty and aërial effects.

Turner never rhapsodised about scenery, but at some dis-tance from his companion—generally much higher—applied himself to work in a silent, concentrated frame of mind. The superior elevation he required for the purpose of obtaining greater distance and more of a bird's-eye view. The sketches were rapid, and with the aid of his tremendous memory were completed subsequently, at leisure, at the inn. He had a horror of what he said Wilson called 'being too mappy.' He used no maul-stick; his touch was so sure and decisive, and his materials were of the rudest—brushes worn away to single hairs, and now thrice as valuable as they were when new.

If you bore with his way, Mr. Munro said, it was easy to get on very pleasantly with him. Indeed, there was a sort of half-resolution come to that the two should visit the East in company.

It was in the course of this tour that the sketch was taken which was afterwards converted into his picture (now in Mr. Munro's gallery) of the 'Avalanche;' one of his grandest and wildest flights of imagination.

When Mr. Munro gave him a commission for a view of

modern Rome from a fine point that included the Tiber and some of the chief antiquities, the artist employed some time in looking for the place indicated, surprising Sir Charles Eastlake, who was with him, by his solicitude to discover the precise spot. He had been particularly anxious to comply with the requirements of 'a copy,' not an ideal picture. A 'copy' was asked for, and a copy he made. So faithful, indeed, has the painter been in this beautiful picture that he has, even at some peril to his success, introduced in the left-hand foreground a long monotonous row of modern houses ; but these he has so cleverly varied with slant shadows that they become pleasing and conduct the eye to where it should go—the matchless distance. It was, I believe, for this painting that Mr. Munro gave the artist his own price, only 300*l.* ; Turner refusing to raise the price beyond that of some other picture Mr. Munro had had. He was full of these punctilious notions of justice.

Turner also went to Venice for Mr. Munro, insisting on his travelling expenses being paid. The commission was for a drawing ; but, on his return, he brought a large, ambitious painting, which Mr. Munro never much took to. The artist, who was greatly mortified at seeing his patron's disappointment, at first declined to sell him the picture ; but at last he consented. When Mr. Munro got tired of it a few years ago it produced 3,000*l.*

Among the Turner pictures in Mr. Munro's collection is a view of the Forum, a beautiful work of genius. Some black goats are in the cool grey foreground ; but the church cupola on the left is rendered unpleasant by being painted in that mustardy yellow which furnished the wits of modern Rome with so many jokes. Another is 'Cicero's Villa,' and a third the 'Wreck Buoy'—an early picture, on which Turner spent six laborious days, quite at the end of his life, much to Mr. Munro's horror; but it came out gloriously with a whitened, misty sky and a double rainbow.

The last special delight of Turner in foreign travel was the Lake of Lucerne and the scenery of Mount St. Gothard. Of these latter works Mr. Ruskin says :—

'The drawing of the St. Gothard was designed from a sketch taken in the year 1843; but with it was made another drawing. Turner made in that year a series of sketches taken in the neighbourhood of the Pass; among others, one of the Valley of Goldau, covered as it is by the ruins of the Rossberg. Knowing his fondness for fallen stones, I chose this Goldau subject as a companion to the "St. Gothard."

'It is a subject which, like the "St. Gothard," is far too full of detail to admit of reduction. [The engravers found Turner's pictures very unprofitable work; they were so full and so subtle.] It is, besides, more than usually difficult to translate this drawing into black and white, because much of the light on the clouds is distinguished merely by orange or purple colour from the green greys which, though not darker than the warm hues, have the effect of shade from their coldness, but cannot be marked as shade in the engraving without too great increase of depth. Enough, however, has been done to give some idea of the elements of Turner's design.

'Detailed accounts of the Rossberg Fall may be found in any ordinary Swiss Guide. The only points we have to notice respecting it are, that the mountain was composed of an indurated gravel disposed in oblique beds sloping towards the valley. A portion of one of these beds gave way and half filled the valley beneath, burying five villages, together with the principal one of Goldau, and partly choking up a little lake, the streamlets which supplied it forming irregular pools among the fallen fragments. . . . Turner has chosen his position on some of the higher heaps of ruin, looking down towards the Lake of Zug, which is seen under the sunset, the spire of the tower of Aart on its shores just relieved against the light of the waves.

'The Rossberg itself, never steep, and still more reduced in terror by the fall of a portion of it, was not available to him as a form explanatory of the catastrophe; and even the slopes of the Righi on the left are not, in reality, as uninterrupted in their slope as he has drawn them; but he felt the connexion of this structure with the ruin amidst which he stood, and brought the long lines of danger clear against the sunset, and as straight as its own retiring rays,'

Turner had a profound sense of the tragic. The beautiful and the terrible were both at his command. His shipwrecks are full of terror ; and from these he is able to pass away into sunshine, or leap up in a rainbow, and so scale heaven. Now he will watch children at play ; and the same evening, perhaps, he will draw Rizpah guarding those shrouded skeletons beside the moon-lit barley-field.

'Turner's imagination was always instinctively in possession of those truths which lie deepest, and are most essentially linked together, in the expression of a scene.'

He did not care for the mere prosaic fact of any place ; he was no local topographer ; he did not draw for the townsmen or villagers. What he tried to do was to crowd into one drawing all the salient features of the whole neighbourhood. Knowing how limited Art was, he sought to extend its frontier. If a steeple is a hundred feet high, it is sometimes necessary to draw it as if it were three hundred, to convey the effect of its real measurement.

One or two points connected with these twin drawings, says Mr. Ruskin, are of yet more touching interest. 'They are the last drawings which Turner ever made with unabated power. The one of the St. Gothard, speaking with strict accuracy, is the last drawing ; for that of the Goldau, though majestic to the utmost in conception, is less carefully finished, and shows, in the execution of parts of the sky, signs of impatience, caused by the first feeling of decline of strength. But the Goldau is still a noble companion to it—more solemn in thought, more sublime in colour, and, in certain points of poetical treatment, especially characteristic of the master's mind in earlier days. He was very definitely in the habit of indicating the association of any subject with circumstances of death, especially the death of multitudes, by placing it under one of his most deeply crimsoned sunset skies. The colour of blood is thus plainly taken for the leading tone in the storm-clouds above the Slave Ship. It occurs with similar distinctness in the much earlier picture of "Ulysses and Polyphemus," in that of "Napoleon at St. Helena," and, subdued by softer hues, in "The Old Téméraire." The sky of this "Goldau" is, in its scarlet and crimson, the deepest in tone of all that I know of Turner's drawings.   Another feeling, traceable in several of his former works, is an acute sense of the contrast between the careless interests and idle pleasures of daily life, and the state of those whose time for labour, or knowledge, or delight, is passed for ever.   There is evidence of this feeling in the introduction of the boys at play in the churchyard of Kirkby Lonsdale, and the boy climbing for his kite above the little mountain churchyard of Brignal Banks.   It is in the same tone of thought that he has placed here the two figures fishing, leaning against these shattered flanks of rock—the sepulchral stones of the great mountain-field of Death.

' Another character of these twin drawings, which gives them especial interest as connected with our enquiries into mediæval landscape, is that they are precisely and accurately illustrative of the two principal ideas of Dante about the Alps.   I have already explained the rise of the first drawing out of Turner's early study of " The Male Bolge ' of the Splugen and the St. Gothard.   The Goldau, on the other hand, might have been drawn in purposeful illustration of the lines [of Dante] descriptive of a " Loco Alpestro." '

During some three years Turner was associated in the production of the ' Rivers of France ' with Leitch Ritchie.   They travelled, however, very little together ; their tastes in everything but Art being exceedingly dissimilar.   ' I was curious,' says his companion, ' in observing what he made of the objects he selected for his sketches, and was frequently surprised to find what a forcible idea he conveyed of a place with scarcely a single correct detail.   His exaggerations, when it suited his purpose to exaggerate, were wonderful—lifting up, for instance, by two or three stories, the steeple or rather stunted cone of a village church—and when I returned to London, I never failed to roast him on this habit.   He took my remarks in good part, sometimes indeed in great glee, never attempting to defend himself otherwise than by rolling back the war into the enemy's camp.   In my account of the famous Gilles de Retz I had attempted to identify that prototype of " Blue Beard " with the hero of the nursery story by absurdly insisting that his beard was so intensely black that it seemed to have a shade of blue.   This tickled the great painter hugely; and his only reply to my bantering was, his little sharp eyes glistening the while, " Blue Beard ! Blue Beard ! Black Beard ! " '

While missing the true spirit of Italy through slender familiarity with classical and mediæval history, while changing and perverting Venice, while robbing the Alps of their sharpness and even of their snows, Turner thoroughly enjoyed and appreciated the hitherto despised scenery of France. The feeling of association that some men derive from long reading was not strong in him; but certain places affected him deeply. From his childhood France must have been much in his mind. She was our old, steadfast enemy ; and our victories over her had been the subject of his juvenile conversation. Napoleon's wonderful career had imparted a deep interest to France ; and he wished to convey to Englishmen a sense of its outward aspect, for as yet it had had no landscape painter. On this subject Mr. Ruskin pronounces—

' Of all foreign countries Turner has most entirely entered into the spirit of France ; partly because here he found more fellowship of scene with his own England, [1] partly because an amount of thought which will miss of Italy or Switzerland will fathom France, partly because there is in the French foliage and forms of ground much that is especially congenial with his own peculiar choice of form. To what cause it is owing I cannot tell, nor is it generally allowed or felt ; but of the fact I am certain, that for grace of stem and perfection of form in their transparent foliage the French trees are altogether unmatched ; and their modes of grouping and massing are so perfectly and constantly beautiful, that I think, of all countries for educating an artist to the perception of grace, France bears the bell ; and that not romantic nor mountainous France, not the Vosges, nor Auvergne, nor Provence ; but lowland France, Picardy, and Normandy, the valleys of the Loire and Seine, and even the district so thoughtlessly and mindlessly abused by English travellers as uninteresting, traversed between Calais and Dijon ; of which there is not a single valley but is full of the most lovely

---

[1] And partly because France was the cheapest country to visit, and the most accessible.

pictures, nor a mile from which the artist may not receive instruction; the district immediately above Sens being perhaps the
most valuable, from the grandeur of its lines of poplars and the
unimaginable finish and beauty of the tree-forms in the two
great avenues without the walls. Of this kind of beauty Turner
was the first to take cognizance, and he still remains the only,
but in himself the sufficient, painter of French landscape.'

Mr. Ruskin ranks many of the subjects included in the
'Rivers of France' among Turner's most successful works of
the class, and refers to them as helping very materially to illustrate the principles of his art. We transcribe a few of his
remarks :—

'"Château Gaillard." Black figures and boats; points of
shade; sun touches on castle and wake of boat; of light. See
how the eye rests on both, and observe how sharp and separate
all the lights are, falling in spots edged by shadow, but not
melting off into it.

'"Orléans." The crowded figures supply both points of
shade and light. Observe the delicate middle tint of both in
the whole mass of buildings, and compare this with the blackness of Canaletti's shadows, against which neither figures nor
anything else can ever tell as points of shade.

'"Blois." White figures in boats, buttresses of bridge,
dome of church on the right for light; woman on horseback,
heads of boats, for shadow. Note especially the isolation of
the light on the church dome. "Château de Blois." Torches
and white figures for light; roof of chapel and monks' dresses
for shade. "Beaugency." Sails and spire, opposed to buoy
and boats. An exquisite instance of brilliant, sparkling, isolated
touches of morning light. "Amboise." White sail and clouds;
cypresses under castle. "Château of Amboise." The boat in
the centre, with its reflections, needs no comment. Note the
glancing lights under the bridge. This is a very glorious and
perfect instance.

'"St. Julien, Tours." Especially remarkable for its preservation of deep points of gloom, because the whole picture is
one of extended shade.'

From the same series of plates Mr. Ruskin enumerates a

few examples of chiaroscuro more especially deserving of study
—namely, 'Scene between Quillebœuf and Villequier;' 'Honfleur;' 'The Scene between Nantes and Vernon;' 'The Lantern of St. Cloud;' 'Confluence of the Seine and Marne;' and
'Troyes.' He also instances the following:—

'"Jumiéges." The haze of sunlit rain of this most magnificent picture, the gradual retirement of the dark wood into its
depth, and the sparkling and evanescent light which sends its
variable flashes on the abbey, figures, foliage, and foam, require
no comment. They speak home at once. But there is added
to this noble composition an incident which may serve us at
once for a further illustration of the nature and forms of cloud,
and, for a final proof, how deeply and philosophically Turner
has studied them. We have on the right of the picture the
steam and the smoke of a passing steamboat. Now, steam is
nothing but an artificial cloud in the process of dissipation; it
is as much a cloud as those of the sky itself—that is, a quantity
of moisture rendered visible in the air by imperfect solution.
Accordingly, observe how exquisitely irregular and broken are
its forms, how sharp and spray-like; but with the convex side
to the wind, the sharp edge on that side, the other soft and
lost. Smoke, on the contrary, is an actual substance, existing
independently in the air, a solid opaque body, subject to no
absorption but that of tenuity. Observe its volumes: there is
no breaking up or disappearing here; the wind carries its
elastic globes before it, but does not dissolve nor break them.
Equally convex and void of angles on all sides, they are the
exact representations of the clouds of old masters, and serve at
once to show the ignorance and falsehood of the latter, and
the accuracy of study which has guided Turner to the truth.'

Mr. Ruskin also instances the following subjects from plates
contained in the same volume, as remarkable examples of the
varied effects of light given by Turner:— 'Beaugency,' as
representing the sun half an hour risen; cloudless sky. 'Lantern of St. Cloud;' midday, serene and bright, with streaky
clouds. 'Amboise;' sun setting, detached, light cirri, and clear
air. 'Troyes;' sun setting, cloudless; new moon. 'Caudebec;'
sun just set; sky covered with clouds; new moon setting.

'Montjean;' sun five minutes set, serene; new moon. 'Château de Blois;' sun a quarter of an hour set, cloudless. 'Clairmont;' sun half an hour set; light cirri. 'St. Julien, Tours;' an hour after sunset; no moon; torchlight. 'Nantes;' the same hour, moon rising. 'Calais;' midnight; moonless, with lighthouses.

For grand simplicity of treatment he refers to Honfleur, and the scene between Clairmont and Mauves; the latter more especially for its expression of the furrowing of the hills by descending water, the complete roundness and symmetry of their curves, and the delicate and sharp shadows which are cast in the undulating ravines; 'Caudebec' being cited particularly as an example of the mode by which the height of the observer above the river is indicated by the loss of the reflections on the banks.

Turner's illustrations to Rogers's 'Italy' have never been equalled. The poet-artist's best work is there engraved in the best manner and printed on the costliest paper. The figures and animals—such as the banditti, the dogs, and the monks, the boating party on Como, the goats on the Campagna, are among the best he ever drew; the Alps and the Lake of Geneva, his Moonlight and his Rome, are gems. All that he liked to do best he seems to have done then. The Moonlight is serener, the Rome more solid, and the Venice more fairy-like than anyone else's Rome, Venice, or Moonlight ever were.

CHAPTER XII.

TURNER AT HAMMERSMITH AND TWICKENHAM.

IN 1808, the year in which Turner was appointed Professor of Perspective in the Royal Academy, he removed to the Upper Mall, Hammersmith, but without giving up the old house in Harley Street. His attachment to the river no doubt led to this westward flitting, and it is surmised that he also desired to be near Loutherbourg, a German artist, whose daring effects of fire and storm he much admired.

Loutherbourg, who was born at Strasbourg in 1730, came to

CALAIS HARBOUR

England in 1771; was made Academician in 1779, when his future admirer was only four years old; and died in 1812, a year or so before Turner went to live at Twickenham. His most famous pictures were 'The Destruction of the Armada,' 'The Fire of London,' and 'Lord Howe's Victory' (1794). His drawings are neat and correct, and often shaded in blue.

Loutherbourg was a book-illustrator, a landscape-artist, and Garrick's chief scene-painter. His effects of tempest and fire led to many of Turner's efforts in the same manner. Wright of Derby, in his lamplight effects, was merely imitating in a vigorous way Schalcken and other Dutch painters; but Loutherbourg was one of the first to carry such effects into the regions of landscape-painting; and Turner, who was too cautious to tell many secrets, was not too proud to learn of anyone.

Loutherbourg's greatest effort was a combination of scene-painting and landscape, which he exhibited under the designation of the 'Eidophusikon.' It was the panorama of that day, and attracted the popular favour first, I believe, in Panton Square, and latterly at Exeter Change. It followed Hubert Stoppelaer's Patagonian Theatre, for which Dibdin wrote pieces, and which succeeded Powell's puppet-show, whose performance in Salisbury Square is so often mentioned in the early numbers of the 'Spectator.' The origin of the Eidophusikon is to be sought in the reduction of De Loutherbourg's salary as scene-painter for Covent Garden on Garrick's retirement from the stage.

Gainsborough was a passionate admirer of this exhibition; and Reynolds, who was a frequent visitor, recommended all his lady sitters to take their daughters there to observe the wonderful effects and to improve their taste. De Loutherbourg, who had studied in the Alps, the Pyrenees, and his own Alsatian mountains, was the first foreigner who had the courage to proclaim that 'no English landscape-painter needed foreign travel to collect grand prototypes for his study.'

In his curious book entitled 'Wine and Walnuts' Mr. Pyne describes the stage as little more than six feet wide and eight deep; yet the horizon seemed miles distant. The opening scene represented the view from the summit of One Tree Hill, in Greenwich Park, looking up the Thames towards London, On one side rose Flamstead House ; on the right was Greenwich Hospital, with its cupolas cut out of pasteboard ; and in the rear of scattered groups of trees were the towns of Greenwich and Deptford, with the long shores stretching from Poplar to Chelsea. Behind were the hills of Hampstead, Highgate, and Harrow, with the Port of London, crowded with shipping, in the middle distance. The heathy foreground, the sand-pit, and lichens were formed of broken cork. At first the scene was dim ; then came daybreak, with a faint vapourish-grey and a gleam of living saffron, brightening by degrees till at last the sun rose, lighting the tree-tops and gilding the vanes, and the whole scene was bathed in the light of day.

The clouds, which waved with the appearance of nature, were painted in semi-transparent colours, and could be lighted by Argand lamps behind and before. The linen on which they were painted, it may be explained, was stretched on large frames, which rose diagonally by a winding-machine. De Loutherbourg excelled in representing clouds ; and in this exhibition their varied motion and density were accurately reproduced. The lamps on the stage were above the proscenium, invisible to the spectators ; and before them were introduced slips of stained glass, by the shifting of which natural or supernatural tints could be thrown over the scene.

The 'picturesque by sound' was also theatrically called in to aid the effect of the scene. In the 'Storm at Sea and Loss of the Halsewell Indiaman' Loutherbourg imitated the signals of distress, which he produced from a large tambourine, with a whalebone spring attached to it headed with sponge. The thunder was imitated by shaking a large sheet of thin copper hung to a chain ; and the waves, carved in soft wood, were coloured and varnished so as to reflect the lightning. A machine regulated the speed of their revolution, and each one turned on its own axis, and in a contrary direction to its neighbour. The vessels were beautifully modelled and correctly rigged, those to the rear being coloured to suit the required aërial perspective. The rush of the waves was simulated by an octagonal pasteboard box full of shelves, which, charged with shells and peas was ground round. The wind was imitated by silk strainers, that gave out a sort of hollow whistling sound ; and the rain and hail, by revolving tubes filled with small seeds and beads.

One of the most interesting scenes represented an Italian seaport ; the waves calm, the moon pure and cold, and the mountains and water contrasting with a picturesque lighthouse situated on a jutting promontory of broken rock. The red light of the lantern lit one-half the water, while the moon silvered the other half ; in the foreground was moving shipping, and a fleet in the offing, which slowly melted into air. The clouds, which at intervals were painted opaque, rolled now luminous, now obscure. But the grandest tableau was reserved for the conclusion. It represented Hell, with Satan arraying his troops on the banks of the Fiery Lake, and Pandemonium rising as described by Milton. De Loutherbourg had already been very successful with effects of fire in Garrick's Theatre. First the spectator saw rising an immeasurable vista stretching between snowy mountains, and a dark chaotic mass, which gradually assumed form till it appeared a vast and gorgeous temple of molten brass. It changed to a sulphurous blue, next to red, then to a lurid paleness, and ultimately to the dreadful white heat of a raging fiery furnace ; and all this time the room was filled with groans and thunder, and the sounds of rain and of lashing waves.

De Loutherbourg, however, was beyond his age ; the exhibition lasted only two seasons ; and the painter degenerated into a disordered enthusiast who conceived he could cure all diseases by prayer. On a certain occasion he invited by advertisement the sick of London to come at a day and hour named, and be healed. They responded to the invitation in hundreds ; but, finding after some time that they remained uncured, they commenced a riot, and all but pulled the house down about the madman's foolish ears.

It is said that Mrs. Loutherbourg grew very jealous of Turner's frequent visits to her husband, and that at last, suspecting the young painter was obtaining all her husband's secrets from him, she shut the door in his face and roughly refused him admittance.

'At the beginning of the century Turner had a place at Hammersmith Mall,' writes a friend. 'The garden, which ran down to the river, terminated in a summer-house; and here, out in the open air, were painted some of his best pictures. It was here that my father, who then resided at Kew, became first acquainted with him; and expressing his surprise that Turner could paint under such circumstances, he remarked that lights and room were absurdities, and that a picture could be painted anywhere. His eyes were remarkably strong. He would throw down his water-colour drawings on the floor of the summer-house, requesting my father not to touch them, as he could see them there, and they would be drying at the same time.'

It was here Mr. Trimmer remembers walking, when a child, with his father and Turner at night under the blaze of the great comet. Turner was fond of children; and children reciprocated the affection.

In 1813 or 1814 he secured a cottage at Twickenham, which was introduced by Havell into one of his drawings for the issue of Cooke's 'Thames Scenery' for the latter year. He lived in it more or less until 1826, when he sold it to a Mr. Ford. Probably he found it inconvenient to be so far from the Academy, and from the engravers, and his patrons the Art publishers. A born Londoner always grumbles at London, and yet, when absent, pines for it.

The powder tax that the Tories imposed in 1795 (when Turner was twenty) drove out wigs, for the simple republican manners of the Revolution had already undermined and spoiled the barber's foolish trade. The paternal Turner gave up his shop some time between this and 1800, in which year his son went to live in Harley Street, and removed with him to Twickenham. 'The old man latterly,' says Mr. Trimmer, 'was his son's willing slave, and had to strain his pictures, and varnish them when finished; which made Turner say that his father began and finished his pictures for him. But I doubt if he varnished many pictures; few of them, I believe, were varnished at all; still he was of great assistance to his son, and I think it was Mr. Turner the engraver who told me that, once making bold to enter Turner's studio, he found the old man on his knees colouring a canvas, when Turner made his appearance, and good-humouredly trundled out the visitor, telling him he was on forbidden ground. Turner was much attached to his father, and at his death stayed with us a few days at Heston for change of scene. He was fearfully out of spirits, and felt his loss, he said, like that of an only child. When at Sandycomb Lodge, Turner senior was much respected, and I was told by the vicar that he was a regular attendant at the parish church. As he advanced in years, his son had him with him in London, and sold the place at Twickenham, much to the old man's dislike. I have heard Turner censured for it; but he told my father that 'Dad' was always working in the garden and catching cold, and required looking after. Turner never appeared the same man after his father's death; his family was broken up. Phrenologically speaking, the father had the better skull of the two.'

The father is described to me as very like his son in the face, particularly as to the nose. He was a little, thin, common-looking old man, very short, and endowed with all the tonsorial loquacity. He had a habit of nervously jumping up on his toes every two or three minutes (St. Vitus !), which rather astonished strangers. The father and son lived on very friendly terms together ; and the elder attended to the gallery, showed in visitors, and took care of the dinner, if he did not himself cook it. That he ever received the shillings at the door is, I believe, entirely untrue, though, had they been offered to him, I fear the temptation might have been too much for him to resist.

Soon after Turner first went to Solus Lodge at Twickenham a friend met the old man, very disconsolate, in Queen Anne Street. The cost of coming up daily to open the gallery was weighing heavily on his heart, and life was embittered to him by thought of the expenditure. A week after the same friend met him again, but he was in another frame of mind. He was gay, happy, and jumping up on his old toes ; and when asked the reason of the sudden change in his spirits he replied, 'Why, lookee here, I have found a way at last of coming up cheap from Twickenham to open my son's gallery. I found out the inn where the market-gardeners baited their horses; I made friends with one on 'em; and now, for a glass of gin a day, he brings me up in his cart on the top of the vegetables.' Even after his removal to Twickenham he used to come up at stated times to dress the wigs of his old customers round Maiden Lane. He died in 1830, and was buried in St. Paul's Church, Covent Garden, where the son erected a monument, for which he himself wrote the following confused epitaph :—

In the vault
Beneath and near this Place
are deposited the remains of
WILLIAM TURNER,
many years an inhabitant of this parish,
who died
September 21st, 1830.
To his memory and of his wife,
MARY ANN,
Their son, J. M. W. TURNER, R.A.,
has placed this tablet,
August 1832.

Always fond of architecture from the period of his service as a draughtsman to architects, Turner several times essayed the arduous task of designing a house. Thus he designed his own house, Solus Lodge, at Twickenham; he designed his own doorway in Queen Anne Street; and he made designs for portions of his friend Fawkes's house at Farnley. The title of *Solus* Lodge—bestowed, I suppose, in commemoration of its owner's desire of solitude—he afterwards changed into Sandy-comb Lodge, which has a sort of Devonshire flavour about it. Here he once entertained some Academicians, including Mr. Mulready, at tea; and here he once feasted Mr. Pye, his celebrated engraver and the great opponent of Academic abuses, with cheese and porter. It was here that he used to protect from birds'-nesting boys the blackbirds who sang and cheered him after his day's work; for which act of ornithological kindness they christened him 'Blackbirdy;' and it was here, in his rude tangle of a garden, that he grew the water-plants which he loved to introduce into his foregrounds. To be near

Reynolds's old house at Richmond is said to have been one of his chief reasons for building Solus Lodge. More probably it arose from his wish to be undisturbed, to study the Thames, and to be near his old schoolboy home at Brentford.

Chantrey's early days were mostly spent at Twickenham, says Mr. A. Watts, where the famous sculptor's future wife resided with her parents in a fine old house, subsequently known as Jonas Burdett's, in which a room was allotted to him as a studio ; and this vicinity to Turner, combined with their mutual love of angling, brought them for some years into constant companionship. They used to hire a boat at Isleworth, and, after an early lunch of bacon and eggs, would angle out the day.

Let into the wall over the dining-room chimney in Turner's villa at Twickenham is a pretty little piece of sculpture, the subject being Paul at Iconium, from the cartoon, but with variations. This is supposed to have been the gift of Chantrey.

And here I gladly introduce some reminiscences of Turner when at Twickenham, which have been furnished me by the eldest son of his oldest friend the Rev. Mr. Trimmer, rector of Heston, near Brentford. They do not exclusively relate to this period of Turner's life ; but I give them in full to preserve the interest of their sequence.

'About this time,' Mr. Trimmer deposes, 'Turner removed to Twickenham, where he purchased Sandycomb Lodge, near Richmond Bridge. It was an unpretending little place, and the rooms were small. There were several models of ships in glass cases, to which Turner had painted a sea and background. They much resembled the large vessels in his sea pieces. Richmond scenery greatly influenced his style. The Scotch firs (or stone-pine) around are in most of his large classical subjects, and Richmond landscape is decidedly the basis of " The Rise of Carthage."

' Here he had a long strip of land, planted by him so thickly with willows that his father, who delighted in the garden, complained that it was a mere osier-bed. Turner used to refresh his eye with the run of the boughs from his sitting-room window.

'At the end of his garden was a square pond—I rather think he dug it himself—into which he put the fish he caught. The surface was covered with water-lilies. I have been out fishing with him on the Old Brent, with a can to catch trout for this preserve; but the fish always disappeared. At last he discovered that a jack was in the pond; and Turner would have it that it had been put in to annoy him.

'I have dined with him at Sandycomb Lodge, when my father happened to drop in, too, in the middle of the day. Everything was of the most modest pretensions; two-pronged forks, and knives with large round ends for taking up the food; not that I ever saw him so use them, though it is said to have been Dean Swift's mode of feeding himself. The table-cloth barely covered the table, and the earthenware was in strict keeping. I remember his saying one day, "Old dad," as he called his father, "have you not any wine?" whereupon Turner senior produced a bottle of currant, which Turner smelling said, "Why, what have you been about?" The senior, it seemed, had rather overdone it with hollands, and it was set aside. At this time Turner was a very abstemious person.

'I have also dined with him in Queen Anne Street, where everything was of the same homely description. I should say that he never altered his style of living from his first start in Maiden Lane; not that I think him censurable for preferring the frugal meals of past times. You were welcome to what he had; and, if it was near his dinner-time, he always pressed us to stay, and brought out cake and wine. The cake he would good-naturedly stuff into my pocket. I mention this for the benefit of those who think Turner destitute of humanity.

'When, as a child, I have been out fly-fishing with him on the Thames, he insisted on my having the fish, which he strung on some grass through the gills. He seemed to take more pleasure in giving me the fish than in taking them himself. These little incidents mark character. He threw a fly in first-rate style, and it bespeaks the sportsman wherever the rod is introduced into his pictures.

'He had a boat at Richmond, but we never went farther

than the water's edge, as my father had insured his life. I have, however, seen him start on his sketching expeditions. From his boat he painted on a large canvas direct from Nature. Till you have seen these sketches, you know nothing of Turner's powers. There are about two score of these large subjects, rolled up, and now national property. In my judgment these are among his very finest productions : no retouching, everything firmly in its place. If the subject had been photographed, there would have been greater exactitude, but Turner's would have carried the bell in elevation of sentiment and mind. This is the perfection of the art ; but Turner's mind was so comprehensive that he could not carry out the detail, though he was far from despising it ; and I was told by Howard he would spend hours sketching a stone. There is a red sunset (simply the sky) among the rolls ; the finest sky, to my mind, ever put on canvas. Probably these are thrown aside as worthless, and not popular ; but what studies for young painters ! Reynolds has said that no painter has ever made above one or two designs ; and, when Wilson hit upon one of these, he varied them and called them breeding subjects ; but Turner, like Nature, never reproduced himself.

'Besides his boat, he had a gig and an old horse ; an old crop-eared bay horse, or rather a cross between a horse and a pony. In this gig he used to drive out sketching, and take my father and myself with him. His sketching apparatus was under the seat. I remember once going on an expedition of this kind to Staines, and thence to Runnymede, where he made some sketches. From there he painted a picture which strongly resembles the place to this day. We went, I remember, at a very steady pace, for Turner painted much faster than he drove. He said, if when out sketching you felt at a loss, you had only to turn round or walk a few paces farther, and you had what you wanted before you.

'He has immortalised his old crop-ear in his " Frosty Morning," which is now exhibited. There are two horses, but they are both taken from Crop-Ear. Turner could not paint a horse ; still, he has been very happy in catching the stiffness of old Crop-Ear's fore legs. And, on the subject of horses, I once asked him, long afterwards, if Gilpin had not painted the horse in " Hannibal Crossing the Alps." It was his own design, he said ; no painter had ever touched any picture of his.

' The " Frost Piece " was one of his favourites. Once he talked of giving it to my father, who greatly prized it. He said he was travelling by coach in Yorkshire, and sketched it *en route* ; and the coach is introduced in the distance in the picture. My father told me that when at Somerset House it was much brighter, and made a great sensation. It was over the fireplace in his gallery. The girl with the hare over her shoulders, I have heard my father say, reminded him of a young girl whom he occasionally saw at Queen Anne Street, and whom, from her resemblance to Turner, he took to be a relation. The same female figure appears in his " Crossing the Brook." This picture I consider one of Turner's happiest productions, and totally distinct from Cuyp, with whom it is injudiciously confounded.

' Henry Howard, R.A., was an early friend of my father's ; and he and Turner have stayed with us at Heston. I remember, when I was about five years old, going to Penn, in Buckinghamshire, with Howard, Turner, and my father ; all of them in search of the picturesque. We went in a postchaise, and, when tired, my father carried me pick-a-back. We came to a halt in a grove or copse where luxuriated wild flowers in profusion. It was a charming day ; and, though so many " years bygone," I can see now vividly before me my father and Howard, both standing legs a-straddle, and Turner at a little distance in a ditch, all hard at work at the æsthetical. After a while Turner emerged from his retreat with a capital water-colour, with which Howard and my father were in raptures. He said he got into the ditch to avoid the sun, but Howard whispered my father that it was to avoid showing his *modus operandi*. I have heard this from my father subsequently ; but I remember after this going up Penn steeple on my father's back, part of the way up a ladder, then on the leads. The great Turner, Howard, my father, and myself were there fifty years ago ; but Death has mowed them all down but myself. I dare say Turner did not think that that little child would be telling about it half a century afterwards, or that he would ever be the subject of such homage.

'Turner was strong in the creative faculty, and his power of invention was exhaustless. His remarks on pictures were admirable ; no beauty and no defect escaped him.

'Howard, inferior though he was to Turner as an artist, was his superior in education ; and, though he did ample homage to his genius, he often got into warm professional disputes with him. But Turner was mostly in the right. They once, I remember, had a very hot dispute, and for the time being lost temper. Howard maintained they should paint for the public ; Turner, that public opinion was not worth a rush, and that one should paint only for judges. But, according to all artists, no one but an artist can judge of the difficulties of painting, and consequently of the merits of a picture.

'Whether the instincts of mankind are to be pitted against the taste of the cultivated few, I am not prepared to discuss. The vulgar, on the whole, would understand form better than colour, and low subjects better than cultivated ones ; so that Turner argued wisely, with reference to himself, in painting for the cultivated few. Still no one felt more keenly the illiberal strictures of the newspapers ; and I have seen him almost in tears, and ready to hang himself, though still only valuing their opinions at their worth. Independently of his artistic powers, his ability was over the average of his brother artists.

'Turner was very communicative to my father, and would point out to him any defect in sketching. I think he fairly instructed my father in painting in his own method ; which was to lay the dead colours as nearly as possible in the forms you wished, leaving as little as possible for finishing, using as a vehicle nothing but linseed oil, diluted as required in spirits of turpentine. I forgot to say that, in his picture of " Æneas and Dido Hunting," the *equi effrenati* are without bridles. My father told him the Libyan horses had no bridles, and Turner said he knew it, though I doubt if their views are borne out by modern critics.

'Turner, when beginning his great classical subjects from the " Æneid," regretted his ignorance of Latin ; and my father undertook to teach him for instruction in painting in return. My father, who was accustomed to teaching, has told me Turner sadly floundered in the verbs, and never made any progress—in fact, he could not spare the time. But, though his early education was deficient, Turner was never idle or unemployed; he had always a brush or pencil in his hand; in the evening he latterly went from home, mostly to the Academy.

'Turner told my father that he had painted a certain picture on a tablecloth; but, having once had an opportunity of examining it, I found it must have been some other picture that he meant.

' At this early time my father has seen his pictures in progress, and considered that he availed himself largely of body colours. A picture dealer who repaired one of his large pictures, and whose name I forget, told me that Turner came and worked over it with body colours, and then varnished them. At Somerset House I have been told by Howard that he worked over his pictures with body colours, using brushes with very small handles, and painting from little jars.

' From the examination I made of his half-finished pictures after his death, I could find no traces of body colour; everything was firmly put in in oil; and I extend this remark to an unfinished picture of Titian's I once examined. In my opinion, Turner painted all his early pictures in oil, and used body colours very sparingly in his later ones. In fact, I never detected any traces of body colour in any picture of his, nor did I see any body colours in his studio, although he might have employed dry colour. I believe Turner (like Reynolds) never kept to one plan for any length of time; I mean latterly, when he began to paint Italian subjects, and was striving to get more vivid effects. He was ignorant of chemistry and the affinities of colour; and I have heard him say that no one could tell if a method would answer, as he would be dead before it could be proved. He was far from satisfied with his own method, and would gladly have changed it for a better. My father, who was fond of experiments in colours, often talked the subject over with him. Turner was always impressed with the idea that the old masters had a much better method than the moderns. He considered old Ward's method a good one ; and my father tried through a friend to obtain his vehicle, but obtained a false one. I had it afterwards from a pupil of Ward's ; it was a preparation of spirit varnish, but difficult to manage.

'He once told my father he had gone nine times over one of his large skies. My father one day said to him, "Nothing is to be done without ultramarine." "Cobalt is good enough for me," was Turner's reply. Mr. Jones, his executor, told me that at his suggestion Turner introduced Prussian blue into his skies, as nearer Nature ; and Mr. Danby, who prepared his palette, informed me he also used smalt largely. On the subject of skies, the "Carthage" in the National Gallery had an entirely new sky painted at the desire of Lawrence and other brother artists, who, when he had altered it, said the picture was ruined. The sun was yellow in Turner's gallery ; it is now white.

'Looking at a black cow against the sun, in the course of a walk out with me, he observed, "It is purple, not black, as it is painted." In his later pictures he employed blue-black freely, and had no fear of the canon, "Don't use black when painting a blackamoor."

'Yellow, he said, was his favourite colour, "for pictures wanted colour." In his walks painting was seldom from his thoughts ; he would point to a piece of moss or a weed growing out of a wall, and observe, "*That is pretty.*" He made his observations in a low voice; or, rather, he half made them, leaving your suggestive faculty to supply the gap.

'He never appeared illiberal when speaking of the great masters. When he called on me once, he spoke in raptures of a picture of (I think) Poussin's—"Jonah Cast on the Shore," then exhibited in Pall Mall—calling it a wonderful picture, and despatching us to see it. I have heard him speak most enthusiastically in praise of Gainsborough's execution and Wilson's tone, and he plainly thought himself their inferior. My father had some admirable oil sketches of Gainsborough ; and these Turner one evening examined by candle-light so closely that the next morning he complained of having hurt his eyes.

'We were one day looking at a Vandervelde, and on some one observing, "I think you could go beyond that," he shook his head and said, " I can't paint like him." I never heard him speak highly of modern pictures; and he told me once that he considered the art at Rome at the lowest ebb. I think he hardly did justice to his brother landscape-painters, most of whom, I fear, he considered beneath criticism; and when one considers that such painters as Glover were placed above him, not only by the public but by the press, his sensitiveness is hardly to be wondered at.

'When at the height of his fame he admired the *leafage* of some landscape painter whose name he did not mention, and asked him to let him see him work, which he did; but Turner said it was so tedious it was of no use to him. Nothing angered Turner more than *piracy*. Owen, the water-colour painter, had been imitating him; on which he wrote him a very brisk note, requesting him in future to draw from his own resources, and not from his. Once observing some one making a memorandum of his pictures in the Queen Anne Street gallery, he walked up to him and whisked him out forthwith, greatly to the surprise of the individual.

'Having on one occasion forgotten to take the bait with us when we went out fishing, we had to send back for them. Turner gave the messenger a shilling; he would not let me give it. This was about twenty years ago. He had taken Campbell's " Pleasures of Hope " with him; and, indicating one of the prints, he remarked, " *That is pretty*." " Nothing first-rate," I interposed, " is it? " " It is *pretty*," was the reply; " and he is a poor man with a large family." This he said with much good feeling.

'The funeral of Sir Thomas Lawrence was in winter, and there had been a fall of snow that day. During the service Wilkie, who was next to Turner, whispered into his ear, " Turner, that's a fine effect! " but from the untimely observation he turned away with disgust. This I had from Constable, who was on the other side of him, and who, when telling me the anecdote, remarked that Turner had a great deal of good feeling about him.

'My father was Turner's eldest executor; they had known each other many years. When Mrs. Danby read from the

"Times" the decease of a namesake of my father's, whom they mistook for him, Turner was very much affected, and exclaimed, "Ah, poor fellow; so he is gone!" This my father learned when he called at Queen Anne Street to make enquiries touching his last moments, when Mrs. Danby, who opened the door, started as if she had seen an apparition. I mention these as instances of Turner's kindness of heart and sincerity in friendship. Mrs. Danby was his housekeeper, and had lived with him many years. She had some fearful cancerous malady which obliged her to conceal her face, which did not add to the charms of his domicile.

'At first sight Turner gave one the notion of a mean-looking little man. In descending a hill while out once on a sketching ramble, he snapped a tendon Achilles, and the enforced limping about thereafter with a stick did not add to his appearance; but all this wore off. To be appreciated, he required to be known. Though not polished, he was not vulgar. In common with many men of genius, he had not a good flow of words; and, when heated in argument, got confused, especially, I am told, in his lectures on Perspective, though he was master of his subject. He was rather taciturn than talkative. His hair was dark brown, bordering on black; and his complexion sallow.

'There is a picture of a windmill, a yellow picture, etched in the "Liber Studiorum;" which hung in Turner's gallery over the "Bligh Shore," and was purchased by one of the executors. He made the sketch one evening returning from my father's. It was "Hanwell Windmill," since pulled down, near the site of the present asylum. It is a most charming picture; though highly ideal, one of the most realistic representations of the spot. How modern critics can prefer "Napoleon Standing on the Shore" to such charming productions is to me incomprehensible. His "High Street, Oxford" is a well known subject, and displays his architectural knowledge. This, he told my father, he drew in a postchaise in High Street, I think opposite the corner print-shop.

'Turner once went with my father and mother to see the pictures at Osterley House, collected by Mr. Child. There was a splendid Gainsborough my father had once rescued from a garret. Of this picture Turner made, *memoriter*, a small pencil drawing in the evening, and also a sketch of a woman gathering water-cresses whom they had seen on the way, on which he had written, " *Checked blue apron.*" "These," said my mother, when he had finished them, " are for me." " If you take them," said Turner, " I must do two more." These were sold at my father's sale. However, once at my uncle's he made a very clever water-colour drawing, which they have now, of two of my cousins playing on the floor. I never heard of another instance of his giving away his drawings.

' He once said to my mother, who was looking at "The Building of Carthage," " That picture shall be my winding-sheet ; " but the remark, I am told, was often repeated. He also said at the same time, pointing to the " Fall of Carthage," " That is the better picture of the two, but they do not understand it." Shifting to another subject, I rather think he was much smitten by a sister of my mother's. Singularly enough, my father had written two letters of proposal for rejected suitors, and Turner wrote to my father a mysterious letter when they were on the Eastern coast. It is of about the date 1813. I give it elsewhere.'

Turner at this time was thirty-eight ; and this was his second disappointment in love. Henceforth the devotion of his soul was directed exclusively to the idol Fame.

CHAPTER XIII.

TURNER IN WALES AND SCOTLAND.

THAT Turner should soon set his face towards Wales was the most natural thing in the world. He went there in search of lake and mountain, and of the old abbeys and castles Hearne had drawn so well ; and the result of these sketching rambles, undertaken in 1793, when he was twenty years of age, were incorporated in the pictures exhibited by him in the succeeding year—' The Devil's Bridge, Cardiganshire,' and the interior of

EDINBURGH FROM ST. ANTHONY'S CHAPEL

the beautiful Abbey of Tintern. In 1795 he exhibited a scene in Derbyshire, another view of Tintern, and a second view near the Monach's Bridge, in Cardiganshire. A second or third Welsh trip in 1796 results in a study of 'Llandaff Cathedral;' and next year we find him painting 'Ewenny Priory, in Glamorganshire.' He had long before discovered that Hearne and Sandby had not exhausted the picturesque wealth of Great Britain.

As British and Welsh proclivities had led him to Wales, so Yorkshire rambles and the Lakes soon lured him on to Scotland. In 1797, probably, he drew his favourite study of 'Norham Castle, on the Tweed,' to which he attributed so much subsequent good fortune; and some time during 1801 it must have been that he made his first appearance in Scotland; for in 1802 he exhibited pictures of the 'Falls of the Clyde' (afterwards used in the 'Liber'), 'Kilchern Castle, with the Cruchan-Ben Mountains,' and 'Edinburgh from Leith and Ben Lomond.' But his two great visits, severally undertaken for the purpose of illustrating Sir Walter Scott's works, were in 1818 and 1831; the first being the year of his Waterloo picture, and the second that of the exhibition of 'Caligula's Palace and Bridge.'

Lockhart, in his delightful Life of Sir Walter, describes his father-in-law as busy in 1818 collecting and revising for publication his 'Topographical and Historical Essays,' which had originally appeared in the successive numbers of that splendidly illustrated work entitled 'Provincial Antiquities of Scotland.' He did this partly to gratify his own love of the subject, and partly because, well or ill, he must be doing something. He even generously declined all pecuniary recompense for his labour of love; but afterwards, when the success of the work was secure, he accepted from the proprietor some beautiful drawings by Turner, Thomson of Edinburgh, and other artists, which had been prepared to accompany the rest; and these were hung in the little breakfast-room at Abbotsford, the same which had been constructed for his own den.

In 1818, when Turner first visited Edinburgh to make drawings for the 'Provincial Antiquities,' for which Scott wrote the letter-press, that emperor of novelists was in his prime.

The wonderful novels were then bringing in 10,000*l.* a year. Eighteen hundred and eighteen was the year in which the 'Heart of Midlothian' appeared, and that in which he began the 'Bride of Lammermoor,' two of his most tender and noble works ; and it was the very year in which Lockhart describes meeting Home Drummond in Scott's study in Castle Street, a small room behind the dining-parlour.

In this house it was that Kirkpatrick Sharpe, the Skenes, Terry, Constable, and the Ballantynes—all Scott's cronies—met to barter wit and anecdote over whiskey toddy and good claret. The one window of this den looked out on a small patch of turf; and the floor was strewn with folios and octavos (Comines for 'Quentin Durward' and Pepys for 'Peveril'), while Scott sat at a desk with drawers, the top of which was covered with sessions papers, letters, proofs, red tape, and green tin-boxes. Maida sat watching his master ; on the book-ladder perched a large favourite cat ; and the walls were adorned with Highland targets and dirks that encircled a portrait of Claverhouse.

This was the year in which, attended by his sarcastic and haughty son-in-law, whose pride vanished in Scott's presence alone, the Wizard of the North (still hoarding his secret with proud humour) visited with him Holyrood, the Grassmarket, the Cowgate, and Canongate—scenes that he has invested with a magic light, a light that can never fade. It was also the year in which, in Lockhart's company, we find Scott consulting with Tom Purdie about laying down the bowling-alley at Abbotsford, which was rising fast like a dream-castle, or ascending the turrets to muse over the distant Eildons, and to see Melrose gleam like alabaster in the twilight.

'Peter's Letters to his Kinsfolk,' published about 1818, contains several eulogies of Turner. We read therein : 'For the first time is Scotland now possessed of admirable landscape painters, as well as of historical painters. With regard to landscape painting, it is very true that she has not yet equalled the present glories of the sister kingdom ; but then the world has only one Turner, and Scotland comes far nearer to the country which has had the honour of producing that great genius than any other country in Europe.' [1]

[1] Vol. iii. p. 280.

Then follows a long critique on Mr. Williams, and the writer proceeds—

'But there is no want of admirable artists in the same department of this city. . . . . . There is Mr. Thomson, the clergyman of Duddingston, a village in the immediate neighbourhood of Edinburgh, whose works, in masterly ease and breadth of effect, seem to me to approach nearer to the masterpieces of *Turner* than those of any other artist with whom I am acquainted, and who, you will be happy to observe, is engaged along with that prince of artists in Mr. Scott's great work of the "Provincial Antiquities of Scotland."'

This shows in what high estimation the Scotch people held Thomson at that time.

Turner is mentioned again with sincere appreciation :—

'When I passed by this fine ruin (Borthwick Castle and Keep), the air was calm, the sky was unclouded, and the shadow of the square masonry pile lay in all its clear breadth upon the blue stream below ; but *Turner* has caught or created a perhaps still more poetical accompaniment. You may see it to at least as much advantage as I did in his magnificent delineation.'

I do not know whether it is of this or of the second visit that Scott wrote that he should have liked Thomson, but as they had engaged Turner, and as he was all the fashion, he supposed he must acquiesce in the arrangement.

In the autumn of 1831 Turner was employed by Mr. Cadell to make a collection of twenty-four sketches for a new edition of Scott's poems, with the condition that the publisher was to retain the drawings. He had not seen the Trosachs or Loch Katrine till this year ; but, after visiting the scenes immortalised by Scott, he expressed his increased admiration of the fidelity of his descriptions. Corriskin, in the Isle of Skye, he used to say, was the grandest scene he had ever beheld ; and it was at Corriskin that he all but perished while clambering about the crags.

On the passage ending with the line 'the bleakest mountainside,' in the 'Lord of the Isles,' the following note occurs :—

'The "Quarterly" reviewer says, This picture of barren desolation is admirably touched ; and, if the opinion of Mr.

Turner be worth anything, no words could have given a truer picture of this, one of the wildest of Nature's landscapes. Mr. Turner adds, however, that he dissents in one particular—but *for one or two tufts of grass* he must have broken his neck, having slipped when trying to attain the best position for taking the view which embellishes this volume.'

When Turner went to Scotland the second time, Lockhart writes of his visit—

' I am not sure whether the Royal Academician *Turner* was at Abbotsford at the time of Mr. Adolphus's last visit ; but several little excursions were made in the company of this great artist, who had come to Scotland for the purpose of making drawings to illustrate the scenery of Sir Walter's poems. On several such occasions I was of the party, and one day deserves especially to be remembered. Sir Walter took Turner that morning, with his friend Skene and myself, to Smailholm Crags ; and it was while lounging about them, while the painter did his sketch, that he told Mr. Skene legends of the place. He then carried us to Dryburgh, but excused himself from attending Mr. Turner into the enclosure. Mr. Skene and I perceived that it would be better for us to leave him alone, and we both accompanied Turner.

' Lastly, we must not omit to mention Bemerside. For that ancient residence of the most ancient family [the Haigs] now subsisting on Tweedside he was resolved there must be a fit memorial by this graceful hand. The good laird and lady were of course flattered with this respect ; and, after walking about a little while among the huge old trees that surrounded the tower, the artist made his sketch.'

The sketch of this picturesque Peel, and its ' brotherhood of venerable trees,' is probably familiar to most of my readers.

With true Scotch clannishness, Sir Walter (as we have seen) had, before Turner's arrival, expressed his preference for his countryman Thomson ; but he yielded at last with a good grace to having the man who was the fashion. Sir Walter was a great novelist and a great poet ; but he knew nothing of Art, or he would have at once realised the importance of securing one who was likely to prove so great an ally. In Scott's delightful com-

DUNFERMLINE

pany Turner went to several of the scenes around Edinburgh that he had selected for his illustrations. Foremost amongst these was the scene of his fine ballad the 'Eve of St. John,' a spot specially dear to the poet-novelist. It was here he had been sent, the poor lame son of the Edinburgh lawyer, for health ; and here, on the turf under the ruins, he had played among the sheep and listened to the cow-bailie's legends. From this spot there is a view of nearly half the region immortalised in his novels and poems. Every field you see has been a field of battle, and every rivulet has been immortalised in song.

> The lady looked in mournful mood,
> Looked over hill and vale,
> O'er Mertoun's wood, and Tweed's fair flood,
> And all down Teviotdale.

The panorama here, as Lockhart says, is beautiful. Dryburgh and its yew trees are at your feet ; opposite rise the purple peaks of the Eildons, where Thomas the Rhymer met the Queen of the Fairies. Yonder are Ercildoun, and the black wilderness of Lammermoor. Eastward the desolate grandeur of Hume Castle breaks the horizon ; and as the eye travels on to the blue range of Cheviot, a few miles westward, Melrose rises like a tall rock, clasping the windings of the Tweed ; while in the distance are Gala, Ettrick, and Yarrow.

In the epistle to Erskine, Scott has sketched Smailholm with an intense and loving truth. He shows us the naked cliffs with occasional velvet tufts of green ; the broken arches, overgrown with wall-flowers and honeysuckle ; and the rusty window-bars through which he fancied so often that he saw grim, scarred faces peering. In this farm-house, overhung by the crag on which the ruined tower stands, Scott felt the first consciousness of existence ; and he told the painter that 'the habit of lying here on the turf among the sheep and lambs, when a lame infant, had given his mind a peculiar tenderness for those animals, which it had ever since retained.' This was in the autumn of 1830, when Scott must have been in one of his saddest and most reflective moods, for the turbulent state of the people agitated him, and his health, too, was failing.

1831 was the year in which he was pelted by the Selkirk electors; in which he broke down in a fit of apoplexy over 'Count Robert of Paris;' and in which eventually, both mind and body worn out by his desperate efforts to pay his debts, he went abroad, to be brought home, alas! only to hear the dear Tweed murmur once more to him, and then to die. Turner caught all the mournful poetry of the old poet's reveries. In how many of the scenes does he give us the moonlight rising and the cows pacing homeward!

He ransacked the Borders of Scotland with a design very different from that of Sir Walter, whose poems and historical narratives he was illustrating. Scott, charged to overflowing with old romance, had galloped through the Border country in search of ballads and legends, caring little for any place if it had not been hallowed by tradition. He had ransacked Scotland with the patience of an antiquary and the fervour of a poet. But Turner knew little of Scotch history, and cared, I should imagine, less. What were the Elliots and Johnstones to him but cattle-stealers of three hundred years ago? What he wanted was to paint beautiful dreams of quiet lakes, and of calm old castles mouldering majestically away to the dust from which they sprang; and so he could do that, and carry off a good bagful of guineas to boot, he cared not for the Douglas of the Bleeding Heart, nor for Bruce of Bannockburn himself. I do not say (far from it) that Turner had not read Scott's poems. No doubt he had, and enjoyed heartily the vigour and truth of their mediævalism; but still his works betray no especial appreciation of the poet. They are distinct creations, with a tender and exquisite beauty of their own; showing us the scenes, not as they were, but as they are—contrasting the feudal and the past as much as possible, and as sadly as possible, with the present. Take, as an example, 'Unroofed Jedburgh Abbey,' with the bare-legged hizzies washing clothes; and 'Smailholm Tower,' with the kye coming home to the byre at moonrise. One thing Turner will always show us in a ruined castle, and that is, that it is the work of a far receding and contrasting age. At Lochmaben Castle he gives us fishermen dragging in their nets; and at Caerlaverock,

SMAILHOLME TOWER

where Kirkpatrick was murdered by his guest, the artist, uninterested in a crime many hundred years forgotten, is intent on the reflective dazzle of the moon, the net circling in the lake, the sheep flocking home, or the plaided man and his noisy, faithful collie. Bemerside, where the Haigs are and will be for aye, he quite disregards, to pay a compliment to Scott as 'Thomas the Rhymer,' and to introduce Sir Walter and the old laird.

Very often he evidently dislikes his subjects, as in his drawings of 'Ashestiel,' where Scott wrote 'Marmion.' The cottage is a mere rude square box; but Turner takes refuge in the hills above, where he can escape to the distance. Occasionally, however, as in Carlisle, where from the wooded scaur he sees the town fair and bonny, he is reasonably contented; so he clothes it in sunshine, or throws up a rainbow, and is happy with the beauty before him, though it may not be quite the beauty he is then specially in the mood for. He is contented in his way with Newark Castle, where the minstrel sang his last lay to the Duchess of Buccleuch. He is more than usually pleased with Johnny Armstrong's tower, seen from the bridge the Carlisle coach traversed, as it stands bold and unroofed on the bare hill; and at Kelso he contrasts pigtailed men with the staring white Grecian bridge to which he gives quite a dignity. But these are not his moments of supreme genius. No; he always soars highest (as all men do, genius or no genius) when he loves his work, when he can convey a sense of infinity, carrying the eye up to the farthest range of a telescope.

Turner's greatest triumph was when he depicted the intense wildness and savage desolation of the Hermitage Castle, where wicked Lord Soulis suffered. The mountains there are terrible; the wilful torrent in the foreground is passionately reckless; even the tone of colour is lurid and sad. It might be a glen in the 'Inferno' for all the happiness Turner has thrown over air, earth, and water. The sadness is the sadness of the old ballad :—

> He looked over fell ; he looked over flat ;
>   But nothing he wished he saw,
> Save the pyot on a turret that sat,
>   Beside a corby craw.

'Glencoe' and 'Killicrankie' are both fine; but they are as nothing, though stern and bold enough, to the 'Edinburgh' in 'Marmion,' and the 'Loch Corriskin' in the 'Lord of the Isles.' The first is full of ambition and enjoyment. To give importance to the drawing, he has represented himself helping Scott up Arthur's Seat. He has followed the poet, too, with delight in giving us the strong spine of the Pentlands, and far beyond the castle the Ochil Mountains, the shore of Fife, the Frith, Preston Bay, and Berwick Law. The amethyst and emerald of the poet's distance are shown by the artist; and so are the lesser beauties of those heroic and passionate lines :—

> Such dusky grandeur clothed the height
> Where the huge castle holds its state,
>   And all the steep slope down,
> Whose ridgy back heaves to the sky,
> Piled deep and massy, close and high,
>   Mine own romantic town!

Loch Achray, with its sheet of living gold, its empurpled islands and grand sentinel mountains, is not unworthily depicted; neither is Dryburgh, with its vassal wood of trees, and the great silver loop-chain of the Tweed; nor Staffa, with the moon shining through the wave-wasted arch of basalt; but perhaps the *chef-d'œuvre* is that tremendous scene 'Loch Corriskin, in the Isle of Skye :'—

> For rarely human eye has known
> A scene so stern as that dread lake,
> With its dark ledge of barren stone.
> Seems that primeval earthquake's sway
> Hath rent a strange and shattered way
> Through the rude bosom of the hill :
> And that each naked precipice,
> Sable ravine and dark abyss,
> Tells of the outrage still.
> The wildest glen but this can show
> Some touch of Nature's genial glow.
> But here above, around, below,
> On mountain or in glen,
> Nor tree, nor shrub, nor plant, nor flower,

Nor aught of vegetative power,
The weary eye may ken.
For all is rocks at random thrown,
Black waves, bare crags, and banks of stone,
As if were here denied
The summer sun, the spring's sweet dew;
That clothe with many a varied hue
The bleakest mountain-side.

In the upheaved waves and pinnacles of rock Turner revels, as he does in the mist that rolls up the receding glen, and darkens the small black grave of the Goblin's Lake. The danger of the scene is hinted by the precarious seat in which the painter sits, while his guide lies down and waits. 'Bare as Cheapside,' says one traveller; 'all but a few shrubs of juniper.'

Among the lesser beauties of his illustrations to Scott should be mentioned 'The Junction of Greta and Tees,' with the countless billows of tree-tops, and the painter's favourite subject of 'Norham Castle, the Lord Warden's Castle,' so beautifully lit up by the moon, with its cliffs, nets, mills, and other objects.

The Scotch drawings, both for the Poems and the 'Life of Napoleon,' which are nearly all in the possession of Mr. Munro of Hamilton Place, are beautifully executed. They are small vignettes, painted in water colours (drawn through a reducing-glass), of the size required by the engraver; which was one of the conditions imposed by the publisher. The most beautiful for colour that I have seen is the 'Inverness Bridge.' In many of them the figures and adjuncts are exceedingly careful and expressive, through microscopically small—such, for instance, as the mounted farmer and the reaper in the 'Dunfermline;' the schoolboys in 'Ashestiel;' the girl and the dog in the 'Dumbarton Castle;' the steamer and boats in the 'Dunstaffnage' (notable for motion); the lovers in the 'Craigmillar;' and Scott's open book and stick on the seat in the 'Rhymer's Glen.' Nor are some of the illustrations to Scott's 'Life of Napoleon' and the French 'Tales of my Grandfather' less admirable.

We have no space to dilate on the savage grandeur of the

'Château d'Arc,' or the cocked-hat men who repair the road outside Rouen; but we must rest a moment at the 'Simplon,' the 'Fontainebleau,' and the 'Bellerophon.'

In the 'Simplon' he has succeeded in conveying a sense of the wonder and danger of Napoleon's mountain road by means of a corner rock in profile, with soldiers entering one of the galleries. The firs, though small as weeds, are beautifully painted. In the two other scenes he has given us wonderful figures—small as pins' heads, but expressing everything. In neither is the figure of Napoleon larger or thicker than a gnat's body; yet it is seen directly, and tells a complete story. The sentiment, too, of the 'Fontainebleau,' though produced as usual by an unjustifiable exaggeration of the height of the building, is truly poetical; so ghastly and fading does the vast pile of palace seem by the light of a sullen moon.

The figures in the 'Murder of the Duc d'Enghien' are especially admirable; and so is the Napoleon in the sketch of his early lodgings in the Quai de Conti. But in these foreign works Turner is unequal. Nothing can be worse, for instance, than the figures in the foreground of the 'Verona,' or the architectural ornaments in the 'Venice.' The 'Jerusalem' is very unoriental, and 'Mayence' very shaky about its towers. Then, again, he is often disappointing; the drawing of Shakespeare's tomb is far inferior to that of Dryden's monument, and neither 'Waterloo' nor 'Hougoumont' is very grandly treated. The 'Malmaison' is crowded with incomprehensible figures. The 'Milan Cathedral' is not far enough off; 'Père-la-Chaise' is confused and uncomfortable; and the 'Brussels' is taken from a bad point of view. All these faults are forgotten, however, when you look at 'Brienz' or 'Piacenza.' The latter especially is remarkable for its headlong, scouring flight of despairing men and tired horses.

Turner and Thomson of Duddingston, whom he met at Edinburgh, belonged to the same set of artists and painters, and used to go out sketching and painting together. At the meetings of the clique Turner would constantly battle with them upon the subject of light, trying to gain from Brewster and other *savans* information thereon; and it is supposed that the discussions contributed to form a theory which enabled him to create the varied effects he has displayed in his works. To such a height, indeed, did he carry the verbal contests that the subject, it is said, finally was prohibited ; and he then became more earnest to discover what combination of colour would produce light.[1]

Turner once called upon Thomson, by appointment probably, for the express purpose of seeing the painter-parson's works. Thomson, of course, was delighted to receive the great landscape painter, and naturally expected his own pictures would receive some notice and even praise ; but, after Turner had taken a survey, the only remark he made was, ' You beat me in frames.' Some of Thomson's admirers had gone so far as to say that at times he was equal to Turner. This Turner may have heard, and felt piqued at the fulsome flattery. Thomson, it is easy to understand, was sadly mortified on the occasion.

Many years ago, when he was making sketches for the ' Provincial Antiquities,' in the company of Cadell, the Edinburgh bookseller, as they passed Norham, Turner took off his hat and made a low bow to the ruins. Observing this strange act of homage, Cadell exclaimed, ' What the Devil are you about now?' ' Oh,' was the reply, ' I made a drawing or painting of Norham several years since. It took ; and from that day to this I have had as much to do as my hands could execute.' Many of the sketches he made on this trip he opened with the foreground ; and he often sent some of the party forward to see if there was any rock, or other object, which from his position could not be seen ; all being duly noted down. After they were engraved, the drawings made for Scott's works were sold

---

[1] The story communicated by Mr. Birch is correct in the main ; but Sir David Brewster himself could not have been among the *savans* with whom Turner discussed optics, for, on being applied to, Sir David says : ' The only time I ever saw Turner was at a dinner given to Lord Grey, at Edinburgh, in 1834 [?], when I sat between Turner and Sir Charles Bell. On that occasion he exhibited none of his peculiarities.' In a later chapter, treating of Turner's interest in photography, I bring forward many instances in point of his intense desire to understand the law of colours.

by Cadell for 500*l.* They were nearly all in the hands of Mr. Munro of Hamilton Place.

Most probably his earliest Scotch tour produced the 'Norham Castle' ('Summer's Morn') which was exhibited at the Royal Academy in 1798, and used again in the 'Liber' in 1816. It also served as an illustration to 'Marmion.' In several drawings of it by him, which have come under my inspection, it is to be noted that he generally sets the castle as a dark mass against the rising sun, with cattle and boats in the foreground.

Turner always cherished a kind remembrance of Scotland. Upon Mr. Munro's periodic return from Edinburgh, it was his wont to enquire how they got on at 'Modern Aythens,' and whether 'Thomson and that set had discovered Titian's secret yet.'

CHAPTER XIV.

TURNER'S HOME TOURS.

THERE are few places in England where I do not seem to see Turner. I find him on the Derbyshire hills, and among the ruins of Yorkshire abbeys. I meet his ghost on the banks of the Wharfe, and on the sea-shore at Dover. I come across him in the green hop-fields of Kent, and in the marshes of the Thames. I see his short, stalwart spirit pacing about the Scotch moors, and around the pebbly margins of Scotch lakes. I never go on the Thames, and look at St. Paul's, but his boat goes by me in the direction of dear old Chelsea. In Wales, at Oxford, in Sussex, in Wiltshire, I still cannot disengage myself from his apparition. He haunts Fonthill, Petworth, and Tabley; he emerges at every old castle and abbey in England; he has been on every river, and in every county.

A careful study of the catalogue of pictures exhibited by him at the Royal Academy yields the following results as to the dates of some of his home and foreign tours :—

In 1789 he was painting with Girtin on the Thames; in 1790 he was at Eltham and Uxbridge; in 1791 at

Malmesbury ; in 1792 at Bristol and in Wales ; in 1792–3–4–5 in Wales, Worcestershire, Staffordshire, Essex, and on the sea-coast ; in 1797 in Yorkshire, at the Lakes, on the Border, and in Scotland ; in 1798 probably again in Wales, where he got materials for his diploma picture ; in 1799 in Wiltshire ; and in 1801 in Scotland. His first Continental tour to France and Switzerland was undertaken in 1802. In 1809 he was painting at Petworth ; in 1812 in Devonshire ; in 1818 in Scotland ; in 1819 on the Rhine ; in 1828 in Italy ; in 1832 in France ; in 1838 in Switzerland ; and in 1843 in Switzerland.

When on the Northumberland hills, making those beautiful drawings of the Chain Bridge and the High Force, he one evening got ten miles out of the way, and was all but benighted. In his drawing he has introduced a solitary grouse-shooter, and in the foreground, not far from himself, some timid birds cowering under the heather.

An intimate friend, while travelling in the Jura, says Mr. Lovell Reeve, came to an inn where Turner had only just before entered his name in the visiting-book. Anxious to be sure of his identity, and to be in pursuit of him, he enquired of his host what sort of a man his visitor was. ' A rough, clumsy man,' was the reply ; ' and you may know him by his always having a pencil in his hand.'

He was in Keswick many years ago ; and a guide used to point out a small but beautiful waterfall in the great wood, where he spent many days sketching one bit of rock. Turner's materials were not worth half a crown, he adds, though he was not shabby ' *his sell.*'

He visited Wiltshire in 1800, when he was thirty-two. The date may be determined by the aid of one[1] of five sketches of Fonthill Abbey he made that year for Beckford, which I have carefully examined. The abbey was then in course of erection for that great voluptuary and millionaire. They severally were— an afternoon effect ; morning ; south view, evening ; east view, noon ; and north-east view, sunset. Of these Mr. Allnutt has two, and two others are the property of Mr. A. Morrison and his brother. They are large, ambitious drawings, of a mellow,

[1] Now in possession of Mr. Morrison, of Fonthill-Bishop, Wiltshire.

subdued tone, and remarkable for a rather careless breadth. The foliage of the ash trees in the foreground is not at all made out, but is washed in in low-toned flat tints, with hardly any details ; and here and there it is touched with white. The sky is not very good ; the clouds are hard in the edges, and rather stiff in shape. As is too common with him, little attention is devoted to fidelity, cottages and water being introduced where cottages and water do not exist ; and there are rough prints of figures, subsequently obliterated, and some half-shaped out animals—deer, I think. The sky is serene ; but the great aim of the artist seems to have been to shed a flood of white light on the tower, which stands like a beacon on the crest of the wooded hill. The fir trees, that stretch in ranks up the sides of this slope, are but rudely indicated by small, shapeless dashes of green. The fir Turner could seldom manage, and probably he disliked it.

Mr. Morrison also possesses a small water-colour sketch, somewhat opaque, made on the spot. Taken from the quarry whence the stone for the abbey was hewn, it is true in its details. A well-known picture dealer, now living, remembers being down at Fonthill, during Turner's stay with Beckford, when the three had luncheon together in a tent pitched near the spot selected by the artist.

In the first picture the tone is very subdued, nearly all of a reddish-yellowish brown, or greenish blue ; the lighter parts of the sky are rather pale, and the atmospheric effect of distance on the hill is expressed by a vague softness and absence of outline. The manner is a strong imitation of Girtin's, even to the dots of dark colour on the trees and foliage.

Mr. Cyrus Redding, who met Turner in 1812 on one of his Devonshire tours, remembers that his sketches were not larger than sheets of letter-paper. From his autobiography, which contains most characteristic traits of Turner in his home tours, I submit some passages, written in so hearty, amiable, and gossiping a style, and withal so full of interest, that it would be quite unfair to the writer to paraphrase them. I therefore quote them in full. They reveal Turner as a vigorous pedestrian, joyously roughing it at a homely Devonshire inn, and as much at his ease there as amid the princely splendour of an English nobleman's house ; frank and merry at the picnic as the hospitable giver of the feast ; and stealing from his friends to climb a cliff and take eager notes of a stormy evening sea. We see him, too, that brilliant dewy morning, sketching the bridge that he afterwards idealised and lighted up with an Italian sky in one of his noblest pictures.

'Turner, the landscape painter,' says Mr. Redding, 'had arrived in the West on a professional tour. Among those who entertained him with admiring hospitality was Mr. John Collier, whom I have mentioned among my own most respected friends, and as having preceded Turner to the grave.

'The unprepossessing exterior, the reserve, the austerity of language, existed in Turner in combination with a powerful, intelligent, reflective mind, ever coiled up within itself ; he had a faculty of vision that seemed to penetrate the sources of natural effect, however various in aspect, and to store them in memory with wonderful felicity. His glance commanded in an instant all that was novel in scenery, and a few outlines on paper recorded it unintelligibly to others. He placed these pictorial memoranda upon millboard, not larger than a sheet of letter-paper, quite a confused mass. How he worked out the details from such sketches seemed to me wonderful. His views around Plymouth, in the engravings from his pictures, were marvellously varied in effect, as well as faithful representations. His first sketches showed little of the after picture to the unpractised eye ; perhaps he bore much away in memory, and these were only a kind of shorthand, which he deciphered in his studio.

'We once ran along the coast to Borough, or Bur Island, in Bibury Bay. There was to be the wind-up of a fishing account there. Our excuse was to eat hot lobsters, fresh from the water to the kettle. The sea was boisterous, the morning unpropitious. Our boat was Dutch built, with outriggers and undecked. It belonged to a fine old weather-beaten seaman, a Captain Nicols. Turner, an artist ; a half-Italian, named Demaria, an officer of the army ; Mr. Collier, a mutual friend ; and myself, with a sailor, composed the party. The sea had that dirty, puddled appearance which often precedes a hard gale. We kept towards Rame Head to obtain an offing, and when running out from the land the sea rose higher, until off Stokes Point it became stormy. We mounted the ridges bravely. The sea in that part of the Channel rolls in grand furrows from the Atlantic, and we had run about a dozen miles. The artist enjoyed the scene. He sat in the stern sheets intently watching the sea, and not at all affected by the motion. Two of our number were sick. The soldier, in a delicate coat of scarlet, white, and gold, looked dismal enough, drenched with the spray, and so ill that at last he wanted to jump overboard. We were obliged to lay him on the rusty iron ballast at the bottom of the boat, and keep him down with a spar laid across him. Demaria was silent in his suffering. In this way we made Bur Island. The difficulty was how to get through the surf, which looked unbroken. At last we got round under the lee of the island, and contrived to get on shore. All this time Turner was silent, watching the tumultuous scene. The little island, and the solitary hut it held, the bay in the bight of which it lay, and the dark long Bolt head to seaward, against the rocky shore of which the waves broke with fury, made the artist become absorbed in contemplation, not uttering a syllable. While the shell-fish were preparing, Turner, with a pencil, clambered nearly to the summit of the island, and seemed writing rather than drawing. How he succeeded, owing to the violence of the wind, I do not know. He probably observed something in the sea aspect which he had not before noted. We took our picnic dinner and lobsters, and soon became merry over our wine on that wild islet. Evening approached ; the wind had rather increased than diminished in violence. The landsmen did not approve of a passage back that must run far into the night, if not the morning. Some one proposed we should walk to Kingsbridge and sleep. Captain Nicols declared he would return ; his boat would defy any sea. We ought not in good fellowship to have separated ; when it was low water we could reach the main land over the sands. We left the boat, and the captain with his man set sail back alone, and was obliged to run off the coast nearly to the Eddystone to make the Sound. Some of the men-of-war there were firing guns to give notice that they were dragging their anchors. We slept at Kingsbridge. Turner and myself went early the next morning to Dodbrook to see the house in which Dr. Wolcot (Peter Pindar) was born, of which the artist took a sketch. We walked a good part of the way back.

    ✴   *   *   *   *   *

'I was one of a picnic party of eight or nine ladies and gentlemen, which he gave in excellent taste at Mount Edgcumbe. There we spent a good part of a fine summer's day. Cold meats, shell-fish, and good wines abounded. The donor of the feast, too, was agreeable, terse, blunt, almost epigrammatic at times, but always pleasant for one not given to waste his words, nor studious of refined bearing. We visited Cothele on the Tamar together, where the furniture is of the time of Henry VII. and Henry VIII.

'The woods are fine, and the views of some of the headlands round which the river winds are of exquisite beauty. In one place he was much struck, took a sketch, and when it was done said, "We shall see nothing finer than this if we stay till Sunday ; because we can't." It was the last visit he paid to the scenery of the Tamar before he quitted the West. It was to the honour of several of the inhabitants of Plymouth that boats, horses, and tables were ready for his use during the time he remained. Everybody felt that in paying him attention they were honouring a most extraordinary genius, whose artistic merit had not been exaggerated.

'I remember one evening on the Tamar ; the sun had set, and the shadows become very deep. Demaria, looking at a seventy-four lying under Saltash, said, " You were right, Mr. Turner ; the ports cannot be seen. The ship is one dark mass." " I told you so," said Turner ; " now you see it all is one mass of shade." " Yes, I see that is the truth, and yet the ports are there."

' " We can take only what we see, no matter what is there. There are people in the ship : we don't see them through the planks." " True," replied Demaria.

'There had been a discussion on the subject before between

the two professional men, in which Turner had rightly observed that after sunset, under the hills, the port-holes were undiscernible. We now had ocular proof of it.

*   *   *   *   *   *

'When we came to the Lara passage we met Lord Baringdon (afterwards Earl of Morley), who invited Turner, Demaria, and myself to Saltram, to dine and sleep, the following day. We went accordingly. In the morning we ascended the high ground in the park, where there is a fine view. There is also some fine scenery near the eastern entrance, at the mouth of the Plym; and Turner made some sketches there.

'Among the guests at Saltram was Madame Catalani, who sang some of her favourite airs. Zuccarelli's best paintings adorn this hospitable mansion, but I could not extract from Turner any opinion regarding them. In the billiard room was Stubbs's fine picture of "Phaeton and the Horses of the Sun," with which, I remember, the artist was much pleased, as indeed everybody must be ; but it elicited no further remark than the monosyllable "Fine !" Turner, on retiring to rest, had to pass my bedroom door, and I remarked to him that its walls were covered with paintings by Angelica Kauffman—nymphs, and men like nymphs, as effeminate as possible. I directed his attention to them, and he wished me " Good night in your seraglio !" There were very fine pictures at Saltram by the old masters, but they seemed to attract little of his attention, though they might have done more than I imagined, for it was not easy to judge from his manner what was passing in his mind.

'On looking at some of the wonderful fancy works of this artist painted a little subsequently, I perceived that several were composed of bits of scenery we had visited in company. He told me afterwards, in London, that if I would look into his gallery I should see a picture ["Crossing the Brook"] some of the features of which I could not fail to recognise. I went accordingly, and traced three distinct snatches of scenery on the river Tamar, especially a spot near Newbridge. It was a beautiful work. Though I cannot recollect what name he gave it, I recognised a scene on that river which he told me on the spot he had never observed in Nature before. I know that the Headlands of Plymouth Sound closed the distance twelve miles off, and that the intervening objects were those to which he alluded. In his gallery at that time I first saw, too, his picture of " Hannibal Crossing the Alps." Another picture which was in the Exhibition he told me was the fruit of our expeditions. I speak of his fancy compositions, for his pictures of existing scenery in the West cannot be mistaken, so faithful are they, so true to nature, and so deeply imbued with the magic of his genius. I was with Turner when he sketched Plymouth Sound, with part of Mount Edgcumbe ; when he visited Trematon Castle, Saltash ; the Wear Head, Calstock— in fact, all the views he made on the banks of that picturesque river which have been since engraved.

'We had one day reached the Wear Head of the Tamar, no great way below the Duke of Bedford's cottage at Endsleigh, when night came on. Turner was struck with admiration at the bridge above the Wear, which he declared altogether Italian. Our party consisted of four. To go down the river in the night was impracticable, on account of the chance of getting on shore upon the mud-banks. There was an inn hard by, at which beds could not be obtained ; and some course must be resolved upon. We might walk to Tavistock, three or four miles off ; but a vehicle which had come from Plymouth that day with two of our party could do no more than carry two to the town. Turner said that he would rather stay until the morning, on the spot where we were debating the subject. He did not mind sitting up. Would anyone volunteer with him ? The horse would come over fresh in the morning with those who might then leave. I volunteered. Our friends drove off, and the painter and myself soon adjourned to the miserable little inn. I proposed to " plank it," in the sailor's phrase— that is, to go to sleep on the floor—but some part of it was damp, and the whole well sanded, so that it was not a prac- ticable couch, however hard. Turner said, before he considered any other matter, he must have some bread, cheese, and porter. Very good bread and cheese were produced, and the home- brewed suited Turner, who expatiated upon his success with a degree of excitement which, with his usual dry, short mode of expressing his feelings, could hardly be supposed. I pleased him further by enquiring whether bacon and eggs could be obtained ; and, getting an affirmative reply, we supped in clover, and sat up until midnight in conversation. I found the artist could, when he pleased, make sound, pithy, though somewhat caustic, remarks upon men and things, with a fluency rarely heard from him. We talked much of the Academy, and he admitted that it was not all which it might be made in regard to Art. The "clock that ticked against the wall" sounded twelve; I proposed to go to sleep. Turner leaned his elbow upon the table, and, putting his feet upon a second chair, took a position sufficiently easy, and fell asleep. I laid myself at full length across three or four chairs, and soon followed his example.

'Before six in the morning he rose, and went down towards the bridge. The air was balmy ; the strong light between the hills, the dark umbrage, and the flashing water presented a beautiful early scene. Turner sketched the bridge, but appeared, from changing his position several times, as if he had tried more than one sketch, or could not please himself as to the best point. I saw that bridge and part of the scene afterwards in a painting in his gallery. He had made several additions to the scenery near the bridge from his own imagination. The picture was poetical ; and, if I remember rightly, he had introduced into it some of the fictitious characters of the heathen mythology ; he had bathed it in the gorgeous glories of the southern sun, clothed it in barbaric pearl and gold—in fact, enriched it with that indefinable attraction which true genius confers on all its works. In delineating ocean, storm, or calm, the effulgence of southern glory on the chaste and highly decorated, but soberer scenery of his native land, Turner seemed to me then, as still, without a compeer. His sea pieces far excel those of the higher Dutch painters. His pictures of Italy's sunny clime, her melancholy ruins, and the unsullied azure of her blue heaven, have received from Turner a charm which is scarcely to be found in any other painter. He was truly the poet of painting.

'Turner said that he had never seen so many natural

beauties in so limited an extent of country as he saw in the vicinity of Plymouth. Some of the scenes hardly appeared to belong to this island. Mount Edgcumbe particularly delighted him, and he visited it three or four times. I have now in my possession a pencil sketch, of the roughest kind, which he drew. It is from the side of that fairy spot which looks into Cowsand Bay. There is the end of the seat, over which projects a thatched roof, the table, the bottle of wine, and a full-length of myself in the foreground—not the most flattering of his little-flattering impersonations. In the bay are several line-of-battle ships at anchor. This, a mere scrawl, is as full a representation as he took of many scenes of which he made some of his finest pictures. His slender, graphic memoranda induce me to think that he possessed the most extraordinary memory for treasuring up the details of what he saw in Nature of any individual that ever existed, and that such outlines were to him what the few heads of a discourse would be to a person who carried them away with a good memory. Some have said that he was not conscious of his own superiority ; I believe that he was, and enjoyed the reflection as much as a nature would permit that did not participate in common susceptibilities, nor build its satisfaction upon such pleasures as the common mind most esteems. His habits were of the simplest character ; he had no relish for the tawdry displays that obtain so much conventional estimation. A splendid house and large establishment would have been an encumbrance rather than a luxury to Turner ; his mind was set on higher objects. If he desired what everyday people estimate highest, it was at his command. He was called close and niggardly ; but he had no desire to live and enjoy beyond the style of living and enjoying to which he was habituated. His mind lived in his art ; he did not wish to appear other than he was. His wealth he had long determined to devote to a better purpose than giving dilettanti dinners, or assembling in a drawing-room the customary bevy of visitors that come and go to no good purpose, either as regards themselves or others. He was rather content to follow the path of most great men who have devoted themselves to a pursuit to which they have given their whole hearts. He did not fawn, as artists continually do, in the crowded rooms of men of rank and fortune for interested ends, while he did not shun an occasional intermixture in good society ; his own time was too precious to be wasted as too many waste theirs.   Turner felt that he bore, and desired still to bear, no surreptitious name in coteries ; but to leave behind enduring renown as an artist.   Concealed beneath his homely exterior there was much that was good and aspiring.   Who with such ideas, humbly born as he was, so pre-eminent in Art, destitute of fluency in language, though always speaking to the point—who with such ideas has ever existed without being an object of attack from some quarter or other ?

'He was charged with being close in money matters.   If he satisfied his simple personal wants, who has a right to call him niggardly when he preserved his wealth for a noble purpose? I denied to several artists who told stories of his love of money that his character was as they represented it.   The most miserable of wretches is he who makes life a burden in order to move in the track of other people's ideas.   When I was out with Turner in Devonshire, he paid his quota at the inns with cheerfulness ; and some of our bills were rather higher in amount than bread and cheese would have incurred.   Turner accommodated himself as well as any man I ever saw to the position of the moment.

'I chanced to relate to one of his brother Academicians that I was of a party to whom Turner had given a picnic in Devonshire, but I was scarcely credited.   Never was there more social pleasure partaken by any party in that English Eden.   Turner was exceedingly agreeable for one whose language was more epigrammatic and terse than complimentary upon most occasions.   He had come two or three miles with the man who bore his store of good things, and had been at work before our arrival.   He showed the ladies some of his sketches in oil, which he had brought with him, perhaps, to verify them.   The wine circulated freely, and the remembrance was not obliterated from Turner's mind long years afterwards. My opinion is, that this great artist always understood the occasion, and was prepared to meet it as any other individual would do. At home he led the life he preferred ; he was not calculated for any but his own pursuit, and in that he shone ; he knew and felt it. When I see a deviation from the common track in such a man, I feel persuaded that it is the result of a preference or inclination that should be respected. He had a great regard for his own fame.

*   *   *   *   *   *

'Suddenly a battery of twenty-four pounders opened only four or five feet above our heads. I was startled with the shock, but Turner was unmoved. We were neither of us prepared for the concussion ; but he showed none of the surprise which I betrayed, being as unmoved at the sudden noise and involvement in the smoke as if nothing had happened.

'We visited Cothele together, where the furniture is of the date of the reigns of Henry VII. and Henry VIII. Turner did not seem much interested in the building ; but with the woods and the views from some of the headlands round which the river winds he was so much taken that, following him with a gig, we could not return, and were obliged to take out the horse, and lift the vehicle over a hedge by main strength. In doing this and getting upon the hedge, there burst upon the view a noble expanse of scenery, which we had not anticipated. Here the artist became busy at once, but only for a short time. " Now," said he, " we shall see nothing finer than this, if we stay till sundown ; because we can't. Let us go home." It was the last visit we paid to the scenery of the Tamar together. We subsequently had a picnic on the romantic banks of the Plym, and visited the crags and precipices of Sheep's Tor together. This visit closed nearly three weeks for the most part spent in similar rambles. It was during these rambles that I imbibed higher ideas, not only of the artist, but of the man, than I had previously held, and still hold, now death has closed his shining career.

'Many years afterwards he spoke to me in London of the reception he met with on this tour, in a strain that exhibited his possession of a mind not unsusceptible or forgetful of kindnesses. Among his entertainers some preceded him to the narrow house, and foremost among them the late John Collier,

then resident at Mount Tamar, and subsequently member of
Parliament for Plymouth.

'As the birthplace of Turner has recently appeared to some
persons a matter of doubt, I may here observe he was born at
Barnstaple, and neither in Maiden Lane nor at South Molton,
if his own words go for anything. The latter place, it is true, is
but twelve miles from Barnstaple. We were sailing together in
a boat on the St. Germains river, near Ince Castle ; I recollect
it as well as if it occurred yesterday. Turner, Collier, and
myself were the only persons present, except the boatmen. I
was remarking what a number of artists the West of England
had produced, particularly Devon and Cornwall. I enumerated
all I could remember from Reynolds to Prout. When I had
done, Turner said, " You may add me to the list; I am a Devonshire man." I demanded from what part of the county, and he
replied, "Barnstaple." I have many times since repeated the
incident to others, who would insist that the artist was a Londoner. His father was of the same trade as the parent of the
distinguished equity lawyer Sugden, and came to London when
Turner was young. I remember the little, plain, but not ill-
made old man letting me into Turner's house, or rather gallery,
in Queen Anne Street more than once. He was not as stout nor
as bluff-looking as his son, allowing for the difference in years.'

The following interesting communication, relative to probably
the same tour, was kindly supplied by the late Sir Charles Eastlake :—

' Turner visited Plymouth (my native town) while I was
staying there in the summer of 1813, or perhaps 1814 (1812 ?),
painting portraits. As he wished to see the scenery of the
river Tamar, I accompanied him, together with Mr. Ambrose
Johns, of Plymouth (a landscape painter of great merit, lately
deceased at a great age), to a cottage near Calstock, the residence of my aunt, Miss Pearce, where we all stayed for a few
days. From that point as a centre Turner made various excursions, and the result of one of his rambles was a sketch of
the scene which afterwards grew into the celebrated picture of
" Crossing the Brook." The bridge in that picture is Calstock
Bridge ; some mining works are indicated in the middle dis-

tance. The extreme distance extends to the mouth of the Tamar, the harbour of Hamoaze, the hills of Mount Edgcumbe, and those on the opposite side of Plymouth Sound. The whole scene is extremely faithful.

'Turner made his sketches in pencil and by stealth. His companions, observing his peculiarity, were careful not to intrude upon him. After he returned to Plymouth, in the neighbourhood of which he remained some weeks, Mr. Johns fitted up a small portable painting-box, containing some prepared paper for oil sketches, as well as the other necessary materials. When Turner halted at a scene and seemed inclined to sketch it, Johns produced the inviting box, and the great artist, finding everything ready to his hand, immediately began to work. As he sometimes wanted assistance in the use of the box, the presence of Johns was indispensable, and after a few days he made his oil sketches freely in our presence. Johns accompanied him always; I was only with them occasionally. Turner seemed pleased when the rapidity with which those sketches were done was talked of; for, departing from his habitual reserve in the instance of his pencil sketches, he made no difficulty of showing them. On one occasion, when, on his return after a sketching ramble to a country residence belonging to my father, near Plympton, the day's work was shown, he himself remarked that one of the sketches (and perhaps the best) was done in less than half an hour.

'When he left Plymouth he carried off all the results. We had reckoned that Johns, who had provided all the materials, and had waited upon him devotedly, would at least have had a present of one or two of the sketches. This was not the case; but long afterwards the great painter sent Johns in a letter a small oil sketch, not painted from Nature, as a return for his kindness and assistance. On my enquiring afterwards what had become of those sketches, Turner replied that they were worthless, in consequence, as he supposed, of some defect in the preparation of the paper; all the grey tints, he observed, had nearly disappeared. Although I did not implicitly rely on that statement, I do not remember to have seen any of them afterwards.'

CHAPTER XV.

ENGLISH ENGRAVERS.

So limited was the number of good engravers in England in 1703 that, to procure plates for his folio 'Cæsar,' Tonson had to go to Holland in search of artists.[1]

In George II.'s reign Vandergucht and Faber, the one a Fleming, the other a Dutchman, engraved a few plates ; but, in 1725, the thirteen octavo volumes of Rapin's 'History of England,' translated by Tindal and illustrated with George Virtue's portraits, drew much attention to native talent. In 1732 a folio edition of this work was published in weekly numbers, and sold by thousands.

To this followed Picart's 'Religious Ceremonies of all Nations,' illustrated by Gavelot and Scotin ; whom Hogarth also employed, together with Ravenel, Grignon, and Walker. In 1719 Dorigny completed his plates from Raphael's Cartoons ; and in 1751 Messrs. Knapton published a series of historical prints after the English artists Hayman and Blakely ; while in the same reign Dubosc brought out 'The Battle of Blenheim,' and Pine his copies of 'The Tapestry in the House of Lords.' In fact, between 1740 and 1750 engraving began to develope English talent ; mezzotint portraits became common, and the printsellers commenced to exhibit likenesses of distinguished characters.

Illustrated editions of English works now increased in number, and the magazines rivalled each other in their engravings and increased the taste for Art. Reckless Hayman, Hogarth's friend, who decorated Vauxhall, drew largely for the booksellers at two guineas a drawing ; inferior artists received only one

---

[1] Our earlier engravers were—Faithorne, who died 1691 ; Whister, who died 1704 ; Smith (mezzotint), who died 1720 ; Boydell, born 1719, died 1804 ; Strange, born 1721, died 1792 ; Basile, born 1730, died 1802, Ryland, born 1732, died 1783 ; Woollett, born 1755, died 1785 ; Sharp, born 1740, died 1824 ; Rooker, born 1748, died 1801.

guinea, though Lownes, the publisher, gave Wale for each of his designs to 'Clarissa Harlowe' half a crown extra. Hayman illustrated Moore's 'Fables' in 1744, Hanmer's 'Shakespeare' in 1744, and Milton's Works in 1749. Gavelot also drew antiquities, designed for upholsterers, and illustrated books between 1735 and 1745. His best work is the 'Decamerone,' 1757—a work published, however, after his return to France.

In 1741 Boydell, a young English engraver, began to publish a series of views in and about London, the size folio and the price one shilling; which were placed for sale in toy-shop windows. Encouraged by success, he extended his tours to the whole of England and Wales between 1741 and 1755.

From 1780 Rooker, Ryland, Strange, and Woollett began to get patronage. In 1751 Strange commenced his series of copies from the old masters; and in 1752, the year that Reynolds returned from abroad, and Zuccarelli came to live in England, Knapton and Dodsley published some historical prints. At the same time Dalton's work on Greece and Egypt employed the talent of Basile, Mason, Chatelain, and Vivares. In 1753 Cipriani came to England; and in 1755, the year Wilson returned from Italy, Stuart returned from Greece, and commenced a folio work on Athens, illustrated with engravings by Basile, Rooker, Strange, Walker, Grignon, and others.

In 1754, through the exertions of Mr. W. Shipley, a Northamptonshire gentleman, a Society for the Encouragement of Art was founded in London, in imitation of one founded by Dr. Madden in Dublin in 1740. About 1755 Mr. Wedgwood, the Staffordshire potter, began to introduce high Art into ceramic manufacture.

Among the early engravers we may reckon—F. Legat, a Scotchman, and pupil of Runciman, who engraved for Boydell Northcote's 'Children in the Tower,' Stothard's 'Fall of Abercromby,' West's 'King, Queen, and Laertes,' 'Cassandra,' after Romney, and the 'Death of Cordelia,' after Barry; and who died of disappointment in 1809. Hall, a pupil of Ravenet, who engraved, among others, West's pictures of Penn's 'Treaty with the Indians' and 'Cromwell Dissolving the Parliament,' became historical engraver to George III. Robert Strange, chiefly an engraver of the old masters, born 1721, died in 1772. Vivares, a Frenchman, originally a tailor, was a beautiful etcher of trees, and was often assisted by Chatelain, who lived in Great New-port Street ; he was born in 1709 and died in 1780. And last, yet first of all, Woollett, who engraved Wilson's 'Niobe.' He was born at Maidstone in 1735, and died in 1785. He also engraved the 'Phaeton,' 'Celadon and Amelia,' 'Ceyx and Alcyone.' Gavelot, who kept a drawing-school in the Strand, also drew for Grignon. MacArdell engraved much for Rey-nolds, and also fine mezzotints of Hogarth's 'Captain Coram.' Luke Sullivan, who etched the 'March to Finchley,' was also a miniature painter ; he died in poverty. Nor must we forget the unfortunate Sherwin, who engraved portraits of Mrs. Robinson, Mrs. Siddons, and others.

For the 'Death of General Wolfe,' 1776, Woollett received some 6,000l. or 7,000l., participating in the profits of the pub-lisher ; nor was the 'Battle of La Hogue,' published in 1781, less popular. They were both copied in Paris and Vienna. The mezzotints of Earlom helped to swell the 200,000l. re-ceived by the English in one year for engravings from foreign customers.

Gradually topographical works became more numerous, and began to improve in merit. Our artists were few, especially landscape artists, and even of these not many there were who cared to go and see Nature for themselves. The brown tree, the upas tree of Art, flourished in every studio. Spring and autumn had never yet been painted, and green grass was despised as mere salad ; the real high-Art grass being of the colour of an old violin.

In 1780 illustrated works made a considerable advance in the shape of Harrison's 'Novelist's Magazine ;' for which Stot-hard's first drawing was one to illustrate 'Joseph Andrews,' the remuneration being half a guinea, and for later drawings a guinea. For engraving one of these Heath received five guineas.

From about 1780 Heath stood high among English line-engravers ; and after the French Revolution arose Raimbach and Warren. It is not known exactly when steel engraving superseded copper, but Pye tells us that in 1811 Raimbach engraved a steel plate for the Bank of England, and that steel engraving was then a proved thing.[1]

In 1786 Boydell, growing wealthy, determined to encourage historical painting by publishing by subscription a series of prints illustrative of Shakespearian scenes ; and the pictures painted for the work were exhibited in a gallery built expressly for their reception in Pall Mall (now the British Institution). For this collection Northcote painted his ' Death of Wat Tyler,' and Reynolds his ' Robin Goodfellow,' the ' Vestal Tuccia,' the ' Holy Family,' the ' Gleaner,' ' Cardinal Beaufort,' and the ' Caldron Scene in Macbeth.' [2]

[1] The following record of engravers' prices is valuable:—For Duroveray's plates after Westall and others, sixteen and twenty guineas each ; Warren twenty, and Heath eighteen ; for *Sharpe's Classics*, 1308, fifteen guineas each, but eighteen to Bromley, Raimbach, and Warren ; two plates by P. Sharpe, in the *Spectator*, twenty guineas each ; and the *Rival Beauties*, by Parker, twenty-five guineas. Warren received for *The Heiress* and *Dr. Sangrado*, in *Inchbald's Theatre*, after Smirke, thirty guineas each ; for the plates in *The Arabian Nights*, after Smirke, thirty-eight guineas each ; for the *Broken Jar*, after Wilkie, fifty guineas. Raimbach received for his four beautiful plates for *Suttaby's Spectator* after Stothard, one hundred guineas ; for the plates for the *World*, twenty-five guineas ; for Smirke's *Don Quixote*, fifty guineas. Cook, for the illustrations to his edition of the Poets, gave but six or seven guineas each.

[2] Among the artists employed by Boydell were—

Angelica Kauffman	Highmore	Smirke
Barry	Hodges	Stothard
Beechey	Howard	West
Farington	Northcote	Westall
Fuseli	Opie	Wheatley
Hamilton	Reynolds	Wilson
Hearne	Romney	

And among the engravers were—

Aliamet	Fittler	Picot
Bartolozzi	Grignon	Ravenle
Baron	Val. Green	Schiavonetti
Brown	Hall	Sharpe
Byrne	Heath	J. Smith
Carnot	M'Ardell	Vivares
Chatelain	Mason	Woollett
Earlom	Middiman	

In 1803 the catalogue published by Boydell of the plates forming his stock extended to forty-eight volumes.[1]

In 1804 Boydell obtained the sanction of Parliament to dispose of his Art property by lottery ; when the gallery fell to the share of Mr. Tassie, a modeller, of Leicester Square, who died in 1861. Boydell had spent 500,000*l.* in plates for prize prints, 46,266*l.* in pictures and drawings, and 30,000*l.* in the Shakespeare Gallery. The lottery was drawn in 1805. Boydell had died in the previous year.

In 1811 the bequest of the Desenfans pictures to Dulwich College by Sir Francis Bourgeois contributed largely to advance English Art. In 1819 Mr. J. O. Robinson purchased the Boydell stock, and in connexion with Mr. Hurst carried on the trade of print-selling and publishing. In 1822 they entered into an agreement with Sir Thomas Lawrence to give him 5,000*l.* per annum for the exclusive privilege of engraving plates from his pictures ; and for the right of engraving the portrait of the Duke of York, the two children called 'Nature' (by G. D. Doo), the 'Little Red Ridinghood' (by Lane), and the portrait of George IV. (by Finden), with two or three others never finished, they paid him 10,000*l.* From Messrs. Moon, Boys, and Graves, who purchased Messrs. Hurst and Robinson's stock in 1825, Wilkie received 1,200 guineas for the right of engraving the 'Chelsea Pensioners,' which he had painted for the Duke of Wellington.

About 1824 the frivolous Keepsake mania, though originating mere literary confectionery, gave an impetus to modern Art. Keepsakes are said to have originated in an idea suggested by Mr. Alaric Watts, the poet, at that time the editor of a Manchester paper. He proposed to Messrs. Hurst and Robinson, Sir Walter Scott's London publishers, to start an annual volume (half art, half literature) in imitation of the German pocket-books. Scott, Byron, Lady Blessington, Mrs.

---

[1] After Boydell's enterprise followed Macklin's *Illustrations of the Poets of the Bible*, and Bowyer's *Illustrations o the History of England*.

Shelley, Wordsworth, Southey, Praed, and the like were to contribute ; Turner, Leslie, Newton, Stothard, Alston, Lawrence, Collins, Danby, and Martin were to furnish drawings ; and Hall, Finden, Watt, Goodall, and Pye were to engrave. The 'Literary Souvenir' appeared in 1824, and was followed by the 'Amulet' and 'Keepsake,' the latter of which ran its course for ten years. Thousands of these ephemeral productions were sold ; of some editions as many as 14,000 copies ; and a single speculator is said to have spent some 50,000*l.* thereon ; the engravers receiving between 150*l.* and 200*l.* each. Finding, however, that these butterflies injured the Christmas sale of their books, the authors clubbed to put them down.

Like all great movers of the world, Turner was born at the precisely right moment. The planets were in due conjunction over his house of life. Illustrated books began to be popular, and engraving flourished, just as Turner's talent began to be known. We have already seen that in 1778, when he was three years old, appeared 'Hearne and Byrne's Antiquities,' some of the drawings in which, as a boy, he copied and revised. In 1779 came out Harrison's 'Novelist's Magazine,' which Stothard, a young apprentice to a Spitalfields pattern-drawer, began to illustrate with great elegance and poetry. Then came out in rivalry 'Paul Sandby's Views,' the 'Virtuoso's Museum,' 'Watt's [one of Hearne's engravers] Views of Gentlemen's Seats,' 'Milton's Views in Ireland,' 'Middiman's Views,' and in 1782 Bell's illustrated edition of the 'British Poets.' Turner was then eight years old.

In 1793, when he was eighteen, Turner was engaged by Walker to make his earliest tours to Kent, Staffordshire, Derbyshire, and Cheshire.

We have already seen that Turner was a bitterly disappointed man. He had been cruelly frustrated in love, and his nature was one that could not forget. In Art, too, he had had hard struggles. His oil pictures did not sell at first : the engravings from his works were unlucky. The 'Liber' was stopped because it was at first partially a failure ; and his plates to the 'History of Richmondshire' were a great loss to the publishers. Was it any wonder, then, that he learnt to despise a public who could not understand his genius, and would have let him starve had he been less fertile in resources? Even his drawing-lessons missed success. An authority pronounces that the 'plates from " Cologne " and " Dover " were not successful; whilst Whitaker's " History of Richmondshire," containing twenty engravings from some of the finest of his designs, entailed a heavy loss on its proprietors. All these works, however, are now sought with the greatest avidity, and fetch, when the impressions are really good, prices greatly beyond their original value.'

A review of Mr. Stokes's elaborate index of the engravings from Turner presents some view of his Art progress in conjunction with his paintings, and enables us to see that his fame as a painter profited largely by the reputation he acquired through his engravings.

In 1794, when Turner is nineteen, he is drawing Rochester and Chepstow for Walker's 'Copperplate Magazine;' his tours have been as yet chiefly in the home counties and on the coast, and in Wales. In 1795 he makes drawings of Nottingham, Bridgenorth, Matlock, and Birmingham for the same periodical; the Tower of London and Cambridge for the 'Pocket Magazine;' and Worcester and Guildford for Messrs. Harrison. In the next year, for that and other magazines, from previous tours he makes drawings of Chester, Leith, Peterborough, Tunbridge, Bath, Staines, Bristol, Wallingford, and Windsor. In 1797 he sketches in Flint, Herefordshire, and Lincolnshire; and the first illustrations of his to a genuine topographical work, the 'Views of the County of Lincoln,' appear.

In 1798 the 'Itinerant' contains his 'Sheffield' and 'Wakefield;' and in 1799, when illustration work seems unusually scarce with him, he begins the first of his nine years' drawings for the 'Oxford Almanac.' In 1800 work apparently comes with a rush, and he furnishes numerous drawings of abbeys and gentlemen's mansions to Angus's 'Seats' and Whitaker's 'Parish of Whalley.'

In 1801 he contributes his only drawing to the 'Beauties of England and Wales;' and in 1803 to Byrne's 'Britannia Depicta.'

In 1807 he issues the first volume of his 'Liber Studiorum,' and does little else for the engraver till 1812, when he contributes a drawing of Fountains Abbey to Whitaker's 'History of Craven.' He had now become sufficiently known to venture on single plates engraved from his drawings. The first was 'Brocklesby Mausoleum;' the next was 'Dunster Castle' (in 1800, when he was twenty-five). This was a great step. Not until 1814, however, did he find full scope for his ambition in Cooke's 'Southern Coast,' the first number of which contained the following drawings :—'St. Michael's Mount,' 'Poole,' 'Land's End,' 'Weymouth,' and 'Lulworth Cove.' This work employed him regularly till 1826. In the meantime he had begun to progress. In 1820 and 1821 he contributed some of his finest works to Whitaker's 'History of Richmond.' Of this series the most matchless are the 'Ingleborough' and the 'High Force;' the 'Kirkby Lonsdale Churchyard' and the 'Wycliffe;' the 'Junction of the Greta and Tees;' and the 'Hardraw Fall' (engraved by the inimitable John Pye).

In 1820 he completed some drawings from camera-obscura sketches for Hakewell's 'Picturesque Tour in Italy,' from which country he had recently returned. They are careful, but rather blue in tone. One of them was privately published on a large scale by Mr. Allnutt, who became the owner by purchase.

In 1824 appeared Turner's 'Rivers of England,' published by W. B. Cooke, including the 'Norham Castle,' which he had always considered the turning-point in his career. Worn out, I believe, by the exactions and petty tyranny of Cooke, he began in 1827 his 'England and Wales.' The alphabetical plan of this series, which lasted eleven years, indicated the desire for comprehensive unity that specially distinguished Turner's mind. When his later Venetian pictures were bought, he was always saying, 'What do people want with such scraps?' His study in the 'Liber' had been to epitomise all landscape ideals; his study in the 'England and Wales' was to epitomise all the beauties of his own country.

In 1826 he took a higher flight, proceeding to illustrate the greatest poet of the age, Lord Byron, for Murray's octavo edition. The sketches were not always over-accurate ; the 'Athens' is specially bad. In 1833 he contributed some similar drawings to Finden's 'Landscape and Portrait Illustrations of Byron.'

In 1829 he executed several drawings of Fonthill for the 'Anniversary ;' and from 1828 to 1837 extended a series of drawings for the 'Keepsake,' beginning with 'Florence,' and ending with 'The Sea—the Sea.' About this time, I think, came out his very unequal engravings to Finden's 'Illustrations of the Bible.'

In 1830 and 1834 he executed some of his most charming drawings for Rogers's beautiful edition of his 'Italy ;' and, in the latter year, others for his complete Poems. In the 'Mont St. Bernard' the figures were by Stothard, and the dogs by E. Landseer. The moonlight in the 'Villa Madonna' is steeped in the most delicious poetry ; the figures in the 'Scene with Banditti' are full of spirit.

Nor does this lengthy enumeration of his labours exhaust the list of the engravings from Turner's pictures and drawings. In my Index will be found a long list of subscription plates, conspicuous among which are the 'Dido and Æneas,' the 'Caligula's Bridge,' the 'Mercury and Herse,' the 'Crossing the Brook,' the 'Ancient and Modern Italy,' the 'Cologne' and 'Ehrenbreitstein,' the 'Golden Bough,' the 'Lake of Narni,' and several Venetian pictures. To these we must add a long series of single plates.

In 1834 appeared further illustrations to Byron's works ; and the same year was marked by a succession of Scotch and French landscapes in the edition of Scott's 'Prose and Poetical Works' published by Cadell of Edinburgh.

Turner's tours in 1833-4-5 embraced the rivers of France, including châteaux, bridges, and towers innumerable. In the last year were published his seven illustrations to Macerone's edition of Milton's works, the least successful of all his book illustrations. In 1837 he rendered service to Campbell ; and, in 1839, to Moore's 'Epicurean.' These also were feeble, strained, and misunderstood productions.

HÔTEL DE VILLE. PARIS

In 1836-7 he had prepared for the engraver some careful drawings of views in India, from sketches by Lieutenant White.

His single plates commenced with the ' Brocklesby Mausoleum,' ' Norham Castle,' and ' Ivy Bridge ' in 1827, and ended with a frontispiece for ' Pilgrim's Progress ' in 1847. There are also some mezzotints after Turner, such as ' Whiting-Fishing off Margate,' the ' Eddystone Lighthouse,' the ' Wreck of the " Minotaur," ' the ' Wreck,' a ' Shipwreck,' and the ' Burning Mountain ' (engraved in colours). To these we must add the ' Ports of England ' and ' Views in Sussex.'

This constant issue of engravings was the real secret of Turner's wealth, and explained the two cart-loads of proofs that he left behind him. From some of them he must have reaped large sums. No one knows, moreover, how many of the ' Liber ' were sold ; probably at least three times as many copies as the ' coppers ' ought to have produced. He was always furbishing them with new effects.

CHAPTER XVI.

TURNER'S WORK FOR THE ENGRAVERS.

THE sixteen interesting letters which are introduced in the following chapter were addressed to Mr. J. Wyatt, a carver and gilder of Oxford, who was also an artist, and to Mr. F. Millar, of Edinburgh, who was Turner's favourite engraver. They possess considerable value, as containing the *ipsissima verba* of a very reserved and taciturn man, and as revealing the kindness of his heart and the ceaseless and anxious care with which he followed the development of his engraved works. If Reynolds was correct in his definition of genius as only ' well applied industry,' an argument in support of his dictum might be derived from these letters. Indeed, in all Turner did there was a restless aspiration after supreme excellence, a sleepless care, an untiring watchfulness to discover and to unite the beautiful with the true.

In 1809, the date of these letters, Turner—at the time Professor of Perspective at the Royal Academy—exhibited ' Boatmen Recovering an Anchor off Spithead;' two views of Tabley, in Cheshire, the seat of Sir J. F. Leicester, Bart.— one 'A Windy Day,' and the other 'A Calm Morning'—and also one of his few figure pictures, 'The Garreteer's Petition'—a faint echo of Hogarth's 'Grub Street Post.'

The first letter runs thus :—

> 'West End, Upper Mall, Hammersmith :
> 'Friday, November 23, 1809.

'Sir,—I will do what I can in respect to size, time, &c., considering your last letter's conclusion as to choice of price. But, concerning the engraver, it is a difficult thing to know who to choose; their prices are as different as their abilities, and therefore that point must remain with you. But if Mr. Warren will undertake a large plate, surely his abilities may be said to equal to the task; or Middiman, Lowry, young Byrne, or Miton, &c. The question is certainly of the first importance to me; but you must decide; and all I can do respecting *advice, &c.*, to whomsoever you may ultimately choose, shall be at his or your service.

> 'Your most truly obedient
> 'J. M. TURNER.

' " Britton's Antiquity " contains some good specimens of engraving for depth, clearness, and well-laid lines, but [I] cannot recollect their names.

> 'Mr. J. WYATT,
>   Carver and Gilder,
>   High Street, Oxford.'

> 'December 9, 1809: 9 o'clock, Saturday.

'Sir,—By some accident or other your letter arrived but just now, and therefore I shall despatch this answer by the coach to-morrow morning, for to wait for the next post would prevent your getting the proposal printed by Tuesday, and which even now appears to be doubtful.

'I think that a *print* or an engraving should follow the words " proposal for subscription " (which you think best), and that it is so near the size of " Niobe " that to mention it would perhaps induce some to think of yours as a comparison print. Another thing, you should by all means particularise how many *proofs* you intend to take off, and at what price, for the public like to have more than assurances; they now want particulars, and which leads me to hope that you will be very particular about mentioning Mr. Middiman's name; for to insert it in the prospectus without being *sure* of his co-operation would mar your endeavours in the eye of the public, for the least deviation from a proposal renders all subscriptions void. Be pleased to accept this hasty advice; and am glad to hear Mr. M. is inclined to engrave the picture. Respecting your sketches, I only want the honour to judge whether or not they are worth introducing; but you have not said or hinted at a second view, and therefore it is not of so great a consequence of taking in the corner of Queen's College.

'However, I have no objection to a trip to Oxford, but could wish it warmer weather.

'Your most truly obedient

'J. M. TURNER.

'Mr. J. WYATT, West End, Upper Mall.'

'December 26, 1809.

'Sir,—I cannot but think it very unhandsome of Mr. Taylor, and therefore will do all that is within my power to accommodate your wishes. .Will leave here some day this week for Oxford. I therefore wish you to get me a sheet of paper pasted down on a board in readiness, about two feet by one foot.

'I think of coming by the Shrewsbury or Birmingham coach, and therefore hope to be at Oxford by twelve at night. Could wish you, if possible, to secure me a bed at the inn.

'Yours most truly,

'J. M. TURNER.'

In the next year the Academy Catalogue enables us to determine Turner's residence to have been at 64 Harley Street, in conjunction with his rural retreat on the Upper Mall, Hammersmith. 1810 was the date of his exhibition of two fine views of Lowther Castle, the seat of the Earl of Lonsdale, one being a morning effect, and the other an evening; and also 'A Dewy Morning,' the scene taken from his favourite Petworth, painted for his close friend the good-natured Earl of Egremont.

'February 28, 1810.

'Sir,—I did not receive yours yesterday early enough to answer by post. But with respect to the picture, I have continued it on the same size, only 2 feet $3\frac{1}{4}$ inches by 3 feet 3 inches at most measures; yet the sky, I do think, had better be an inch at least under the top rabbet. Therefore I should advise you to make the rabbet deep, so that it can be hid; therefore the right measures may be as follows:—3 feet $2\frac{1}{2}$ inches by 2 feet $2\frac{1}{2}$ inches.

'The picture, you may inform Mr. Middiman, can be seen if he will favour me by calling, and with a time when it will so suit him, that I may be sure to be at home. I am afraid it will not be finished as early as you mentioned, but I shall not long exceed that time (March 7), for it certainly would be desirable to you to have it while Oxford is full.

'The figures introduced are as follows:—Two clericals, one in black, with a Master of Arts gown; the other with lawn sleeves for the bishop (being in want of a little white and purple scarf),   and followed by a beadle. Now arises some questions—First, is it right or wrong to introduce the bishop crossing the street in   with his robes? Whether he should wear a cap? What kind of a staff the beadles use, and if they wear caps? In short, these are the principal figures, and if you will favour me with answers to the foregoing questions, and likewise describe to me the particularity of each dress, I should be much obliged to you, for I could wish to be *right*.

'I am your most obedient

'J. M. TURNER.

'P.S.—A Proctor's gown has, I think you said, velvet sleeves?

'Mr. J. WYATT.'

'March 4, 1810.

'Sir,—I have not heard or seen Mr. Middiman, and not being so fortunate as to meet with him at home yesterday evening, I now write to ask how to proceed, *the picture being finished*, and in a day or two can be varnished for the last time. The packing-case is likewise ready; therefore be so good as to say what con-

veyance you wish me to use to send it by, and whether you positively wish Mr. M. to see it first, in which case you had better
write to him again; or perhaps my delivering the picture to him
you may consider the same (sending you a receipt for it).

'As to the figures introduced, I have made use of those you
sent, and therefore hope you will find them right; but I took
the hint, for the sake of colour, to introduce some ladies. The
figures taking down old houses are not only admissable, but I
think explaining their loss and the removal of the gateway. In
short, I hope that the picture will *please*, and that you will
find your endeavours seconded and prove ultimately very
advantageous.

'Your most truly obedient
'J. M. TURNER.

' P.S.—The prints shall be returned as you direct, and allow
me to thank you for sending them.

'Mr. J. WYATT.'

'1810.

'Sir,—I am glad to hear the picture is so approved of.
Really I thought of you long before you wrote, and I could not
have rested a day or two more without writing for uneasiness
as to the safe conveyance of it by the coach or otherwise.
However, that is past; and respecting the spires, crosses, and
window, they can be done after the 10th. As you proposed,
you may send it to Mr. Middiman direct; for I shall be in town
about that time to finish: therefore I can do what you wish
there. I feel some concern about the spire of St. Mary's. Many
who look at that spire at the side opposite will, in the street,
think that it should look equally high at the angle, but which
wholly changes its character. It becomes more dignified than
lofty. However, if you can get me the height and
base from the springing or setting off of the spire, or from the
clock, it shall be altered to measure.

'You must be the best judge how far a second print would
meet the support of your friends; but as you ask my opinion, I
should think you could very well try now *conditionally*, by which
you would feel the   of your present friends about it; but I
still think that it should be merely for names, and not to confine

them by a deposit (or a very small one); for in case it should be returned to try the other end of the high spire, it would be at least three or four years before the same engraver could furnish you with the engraving.   'Yours most truly,

'J. M. TURNER.

'The book will be serviceable to me to make some memoranda respecting the dresses. Let me have it a little longer, as I am now so very busy. If you think, or Mr. M. wishes for it, let me know, and I will return it safe to him.

'Mr. J. WYATT.'

In 1812 Turner, then an R.A., living in Queen Anne Street, West, in the course of his unrelaxed efforts to obtain fresh victories over Nature, exhibited 'A View of the Castle of St. Michael, near Bonneville, Savoy;' a view of the 'High Street' of his favourite Oxford; another of the same learned city from the Abingdon Road; and finally that fine picture 'The Snow-Storm, with Hannibal and his Army Crossing the Alps,' to which were appended some grandly obscure lines from that mysterious MS. epic 'The Fallacies of Hope:'—

> Craft, Treachery, and Fraud—Salassian force
> Hung on the fainting rear! Then Plunder seized
> The victor and the captive—Saguntum's spoil
> Alike became their prey. Still the chief advanced,
> Looked on the sun with hope; low, broad, and wan.
> While the fierce archer of the downward year
> Stains Italy's blanch'd barrier with storms.
> In vain each pass, ensanguined deep with dead,
> Or rocky fragments—wide destruction roll'd.
> Still on Campania's fertile plains—he thought,
> But the loud breeze sobbed, 'Capua's joys beware.'

The original idea of this truly great picture was suggested to Turner by a thunderstorm over the Yorkshire hills seen from the terrace of Farnley, where he always found warm welcome.

The correspondence continues:—

'Friday, April 10, 1812.

'Dear Sir,—I received yours last night upon my return from the Royal Academy, where your two pictures are; let me therefore thank you for the enclosed bill it contained. As to the frame, it is very handsome, and makes the picture look very well, but I fear that by the time it gets back to Oxford the centre ornament will be wanting, for it projects beyond the back, so it has no guard.

'Mr. Pye called to-day with proof with the alteration of the pavement, and that has improved it. He talks of sending you *one* down shortly for your inspection, and he hopes approval.

'Your obedient

'J. M. TURNER.

'Mr. J. WYATT.'

'Saturday, November 6, 1812.

'Sir,—First let me *thank* you for the sausages and hare. They were very good indeed. As to the   I understood you that Mr. Pye would have it immediately after the high spire should be finished; therefore I began it at Christmas. But respecting the venerable oak or elm, you rather puzzle me. If you wish either, say *so*, and it shall be done; but fancy to your-self how a large tree would destroy the character—that burst of flat country with uninterrupted horizontal lines throughout the picture as seen from the spot we took it from. The hedge-row oaks are all pollards, but can be enclosed if you wish. As to figures, I have not determined upon them, and even with them, if you have any predilection for any, or *object*, it is the same to me, or if, as I suppose, the   have carved some out for me in order at least; so their opinions may be taken, reserving to myself the use or adaptation of them as most fit or conducive to my subject as to colour, &c.

'Mr. Pye called to-day with a proof; the spire is much better, and it begins to look rich, clean, and full. How long he will be yet I know not; but as to   me to send the picture to the Exhibition, you must make haste with the frames, for the pictures are to be sent on the 5th and 6th of next month. The size is the same as the other picture, only 3 feet 3 by 2 feet 2¾ in the straining frame, and to hide part of the sky with the high p., for it would be scarcely worth while to make the inch in the sky to change the size of frame.

'Your most obedient Servant,

'J. M. TURNER.

'Mr. J. WYATT.'

In 1841, when he was in the full height of his later period, in which everything was sacrificed to colour, and his eye had lost its old far-reaching power, he exhibited his ' Ducal Palace, Dogana, with parts of San Giorgio;' 'Giudecca, la Donna della Salute, and San Giorgio;' 'Rosenau, Seat of H.R.H. Prince Albert of Coburg, near Coburg, Germany;' ' Depositing of John Bellini's three Pictures in La Chiesa Redentore, Venice;' 'Dawn of Christianity: the Flight into Egypt;' and ' Glaucus and Scylla.'

Addressing Mr. Millar, he writes thus :—

' Saturday, October 22, 1841.

' My dear Sir,—So much time (for I only returned from Scotland last night) since your letter and the arrival of the proof (for Mr. Moon has sent only *one*), that I hope you have proceeded with the plate, in which case it is evident you must take off *three*, and mark the two for me, if you adopt the same medium of transfer; but I would say, send them direct.   My remarks would be wholly yours, and some inconvenience to both avoided.   If you have not done anything, take off one for me. So now to business.

' It appears to me that you have   so far that I do think I could now recollect sufficiently without the picture before me, but will now write points out and answer your questions, viz. if the sky you   right you could advance more confidently.   Therefore do not touch the sky at present, but work the rest up to it.   The distance may be too dark, though it wants more fine work, more character of woods, down to the very Campagna of Rome—a bare, sterile flat, much lighter in tone.

' The question of a perpendicular line to the water—pray do not think of it until after the very last touched proof, for it has a beautiful quality of silvery softness, which is only checked by the rock, which is the most unfortunate in the whole plate. How to advise you here I know not, but think fine work would blind the scene with the reflection of it with the water. This is the worst part, and I fear will give us some trouble to conquer, and if you can make it take the water in the middle of the plate, I should like it better.   The houses above, and particularly from the figures, and the parts from and with the boys looking down, are what I most fear about, which range all along the south, and the broken entrance and the shrine want more vigour to detach from the town all the corner figures, &c. The foreground will be required to be more spirited, and bold, open work dashing   like touches, and bright lights. So do all you can in the middle part   town and leave it all for the present in front. The figure in front would be better with the white cloth over the face done by one line only; and perhaps a child wrapped up in swaddling-clothes before her would increase the interest of the whole. The ground on which she kneels break into small pebbles or broken pavement. Now for the good parts, the greatest part of the sky, all the *left side*, the upper castle and palaces and partly round to the Sybil temple, town and   on the right side, and the water in the middle particularly good, and I hope to keep it untouched if possible.

'I am glad to hear you say I can know the picture after the first touched proof, and trust this long letter of directions will be equal to *one*, and you will be able to proceed with confidence. Write if you feel any difficulty, and believe me truly yours,

'J. M. W. TURNER.

'P.S.—Very sorry to hear of the loss you have sustained.'

In 1842 Turner's power of sight and accuracy was fast declining, and even brown sherry could not brace the once dexterous fingers or clarify the clouding eyes. Poor Wilkie's death the year before, and his burial at sea off Gibraltar, had profoundly touched the waning man; and this year he exhibited that fine dream of the scene, now in the National Collection, and also another national picture singularly imaginative and singularly eccentric—' The Exile and the Rock Limpet' (Napoleon at St. Helena), full of strange errors and phantasmagoric reflections of scarlet; allegorical, no doubt, and subtle enough to please even Mr. Ruskin or the wildest of pre-Raphaelites. In the Royal Academy Catalogue for this year the list of Turner's exhibited works stands thus:—

'The Dogano, San Giorgio, Citella, from the steps of the Europa.'

'Campo Santo, Venice.'

'Snow-Storm: Steamboat off a harbour's mouth making signals in shallow water, and going by the lead.' The author was in this storm on the night the 'Ariel' left Harwich.

'Peace: Burial at Sea.'

> The midnight torch gleam'd o'er the steamer's side,
> And Miret's corse was yielded to the tide.
>   MS. *Fallacies of Hope.*

'War: the Exile and the Rock Limpet.'

> Ah ! thy tent-formed shell is like
> A soldier's nightly bivouac, alone
> Amidst a sea of blood . . . . .
> . . . . but can you join your comrades ?
>   MS. *Fallacies of Hope.*

Other letters to Mr. Millar are as follow :—

> '47 Queen Ann Street, West:
> 'June 24, 1842.

'Dear Sir,—I have now nearly done all I have to do before I   for *my trip*; so make all haste possible to get your plate finished *first* and foremost.

'Let me know as soon as possibly you can, and ask your printer what he will print 500   eagle—eagle or columbin—India and plain for (PAPER INCLUDED). Note every proof to be numbered and marked by him when taken off, and all failures in printing or so doing to be   all by marking and *given* up, *but not charged.* What time the 500 will take printing, and all sent to me or in London; and if the number is increased, what reduction per hundred; and if ready money, what discount.

'Your answer as soon as possible, or at your earliest convenience, will oblige,

> 'Yours truly,
>   'J. M. W. TURNER.

'W. MILLAR, Esq., Hope Park, Edinburgh.'

> 'Saturday, July 9, 1842:
> '47, Queen Ann Street, West.

'My dear Sir,—I beg to thank you for the terms of the

printer, and will thank you for your kindness in offering to look to the printing during progress, but your plate is Mr. Moon's; and   for a plate of my own.   Only may I now trouble you further by asking him (the printer) if he allows *discount* for ready money; and how many printing-presses he has ; and if two or more plates were worked at the same time what deduction he could make in proportion ?

'Yours most truly,
'J. M. W. TURNER.

'P.S.—Your box has not arrived ; but have the goodness to get me an answer about the printing at your earliest convenience.   Your proof shall be touched immediately it arrives in Queen Ann Street.   Excuse haste, &c.,   and all to be in time for the post to-night.'

'Saturday, November 5, 1842.

'Dear Sir,—I have received a case left by Mr. Lloyd, the printer, directed to Mr. Moon.   It appears to me, by the direction and handwriting, to be from you.

'I therefore, having no message with it, write to you to know what it contains, and what you wish or want me to do.

'Yours most truly,
'J. M. W. TURNER.'

'47 Queen Ann Street, West:
'Saturday, December 10, 1842.

'Mr. Millar,—I beg to know when and how (as to time) you received the last touched proof, which I touched more copiously to meet your wishes expressed in your last letter.   The box was returned to the parties who left and called twice for it.   You will write if you afterwards sent the amended proofs and touched proof back to me, and how, for none having reached me, and Mr. Lloyd is now printing the plate.

'Therefore I declare that, not having seen your amended proof or my touched proof since that, I consider the plate of " Modern Italy " unfinished.

'Yours truly,
'J. M. W. TURNER.
'Mr. W. MILLAR, Hope Park, Edinburgh.'

The following letters, two of which have unfortunately no date, are all directed to Mr. J. Wyatt, of Oxford, and serve to show Turner's attachment to places which had been the scenes of early and deeply-relished success :—

' Dear Sir,—Your pictures are hung at the Academy, but not to my satisfaction at least. I therefore wrote to you, for as I did not wish to counteract your wishes, or expectation as to the benefits which you suppose might probably result from them by exhibition at the Royal Academy, consequently they were sent ; and if you still think, notwithstanding their situations are as unfortunate as could possibly be allotted them (from the pictures close to them), that their remaining there may be advantageous to you, *there they shall remain* ; but if indifferent about their being exhibited *there with me*, or at the *British Institution next season*, I must confess I should like to have the *option* of withdrawing them. Provided nothing can be done to make them (and another which I have sent) more satisfactory in point of situation to my feelings, I must request an answer by post to Queen Ann Street, West, and beg that you will think of yourself *first* and afterwards

' From your most truly obliged Servant,
' J. M. TURNER.

' Sir,—You may prepare a frame two feet three inches high by three feet three long, but I think it must be cut less, having at present too much sky ; so do not put the frame together until you hear again from me. By way of consolation let me tell you the picture is *very forward*. But I could wish you to send me back the annexed sketch, with information how the several windows are glazed, and those *blank* in the front of the All Souls entrance, particularly those in the *large gable porch*, if they project in a bow like the two by the gateway, as I find two marked in my second sketch more than in my first, and therefore suppose some alteration has taken place since the first was made.

' Pray tell me likewise of a gentleman of the name of Trimmer, who has written to you to be a subscriber for a print.

'Your most obedient Servant,

' J. M. TURNER.

' West End, Upper Mall, Hammersmith :
    ' Saturday, February 4, 1810.'

       ' West End, Upper Mall : Friday afternoon.

' Sir,—The approaching election for the Chancellorship should not pass without a *prospectus* ; and, therefore, as far as relates myself, to say that I will do you a drawing or painting, but must apprise you that there is no possibility of reaching your size frame, for my pictures are all three feet by four feet, 200 guineas, half which size will be 100, but shall not mind an inch or two a drawing.

' I will do you for 80 guineas. You will be pleased to turn in your mind which will suit your purpose best ; and if you print a *prospectus*, will thank you to let me see *it* before you print off a number for delivery.

' The size of the engraving you had better settle with your engraver about, for it is rather difficult to get a large one done, for many engravers think the print of *Wilson's Niobe* large, but it appears to me the proportion should be about 3 to 2, or 18 inches by 30 inches.

'Your most obedient Servant,

' J. M. TURNER.'

' I acknowledge the receipt of the draft for 105*l.* upon Messrs. Ham—for the picture, and beg to add my thanks, and am glad to find that yours have answered *finally* with Mr. Middiman and Pye, for I greatly feared Mr. M. would decline, because the subject proved more architectural than he expected.

' I shall varnish it for the last time this evening, and on Saturday morning 9 o'clock, by Gilbert Coach, it shall be forwarded to Oxford.

'Sincerely trusting that every idea you

'I am, &c. &c., with haste,
            'Your most truly obliged,
                        'J. M. TURNER.

'P.S.—I shall be ever ready to assist in advice or otherwise
in your undertaking with Mr. M. or Mr. Pye.'

CHAPTER XVII.

TURNER'S PRICES.

FROM some of Mr. W. B. Cooke's account books, kindly lent
me by Mr. Lupton, I derive a very clear view of the prices
Turner obtained for drawings from 1817 to 1824. As all the
figures are given in the Appendix, here I will only select a few
of the leading items to comment on.

For such drawings (prepared for the engraver's use) as
'Brixham,' 'Fowey,' and 'Ilfracombe' he received 10l. 10s. ;
and for the loan of drawings for the 'Rivers of Devon,' such
as the 'Eddystone' and the 'Junction of the Tamar,' presum-
ably not made specially for the work, but lying by him in his
portfolio, 5l. 5s. But the charges vary, I suppose, according
to certain degrees of finish and goodness, since 31l. was the
price paid for two drawings of Vesuvius for some work on
Pompeii, while drawings of Battle Abbey (1818), and Winchelsea (1817), obtained only six guineas. Then come, on
the creditor side, in August 1818, charges for copper supplied
for the 'Liber Studiorum.'

In the same year 'Hastings, from the Sea,' for Mr. Fuller's
work, is charged at 42l. This sum represents, I presume, the
purchase money for a work perhaps in oil ; and farther on
189l. is paid for 'Dover Shipwreck' (large drawing for Exhibition, 1823), and 'Margate—Sunrise.' In 1822 occur charges
of 2l. 2s. for touching Tomkinson's 'Cuyp' and Girtin's

' Kirkstall ; ' the drawings of Colne, Rochester, and Norham are charged 8*l*. 8*s*. each ; and three of the Rhine, 85*l*. In 1824 a large drawing of ' Smugglers Fishing Gin ' is marked 63*l*. Then comes a counter item of fourteen numbers of the ' Liber Studiorum,' at 1*l*. 1*s*. each, 20 per cent. allowed ; making a total of 11*l*. 15*s*.

In 1824 Turner's charges for lending drawings increase. He now receives 25*l*. for the loan of ' Brougham Castle, Totnes,' and ' Oakhampton Castle,' for the ' Rivers ; ' and for the first two drawings, for the continuation of the ' Coast ' (bought by Mr. Tomkinson), he obtains 52*l*. 10*s*. His oil pictures might not sell ; but he was still getting money in many ways — by making drawings and lending drawings, by publishing the ' Liber,' and by retouching paintings.

The ' Times ' of 1851 records that 120 guineas have not unfrequently been given for a small sketch of Turner's in water colours ; and a small sketch-book containing chalk drawings of one of his river tours on the Continent has lately fetched the enormous sum of 600 guineas.

The prices of his more finished oil paintings have ranged, in the last few years, from 700 to 1,400 guineas. All his works have now acquired triple or quadruple the value of the sums originally paid for them.

A propos of prices, we are told that one day Mr. Gillott, the well-known manufacturer of Birmingham, sallied forth from his hotel, determined at any price to obtain admission to the enchanted house in Queen Anne Street. He was rich ; he was enthusiastic ; and he believed strongly in the power of the golden key to open any door. Arrived at the blistered, dirty door of the house with the black-crusted windows, he pulled the bell, which answered with a querulous, melancholy tinkle. After a long, inhospitable pause, an old woman with a diseased face having looked up from the area, presently ascended and tardily opened the door. She snappishly asked Mr. Gillott's business ; and when he told her in his blandest voice, ' Can't let 'e in ' was the answer ; after which she tried to slam the door. But during the parley the crafty and determined Dives had put his foot in ; and now, declining further interruption, he pushed past the feeble, enraged janitress, and hurried upstairs to the gallery. In a moment Turner was out upon him with the promptitude of a spider whose web has been invaded by another arachnid. Mr. Gillott bowed, introduced himself, and stated that he had come to buy. 'Don't want to sell,' or some such rebuff, was the answer; but Gillott shut his ears to all Turner's angry vituperations. 'Have you ever seen our Birmingham pictures, Mr. Turner?' he enquired with un-ruffled placidity. 'Never 'eard of 'em,' was the answer. Gillott now drew from his pocket a silvery, fragile bundle of Birmingham bank-notes (about 5,000*l.* worth). 'Mere paper,' observed Turner with grim humour; a little softened, however, and evidently enjoying the joke. 'To be bartered for *mere* canvas,' said Gillott, waving his hand at the 'Building of Carthage' and its companions. This tone of cool depreciation seemed to have a happy effect. 'You're a rum fellow!' exclaimed the painter; after which he was induced gradually to enter into negotiations, which finally resulted in the deportation in Gillott's cab of some 5,000*l.* worth of Turner's pictures. It was the manufacturers, as I have said, and not the noblemen of England, who were Turner's best patrons.

Mr. Britton is our authority for another characteristic story. In his early days Turner was busy one morning in the bed-room at Maiden Lane, working at some drawings for one of Britton's patrons—I think for the Earl of Essex—when the door suddenly opened, and Britton entered, nominally to enquire how the drawings progressed, but really to spy out all he could of the artist's professional secrets. In an instant Turner covered up his drawings, and ran to bar the crafty intruder's progress. 'I've come to see the drawings for the Earl.' 'You shan't see 'em,' was the reply. 'Is that the answer I am to take back to his Lordship?' 'Yes; and mind that next time you come through the shop, and not up the back way. I allow no one to come here;' and so, shutting the door on his visitor, the artist returned to growl at him over his work.

Turner often was unjustly accused of being extravagant in the prices he demanded for his drawings; but the complaining purchaser forgot that he was buying something which in a few

years would be worth perhaps double the money given for it.
Mr. Cockerell, for instance, on his return from Greece, engaged
Turner to execute for him a drawing of a temple in Ægina
from rough hints furnished him. It was a troublesome task,
and probably uncongenial to the artist, whose mind it diverted
from its own channels; for he had to paint a country and
people he had never seen. However, he set to work, and
executed his task with a patience and care worthy of one who
had to win his spurs; the result being that he produced in the
given time a beautiful and elaborate water-colour drawing fit for
the engraver, and highly finished enough to afterwards adorn a
gallery. The sum of thirty-five guineas, which he asked for it,
was thought by Mr. Cockerell to be an exorbitant demand
from an old friend. A few years after, however, the drawing
was sold for fifty guineas. It is now in the possession of Mr.
Munro, and would most probably fetch, if it were submitted to
auction, at least · some sixty guineas. So, again, for a picture
which one of his patrons preferred to forfeit a hundred pounds
rather than take, the offer of a thousand pounds was subsequently declined.

Induced thereto by the recommendation of a R.A., Chantrey, without even seeing it, purchased one of Turner's early
Venetian pictures, on a varnishing day, for 250*l.* At the sculptor's death this picture, though much damaged by an ignorant
dealer, was secured at Christie's, by one who also had not seen
it, for the enormous sum of 1,500*l.*

Mr. Ruskin represents that if Turner disliked his theme, he
painted slightly, and let the purchaser take his chance; whereas,
if he liked his theme, he would give three hundred guineas'
worth of work for a hundred, and ask no thanks. He also
altered the engravings from his drawings to suit the public
taste. Sometimes, it is said, when an engraver came with a
plate to be touched, he would take a piece of chalk (or whiting)
in his right hand and of black in his left, with the enquiry, 'Which
will you have it done with?' The engraver having chosen either
black or white, according as he thought his plate weak or heavy,
the other piece of chalk would be thrown down, and the plate
reconstructed with the added lights or darks in ten minutes.

' He was never troublesome about detail,' writes one engraver to me; 'yet I remember that in one small engraving he took enormous pains to get a little doe's head in the foreground exactly true to Nature.' His touched proofs he sometimes worked on with pencil.

' He never broke a promise or failed in an undertaken trust,' is the emphatic testimony of Mr. Ruskin. His sense of justice, indeed, was strangely acute. One of my friends had long desired to possess a picture which Turner resolutely declined to sell. Originally it had been painted as a companion to another; but, while its fellow was sold, this was reserved. After the lapse of several years, however, he consented to part with it. In the interval the value of canvas of the proportions of the picture having doubled, a question arose as what was to be the price. ' Well,' said Turner, ' Mr. —— had the companion for so much; you must be on the same footing.' He had no intention of doing a favour; his sole study was to be just.

Numerous stories are related of Turner's dealings with a merchant (let us call him Mr. Dives) of Liverpool. Whether from sincere regard for the great magician's works, or from pure love of commercial profit alone, it is certain that the hero of these stories came to market with princely liberality. On one occasion he is represented as having offered to buy the whole stock of paintings, drawings, and engravings in Queen Anne Street for 100,000*l.*; and, confident of acceptance of the offer, to have asked for the key of the house, in order that he might forthwith cart off the valuables. But Turner said, ' No, sir; I have refused a similar offer before;' and well he might, for even then the stock was worth far more than that in the market, and in the hands of a monopolist might have realised any sum. ' I'll make it guineas,' was the seductive invitation; but it was resolutely declined. He had willed it all to the nation.

When the same magnificent Dives purchased the ' Mercury and Argus' of Turner, the painter, from some caprice, perhaps from his favourite notion of a series, refused to sell it alone. He insisted upon associating with it another picture of the same kind, at the same price. The eager purchaser made no objection to the arrangement.

On another occasion, according to Mr. Birch, Turner enumerated to Dives various books of sketches that he possessed, and several of which he produced; they are now national property. They were coloured memoranda, valuable as jewels, embracing notes in pencil and chalk; blue gleams of sea and sky, wafts of mist, ochry sails, and white frozen waves of Alps. To the eager merchant these were exhibited with a certain savagely selfish satisfaction, such as that wherewith an ill-conditioned old maid exhibits the family diamonds to her poor but pretty niece, or an affluent antiquary sets forth his cameos before a juvenile collector. Turner's delight was expressed by many a chuckle distributed through the interview, during which it was his study to tantalise the inflamed spectator in every possible way; and such was his amiability on the occasion that he even induced him to make several offers. But it was only playing at business; Turner simply was amusing himself by observing the mercury rise again in the well-known price-barometer. His increased favour with rich purchasers he delighted thus to realise. Each of these books consisted of about a hundred leaves of sketches, and the offers gradually mounted to the large sum of a thousand pounds a piece; when, after deliberately closing them one by one, and laying them aside, he proceeded to enquire, 'Well, would you like to have them?' 'Yes! yes!' was the answer, returned with all the impetuosity characteristic of one burning to secure his treasures. 'I dare say you would!' was the final exclamation, to which a slily malicious laugh lent not a little point by way of aggravation.

Probably Turner took an especial delight in tormenting this particular man; upon whom accordingly he chose to inflict as much annoyance as he possibly could, in satisfaction (as it were) for the wrongs he had himself endured in early days at the hands of trading oppressors. Certain it is, however, that the interview terminated in a quarrel; and having learned that this would-be patron, whom he had fondly regarded as a genuine admirer, had sold some of the pictures that had been painted for him, Turner declined thenceforth to have any dealings with him, and thus the companion to 'Mercury and Argus' was never painted.

We have already seen him refuse a private offer of 2,000*l.*
for the 'Rise of Carthage.' We have now to record in connection with the same picture one of his greatest and most
heartfelt triumphs; when he refused the sum of 2,500*l.* from a
body of eminent public men, who desired to present the picture to the nation. It is to be remembered that all he had to
do was to keep silent; and, forgetting his generous intention,
he might have pocketed the money without anyone being
conscious of his change of purpose; and, besides, he had other
pictures to leave.

At a great meeting at Somerset House, at which Sir Robert
Peel, Lord Hardinge, and others were present, it was unanimously agreed to buy two pictures of Turner for presentation
to the National Gallery, as monuments of Art for the incitement
and instruction of artists and Art-lovers for all time ; and a
memorial was drawn up and presented to the artist by his
sincere old friend Mr. Griffiths, who exulted in the pleasant
task. The offer was 5,000*l.* for the two pictures, the 'Rise'
and 'Fall of Carthage.' When Turner read the memorial his
eyes brightened. He was deeply moved, even to the extreme
of shedding tears; for he was capable, as all who knew him are
well aware, of intense feeling. He expressed the pride and
delight he felt on receiving such a noble offer from such men;
but, directly his eye caught the word 'Carthage,' he exclaimed
sternly, ' No, no; they shall not have it;' and, upon Mr.Griffiths
turning to leave, he called after him and said, ' Oh! Griffiths,
make my compliments to the memorialists, and tell them
" Carthage" may some day become the property of the nation.'

One of his oldest friends tells me that the week in which
Turner sold a picture he invariably wore a look of dejection and
oppression; and, when pressed with enquiries as to the reason,
he would sorrowfully exclaim, ' I've lost one of my children
this week.'

A merchant who had one day expended 10,000*l.* in the
purchase of pictures from Turner, suddenly, as he was on the
point of leaving, made a proposal to him. ' Now, Mr. Turner,
there are three more pictures in your gallery ; I'll give you
5,000*l.* for the three, if you will allow me to pick.' ' Well,'

was the answer, 'tell me which they are.' The merchant began with the 'Rise of Carthage;' but Turner stopped him at once. 'No,' he said; 'it's a noble offer; but I have willed it.' The purchaser then pressed him to let him have two for 5,000*l.* The liberality of the offer seemingly affected Turner; but he merely repeated, 'I have willed it.'

The picture, it is said, was originally painted for 100*l.* for a gentleman who declined to take it when the critics and the press began to attack it; so that we cannot express surprise at the satisfaction with which the artist dwelt on this incident, exclaiming again and again, 'This is a great triumph!' His pride had been deeply wounded by the original rejection of the picture, and the noble revenge he took was to refuse 2,500*l.* for it and leave it to the nation.

Mr. Heath, once seeing some papers lying on the table, asked him what he had got there. 'Oh,' was the reply; 'some old receipts and papers not wanted.' Mr. Heath's attention had been attracted by a bill of exchange for 200*l.*, evidently unpaid, and due on that very day, of the existence of which Turner appeared to be wholly unconscious. This carelessness did not, however, extend to many of his transactions, for never was anyone more rigorous in exacting the last farthing in a contract than he was, or more punctual in executing within the stipulated time whatever he undertook. Mr. Heath was wont to declare that, in spite of his exactions and the difficulty of bringing him to any reasonable terms, he had greater satisfaction in dealing with him than any other artist. When once he had pledged his word as to time and quality, he might be implicitly relied on.

The following letter to Mr. Finden is a good specimen of Turner's business communications. It is like one of Cæsar's despatches, so terse and free is it from all superfluous words :—

'47 Queen Ann Street, West.

'Dear Sir,—I shall want some money before I leave London for my summer tour, which will take place in about a fortnight.

'Yours truly,
'J. M. W. TURNER.

'W. FINDEN, Esq.

'Mr. MacQueen called (to look about printing my plates). I did not see him, but sent down word that I would thank him to send me the remaining proofs belonging to you. His answer [was] that he did not know he had any of Mr. Finden's; if he had, he would send them. This somewhat says that you have not said anything to him for my remaining proofs or book.

'J. M. W. T.'

This question of proofs, indeed, was an endless source of quarrel between Turner and his engravers. Even as an author claims so many copies of his book from a publisher, so an artist claims from his engravers so many proofs. In the author's case this right is generally decided by a written agreement, which is legally binding; but in the case of artists I believe there is no distinct law laid down, the number of proofs depending on the engraver's liberality or good-nature. The artist gets as many as he can. Such, however, was Turner's cupidity and acquisitiveness that he invariably advanced claims which his engravers sometimes refused to concede, whatever loss they might sustain from a quarrel with the great artist. On one occasion words rose so high that a well-known engraver threatened, upon principle, to burn the proofs before his eyes rather than surrender them; another turned him out of doors. Impelled by that love of hoarding which attained almost the gravity of a mental disease with him, Turner would keep the smallest scrap of paper that contained the note of a single hint or thought. In truth, he had dreadful fights with the print publishers. He regarded them as Pharaohs; as cruel task-masters, who thought a few guineas could buy any man's brains; as men who did not care what they got for their money, so it had but a good name appended to it; as men who were hucksters of Art, mental pedlers, costermongers of brain-produce. He viewed them as perpetuators of his serfdom; and, like Blücher at Waterloo with the French, he had to revenge on them the injuries and insults of years. Not that he was insolent to them, but he would have all the money he could get; seeing no reason why the mere interchanger of commodities should derive greater profit from them than those who originally produced them. He knew his value in the market, and he used that knowledge with somewhat exacting severity. Moreover, it must not be forgotten that engraving with Turner was a compulsory and not a voluntary work. He was born a painter, not an engraver. He painted for fame; he engraved for bread.

With Cooke, at whose house the scene of many a story is laid, Turner never seems to have been on really amicable terms; and we now are in no position to determine to which side the blame is to be chiefly ascribed. I have in my possession a most violent letter from the former, dated January 1, 1827, on the subject of the 'Coast' drawing, in which he accuses Turner of misrepresentation and deception. The idea of the 'Coast,' it appears, originated with the publisher, who gave the artist a commission for 400*l.* worth of drawings; to which Turner added a demand of twenty-five sets of India proofs before letters. Seven pounds ten shillings was the price originally paid for each drawing, but eventually it was raised to 10*l.* Turner now claimed the same rate of remuneration for the earlier drawings, which he had contracted to supply for 7*l.* 10*s.* a piece.

There can be no doubt that he had a confused notion of Cooke's intentions, or had been deceived by the keener tradesman. Cooke begins by underpaying him, and then writes to the artist, promising him twelve guineas and a half for the 'drawings for the future "Coast."' Turner chooses to consider this offer as referring to work already done, as well as to that which is in hand. Ever dogged and obstinate when he believes himself defrauded, he goes to Cooke, and says—

'I will have my terms! I will have my terms! or I will oppose the work by doing another "Coast."'

Then Cooke goes on to complain of Turner's giving him a drawing called 'Neptune's Trident' as a present to his wife, and afterwards reclaiming it, with the charge of two guineas for the loan. It is probable that Cooke must have mistaken a loan for a gift, for Turner never could have been intentionally guilty of such meanness.

The indignant engraver concludes by asking insolently if

Hakewell's 'Italy,' the 'Scottish Scenery,' or the 'Yorkshire' work had ever returned the capital laid out on them, asserting that Turner quite over-calculated the profits of the 'Coast' work. But let the letter speak more fully for itself:—

'January 1, 1827.

'Dear Sir,—I cannot help regretting that you persist in demanding twenty-five sets of India proofs before the letters of the continuation of the work of the "Coast," besides being paid for the drawings. It is like a film before your eyes, to prevent your obtaining upwards of two thousand pounds in a commission for drawings for that work.

'Upon mature reflection, you must see I have done all in my power to satisfy you of the total impossibility of acquiescing in such a demand. It would be unjust both to my subscribers and to myself.

'The "Coast" being my own original plan, which cost me some anxiety before I could bring it to maturity, and an immense expense before I applied to you, when I gave a commission for drawings to upwards of 400*l. at my own entire risk*, in which the shareholders were not willing to take any part, I did all I could to persuade you to have one share; and which I did from a firm conviction that it would afford some remuneration for your exertions on the drawings in addition to the amount of the contract. The share was, as it were, forced upon you by myself, with the best feeling in the world; and was, as you well know, repeatedly refused, under the idea that there was a possibility of losing money by it. You cannot deny the result: a constant dividend of profit has been made to you at various times, and will be so for some time to come.

'On Saturday last, to my utter astonishment, you declared in my print-rooms, before three persons who distinctly heard it, as follows:—" I will have my terms! or I will oppose the work by doing another 'Coast!'" These were the words you used; and everyone must allow them to be a *threat*.

'And this morning (Monday) you show me a note of my own handwriting, with these words (or words to this immediate effect):—

' " The drawings for the future ' Coast' shall be paid twelve guineas and a half each."

' Now, in the name of common honesty, how can you apply the above note to any drawings for the first division of the work, called the " Southern Coast," and tell me I owe you two guineas on each of those drawings? Did you not agree to make the whole of the " South Coast" drawings at 7*l.* 10*s.* each? and did I not continue to pay you that sum for the first four numbers? When a meeting of the partners took place, to take into consideration the great exertions that myself and my brother had made on the plates, to testify their entire satisfaction, and considering the difficulties I had placed myself in by such an agreement as I had made (dictated by my enthusiasm for the welfare of a work which had been planned and executed with so much zeal, and of my being paid the small sum only of twenty-five guineas for each plate, including the loan of the drawings, for which I received no return or consideration whatever on the part of the shareholders), they unanimously (excepting on your part) and very liberally increased the price of each plate to 40*l.*; and I agreed, on my part, to pay you ten guineas for each drawing after the fourth number. And have I not kept this agreement? Yes; you have received from me, and from Messrs. Arch on my account, the whole sum so agreed upon, and for which you have given me and them receipts. The work has now been finished upwards of six months, when you show me a note of my own handwriting, and which was written to you in reply to a part of your letter, where you say, " Do you imagine I shall go to John o' Groat's House for the same sum I receive for the Southern part ? " Is this *fair* conduct between man and man, to apply the note (so explicit in itself) to the former work, and to endeavour to make me believe I still owe you two guineas and a half on each drawing? Why, let me ask you, should I promise you such a sum? What possible motive could I have in heaping gold into your pockets when you have always taken such especial care of your interests, even in the case of " Neptune's Trident," which I can declare you *presented* to me; and in the spirit of *this* understanding I presented it again to Mrs. Cooke. You may recollect afterwards charging me two guineas for the loan of it, and requesting me, at the same time, to return it to you; which has been done.

'The ungracious remarks I experienced this morning at your house, when I pointed out to you the meaning of my former note—"that it referred to the future part of the work, and not to the 'Southern Coast'"—were such as to convince me that you maintain a mistaken and most unaccountable idea of profit and advantage in the new work of the "Coast;" and that no estimate or calculation will convince you to the contrary. Ask yourself if Hakewell's "Italy," "Scottish Scenery," or "Yorkshire" work have either of them succeeded in the return of the capital laid out on them.

'These works have had in them as much of your individual talent as the "Southern Coast," being modelled on the principle of it; and although they have answered your purpose by the commissions for drawings, yet there is considerable doubt remaining whether they will ever return their expenses, and whether the shareholders and proprietors will ever be reinstated in the money laid out on them. So much for the profit of works.

'I assure you I must turn over an entirely new leaf to make them ever return their expenses.

'To conclude, I regret exceedingly the time I have bestowed in endeavouring to convince you in a calm and patient manner of a number of calculations made for *your* satisfaction; and I have met in return such hostile treatment that I am positively disgusted at the mere thought of the trouble I have given myself on such a useless occasion.

'I remain, your obedient Servant,

'W. B. COOKE.'

A more inflexible man than Turner, when once the idea of being defrauded or tricked had entered his mind, it would not be easy to imagine.

The following letter contains little of special interest; but it shows us Cooke and Turner again at cross purposes, respecting the beautiful Swiss drawings at Farnley:—

'Saturday morning.

'My dear Sir,—I rather expected you would have called yesterday, as your messenger said there required no answer when he left your letter. However, I have seen Mr. Fawkes this morning, and there appears a great misconception respecting the extent of the drawings offered to you, *for the Swiss drawings are either bound together, or cannot be lent*. I shall be at home all to-morrow, if you can give me a call.

'Yours most respectfully,
'J. M. W. Turner.'

(Pencil note on a slip of paper fastened to the above letter by a pin.)

'I told your brother George, on Thursday or Saturday last, that I expected to have heard or seen you before then, particularly when I had heard you did not go to Brighton, and to tell you so, you having left a message that things must remain until you returned, that the list you sent me had an inaccuracy or two, which required me to see you, and will call to-morrow before twelve, or after two o'clock.

'Yours,
'J. W. Turner.'

The two next letters also relate to the connexion between Turner and Cooke. They refer to the letterpress of the 'Coast Scenery,' written by Combe, the author of 'Dr. Syntax.' Turner has evidently been trying his hand at a description of St. Michael's Mount, probably a favourite scene. Combe cannot understand it, and pronounces it to be the most extraordinary thing he ever read, and to be badly punctuated; upon which Cooke suppresses the contribution with a sort of insolent contempt. Combe, who evidently knew his man, directs Cooke, unless he wishes to drive Turner 'stark, staring mad,' to send him uncorrected sheets of the suppressed article.

'Friday afternoon.

'My dear Sir,—I am really concerned to be obliged to say that Mr. T——'s account is the most extraordinary composition I have ever read. It is impossible for me to correct it, for in some parts I do not understand it. The punctuation is everywhere defective, and here I have done what I could, and have sent the proof to Mr. Bulmer. I think the revise should be sent to Mr. T——, to request his attention to the whole, and particularly the part that I have marked as unintelligible. In my private opinion, it is scarcely an admissible article in its present state ; but as he has signed his name to it, he will be liable to the sole blame for its imperfections.

'Your faithful humble Servant,

'W. C.'

'Friday morning.

' My dear Sir,—When I had just finished the article of St. Michael's Mount, and introduced all I possibly could into it of Mr. Turner's, I received your note requesting me not to insert a syllable of his writing. This has, of course, occasioned a considerable delay, as I must write the whole over again. Mr. Bulmer, however, shall have it to-morrow, and Pool shall follow.

' I enclose the proofs ; but if you do not mean to drive Mr. T—— stark, staring mad, you had better get two uncorrected sheets from Mr. Bulmer.

'Your faithful humble Servant,

'W. C.'

I have no doubt at all Cooke was a timid, time-serving tradesman, with no real appreciation of Turner's genius, and vexed the great man by his small, higgling ways.

It seems to be a general opinion amongst engravers that Turner disliked them as a body. I am afraid he regarded everyone who came to him for money as an enemy ; yet he was very punctual and very just, though never liberal. Some of them refused his work, finding it took up too much time to be profitable. One engraver, whom he accused unjustly of eavesdropping, ordered him out of his house ; but seven years after Turner met him in Regent Street, and nobly confessed his fault by offering him his hand ; for magnanimity was one of the artist's noblest qualities.

I believe that ' Loch Corriskin,' in the Isle of Skye (illustration to Scott's ' Lord of the Isles '), engraved by Le Keux,[1] is almost the only work of Turner's which was not touched or corrected by him. There are lines in the curves of the rocks which, admirable as they are, he would doubtless have altered.

The publishers always treated Turner as a Jew ; and an excellent story is told in point of that conviction. When he went down there to make his drawings for Whitaker's ' History of Richmondshire,' he took with him a letter of introduction from a London publisher to one in Yorkshire, which concluded thus : ' Above all things remember that Turner is A GREAT Jew.'

The intimation was taken seriously and literally to heart, and down came the little man, looking ' the very moral ' of a master carpenter, with lobster-red face, twinkling staring grey eyes, white tie, blue coat and brass buttons, crab-shell turned-up boots, large fluffy hat, and enormous umbrella. The next day happened to be Sunday ; and after breakfast the publisher, signifying his departure to church, expressed a hope that Turner would amuse himself with the books and pictures till he returned. Turner was somewhat nettled at being thus obviously treated as a pagan, but preserved silence until dinner arrived ; in the course of which some apology was made about an unlucky and *mal-à-propos* ham ; whereupon Turner broke out—

' What on earth do you mean, sir ? '

' Why they wrote to me that you were a Jew,' was the explanation of the astonished host.

The engravers were sometimes puzzled with the obscurer parts of Turner's later efforts. In transferring to steel one of the Venetian pictures, some ships were turned into houses ; but, as houses did quite as well, they remained. The picture was meant to be not topographically correct, but a beautiful dream, true in the feeling it conveyed.

He never, if he could help it, gave an opinion on the authenticity of a picture of his own, having once been called,

---

[1] One of the earliest engravers remarkable for imitating crumbling stone, and much employed by Mr. Britton.

to his great vexation, as witness in a case of this kind. It was a severe wound to his pride.

He was thoroughly aware of the necessity of contrast in engraving, and, as Mr. Ruskin thinks, injured himself by unduly aiming at meretricious black and white to please a public he despised—a public who would buy his engravings, but would not buy his pictures.

About his touched proofs he was always quarrelling with the engravers. He required the return of every proof on which he had written directions, and sometimes he was baffled. In this I think he was right, for the law on the subject is only traditional ; and, if he was just, he had a right to be severe and thrifty, though I think it is a pity that, as a rich man, he condescended to wrangle about such trifles : but we must remember that he was doggedly obstinate ; and the desire to retain the touched proofs was rather a matter of pride than of parsimony, for he did not sell them again. He stood on his right ; he felt he was asserting a principle ; and we must not forget that his early life had been embittered by the exactions of employers. These wrongs had hardened him. Goodall, the clever engraver of his ' Caligula's Villa,' was one of those with whom he had a most violent quarrel on the subject.

The ill feeling thus generated flamed out even in public. At a conversazione in Freemasons' Hall a dispute once occurred between Cooke and himself about the return of some drawings (of the ' Annual Tour,' I believe), to which both artist and publisher laid claim. Turner's red face became white with the depth of his rage, while Cooke grew hot and red, and high words ensued even to the extreme of ' rogue,' to the terror of those who unfortunately witnessed the verbal contest.

It was his habit, Mr. Munro told me, to visit Turner on Sunday afternoons, when the painter was often at leisure. In the course of a pleasant chat on one of these occasions—for they were sincere friends—their social privacy was invaded by the irruption of Cooke, who, with all the air of a bullying tailor come to look after a poor sweating journeyman, wanted to know if those drawings of his were never to be finished. When the door presently closed behind him, the big salt tears came into Turner's eyes, and he murmured something about ' no holiday ever for me.'

The corrections marked on the proofs were of enormous value to the engraver, giving reasons as they did for the minutest change even in the curve of a twig. Sometimes, however, to one he trusted great latitude was allowed; the direction being general as to this sky being heightened, or those towers being raised ; and on one occasion he even allowed Mr. Goodall to introduce figures of his own. It is almost certain that many of Turner's proofs, especially of the ' Liber,' were secretly stolen and sold by a workwoman who was trusted with the sewing together of the numbers.

In 1805 the first engraving ever made from an oil picture by Turner was published. The subject was taken from Sir John Leicester's ' Shipwreck.'

As this is somewhat an epoch in Turner's Art life, let me here introduce the prospectus issued upon the occasion, and the terms of his contract with the engraver :—

Proposal for publishing by subscription, with permission of Sir John Leicester, Bart., a print from that celebrated picture of

A SHIPWRECK,

WITH BOAT ENDEAVOURING TO SAVE THE CREW,

By J. M. W. TURNER, Esq., R.A.

To be seen at his Gallery, No. 64 Harley Street, until July 1, 1805 ; and after at No. 50 Warren Street, Fitzroy Square. To be engraved in mezzotinto by C. Turner. Size of the plate will be 33 inches by 23½ inches. Prints, 2*l.* 2*s.* ; proofs, 4*l.* 4*s.* Those in colours to be under the direction of the artist. Half of the money to be paid on subscribing, and the other on delivery, which will be in December next, 1805.

C. Turner has the pleasure to inform his friends, as it will be the first engraving ever presented to the public from any of Mr. W. Turner's pictures, the print will be finished in a superior style ; and, as only fifty proofs will be taken, gentlemen desirous of fine impressions are requested to be early in their application, as they will be delivered in order as subscribed for.

Subscriptions received by the engraver, No. 50 Warren Street, Fitzroy Square.

Terms of Contract.

1. To receive the 31st of Sept. 25 guineas for the loan of the picture.

2. To pay Mr. C. Turner the price of 1*l.* 6*s.*, or trade price, for all I want to colour.

3. The price of the print two guineas, proofs double size of the plate, viz.—

4. For J. M. W. T. not to part with any coloured print under four months after the publishing the proofs.

The plate to be finished by the end of Dec. 1805.   1*l.* 12*s.* trade price for 2*l.* 2*s.*

The following prospectus relating to 'The Ports of England, 1826,' is also interesting, as showing the style in which Turner's engraving ventures were presented to the public :—

Under the patronage and dedicated, with permission, to his Most Gracious Majesty George the Fourth.

PORTS OF ENGLAND,

FROM ORIGINAL DRAWINGS, MADE EXPRESSLY FOR THE WORK,

By J. M. W. TURNER, Esq., R.A.

To be engraved in highly-finished mezzotinto by Thomas Lupton. Size of the plates, 9 inches by 6½, and to be printed on small folio. Price of the work : Prints, 8*s.* 6*d.* ; proofs, 12*s.* 6*d.* ; proofs on India paper, 14*s.*

Notwithstanding the many splendid and useful publications undertaken by various persons within the last twenty years, it appears somewhat extraordinary that in a maritime nation like England, immeasurably indebted to her naval achievements for opulence and glory, a subject so deeply interesting and so intimately connected with her general history as a series of views illustrative of her several seaports and harbours, should have been to this period neglected.

A work of this kind (hitherto unattempted on an extended scale), comprising all the licensed and chartered ports of the country, has been long in preparation, and is now proposed to be published in numbers, the first of which will appear on the 1st of May next, and will contain two views, to be delivered in the order of subscription : twelve numbers to form a volume. At the completion of each volume will be published, in handsome letterpress (detached), an Historical Account of the Rise and Progress of the Ports up to the Present Time ; the whole forming a complete graphic and historical illustration of the British ports.

As the greatest care and attention will be given to the execution of this work, it is determined not to endanger its excellence by a rigid compliance with a fixed period of publication : the intervals between the production of each number will, however, be as short as the requisite attention to the work will allow.

When it is considered how many pleasing associations, how many recollections dear to the well-founded national pride and best feelings of Englishmen, arise even involuntarily on contemplating such subjects—the almost countless host of naval heroes who with well-omened hope have embarked from these ports and have returned to them in glorious triumph, shedding immortal lustre on their country—the magnificence and national importance of the ports themselves, and their immense superiority over those of other nations—it is impossible for the artist to feel otherwise than confident of the patronage of a discerning public.

London : published (May 1826) by Thomas Lupton, 7 Leigh Street, Burton Crescent ; R. Ackerman, Strand ; and Messrs. Colnaghi, Son, & Co., Pall Mall East.

Mr. Millar, the well-known Edinburgh engraver, deposes to his business transactions with Turner in these terms :—

‘ Living at a distance from London, my personal interviews were not many ; and the communications which passed between us during the twenty years or upwards that I was executing engravings from his works were chiefly confined to the margins of the proofs, and were mostly returned to him. When in London, I occasionally met him either at his own house or in company at a friend's. On one such occasion, at the house of W. B. Cooke, the landscape engraver—where were also present Hugh W. Williams (whose talents as an artist Turner respected), Lupton, the mezzotinto engraver, and Geo. Cooke—during the evening, when Turner and Williams were discoursing on some scene, and differing in opinion as to the forms of some lines in the subject, a piece of paper was produced, upon which each artist made a slight sketch in pencil to elucidate his views. At the conclusion Lupton was somewhat slily appropriating the sketch, a proceeding which Turner's keen eye disappointed by transferring it to his own pocket, notwithstanding Lupton's claim of property as having furnished the paper. My friend George Harvey, the artist, relates an amusing and highly characteristic anecdote of an interview between Turner and a gentleman (whom he named) who had recently purchased from a third party a Turner landscape. In the course of the conversation he explained with great glee the mode in which sundry parts of the picture had been got up—in particular that a dog in the foreground was cut out of an engraving and stuck on, and a lady's parasol was in like manner a wafer attached and painted over. The current story of a cap flying through the air has, I think, a reference to the engraving of the "Mouth of the Yare, Yarmouth Roads." There are several articles of clothing apparently in motion in the foreground, and I recollect being puzzled at first about them.'

One of the most painful things that ever happened to any of Turner's engravers occurred to Mr. Lupton, one of the most talented of them. He took great pains in executing a mezzotint of the 'Calais Pier;' but from some reason or other it never satisfied the painter, and after much loss of time and innumerable corrections it was left unfinished. In justice to Mr. Lupton, I append his own manly and straightforward version of the matter; but in my opinion the picture was far too dark to work from :—

'J. M. W. Turner employed Mr. Lupton to engrave his large picture of "Calais Pier" (now in the National Collection), of the same size with the beautiful print of the "Wreck," engraved by Charles Turner. All the engravings Mr. Lupton made from Turner he was in the practice of showing to the painter in their progress (that is, the working proofs from the very commencement of the plates); of course "Calais Pier" being a large plate and an important picture, the engraver presented the second or third working proof off the plate for the painter's inspection. The painter, upon looking at it, instantly exclaimed, "This is not the proportion of my picture ! There is some mistake here." The engraver replied that was impossible, because all engravings from pictures were reduced upon

mathematical principles ; consequently it was a correct reduction, and in true proportions to the picture. The painter
again exclaimed, " Well, if it is so, it won't do. These are
perfect doll's boats ! Therefore the boats, &c. &c., must all be
considerably increased in size, or there must be a large piece cut
off all round the plate to give the boats or objects in the picture
more importance ; at present it is all *sea* and *sky*, and it won't do."

' As the engraver's principal object in undertaking so large
and laborious a work was to produce an engraving equally large
and valuable as a work of Art as Mr. Charles Turner's " Wreck,"
he objected, or refused to have the plate reduced from the original size first intended. The painter then declared the objects
must all be increased. Now, it may be proper here to remark,
in the first place, that beautiful and unrivalled as the picture of
" Calais Pier" is, it is thought by artists to be a little heavy in
colour, or too dark in tone ; and as this character of blackness
in the picture was increased by the early proof shown to the
painter (in mezzotinto), the process of which style is from black
to white, this unavoidable blackness of the proof in its working
state no doubt tended to increase the delusion in the painter's
mind that the picture had not been correctly reduced ; but the
engraver's opinion was, and still is, that if Mr. Turner had
allowed the engraver to proceed and scrape away the superfluous black of the plate up to the light and finish of the picture, the painter would have felt differently about it. But no :
at it the painter went, increasing every boat and sail in the
picture, and this on a plate that had been most elaborately and
carefully worked towards completion. The two principal boats
in the picture—a lugger going out and a passage boat coming
into the harbour—were first operated upon. In the former (the
lugger) the mainsail was lifted an inch higher on the plate, the
boat itself widened to prevent the sail being too large for the
boat. Then came the Dover and Calais passage boat, the
mainsail of which was both lifted and widened, also the foresail
greatly increased, and, last of all, a large topsail was added to
it ; and, indeed, another boat also was introduced into the
subject. (These various touched proofs, with the alterations,
the engraver believes are in possession of Mr. Dillon.) The

above alterations were made at various times, and each always after a laborious taking out of work and replacing it as well as could be done by the engraver from loosely touched proofs in chalk ; so that at last the engraver found it impossible to follow them satisfactorily to his reputation, and therefore declined proceeding further with the engraved plate until the painter could give him a matured and perfectly finished picture to complete the almost new design which the painter had, *pas à pas*, created on the plate. The engraver regrets to say that this, though contemplated, was never done, which accounts for the engraving never having been finished, and at the same time for the altered state of the subject now on the plate as compared with the original picture in the National Gallery, from which the engraving was commenced.'

CHAPTER XVIII.

TURNER AT PETWORTH.

WITH the exception of Farnley in Yorkshire, there was, perhaps, no place in England which Turner so often visited as Lord Egremont's seat at Petworth, in Sussex, where he spent some of his happiest days, either in sketching with the patient devotion that was his characteristic, or in chatting and fishing with Chantrey and his old friend George Jones, R.A. The cunning, rough, honest old nobleman of Petworth liked Turner, and the pair of eccentric men got on well together.

Petworth House, the old seat of the Percys, does not date back further than 1730, nearly all the earlier buildings having been removed by the Duke of Somerset. The present erection is a large, commonplace-looking building, fronting a park which is fourteen miles in circuit; a long, straight, white structure, full of windows. The interior is fine; the rooms of white and gold are large and light, and the visitor passes through marble halls to carved chambers; from the Duke of Somerset's room to the square dining-room; and from the Beauty Room to the north gallery, delighted and astonished at some of the finest Vandykes and Holbeins that are to be found in England. The grand staircase is decorated with a French version of the classics ; and the fine gallery built by Lord Egremont is full of English pictures, antiques, and some fine specimens of Flaxman's works; the finest among which are the colossal group of the Archangel Michael piercing Satan with his spear, and a study of a shepherd boy, which Wagner pronounces to be one of Flaxman's best works. But in spite of the beautiful landscapes by Gainsborough, Copley Fielding, and Loutherbourg, the pre-eminent pictures in the north gallery are the landscapes painted by Turner for the Earl of Egremont. 'The Thames and Windsor Castle;' 'The Thames at Weybridge;' 'The Thames near Windsor;' 'An Evening Scene, with Men Dragging a Net on Shore;' 'The Thames from Eton College;' 'A Scene at Tabley, in Cheshire;' 'The Tower in the Lake ;'· 'An Evening Scene, with a Pond Surrounded by Willows—Cattle Drinking, and Men Stripping Osiers;' 'A sea View, with an Indiaman and a Man-of-War;' 'Echo and Narcissus;' and 'Jessica,' should all be carefully noted.

Turner's pictures suffer from being surrounded by carvings which are of a light-brown colour; it would be a great improvement to have a black line painted round them by way of relief to the eye. They have also sustained considerable injury from being placed in front of the light. Indeed, the beautiful painting of ' Chichester Canal ' is cracked all to pieces.

'The greater part of the present building,' says my friend Mr. G. Storey, ' was erected by the proud Duke of Somerset, James's favourite, Overbury's mortal foe, and the father of the beautiful angel Lady Ann Carr, whose portrait by Vandyke is so matchless; and here the Duke and Duchess spent their last days, doubtless holding in their hearts many terrible secrets. But to enter upon historical details would transport us too far. Striking, however, are the fine old massive walls, especially by lamplight. The effect of these receding into intense darkness is most impressive ; and in the long passages, or cloisters, one might paint sunny " De Hooghes." '

The following notes were written beside the pictures by Mr. Storey:—

'33. A grand sea-piece by Turner. The waves are full of wind, and the wind full of strength; the sky looks stormy; some small frigates are beating into harbour, a fine old India-man is waiting for a favourable wind; while a man-of-war, lit by a stream of light that breaks through the dark clouds, is lying at anchor, her white masts and giant sides rolling about; and behind her is the black storm.

'5. "The Thames at Weybridge." I mention this picture as most highly finished; the foreground is large and beautiful, and every leaf truly and exquisitely drawn.

'21. "The Thames near Windsor." Has a fine sky; a very sweet little girl carries a baby, which baby is holding out its little joyous arms to its mother. On the river fishermen are engaged with their nets; but the water looks dirty.

'108. "The Thames at Eton." Another very lovely pic-ture, full of peace and poetry, extremely simple, but rather yellow with age. The calm river winds away by the distant college; summer trees are reflected in it, white swans swim in it, and some men in a punt fish in it; but the effect of the picture is subdued, and after the sun ot those in the carved room is little more than darkness.

'46. "Echo and Narcissus." This is simply grand as a line of Homer. The scenery is very true and vivid; a deep blue bay, in the distance pale mountains, and an ancient city built round the brink of the waters; rocky hills rise round the valley in the middle distance, which is full of rich, deep-coloured autumn trees. In front of the wood Narcissus bewails over the image in the stream.

'There are some sweet Gainsboroughs, of course very in-ferior to Turner as regards drawing and knowledge, depth and vigour, but sweet in the extreme. A tree is only a tree with Gainsborough, whereas with Turner it is a willow or an oak besides being a tree. Yet there is such tender sentiment, such harmony of colour and composition, that his pictures are pleasant to the eye as music is to the ear. While Turner lays hold of us with a firm, a giant grasp, Gainsborough steals into our hearts like soft melody, and we can but say, "Play on, gentle musician." 28 is a most charming sketch by this artist. A shepherd and shepherdess meet at a fountain whither they have led their thirsty cattle, while the summer's day, so hot, is soft declining. The fair shepherdess sits on the grass, looking up into her rosy lover's face, and delicate trees, bending gracefully over, enclose this tranquil place of rendezvous. It truly is a pleasant pastoral. There are also many good specimens of the old landscape painters.

'The dining-room has its walls almost covered with carved work executed by Grinling Gibbons and his pupil Selden; the rest being by a Cumberland man named Ritson, who lost his life by saving this carving when the house was on fire. The curiously-worked clusters of leaves, flowers, and birds are the perfection of wood carving, and are quaintly intermingled with fiddles, flutes, and every variety of ornament and trophy that the artists of the Renaissance have heaped together. "There are birds," says Horace Walpole, "absolutely feathered, and two antique vases with bas-reliefs as perfect and beautiful as if they were carved by a Grecian master." Two of the pictures (the panel pictures in the Carved Room) represent the lake in the park. In the one taken from a window of the house, the sun is shining, glowing over the grass, making long shadows of the stags that grow out towards you as you look at them; and some cricketers are enjoying the evening in lusty sport. But it seems to me that the other picture (142) is much grander in subject; it is a nearer and larger view of the lake. Here the glory of the sun is supreme. The autumn trees all cringe before him as he pours his burning light through their trembling leaves.

'A view of "Chichester Canal at Sunset" is full of light, and yet solemn, calm, and almost plaintive. There is even gentle movement in it, for the smooth waters glide along and carry us with them into the picture. We all know that the sun does not go out like a candle, yet the old way of painting it was nearly this. But here the sun, though partly sunk behind the hill in the distance, seems by its intensity to be in front of it, and to burn a fiery gap and hollow in it. I dare say you have often noticed this effect in Nature. I cannot help thinking that I would rather have this picture of the four, but I do not pretend to pass judgment. Turner, instead of trying to make the sun look bright by surrounding it with darkness, has made it look brighter by surrounding it with brightness. So truthful is the effect that we begin to class it with the real sunsets that we remember to have seen, and forget that we saw this one in a picture. Nothing could be simpler than the composition.

'Eight of Turner's early pictures hang in the gallery devoted to British artists, in company with Reynolds, Romney, Leslie, Gainsborough, Hofner, and Wilson. (There is such a lovely "Woman in White," with downcast eyes, by Reynolds.) Compared with his own later works, they are the careful studies of a humble man; yet through this humility alone he was enabled to obtain full mastery over his more profound and daring subjects. No. 39, "Evening," is one of the sweetest landscapes that I ever saw. Some beautiful willows, exquisitely drawn, lean over a quiet pool, where a red cow stands bathing her feet in the water, and her back in the warm rays of the setting sun come through the leaves and branches, filling the whole picture with a rich evening glow. There are four beautiful views on the Thames; one very delicate in colour, and most highly finished. In the foreground a proud peacock, perched on a piece of a ruined palace, seems to typify a poor descendant perched on the forgotten pride of his ancient family. The rest I have not time to describe, nor is there any need. The picture called the "Mustard Pot," Turner's "Jessica," is a roundabout proof that Turner was a great man; for it seems to me that none but a great man could have painted such a mistake.

'I took a most delightful walk,' continues Mr. Storey, 'with a very pleasant guide, who led me over a common, through woods ringing with the music of birds, and bright with countless primroses. We were greeted by the hoarse crow of the pheasant, and by the always distant cuckoo. At every turn some fresh picture opened upon us—now a far-outlying view going miles and miles away; now a quaint old cottage, or a farm with its tumbledown barn and moss-covered walls. Almost every variety of picturesqueness peculiar to Old England seems to abound unmolested either by the artist or the model farmer. Indeed, so delighted was I with all I saw, so fresh and hopeful at this early spring time, that I thought of taking up my abode here for a while, in order to study the great beauty that Nature, left to herself, can bestow upon the meanest object, not only by the delicate working of her moss spreading fingers, her infinite variety of lovely leaf and flower industry, but by the various lights that sun or moon, night or day, cloud or blue sky, cast, altering into a thousand pictures one modest valley. To-night I sauntered almost sadly, and in a somewhat sentimental mood, to that valley where in the morning I had seen the little boys of the last century playing at marbles. The calm moon shone down on the graveyard through the black firs, casting their long shadows down the dusky slope, flowing away in sub-dued mystery over the wide view beyond, sending down another gentle but ample stream behind an outstanding hill; behind it, dark delicate trees, swimming away over to the distant hills, and so softening them with light that they almost mingled with the sky, the glittering sky. There was no sound but that of the little brook, rising clear and constant in the distance. Such scenes teach the artist something of the deep soul of Nature, which unless he can get at, his pictures are but worthless, cold, material pieces of cleverness; forgotten as soon as left; admired, perhaps, but never loved. I once heard a remark from a refined and witty lady which struck me at first as odd, but of which I have often felt the truth. She said that she did not care for any landscape that could not make her cry. I remember noticing two drawings of the same old castle (I forget which), one by Turner, and the other by a very ordinary drawing-master. The latter had painted it in its cold, everyday reality —had almost photographed it—and we turned it over at once. But the other was by Turner; he had gone down to the other side, where there was a river; he had gone there when the calm light of evening was lying along at the back of the black ruin; the waters were still; the sullen walls were reflected clear and deep in the stream; the castle itself towered high above, and one seemed to look up to it with reverence and with sadness. The day departing, the strong walls broken down by time, and the deep, still-flowing river, flowing on through the dark night of the future, made me think of the littleness of everyday life, and

the greatness of that other life that only the soul can understand.   And all this beauty, all this solemn majesty, depended
on Turner's choosing his time and his place, and on his feeling
that the sentiment of Nature was her noblest attribute.

'There is a pretty little lake in the park where Turner was
so fond of passing hour after hour with his fishing-rod.   It is a
pleasant place, especially on a summer's day; full of tranquillity and delight, little troops of ducks swimming on its sparkling
waters, timid fawns nibbling on its green banks, and birds
whistling out of the reach of bird-nesters, enjoying their own on
the very tiny islands that dot its surface, and are hardly large
enough for the many roots of the trees that grow out of them,
some standing in the water, and dabbling in it with the ends of
their delicate drooping branches.'

It is from the upper park of Petworth that the bolder views
of Sussex scenery are to be obtained.   The lower is somewhat
tamer after the highlands of Surrey; but from the Prospect
Tower a grand expanse opens before the eye.   A steep, heathery
descent leads to the Stag Park, and beyond that the view
stretches away to the precipitous crests of Farnhurst and Hey-
shott, with the line of black Down, extending beyond them.   On
the other side are the South Downs, with Chanctonbury Rings ;
east is a wide range of woodlands, the heart of the Weald ; and
from the Raven's Clump there is also a fine view of sketching
scenery extending towards Hindhead.

CHAPTER XIX.

TURNER'S POETRY.

TURNER was a dumb poet.   His brush was a lightning conductor, but his pen a torpedo.   Perhaps no one ever more vigorously wrestled for a blessing with the Angel of Poetry ; perhaps
no unlucky bard, not even Tate or Brady, got more unlucky
throws and more vexatious falls.   All his life, as his sketch-
books prove, he seems to have beguiled his time by efforts at
verse, generally utterly destitute of rhyme, and always lacking

and stammering in sense.   True rhythm, harmony, music, variety, everything is wanting; though occasionally a grand sounding line occurs; sometimes a happy epithet offers a sustained dull clock-beam cadence imitative of Pope, showing that in Turner's brain the organ of 'tune' was not altogether undeveloped; and at intervals come imitations of Crabbe and Thomson.

The following extracts[1] from the longest fragment found among Turner's papers will convince even the most sanguine enthusiast of the utter hopelessness of the painter's ever attaining to the rank of a great poet, ambitious as he must always have been of such an honour :—

> ' To that kind Providence that guides our step
> Fain would I offer all that my power *holds* (?),
> And hope to be successful in my weak attempt
> To please.   The difficulty great, but, when nought
> Attempted, nothing can be wrought,
> Though (?) thankful for the mental powers given,
> Whether innate or the gift of Heaven.
> Perception, reasoning, *action's slow ally* (?),
> Thoughts that in the mind *awakened* (?) lie,—
> Kindly expand the monumental stone,
> And, as the . . . . continue *power* (?).'

> ' A steady current, nor with headlong force,
> Leaving (?) fair Nature's bosom in its course,
> But, like the Thames, majestic, broad, and deep,
> Meandering *quickness* (?) in each circling sweep,
> Through *variegated Chelsea's* (?) . . . . meads,
> To *Twickenham bowers* that . . . . *reads* (?),
> In humble *guise* (?) should *each my* (?) . . . . assume
> My *self-reared* (?) willow, or the grotto's gloom,
> 'Twould be my pride to hold from further scorn
> A *remnant* (?) of his . . . . which once the bank adorn.
> What once (?) was his can't injure, but—'

> ' If then my ardent love of thee is said with truth,
> Agents (?) the *demolition* (?) of thy house, forsooth,
> Broke through the trammels, *doubts* (?), and you, my rhyme,
> Roll into being since that fatal time.'

[1] Mr. W. Rossetti complains that these extracts are not made the best of. I wish he would kindly sew them together, for I cannot.

' Lead me along with thy armonuous verse,

Teach me thy numbers, and thy $\begin{bmatrix} \text{style} \\ \text{idyls} \end{bmatrix}$ rehearse

Throughout the *lingering* (?) night's careers to *stand* (?),
And . . . . *incidents* (?) to write by Nature's hand,
The passing moments of a chequered life to give,
To cheer a moment's pleasure that we live ;
To call what's *heroic* (?) into force and *show*,
But *inimitable* alas ! (?) the glow-worm's *fire* (?).'

' From thy famed banks I'll make way (*make my way ?*),
And with regret must leave, and leave to stray,
Traverse the gloomy heath of Hounslow *wild* (?)
Render (?) more dreary *the remembrance side* (?)
That by the . . . . *nettles nowhere tell* (?)
Do sore-fraught grains . . . . rebel
And wreak full mischief stand around
And air blackens, horribly resound
The rains around, who *beat* (?) the silver Thames.'

' Put (?) arts and the love of war at mortal strife,
Deprives (?) the needy labourer of his life,
Until those days when *leaguèd* (?) barons strong
Dared to tell their monarch acted wrong,
And wrung a charter from his fallen pride,
And to maintain its freedom all have died,
The parchèd tracks of Memphis . . arid sands,
And *planted* (?) laurel-wreath in hostile lands.
Thus Nature *bravely* (?) liberty decreed,
Received the stimulus-act from Runnymede :
A little island still retains the name,
Saved (?) by its *parent* (?) . . . . *Fame* (?).'

' Ah ! little troubled seems the humble cot
That marks the *island* (?), and its inmates' lot !
The meshy nets bespeak the owner poor,
Like (?) to the spider-web in evil hour,
The finny tribe and *fancy* (?) playful webs
Within its mazes struggles but to die.
Westward the sandy tracks of Bagshot rise,
And wonder . . . . have the circling skies
Alas ! the gloomy care . . . . create
. . . . a *princely* (?) state
Should hang so long to a clear . . . . coy.'

' Oft changes on the moon the gleam of joy
So fair, so gay, assumes a gloom and woe,
And prince and peasant feel alike the blow.
But distant rising through the darkling skies
The bleak expanse of Sarum's plain arise,
Where mouldering tumuli sepulchral sleep
Gives but a niggard shelter e'en to sheep ;
The stunted . . . . and holly barely live,
And Nature asks of Heaven a short reprieve ;
The scudding clouds distil a constant dew,
And by the high *exposure* (?) life renews.'

' Hill after hill incessant cheats the eye,
While each the intermediate space deny.
The upmost one *long* (?) call to attain,
When still a higher calls on toil again.
Then the famed . . . . street appears a line,
Roman the work and Roman the design.
Opposing hill or streams alike to them ;
They seemed to scorn impediments ; for when
A little circuit would have given the same,
But conquering difficulties cherished Roman fame.'

' There on the topmost hills exposed and bare
Behold you . . . . court the upper air,
To guard the road, maintain the watch and ward ;
'Twas (?) then Old Sarum knew their high regard,
The . . . . ditch ; but here where Earth denied
Her kind assistance they by *will* (?) supplied :
Witness the inmost mount of labour all,
And still remains a monument and wall,
What perseverance can attain and bind
The unconquerable germ that sways the human mind ;
Power on *abettance* (?) thus by *mutual* (?) strife
Of priests and soldiers . . . . to life.'

Peaceful the streams lave now the . . . . hills,
No warlike clans of hostile armies thrill
The timorous female with dire alarms,
Or tear a vassal husband from her arms.
Now roams the native o'er the wide domain,
No feudal rights demands or claims,
The recompense of labours all his own,
Content and pleasure crown his humble home

That, by the prattling murmur of the rill
Which, rushing onwards, feeds the valley (?) mill,
Whose stores the neighbouring farms supplied,
And *roll* (?) a *justice* (?) newer ear denied.
Close to the mill-race stands the school,
To urchin dreadful on the dunce's stool :
Behold him placed behind the chair,
In doleful guise twisting his yellow hair,
While the grey matron tells him not to look
At passers-by through doorway, but his book.
Instant the . . . . goes round the *louder* (?) throng,
Who *meet* (?) . . . . *we dash* (?) along.'
' Close to the household way-worn stone
Her coifs hang bleaching on the . . . . thorn—
Her only pride besides the thread and reel,
For time had steeled her bosom even to feel ;
Though once, in May of life, that half-closed eye
Had taught the proudest of her time to sigh ;
But mutual impulse only triumph gained,
And homely love to higher thoughts maintained.
But here again the sad concomitant of life,
The growth of family, producèd strife.
Roused from his long content cot he went
Where oft he labour and the . . . . *bent* (?)
To form the snares for *lobsters armed in mail* (?),
But man, more cunning, over this prevail,
Lured by a few sea-snail and whelks, a prey
That they could gather on their watery way,
Caught in a wicker cage not two feet wide,
While the whole ocean's open to the pride.
Such petty profits could not life maintain ;
From his small cot he stretched upon the main :
And, by one daring effort, hope to gain
What hope appearèd ever to deny,
And from his labours and his toil to fly.
And so she proved, entrapped and overpowered,
By hostile force in Verdun dungeon cowered,
Long murmured 'gainst his hard-thought lot,
Rebelled against himself, and even his wife forgot.
But she, *returned* (?) yet hoped, no tidings gained
And, fondly cherished, *chid* (?)—yet hope remained ;
Would sighing pass delusive many an hour.'

' By Cross (?) Church ancient walls and . . . . frowned
That Nature gave by verdant greensward ground,
Amidst a marsh of pashes (?) saved by mounds
That irrigate the meadows, serve for bounds
To the overwhelming influx of the sea,
Which makes the marsh appear an estuary.
Westward the sands by storms and drift have gained
A barrier, and that barrier maintained,
Backed by a sandy heath, whose deep-worn road
. . . . the groaning wagon's ponderous load.
This branches southwards at the point of Thule,
Forms the harbour of the town of Poole.
A little "headlong" on a marshy lake,
Which probably contemptuously was given
That deeps and shallows might for once be even.
The floating sea-weed to the eye appears,
And, by the waving medium, seamen steers.
One straggling street here constitutes a town ;
Across the gutter here ship-owners frown,
Jingling their money,—passengers deride,
The consequence of misconceivèd pride.'

' Southward of this indentured strand
The ruins of Corfe's ruined turrets stand,
Between two lofty downs whose shelving side
The *upper* (?) mountain for her towers supplied,
Caused by two slender streams which here unite,
But early times give . . . . of her might.
The archèd causeway . . . . towering keep,
And yet deep fosse, scarce fed the straggling sheep,
While overhanging walls, and gateway's nod,
Proclaim the power of force and Time's keen rod :
Even earth's inmost caverns own his sway,
And prove the force of Time in *Scudland* (?) Bay,
Where massy fragments seem disjoined to play
With sportive sea-nymphs in the face of day,
While the bold headlands of the sea-girt shore
Receive (?) ingulphed old ocean's deepest store.
Embayed the unhappy Halswell toiled,
And all their efforts Neptune *herewith* (?) foiled :
The deep-rent ledges caught the trembling keel,—
But Memory draws the veil, where Pity soft doth kneel,

And ask St. Alban why he chose to rest
Where blades of grass seem even to feel distressed
'Twixt parching *sun* (?) and raging wind,
And others *here* (?) a . . . . *waters* (?) find.'

' Disjointed masses breaking fast away
Tell the sad *news* (?) . . . . and the sway
Of wintry billows foaming o'er ;
In fell succession, waves incessant roar,
Denying all approach.   Ah ! happy they
Who from mischance . . . . *means convey* (?)
Or jutting headland for another takes,
For Nature's jealous—has allowed no breaks
Of streams or valleys sloping, save but one,
And there she still presents a breast of stone :
Above are downs where *press* (?) the nibbling sheep,—
Below, the seamews full possession keep.
A little hollow, excavated round,
To a few fishing-boats give anchory ground,
Guarded with bristling rocks, whose strata rise
Like . . . . scoria to southern skies,
Called Lulworth Cove,—but no security to those
Who wish from storming sea a safe repose.
Whoever lucklessly are *driven* (?)
From Portland seeks an *eastern* (?) haven
Must luff against the south-west gale
And *strike* (?) for Poole alone the *tortured* (?) sail ;
For Wight again the safe retreat denies,
The Needles brave the *force* (?) of southern skies.'

' The long, long winter months, but summer skies
Permit the quarry to give up its prize,
The tinkling hammer and the driving bore
Detaching fragments from the massy store :
Then, squared or rough, in a shallow yawl
The *wadding* (?) workmen by mere strength do hawl
Invention, kindest friend to weak-formed man,
Taught him the lever, accumulating span.
Seems palsied, paralyzèd, hopeless, here,
Even Swanage Dock (?) can't boast a pier,
A single cart conveys a single stone
Into *deep water prejudice must* (!) own.'

' But . . . . alas ! follow, and we find
  That each excuse most savours of the kind.
  Hence rugged Portland steps upon our view
  And the same efforts tracing but anew,
  The ponderous shaft each track contains
  Unless a load drags on a lengthened chain,
  As down the track-worn step it glides,
  And, by its dragging weight, even serves to guide ;
  Keeps the poor horse beneath the ponderous load
  From overpowered adown the shelving road.
  Some small endeavours of mechanic still
  To ship they cheer *overhangers* (?) at the *will* (?)
  Of tackle (*fixed*) place by the jetties ride,
  But here no depth of water even at tide
  Allows what Nature all around has thrown
  With (?) great profuseness : here alone is stone.
  Along the south and west no creeks appear,
  No bay or harbours, labouring eyes to cheer,
  Who, vain watching, throng the creaking shrouds,
  When night and darkness mix the gloomy clouds—
  Chaotic warfare ! surges tell *alone* (?)
  The trembling pilot to beware, nor hold
  An onward course, *nor* (?) while the cable holds
  The struggling ship her bows into the wind,
  Nor rush on danger by the hope to find
  Upon the iron coast the Portland race.'

' Nor hope amongst direful (?) reefs a resting-place.
  Indented (?) west and north a bank extends :
  Now to the utmost stretch the eye.
  Loose shelving beach thrown up by restless waves
  A useful, barren, careful nature craves.
  Beneath the western waves the marshes lie,
  Luxuriant, bearing every varied dye :
  Even Melcombe sands their safety owes,
  Melcombe, whose sands oft bear the *lover vows* (?),
  Whose yielding surface tells the lovèd name,
  But Neptune, jealous, washes out the same.
  Alas ! the yielding type commixing gives
  Its tender hope and then coquettish leaves.
  So hopeful fancy leads us through our care,
  Stretch wide our visionary minds, on air

Builds all our inmost wishes could attain,
Even to the sandy frailty of the main.
And ask the blessing which we all desire
To give what Nature never could inspire,
What madness asked, or passion fans the flame,
At once our pilot and our early bane :
Enrapt we wish the object not in scope,
And prove a very libertine to hope.
Can *ardour* (?) . . . . *our of* (?) youthful fire,
Check for a *moment* (?) all our warm desire.'
' Tempts us to declare to all who view
The name we hold most lovely and hope true.
But thought created by the ardent mind
Proves oft as changing as the changing wind.
A great . . . . renders all our care
A *short* (?) to others who are thought more fair.
Absence the dreadful monster to delight,
Delusion like the silent midnight blight,
Frailty, that ever courted, oft beloved,
And modesty though slighted, most approved,
All give and urge the intolerable smart
Of loves when absent, rankling at the heart.
Moreover (?) the . . . .
No church and meads in (?) . . . . *as the road* (?)
Or anxious shivered in (?) . . . . *bands* (?)
And longed (?) . . . . *on the oozy sands* (?).
She tended oft the kine, and to the mart
Bore all the efforts of her father's art ;
And, homeward as she bore the needful pence,
Would loiter careless on, or ask through mere pretence—
To youth much *mischief* (?) ; for, maturely grown,
It proved, alas ! a mischief all her own.
Guileless and innocent she passed along,
And cheered her footsteps with a *morning* (?) song ;
When craft, and lechery, and . . . . combined
Proved but to triumph o'er a *spotless* (?) mind.
To guard the coast their duty, not delude
By promises as little heeded as they're good :
When strictly followed, give a conscious peace,
And ask at the eve of life *a* (?) just release.
But idleness, the bane of every country's weal,
Equally enervates the soldier and his steel.

Lo ! on yon bank beneath the hedge they lie,
And watch with cat-like . . . . each female by :
One sidelong glance or hesitating step
Admits not of recal who once o'erleap.
The deep-ploughed sands are . . . . up by the main,
But time denies the *cure* (?) of love or gain :
Deep sinks the (curse ?) of *lucre* (?) at the heart,
And virtue stained o'erpowers the greater part.
Wan, melancholy, sits the once full-blooming maid,
Misanthrope stalks her soul in silent shade :
On the bold promontory thrown at length she lies,
And sea-mews shrieking are her obsequies.
Or on the blasted heath or far stretched down
Exposing still the field by iron sown,
Barrow after barrow ; till with silent awe
The dreadful cause pervading Nature's law,
That the rude hands of warfare (*feudal ?*) strife,
Denying peace, and oft denying life
Along the topmost ridge, the *narrow* (?) way,
The work of Norman prowess braves the day,
With triple ditch and barbican arise
Defying the hand of Time and stormy skies
Which from the wide . . . . *drawing o'er* (?)
Pour o'er those bulwarks . . . . clouds or showers.'

' Oh ! powerful beings, hail ! whose stubborn soul
Even o'er itself to urge *even* (?) self-control.
Thus Regulus, whom every torture did await,
Denied himself admittance at the gate
Because a captive to proud Carthage power,
But his *fierce* (?) soul would not the Romans lower.
Not wife or children dear, or self, could hold
A moment's parley,—love made him bold,
Love of his country ; for not aught beside
He loved,—but for that love he died.'

' The same inflexibility of will
Made them to choose the inhospitable hill ;
Without recourse they stood supremely great,
And firmly bid defiance even to fate.
Thus stands aloft this yet commanding[1] fort,
" The Maiden " called, still of commanding port.

> [1] Another word substituted, perhaps ' encinctured,'

So the famed Jungfrau meets the nether skies
In endless snow untrod, and man denies,
With all his wiles ; precipitous or bold,
The same great characters its summits hold :
Thus *graves* (?) o'er all the guarded area tell
Who fought for its possession, and who fell.'

' The chieftain's tumule, and the vassal's sword,
Own the dread sway of Death, tremendous lord.
On every side, each hill or vantage ground,
The awful relics everywhere abound,
And feelingly its ancient prowess own,
Though power, and arms, and carnage, roam
O'er other lands ; yet still, in silent pride,
It looks around, majestic, though decried
And useless now.   So on the sea-girt shore
Where Abbotbury cliffs re-echo to the roar,
Another guards the passage to the main,
And on the right in-land some vestige yet remain.'

' Where the soft . . . . flowing gives renown,
'Mid steep worn hills and to the low-sunk town
Whose trade has flourished from early time,
Remarkable for thread called Bridport twine,
Here (?) roars the busy *mell* (?) called breaks
Through various processes o'ertakes
The flax in dressing, each with one accord
Draw out the thread, and meet the just reward.
Its population great, and all employed,
And children even draw the twisting cord.
Behold from small beginnings, like the stream,
That from the high-raised downs to *market breem* (?).'

' First feeds the meadows where grows the line,
Then drives the mill that all its powers define,—
Pressing (?), dividing all *vegetating pass* (?) [1] ⎱
Withdrawn, high (?) swell the *shiny* (?) mass— ⎰
On the peopled town who all combine
To throw the *many* (?) strands in lengthened twine ;
Then onward to the sea its freight it pours,
And by its prowess holds to distant shores ;
The straining vessel to its cordage yields :
So Britain floats the produce of her fields.

[1] Uncertain whether these lines come here.

Why should the Volga or the Russians
Be coveted for hemp? Why thus supplied
The sinew of our strength, our naval pride?
Have not we soil sufficient rich? or lies
Our atmosphere too temperate, or denies
The Northern . . . . to harden, or mature
The vegetable produce? or can it not endure
The parching heat of summer's solstice o'er?
Weak argument? Look round our shore.
Sterile and bleak our uppermost appear,
And barren left through all the varied year,
With *whinns* (?) and gorse alone possessed.
Would here the seedling hemp then be distressed?
Look farther—north of *vaunted* (?) Scotia's heights,
With firs, and snows, and winter's full delights :—
Not—North enough, then, transatlantic lay
Some vast-extended land of Hudson's Bay.'

' If heat is requisite more than our suns can give,
Ask but the vast continent where Hindoos live—
More than the mother-country ten times told,
Plant but (?) the ground with seed instead of gold.
Urge all our barren tracts with agricultural skill,
And Britain, Britain, British canvas fill ;
Alone and unsupported prove her strength
By means her own to meet the direful length
Of Continental hatred called blockade,—
When every power and every port is laid
Under the proscriptive terms themselves have made.'

' O'er the Donetian downs that far-expand
Their scathed ridges into Devon's land
The mounting sun, bedecked with purple dyes,
As o'er their healthy summits beaming flies.
The gilding radiance on the upmost ridge
That, looking eastwards, on rocky rampart stood
A garden once, like others, through the land
Where native valour dare to make a stand
Against [despotism ?] and Rome . . . . taught
The prayer of valour, *gained* (?) though dearly bought
Thus wrought *through habit* (?) by *prorogued* (?) disease,
As morning fogs that rising tempt the breeze,

Grey and condensing, hovering o'er the swamp
Of deep-sunk woods, or marshes dull and dank,
Crowd like tumulous legions beneath the hill,
Like congregated clouds, and eddying reel
This way or other, as the air incline,
Till the all-powerful doth on them shine,
Dispersed, and showing on their edge its power
In varied lights.   Sometimes, in force combined,
It seems to have the force of sun and wind ;
Blotting the . . . . (?), sheds a doubtful day,
Besprinkling oft the traveller on his way.
As others, stealing 'neath each down of hill,
And, scarce diaphanous, the valley fill :
Then day brings on his coursers and sultry car,—
All Nature, panting, dreads the ruling star,—
Along the narrow road whose deep-worn track ;
Till, up with heavy dusk, the *usual* (?) burdened pack
Plods heavily and dull, with heat oppressed,
And champs of snorting tell his great distress,
Burdened with stone or sand, where the steep ascent
Prevents the *East* (?) or slides ; whose quick descent
Makes o'er a load of nothing endless toil,
And to the *o'erladen path ever quick* (?) recoil
Upon its galled withers ; and the heavy band,
Upheld by pegs, within the panniers stand
Relieved from its load the other flies,
When (?) Satan scales aloft in *nether* (?) skies,
Or sulphurous cloud at open east foretels
Where atmospheric *contraries* (*contraction ?*) doth dwell ;
And the warm vapour, condensing from the main,
O'er the wide welkin darksome clouds remain :
Till, borne by various currents, dimly spread,
The *sickening* (?) rays of the wan sunbeam's head.
A gloomy lurid interval succeeds,
As from the *high* (?) , ... noon the orb recedes.
Spotty as partial, quenches (?) the evening sky
In . . . . of clouds of every shape and dye.
Meantime an *ever inwards* (?) rolls around the clouds,
And bear against the blast the thunders loud,
Breaking on the upmost hills ; then *quick ascends* (?)
The scattered . . . ., and conquering *tends* (?)

To the full-charged elementary strife—
To man even fears, and oft . . . . life.
A corse tremendous, awful.   Dark indeed
Died (?) the smitten *wretch* (?) not doomed to bleed,—
The current *dread charred* (?) with the veins,
Sulphurous (?) and livid, still the form retains.
Most dreadful visitation !   *Instantaneous* (?) death
Of supreme goodness allows the fleeting breath
To fall, apparently without a thought of pain.

' Exalted sat St. Michael in his chair
Full many a fathom in the *circling* (?) air.
Scarce can the giddy ken of mortal sight
Behold the dreadful chasm but in height.'

The tenacity with which Turner held on to a resolve could
not be exemplified better than by these painful and stammering
efforts of his muse.   Now he seems to be thinking of Shenstone
and Thomson, then of Crabbe, and next of Pope ; yet never,
in any form of imitation, does he spell well or carry on a clear
and consecutive meaning for ten lines together.   There is never
a perfect picture, never a continuous strain of thought.   The
impulse for verse is there, but not the power of expression.   It
is the dumb man making noises, and fancying himself an
eloquent speaker.   Let us review this poem.   At Bridport our
struggling poet becomes more than usually obscure and more
than usually didactic.   He introduces to us amid steep worn
hills ' the low sunk town,'

from early time
Remarkable for thread called Bridport twine.

The practical bard rejoices much in the large population
employed in dressing flax and twisting cord.   He then suddenly
grows interrogative and argumentative.   Why, exclaims he,
should the Russians grow hemp, ' that sinew of our strength,'
for us ?   Have we not soil sufficiently rich, or is our atmosphere
rather too temperate ?   Are there not sterile and bleak cliffs on
our shores, now overgrown with whinns and gorse, where hemp
might be sown ?   Or, if more cold is wanted, are there not
' Scotia's heights,' with their firs and snows ; and, further still,

is there not the ' vast extended land of Hudson's Bay '? If heat is required, there is 'the vast continent where Hindoos live.' Indeed, pursues the bard, if all our barren tracts were but sown, Britain, alone and unsupported, might prove her strength against Continental hatred and Napoleon's direful ' blockade' of the foreign ports.

At Corfe Castle the poet stops, and depicts to us the arched causeway and the towering keep ; the overhanging walls, the nodding gateway, and the deep fosse where the straggling sheep obtain their scanty meal. Presently he passes on to Roman camps, and jolts out the story of Regulus, one of those ' powerful beings' and ' stubborn souls' the poet seems to sympathise with ; for he instantly goes on to sketch another Roman fort on the coast, and says—

> The same inflexibility of will
> Made them to choose the inhospitable hill.

And he proceeds to compare it to the ' Jungfrau.'

It is curious, however, to trace everywhere in these verses the sympathy of the writer with a sea life. From stories of seductions by coast-guard men, and a rather prosaic description of the stone quarries of Portland, he turns to painting shipwrecks and sketching the embayed ' Halswell,' whose 'trembling keel' is caught by the ' deep-rent ledges ;' and, when he gets to Lulworth Cove, he writes indeed more like an examiner of pilots than a simple poet :

> ' No security to those
> Who wish from stormy sea a safe repose.
> Whoever lucklessly are (fiercely) driven
> From Portland, seeking (then) an eastern haven,
> Must hit against the south-west gale,
> And strike for Poole, where the tortured sail
> For Wight again the safe retreat denies.
> The Needles brave the force of Southern skies.'

These directions certainly are honest and earnest ; but they are not altogether remarkable for perspicuity.

What this work was meant for, I cannot tell. It reads like

an attempt at a rhymed gazetteer of England, or a new Polyol-
bion. In one place he talks of wishing

> The passing moments of a chequered life to give ;

and then he wanders to descriptions of Hounslow and Bagshot
heaths—as if they were the first stages of some journey he had
tumbled into rhyme. Presently we find him at Poole, in Dorsetshire, which he sketches sarcastically in the following lines :—

> One straggling street here constitutes a town ;
> Across the gutter here ship-owners frown,
> Jingling their money,—passengers deride,
> The consequence of misconceivèd pride.

Now, the first three lines are tolerably terse ; but the last is
merely a hint at sense, and sadly wants beating again on the
anvil.

In one place, it is true, he sketches a village school with
some eye to character ; he shows us the dunce's stool, and the
grey matron chiding the boy, 'who twists his yellow hair,' and
bidding him look at his book and not at the passers-by. Close
by the school, upon a thorn, the dame's caps hang bleaching ;
and these are her only pride, besides her spinning-reel. The
dame was once a village beauty, and made 'the proudest of
her time to sigh.' Then follows a line or two of chaos, from
which we gather that after all she married a fisherman, who,
disdaining lobster-catching when the whole ocean was opened
to him, turned privateer, because he

> By one daring effort hopes to gain
> What hope appeared ever to deny.

For once the balance of the lines is preserved ; but the unlucky adventurer is caught by the French, and thrown into
Verdun's dungeon. His wife, who can gain no tidings of him,
still hopes on and passes the delusive hours in sighing.

In one of his note-books I find these lines of Cunningham's
copied :—

> O'er the Heath the Heifer strays
> Free—the Furrow'd task is done.

Now the village windows Blaze
Burnish[ed] by the setting sun.

Now he sets behind the Hill
Sinking from a Golden sky ;
Can the pencil . . . . mimic skill,
Copy the refulgent Dye . . . .

Shivered by a thunder stroke
From the Mountain . . . . misty ridge
O'er the Brook a ruined oak
Near the Farm House forms a Bridge.

They attest at least the copyist's intense enjoyment of new
and grand objects, of clear, calm sunsets, of mountains and
misty ridges, and of rude bridges formed by lightning-rent oaks.
The last verse seems to be his own. There is, too, an instructive sense of Art in the word *free*, so strongly placed with a full
emphasis on it as the commencement of a line. The spelling,
as usual, is wanting in finish and detail. On the whole, I think
that for 1792 the verses are rather an anticipation and a prophecy of the restoration of poetry by the Lake school, some
twenty years later. Bad as they are, they are better than pastoral sentiment, punning epitaphs, or ribald epigrams.

There is hardly much hope for a poet who cannot even
spell correctly. Turner felt poetry and painted poetry, but he
could not write it. Persevering and yet indolent, he never took
the trouble to learn the commonest laws of metre or rhythm.
This desire to write verse was one of the ' Fallacies of Hope ;'
a poem which, if it ever did exist, was not found among his
sketches or papers after his death.

In early years his pictures at exhibitions were accompanied
with various quotations, descriptive of atmospheric effects, from
Thomson, interspersed with two or three from Milton, and one
from Mallet.

' In 1800,' says Mr. Ruskin, ' some not very promising
" Anon." lines were attached to views of Dolbadern and Caernarvon Castles. Akenside and Ossian were next laid under
contribution. Then Ovid, Callimachus, and Homer. At last,
in 1812, the " Fallacies of Hope " begin, *à propos* of " Hannibal's

Crossing the Alps ; " and this poem continues to be the principal text-book, with occasional recurrences to Thomson, one passage from Scott, and several from Byron. The " Childe Harold " (picture) is an important proof of his respect for the genius of Byron.'

Secretive by nature as Turner was, he no doubt enjoyed the mysterious rumours constantly circulating about this poem, which he knew he should never print.

CHAPTER XX.

TURNER'S FRIENDS.

TURNER was neither an ascetic, nor a miser, nor a misanthrope. He loved his friends with deep tenderness ; he left the nation that neglected him 140,000*l.* ; and he was one of the most social of men. Nor was he unaccustomed to the society of men of wealth and rank. Lord Egremont delighted to have him at his table ; Lord Harewood knew him well in the easy intercourse of life ; at the houses of his friends, the Rev. Mr. Trimmer, Mr. Ruskin, Mr. Stokes, Mr. Griffith, Mr. G. Jones, and others, he was ever welcome. At Royal Academy dinners or private meetings he was the gayest and merriest of the band. He was fond, too, of water excursions ; and when down in Yorkshire with his old friend Mr. Fawkes, of Farnley, he shot grouse and fished with the enjoyment of a boy.

Of the suspiciousness which was an unpleasing part of his character Mr. G. Jones testifies—

' In early life every hand extended to him sought to profit by his talent at the smallest expense possible ; he encountered extortions of time and work ; he discovered that he was unjustly used to fill the purses of others rather than his own. He became by degrees so suspicious and sensitive that he dreaded the motives of all by whom he was surrounded. He desired to be wealthy, and took every honourable means to become so ; not to indulge in luxury or ostentatious display, but to be independent of the world.'

Turner was too reserved to be often praising, but he never uttered a word of critical disparagement or detraction. The poisonous distilment of envy never flowed perpetually from his tongue. Stothard, however, he frequently praised, for he loved the gentle poetry which suffused all that good man did; the pastoral grace, the beautiful simplicity (as of 'The Golden Age'), that irradiated with a foretaste of heaven the happy pictures of 'the English Watteau,' as he was truly called. It is true that he painted his Boccaccio picture in distinct rivalry of Stothard; but he openly expressed his desire that Stothard, above all men, should like his pictures. Etty, I believe, he did not like; for Constable personally he had no relish; and Constable, I fear, had an aversion for Turner's works. I have been told he has been seen to spit with disgust at the very sight of some of them.

Of Girtin, the companion and rival of his youth, he was, as I have said, never tired of speaking. 'If Girtin had lived,' he used to say with true generosity and pathos, 'I should have starved.' All through his life, the sight of one of Girtin's yellow drawings made his eyes sparkle, and often would he earnestly declare that he would lose a finger willingly, could he learn how to produce such effects.

Mr. Field, author of 'Chromatics,' was a friend of Girtin's, and it is on his authority I give the following anecdote. Girtin had finished a water-colour drawing of St. Paul's, looking up Ludgate Hill. Turner, after inspecting it first closely, and then at a distance, turned to Girtin and observed, 'Girtin, no man living could do this but you.' In later life he often expressed to Mr. Trimmer and Mr. Field his high opinion of Girtin's power. 'We were friends to the last,' he used to say, 'although *they* did what they could to separate us.' How much of regret and tenderness is summed up in these words!

Mr. Lupton, the celebrated engraver, says—

'Turner was a man who not only considered that time was money, but he acted upon it, and worked from morning till night; indeed, it would be correct to say he laboured from sunrise to sunset. He would often ask his brother artists, sarcastically, if they ever saw the sun rise. These industrious habits, and his love of his profession, gave him a very long life, and account for the great number of works he left behind him, for it may be truly said he worked as many hours as would *make the lives* of two men of his own age. He was a great observer of all that occurred in his profession. Of reserved manners generally, but never coarse (as has been said), though blunt and straightforward, he had a great respect for his profession, and always felt and expressed regret if any member of it appeared to waste or neglect his profession.

' In the sale of his pictures he always took a high moral position. When asked the price of a picture by a purchaser (for instance), he would say, " Two hundred guineas." The reply has been, " No ; I will give you one hundred and seventy-five." " No ; I won't take it." On the morrow the applicant for the picture has come again. " Well, Mr. Turner, I suppose I must give you your price for that picture : the two hundred guineas." Mr. Turner has been known to reply, " Ah, that was my price yesterday, but I have changed my mind also ; the price of the picture to-day is two hundred and twenty-five guineas." The applicant went away, and perhaps the next day was glad to have the picture at another increased price. Turner among his social friends was always entertaining, quick in reply, and very animated and witty in conversation. He was well read in the poets.'

It is generally supposed that Turner never painted a picture in conjunction with any other Academician ; but the following story will show the contrary. On occasion of a visit to the house of his old friend the Rev. Mr. Trimmer, by whose children he was much beloved, as a kind, funny old gentleman, Turner was present while Mr. Howard painted the portrait of one of the children. The poetical painter of Venuses and Hebes had got into a hobble ; the picture would not come right. Turner, who was called in as consulting physician, cast his eagle eye instantly on the fault. There being want of warm colour in the foreground, he advised the introduction of a cat wrapped up in a red handkerchief. The now forgotten poet was horrified at the suggestion, and confessed his inability to work it out ; whereupon Turner instantly took up his brushes, and painted in the ingenious expedient. The picture was saved by the alteration; and, thus saved, it still exists at Mr. Trimmer's house, an interesting relic of Turner's sagacity.

Mr. Trimmer himself was not unskilled in Art, having painted landscapes, I am told, with great skill. A picture dealer opposite Furnival's Inn once showed him a portrait by Sir Joshua Reynolds with a tree in the background, which in the sale-room had been compared for breadth and knowledge to Titian. It was well known Reynolds had made fine sketches of the sea in Devonshire, and had once or twice painted landscapes that lay round his villa at Twickenham; but this tree!—Mr. Trimmer smiled at the pedantic cant of the trade, for he had himself added that object to the portrait, which had once been his own property.

Turner on one occasion was much struck by a picture in which a sea-fog had been cleverly and truthfully introduced. The mystery of it delighted him, for he had found such effects most difficult. When, however, Mr. Trimmer stood up and explained that it was painted by himself, Turner was quite angry, and never praised anonymous pictures again. His 'Mill and White Horse' in the 'Liber' he took from a sketch made by Mr. Trimmer from a lock near Brentford.

Mr. Trimmer's sons, who are still living, remember Turner as an ugly, slovenly old man, with rather a pig-like face; in fact, somewhat of 'a guy;' and describe how he made them laugh, and how pleasant and sociable he was. They recollect him mixing some sort of paste with his umbrella, and their mother, on one occasion, in fun, carrying off one of his sketches against his will, for he was by no means a member of 'the give-away family.' He liked to be at Heston, not merely for the fishing and fresh air, but because Mr. Trimmer was an old friend and a lover of Art, and because he was close to his old school at Brentford Butts, now a public-house, near the 'Three Pigeons.' During these visits to Mr. Trimmer he always behaved with great decorum, and regularly attended church. Indeed, I have a strong belief that the interior of a church in the 'Liber' is taken from Heston. It is almost the only church interior painted by him; and he did it twice, once by daylight and once by lamplight. It was with this friend that he bartered lessons in painting for lessons in Greek. Mr. Trimmer was remarkable for a habit of keeping all letters that he ever received ; and the result of this literary accumulation was that, after his death, his son, exhausted by the labour of reading a packet or two of crabbed MS., set to and with ruthless hands burnt some twenty sacksful of original and unpublished letters, including, no doubt, some hundreds of Turner's. When I first heard this, I thought of the fatal fire at Warwick that destroyed Shakespeare's relics, and of the great conflagration that Amrou made in Egypt of the vast Alexandrian Library ; but Mr. Trimmer consoled me by telling me that Turner never wrote often or at any great length to his father, because he was then living at Solus Lodge, within walking distance ; and, moreover, like most artists, he did not like writing. He firmly believes, however, that some verses perished, and is not sure that such destruction was a loss to the world.

One letter, however, which he found and preserved was of interest. Penned when Turner was about forty, it described him as being deeply in love with a lady, a relation of Mr. Trimmer's, staying in the house at Heston. It was the letter of an affectionate but shy and eccentric man ; imploring his friend to help him at his need ; talking of soon coming down again, but expressing his fear that he should never find courage to pop the question unless the lady helped him out. But no ; cruel Fate stepped in ; some small pebble turned the painter's foot aside ; and he died unmarried, with no hands save those of mercenary Love to close his eyes and smooth his dying pillow.

Of this second attachment I know no more than the following singular letter discloses. We may presume, however, that the lover lacked courage ; that fresh ambitions arose, and more daring suitors ; and so Turner was left to sink into the cheerless, selfish old bachelor, with no children to prattle round his knees, and no kind heart to double his joys and halve his sorrows.

[*Redirected.*

'Rev. Mr. Trimmer,
'Southwold,
'Suffolk]

Q

'Tuesday, August 1, 1815:
'Queen Ann Street.

'My dear Sir,—I lament that all hope of the pleasure of seeing you, or getting to Heston, must for the present probably vanish. My father told me on Saturday last, when I was, as usual, compelled to return to town the same day, that you and Mrs. Trimmer would leave Heston for Suffolk as to-morrow, Wednesday. In the first place, I am glad to hear that her health is so far established as to be equal to the journey, and to give me your utmost hope for her benefiting by the sea air being fully realised ; 'twill give me great pleasure to hear, and the earlier the better.

'After next Tuesday, if you have a moment's time to spare, a line will reach me at Farnley Hall, near Otley, Yorkshire, and for some time, as Mr. Fawkes talks of keeping me in the North by a trip to the Lakes, and until November. Therefore I suspect I am not to see Sandycombe. Sandycombe sounds just now in my ears as an act of folly, when I reflect how little I have been able to be there this year, and less chance (perhaps) for the next. In looking forward to a Continental excursion, and poor Daddy seems as much plagued with weeds as I am with disappointment—that if Miss —— would but waive bashfulness, or, in other words, make an offer instead of expecting one, the same might change occupiers ; but not to trouble you further, allow me, with most sincere respect to Mrs. Trimmer and family, to consider myself

'Yours most truly obliged,
'J. M. W. TURNER.'

Mr. Trimmer's eldest son, who was very fond of drawing, one day scrawled a man with his legs close together. 'Why do you draw the legs together?' was Turner's question. Stimulated by the rage of the day, the boy then took to battle-pieces —little queer men, all swords and plumes, men slashing, and horses kicking. Turner loved to run over these, observing with a good-humoured grin at each of them, 'That's better;' 'Not so good;' 'He'll never hit him,' and so on ; and he advised the tender aspirant to change his style, there being no play for talent in military costume. In fact, '*I commenced as battle-painter myself,*' was his emphatic declaration. He even lent him some sketches done by a military friend on the field of Waterloo during the action, which he considered to be very spirited ; but later on he dissuaded him from being an artist, for which profession he had a great bent, telling him it was the most wretched calling he could turn to.

Mr. Field having sent Turner his treatise on 'Chromatics,' when they next met, asked him his opinion of it. 'You have not told us too much,' was Turner's dry remark. Almost the last conversation Mr. Trimmer had with him was respecting colours, which he did not consider were reducible to scientific rules ; and on that occasion he pronounced Field's book to be fallacious. Genius, Mr. Trimmer observed, was the unconscious pursuit of rule ; and, even as oratorical canons had been deduced from Cicero's orations, of which the orator was not aware, Turner's pictures might form the basis of a scientific system of colouring. Field used to maintain that Turner's most extravagant conceptions were in perfect harmony ; Nature in a very high key, as seen through a prism ; the painting being off-hand, and the most inimitable effects produced without the slightest effect. An oil painter should never paint but in oil, said Constable, who held that Turner's pictures were only large water-colours, after testing them with a diminishing-glass, writes Mr. Trimmer.

Many years ago two of Turner's friends were standing at the door of an exhibition where some of his water-colours were on show, and were debating about the entrance fee. Suddenly a little man dashed up to the astonished custos and snatched two tickets from him, having given which to the applicants, he set off instanter. It was Turner, who had that morning met them in the street, and asked them if they would like to see the drawings.

Mr. E. Swinburn, himself an accomplished artist, was very intimate with Turner ; who, I have heard, used to stay in Northumberland, at the seat of Sir John Swinburn, Bart.

Mr. Allnut, of Clapham, I think, bought many of Turner's

drawings, one of which, the 'Fall of Terni,' he published. G. F. Robson, the eminent water-colour painter, who met him there, found him to be 'civil and communicative.'

Turner and Carew were once fishing in the pond at Lord Egremont's at Petworth, when the latter, in his blunt, honest, Irish way, broke silence, and said, 'Turner, they tell me you're very rich.' Turner chuckled and enquired, 'Am I?' 'Yes; everybody says so,' was the observation. 'Ah!' replied he; 'I would give it all up again to be twenty years of age again.' 'What!' exclaimed the other, 'do you like it so well as all that?' 'Yes, I do,' was the response.

Mr. David Roberts, his old friend, bears the following testimony to Turner's kindness of heart and general sociability :—

'I afterwards became well acquainted with him, being in the habit of meeting him at the dinner table of General Phipps, in Mount Street, where one was always sure to meet the best artists of the day—Wilkie, Chantrey, Calcott, Collins, Mulready, Etty, &c. &c. Although reserved, he was ever kind and indulgent to younger men : I mean such as myself. I write more especially of my own knowledge, as, besides meeting him at General Phipps's, I had many other opportunities of meeting at dinner, particularly at Munro's, of Novar, and the Rev. E. Daniel's, to whom he was much attached. Poor Daniel, like Wilkie, went to Syria after me, but neither returned. Had Daniel returned to England, I have reason to know, from Turner's own mouth, he would have been entrusted with his law affairs.

'Turner, though kind to younger men, could frown, and show his contempt fearlessly for those whom he considered unworthy his friendship. He was ever modest of his own abilities, and I never remember him uttering a word of disparagement of others. Of a contrary disposition was Constable, ever talking of himself and his works, and unceasing in his abuse of others. We had met one night at the General's, shortly after the hanging of the Royal Academy. Constable was, as usual, lavish of the pains he had taken and the sacrifices he had made in arranging the Exhibition. But, most unfortunately, he had, after placing an important work of Turner's, removed it, and replaced it by one of his own. Turner was down upon him like a sledge hammer ; it was of no use his endeavouring to persuade Turner that the change was for his advantage, and not his own. Turner kept at it all the evening, to the great amusement of the party ; and, I must add, he (Constable) richly deserved it, by bringing it on himself.

'It would be useless to add his many personal acts of kindness to myself, and of confidence he placed in me, which led to my seeing much of him towards the latter part of his life. When he dined with me, I always contrived to get those to meet him that I knew would be agreeable ; a very simple method of making your friends happy. I was myself too much occupied to trouble myself about his private affairs, for his life partook of the character of his works. It was mysterious, and nothing seemed so much to please him as to try and puzzle you, or to make you think so ; for if he began to explain, or tell you anything, he was sure to break off in the middle, look very mysterious, nod, and wink his eye, saying to himself, " Make out that if you can ; " and it no doubt was this love of mystery that led, at last, to the sad muddle in which he left his affairs. No doubt, like many others, he intended some day to put them all right, but the grim gentleman stepped in before he could make up his mind.

'I and others knew he had another home besides Queen Anne Street, but delicacy forbade us prying further. We all knew that whoever he lived with took great care of him, for he was not only better dressed, but more cleanly and *tidy*, than in former years. He was ever constant in his attendance at all meetings of the Academy, and at such meetings he usually took a part in the debates ; but such was the peculiar habit of his thoughts, or of his expressing them (the same *aerial perspective* that pervades most of his works pervaded his speeches), that when he had concluded and sat down it would often have puzzled his best friend to decide which side he had taken.

'I might mention instances of his kindness to myself, but they are of little interest to others. Suffice it to state one, on my first exhibiting at Somerset House a picture of the front of Rouen Cathedral, painted for the late Lord Northwick. He took Sir William Allan out of the Great Room (where they were at work on varnishing day) to the School of Painting, where my picture had been placed, and said, " Here is a man we must have our eye upon." This, Sir William gave me to understand, was no trifling compliment from the great painter.

'After all, much may be said in mitigation of his reserve and love of mystery. Uneducated as he was (a thing not unusual with men of genius), he would naturally avoid society, where he knew he would be seen to a disadvantage. But that he was not the recluse Ruskin has pictured him, is *well known to all who knew anything about him*, for he loved the society of his brother painters, and was in reality "a jolly toper," never missing a night at the meetings of the Royal Academy Club, usually then held at the "Thatched House;" and, as a proof that he loved them and these jolly parties, he *willed* that 50*l.* annually should be spent expressly for that purpose on his birthday; but I regret to add, it has not been fulfilled, although the Academy have it in contemplation to do so from the 20,000*l.* awarded them by the Court of Chancery. Meantime the interest, 600*l.*, is distributed amongst certain old painters, not members of the Academy, but whose necessities are such as compel them to ask charity, in annual grants of 50*l.* each ; so that, after all, his wish has in some measure been realised.'

'Jack Fuller,' as he was generally called—one of Turner's patrons and friends—was an eccentric, blunt old bachelor, who had considerable property in Sussex, as well as some West Indian estates. He lived at Rose Hill, in the neighbourhood of Battle, and represented the county of Sussex for many years. He was much beloved by his friends and tenantry in spite of his rough manners ; and as an Art amateur he became known as a purchaser to Turner.

It is of Jack Fuller, the boisterous English country gentleman of the Lord Egremont stamp, that one of the best stories connected with debates in the House of Commons is related. It is well known that an Irish reporter, under the influence of too much whisky and water, once had the audacity to call out from the gallery, 'A song from Mr. Speaker!' This is reckoned an outrage of the grossest character ; but Jack Fuller, it is said, was even more audacious. The story is that once upon a time —it was *after* dinner—he was guilty of some indecorum in the House of Commons, and the Speaker was obliged to administer a rebuke, beginning, 'It has been brought to my notice that an *honourable member*;' when Fuller burst out with, 'What's the use of beating about the bush? My name is honest Jack Fuller, and everybody knows it!' Thereupon he snapped his fingers at the majestic presence, called him a little man in a great wig, and eventually was committed to the custody of the sergeant-at-arms.

Turner knew Tom Moore, from whose 'Journals and Correspondence' (vol. vii. p. 77) I take the annexed interesting extract:—

'*March* 1.—Wretchedly wet day. Hard at work in Paternoster Row, as was also Tom at his Sunday exercise, I occasionally helping him. Dined at Rogers's, to meet Barnes; an entirely clandestine dinner, none of our Whig friends in the secret; and R. had been a good deal puzzled as to whom he should ask to meet him. Tried Lord Lyndhurst, with whom Barnes is intimate; and he would have come had he not been engaged. Could then think of none but Turner the painter; and he, Barnes, and myself formed the whole of the guests. . . . Had some talk with Turner in the evening. Mentioned to him my having sometimes thought of calling in the aid of the pencil to help me in commemorating, by some work or other, the neighbourhood in which I have now so long resided. The recollections connected with Bowood (where so many of the great ones of the time have passed in review before us— Byron, Madame de Staël, Mackintosh, &c.), the ancient and modern associations that give such a charm to Lacock Abbey, the beauty and music of Farley Castle, the residences of Bowles and Crabbe, the Druidical vestiges in so many directions,—all would afford subjects such as might easily be rendered interesting, while the natural beauties of this immediate neighbourhood, though hardly worthy, perhaps, of the pencil of a Turner, would supply scenes of calm loveliness to which his fancy could lend an additional charm. All this I now put down here rather as what was in my mind to say to him than as what I actually did say; for he interrupted me by exclaiming, "But Ireland, Mr. Moore, Ireland! There's the region connected with your name! Why not illustrate the whole life? I have often longed to go to that country, but am, I confess, afraid to venture myself there. Under the wing of Thomas Moore, however, I should be safe." . . .'

It was Wilkie who teased Turner about his titles, and nicknamed him R. A. P. P.; and who used to observe of his change of style that he was 'getting into a weak and vapid tone of painting.' Beaumont called it 'innovation;' and his clique of protégés sneered at the daylight manner as 'the white and yellow school;' so Turner and Wilkie quarrelled. When Wilkie, on a hanging-day, maliciously suspended a Rembrandt among the modern pictures, with the remark that it looked like 'a hole in the wall,' it must have been to deride the Turnerians.

From his dislike of Beaumont sprang Turner's jealousy of Wilkie. Sir John Beaumont, who was born in 1782, seven years after Turner, died in 1827, the year Turner exhibited his 'Now for the Painter!' He never understood Wilson; he patronised Wilkie; and he tried to sneer down Turner. He was a type of the unoriginal, conventional amateur, and did great injury to English Art.

'Mr. Rogers gave Turner a commission to illustrate his "Pleasures of Memory" and his "Italy." Turner was so satisfied with the elegant way the works were published that he would only receive five guineas a piece for the loan of the drawings. Campbell, the poet, desired Turner to make a set of drawings for an edition of his works, for which Campbell's circumstances did not allow him to pay, and he had the honesty to confess that it would be inconvenient for him to discharge the debt; on which Turner, with kind sympathy, told the poet to return the drawings, which he afterwards gave to a friend.'

Mr. Cyrus Redding, however, after mentioning Turner's complete exemption from nervousness, and the resolute way in which he laid on his touches, gives quite a different version of this story of Campbell, which certainly reflects more credit on the painter than on the poet:—

'Within two years of the decease of Campbell, the poet, I met him in Cavendish Square. "I am coming," he said, "from your quondam acquaintance, Turner. I have just played him a trick." "What do you mean?" "Why," observed Campbell, "I had gone to a great expense for Turner's drawings, to be engraved for my illustrated poems." (I forget the number he said, for each of which he had paid twenty-five guineas.) "I was also told not to mind the expense; the drawings would sell, being Turner's, for what I had paid for them, as soon as the engravings were finished. They could not be disposed of at anything like the price. It was said they were not in his best style; in short, I thought I should be compelled to keep them. One day I saw Turner, and told him what had occurred, and that I had hoped to make something of them. I added, in joke, that I believed I should put them up to auction. Turner said, feeling annoyed, I suppose, at my remark, 'Don't do that; let me have them.' I sent them to him accordingly," said the poet, "and he has just paid me for them." I think Campbell said twenty guineas each, but I am not sure of the sum, my recollection failing me about the precise amount. I could not help saying, "Turner does this because he is tender about his reputation; he will not have them in the market." Campbell had just before been censured for lending his name to books written by other people, which struck me when I made the remark. The poet, however, was too joyous about his bargain to apply the remark to himself. I have since thought whether Turner did not do this with a desire to befriend Campbell. He was just the character to do such an act silently and bluntly.'

One of Turner's oldest friends writes—

'The late Earl of Egremont was much attached to him, and well did he merit sincere attachment when he was known. He has and had many to disparage him. He was much used, and much abused, because he knew not how to make use of others, and so became the victim himself. Although unaccomplished in manners, he was as sound in heart and as good as any man I ever knew.'

Mr. Fawkes, of Farnley, deposes—

'When Turner was so much here in my father's lifetime, I was but a boy, and not of an age to appreciate or interest myself in the workings of his mind or pencil. My recollection of him in those days refers to the fun, frolic, and shooting we enjoyed together, and which, whatever may be said by others of his temper and disposition, have proved to me that he was, in his hours of distraction from his professional labours, as kindly-minded a man and as capable of enjoyment and fun of all kinds as any that I ever knew.

'Though often invited, Turner never came here after my father's death; and, as I have seldom gone to London, our meetings since I had learnt his value had been few and far between : but up to the last time that I saw him, about a year before his death, he was always the same to me that I had known him in my boyhood, always addressed me by my boy name, and seemed ever anxious to express in his kindness to me his attachment to my father, and still glowing recollections of his " auld lang syne " here.'

From Mrs. Wheeler, the daughter of Mr. Wells, the artist, I have received the following interesting record of their friendship :—

'I had a life-long acquaintance with the late Mr. Turner, my father being one of his earliest and most esteemed friends.

'It is over sixty years since a friendship began which ended only at the death of Mr. Turner, who, in very early life, was a constant and almost daily visitor at my father's house, whom he regarded as an able counsellor in difficulties. He usually spent three or four evenings in every week at our fire-side; and, though very much more than half a century has elapsed, I can still vividly recall to mind my dear father and Turner sketching or drawing by the light of an Argand lamp, whilst my mother was plying her needle, and I, then a young girl, used to read aloud some useful and entertaining work. These and many such recollections of my dear departed friend often present themselves to my mind, and are cherished as the dream of days long passed by. Indeed, there was more hidden good and worth in his character than the world could imagine. He had a tender, affectionate heart, such as few possess. Like all great men, his faults were largely published to the world, and greatly exaggerated, while, from his very reserved disposition, his many virtues were known only to a very few, though they clearly show forth the noble mind of the man who devoted the whole of a long life to one end and aim, and that the generous wish of providing an asylum in old age for the decayed members of his own profession. Unhappily, either through ignorance or carelessness, or something worse, this noble design has been frustrated ; but surely the man is to be honoured who, denying himself almost the comforts of life, could steadily devote the accumulated wealth of long years of toil to so noble a purpose ; and let it not be thought that Turner's heart was closed to the many appeals to his benevolence which came before him. I know he gave un-grudgingly, but he was no boaster of his good deeds. Another trait of character, which ought to be named, is the liberality with which he viewed the works of other artists. If he could not speak a word of praise, he carefully abstained from giving any opinion. I never heard him utter a syllable in dispraise of any artist.

' Though thoroughly modest and unpretending, yet he had a full appreciation of his own merits, and no one so much enjoyed his exquisite pictures as he did himself. It was a matter of real sorrow to him to part with any favourite picture, and on more than one occasion, when he has been looking graver than usual, and I have asked if anything vexed him, he has said, " No, only I have been sending some of *my children* away to-day."

' His art was his life's employment and his leisure's charm.

' His painting-room was emphatically his sanctuary, his harbour of refuge.

' In early life my father's house was his second home, a haven of rest from many domestic trials too sacred to touch upon. Turner loved my father with a son's affection ; and to me he was as an elder brother. Many are the times I have gone out sketching with him. I remember his scrambling up a tree to obtain a better view, and there he made a coloured sketch, I handing up his colours as he wanted them. Of course, at that time I was quite a young girl. He was a firm, affectionate friend to the end of his life ; his feelings were seldom seen on the surface, but they were deep and enduring. No one would have imagined, under that rather rough and cold exterior, how very strong were the affections which lay hidden beneath. I have more than once seen him weep bitterly, particularly at the death of my own dear father, which took him by surprise, for he was blind to the coming event, which he dreaded. He came immediately to my house in an agony of grief. Sobbing like a child, he said, " Oh, Clara, Clara ! these are iron tears. I have lost the best friend I ever had in my life." Oh ! what a different man would Turner have been if all the good and kindly feelings of his great mind had been called into action ; but they lay dormant, and were known to so very few. He was by nature suspicious, and no tender hand had wiped away early prejudices, the inevitable consequence of a defective education. Of all the light-hearted, merry creatures I ever knew, Turner was the most so ; and the laughter and fun that abounded when he was an inmate in our cottage was inconceivable, particularly with the juvenile members of the family. I remember one day coming in after a walk, and when the servant opened the door the uproar was so great that I asked the servant what was the matter. " Oh, only the young ladies [my young sisters], ma'am, playing with the young gentleman [Turner]." When I went into the sitting-room, where Turner was seated on the ground, with the children winding his ridiculously large cravat round his neck, he exclaimed, " See here, Clara, what these children are about ! "

' Turner, who was greatly interested in the science of geology, met Dr. M'Cullock, the celebrated geologist, at our house. The Doctor was delighted with his acute mind, and observed, " That man would have been great in any- and everything he chose to take up. He has such a clear, intelligent, piercing intellect." I have often heard Turner say that, if he could begin life again, he would rather be an architect than a painter.'

One of his oldest and dearest friends was Mr. Fawkes of

Farnley Hall, near Otley, in Yorkshire. With this kind and hospitable squire he became acquainted about 1802, in the course of an early topographical tour in the district, when he was visiting Richmond for Whitaker, or sketching for Lord Harewood, whose seat was in the vicinity of Farnley.

Some ten thousand pounds' worth of his water-colour drawings and oil pictures still adorn the walls of the house. In the drawing-room, shining yet like a sun, is the great picture of 'Dort,' while on the surrounding walls are the 'Red Cap,' 'Rembrandt's Daughter,' a most poetical figure-picture, and an oil painting representing the 'Victory,' with the body of Nelson on board, in three positions, as she was seen approaching Portsmouth.

Farnley Hall looks down on the Wharfe, the river that flows beneath the walls of Bolton Abbey, one of Turner's favourite scenes. Those rounded scaurs that he all his life delighted in, and to some semblance of which he even moulded the eternal Alps, stretch in a misty and sun-barred line opposite the peacock-guarded terraces of the fine old Carolan hall.

At Farnley he delighted to be ; there he shot and fished, and was as merry and playful as a child. An exquisite water-colour drawing by him still survives of a grouse that he himself shot and then immortalised. There is also a drawing by him of Mr. Fawkes's tent on the moors, some six miles off ; the servant is drawing corks, and the luncheon is being prepared. It was on one of these occasions that, on the return from shooting, nothing would satisfy Turner but driving tandem home over a rough way, partly through fields. I need hardly say that the vehicle was soon capsised, amid shouts of good-humoured laughter ; and thenceforward Turner was known at his host's by the nickname of 'Over-Turner.' A caricature of him by Mr. Fawkes still exists at Farnley, which is thought by old friends to be very like. It shows us a little Jewish-nosed man in an ill-cut brown tail-coat, striped waistcoat, and enormous frilled shirt, with feet and hands notably small, sketching on a small piece of paper held down almost level with his waist.

The Farnley portfolios abound with his sketches of the

house and estate, all rapidly but beautifully wrought. Some are rough, while others are *chefs-d'œuvre*, particularly a brook-side with wood-flowers, and a water scene. He drew the oak-panelled study and the white drawing-room, the Cromwell relics, and the staircase; the porches (one designed by himself), and the conservatory; the latter a beautiful fairy-like drawing of a greenhouse studded with grapes, hung with gay Chinese lanterns, crossed with errant sunbeams, and wonderfully elaborate in execution.

The Farnley collection also includes a matchless series of drawings, representing a complete Rhenish tour. They number, I think, fifty-three; and, though they were done at the prodigious rate of three a day, they are miracles of skill, genius, and industry. On his return from this particular tour Turner landed at Hull, and came straight to Farnley; where, even before taking off his great-coat, he produced the drawings, in a slovenly roll, from his breast pocket; and Mr. Fawkes bought the lot for some 500*l.*, doubtless to Turner's delight, for he could not bear that any series of his should be broken. Then saying that Mr. Fawkes should have no expense in mounting them, he stuck them rudely on cardboard with wafers, to the infinite detriment of the drawings, as it was found when they came to be remounted.

These Rhenish drawings are most exquisite for sad tenderness, purity, twilight poetry, truth, and perfection of harmony. They are to the eye what the finest verses of Tennyson are to the ear; and they do what so few things on earth do: they completely satisfy the mind. Few of them are gorgeous in colour; most are in a minor key, somewhat subdued and regretful, as if the present Rhine were not quite the Rhine of his earlier days. There is one, I remember, I christened 'The Primrose,' from the pale, tender yellow atmosphere that enwraps the whole scene. Perhaps one of the most matchless is the saddest of all—'Twilight in the Lorelei;' all grey and dim, but with just a speck of light here and there from boats on the river.

Turner was so sensitive that he could never make up his mind to visit Farnley after his old friend's death; but his successor once brought the Rhine drawings to London for the purpose of showing them to Turner. When they came to the grey Lorelei, tears sprang out of the old man's eyes ; and glancing his hand over the faint light in the sky and water, as if he were working, he groaned, ' But Hawkey ! but Hawkey !' as much as to say—

> When, ah ! woful *when*,
> How far unlike the now and then.

' One stormy day at Farnley,' says Mr. Fawkes, ' Turner called to me loudly from the doorway, " Hawkey ! Hawkey ! Come here ! come here ! Look at this thunder-storm. Isn't it grand ?—isn't it wonderful ?—isn't it sublime ? " All this time he was making notes of its form and colour on the back of a letter. I proposed some better drawing-block, but he said it did very well. He was absorbed—he was entranced. There was the storm rolling and sweeping and shafting out its light-ning over the Yorkshire hills. Presently the storm passed, and he finished.

' " There ! Hawkey," said he. " In two years you will see this again, and call it " Hannibal Crossing the Alps." '

At Farnley is a drawing of a man-of-war, complete, elaborate, and intricate, with a fine frothy, troubled sea in the foreground. This Turner did, under Mr. Fawkes's observation, in three hours ; tearing up the sea with his eagle-claw of a thumb-nail, and working like a madman ; yet the detail is full and delicate, betraying no sign of hurry. There is also a large fir in one of the Farnley drawings, so true, so vigorous, so matchless, that it shows not only that Turner could draw the fir when he chose, but that he might have been one of the finest painters of trees the world ever saw.

When Mr. Fawkes visited London, he would go and sit in the Queen Anne Street Gallery for hours, but he was never shown the painting-room. On one occasion he invited Turner to dinner at a London hotel, when he took, as was his wont latterly, a great deal too much wine. For once he became vain, and, staggering about, exclaimed, ' Hawkey, I am the real lion—I am the great lion of the day, Hawkey.'

In the course of one of his foreign tours, Mr. Fawkes, in his travelling carriage circling round the Simplon past those blessed hospices and through those wonderful rock-galleries, suddenly met a well-known little thickset man walking, with no luggage except a large faded umbrella. It was Turner.

The Farnley collection of Turners, specially valuable (apart from their intrinsic worth) as consisting of ungraved pictures, has for its sun the luminous 'Dort,' a favourite picture of the painter's. It includes some almost monochrome but powerful water-colour Swiss scenes of 1804. One of a jagged glacier with shattered pine and goats is especially fine. There are sketches also of the Colosseum and St. Peter's, somewhat wanting in solidity; a fine fancy sketch of the Pyramids, and a poetical but rather flimsy one of Stonehenge.

A very beautiful cold, bright, frosty morning scene, 'Flounder-Fishing off Battersea,' is remarkable for two large and very humorous figures of old boatmen, excellent for character. The name of the boat is 'The Owner's Delight ;' one little triangular white flounder glitters in the net, and the frost lies white on the rueful old man's beard.

For poetry of time and place, and graceful appropriateness, the 'Ulverstone Sands' delights me ; the water on the sands is so transparent—the distance is so truly admirable. The accident to the diligence on Mont Cenis is equally wonderful for local effect, especially for the dazzle and glimmer of snow. The 'Scarborough' is radiant with golden colour; the Swiss scenes are full of graceful figures. The sea in the 'Red Cap' (an oil picture) is perfect for motion and sweep.

The 'Rembrandt's Daughter' is a beautiful day-dream, and there is a comely, plump prettiness and poetry about the Dutch girl as she stands by her bedside, blanched in the sunshine, and reading the love-letter, which her majestic father, coming in behind, is about to detect.

For twenty-four consecutive years one of those wonders of the North, a goose pie, was sent to Turner from Yorkshire. The twenty-fifth pie was already packed when news reached Farnley of the painter's departure from the reach of his friend's kindness. One of the letters acknowledging the annual present

I am enabled to give, through the kindness of Mr. Fawkes. It is dated December 24, 1849, two years before his death. It is curious, as an intelligent friend of mine remarks, to observe the quaint and somewhat contradictory ceremoniousness of the letter, which, beginning with 'Dear Hawkesworth,' ends with 'your obliged servant;' a conventional deference that is almost royal. The letter, on which the postmark is 'Queen's Road, Chelsea,' runs thus :—

'Dear Hawkesworth,—Mother Goose came to a rehearsal before Christmas Day, having arrived on Saturday for the knife, and could not be resisted in my drinking your good health in a glass of wine to all friends at Farnley Hall, also wishing happiness and the *comp^ts of the season to all.* The pie is in most excellent taste, and shall drink the same *thanks* on Christmas Day. Many thanks for the brace of pheasants and hares—by the same train—indeed, I think it fortunate, for with all the strife and strike of pokers and stokers for the railroads—their commons every day growing worse—in shareholders and directors squabbling about the winding up of the last Bill, to come to some end for those lines known or supposed to be in difficulty.

'Ruskin has been in Switzerland with his whife this summer, and now said to be in Venice. Since the revolution shows not any damage to the works of high Art it contains, in Rome not so much as might have been expected. Had the "Transfiguration" occupied its old situation, the St. Pietro Montoreo, it most possibly must have suffered, for the church is completely riddled with shot and balls. The convent on Mount Aventine much battered with cannon balls, and Casino Magdalene, near the Porto Angelino, nearly destroyed ; occurred by taking and storming the Bastion No. 8.

'This is from an eye-witness who has returned to London since the siege by Gen. Oudinot.

'I am sorry to say my health is much on the wain. I cannot bear the same fatigue, or have the same bearing against it, I formerly had—but time and tide stop not—but I must stop writing for to-day, and so I again beg to thank you for the Christmas present.

> ' Believe me most truly
> ' Your oblidged Servant,
> ' J. M. W. TURNER.

W. H. FAWKES, Esq., Farnley Hall.'

The letter is curious also as showing that an involved and confused style, and uncertain spelling, were characteristic of him down to the very close of his days.

Amongst the wonderful examples at Farnley of the versatility of Turner's genius, I must not forget to particularise the Civil War illustrations—elaborate vignettes, full of thought and poetry ; and the drawings of birds, wonderful for minute truth and gorgeously delicate in colour. There is a heron's head ludicrously forcible, a peacock that is all green velvet and amethyst, a game-cock that is a perfect constellation of warm colour, and doves all opaline and mother-of-pearl, with varying green, glances of rose and glimmers of purple.

Another old friend of Turner's, Mr. Rose of Jersey, furnishes me with the following reminiscences of Turner *en famille* ; memories undimmed by the flight of twenty-six years :—

' I fancy I can see him trudging down the avenue something after the manner of Paul Pry, by which I mean that an umbrella invariably accompanied him. Rain or sunshine, storm or calm, there was that old faded article tucked under his arm. Now, the umbrella answered a double purpose, for by some contrivance the stick could be separated from the other parts ; this then formed a fishing-rod, being hollow, with several joints running one into the other. I have seen him sitting patiently for hours by the side of a piece of water belonging to the property, his piscatory propensities keeping up his excitement, though perhaps without even a single nibble ; yet it must not be understood that he was always unlucky, for when fortune favoured him in securing any of the finny tribe, it was not long before we were made acquainted with his success, at which he appeared as much pleased as a boy from school.

'Cowley Hall is about fifteen miles from London. This distance he generally walked, coming in heated and tired, carrying a small carpet-bag, which was kept like a sealed book, never allowing the key to go out of his possession. The ladies tried various means to induce him to give up its possession, ostensibly to arrange his articles of clothing which they presumed it contained, though it must be confessed that female curiosity was the predominating cause; but he clung as tenaciously to his key as a miser to his gold. On one occasion, on his returning from fishing, he came in wet and tired—a sudden shower of rain having fallen when his umbrella had been metamorphosed into a fishing-rod. The servant was sent to the bedroom for his slippers; only one was to be found. Here was an opportunity not to be missed. The ladies ordered the servant to bring down the carpet-bag, hoping doubtless to obtain a glimpse of its contents; but a sly look from our friend, with a peculiar shrug of his shoulders, and the two monosyllables "No, no," effectually put to flight their hopes. As a *dernier ressort*, one then offered to take his key and bring down the slipper. To that he replied, "I never give it up;" and they never learnt its contents. "The man with the carpet-bag" was not then known, or doubtless he would have obtained that *sobriquet*. The name, however, by which he was known at our house was certainly not very euphonious. How it was obtained I can scarcely surmise, unless it was from his manner and his figure, which was short and thick; but it was a common expression on seeing him approach the entrance to cry, "Here comes Old Pogey."

'Mrs. R—— one day had a pet spaniel lying in her lap, while Turner sat close by her, reading. A sudden impulse induced her to ask him to make a drawing of her favourite. The R.A. opened his eyes with astonishment, at the same time replying, "My dear madam, you do not know what you ask." The lady ever after went by the name of "My dear Madam," given her by her friends who were present at the time.

'On one occasion, after the ladies had retired, Turner and myself were left alone. On the table stood a large jug of water and a bottle of cognac. Turner never having been very communicative, I could hardly anticipate what was going to take place (and here I must express my regret at not noting down what would have been highly interesting) ; but he gave me a slight sketch of his travels, adverted to during the course of the evening, but of which, from the lapse of time, I have but a very faint recollection. He took me up and down the Pyrenees, describing various scenes. I recollect asking him if he had seen the Falls of Gavarnie, to which he replied in the negative. He then branched off to various places ; one was the Fall of Foyers, in Scotland. This is brought to my mind by the umbrella, for I recollect his stating he had one blown out of his hand by a sudden gust of wind, and whirled down some great depth. During the evening I mentioned my intention of spending a few months in Jersey the ensuing summer. He remarked that, should I cross over to St. Malo, I was to be sure to proceed by the Rance to Dinan, as that river afforded many picturesque scenes, and the views were the most pleasant in that neighbourhood. During the course of the evening his tumbler had never been emptied ; first a dash of brandy, then an addition of water, and thus he continued, never entirely exhausting its contents, until it struck two in the morning, when, quietly remarking it was getting rather late, we separated each to our domiciles.

'On one occasion I had the audacity to ask him if he painted his clouds from Nature. One has heard of "calling up a look." The words had hardly passed my lips when I saw my *gaucherie.* I was afraid I had roused a thunder-storm ; however, my lucky star predominated, for, after having eyed me for a few moments with a slight frown, he growled out, " How would you have me paint them ? " Then seizing upon his fishing-rod, and turning upon his heel, he marched indignantly out of the house to the water's edge.

' Two ladies, Mrs. R—— and Mrs. H——, once paid him a visit in Harley Street, an extremely rare (in fact, if not the only) occasion of such an occurrence, for it must be known he was not fond of parties prying, as he fancied, into the secrets of his *ménage.* On sending in their names, after having ascertained he was at home, they were politely requested to walk in, and were shown into a large sitting-room without a fire. This was in the depth of winter ; and lying about in various places were several cats without tails. In a short time our talented friend made his appearance, asking the ladies if they felt cold. The youngest replied in the negative ; her companion, more curious, wished she had stated otherwise, as she hoped they might have been shown into his sanctum or studio. After a little conversation he offered them wine and biscuits, which they partook of for the novelty, such an event being almost unprecedented at his house. One of the ladies bestowing some notice upon the cats, he was induced to remark that he had seven, and that they came from the Isle of Man.

'On the first occasion of Turner visiting at Cowley Hall, on the morning after he had left, one of the servants came to Mrs. R—— with several shillings in her hand, stating she had found the silver under the pillow where Mr. Turner had slept, and asking her mistress what she should do with it. She was told it was doubtless intended for herself, but on his next visit she would soon learn if it had been left in mistake. Such, however, did not appear to be the case, for under the pillow was always a little mine of the *argentum vivum*, or silver that will slip through the fingers.'

Here I may suitably introduce several extracts from the letters of a lady in Jersey referring to Turner :—

'*Sept.* 23, 1831.—Mr. Turner is returned from Scotland, where the weather has been very boisterous, and his health not improved by the excursion. He is building in the neighbourhood of Rickmansworth, and I believe he will be there before we leave.

'*Jan.* 10, 1840.—The Maws are at Hastings. They invited Turner down, but he did not go to pass the Christmas. He always inquires after you, and desires his kind regards.

'*April* 18, 1840.—I have not seen Mr. Turner lately. He has been fully occupied preparing for the opening of the Academy.

'*Jan.* 7, 1842.—J. M. W. T. is very well. He was very much shocked at the demise of his old friend Sir F. Chantrey ; but grief will not long hang upon his mind ; and so much the better, as it answers but little purpose.

'*April* 14, 1842.—I think I wrote you Turner had been very ill. He is now better, but it has shook him a good deal. He is living by rule.

'*Oct.* 6, 1843, *Brighton.*—J. W. T. did not go with us or join us this year, but I hear he is safely landed on this side the water again.'

CHAPTER XXI.

TURNER'S PREDECESSORS AND EARLY CONTEMPORARIES.

To Mr. Trimmer I am indebted for the following communication, which embraces some valuable reminiscences of Turner's early and later contemporaries :—

'Thomas Gainsborough was a native of Sudbury, in Suffolk, where his father was a tailor. As a child he went to the local free school, where he distinguished himself by making ink drawings on the desks instead of writing his copies.

'Joshua Kirby, my father's grandfather, was one of his earliest friends ; and, as is well known, Gainsborough's last request was to be laid beside his old friend in Kew churchyard. He was an architect, who was acquainted with the artists of the day ; and, on their forming themselves into a Society of British Artists, he was elected as president, and it was by his instrumentality that the Royal Academy was formed, under the auspices of George III., whom he had the honour of instructing in drawing and perspective. Kirby, who was a Suffolk man, first became acquainted with Gainsborough at Ipswich, whither he had removed from Sudbury, as a place better adapted for his profession ; and it was by his urgent persuasion that the latter left his native county and went up to London.

'Gainsborough was notoriously liberal in giving away his productions, and Kirby came in for the lion's share. Besides painting his portrait twice, and that of his wife, he gave him his first drawing (now in my possession), and his first sketch in oils, sold at my father's sale, after the manner of Waterloo, whom in his early days he much studied ; and whose etching, Gainsborough's gift, I have in my possession. He also gave him above a hundred drawings in pencil and chalk, most of which I still have ; and six or seven small landscapes in oil, among which was his original or first picture of the Gipsies ; so that my family possessed the best collection of his early or Suffolk productions I have ever seen. There is a full-length portrait of himself reclining on a bank, looking at a sketch on a stretching-board on which he is engaged. It was sold at my father's sale as an unknown figure (the catalogue having been got up in a hurry), but it fortunately was lithographed by Lane, his nephew. Gainsborough was very personable in his youth, and in this sketch he presents a remarkably fine figure. A sketch of himself and his wife on a small piece of paper before they were married is among my treasures. She was very pretty. They are both strong likenesses, as I was told by a sister of my father's who knew them.

' I have also a crayon painting (a head) of Gainsborough by himself, apparently at the age of twenty. He has on a dingy yellow coat, black neck-handkerchief, and small collar ; with dark-brown hair, brown eyes, and full under-lip, as in a portrait I once saw of his daughter. The features are delicately chiselled, and his complexion delicate ; the forehead by no means highly developed ; but in the two others, which are profile, his Roman nose shows a face full of intelligence. There are, I believe, no other portraits of Gainsborough in his best days ; the one he is known by is that of a faded middle-aged man.

' There is a celebrated engraving, by Wood, of Gainsborough's Gipsies ; the etching, which is by Gainsborough, I have. It is first-rate : I merely mention this because he has been said to have failed in his etchings, which is not untrue as regards a few late aquatints. He had a commission from a gentleman near Ipswich to paint a group of gipsies. When about two-thirds of it were finished—for Gainsborough in his early works, owing to his great execution, finished as he went on—he came to see it, and was not pleased with it ; he said he did not like it. "Then," said Gainsborough, "you shall not have it ;" and, taking up his pen-knife, he drew it directly across it. In this state Joshua Kirby begged it ; my father had it mended, and it was sold at his death.   It was a terrific gash, and Gainsborough must have been in a flaming passion when he did it.   After this he painted for the same person the picture from which the engraving is taken ; but I never could hear of this picture in Suffolk, though I have had good opportunities for inquiry.

'I have heard my father's sister, who knew him when she was young, say that he was an odd, droll man, excessively fond of music, and that he played on the violoncello.   In fact, there is no doubt of his understanding music, from the masterly way in which his figures hold their instruments, as Turner's figures do the fishing-rod.

'Gainsborough painted an oil picture of Joshua Kirby, on seeing which long afterwards at his daughter's (Mrs. Trimmer), he exclaimed, "Ah, there is old Kirby in one of his brown studies."   Hanging near this was a painting by Kirby, almost the only one he ever did, on which Gainsborough remarked, " He would have made a good painter if he had gone on with it."

'As I have said, he gave Joshua Kirby eight landscapes in oil, most admirable specimens.   Thirty years ago Emerson, the picture dealer, offered my father fifty guineas a piece for them, and pronounced them unique.   These Turner, as I have said elsewhere, examined so carefully one evening that the next morning he said he had hurt his eyes ; and Constable used to say it made him cry to look at them, and that no one at the present day [twenty years ago] could approach him.   These were sold at my father's sale for a mere song, though inferior pictures made large sums.

'As my mother came close from Sudbury, in my youth I knew Gainsborough's sketching grounds well.   Thirty years ago, before the oaks were cut down and the thatched cottages done away with, every step one took reminded one of him, not the least the slim-formed though rustic figures ; and my relative Captain Syce, who was one of his admirers, has told me that the village churches around are those introduced in Gainsborough's early pictures.

'I have dwelt on his early works, because picture dealers,

through his figure subjects being more saleable, always decry them, and say he never painted a picture fit to be seen till he left Suffolk—men who, place them in the green fields, cannot tell one tree from another. It is true his early works are less artificial and less academical, but they are far truer to Nature, to elevated Nature. His early pictures exhibit a remarkable variety of form in his trees ; his oaks are inimitable ; latterly, all his trees assumed one form ; for he mistook system for Nature.

'Joshua Kirby's son was brought up a painter and died at Rome. He was some time with Gainsborough, but did not, I have been told, like him as an instructor. He often had disputes with his brother artists ; but artists are proverbially quarrelsome.

'When I was a boy, I remember Miss Gainsborough, his daughter, who had a house at Acton. He had another daughter, who was deranged ; an additional proof that genius often passes into mental aberration. Mrs. Lane, the mother of Lane the engraver, was (I think) another daughter. Both the young ladies were remarkably handsome, and, when young, were constantly introduced by him into his pictures. There is a fine cattle piece, painted for Mr. Child of Osterly House, now at Middleton, Lord Jersey's place ; in which one of them is so introduced. At Acton, opposite Miss Gainsborough, lived a Mr. Briggs, a young amateur artist, to whom she was very partial, insomuch that she left to him all her father's pictures and sketches. Among these was a charming portrait of herself, which, as I have said, so far as I recollect, strongly resembles my crayon of her father about the lips. She was accustomed to sit in her father's painting-room. His colours were very liquid, she said, so that if he did not hold the palette right they would run over.

'There were several admirable landscapes and studies from Nature among Mr. Briggs's collection ; a very clever study of sheep, equal to one by a professed animal painter ; but the masterpiece was some cows, which was lithographed by Lane, and called by him "Repose ;" a warm, glowing picture. Still one would hardly have expected a countryman to have made cows recline while feeding of an evening, unless he looked upon it as an artistic license. This (like Turner's "Carthage") was one of Gainsborough's favourite pictures ; and, not to be tempted to part with it, he had it hung in a dark passage, where it remained for many years. It underwent sundry glazings, and was a long time in hand. If I remember aright, Mr. Briggs told me it had a wash of tobacco water. It was subsequently cleaned by Cobbett, when it came out blue ; Cobbett told me the yellow coating was merely the varnish turned, but after this it lost value in Mr. Briggs's eyes, and he sold it. I remember this from the circumstance of my father having recommended Cobbett to Mr. Briggs.

'Many years ago there resided at Heston a Mr. Nesbitt, a person of substance, who in his younger days was a companion of George, Prince of Wales, who once possessed Gainsborough's "Blue Boy." He acquired it thus :—" Nesbitt," exclaimed the Prince at one of his entertainments, " that picture shall be yours." At first he was disposed to treat the matter as a joke, but when he saw that it was in earnest, Nesbitt, being an old beau of the very first water, made all due acknowledgments for his Royal Highness's generosity. Next morning the "Blue Boy" arrived at his residence, followed in due time by a bill of 300*l*., which he had the satisfaction of paying. I heard him many years ago tell the story at my father's table.

'*Gainsborough's Palette.*—This I had from Mr. Briggs, but have lost it ; still, as I have copied several Gainsboroughs, I think I can furnish you with it. Yellow : yellow ochre, Naples yellow, yellow lake, and for his high lights (but very seldom) some brighter yellow, probably some preparation of orpiment, raw sienna. Reds : vermilion, light red venetian, and the lakes. Browns : burnt sienna, Cologne earth (this he used very freely, and brown pink the same). He used a great deal of terra verte, which he mixed with his blues, generally with ultramarine. His skies are ultramarine. In his early pictures I could never trace other colours. Latterly he used Cremona white ; this he purchased of Scott in the Strand, who on retiring from business gave me what remained. It was the purest white I ever used, and accounts for the purity of his carnations. His early pictures are painted on oil-non-absorbent grounds of a yellow tint, and in the greys of the sky he availed himself of the yellow of the ground. His later pictures are on absorbent grounds of a dark chocolate colour. In the leafing of his trees he employed gold size ; also sugar of lead, as I have detected by a magnifier, both late and early. In his early pictures he used wax. The application of the iron, though not hotter than usual, to a picture my father had lined, destroyed all the foliage. Turner tried wax ; but, if it facilitates working, it turns yellow, and is highly objectionable.

'From what I have said of Gainsborough you will perceive that I rank him with the non-terrestrials. "O deus certe !" I place the English school thus :—Gainsborough, Wilson, Turner, Reynolds,[1] and then ten abreast at random.

'To Gainsborough I assign the first position because of his great originality. No one can copy him with success, and his genuine pictures pronounce themselves unmistakably. It is a mark of the genius of Turner, Wilson, and Reynolds that they have left their impress on the art subsequently. They have not only had herds of imitators, but painters have not been able to paint from Nature without introducing their feelings into their works ; yet, although it may seem paradoxical, it is perhaps even a greater mark of Gainsborough's powers that so little of him is seen in other paintings. This has arisen from his fine execution and exquisite delicacy of sentiment. As in rifle-shooting the first sight is the most correct, so Gainsborough's first outline admitted of no improvement, and this is probably the reason that his drawings are considered even superior to his paintings. How rare the talent to select from Nature her choicest forms, and embody them with all the certainty of instinct !

'In the estimation of Gainsborough's powers, the striking exactitude of his likenesses is not to be overlooked. There are

[1] ' I exclude Hogarth by reason of the nature of his subjects ; his end is the comic, not the beautiful. In his department he stands alone, and foreign schools have nothing to compete with him. I know of no English painter who has so completely the command of his colours, and the texture of his pictures is unrivalled.'

portraits of his three generations back, family features of which are still seen in their descendants. It is painful to see the clumsiness and incorrectness of outline in Reynolds, and the tameness of Lawrence, when placed by the side of a Gainsborough. Whether he painted childhood, youth, adolescence, or age, male or female, a nobleman or a ploughboy, a rustic girl or a courtly dame, humanity became elevated under his plastic fingers. Gainsborough has also restricted himself to home subjects, which is another of his excellences. I believe it to be no less impossible to paint foreign subjects than it is to speak a foreign language well without having been familiarised to it from childhood. How do Dutch painters handle Italian subjects, or French caricaturists English ones—John Bull, for instance? They are themselves pleased, while to English eyes it is merely a burly Frenchman. I never heard of an Italian recognising Turner's Italian subjects, or a German his German ones; and his crossing the Channel is, in my opinion, the date of his decline; and, although it has been objected to Gainsborough that he never had the advantage of going abroad, it is, I believe, this very circumstance which makes him our great English painter.

'The texture of his pictures has been objected to. There is said to be a washiness and want of solidity in them not desirable to imitate. This may be true as regards imitation; but, with Gainsborough's masterly execution, the thinness and docility of his vehicle is no small part of its merit. Had he painted in a fat, unyielding material, the delicacy and playfulness of his pencil would have been lost, though it must be owned that unsuccessful attempts to obtain a good vehicle mark his period. He is also charged with mannerism; but this is only true of his later productions, where for the wild beauty and untrammelled variety of Nature, as seen in his early works, he seems to have fallen into Hogarth's line of beauty and other fallacies of the day. In some of his later portraits he has followed Vandyke, where he would have done better to have relied upon himself.

'As I have said, Turner did not believe that colour was reducible to system; and Gainsborough, when painting his

" Blue Boy," seems to have been of the same opinion. I think it was the remark of Mr. Field, when we were looking at that celebrated picture, that Gainsborough's eye was truer than his head, since against his theory he had introduced a sufficiency of warm colours into the flesh tints to balance the predominating cold of the picture ; and this reminds me of a dictum of Gainsborough I had forgotten. Joshua Kirby was strong in perspective, of which Gainsborough made very light, and used to say in his joking way that the eye was the only perspective master needed by a landscape painter.

'No one is perfect ; yet, whatever his defects, I place Gainsborough at the head of our English painters ; and he must be an able hand who gets beyond him.

'Among the relics bequeathed by his daughter to Mr. Briggs, besides a model of an old horse, was the bust of Mrs. Sheridan, the charming Miss Linley. It is considered a masterpiece equal to his paintings, as showing his versatility of talent. Of this my father had a cast from Mr. Briggs, but I think it is before the public—quite small. Some of the Gainsborough Du Ponts, of Sudbury, have some pictures of his.'

Of Sir Thomas Lawrence Mr. Trimmer writes—

'Lawrence had the reputation among his friends of being " the finished gentleman," which in the George IV. period consisted in certain conventionalities one could scarcely practise now without being remarkable. This was outréed in successful professionals, as Halford, Astley Cooper, &c. ; in fact, it was thought to chalk out the line between the base and the noble, and its absence precluded all access to the higher castes. We are apt to confound it with sycophancy, but in Lawrence it was considered among his enviable qualities ; and that pliant manner was perhaps in some degree natural to him.

'Up to the day of his death Lawrence enjoyed unbounded popularity ; but, the moment he dropped, his works sank and he seemed to be forgotten. If he was overrated during his life, he has certainly been underprized since. As President he was much esteemed by his brother artists, and was as much flattered by them as by the public. It was greatly to his credit that he painted not for gain, but for reputation. He parted with his money faster than he could make it. He was devoted to the advancement of the Fine Arts, and laid out large sums in collecting Rembrandt's etchings, for many of which he gave, or perhaps undertook to give, greatly more than their value. I have heard that he was much in debt to a printseller in St. Martin's Lane, whose portrait he painted in consequence, and a most striking likeness it was. I doubt if Lawrence had painted a head so far removed from royalty for many a year.

'He was very liberal in showing his etchings, and my father once passed a whole day in looking them over with some artists. This was before we had a National Collection. Neither was there any difficulty in seeing his rooms, which were well worth the inspection. There were pictures in all stages of progress and of all dates, canvas behind canvas ; some merely the first sitting, merely the first coat on the features, laid in with the greatest care and delicacy, the rest in chalk or oil outline. I have been told by Howard (a good authority) that he always made a crayon drawing of the sitter, from which he did his oil ; but, if this had been the case, the drawings would now be in existence. At first there is no doubt he was a crayon painter ; and hypercritics, even as they have pronounced Turner's oils large water-colours, have called Lawrence's oils large crayons, the old chalky manner still adhering. At Etwall Hall, Staffordshire, are two of his early crayons in small. They are well-finished, but he had not at that time mastered the ear.

'In his painting-room was head after head painted years before, lovely angelical faces which had long cruelly left their owners. A lady's portrait done some twenty years before, was pointed out to me—a charming, faultless face, which most decidedly at that later time could have given no inspirations for a second sitting. So fleeting are our complexions, though happily we are not aware of it! As is customary, all these first sittings were half paid for ; and it was said Sir Thomas would gladly give one a first sitting, and then came the hitch. But this, I believe, was not correct. There was a rush of pretty faces, and of others as well, and poor Sir Thomas was fairly beset. It was impossible he could meet so many claimants.

'There is a celebrated print of young Lambton (I think)

sitting on a rock, engraved by Lane, which at the time made a great sensation. His father presented himself at Sir Thomas's with the request that he would paint his son. Lawrence flatly refused ; it was out of the question. " If you saw my child I think you would relent," was the paternal suggestion ; and such was the child's beauty that, when he saw him, the painter yielded. Lawrence was so pressed that, unless for high rank or great beauty or celebrity, he would execute no commissions. I doubt if ever any painter in this country, unless it were Vandyke, had such a run as Lawrence. His full-lengths, first of Lady Agar Ellis (late Lady Dover), and that of her sister, Lady Gower (Duchess of Sutherland), carried his popularity to the height. People who cared nothing about painting flocked to the exhibition to see his pretty women, and Lawrence was on everybody's lips ; while his praises were sung by all the charming daughters of the aristocracy, which in those days made up humanity, strictly so called, not to mention the homage of his brother artists. If under these circumstances he found his head whirl, whose was the fault, his or theirs ? Certainly he was vain, as we should have been ; and one of his vain fancies was to paint his own portrait as near like that of Canning as the original would admit of. He was said to be like Canning. Napoleon, Wellington, Canning, Lawrence, and others not worth naming were all said to be born at the same batch—the year I have forgotten.

' Henry Howard, Secretary to the Royal Academy, was an unbounded admirer of his, and belonged, I was told, to what was called the Lawrence party in the Academy ; and Frank Howard, his son, was one of his pupils. " I shall teach you till you beat me," was the remark addressed by the teacher to the pupil. Howard once showed some of my landscape sketches to Lawrence, who very kindly promised to assist me with his advice, if I followed the profession.

' They used to say that he made ten guineas a day. He worked slowly, everything neat and exact, with the absence of all dash. He finished feature by feature, and would work a whole day on an eye. He had a great many pupils, who made duplicates of his pictures. I once saw a duplicate, a head of the Duke of York, done by Frank Howard ; and, after his father had worked over it, it looked very like Lawrence ; Howard, however, told me that Lawrence would go completely over it, which would make a great alteration in it for the better.

' He was choice in his pigments, and had his madders from Field,[1] which he used freely. A preparation, I think of mercury, called orange vermilion, was first prepared by Field at the desire of Sir Thomas, who was in want of a flesh tint ; and with it he was much pleased. I owe this item of information to Field himself.

' At one time he considered white out of harmony with other colours, and used cream instead. After his death there was an exhibition of his pictures in Pall Mall, some of which bore traces of this error. There was also a large picture of Satan at one end, the largest and perhaps the worst picture he ever painted.

' I exclude Lawrence from the great portrait painters— Titian, Rubens, Vandyke, and the like. Perhaps in genius he was inferior to his contemporary Jackson. He had no difficulty in carrying out his conceptions, but then they were not first-rate. A tameness and want of spirit pervades his works. Still Lawrence is but a face painter. There is an absence of vulgarity and coarseness, and his likenesses are photographically exact. But for Reynolds and Gainsborough we might feel nationally proud of him. In private life he fell a victim to the extravagance of the times, and sank under pecuniary embarrassment.

' A couple of anecdotes of Lawrence and George IV. are, I think, worth preserving.

' The first has reference to the time when a gold chain was placed by the sovereign on Lawrence's neck—I conclude at the inauguration to the Presidency. Quoth the monarch, " I give this chain to you and yours," &c. (I forget the exact terms.) " Sire," said Lawrence, " does your Majesty mean my family or my successors ? " " Your successors," answered the King. The

---

[1] Field resided at Little Lyon House, Isleworth, and supported himself by his pen. He also devoted his talents to pigments, and his madders were then unrivalled. He was well known by the leading artists.

King turned red ; and, when it came to the unrobing, he broke
out as follows : " Damn the fellow ! what does he mean ? Damn
his family ! What do I care for his family ? " I think it was
before this that he had given offence. Among the drawings
contained in the portfolio taken for royal inspection was one
of the young Duc de Reichstadt, who is said to have been
poisoned ; which Lawrence had taken from life, I think in Germany. " Lawrence," said the King, " I must have this." Lawrence
bowed low in acquiescence. " If your Majesty will permit me,
as it is not quite finished, I will return with it in the morning."
The fact was that Lawrence had no inclination to part with it ;
so he forthwith set about making a copy, which he took to the
King the next day. " It is not the same," was the angry exclamation upon seeing it ; and, thrusting his nails into it after the
manner of a cat, he drew them deeply across the face. Thenceforth Lawrence was in disgrace.

'These two anecdotes I had from Lane, nephew to Gainsborough ; the last being derived by him from Lawrence himself, who showed him the scratches.'

Of Flaxman Mr. Trimmer writes—

'Flaxman was acquainted with my father's family, and my
father, as a boy, always received great kindness from him on
the score of his attachment to Art. Flaxman wished him to be
a sculptor, and offered to teach him modelling, but taught him
drawing instead. A number of anatomical studies in red chalk,
taken from life, and the finest I have seen, he lent my father. I
rather think they have been published of late years.

'Flaxman had two sisters, who, like himself, were most
ordinary figures, not to say deformed. How often does a
beautiful mind take its lodgment in such an abode ! What
other Englishman, or rather what modern, possessed so fine a
feeling of the antique ? His illustrations of the Greek tragedians
display a variety of design which is wanting even among the
Greeks. These were drawn by him of an evening with a crow-
quill in Indian ink ; generally one of an evening, his sisters
sitting as models. One of his sisters, who told my mother this,
threw out her long, distorted arms in the way she had sat for
these rare conceptions of modernised Greek. It seemed quite

laughable to my mother that anything so misshapen could supply a hint for such charming creations. But no doubt there are " sermons in stones."

' My father always spoke of Flaxman as an estimable person. From his brother artists I have heard that he was partial and an oppositionist.'

Of Zoffany we learn—

' He lived at Chiswick, and, as my father lived at Kew, they were friends—that is, my father as a boy was often at Zoffany's. But all I remember to have heard from my father, who was constantly in his painting-room, was that he had a good method of laying on his colours. He used his brush as if he were shading with a pencil, thus showing the drawing in his pictures ; but this probably was the German method. Like Fuseli and West, he is hardly to be claimed as an English celebrity.'

Of Henry Howard Mr. Trimmer writes—

' Henry Howard, R.A., 5 Newman Street, Secretary to the R.A., was of the same age as Turner. His father was, I think, an heraldic painter ; which accounts for his great neatness. He gained the prize at the R.A. for drawing, and was told, on being presented with it by the President, Sir Joshua Reynolds, that it was the best design that had received the award of the Academy. This eulogium, I have no doubt, was just. His early sketch-books and academical studies shew a perfect command of the human figure, and great promise.

' Howard was sent by the Academy to study at Rome, where he remained several years. Here he made great progress, and his outlines from the antique are admirable. He also made copies in oil from the old masters, besides oil sketches from Nature in the environs of Rome, full of taste and talent. On his return from Rome, he copied some pictures at Chiswick House, where my father made his acquaintance, which continued through life. He married a daughter of old Reinagle's, a most amiable person. They had a large family, and lived happy and united. He died at an advanced age from paralysis, occasioned, it was supposed, by the absorption of white lead into his system while painting a cartoon for the House of Lords.

'Howard was an ardent admirer of the antique, and believed that all excellency came from Greek statuary. He was very well read in heathen mythology, and his early pictures on his return from Italy have a fine classical feeling. His genius lay in floating female figures and fairy scenes. He also painted subjects from early Greek and Roman history.

'It appears to me that to paint classical subjects one should have that race of humanity for models. And certainly this view is borne out by Howard, whose classical feeling declined from the time of his leaving Rome, and partook more and more of the Saxon or home type amid which he lived.

'His first sketches for his pictures, which he made small in oils, are always his best, and are (in my judgment) the finest mythological subjects I have seen by an English hand, not excepting Etty. I do not suppose that, had he carried out his style to his utmost wish, his pictures would have been saleable, incompatible as they were with public taste. To earn a livelihood he fell back on portraiture; in which he was not so happy. His heads are always in good drawing, in which respect he stood next Lawrence; and his method of painting was safe and durable, he being averse to all experiments; but still his portraits are not atttractive, and his colouring is dull, and too brown.

'Not holding the first position, he laboured under the great disadvantage of having ordinary models; of which I have heard him complain bitterly. He had to paint vulgar people with disgusting features, before which the genius of a Gainsborough must have quailed. But, when he obtained a pretty sitter, his pictures were admired. He often exhibited pictures of two of his daughters in fancy costume, that always sold. When a child, I remember being painted by him myself, running barefoot between two country girls in a shower of rain. This was purchased by some nobleman. But his heart was in "fairy-land;" and some of his scenes, especially his early ones, if not first-rate, at least possess great merit.

'His pictures stand well. They were painted in macgilp (he made it himself by pouring oil on litharge), and look brighter now than the pictures which eclipsed them in Somerset

House. He was a better draughtsman than a colourist, and, like Constable, was fond of altering. He never knew when to stop, and made bad figures wooden and spiritless by working on them too long. When one is unpopular, one gets out of heart and loses confidence in oneself.

'It is pleasing to think how many painters of that time, careless of gain, devoted their talents to their profession, and strove to improve public taste. Howard was one of these. He was a most amiable person, bore an unblemished character, and served the office of Secretary to the Royal Academy with much credit and ability. One wishes he had been more successful.'

Of John Constable, R.A., Mr. Trimmer writes—

'It is said you may tell a man by his paintings as you may one by his handwriting. I knew Constable's paintings long before I knew Constable himself, and formed a very wrong estimate of his character. His paintings give one the idea of a positive, conceited person, whereas anyone more diffident of his own powers could not be. Once, not long before his death, when I was with him on Heston steeple, he scratched on the leads those well-known lines of John Milton where he describes Fame as the last infirmity of noble minds, and introduces the Fury with her abhorred shears. Constable could not have described his own character better.

'From his first start in life he was always making some great preparation to render himself worthy of notice ; a point from which in his own eyes he seemed always receding. He seemed to think his works would never live ; and very few of his brother artists either. He certainly underrated himself. Landscape painters are never popular, and, had he carried his own style to the extent of his desire, it may be questioned whether his admirers would have been increased.

'It was one of the dicta of that time that, in proportion as you individualised, you lost in general effect. Constable's great aim was breadth, tone, and moral sentiment ; meaning by the latter that a good picture is calculated to produce a humanising effect ; and to these ideas probably he sacrificed detail and correct drawing.

' It was his persuasion that you should always work in one material : if a water-colour painter, that you should take Nature in water colour ; if an oil painter, in oil. Not that he rigidly carried out his own views, as he always had a small sketch-book with him in which he noted down anything that struck him ; but his sketching, both in water colour and pencil, was very inferior to his oils.

' When a young man in Essex, he did a number of oil sketches, which have much of the fine feeling of Gainsborough, of whom he was an enthusiastic admirer, and at that time an imitator. Later he aimed exclusively at originality. There were a great number of oil sketches sold at his sale, done on the principle that there is no outline in Nature. They are full of truth and genius, and possess more variety than his pictures. That such productions did not find admirers was not the fault of the artist ; but they required to be seen not simply by the eye, but by the mind.

' His great aim, as I have said, was originality, and to take something fresh from Nature ; holding the opinion that young artists greatly impaired their original powers by copying from prints instead of Nature. It is not easy—perhaps it is impossible—to divest oneself of surrounding influences ; and all painting, like all writing, seems stamped with the impression of its own times. It is not to be denied that Constable was an original painter, but he would take objects, as vistas of trees, in ordinary points of view, which proved less unlike others than he was apt to imagine.

Spring and Midsummer he regarded as the stirring times for the landscape painter, and not Autumn. In his opinion an old tree, half decayed and almost leafless, presented no fitter subject to the painter than an old emaciated man. The idea of taking Nature in its full blood is strongly urged by Laresse ; yet surely Nature has a charm under every point of view. If fine old oak scenery is not the picturesque, it seems hopeless to seek it. Still Constable was the first, I believe, in this country who ceased to paint grass yellow ochre, although it appears to me that we are now in the other extreme ; for by the non-employment of yellow, green pictures show a want of sunlight, and allowance is not made for the yellow of the frame, especially at the edge of the picture ; yet Constable is entitled to great praise for having brought the art back to a truer standard. Green is the colour for trees, and the Midsummer shoot gives the green in its greatest variety.

'It has been well said of photography that it strikes Nature dead. Constable's great aim was to give freshness and motion. I have seen him lying at the foot of a tree watching the motion of the leaves, and pointing out its beauty. He would also stand gazing at the bottom of a ditch, and declare he could see the finest subjects for painting.

'By the French he has always been considered our best landscape painter ; and he was much admired by Louis Philippe, who purchased one of his best pictures—a waggon and three horses passing a brook—of which Constable used to relate that the old attendant at Somerset House pronounced, "That's a good picture, sir ; so natural, all the frost on the trees ;" whereas the picture represented Midsummer. People always mistook his dog-days for Christmas. Fuseli used to say, "Where is my great coat ? I am going to see Mr. Constable's pictures." This anecdote is also told of Turner. As I have heard Constable say, " Do away with this crispness, and all the merit of my painting is destroyed."

'His great object was to obtain the glitter and sparkle of Nature after a shower ; and for this purpose, passing by the oak and elm, our two first trees, he took the white poplar and the ash—the one for the leaf, the other for the bark. This I had from himself, and it is a key to his pictures. A French *paysagiste* once came from Paris to request him to show him his method of painting. Constable said he should have been most happy to meet his wishes, but that unfortunately he had no method, and got his pictures up he did not know how. This I had from Mr. Field, who was present. Yet certainly a method he had, and very unlike that of other people, which inclined to dead colour in white and black, or vermilion and Prussian blue. He used the spatula freely, and the vehicle he employed enabled him to plaster. This was copal varnish and linseed oil diluted in turpentine. His sketches were of equal size with his pictures, and some of these sketches are more spirited than his pictures from them. His fault was working too much, and, like many another not appreciated by the public, mistaking alteration for improvement.

'He had his colours from Field, who was celebrated for his madders, which he used freely, as well as ultramarine. The madder and blue form a purple, and his clouds are purple instead of grey ; but time may improve them in this respect. In his early pictures, where I consider he is true to Nature as regards colour, he employed vermilion and light red.

'When at work, he was life and soul in his subject ; and the last time I saw him he told me he once put on his great coat, and sallied forth in a snow-storm to Hampstead Heath, to sketch an ash for some picture he was about.

'He was acquainted with Archdeacon Fisher, and painted for him Salisbury Cathedral and several views in that neighbourhood. I have stood on the exact spot from which he took the cathedral, which is very like, though not sufficiently confined for his style of painting. "Old Sarùm," too, is among his most interesting productions.

'I knew David Lucas, the engraver, well. He was almost exclusively engraver to Constable ; at least, Constable was out of temper if he took a plate from elsewhere. While Constable lived this was well enough, but at his death Lucas had to make fresh connexions. Always soaring to the unattainable, Constable was never satisfied with the plates ; and after having once kept Lucas at alterations on a large plate (I think "Salisbury Cathedral"), his final exclamation was, "Lucas, I only wish you could bring it to the state it was nine months ago."

'Of the plates by Lucas, two small ones are the best ; and of these one of the most successful is "Clearing up of a Storm." Though admirable for chiaroscuro, in which he excelled, they are all on too dark a scale ; but this was much against the better judgment of the engraver. He did one etching, of which I have an impression, but in his work there is a want of lightness of touch, and it is simply a curiosity. It must be conceded that these plates, though somewhat dull, are most original, and must always stand high in the estimation of the lovers of English landscape.　Constable lost a large sum by them.　I doubt if he ever supported himself by his profession ; but he painted simply for fame, and not for remuneration.　He has left some half-finished lectures on landscape painting, but they contain little new matter, and do not exceed mediocrity.

'Constable was born at East Bergholt, Essex, and, like Rembrandt, was the son of a miller, but in easy circumstances. He was highly respectable, and a most agreeable person ; by far the most agreeable artist I ever knew ; endowed with a great flow of words, and well informed.　He was devotedly attached to his wife, who married him, I have heard, against her father's approval.　Her death by consumption threw a gloom over his after life from which he never rallied.　His own death was sudden.　In height he was above the average ; with dark hair and eyes, a Roman nose, and a pleasing expression. The likeness of him taken after death by his friend Mr. Leslie is not unlike, but there is an expression of death about it which makes it unpleasing.　As I write (June 10, 1861) John Constable stands next to Gainsborough as a painter of English landscape.　Whoever passes him will paint well indeed.'

Of Sir Joshua Reynolds we are informed—

'Years ago I knew a Devonshire lady who knew Sir Joshua. She did not endorse my suggestion that he must have been a very interesting person.　His deafness, she said, made him unfit for society ; and she seemed to describe him as a bore.'

CHAPTER XXII.

TURNER AND THE ROYAL ACADEMY.

TURNER was devoted to the Academy, with all its faults.　It had been quick to see his genius, and to confer on him honours. He had been a student thereat, and was now an Academician ; and he felt for it, therefore, the affection a child feels for its mother, for his great heart was most susceptible of gratitude. There is a singular story in confirmation of this view of his character,　The day poor wrong-headed Haydon ended his untoward life Maclise called upon Turner to tell him of the horrible catastrophe. The narrator's imagination was roused to the uttermost by the suddenness and ghastliness of the event; but to his astonishment his hearer scarcely stopped painting, merely growling out between his teeth, ' He stabbed his mother; he stabbed his mother.'

' Good heavens!' said Maclise, so excited that he was prepared for any new terror. ' You don't mean to say, Turner, that Haydon ever committed a crime so horrible ? '

Making no other reply, Turner repeated in a deep, slow voice, ' He stabbed his mother; he stabbed his mother.' Nothing but this could his startled friend wring from him; and, as he left the house, ' He stabbed his mother; he stabbed his mother' still pursued Maclise down the passage. It was not till he reached home, and before spreading the story sat down quietly to think over what Turner could mean by such a horrid charge, that he came to the true conclusion that it merely was a figurative allusion to the ingratitude of Haydon's attacks on the Academy that had educated him.

In Academic matters Turner was essentially conservative. It is not for me to impugn the motives of his steady fidelity to the Royal Academy. Naturally one of the most generous and grateful of men, he could not forget the fact that from that body he had obtained early recognition of his genius. Moreover, he had enjoyed the dignity of an Academician for nearly half a century; and from his brethren he had received neither check nor injury. His relations to them therefore were of the pleasantest class. In Art, however, he owed nothing to them— but his imperfect drawing of the figure.

Let us review the origin of the Academy.

In 1711 Sir Godfrey Kneller instituted a private academy; and in 1724 Sir James Thornhill built one at the back of his own house in Covent Garden, giving tickets to all who applied for them. The artists disliking, however, this sense of obligation, turned an old meeting-house into a School of Art, but it lasted only a few years. In 1734, on Sir James's death, Hogarth bought the apparatus of the abandoned academy, and founded a school of thirty or forty persons, first in Arundel Street, then in Peter's Court, St. Martin's Lane. A committee of sixteen members, chosen annually, collected the subscriptions and managed the affairs. The 'Turk's Head,' Gerrard Street, Soho, became then a rendezvous for artists and a nucleus for future union.

As early as 1753 an attempt was made by the St. Martin's Lane Society to found an Academy, but the scheme failed. In 1755 the plan was renewed.

The Dilettanti Society were then negotiated with; but the members, being refused all share in the government of the new Academy, withdrew their aid, and so the affair again dropped to the ground.

In 1759 the artists, at a meeting at the 'Turk's Head,' agreed to institute an Annual Exhibition, the funds obtained by which were to be devoted to the relief of aged and infirm brethren; and accordingly in 1760 the first exhibition was held at a room in the Strand, opposite Beaufort Buildings, belonging to the Society of Arts. To this exhibition sixty-nine artists contributed a hundred and fifty works.

Some disagreement ensuing in 1761 between the members, some of them exhibited at an auction room in Spring Gardens, and others in the room of the Society of Arts. The Spring Gardens faction called themselves the 'Society of Artists of Great Britain;' Hogarth aiding them, exhibiting with them, and illustrating two of their catalogues.

In 1767 Mr. Dalton, a librarian to the King, obtained the King's name for the Spring Gardens Society, took premises in Pall Mall in the name of the Royal Academy, and removed all the figures from St. Martin's Lane.

In 1765 the Strand Society, now enrolled as the 'Free Society of Artists,' exhibited in a large room in Maiden Lane; and, in 1767, at the bottom of the Haymarket. This association lingered till 1779, exhibiting first at Cumberland House, Pall Mall, and subsequently in St. Alban's Street; while the rival Society languished at the Lyceum, and finally died out in 1791.

The quarrels of the artists continuing, in November 1768

eight directors sent in their resignation, and co-operated with sixteen others who had been ejected. These eight were—

J. Wilton	W. Chambers
E. Penny	G. M. Moser
R. Wilson	P. Sandby
B. West	F. M. Newton

The King promising his support, which had been intrigued for by West, a meeting was called, laws were drawn up, and on December 10, 1768, the Royal Academy of London was founded: Reynolds being President; Chambers, Treasurer; Newton, Secretary; Moser, Keeper; Penny, Professor of Painting; and Dr. William Hunter, Professor of Anatomy. The incorporated society instantly started a studio over the famous 'Cider Cellar' in Maiden Lane. Woollett, the engraver, was their secretary till 1773; when he was succeeded by John Hamilton, landscape painter; and in 1774 by Isaac Taylor.

The British Institution for Promoting the Fine Arts was established in 1805, the year in which the Society of Painters in Water Colours started in 20 Lower Brook Street, Bond Street. The Associated Artists in Water Colours originated in 1808.

In Buckingham Palace is a picture, painted for George III. by Zoffany, which contains portraits of all the early Academicians. It was engraved in mezzotinto by Earlom in 1773. In the centre is Reynolds, with his speaking-trumpet, talking to J. M. Newton, the Secretary; and between them is Sir William Chambers, listening; while at the back of Newton are John Richards, William Tyler, and Thomas Sandby, the last of whom is talking to Paul Sandby. Behind him are Dominic Serres, Jeremiah Meyer, and Tan-Chet-Gua, a Chinese artist; and in front of these are Wilton the sculptor, and George Barret. In the left corner are Benjamin West, John Gwynn, and J. B. Cipriani. In the front is Zoffany; to the right, leaning on a drawing-board, is Mason Chamberlin and, next him, Francis Hayman, Hogarth's friend, looking at the model. On the right from Reynolds are Dr. W. M. Hunter, Bartolozzi, and Carlini; and above them is Wilson. In front are Charles Cotton, the carriage painter ; Richard Geo. Samuel Wale, the sign painter Edward Penny, the drawing-master ; and Peter Toms, Reynolds's drapery painter. Moser is placing the model. Zuccarelli, Hone, Cosway, William Hoare, and Nollekens also are of the company. On the wall are the portraits of Angelica Kauffman and Mrs. Moser.

A picture by Ramberg represents the Royal Academy Exhibition of 1789. In the centre is George III., attended by Reynolds and West, and beside him is some bishop or archbishop ; on the left-hand wall is Opie's ' Death of Rizzio,' and facing it Northcote's ' Death of Wat Tyler ;' both of which now are in the Council Room of the Guildhall. Beneath the Opie is Reynolds's picture of the ' Heads of Angels,' now in the National Gallery. In the middle wall, high up, is Black's portrait of Tattersall, the horse dealer ; and beneath is Lady St. Asaph, by Reynolds. In the centre is West's ' Shipwreck of St. Paul ;' afterwards painted on a larger scale for the altar piece of the chapel at Greenwich Hospital.

In Brandoin's picture of the Exhibition of 1771 the chief centre picture is Barry's ' Adam and Eve ;' and Dr. Johnson and the King are again introduced.

Turner objected to leaving Somerset House, and hoped to see the day when the Royal Academy would be rich enough to construct a building for itself. This feeling made him careful in the extreme as to the expenditure of the establishment, save in the cause of benevolence, to which he never shut his ear or his heart. He was long one of the auditors of the accounts ; and in the discharge of that office he was as zealous as he was useful. His anxiety to honour and reward meritorious officers was evinced when Sir Robert Smirke first tendered his resignation of the post of treasurer. Turner rose in the general meeting, and would not sit down until he had persuaded the members not only not to accept the tender, but to beg the worthy treasurer to continue in office ; which proposal was gratefully acceded to by Sir R. Smirke, who retained the office for many years after.

Turner liked much to be in temporary office as visitor to the Royal Academy. He enjoyed the authority, as he did the companionship ; yet it was always difficult to get him to receive the usual pecuniary remuneration.   He took it, it is true ; but he took it with a protest, for money had not in this instance been his object.

Turner's speeches, according to Leslie, were 'confused and tedious,' while Mr. G. Jones describes him as irresolute in business details.   There is no doubt that his speeches at the Academy councils were extremely difficult to follow, for he spoke in a deep and, latterly, in an indistinct voice.   You saw the great man's mouth move, and imperfectly heard certain sounds proceed therefrom ; but out of these you seldom caught more than 'Mr. President' and 'namely,' the two verbal forms to which the speaker had recourse when he had hopelessly entangled himself in the subtleties of his own rhetoric.   To add to the darkness of all this mumbling confusion, Mr. E. Ward tells me, the bells of St. Martin's used to break in, merrily and mischievously, with their

ONE TWO—THREE FOUR —— FIVE SIX—SEVEN EIGHT
ONE THREE   TWO FOUR
FIVE SEVEN   SIX EIGHT ;

and then came a lull, through which you heard again 'Mr. President' and 'namely.'

Of Turner's Academic speeches, opaque as they were, little indeed can be said.   Most impartial people thought that, though undeveloped and obscure, they nearly always tended to the right thing.   His opinions on Art were listened to with respect, but his judgment on business matters secured little attention. Sometimes it was really difficult to know what he did mean ; but the haze, as in his pictures, generally enveloped some great or beautiful reflection, grotesque and painful as was the delivery. His thoughts invariably were deep beyond the range of his vocabulary ; the faculty of expression was entirely absent in this dumb poet.   Chantrey used to say that both Turner and Wilkie had great thoughts, if only they could express them.

When he lectured on Perspective, Turner often was at a loss for words to express the ideas he laboured to communicate. To aid his memory, he occasionally would commit passages to writing ; but even these, upon consultation, he could not readily read. Sometimes he would not make his appearance at all, and the disappointed students were sent away with the excuse either that he was ill, or that he had come from home without his lecture. But when the spirit did stir within him, and he could secure utterance to his thoughts, he soared as high above the common order of lecturers as he did in the regions of Art. His language was often elegant, while his ideas were original and most attractive ; and it is to be regretted that copies of his graphic diagrams, as sketched on the lecture boards, were not preserved with his notes.

This painful lack of expression rendered him almost useless as a Professor of Perspective, in spite of the great trouble he took to prepare the most learned diagrams. His sketch-books contain many drawings evidently made in preparation for these lectures ; but he honestly confessed that he knew more than he could communicate. On one memorable occasion the hour had come for his lecture. Soon the Professor appeared, and the buzz of the students subsided. The Professor mounted his desk, and every eye was fixed on him and his black-board. The Professor, however, betrays signs of confusion and perturbation. He dives now into one pocket and now into another—no ! He proceeds to open his discourse ; but what he says is, 'Gentlemen, I've been and left my lecture in the hackney coach.' I have no doubt he would rather have painted five epical pictures than have had to deliver one lecture on Perspective.

On this subject of Turner's lectures Mr. Ruskin writes : 'The zealous care with which Turner endeavoured to do his duty is proved by a large existing series of drawings, exquisitely tinted, and often completely coloured, all by his own hand, of the most difficult perspective subjects—illustrating not only directions of line, but effects of light—with a care and completion which would put the work of any ordinary teacher to utter shame. In teaching generally—he would neither waste time nor spare it—he would look over a student's drawing at the Academy, point to a defective part, make a scratch on the paper at the side, say nothing. If the student saw what was wanted, and did it, Turner was delighted ; but if the student could not follow, Turner left him.'

Turner himself used Hamilton's Perspective. He was fond of puzzling over problems in this science ; and one special difficulty with some domes he never surmounted ; but he used to say to a friend in his dogged way, ' I think somehow I could do that yet.' He was lecturer for nearly thirty years (up to 1837) ; but he lectured only during two or three ; which caused, says Mr. A. Watts, some dissatisfaction.

' Turner,' says one of his Academic friends in reference to the council meetings, ' was ever anxious to allay anger and bitter controversy. Often I have heard him, in subdued tones, try to persuade the excited to moderation ; he would do this by going behind the speaker, and by a touch or word soothe an acrimonious tone by his gentleness. He was unable to speak, but would by his attempt to express himself delay a question until it received more serious and calm consideration.'

When George III. sold Somerset House to the Government, it was on the condition that his pet chicken—the infant Royal Academy, which he had hatched under his own wings—should not be disturbed ; no cast was to be removed, no picture taken away. Years went on ; in due rotation the schools opened ; and the annual exhibitions flung wide their doors. By-and-by the exhibitors increased, says an old Academician, who furnishes me with particulars of Turner's Academic habits. Space was required for displaying the works of Art, and the steep ascent to the upper rooms was found to be an inconvenience. At length the Government saw the difficulty in which the Academy was placed, and, wishing to appropriate the rooms at Somerset House to public offices, suggested the building of a National Gallery ; and offered the Royal Academy accommodation in the same building. This was a most rational project, for the schools assuredly should be where the best examples for study and imitation are to be found. The proposal therefore was readily entertained by the majority of the Academicians ; but there were those who dreaded the interference of the Government or of the House of Commons if the Academy were established in a building erected at the cost of the public. Long before this period Turner and several other members had dwelt upon the prospect of an Academic home that should be the property of the institution, and, to realise it, had endeavoured to amass a sum adequate for the purpose. New members, however, brought with them fresh opinions, and dependence was finally preferred to independence.

Like Chantrey, for whom he had a great affection, Turner was exemplary in the discharge of his duties as councillor, visitor, or auditor. Always zealous and watchful, he was present at all the general meetings; and, to enable him to do this, he postponed his excursions abroad until the business of the Academy was suspended by the vacation. At the social meetings of the members, unfrequent as they were, he never failed to appear. Both the great dinner before the opening of the exhibition, and the exhibitors' dinner at its close, he invariably attended. The latter he deemed a most important opportunity of becoming acquainted with artists likely to associate themselves with the institution as members. This dinner unfortunately has been displaced by a *soirée*, which is unproductive of the advantages proposed to be secured by the gathering around the social board.

During the forty-nine years of his membership—we have the authority of Mr. A. Watts for the statement—Turner failed to exhibit at the Academy only four times ; namely, in 1815, 1821, 1824, and 1851.

CHAPTER XXIII.

TURNER'S CHARACTER.

WHEN Bird, the son of a Wolverhampton clothier, first (about 1811) sent a picture to the Royal Academy—it might have been 'Good News,' or 'Choristers Rehearsing,' or some other of those early anticipations of Wilkie and Webster—Turner was one of the ' Hanging Committee,' as it was opprobriously called. Everyone pronounced the picture of the new man to have great merit, but no suitable place for it was left unoccupied. The guest was desirable, but the inn was full. The R.A.'s looked stolidly content, like people inside an omnibus on a wet day when the conductor enquires at the window if any gentleman would like to go outside and make room for a lady. The R.A.'s joked and talked, undisturbed by the event, for the days of chivalry are no more ; but Turner was otherwise affected. He growled out his displeasure, and protested that, come what may, the young man's picture ' must have a place.' Thereupon arose the cry of ' Impossible,' and members proceeded to discuss other topics. But Turner adhered to his point. He was not to be lightly overcome. He had genuine, honest stuff in him, with not a little of the resolute indomitability of the bull-dog.

While his brethren indulged in gossip he subjected the picture to a severe scrutiny ; the result of which was that it won his approbation completely. In generous recognition of its merits he shouted aloud, ' We must find a good place for this young man's picture.' ' Impossible—impossible,' was the official deliverance, this time made with unusual emphasis. Turner said no more, but quietly removed one of his own pictures and hung up Bird's in its place.

The memory of this event recurred to me when last I went to South Kensington. Standing before his swarthy crimson picture the ' Fiery Furnace,' the heat of which is so blinding, and the black luridness of which is so intense, I could not help thinking of his noble unselfishness, one April, in proposing to remove this, which was hung in a good place, in order to accommodate a little picture by his friend Mr. G. Jones, also in the same collection, to which was assigned a far inferior position. The removal was interdicted by authority; but the generous spirit of self-sacrifice which dictated the offer is none the less admirable. It bespeaks the fundamental kindliness of his character. The fact is that, while he studiously refrained from depreciation of his contemporaries, Turner never lost an opportunity of doing a kindness. Unlike Dr. Johnson's noble patron, he endeavoured to rescue the drowning man ; he did not await his safe arrival ashore, in order then to encumber him with help. Turner had the brave self-confidence that genius always has ; he never flattered, and he never liked to be flattered. But he was often generous with hints and friendly counsel even to the young and unknown. Of his kindness in this respect my friend Mr. Hart, R.A., favours me with an excellent example. Mr. Hart, as a

young man, had sent to the Academy a clever representation of
' Galileo in the Dungeon of the Inquisition.' It was a thoughtful
picture, telling a fine moral of the ingratitude and blindness of
his generation to that great benefactor of mankind. Turner,
whose heart was too large for the nursing of envy, evidently
was pleased with it ; and he expressed his gratification in a
marked manner. After looking at the picture for a moment,
he swept in with a twirl or two of the brush some concentric
spheres upon the prison wall. The operation was a brief one ;
yet those simple circles were worth twenty guineas to the young
aspirant.

Fond of money as he was, and of the pleasant freedom from
worldly cares derived from its possession, Turner never expressed envy of the wealth of other artists, or sought to
supersede them in obtaining commissions. When he met
them in the public lists, he met them smiling and with open
face.

When his picture of ' Cologne ' was exhibited in the year
1826, it was hung between two portraits, by Sir Thomas
Lawrence, of Lady Wallscourt and Lady Robert Manners. The
sky of Turner's picture being exceedingly bright, it had a
most injurious effect on the colour of the two portraits, and
Lawrence naturally felt mortified, and openly complained of the
position. Artists at that time, it should be added, were permitted to retouch their pictures on the walls of the Academy.
At a private view on the morning of the opening of the Exhibition, a friend of Turner's who had seen the ' Cologne ' in all
its splendour led a group of expectant critics up to it. He
started back from it in consternation. The golden sky had
changed to a dun colour. He ran up to the artist, who was in
another part of the room. ' Turner, Turner, what have you
been doing to your picture?' ' Oh!' muttered Turner, in a
low voice ; ' poor Lawrence was so unhappy ! It's only lampblack. It'll all wash off after the Exhibition !' He had actually
passed a wash of lampblack in water-colour over the sky, and
utterly spoiled his picture for the time ; and so he let it remain
through the Exhibition, to gratify Lawrence.

For many years, while the Exhibition was held at Somerset

House, Turner was daily indebted to groups of admiring artists, who generously occupied themselves in teaching the public to feel the poetry of his original style. An instance of his own unselfish recognition of the merits of others occurs to me here. On being told that Calcott had painted one of his finest scenes on the Thames on commission for two hundred pounds, he observed, in the presence of several patrons of the Fine Arts, 'Had I been deputed to set a value upon that picture, I should have awarded a thousand guineas.'[1]

I cannot permit myself to alter one word of the narrative communicated to me by Mr. Hammersley, the well-known painter. Its style is so unaffected ; it is so full of generous humility, poetry, and feeling, and does so much credit to the writer's heart that no paraphrase is permissible.

Mr. Hammersley writes—

'Many years ago—I should certainly hesitate saying how long, did not the following letter from Turner to my father betray the date—I was supposed to have obtained all the instruction that local artists could give me. My father, with more affection for me—more warmth of hope for me—than perception of the audacity of his proceedings, wrote to ask Turner to give me further instruction ! I knew nothing of this at the time, nothing for years ; indeed, absolutely nothing until I lost a parent whose every thought, word, act, and feeling evidenced perpetual self-sacrifice for my advantage. However little I may have attained towards the ideal he had pictured for me, this much I have obtained—an undying reverence for his truth and love.

'The following is Turner's answer, which I copy verbatim :—

'"47 Queen Ann Street, West, London :
"Dec. 4, 1848.

'"Dear Sir,—I have truly, I must say, written three times, and I now hesitate ; for did I know your son's works, or, as you say, *gifted merit*, yet even then I would rather advise you to think well, and not be carried away by the admiration which

[1] *Wine and Walnuts*, p. 295 (1823).

any friendly hopes (which ardent friends to early talent) may assume : they know not the difficulties or the necessities of the culture of the *Fine Arts*, generally speaking. In regard to yourself, it is you alone can judge how far you are inclined to support him during perhaps a long period of expense ; and particularly if you look towards tuition, the more so ; for it cannot insure success (however much it may facilitate practice), and therefore it behoves you to weigh well the means in your power before you embark in a profession which requires more care, assiduity, and perseverance than any person can guarantee.

' " I have the honour to be,

' " Your humble Servant,

' " J. M. W. TURNER."

' *Directed*—

 ' " John Hammersley, Esq.,

   " Liverpool Road,

     "Stoke-upon-Trent,

      " Staffordshire Potteries."

' I leave you to comment upon the latter portion of this letter, which appears to me to contain a world of thought and appreciation of the hugeness of the work Turner had always before him, and of his sense of the responsibility of the artist ; contrasting this with the flippancy and self-satisfaction with which outsiders, and *some painters*, look upon the practice of Art.

'Later in life, and while holding a Government situation in relation to Art, I became acquainted, quite accidentally, with Leitch Ritchie, the author of the text to Turner's " Rivers of France." From this acquaintance several incidents arose relating to Turner, which I will detail to you. It is due to myself, still more to the memory of Turner, to say at once that I am not writing from memory, with a huge interval of time between the circumstance and its narration here. *At the time* I entered the following particulars in my journal, and you may rely upon the precise accuracy of the language. Many hard things have been said of Turner's want of feeling, of his moroseness, of his parsimony, and of his want of sympathy with others pursuing Art through all its doubts and difficulties.

What I am about to relate may illustrate some of these points of character ; and that one of parsimony is somewhat met by the fact that he was in no hurry to accept whatever my father would have given him for lessons to me, and this would have been whatever Turner might have chosen to ask within any reasonable limits. Turner, in this matter of instruction, was right, as he was right in most other things. He knew well enough that all technical and practical matters could be taught by fifty men as well as, or better, than he could have taught them ; and no less certain was he that those things which evidenced thought, personal feeling, and the giving out of soul, were altogether incommunicable ; and he would not lend himself to a huge imposture for lucre. He decided to advise honestly rather than gain meanly.

'I had lived something like a year in London, during which period I had heard much of Turner's gallery in Queen Anne Street. I had heard this from persons who, from their literary or artistic position, had some right of *entrée* within its sacred precincts. I had never for a moment thought it likely that I should gain admission, and had no thought whatever of seeking the privilege, when one evening Leitch Ritchie voluntarily said that he would ask Turner if he would permit me to see his pictures, adding the further proposal that he would ask Turner to meet me. With my feelings then, and, I am happy to say, with my present feelings, this suggestion was received by me with a reverential awe, yet delight, which I will make no attempt to describe. Those who read and think—those who have feeling duly urging—of God's ways of manifesting Himself, will feel with me that it was like suggesting meeting Homer, Dante, or Shakespeare.

'In a few weeks after Ritchie made the proposal I received a short note from Turner, to the following effect :—

' " Dear Sir,—Mr. L. Ritchie intimates to me that you desire to see my pictures. The weather is fine, and if you will call here either on Thursday or Friday this week, not earlier than eleven o'clock, I shall be glad to see you.

' " Your obedient Servant,
' " J. M. W. TURNER."

'Thursday was not very fine, but I found it quite impossible to wait until Friday. I wrote a note to Turner, in due acknowledgment of his communication, and precisely at eleven o'clock I found myself at his door. I left the door, walked across the street, looked at the house, gained breath, for I had nearly run all the way from Somerset House, and, foolish as it *will* appear, I could have worshipped the dirty windows that let in light enough to one whose soul saw at all times the whole brilliancy of Nature. After a short time I became steady enough and calm enough to walk to the door again. I rang, and tardily enough the well-known old housekeeper opened the door to me, and I was placed in what I suppose was Turner's dining-room. I waited there for a short time, all eyes, all ears, when I heard a shambling, slippered footstep down a flight of stairs—slow, measured, yet as of one who was regardless of style or promptitude—what the world calls shambling, in fact. When the door opened, I, nobody, stood face to face with, to my thinking, the greatest man living. I shall attempt no description; you know how he looked. I saw at once his height, his breadth, his loose dress, his ragged hair, his indifferent quiet —all, indeed, that went to make his *physique* and some of his mind; but, above all, I saw, felt (and still feel) his penetrating grey eye !

'Remaining only a moment longer in the cold and cheerless room, at his request I followed him into his gallery, which you, doubtless, remember well. The room was even less tidy than the one we had left—indeed, was an Art chaos, all confusion, mouldiness, and wretched litter—most of the pictures, indeed all those resting against the wall, being covered with uncleanly sheets or cloths of a like size and character. Turner removed these protections to his pictures, and disclosed to my wondering and reverent observation many of those works which are now known so generally ; among them, and the most prominent, being the " Opening of the Walhalla." I make no remark about any of the pictures which I found in the gallery. Far abler hands than mine have given to the world a whole body of the noblest criticism, based upon the great painter's labours ; it merely rests with me to detail any traits of character presented to my observation. Turner and I walked many times from end to end of the apartment, he occasionally giving brief descriptions of the pictures, and asking after my proceedings at the institution with which I was connected. Generally I may say that he was taciturn, though still sufficiently chatty to remove all idea of inattention or discourtesy. After we had been so occupied for, say, five minutes, he turned somewhat quickly towards me and said, " Mr. Hammersley, this gallery is cold ; pray keep your hat on." I moved in acknowledgment of his solicitude, but did not obey him ; I kept it off quite involuntarily, I am sure, and, I trust, as a perfectly natural action. In a few minutes he turned to me again, reiterating his request, when, quite honestly and naturally also, I told him that I "could not think of being covered in his presence." He looked at me very steadily for a few seconds, and then said, " Mr. Hammersley, I shall feel much more comfortable myself if you will comply with my wishes in this respect." I put on my hat at once, seeing that he believed in my sincerity, and feeling how undoubtedly he was speaking his real wishes. This is but a small matter ; but it seems pregnant to me of a kindly and most considerate mind, and, as so much evidence that way, is worth preservation.

'On the 26th of November, 1844, I paid my second visit to the Turner Gallery. I shall not readily forget this visit, though it began and ended in something less than ten minutes. I entered the dingy dining-room as before, and was immediately joined by Turner, who, as before, led me up to his gallery. Our proceedings then resembled our proceedings on the former visit, distinguished from it, however, by the exceeding taciturnity, yet restlessness, of my great companion, who waved about and occasionally clutched a letter which he held in his hand. I feared to break the dead silence, varied only by the slippered scrape of Turner's feet as we paced from end to end the dim and dusty apartment. At last he stood abruptly, and turning to me, said, " Mr. Hammersley, you *must* excuse me. I cannot stay another moment ; the letter I hold in my hand has just been given to me, and it announces the death of my friend

Calcott." He said no more. I saw his fine grey eyes fill as he vanished; and I left at once.'

To me there is something very beautiful and touching in this interview between the young artist and the veteran ; and it is easy to see how impressed the great disappointed genius was with the simple-hearted respect and veneration of his visitor. Let us note also that the letter of advice to the father on his son's choice of a profession is at once wise and sad. How thoughtfully he speaks of the anxieties he had himself felt, and how modestly of 'the care, assiduity, and perseverance' requisite for success !

When his friends were in ill health Turner was all consideration. He was as anxious as a mother or a wife, and as careful as a nurse. In this respect they used to compare him to his patron Lord Egremont. To be ill was to secure a visit from the owner of Petworth. Such was the strength of local associations in the case of some of his friends that Turner could not be prevailed on to enter their houses after their death. As I have already explained, he never went to Farnley after the death of its proprietor.

'I well remember,' says Mr. Jones, 'the morning after Chantrey's death, that he came to the house of our deceased friend. He asked for me, and I went to him, when he wrung my hands, tears streaming from his eyes, and he rushed from the house without uttering a word. Turner's executors discovered that the rents for houses in Harley Street had not been paid during some years. On application to the lawyer, the answer was that "Mr. Turner would not allow him to distrain."'

On occasion of a visit to Petworth, Mr. G. Jones, Turner's great friend and crony, hurt his leg. Nothing could surpass Turner's kind anxiety, and almost womanly tenderness and consideration. He was untiringly assiduous in obtaining everything that could tend to recovery, and he took the greatest pains to enlist every member of the household who might be useful, and that with an unselfish, hearty effectiveness that was as zealous as it was warm-hearted.

Cowper, with almost morbid sensitiveness, declared he would

renounce the friend who would willingly set his foot upon a worm. Of this I am assured, that genuine goodness of heart is most frequently revealed in a love and guardianship of animals, in sympathy with their wants and in pity for their sufferings. Turner was very fond of animals. Even early in life, when he lived at Sandycombe Lodge, Twickenham, he was known to the boys of the place as 'Old Blackbirdy,' because he would not let them take birds' nests in his garden hedges. He was the angry guardian of the little black choristers, and loved to hear the little scraps of heaven's music that the angels had taught them. His house in Queen Anne Street was full of tailless Manx cats. Mercy regulated even his piscatorial pursuits. His old angling companion Mr. Jones says—

'I was often with him when fishing at Petworth, and also on the banks of the Thames, when we were making our annual visit to Sir J. Wyattville at Windsor Castle. His success as an angler was great, although with the worst tackle in the world. Every fish he caught he showed to me, and appealed to me to decide whether the size justified him to keep it for the table or to return it to the river ; his hesitation was often almost touching, and he always gave the prisoner at the bar the benefit of the doubt.'

Now this, I think, is a striking testimony to Turner's tenderness, for fishermen generally are not over-considerate. Even good old Izaak Walton, indisposed as he was wantonly to hurt a fly, would nevertheless, when transported to the banks of the Lea, disembowel and draw and quarter, like any red-handed butcher. A kind heart is not exactly identical with sensitive tenderness. There are those who relieve their poor friends with bank notes ; but they convey their benefits with so little regard to the feelings of their recipients that they make pellets of the salutary missives. If they give a beggar a shilling, they slam the door in his face, and knock him off the door-step in the operation. If they rub oil into your wounds, they do it with an emphasis utterly removed from gentleness. This was not Turner's way. He was full of sensibility ; and his sensibility was all the more real for its un-obtrusiveness. A few stories will prove this as well as a thousand. While down at Petworth he hears his noble host mention a friend's name several times and in rather a hurt tone. ' I have written to ask him, but he won't come,' repeats blunt but sound-hearted Lord Egremont. Turner, as he paints, thinks over this ominous remark, and sees mischief in it. He probably will have to pen another ' Fallacy of Hope ' if his friend declines any more invitations. He writes to him forthwith in a strain of warning ; his kindly meant and sensible advice is taken, and all is well. (*Aphorism*—The only thing a man never forgives is your declining an invitation ; the only thing a man never believes is a friend's excuse for not coming to dinner.) Mr. Jones came ; and within three weeks Lord Egremont died.

To his intimate friends Turner was most affectionate ; and he did not attempt to conceal his affection. One of his dearest friends he used to call ' Georgey ' and ' Joney ' alternately; but, though I believe he was a Tory, he loved liberty and those who fought for it ; so, when his friend's villanous namesake betrayed the Hungarians, he said to Jones, ' I shall not call you Georgey any more.' The name thenceforth was hateful to him.

Stumpy, slovenly, lame, often not over-clean in dress, awk-ward and unconciliatory in habits, and suspicious of pseudo-friends, greedy relations, selfish legacy-hunters and concealed enemies, he had not the manner of one who either could or cared to win the favour of the general world ; but by those who really knew and understood him he was beloved. In the circle of his friends he was ever cheerful and social, delighting in fun, and a most welcome companion at all times. How could one expect courtly demeanour from Turner? He was scantily educated ; his early life was spent in bitter struggles for bare subsistence; and his middle life was passed in drawing for engravers, and in struggling for fame with the black ghosts of the old masters that then filled the galleries of English noble-men ; while his latter days, uncheered by the companionship of a wife, were consumed in the pursuit of various ideals. Now his acquired habits of parsimony had grown inveterate, and he could not unfreeze himself into hospitality. Let us not forget that no man ever endured more that was qualified to petrify the heart than Turner. A cruel deception robbed him of her he was about to make his wife. That was the blight upon his opening career, which permanently affected it to its close. Destitute of the nourishing aid of patronage, his supreme genius next was expended in the service of, and in contests with, engravers, while he was fully conscious that he had outshone Cuyp, distanced Vandervelde, beaten Ruysdale, rivalled Canaletti, and transcended even Claude ; that he had founded English Landscape, that he had advanced Art beyond the utmost limits it had ever attained. When old age arrived, it found him rich but hopeless ; without faith and without solace, save that imparted by his art. The domestic element that might and would have humanised him was wanting to his household, With wife and children to comfort him, a healthier spirit would have been infused into his being ; his thoughts would have been diverted from their ordinary channels ; the solitariness of self would have been exchanged for the expansive geniality of society. Terrible in its severity was the discipline to which he was subjected : but even that did not avail to extinguish his native benevolence. No ! The one great thought that ceaselessly occupied his mind was as to how he could best consecrate the hard earnings of a long and laborious life to the cause of charity. Scant as was the measure of consideration he had meted to him by the world, yet he loved his kind with silent ardour. He might perhaps have been gratified to think that the poor barber's son would be entombed among the magnates in St. Paul's. Assuredly he might well have been proud of the reflection that a national collection of pictures bearing his name would delight the English people for generations to come.

His sarcastically quiet love of mystification was mistaken for wilful deception ; his self-denying and sparing habits were taken to exemplify the greed of avarice. Every story raked up from the familiar lives of Elwes or of Guy (who was his historic prototype) was believed of him when he was not present to contradict them ; but the moment he died, and it was found that he had bequeathed an enormous fortune for the benefit of his poor comrades in Art, the vast edifice of lies so industriously erected crumbled to fragments before the astounding disclosure. Here was the cold, sullen, misanthropic miser, who had consumed his miserable, lonely years in higgling like a Jew pedlar about the odd penny to be paid for his pictures, dying and leaving the whole earnings of his life to found a charity that would last while England endured. How many hours had those black tongues spent in defamation of him ; and all their malicious expenditure had been in vain !

The sole aim proposed to himself by Turner was to benefit Art, and to found almshouses, near where he had once lived, for the relief of the poor foot-sore soldiers in the mighty army of Art. It was no paltry vanity that filled the mind of this large-hearted, yet I fear unhappy, man. To execute this cherished design he had lived like the half-starved steward of a miser's property. For this he had let his house grow into a den, and had worked like a miner amid a sordid gloom. It was in behalf of those whose talents could not command success, for the world's failures, that he had ground down insolent publishers. It was for weeping widows and orphans that he had wrangled about additional shillings for picture frames and cab hire. It was to pay for poor artists' funerals that he had toiled and travelled. It was to chase the wolf from other men's doors that he had patiently submitted to be vilified as 'miser, Jew, and dog.'

One of Turner's executors, who also was one of his oldest friends, one whom he loved and whom he had known for years, tells me solemnly and without reserve that he believes his character to have been entirely without stain. ' I never knew a man,' says he, ' freer from guile or of a kinder nature, notwithstanding his occasionally rough demeanour ; but envy, jealousy, and cupidity made him their victim as far as they were able.'

Turner was unlucky enough to have enemies of various kinds. First came his professional rivals ; men of inferior qualifications who hated their conqueror and monarch.

Next were the legacy-hunters, who felt that they had made no progress in his favour, and therefore hated him with a virulent hatred. And these were reinforced by the mere loose-tongued chatterers of the clubs, who partly invent and partly enlarge the current malice of the day, and who love to get a typical character to hang their gossip upon. Some of these magpies' stories may have found admission into these pages; but I trust they are but few. Unluckily it is impossible to verify every line in a biography.

And now, before I proceed to sum up Turner's character, let me adduce some proofs of his undeviating kindness and amiability.

All his surviving friends testify with one voice to the benevolence and compassion he displayed whenever an occasion arose for charity or sympathy. The rough and unforbidding exterior concealed the warm heart. His speech might occasionally be harsh, but the harshness was only verbal; and he was most careful not to wound the feelings of anyone.

Turner rarely gave away pictures.[1] His closeness in this respect was of course ascribed by his enemies to avarice. But the fact was that he regulated himself by a principle derived from his observation of human nature, that men never value presentation pictures as highly as pictures to obtain which they have expended money or made some sacrifice. He was solicitous of increasing the estimation of his work, which involved the advance of his fame; and, after all, was he not hoarding his best pictures, and refusing thousands for them, that he might leave them to the people whose nobles had neglected him?

Mr. Wilkie Collins tells me, in illustration of Turner's tenderness, that on the occasion of the last visit paid by his father, then dying of disease of the heart, to the Exhibition of the Royal Academy, when his numerous friends and fellow-Academicians were pressing forward to offer him help, Turner was the first to give him his arm and lead him in with all the consideration due to his enfeebled condition. Nor was he less kind in money matters, though to most men he falsely seemed so grasping and obdurate. He once returned to Mr. Charles Heath bills representing 1000*l.* advanced to him for work done for the Keepsakes, with the intimation of his willingness to allow the payment to be determined by the state of Mr. Heath's

---

[1] He seldom visited Mr. Griffiths without bringing him touched proofs as a present; and those, too, of a set his friend was collecting.

affairs. But this is a very trifle in comparison with another less known but thoroughly proved instance of his large heart and generous disposition. I tell the story, but suppress the names. An early patron of Turner, when he was a mere industrious barber's son working at three-shilling drawings in his murky bedroom, had seen some of them in a window in the Haymarket, and had bought them. From that time he had continued his purchases and his kindness to the rising artist; and Turner was not insensible to his patronage. Years afterwards he heard that his old benefactor had become involved, and that his steward had received directions to cut down some valuable timber on the estate, to relieve the pressure. Instantly Turner's generous impulses were roused. Shaking off his habitual parsimony (all, be it noted, directed to one great object), he forthwith wrote to the steward, enjoining him to conceal his real name, and sent him the amount required; many, many thousands—as much as 20,000*l.*, I believe. The gentleman never knew who in truth his benefactor was; but in the course of time his affairs rallied, and he was enabled to repay the whole sum through his agent, who kept the secret strictly. Long years thereafter, the son of Turner's benefactor became involved. When the birds of the air brought the news to the guardian angel of the family, again he forwarded the necessary thousands anonymously; and it is intensely satisfactory to add that the generous advance enabled the gentleman to recover himself and to return it with his warmest acknowledgments through the same channel.

One element in Turner's success Mr. Lovell Reeve judges to have been his indifference to praise. Though proud of his works, he was not a vain man; and he never suffered from the disappointments arising out of a premature desire for fame. According to Peter Cunningham, Mr. Ruskin's superlative eulogies did not gratify him. 'He knows a great deal more about my pictures than I do,' was the semi-protesting exclamation; 'he puts things into my head, and points out meanings in them that I never intended.' Nor was it easy to direct him to admiration of his own pictures. A well-known collector, with whom the artist had long been intimate, once invited him to be present at the opening of a new gallery which was hung round with his most beautiful drawings. To the disappointment of the connoisseur, Turner scarcely noticed them, but kept his eyes fixed upon the ceiling ; which was panelled and neatly grained in oak. 'What are you looking at so intently?' enquired the host. 'At these boards,' was the reply ; 'the fellow that did that must have known how to paint.' And he could not be induced to turn to the magnificent pictures that sparkled on the walls. He never talked about his own pictures, says Mr. Reeve ; but he occasionally would favour artists with hints, which invariably proved upon adoption to be improvements ; and the same authority emphatically records that he never heard of Turner saying anthing likely to give pain, though he felt keenly the ignorant criticisms and ridicule with which his own pictures were sometimes assailed.

So far from being the sordid hunks and miser he was misrepresented to be, Turner was of a tender and kind nature. How could generosity express itself more adequately than in the representation he was wont to address to an intimate friend—

'Don't wish for money ; you will not be the happier ; and you know you can have any money of me you want'?

There is good authority for the statement that a poor woman once interrupted his day's painting by teasing him with a begging petition. He roughly chid her and dismissed her ; but before she had got to the hall door, his conscience goading him, he ran after her and presented her with a 5*l.* note—a large sum for a closely thrifty man to give away thus on a sudden impulse.

Another incident bears overwhelming testimony against the traducers of Turner's character.

The death of a drawing-master deeply affected him, and his regard for the memory of his old friend was manifested by kindness to the widow. He had lent her sums of money at various times of need until the total was considerable. Fortune, however, favoured the exertions of the poor woman, and she waited upon him for the purpose of repayment. But Turner would not accept it. Resolutely keeping his hands in his pockets, he desired her to apply the amount to the education of her children. In the same spirit he cancelled many a debt, and of magnitude too ; for of cruelty or rapacity he was incapable.

Many stories, says Mr. G. Jones, are told of Turner's parsimony and covetousness, but they are generally untrue.   He was careful, and desired to accumulate.   This he acknowledged ; and, often adding to the jokes against himself, he would say with an arch expression of countenance, when congratulated on the successful sale of a picture, ' Yes, but there is the frame, or the carriage, or the time spent in alteration or varnishing.' These, however, were indulgences in the ridiculous, which always excited mirth and gave him pleasure.

When Turner was engaged on his picture, formerly in St. James's Palace and now at Greenwich, he was criticised and instructed daily by the naval men about the Court.   During eleven days he altered the rigging to suit the fancy of every fresh critic ; and he did it with the greatest good-humour.   In fact, he always joked about having worked eleven days without any pay or other profit.

Several who employed Turner (proceeds the same authority) complained that he had not completed the commissions as they expected.   Probably Turner could not or would not work as they desired ; yet he never scrupled to retain the pictures or drawings objected to, though he often declined to make another effort to give satisfaction.   The drawings he executed for Mr. Rogers's work were in his possession at the time of his death, he having received only a small sum as copyright for the designs made expressly for the poet.

Turner, as we have seen, was very fond of fishing.   He seldom went to visit a country friend without binding up a rod with his pilgrim's staff and the inevitable umbrella.   He was an intensely persevering fisherman too ; no bad weather could drive him from his post, or ill-luck exhaust his patience.   Even here we discern the elevation of his character.   The bodily frame that endured the long day's rain was animated by the soul that wrestled manfully for fame.   The hand that for hours without repining held the unlucky rod was the hand that for years continued to paint pictures, though they would not sell. At Petworth he pursued his angling with systematic ardour; and, when he went to revisit the scenes of his childhood at Brentford, or walked over from his house at Twickenham to call upon his friend Mr. Trimmer at Heston, he invariably appeared carrying his rod. One of Mr. Trimmer's sons, still living, well remembers seeing Turner sit on the lawn at Brentford, fishing in a pond for carp. It was a raging wet, dreary day; but the indomitable sportsman mitigated its severities by adopting a kitchen chair for his seat and a board for resting his feet on; and, thus equipped, with one hand he held his huge umbrella, and with the other his rod. The weather was as undesirable as it possibly could be; but there he sat till the dinner bell rang, with the quiet fortitude of a hero, not to be lightly turned from his piscatorial purpose.

It is highly probable that the melancholy monotony of sport under such uninviting conditions was relieved to Turner by the sense of being amid Nature; and it is not unlikely that even on that wet day he carefully noted its special features—the ripples, reflections, and eddies of the water, the gleams of green weed and the silvery glances of the sullen fish. All these, it may be, were garnered up in that vast and tenacious memory which no note-taking habits could weaken.

Turner sometimes, I believe, ventured a little money at cards.

Leslie relates a story of the mode in which he once surprised a large party of brother artists who were dining together at Blackwall. Whitebait and champagne had been copiously associated on that occasion, to the serious amplification of the bill, which in due time was handed in with all fitting solemnity to the chairman of the feast. That officer happened to be Chantrey, the jolly and the fat; and he in pure mischief passed it on to Turner. Great was the admiration of the company when he not only discharged it instantly, but would suffer no contribution towards the amount.

Turner, who liked society, particularly that of his brother artists, often lamented that he could not be hospitable. He was a member of the original club of Academicians; and, when that club was revived by Mr. Pickersgill, he joined it with infinite pleasure. He also once set an example of social kindliness at the Athenæum, by defraying the expenses of rather a large dinner enjoyed by his brethren of the Academy. He did so in the hope that his example would be followed; but the project failed after one or two successive meetings. Nor are these solitary instances of his social spirit. Reluctant as he generally seemed to be in parting with his money, yet, when he dined with two or three at some place of amusement, his companions often found, when the bill was called for, that he had already defrayed the expense.

Turner, in truth, was no sour-blooded recluse. According to Leslie, who knew him well, 'in careless conversation he often expressed himself happily, and was very playful; at a dinner table nobody was more gay and joyous.' He was a social man by nature, and his habit of solitude arose from the wish to have more time to devote to Art.

Here I transcribe Leslie's estimate of Turner :—

'On December 19, 1851, died the greatest painter of the time, by some thought the greatest of all the English painters. By many, however, and perhaps by the best judges, Turner will be placed in that class

> 'Whose genius is such
> That we can never praise it or blame it too much.

'The artists, with scarcely an exception, had from the beginning of his career done him justice; but he passed through life little noticed by the aristocracy (Lord Egremont being, as he had been in the case of Flaxman, the principal exception), and never by royalty. Calcott, and other painters immeasurably below him, were knighted; and, whether Turner desired such a distinction or not, I think it is probable he was hurt by its not having been offered to him. Probably also he expected to fill the chair of the Academy on the death of Sir Martin Shee; but, greatly as his genius would have adorned it on almost every other account, he was incapable of occupying it with credit to himself or to the institution, for he was a confused speaker, wayward and peculiar in many of his opinions, and expected a degree of deference on account of his age and high standing as a painter which the members could not invariably pay him consistently with the interests of the Academy and the Arts.

'Having said that he received but little notice from the nobility, with the exception of Lord Egremont, I must not omit to mention that he painted one of his largest and grandest pictures for Lord Yarborough, and another as fine for the Marquis of Stafford. Mr. Rogers, with less means of patronage, was always his great admirer, and has associated his name with that of Turner in one of the most beautifully illustrated volumes that has ever appeared.

'It is remarkable that the poet was equally the friend and admirer of Flaxman and Stothard, while the titled and wealthy of the country lost for themselves the honour of connecting themselves with names that will probably outlive their own.

'Sir George Beaumont was a sincere friend to the Arts, but in many things a mistaken one. He was right in his patronage of Wilkie and Haydon, but he ridiculed Turner, whom he endeavoured to talk down. He did the same with respect to Stothard ; and, though personally very friendly to Constable, he never seems to have had much perception of his extraordinary genius.

'In the year 1822 Constable thus wrote :—" The art will go out ; there will be no genuine painting in thirty years." And it is remarkable that within a few months of the date thus specified Turner should have died : almost literally fulfilling, as some of his admirers may think, Constable's prophecy.

'It is difficult to judge of the condition of Art in our own time, but I think it cannot be denied that painting is in a much lower state in this country now than in the year 1822. At that time Stothard, Fuseli, Wilkie, Turner, Lawrence, Owen, Jackson, Constable, and Etty were living ; James Ward was in the full possession of his great powers, as were also most among the present eminent painters. But those who have since come forward, however they may hereafter rank, cannot, I think, at present be considered as forming anything like such an assembly.'

In the original sketch of Elgin Cathedral made by an

amateur, the windows in the nave were closed or built up ; but the revised drawing by Turner represented them as open. When his attention was invited to this matter a few years after, he protested that the alteration was as it should be : 'How much better is it to see the light of day in God's house than darkness !'

Quaintness was inseparable from the reasons he was ready to allege in behalf of all he did. When the plate of Wickliffe's birthplace was being engraved for Whitaker's 'Yorkshire,' in touching the proof he introduced a burst of light which was not in the drawing. To the engraver's enquiry as to why he had done so he replied, 'That is the place where Wickliffe was born, and there is the light of the glorious Reformation.' The explanation so far was satisfactory. 'But what do you mean by these large fluttering geese in the foreground?' Not a little ingenuity was demanded to justify the anserous prominence; but he was equal to the occasion. 'Oh ! those—those are the old superstitions which the genius of the Reformation is driving away.'

Equally happy was the reply he made to Mrs. Austin, who subsequently became the aunt of Mr. Layard, of Nineveh renown. 'I find, Mr. Turner,' said that lady, 'that in copying one of your works touches of blue, red, and yellow appear all through the work.' He answered, 'Well, don't you see that yourself in Nature? Because, if you don't, Heaven help you!'

As the writer of the obituary notice in the 'Times' accurately observed, this shrewdness of observation and playfulness of wit were displayed only in the familiarity of close intercourse. 'Everywhere he kept back much of what was in him ; and while the keenest intelligence, mingled with a strong tinge of satire, animated his brisk countenance, it seemed to amuse him to be but half understood. His nearest social ties were those formed in the Royal Academy, of which he was by far the oldest member, and to whose interest he was most warmly attached.'

On one of those pleasant varnishing-days which were productive of so much unrestrained mirth, Mulready had the jocular audacity to liken a cow in the great landscape painter's foreground to one of those little dough pigs with currants for eyes that they sell to children at country shops. Turner, whose appetite for joke was of remarkable keenness, relished this sally hugely, and continued to chuckle over his painting for some time, the while chewing the cud of Mulready's quiet humour as only a great man entirely free from vanity could do. On varnishing-days Turner would arrive at a very early hour with his dirty chest of colours and worn-out brushes, and a palette of which the uncleanliness was sufficient to shock a Dutch painter; and he would sit on steps, or erect himself upon a pile of boxes, if his picture happened to hang at an elevation.

Not seldom he directed his fun against the profession.

In 1826 Stanfield, whose artistic dominion was over the sea, painted a picture of a calm, which he named 'Throwing the Painter,' but unfortunately was unable to complete it in time for the Exhibition. Calcott, hearing of it, produced one which he jocularly entitled 'Dutch Fishing-Boat missing the Painter.' Studio jokes of this sort appealed to Turner's sense of fun, and it was his wont to chuckle over them with amazing satisfaction. He now secretly resolved to put the finishing stroke to the contention. Accordingly he came out next year with 'Now for the Painter,' with the radiant triumph of a boy who at leapfrog takes the last and highest back. It is easy to see that this was but conducting the joke started by Calcott to a further stage; yet detractors perverted it to Turner's defamation.

'Seclusion was Turner's own fault,' says Leslie. 'No death-bed could be more surrounded by attentive friends than his might have been, had he chosen to let his friends know where he lived. He had constantly dinner invitations, which he seldom even answered, but appeared at the table of the inviter or not as it suited him. It may well be supposed that a man so rich, admired in life, and, as it was thought, without near relations, would be much courted. He had for many years quoted in the Academy catalogues a MS. poem, "The Fallacies of Hope;" and I believe that among his papers such a MS., though not in poetic form, was found by some of his friends to be his will.'

'I met Turner,' writes a friend of mine, 'at Sir Richard Westmacott's. One of the party was about to start for Italy, and asked Turner if he could do anything for him. "No," was the playful reply, "unless you will bring me some Naples yellow."'

He had a singular aversion to disclosing the date of his birth. A fellow-student at the Academy, who had been his companion from boyhood, once said to him, 'William, your birthday can't be far off; when is it? I want to drink a glass of wine to my old friend.' 'Ah!' was the growling response; 'never mind that; leave your old friend alone.'

It is worth noting, as an illustration of the double disadvantage under which Turner's memory labours, that, while sheer ignorance of the facts gave birth to the incessant complaints that he never did a generous act in his life, and that he was especially ungrateful to the engravers by whose aid he had earned so many thousands, crass stupidity was ever ascribing to avarice what was simply due to drollery. It is not necessary to challenge the accuracy of stories like the following. Their blundering interpretation, however, may fairly be complained of. Thus runs one of this class :—

'Turner once refused a sum which he had lent; but that was after a sumptuous dinner to which he had been invited. While enjoying the dessert, the host, all at once remembering the transaction, said, "Let me see, Mr. Turner, I owe you a little money." "What for?" said Turner, setting down the wine which he was just raising to his lips. "You paid sixpence for the gate when I drove you down," answered the host. "Oh!" said Turner with a look of disappointment, as he again had recourse to the glass, "never mind that *now*."'

The dulness of malice could not be more aptly exemplified than by this painful straining of the matter. The slightest knowledge of Turner's style would have sufficed to reveal the grotesque emphasis he would lay upon 'now,' and the chuckle with which he would accompany it. So much for malicious misinterpretation of an ordinary incident.

With regard to Turner's ingratitude to the engravers, it is very remarkable that I have failed to obtain from anyone of those whom he employed a single example of wrong or in-justice. That he was exacting in his engagements is notorious; but let it be remembered to his credit that he was unflinchingly true to the terms when once settled.

Under this head I give frankly—for I desire nothing but the truth—some of the most reliable stories I can gather together of Turner's parsimony.

Mr. Alaric Watts relates that Turner once offered, to the amazement of the whole body of Royal Academicians, to pur-chase cloth for re-covering the seats in the room where one of his pictures was hung. 'No one divined the reason for this apparent generosity and most unaccountable act. He was always very particular that everything should aid the effect of his pictures, even to the hanging of those placed around them. To keep up this colour, he would continue painting on his pictures after they were hung, during the varnishing-days. On one occasion, however, he was "checkmated;" and, as he could not produce the effect he wanted by paint, he set about accomplishing it by policy. He studied how it might be done by a foil, and soon found that, if he got a mass of bright red in the foreground, his object would be accomplished.' 'The seats are not fit to sit on,' protested Turner to the hangers; 'they are very shabby; they must be re-covered.' He was re-ferred to the Council; and, as there was no Council, he called upon the President. But some forms had to be complied with which would involve delay, and delay did not suit his secret purpose. Impatiently he denounced the whole affair as disgrace-ful to the Academy, and finally he exclaimed, 'I'll do it at my own expense.' To this proposal, which provoked his laughter, Sir Thomas made no objection; and accordingly Turner lost no time in executing his self-imposed commission. Seeking the President, he said, 'Well, I've got the cloth! Suppose I may charge for the men's time and nails?' Sir Thomas, observing his determination, obtained the necessary permission to incur the whole expense, and the seats were covered with the cloth which Turner had selected. Not until completion of the first form, however, was his deep design made manifest. He then placed the foil in the foreground of his picture, and the chuckle of satisfaction in which he inwardly indulged betrayed the whole secret.

Another story recounts how he once was 'very near' giving a dinner.

Having received many civilities from Mr. Thomson of Duddingston, whose house in Edinburgh he had made his home, Turner, on leaving, pressed the reverend artist to return the compliment if he ever came to London. This Mr. Thomson unexpectedly did, much to the surprise of Turner; who, however, invited his visitor to dine with him, when it is represented that he was delighted to find the gentleman had an engagement. Next day, therefore, was determined upon. Now, it happened that Mr. Thomson in the course of the day called upon a nobleman, who also asked him to dine. He pleaded the excuse of pre-engagement; but, when the nobleman learned that it was Turner who proposed to entertain him, he directed Mr. Thomson to bring the artist with him. 'He will not be sorry for the change,' was the comment. Then he thought it would be better for him to call upon Turner, and tender the invitation in person, more especially as that would enable him to gratify his desire to see the pictures. Turner accordingly was waited upon, and accepted the invitation after a little demur. 'Well, if I must, I s'pose I must; but'—— Before he had time to complete the sentence his father, who had been listening while preparing a canvas for the son, perhaps dreading lest any hesitation should necessitate the dinner at home, thrust open the door, and, without any disguise of his own feelings, exclaimed, 'Go, Billy! go! The mutton needn't be cooked, Billy!' A dinner cooked in Queen Anne Street, proceeds the criticism, would have caused an alarm in the neighbourhood; for to have seen anything beyond the feeblest curl of smoke attempting to struggle and escape from Turner's chimneys would have raised an alarm of 'Fire!'

Another story goes that a friend of Sir Thomas Lawrence's, who resided at Clapham Common, commissioned the amiable President to order of Turner a picture at a most liberal price. When it was finished both Lawrence and Turner were invited to dinner to see to its proper hanging; but the former was summoned to Windsor on the morning of the appointed day. Turner, however, arrived with the picture, which was greatly admired; and when the ladies retired after dinner, the gentleman, noting Turner's uneasiness, said, 'We will now to business. Excuse me for a moment while I write you out a cheque.' The cheque was written and handed to Turner; but, instead of putting it into his pocket, he kept turning it over, eyeing first the gentleman and then the cheque. Apprehensive of error, the gentleman now observed, ' I have made it guineas, I believe ? It was to be guineas; was it not ? ' ' Yes; the guineas are right enough,' was the gruff return; ' but I paid six shillings for the coach; and that's not down ! '

Another story relates to the erection of the tablet to his father in St. Paul's, Covent Garden. Mr. Cribb, the churchwarden, had paid the sum of seven shillings and sixpence for some mason's work done to it, relying upon repayment of the same by Turner when he came to look at the tablet. Turner attended to view it, and expressed satisfaction with all the details up to the point of the last item being mentioned, when he directed the churchwarden to call on him some day with a receipt for the money, without which he should not pay it. The money not being worth the trouble, says the narrator of the story, Turner got the mason's work without paying for it.

That these stories are not altogether unfounded I readily admit; but they have been maliciously accentuated; they have been ingeniously framed so as to present Turner in the most unamiable light; and they betray their issue from a concealed enemy. Take the story of the cloth at the Academy. I maintain that an elaborately malicious construction has been put upon the transaction. In the first place, the painter's anxiety to avoid the neutralising effect of dull-coloured seats upon the production of his brush needs little justification; next, the whole affair was one of those strokes of sly humour upon which I am sure he must have expatiated with delight for many a day.

The story of the tablet is equally susceptible of explanation. Turner may have forgotten about the small bill, for, with all his thrifty habits, he was careless about money; or it may have

been his desire to rebuke the insolence of a pompous official
by insisting on his waiting upon him with the receipt for the
paltry sum.

The story of his demanding the coach fare may well be
credited, for he often asked for small extras, and even made his
pertinacity in this respect the subject of a standing joke with
his friends. He would have his due, down to the last penny,
both because he was a sturdy asserter of what he took to be
his rights, and because thrift was indelibly imprinted on his
character ; but he was restrained by native sagacity and humour
from carrying the love of money too far. Indeed, his own
peculiarities served to supply him with material for satire
directed against himself.

Turner was not a wit, but he had a sarcastic humour of his
own that vented itself most disagreeably against those he disliked. One memorable encounter with Fuseli, however, in
which he was worsted, I must not omit to record.

Turner had sent a canvas to Somerset House with the
subject so undefined that it caused considerable speculation
among the Royal Academicians, when they assembled on the
morning of the first varnishing-day, as to what he intended to
represent. One suggested a ' Moonlight ' another a ' Storm.'
At last Howard submitted it might be an ' Allegory.' ' Yes,'
remarked Fuseli, ' the allegorie of Blazes at a *déjeuner à la fourchette*, wid molten lead !' Turner, who had arrived just in time
to hear the keeper's remark, retorted, ' No, that's Limbo ; where
they are going to send your " Sin and Death "' (a celebrated
picture). Thereupon Fuseli, throwing himself into an attitude
of mock terror, exclaimed, ' Gentlemen, we are ondone ; we all
know *Tourner* to be an imp of de old one transformed into an
angel of light by his double shadow.' ' Yes,' put in Beechey ;
' but Turner's shadows are only double when he sees double.'
' Ah !' added Fuseli, with an affected sigh ; ' gentlemen, it is
what Turner sees dat concerns us, now he is in his fader's
confidence, and he tells him all about de beesiness in his great
fire-office below.' The picture was altered, but Turner never
again ventured on a joke with Fuseli.

And yet there was something absurd in Fuseli, who lived in

a murky world of dreams, ridiculing the poetical obscurity of Turner, which, after all, was at that time only a temporary fault with him.

Destitute of epigram or *bon-mot* as he might have been, Turner had his own quiet way of annoying the enemy. Even that most courtly landlord's son Lawrence did not escape an occasional hit, as the following story will manifest.

Turner, who was at first a stern opponent to engraving on steel, and had no notion of supplying plates for 'the million,' called upon Sir Thomas Lawrence one day just as he had received a proof with which he was highly pleased. Showing it to Turner, Sir Thomas said, 'By the way, Turner, I wonder you don't have some of your drawings engraved on steel.' 'Humph! I hate steel.' 'But why?' 'I don't like it. Besides, I don't choose to be a basket engraver!' 'A basket engraver! A basket engraver, Turner! What is that?' enquired the President. Regarding Lawrence with a malicious leer in his little penetrating eyes, which heralded the advent of some mischievous saying, he explained, 'When I got off the coach t'other day at Hastings, a woman came up with a basketful of your Mrs. Peel, and wanted to sell me one for sixpence.'

Of the cheap sale of his works he had a mortal horror; which is accounted for by the circumstance that he was most acutely sensitive to anything likely to lower his reputation. He was even reluctant to sit for his portrait, from an apprehension that people who saw his portrait would be induced to think less of his paintings. Of this over-solicitude for his fame a striking example is attested by an eminent printseller, whose shop he once entered to purchase, if possible, an engraving made many years before from one of his pictures. It is a curious illustration of the value he attached to the veriest trifle from his own hand, and of his nervous fear lest it should be turned to account somehow. His description of the subject he aided by a few rude lines scrawled with a pen on a fragment of paper; and this slip in the process of turning over the portfolio in quest of the print was blown behind the counter. The print was ultimately discovered, but, the scrap of paper being now missed, it was eagerly demanded from the unconscious printseller, whose confusion only served to redouble Turner's anxiety; which was not to be appeased until the fragment was recovered from a dark corner, when it was carried away carefully wrapped with the engraving.

Turner generally bought in his own works when they were put up for auction. If time pressed and he was unable to attend in person, he would sometimes entrust his commission to the auctioneer ; but his ordinary practice was to send an agent, with written instructions, to bid in his behalf, and he was not always very fastidious in his selection of one. At the sale of the pictures of Mr. Green, the well-known amateur of Black-heath, two by Turner were among the most attractive lots, though they were neither important in size nor of his best time. In those days their market value might have been about eighty guineas each. They would, however, have been knocked down for considerably less, but for the impetus given to the biddings by his representative, whose personal appearance did not warrant the belief that he was in search of pictures of a very high order. He was, in fact, a clean, ruddy-cheeked butcher's boy, in the usual costume of his vocation, and he had made several ad-vances, in five-guinea strides, before anything belonging to him, excepting his voice, had attracted Mr. Christie's notice. No sooner, however, did the veteran auctioneer see what kind of customer he had to deal with than he beckoned him forward, with a view, no doubt, of reproving him for his impertinence. Nothing daunted, however, the boy put a small piece of greasy paper into his hand ; it was a credential from the painter him-self. The auctioneer smiled, and the biddings proceeded. Both pictures brought high prices, and the object of the painter was as successfully achieved as if Count d'Orsay had been his representative.

When the son of Charles Turner (the late eminent engraver) was dying, the subject of this biography was most regular in his visits to the house for the purpose of learning the condition of the youth and of the family. He never, however, left his name ; and this constant solicitude was not known to the parents until after the son's death, when the servant reported that a short gentleman, of odd manners, had called every evening enquiring tenderly after the sufferer. Such was the character of this misappreciated man ; and numerous examples of the sort doubtless were similarly concealed. I know that in one instance he cancelled a bond for 500*l.*

Turner carried the same secretiveness into his professional sphere. He resolutely refused to disclose the process by which he obtained breadth and depth in his water-colour painting. He generally painted with his door locked, if he was at a stranger's house ; and if anyone approached him, or idlers tried to over-look him, he covered his drawing. He had no special secrets to hide ; for Turner's colours were of little use to men who were not equally gifted to employ them. But he had been accus-tomed, as a boy, to paint up in his bedroom, and he could not shake off the solitary habit. He did not like imitators, and did not desire idle tales to be spread of his mechanical artifices. Moreover, there was in this isolation a special gratification of his innate love of mystery and concealment. Strange to say, however, at Edinburgh he communicated all he knew to a struggling artist, at a time when the secret of his modes of sponging and bistre washing was worth 100*l.* to anyone.

CHAPTER XXIV.

TURNER'S CHARACTER—*(continued).*

JUST about the time (1843) when Mr. Ruskin had been herald-ing Turner as the apostle of Nature the latter was seen on a Margate steamer, eating shrimps out of an immense red silk handkerchief laid across his knees. 'An apostle, surely,' ex-claimed a bystander, 'in the strangest guise.'

In summer he often went to Margate on Saturday morning by the 'Magnet' or 'King William' steamer. Most of the time he hung over the stern, watching the effects of the sun and the boiling of the foam ; but about two o'clock he would open his wallet of cold meat in the cabin, and, approaching anyone with whom he was in the habit of chatting, would beg a clean plate and a hot potato ; nor was he above accepting one glass of wine. He would not, however, take a second. It need hardly be added that he was no favourite with the waiters.

When some one told him of Mr. Knight's house having been broken into, 'That's the worst of being rich' was his comment.

A friend of his remembers Turner coming to see a water-colour drawing he had purchased of him. After looking at it a long time (I think it was a view of Windermere) he pulled a box of colours out of his pocket, and set to work at it again for some hours 'like a tiger.' When people called upon him, he would sometimes come down quite dizzy 'with work.' But I fear that latterly he drank sherry constantly while he painted.

There are men living who have seen him in bitter anger about the neglect shown to his exhibited pictures. Pointing to a stack of them against the wall, he would say, 'Don't talk about 'em; all of them came back. They might have had 'em; now they shan't have 'em.'

When he was visiting once at some grand place in York-shire, he paid the gardener 2s. 6d. for putting him up a small hamper of plants for his London garden. On his next visit he made a point of seeing the gardener, and informing him 'Those plants of yours all died.' Bystanders were cruel enough to think he rather hoped that the gardener would return the bit of silver in consideration of the vegetable failure.

Turner never would verify a picture. He had done so once, he told a friend, and the result was that he was put in the witness box at a trial. 'It was the first,' he said, 'and it shall be the last time.' Among his papers were found the leaves of flowers and careful notes of their times of opening. It is said that letters remained unopened on his table for months. 'They only want my autograph,' he used to say.

'Turner's manners,' says one of his friends, 'were odd, but not bad. He was fond of talking of poetry.' Those friends to whom Mr. Jones introduced him always liked him, and were delighted to have him at their tables. 'My own admiration of him,' says Mr. Ruskin in his last volume, 'was wild in enthusiasm ; but it gave him no ray of pleasure ; he could not make me, at that time, understand his main meanings. He loved me, but cared nothing for what I said, and was always trying to hinder me from writing, because it gave pain to his fellow-artists. To the praise of other persons he gave not even the acknowledgment of this sad affection.'

He had a great aversion to appearing kind. ' Drawing,' says Mr. Ruskin, ' with one of his best friends (Mr. Munro) at the bridge of St. Martin's, the friend got into great difficulty with a coloured sketch. Turner looked over him a little while, then said in a grumbling way, " I haven't got any paper I like ; let me try yours." Receiving a block-book, he disappeared for an hour and a half. Returning, he threw the book down with a pout, saying, " I can't make anything of your paper." There were three sketches in it, in three distinct stages of progress, showing the progress of colouring from beginning to end, clearing up every difficulty into which his friend had got.'

Of the same person, who produced a sketch which had no special character, he enquired, ' What are you in *search of ?*' Sometimes the advice would come with startling distinctness. A church spire having been left out in a sketch of a town, ' Why did you not put that in ? ' ' I had not time.' ' Then you should take a subject more suited to your capacity.'

Of Turner's character Mr. Ruskin writes : ' ·He had a heart as intensely kind and as nobly true as God ever gave to one of His creatures. . . . Having known Turner for ten years, and that during the period of his life when the brightest qualities of his mind were in many respects diminished, and when he was suffering most from the evil-speaking of the world, I never heard him say one depreciating word of living man or man's work. I never saw him look an unkind or blameful look. I never saw him let pass, without some sorrowful remonstrance, or endeavour at mitigation, a blameful word spoken by another. Of no man but Turner whom I have ever known could I say this; and of this kindness and truth came, I repeat, all his highest power ; and all his failure and error, deep and strange, came of his *faithlessness.*' [1]

[1] A word Mr. Ruskin uses, I suppose, for ' despair.'

Turner was indifferent, utterly indifferent, to praise, even when it came from the most appreciating. ' In silence, with a bitter silence, Turner only indicated his purpose,' says Mr. Ruskin, ' or by slight words of contemptuous anger. When he heard of anyone's trying to obtain this or the other separate subject, as more beautiful than the rest, "What is the use of them," he said, "but together?" The only thing he would sometimes say was, " Keep them together ; " he seemed not to care how they were injured, so that they were kept in the series which would give the key to their meaning. I never saw him at my father's house look for an instant at any of his own drawings. I have watched him sitting at dinner nearly opposite one of his chief pictures ; his eyes never turned to it. But the want of appreciation touched him sorely, chiefly the not understanding his meaning. He tried hard one day, for a quarter of an hour, to make me guess what he was doing in the picture of " Napoleon," before it had been exhibited, giving me hint after hint in a rough way ; but I could not guess, and he would not tell me.'

On one occasion, at a dinner party at Mr. Hardwick's, Turner and another guest took and wheeled his friend, who had been pertinacious in some argument, into an inner room, and locked him in, amid roars of good-natured laughter. No one enjoyed a joke more than Turner when he liked his company.

Many of his pictures have cracked ; many are faded ; others are but ghosts of what they once were. The sky of the ' Bligh Sands,' an artist friend tells me, has lost its beauty ; the sugar of lead used in the clouds having turned to a rusty brown. The varnish, too, has suffered from time. He latterly used copal, which is a quick dryer, in order to promote expedition. Some of his later pictures were half in distemper, and were sometimes washed out in cleaning.

He was a great observer and appreciator of the thoughts and ingenuities of other painters. On one occasion the Rev. Mr. Judkins, an amateur artist friend of considerable merit, exhibited a landscape, in the foreground of which, to convey a sense of solitude, he had put a robin upon a post. The next time Turner met him, his sly greeting was ' I saw your robin.'

To some one who once complained that Turner was ungenerous, his friend answered, 'No; for he once paid the toll over Waterloo Bridge for me.'

The Rev. Mr. Judkins once saw him in St. Paul's Church-yard, wrangling with an omnibus conductor who had promised to take him to the Bank. 'If you don't do as you promised, I don't pay,' said Turner; and the artist sturdily walked off un-impeded.

He was not a rash man, and no fair sarcasm moved him at all. 'Your "Rome" is cracked,' said Mr. Judkins to him one day at the Exhibition. 'I will soon doctor that,' was his laughing reply. But perhaps he had his revenge, for he could be sarcastic. Mr. Judkins one day was speaking in a depre-cating tone of a work of his in the Exhibition Room. 'If you can paint better, why not send it?' was Turner's searching inquiry.

At Lawrence's sale he stepped forward and forbade a drawing of his, which he had lent to the dead artist, being put up for auction.

His pride, when hurt, was unappeasable. When Mr. Griffith published some of his great Carthaginian pictures, and they began to sell after their first failure, he would not allow any more to be disposed of. When the prices of the 'Liber' began to improve, he one day came suddenly into Mr. Col-naghi's shop, and said oracularly, 'I give no more discount to the trade.' 'Very well, Mr. Turner,' was the deprecating answer; but it did not allay his wrath. When he found that Mr. Windus had re-sold some of his drawings at higher prices, he refused to make him any more, though offered his own price; for Turner was as proud and sensitive as he was obstinate. In the same way, when Mr. Allnutt had a drawing of Tivoli by him engraved, he wanted additional money for the copyright; and, on being refused, he declined to sell him some sketches on the Rhine. Nothing could pacify him when he once thought himself ill-treated.

If he was firm, he always was tremendously obstinate.

One day at Petworth, Lord Egremont and he had a dispute as to the number of windows in the front of a show-house in the neighbourhood. 'Seven,' said the lord. 'Six,' maintained Turner; 'I counted them.' As neither of them would yield, Lord Egremont instantly rang the bell, and ordered a post chaise to the door. Off they went accordingly, when the windows were counted, and Turner was found to be in error.

He was rough in his manner to applicants for charity; but it was after the mode of Abernethy—only assumed to conceal his true feelings. 'He often,' says one of his most intimate friends, 'would give half a crown where others would only have offered a penny.'

The injustice of the low prices he got in his early career had been deeply felt by him. It hurt his pride, and even checked his desire to save. To the injury of his pocket and the reduction of his fame, he became suspicious of all business men, because they had pinched and ground him, and bated down the produce of his mind. His thirst for revenge on these money spiders was most keen. He would sell nothing but at his own rate; he would save up his money for royal deeds of posthumous charity. As to his ceaseless thoughts on charitable objects, we have the testimony of his friend Mr. Jones, who says—

'During twenty-five years he indulged the pleasing hope that he should leave a testimony of his goodwill and compassion for unfortunate artists. To his intimate friends he constantly talked of the best mode of leaving property for the use of the unsuccessful; he wished his survivors to employ his property in building houses for the above-named purpose; he did not like to call them almshouses, but had selected the denomination of "Turner's Gift." His benevolence was conspicuous whenever he was tried, though he often used terms of harshness in which his feelings had no part; but he hated idleness, extravagance, and presumption. He thought that artists had not time for the duties and pleasures of domestic festivity, yet believed that they should often meet to strengthen fraternal feeling without much expense; therefore he was zealous in support of the Academy Club, tried to establish an artists' dinner at the Athenæum, and left 50*l.* in his will to be expended annually on a dinner for the members on the anniversary of his birthday. It is very probable that Turner's hint about leaving property for the benefit of his brother artists suggested to Chantrey and to Mr. Vernon the desire to raise their names by their benevolence. The first has done so ; the last intended to leave 70,000*l.* to secure his reputation for taste, liberality, and charity ; but in the end preferred seeking his commemoration by leaving his name as a county man in Berkshire, in lieu of being immortalised by the godlike attribute of benevolence.'

Turner, who was as fond of amusement, good cheer, and fun as his affectionate friend Chantrey, often expressed his sincere regret at his not being able, from his solitary and rude life, to follow the example of the lavish hospitality of Sir Francis. He had no servants, and no appliances for large dinner parties ; but he was always ready to contribute his share to get up a professional party, and enjoyed it more than anyone. He was not averse to joining in jokes directed against his own close and careful habits. He would even originate them, and extend those launched by others beyond their original bounds, for his humour was free from all fretful or malicious vanity.

He never appeared morose and displeased but when people had been trying to cajole or defraud him, or when he observed in anyone an unbecoming desire to pry into his private affairs. This he never forgave. Mr. Jones deposes—

' My great intimacy with him arose from his confidence (that I had his confidence Turner proved by his appointing me his executor in 1831, without my knowledge) that I had no desire to know his secrets, control his actions, or suggest changes in his course of life. He never interfered with nor condemned the habits of others. If he thought them incorrect, he was silent on the subject ; and, if any excuse or palliation could be made, he was always ready to accept, adopt, and promulgate the excuse. I never heard him speak ill of anyone.'

By his enemies, whether simply rivals or the detractors who swarm, small and poisonous as gnats, round all great men, the wildest exaggerations of Turner's reserve and love of solitary study were spread ; yet, singularly enough, of what was bad in him they were ignorant ; and it was what was purely good in him that they blackened and defamed. That his love of pleasure was inordinate and unrestrained they did not know ; but they accused him of shunning mankind and avoiding society, of which he was not guilty. They did not know that in old age pleasure had still, unhappily, but too irresistible a magnetism for him. Whereas they accused him of being a flint-hearted miser, his whole life was one long, unchanging scheme of benevolence. Everything he did was perverted by these men industrious and ingenious in evil alone. His sturdy determination not to let his great works be bought at insufficient prices was disfigured into the habit of griping meanness.

He was intensely obstinate. I think it was during a visit to Petworth that a discussion ensued between Lord Egremont and Turner as to whether carrots could float in water. I suppose he introduced some in one of the Petworth pictures.

' Carrots don't swim.'

' They do.'

' They don't.'

' They do.'

Lord Egremont thereupon rings the bell, and calls for a bucket of water and some carrots. The water is brought, and the carrots are thrown in ; when the obstinate painter is discovered to be correct in his affirmation.

Turner's conversation was sprightly, but desultory and disjointed. Like his works, it was eminently sketchy. He would converse in this manner for half an hour, and then be amazed at finding his companions in doubt of what he had been talking about. He knew that his ideas were original, and he could not understand that they never reached his tongue. He was like a man with a wonderful Cremona, which he cannot play. He was poetical, he was scientific, he had travelled, he had observed, he was fond of humour ; and yet he could not give these thoughts and fancies expression. The winged soul which was imprisoned in his body could speak only by the medium of pencil. He felt deeply—he saw deeply— he knew deeply ; yet he could find no voice to utter his dreams and oracles.

' He wrote few letters,' says Mr. Lovell Reeve, and these

were, like his conversation, abrupt, and referred little to Art. The following, accepting an invitation to dine with his valued friend and patron Mr. Windus of Tottenham, on the occasion of his birthday, is characteristic :—

'My dear Sir,—Yes, with very great pleasure, I will be with you on the B.D. Many of them to yourself and Mrs. Windus ; and with the compliments of the season believe me

'Yours faithfully,

'J. M. W. TURNER.'

Turner did not value the works of Copley Fielding, or of Harding. All imitators he despised, but Pyne he regarded as poetical. I think I have heard that he had a great dislike to the faces of Etty's nude studies ; but he never found fault with or spoke detractingly of anyone.

All his life he had the peculiar love of mystification which is the result of suspicious reserve, when accompanied by humour. As a youth he concealed his processes of water colours from all but special friends with the narrow distrust of a petty tradesman guarding trade secrets ; and, at a later period, he stole backwards and forwards to the Continent with the jealous secresy with which a detective officer effects his silent journeys. As for his 'Fallacies of Hope,' that imaginary and unwritten poem was the standing joke of his life. Latterly in the names and even the subjects of his pictures he sought to puzzle and tease the public. His charitable intentions were mysteries ; his residence was a mystery ; where he had been to, where he was going to, and what he intended to do, were all mysteries ; and so powerful was this habit of reserve that I have no doubt he died absolutely rejoicing in the fact that even his best friends knew not where he lay hid.

Turner had found hope after hope fail him, as rope after rope, sail after sail, blows from a foundering vessel. Only one thing had survived immutable, and that was Nature. On the Yorkshire fells or beside the Swiss lakes he forgot his cares in the love and gratitude he felt for the stainless beauty of God's world. Then alone he trampled all sorrows under foot, and became once more happy as a child.

I am not sure that, apart from everything relating to the Art faculty, his brain was of very great calibre, for even his thirst for scientific knowledge was remarkable chiefly for its leaning towards Art. His forehead, phrenologically speaking, was full but narrow and receding ; the brain projected over the eyes. It rose round and full, but narrowed at ideality, and then sloped backwards.

Either his education was scanty and imperfect, or his mind was singularly unreasoning and inaccurate, else he would not have spelt so badly. The names of French and Italian towns he spelt to the end of his life as they were pronounced, not as they were written. In speaking he never seemed to get quite the right word : he would say ' the internal of a cottage ' for the ' interior.' His will is an extraordinary mash of grammar ; and even his father's epitaph has the awkward expression ' Under and beneath this stone lie.' He was, in truth, a great single-facultied man.

There are two old boatmen still living at Sunbury who well remember rowing him out on his sketching excursions. It is still their unspeakable wonder how ' a man like that,' who always took a bottle of gin out with him for inspiration and never gave them any, could have been a great genius. Turner has many admirers, but these obstinate Sunbury boatmen are not of the number.

Mr. Ruskin bears the following testimony to the general kindness and goodness of Turner's nature :—

' Imagine what it was for a man to live seventy years in this hard world, with the kindest heart and the noblest intellect of his time, and never to meet with a single word or ray of sympathy, until he felt himself sinking into the grave. From the time he knew his true greatness, all the world was against him. He held his own ; but it could not be without roughness of bearing and hardening of the temper, if not of the heart. No one understood him, no one trusted him, and everyone cried out against him.

' Imagine, any of you, the effect upon your own minds, if every voice that you heard from the human beings around you were raised, year after year, through all your lives, only in condemnation of your efforts and denial of your success. This may be borne, and borne easily, by men who have fixed religious principles, or supporting domestic ties. But Turner had no one to teach him in his youth, and no one to love him in his old age. Respect and affection, if they came at all, came too late. Naturally irritable, though kind—naturally suspicious, though generous—the gold gradually became dim, and the most fine gold changed, or, if not changed, clouded and overcast. The deep heart was still beating; but it was beneath a dark and melancholy mail, between whose joints, however, sometimes the slightest arrows found entrance and power of giving pain. He received no consolation in his last years, or in his death. Cut off in great part from all society—first by labour and at last by sickness—hunted to his grave by the malignities of small critics and the jealousies of hopeless rivalry, he died in the house of a stranger—one companion of his life, and one only, staying with him to the last. The window of his death-chamber was turned towards the west; the sun shone upon his face in its setting, and rested there as he expired.

‘ Brother artists ! I will tell you how jealous he was. I knew him for ten years, and during that time had much familiar intercourse with him. I never once heard him say an unkind thing of a brother artist, and I never once heard him find a fault with another man’s work. I could say this of no other artist whom I have ever known.

‘ But I will add a piece of evidence on this matter of peculiar force. Probably many have read a book which has been lately published, to my mind one of extreme interest and value, the life of the unhappy artist Benjamin Haydon ! Whatever may have been his faults, I believe no person can read his journal without coming to the conclusion that his heart was honest, and that he does not wilfully misrepresent any fact or any person. Even supposing otherwise, the expression I am going to quote to you would have all the more force, because, as you know, Haydon passed his whole life in war with the Royal Academy, of which Turner was one of the most influential members. Yet in the midst of one of his most violent expressions of exultation at one of his victories over the Academy

he draws back suddenly with these words : " But Turner behaved well, and did me justice."

'Northcote had a dark picture in the Exhibition, and was
very angry with the arrangers for putting a bright one of Turner's immediately below it. "You might as well have opened
a window under my picture," said the painter. The compliment was as handsome as it was unintentional. But even
Turner has complained of other pictures putting his down. In
1827, when he exhibited his "Rembrandt's Daughter," with a
red robe, it happened that a portrait of a member of Dublin
University was hung alongside of it, with a College gown that
was still redder. Upon finding this out on varnishing-day,
Turner was observed to be very busy adding red lead and
vermilion to his picture, in order to out-rouge his neighbour in
brilliancy. "What are you doing there, Turner?" remarked
one of the arrangers. "Why, you have checkmated me !" said
the painter, pointing to the University gown.

'In a proof impression of a plate lately submitted to me,
the engraver had failed to discern the distant representation of
a village at the base of a hill, and had substituted some unintelligible nothings. Turner had run a heavy pencil line into
the margin of the paper to intimate that these were " houses ; "
and the miniature village seemed to come into focus as if by
magic. Look closely at Turner's pictures, and a few patches,
and dashes, and streaks only are visible, seeming only an unintelligible chaos of colour; but retire from the canvas, and
what magnificent visions grow into shape and meaning. Long
avenues lengthen out far into the distance, and sun-clad cities
glitter upon the mountains, while cloud-illumined space presents itself to an extent that is inconceivable, manifesting a
grandeur of conception and a largeness of style that must serve
to demonstrate and glorify the genius of the painter to the end
of time.

'When at the Royal Academy dinner the gas was turned on,
as is customary on the Sovereign's health being drunk, his
pictures shone like so many ʳuns on the walls. While other
meritorious works looked flat in comparison, there was an
effulgence in Turner's that seemed to grow upon the observer,

making the contrast more apparent. "They seem to represent so many holes cut in the wall," said a veteran connoisseur at one of these Art festivals, "through which you see Nature." This observation was probably suggested, however, by one made some years before by Northcote. Turner's pictures were always the terror of exhibitors, from showing whatever were the defects in colour of those placed nearest them.

' "The Burning of the Houses of Lords and Commons" was almost entirely painted on the walls of the Exhibition. His facility at this period of his life was astounding. He would frequently send his canvas to the British Institution with nothing upon it but a grey groundwork of vague, indistinguishable forms, and finish it upon varnishing-day into a work of great splendour. Likewise at the Academy he frequently sent his canvas imperfect and sketchy, trusting entirely to varnishing-days for the completion of his picture. It was astonishing what he accomplished on those days. . . . Turner was always the first at the Academy on those occasions, arriving there frequently as early as four o'clock, and never later than six ; and he was invariably the last to quit in the evening. He might be seen standing all day before his pictures ; and, though he worked so long, he appeared to be doing little or nothing. His touches were almost imperceptible ; yet his pictures were seen in the end to have advanced wonderfully. He acquired such a mastery in early life that he painted with a certainty that was almost miraculous. Although his effects were imperceptible on a near inspection of the picture, he knew unhesitatingly how to produce them without retiring from his work to test the result. He was never seen, like Sir Thomas Lawrence and others, to be perpetually walking about, but kept hard at work, nose to the canvas, sure of his effects.'

I am sorry to own that I cannot say very much for Turner's moral character A selfish, brooding, solitary life, and naturally strong passions could not be expected to lead to anything but a selfish and vicious old age. Latterly he resorted to wine while he painted, to rouse his imagination ; and at Chelsea I fear he gave way to even greater excess. Nor were these his only excesses. Towards the end of his career he would often,

I am assured on the best authority, paint hard all the week till Saturday night ; and he would then put by his work, slip a five-pound note into his pocket, button it securely up there, and set off to some low sailors' house in Wapping or Rotherhithe, to wallow till Monday morning summoned him to mope through another week.

He left four illegitimate children, and bequeathed money to the mistress with whom he passed the later years of his life. ' I once,' says a friend, ' heard Crabb Robinson (the friend of Wordsworth) casually mention a remark dropped by the late Miss Maria Denman when the two were out for an excursion with Rogers (I think), and had put up at an inn in a village near London. " That," said the lady, pointing to a youth who happened to pass, " is Turner's natural son." '

He was indeed a man whose character was full of contra-dictions. The head of gold was united to feet of clay. Like others of us, he was not all black, nor all white, but of a mixed colour ; a divine genius, yet one not free from human passions; with faults in his art, as in his life. I am not going to construct special pleas for him, after the manner of the hireling advocate who sees only that part of the truth which he is paid to see. I am going to point out the good and the bad, and not merely the good, because my object is not to paint a sham, lying, flattering portrait of him, but to draw his real likeness with the unerring fidelity of a photograph.

We find him mean, grinding, parsimonious, to the degree almost of disease. Here we see innate acquisitiveness nourished by a narrow-minded father, and stimulated by the painful growth of his own struggling ambition. The faculty of generosity never recovered from this early season of frost, never again extruded its leaves confidingly to the sunshine. A devotee to Art, naturally shy and reserved, and cramped by long adherence to habits of close parsimony, Turner in later life, when he grew rich, became incapable of launching into a wider hospitality. But, oh, the contradictions of humanity ! Was all this retirement and penury the result of avarice ? Was it avarice to refuse thousands for a single picture, and to work and pinch and fret, in order to leave 140,000*l.* to found an almshouse for decayed artists—a plan over which he had all his life been brooding?

That all the ordinary opinions of Turner are wrong ; that he was neither unsociable nor misanthropic ; that he was neither a cynic nor an anchorite, neither a miser nor a cheat, the preceding chapters have, I think, already proved to satiety. If it was necessary to clear his genius from the charge that in ordinary life he was a mere stupid, brutal man, half mad, selfish, and friendless, I believe I have succeeded in accomplishing that task.

I have explained that he had a large circle of friends,[1] including noblemen and gentlemen of education and refinement, who loved him sincerely, and in whose memory his name still holds a dear place. I have shown that, though shy, he was most sociable—fond of children and amusement, and delighting in fun and good-natured humour. I have shown that he was unalterable in gratitude, obstinately attached both to persons and to places, and sensitive as a child. I have shown him, too, capable of great and sudden sacrifices of money, even in his lifetime, to rescue friends from difficulty.

I have tried to show him as a disappointed and unhappy man, who yet continued to work with giant industry to develope his genius and display his powers. I have shown that, far from being false and slovenly, he was an artist of extreme, most painful, and extraordinary accuracy. I have shown him to be a brave friend, and a rival whose generosity was without a flaw.

I hope I have shown in a more condensed form what Mr. Ruskin has already proved with such fulness and consummate ability—the vastness of Turner's genius, its depth, width, and elastic versatility ; its great compass ; its comprehension

---

[1] Turner and Rogers got on very well together. Turner liked Rogers's taste and liberality, and Rogers admired (without criticism) the genius of Turner. ' Ah !' he would say, looking through his telescoped hand, ' there's a beautiful thing ; and the figures, too—one of them with his hand on the horse's tail—not that I can make them out, though.' There was always a dash of the lemon about Rogers's sayings. The poet was once expressing his wonder at a beautiful table that adorned Turner's parlour. ' But how much more wonderful it would be,' he exclaimed, ' to see any of his friends sitting round it.'

of all lesser powers ; and its wide range, extending from the
'Lambeth Palace' to the 'Building of Carthage,' from the
Vandervelde imitations to the old 'Téméraire.' Yet can I never
hold with Mr. Ruskin that Art knows any finality. I would
not encourage rising artists to copy Turner; I would bid
them go and study Nature with Turner's patience, industry,
and love. Nor am I at all persuaded, even by Mr. Ruskin's
eloquence, that England has yet seen the greatest of her landscape painters.[1]

---

[1] Mr. E. Goodall tells me that Turner often wrote on his touched proofs
'More figures.' He was glad to have his perspective improved, and would
make rude marks with white chalk where he wished the engraver to
introduce them, as in the 'Bridge of Caligula.' Of Turner's quarrel with
G. Cooke Mr. Goodall gives the following account:—Turner met Cooke
at a meeting of the Conversazione Society (now the Graphic, held at the
'Freemasons' Tavern '), when words ensued about certain touched proofs in
the possession of Mr. Goodall. Turner grew white with rage, and Cooke
red as fire ; and presently Cooke came up to Mr. Goodall and said, 'If you
give them up, I shall call you a mean fellow.' Next day Mr. Goodall went
to Turner's house about a plate, when the storm commenced. Turner
lamented that the Conversazione should have no more pleasure for him
since these quarrels, and demanded the proofs. Goodall refused to give
them up, and even half thrust them into the fire, when the blaze caught
them. In terror of fire, Turner, whose chimney was never swept, ran with
shovel and tongs to save the house, exclaiming, 'Good G——! you'll set
the house on fire !'

Years afterwards Turner, I believe, renewed his acquaintance with Mr.
Goodall, and gave him fresh work to do for him ; and again, in spite of his
previous warning, he demanded the touched proofs. Again Mr. Goodall
resolutely refused. Turner asked to see them, and a large bundle of them
was brought out and shown him. After eyeing them wistfully, he addressed himself to the engraver. He threatened, he coaxed, he argued.
He showed they were useless to others, and uninteresting but to himself ;
he proved they were utterly valueless. Such was his persistency that
eventually he won the day, and went off with the treasure under his arm—
no doubt to throw them into a lumber room, to rot and mildew with some
thousands of others that after his death were found half spoiled.

CHAPTER XXV.

TURNER AT QUEEN ANNE STREET.

TURNER painted in Queen Anne Street in what he called his drawing-room, in which there was a good north light. Here he would be surrounded by water-colour drawings in all states of progress. Once in the presence of Mr. Trimmer's son, then a child, he took up a drawing and said, 'I shall put in some sheep and cattle here.' The quick child, with an innate love of Art, replied, 'Yes; but you cannot put in sheep over grass in water-colours;' upon which Turner smiled at the child's ignorance of the power he had over materials.

The sordid and unhappy-looking room in Queen Anne Street was remarkable for a dusty and dirty buffet, bought at some second-hand Jew broker's. In this he kept the immemorial sherry bottle with the broken cork that served him for a decanter, and which no rallying of friends could induce him to change. This was the identical bottle and buffet of which the old story was current at the clubs. A friend who called upon him was treated to a glass of sherry from the old bottle and the old buffet—one glass. About the same time next year the artist came again, had another glass, and praised the wine. 'It ought to be good,' said Turner; 'it's *the same bottle* you tasted before.'

The 'Bligh Shore,' that hung in the gallery near the fireplace, was a great favourite with him. It served as the blind to a window that was the private *entrée* of the painter's favourite cat, who one day, indignant at finding such an obstinate obstacle in her way, left the autograph of her 'Ten Commandments' on the picture. Did the misanthrope lose his temper and instantly flay her alive? No; all he did was to say to Mrs. Danby, 'Oh, never mind.' He would not have her punished.

'Nobody ever seemed to enter the house,' says Mr. Rippingille; 'and, while all the houses round it from time to time smartened themselves up, this alone remained unchanged.' It looked cold, dirty, and forsaken, like a bankrupt's warehouse;

' nor was anything alive,' says the bitter writer, ' ever seen in it, pass when and as often as you would, but an old tabby cat lying upon a bit of ragged green baize on a table at the area window, and sometimes an old woman in a mob-cap, who looked like a being of the last century, or the other world.' Of course this is a picture darkened by the spirit of the writer, who could see nothing in Turner but a sordid, repulsive miser, and to whose imagination, therefore, the house seemed to be the abode of Despair.

Turner's friends, on the other hand, describe the house as neglected, but not sordid by any means.

Let me here introduce a vivid picture of the house in general, communicated to me by Dr. Shaw (who was a maternal relation of his), who went to claim relationship with the great man; a mode of introduction that Turner regarded with peculiar abhorrence. My informant was not one of the number; but his other relations, no doubt, had ignored him in poverty, and sought to ingratiate themselves with him in his prosperity.

Dr. Shaw says—

' I once had an interview with the great artist, and once only, with a view to claim the relationship. A time was duly appointed for an interview. Accordingly I went to his residence in Queen Anne Street, when I was ushered into a dark room, where the mantelpiece was so covered with dust that I had great difficulty in ascertaining whether it was wood or marble, in the testing of which a large finger-mark remained as an evidence of careless and bad management in house-keeping. The door outside was as shabby as if it had formed part of a ruin ; a circular space surrounding the knocker showed the original grain of the wood, all the paint having disappeared for many years past. This circular space was a remarkable feature of the door, being nearly white, and this vividly contrasted with the dingy accumulated paint and dirt which was visible on every other part of the door. The iron chain communicating with the kitchen bell outside was as thoroughly rusted as if it had lain twenty years in a desert, without shelter from the oxidising influences of rain and dew. It could not have been painted for twenty years at least, perhaps not for forty. As I had to wait some ten minutes at least before Mr. Turner made his appearance, I had leisure to examine the room and its contents. I have now forgotten the kind of furniture, but I well remember the dark, dirty, murky-looking windows. They appeared to me as though they had been cleaned but once, and that must have been when they first came from the hands of the glazier. The room appeared to be less under the influence of the beautiful light of heaven than any other apartment I ever remember to have seen. It was a comparative dungeon with two dark-lanterns for windows. In the midst of various cogitations, which necessarily occupied my mind while alone in this dirty dungeon, on a sudden the great artist made his appearance. I bowed, not too obsequiously nor too low, putting a question to him immediately after the salutation as follows:—" May I ask you if you are the Mr. Turner who visited at Shelford Manor, in the county of Nottingham, in your youth?" "I am," he answered in a tone and manner full of dignity, evidently evincing feelings of an untoward nature. He was clearly paving the way for a magnificent outburst of passion ; the thunder-storm was gathering. To appease him I became somewhat bland in manner ; I tried to throw oil upon the troubled waters. Assuming a manner which perhaps might be denominated one of a more winning kind, I said, " May I take the liberty of asking you whether your mother's name was Marshall?" He replied in a tone of voice, accompanied with the look of a fury, clearly showing that the flash of lightning had appeared to warn me that the storm was about to break. After this I began to feel uneasy. I felt half inclined to say something monstrously uncivil to him for his bearish manners. I wanted, however, for him to begin the attack, which soon followed. He drew himself suddenly into the most dignified attitude I ever beheld even from a clever actor or an infuriated duke. His manner was full of majesty, accompanied with a diabolical look. He said, " I consider, sir, that you have taken a most unwarrantable liberty with me by the manner in which you have obtruded yourself upon me." I immediately apologised ; to which he replied (by one of the most dignified and elegant bows I ever remember to have seen from duke, lord, dancing-master, or actor), " I accept the apology." After humbling myself, I then felt that it was my turn, in justice to myself, to confront the great artist in a very bold and independent manner, accompanied with resentment. " I beg leave, sir, to state to you," I said (at the same time assuming all the dignity of manner at my command), then marching to within a yard of him, and eyeing him as the warrior would look at the man he was about to bayonet, I addressed him as follows : " I am independent, sir, both in spirit and in pocket, and be assured that my whole and sole object in calling upon you was to connect myself with the distinguished name of Turner." The smile that he gave me at this moment I can only compare to the rays of the sun suddenly breaking through dark and stormy clouds. " I hope, sir," he replied, " whenever you come to town, that you will give me the favour of a visit; I shall always be glad to see you." He then preceded me to the door, which he opened, politely bowing. I frequently went to lounge away half an hour in his gallery, without ever obtruding myself upon him; I had also the privilege of taking any other person. This was our first and last interview.'

Turner almost entirely rebuilt his house in Queen Anne Street, and took great care to cut down the architect's bill. He himself designed the doorway ; but neither doorway nor building has any merit or originality. There are several designs for houses in Turner's sketch-books; and he planned a porch in his friend Mr. Fawkes's house at Farnley, in Yorkshire. Had he attempted architecture, Turner would of course have followed the classical school, the Gothic never having much real charm for him.

Everything about the gallery in Queen Anne Street seemed of a piece to those who went with a scornful determination to find there the miser and the philanthropist. The drugget, once red, was grey and threadbare. The screen was made of the black strips of some refuse or 'remainder.' The red cloth on the walls, marked all over with tack holes, had been bought by Turner as a bargain, after having been used at the Abbey for the Queen's coronation. Against the wall there were heaps of dirty frames, and stacks of dusty pictures, with their faces turned inward. As for the sofa, it seemed dangerous to your future

THE CALEDONIAN CANAL

peace to rest on it. The drawing-room was peopled by filthy tailless cats—pets, I suppose, of the old housekeeper. Its chief furniture was a common oak-grained table, once, it is believed, the property of Lawrence ; a huge paint-box, sheafs of uncleaned short brushes in a tin case, and a palette that also once belonged to Sir Thomas.

Those who were familiar with Turner's secretive and suspicious habits took care never to express any of their opinions in a loud voice when left alone in the gallery. Not that he was an intentional, but he certainly was often an accidental, eavesdropper ; and he has been known to go the next day and stormily accuse his acquaintance (sometimes, too, in error) of judgments pronounced there.

The gallery latterly got most dilapidated ; the oiled paper of the skylight hung down in black, sooty, furred slips. The damp here and there had free access ; and it is certain that, while many of the pictures ripened and improved, others were cracked, warped, chilled, and seriously injured. Both the ' Hero and Leander' and 'The Building of Carthage' suffered. Mr. E. Goodall tells me that in one picture, particularly, a great white button of paint that had stood for the sun had dropped off. ' I think some one has picked it off intentionally,' he could not help saying. ' I think somebody has,' replied Turner, quite unmoved.

The gallery had a fire in winter ; but there were times when it wanted supervision more than mere heat. And in this sordid den were all the thirty thousand proofs of engravings rotting and mouldering, uncared for by anyone but the cats, who hid behind them.

From the 'Times' of November 10, 1856, I quote a clever description of that dreary Queen Anne Street house ; which, although not entirely free from exaggeration, yet is valuable as embodying the public opinion of 1856 as to the gloomy and misanthropic way in which Turner had lived towards the end of his career. It runs thus :—

' In that region of dull and decorous streets which radiates to the north and west from Cavendish Square, Queen Anne Street is one of the dullest and dingiest ; and of that dreary

Queen Anne Street the dreariest house any thirty years before 1851 was No. 47. Judging from its weather-stained and soot-grimed walls, its patched windows dark with dust and foul with cobwebs, its wood-work unfreshened by paint, its chimneys from which curled no smoke, its unsound threshold, it might have been in Chancery, it might have been haunted, it might have been the scene of a murder. Yet it was not uninhabited. Not unfrequently a visitor might be seen to knock, and, after long waiting, the door would be half-opened by a withered and sluttish old woman, or, before 1830, by a little, shabby, lean old man. Nay, repulsive as the house might be, and grim as might be its guardians, carriages would sometimes be seen drawn up before its door for hours, while their gay and elegant freight found occupation inside. Could they be prying into the laboratory of an adept, or consulting a wizard, or driving a hard bargain with some sordid old hunks of a money-lender? Truly, neither deep alchemy, nor potent witchcraft, nor hard-fisted meanness was wanting inside that dreary door. But it was the alchemy that coins sunlight from pigments—the witchcraft that evokes beauty out of the brain—the nearness that is capable of life-long self-sacrifice to consummate an intention of noblest patriotism.

'In that desolate house—47 Queen Anne Street, West—from 1812 to 1851, lived Joseph Mallord William Turner, the greatest landscape painter of the English school. Hanging along a bare and chilly gallery on the first floor of that gloomy house, stacked against the walls, rolled up in dark closets, flung aside into damp cellars, the rain streaming down the canvasses from the warped sashes and paper-patched frames of the ill-fitting skylights, were collected some of the noblest landscapes that were ever painted, while piles of drawings even more masterly, and reams of sketches, the rudiments and first thoughts of finished works, were piled away in portfolios, and presses, and boxes, in every nook and corner of the dark and dusty dwelling. Notes for hundreds, cheques for thousands, had been offered again and again in that gallery to the painter of these pictures. He was said to adore money, and yet he refused both notes and cheques—scornfully often, sometimes regretfully and as if by an effort, but always persistingly. Dealers wondered ; patrons were in despair ; artists scoffed, or sneered, or doubted. "Turner was mad ; he meant to be buried with his ' Carthage' for a winding-sheet." '

The writer is correct. The house latterly was indeed dull and dingy ; soot-stained and weather-stained ; and its chimneys emitted no smoke. The door was paintless ; and the area rails were orange-red with rust. It might have been the house of Despair. Death's door could scarcely have been less inviting to knock at.

CHAPTER XXVI.

THE ORIGIN OF SEVERAL PICTURES.

Two of the best stories extant about the motives which led Turner to paint particular pictures are the following, which were kindly communicated to me by Mr. G. Jones, the painter's special crony and comrade. The first relates to ' The Burial of Wilkie,' that funereal picture in which every tone and tint is so attuned to the subject that the whole seems as if it were painted on crape. It dates the time back to when Wilkie, on his return to England, died near Gibraltar, and was buried in the sacred blue water close to Trafalgar ; and it strikingly reveals the depth of Turner's feeling, and his desire, without regard to buying or selling, to paint a monumental picture that might record his esteem for Wilkie's talent.

Shortly after Wilkie's death and burial at sea a conversation took place between Turner and his friend Jones.

' *T.* I suppose nobody will do anything to commemorate Wilkie ?

' *J.* I shall pay a humble tribute by making a drawing representing his funeral.

' *T.* How will you do it ?

' *J.* On the deck of the vessel, as it has been described to me by persons present, and at the time that Wilkie's body was lowered into the sea.

' *T.* Well, I will do it as it must have appeared off the coast.

' The picture by Turner and the drawing by Jones appeared in the ensuing Exhibition ; the former under the title of " Peace : Burial at Sea."

'Turner painted the sails of the steamer as black as he could make them, which occasioned a remonstrance from Stanfield, who justly thought the colour and effect untrue ; upon which Turner said, "I only wish I had any colour to make them blacker." It is very like him to have indicated mourning by this means, probably retaining some confused notions of the death of Ægeus and the black sails of the returning Theseus.'

The second story relates to that swarthily crimson picture ' The Fiery Furnace ;' and the dialogue between the same persons is worthy of notice, as proving Turner's willingness to be on the most social terms with his brethren.

'Turner asked his friend what he intended to paint for the ensuing Exhibition of 1832.

' *J.* The fiery furnace, with Shadrach, Meshach, and Abed-nego.

' *T.* A good subject ; I'll do it also ; what size will you do it ?

' *J.* Kit-cat.

' *T.* I'll paint it Kit-cat size too. Will you have an upright or a long picture?

' *J.* Upright.

' *T.* I'll paint it upright. What will you paint it on?

' *J.* On panel.

' *T.* I'll paint it on panel. Have you ordered a panel?

' *J.* No.

' *T.* Then order two, and tell the maker to send one of them to me ; but remember that, if I come into your room while you are painting that subject, you hide it instantly.

' The pictures were painted and exhibited in 1832. The members of the Academy were surprised to find that they had been executed with the most perfect sympathy.'

These narratives show that Turner was too great a man, and too original, to be afraid of, sometimes from idleness or caprice, borrowing from a friend. The humorous suddenness with which he seized, in the one instance, the notion of painting a picture in remembrance of Wilkie, and, in the other, the quickness with which he made up his mind to imitate his old crony, are eminently characteristic of him. So is the obstinacy with which he resisted Stanfield's advice to make the sails of the funeral vessel lighter. He knew what he wanted ; who should know better? He had the idea of grief to express ; and the expression of that idea was more important to him than the trivial technicalities of Art.

The picture in the Ellesmere Gallery was painted for the Marquis of Stafford as a rival to a Vandervelde. The same evening he received the order he went home, stretched a canvas, and had it all in dead colour before he left it. He worked with the greatest rapidity, commencing at four o'clock in the morning. ' I never saw him idle,' was his old housekeeper's declaration to Mr. Trimmer.

Burnet, the celebrated engraver of Wilkie's ' Blind Fiddler,' supplies the following instance of the strength of Turner's memory of natural effects:—

As he was once driving down with Mr. Woodburn to the latter gentleman's house at Hendon, a beautiful sunset burst forth in all its gorgeous but transitory pageantry. Turner asked if the carriage might be stopped, and remained some time in intense and silent contemplation of the sky. Some weeks afterwards Mr. Woodburn called at the Queen Anne Street Gallery, and saw the identical sky fixed on canvas. He instantly begged to have a landscape added to it. Turner refused the commission; he would not part with it. Wilkie used to call these studies his ' stock in trade.'

He entered one day the shop of Cobalt, the picture cleaner, when he had a fine Cuyp under his treatment. There was one corner where the golden brown, the sherry colour, was so transparent and luminous that you seemed to see deep down into it. Turner exclaimed, ' I would give a thousand pounds to have painted that !' This transparency, it is thought, can be obtained only on panel.

CHAPTER XXVII.

TURNER ON VARNISHING-DAYS.

My kind friend Mr. Wilkie Collins sends me an item of his boyish recollections of Turner.

Mr. Collins used to attend his father with his paint box, and make himself generally useful. On one of these occasions he remembers seeing Turner (not the more perfect in his balance for the brown sherry at the Academy lunch), seated on the top of a flight of steps, astride a box. There he sat a shabby Bacchus, nodding like a mandarin at his picture, which he, with a pendulum motion, now touched with his brush, and now receded from. Yet in spite of sherry, precarious seat, and old age, he went on shaping in some wonderful dream of colour; every touch meaning something, every pin's head of colour being a note in the chromatic scale.

That admirable, frank, and simple writer on Art the late Mr. Leslie also sketches Turner on these pleasant days. He says—

'Turner was very amusing on the varnishing, or rather the painting, days at the Academy. Singular as were his habits—for nobody knew where or how he lived—his nature was social, and at our lunch on those anniversaries he was the life of the table. The Academy has relinquished, very justly, a privilege for its own members which it could not extend to all exhibitors. But I believe, had the varnishing-days been abolished while Turner lived, it would almost have broken his heart. When such a measure was hinted to him, he said, "Then you will do away with the only social meetings we have, the only occasion on which we all come together in an easy, unrestrained manner. When we have no varnishing-days, we shall not know one another."'

In 1822, when Constable exhibited his 'Opening of Waterloo Bridge,' it was placed in the School of Painting, one of the small rooms at Somerset House. A sea piece by Turner was next to it—a grey picture, beautiful and true, but with no positive colour in any part of it.   Constable's picture seemed as if painted with liquid gold and silver, and Turner came several times into the room while he was heightening with vermilion and lake the decorations and flags of the city barges.   Turner stood behind him, looking from the ' Waterloo ' to his own picture; and, putting a round daub of red lead, somewhat bigger than a shilling, on his grey sea, went away without a word.   The intensity of the red lead, made more vivid by the coolness of his picture, caused even the vermilion and lake of Constable to look weak.   On Leslie entering the room just as Turner had left it, ' He has been here,' said Constable, ' and fired off a gun.' On the opposite wall was a rather warm picture, by Jones, of ' Shadrach, Meshach, and Abednego in the Furnace.' ' A coal,' said Cooper, ' has bounced across the room from Jones's picture, and set fire to Turner's sea.'   Turner did not come again into the room for a day and a half; and then, in the last moments that were allowed for painting, he glazed the scarlet seal he had put on his picture, and shaped it into a buoy.

This is a matchless story.   The fact was that Turner did not much like Constable, and was not going to let himself be checkmated.   And what a vast reach of knowledge it involved —this sudden alteration of the whole plan of his picture, and yet not spoiling it.   Constable, in secret, was most severe on Turner's pictures; and Leslie, his worshipper, acquired somewhat of the same prejudice: but his strong good sense soon mastered it.   Once Constable was pacing impatiently before a picture, the effect of which somehow or other did not please him.   It was true to rules, but still there was something wanting (perhaps a mere red cap, a blue apron, or a tree stem); yet what it was he could not for the life of him tell.   It was a line either too much or too little in the composition; evidently it was a speck of colour either redundant or deficient.   At that moment Turner entered.

' I say, Turner,' cried Constable, ' there is something wrong in this picture, and I cannot for the life of me tell what it is.   You give it a look.'   Turner looked at the picture steadily for a few moments, then seized a brush, and struck in a ripple of water in the foreground.   That was the secret; the picture was now perfect; the spell was completed. The fresh, untired eye of the great magician had detected the want at a glance.

CHAPTER XXVIII.

TURNER AS A CORRESPONDENT.

TURNER was notoriously a barred-up man, one who would come to the threshold of his mind and talk to you perhaps, but would by no means throw open the door and usher you as a welcome guest into the palace; yet he was cheerful and social among friends, loving them and beloved by them in turn. I introduce here a batch of letters, trifling enough, but valuable by reason of the scarcity of his letters. They convey a very fair notion of his epistolary manner in 1844. The first is addressed to Mrs. Carrick Moore, 38 Brooke Street, Grosvenor Square:—

'47 Queen Ann Street: Thursday, 18th inst.

'Dear Madam,—Mr. Jenkins will take the benefit of the Act himself, and will (without asking counsel's opinion thereon) appear before the court of Brook Street on Wednesday, the 24th instant, quarter before seven o'clock, and abide by the same.

'I have the honour to be for Mr. Jenkins's case.

'J. M. W. TURNER.'

'Dear Madam,—It is very, very, very unlucky for me that although dear Miss Rogers had induced me to hope for your kind invitation, it should be thwarted in any manner, and particularly by me, against my own inclination; but I have received a summons to attend the Council of the Royal Academy at half-past eight on Saturday evening, to consider on a case which friend Jones will tell you more about if you feel inclined to know why I am constrained to defer (I hope only in the present case) your kind and friendly feelings towards me.

'I have the honour to be, dear Madam,

'Yours most truly obliged,

'J. M. W. TURNER.

'To Mrs. CARRICK MOORE, 1 Saville Row.'

' J. M. W. Turner presents his compliments to Miss Moore, and requests her to make his thanks to Mrs. Moore for the very kind offer of forgiveness to him, which he will avail himself of with very great pleasure on Sunday next, at a quarter past six o'clock.

    ' February 3, 1840: 47 Queen Ann Street.
      ' To Miss H. MOORE.'

                         ' Wednesday, 20th, 1841.

' Dear Miss Moore,—I am very sorry to be engaged on the 29th, Friday, and therefore excluded from the happiness of being in Brook Street on that day.

' Very many thanks for the name of the church,[1] Redentori.
                    ' Yours truly,
                        ' J. M. W. TURNER.'

            ' 47 Queen Ann Street : December 9, 1841.

' Dear Madam,—I am truly sorry in being engaged Tuesday and Wednesday next (out of town), particularly sorry on present occasion of your kind invitations.
              ' Most sincerely,
                    ' J. M. W. TURNER.

' P.S.—Very low, indeed, for our loss in *dear* Chantrey.
' Mrs. CARRICK MOORE, Albemarle Street.'

            ' 47 Queen Ann Street : June 16, 1847.

' My dear Miss Moore,—Very glad to hear Mr. Moore is quite well again, and hope Mrs. Moore will now be better, being relieved from the anxiety attendant on the illness of Mr. Moore.

' Many thanks for the news of the whereabouts of the Jones's, and his piece of your letter sent me enclosed ! ! ! How we all grumble in search of happiness or benefits for others, yet find home at home.
              ' Yours truly,
                    ' J. M. W. TURNER.'

[1] ' He asked me to find the name of the church in Venice which contained three pictures by G. Bellini.'—M.

'J. M. W. Turner begs to present his respects to Miss Moore, and begs to say he is sorry an engagement for Christmas Day will prevent him offering his apology and contrition for his misdeeds and errors, regretted the more by him because he cannot but defer expressing his disappointment in person.

'Respects.

'To Miss H. MOORE.'

'Saturday, January 9, 1847.

'Dear Miss Moore,—Charming weather for the Arts ; they must be fine this weather of uniformity.

'Sorry to be likewise engaged on Sunday next, the 10th; best regards to Mr. and Mrs. Moore, yourself, and all the family.

'Yours truly,
'J. M. W. TURNER.

'Miss MOORE, 11 Grafton Street, Bond Street.'

'Tuesday night.

'Dear Miss Moore,—Jones must have pulled a feather from the wing of Time; so, with your permission, and Mr. and Mrs. Moore's, I will be selfish, and try to borrow it on Saturday; but if I should be beyond a quarter past six pray ask him for the loan (for me), fearing others are like.

'Yours truly,
'J. M. W. TURNER.

'Miss MOORE, 38 Brook Street, Grosvenor Square.'

In a playful strain runs the next :—

'Mr. Avalanche Jenkinson presents his thanks to Mrs. Moore for the kind invitation to Wonhams, which by some mischance he did not find till this morning, because " 'twas not in sight," and he feels his mishap the greater because the chance becomes the lesser, for the Exhibition closes to-day, the anniversary dinner on Monday, and the Spanish Fleet (*alias* pictures) will be removed from their present moorings to be scattered east, west, north, and south, like the Armada.

'Therefore Mr. Jenkinson fears he may be driven before the wind with his passport before the end of next week, but he begs to offer his sincere thanks, though with slender hope of being able to have the pleasure of being at Wonhams until his return from Switzerland. Mr. Jenkinson, with great respect, becoming to all enquiring friends,

'Most sincerely,
'J. M. W. TURNER.'

The explanation of the unusual designation is that Mrs. Carrick Moore used to call him Mr. Jenkinson, as being a common, insignificant name.

These letters, with their pithy brevity and cheerful jokes, are very characteristic of the man. How drolly he rejoices in the nickname of ' Mr. Avalanche Jenkinson,' and throws in here and there a clever thought or kind remembrance. 'The loss of *dear* Chantrey' shows how deeply his heart felt the loss of friends. Chantrey the ' gay ' and the ' good,' as he calls him in the next letter addressed to his friend Jones, he seems especially to have loved.

I here interpolate a letter dated as far back as 1830 (for these communications are too few to be worth arranging chronologically), written to his friend Jones when at Rome; in which he adverts with much feeling to the death of Lawrence and Dawe, and of his father, and to the contingency of his own ; and in which he is quietly sarcastic on the heartless custom of great people sending their empty carriages to public funerals, and hints at Academy intrigues. The conjunction of ' yellow' with Italy refers to the mustard tone of his later Italian pictures, which Chantrey seems good-naturedly to have joked him about :—

'London : February 1830.

' Dear Jones,—I delayed answering yours until the chance of this finding you in Rome, to give you some account of the dismal prospect of Academic affairs, and of the last sad cere-monies paid yesterday to departed talent gone to that bourne from whence no traveller returns. Alas ! only two short months

Sir Thomas followed the coffin of Dawe to the same place.
We then were his pall-bearers. Who will do the like for me,
or when, God only knows how soon. My poor father's death
proved a heavy blow upon me, and has been followed by others
of the same dark kind. However, it is something to feel that
gifted talent can be acknowledged by the many who yesterday
waded up to their knees in snow and muck to see the funeral
pomp swelled up by carriages of the great, without the persons
themselves. *Entre nous*, much could be written on this subject;
much has been in the papers daily of anecdotes, sayings, and
doings, contradictory and complex, and nothing certain, excepting that a great mass of property in the unfinished pictures will
cover more than demands. The portraits of the potentates are
to be exhibited, which will of course produce a large sum.
The drawings of the old masters are to be offered to his
Majesty in mass, then to the British Museum. Thomas
Campbell is to write Sir Thomas's life at the request of the
family, and a portrait of himself, painted lately and engraved,
for which great biddings have been already made. I wish I
had you by the button-hole, notwithstanding all your grumbling
about Italy and yellow. I could then tell more freely what has
occurred since your departure of combinations and concatena-
tions somewhat of the old kind, only more highly coloured, and
to my jaundiced eye not a whit more pure. . . . Chantrey is as
gay and as good as ever, ready to serve : he requests, for my
benefit, that you bottle up all the yellows which may be found
straying out of the right way; but what you may have told him
about the old masters which you did not tell me, I can't tell,
but we expected to hear a great deal from each other, but the
stormy brush of Tintoretto was only to make " the Notte " more
visible. May you be better in health and spirits.

' Adieu, adieu; faithfully yours,
' J. M. W. TURNER.'

Turner's letters to Mr. Ruskin I have not incorporated.
They are very brief, being chiefly friendly answers to invitations. In one of them he alludes bewailingly to the November
fog that stops his painting.

He was fond of Calcott's style of painting, his cool, sober manner; and Mr. Munro has a picture by him of a Dutch town closely after the manner of that artist. A letter from Turner to him is extant in which, in place of his full name, a wild duck (a mallard) is subscribed. Turner was fond of these little good-natured bits of fun, for his spirits were high, deep as were occasionally his fits of melancholy.

The following letters also claim a place here :—

'Dear Sir,—Herewith I submit for your inspection and observations my remarks on your picture of "Pope's Villa;" and, if you wish to make any alterations to the same, I will readily comply with your suggestions. I must beg the favour of you to return *this sheet* by the FIRST post, as I must print the account *immediately*. I am sorry I could not submit it to you previous to your leaving town. Pray inform me if you can make it convenient to oblige me with two or three drawings of Lindisfarne; they shall be engraved in the very best manner.

'Yours truly,
'J. BRITTON.

'November 16, 1811 : Tavistock Place.'

'Sir,—I rather lament that the remark which you read to me when I called in Tavistock Place is suppressed, for it es-poused the part of Elevated Landscape against the aspersio . . . . of map mak . . . . criticism ; but no doubt you are better acquainted with the nature of p . . . . tion, and mine is a mistaken zeal. As to remark, you will find a . . . alteration or colour in pencil. *Two* groups of sheep. *Two* fishermen occur too close ; baskets to entrap eels is not technical, being called eel pots; and making the willow tree the identical Pope's willow (*sic*) is rather strained. (?) Cannot you do it by allusion, and with deference. (?) Mellifluous lyre—seems to deny energy of thought—and let me ask one question. (?) Why say the Poet and Skophite are not often united? for if they are not, they . . . . ought to be : therefore the solitary instance given of Dodsley acts as a *cen*sure. The fourth and fifth line requires, perhaps, a note as to the state of the grotto, that gratfull posterity from age to age may repair what remains. If . . . . will in . . . . I would ask a little more to be added ; but, as it is, use your own discretion (?), and therefore will conclude cavaling any further with Dodsley's lines.

'Your most truly obed.

'J. M. W. TURNER.

' P.S.—Respecting Lindisfarne, we will have some conversation when I return ; and you may see the sketches which will best suit, and I must . . . . know what size, &c., you wish, before I can positively accept of your proposal, as one more I think . . . . bring into " Liber Studiorum." I had not time to return this by post yesterday, but hope that no delay has been experienced in the printing.'

The next two are addressed to Sir Thomas Lawrence :—

'July 1, 1825: Queen Ann Street.

' Dear Sir Thomas,—I have just now received a letter from the Lord Chamberlain's office, stating that the amount for my picture will be paid upon demand. I therefore feel the necessity of again asking you if you do authorise me in demanding the 600 guineas you mentioned ; or, if in your warmth for the service of the Arts, you did exceed (in your wishes) the terms proposed? Do, pray, have the goodness to tell me.

' In regard to the fees, I beg to renew my objections ; but do believe me to be,

'With true regard, yours most faithfully,

'J. M. W. TURNER.'

'Thursday morning.

'J. M. W. Turner presents his respects to Sir Thomas Lawrence, and he feels sorry his engagements will prevent him the pleasure of waiting upon Sir Thomas to-morrow morning ; he called in Russell Square to request he might be excused giving any opinion of the picture, in consequence of his having positively declined so doing to Mr. Wright, a particular friend of Sir W. Pilkington, on the part of Mr. Gray.'

CHAPTER XXIX.

TURNER'S VENETIAN PICTURES.

IT was from the great middle class, and not from the aristocracy of England, that Turner obtained patronage; and to that class, from which Shakespeare and our foremost men have sprung, English Art owes its present flourishing condition. It was only after the Reform Bill had passed both Houses that the national pictures were treated as national property, and rendered accessible to the people. Gradually, as the popular element began to leaven Parliament, and new intellect to quicken it, committees on Art subjects began to sit, and Art was considered as a national question; not as the luxury of the few, but as the birthright of the many. Then good modern pictures rapidly began to assert their claims over third-rate, doubtful, black old masters, and modern Art emerged from the deluge, thanks, not to the nobles of England, but to the great merchants of the North. From them Turner obtained his most generous commissions; for taste that had grown paralysed in drowsy country seats began now to bloom afresh amid factory smoke and the roar and buzz of wheels, amid cotton fluff, and in the vaporous Manchester engine rooms.

Mr. Henry M'Connel was, I believe, one of the first gentlemen to give him commissions for his later Venetian pictures. He was one of the earliest in the Northern district who had the originality of taste to admire and purchase Turner's works; and his collection became one of the best in the whole region. He generally gave commissions to artists direct. In this way he obtained that admirable picture, so full of pathos and interest, Landseer's 'There's Life in the Old Dog yet;' representing a Highland deer-hound that had fallen into a chasm in the ardour of his pursuit. He had also in his gallery Sir Charles Eastlake's 'Slave Market,' and Wilkie's 'Sancho Panza and his Mother at the Fountain,' not the happiest effort of that excellent artist.

Of one of Turner's small pictures of Venice, now in the Vernon Gallery, a pleasant story is told, which shows his good-nature and his love of practical joking. The picture in question, one of those so full of vivid reflections (not always quite true to fact), was hung next a view of Ghent by his old friend George Jones, R.A. On the varnishing-day at the Academy Turner, who delighted in these opportunities of working and chatting amongst comrades, said to his friend, 'Why, Joney, how blue your sky is! But I'll outblue you.' And immediately scrambling upon a box, chuckling audibly, he deepened the sky of his Venice with a scumble of ultramarine. 'I've done you now, Georgey,' he exclaimed, as he passed on to another picture. In his absence Jones, jocularly determined to baffle him, instantly set to work and painted the sky of Ghent a blank white, which, acting as a foil, made Turner's Venetian sky look preposterously blue. Turner laughed heartily, when he returned to his picture the next day, to find himself again checkmated. 'Well, Joney,' was the admission, 'you have done me now; but it must go;' and he went to work briskly and merrily at the water, ships, and fairy-like buildings, but altering the sky no more.

For this dream of Venice Mr. Vernon gave him two hundred guineas; and this price the painter evidently thought extravagant, for he was heard to say, 'If they will have scraps they must pay for them;' by which oracular utterance he meant, I presume, that the picture was only a fragment of an harmonious whole—a merry, fanciful sketch; and it is certain that he despised such studies in comparison with his earlier and more solid, though less poetical works.

In Leslie's Autobiography we have the following account of the first picture by Turner that went to America. He says—

'It fell to my lot to select the first of his pictures that went to America. Mr. James Lennox, of New York, who knew his pictures only from engravings, wished very much to possess one, and wrote to me to that effect. I replied that his rooms were full of unsold works, and I had no doubt he would part with one. Mr. Lennox expressed his willingness to give 500*l.*, and left the choice to me. I called on Turner, and asked if he would let a picture go to America. "No; they won't come up to the scratch!" I knew what he meant; for another American had offered him a low price for the "Téméraire." I told him a friend of mine would give 500*l.* for anything he would part with. His countenance brightened, and he said at once, "He may have that, or that, or that," pointing to three not small pictures. I chose a "Sunset View of Staffa," which I had admired more than most of his pictures from the time when it was first exhibited. It was in an old frame, but Turner would have a very handsome new one made for it. When it reached New York, Mr. Lennox was out of town, and we were in suspense some time about its reception. About a fortnight after its arrival he returned to New York, but only for an hour; and wrote to me, after a hasty first glance, to express his great disappointment. He said he could almost fancy the picture had sustained some damage on the voyage, it appeared to him so indistinct throughout. Still he did not doubt its being very fine, and he hoped to see its merits on further acquaintance; but, for the present, he could not write to Mr. Turner, as he could only state his present impression.

'Unfortunately, I met Turner at the Academy a night or two after I received this letter; and he asked me if I had heard from Mr. Lennox. I was obliged to say "Yes." "Well, and how does he like the picture?" "He thinks it indistinct." "You should tell him," he replied, "that indistinctness is my forte."

'In the meantime I had answered Mr. Lennox's letter, pointing out, as well as I could, the merits of the picture; and concluded by saying, "If, on a second view, it gains your estimation, it will assuredly gain more and more every time you look at it." Mr. Lennox, in reply, said, "You have exactly described what has taken place. I now admire the picture greatly, and I have brought one or two of my friends to see it as I do; but it will never be a favourite with the multitude. I can now write to Mr. Turner, and tell him conscientiously how much I am delighted with it."

'Mr. Lennox soon afterwards came to London, and bought

another picture of Turner's at a sale, and, I think, another of himself, and would have bought the "Téméraire," but Turner had then determined not to sell it.

'It was reported that Turner had declared his intention of being buried in his "Carthage," the picture now in the National Gallery. I was told that he said to Chantrey, "I have appointed you one of my executors. Will you promise to see me rolled up in it?" "Yes," said Chantrey, "and I promise you also that, as soon as you are buried, I will see you taken up and unrolled." This was very like Chantrey; and the story was so generally believed that, when Turner died, and Dean Milman heard he was to be buried in St. Paul's, he said, "I will not read the service over him if he is wrapped up in that picture." I have said that Turner often expressed himself happily. I remember that, when it was proposed that the new Houses of Parliament should be decorated with pictures, he exclaimed, "Painting can never show her nose in company with architecture without being snubbed."'

Some of Turner's enemies accuse him (very unjustly, as I hold) of latterly taking advantage of his name, and selling at large prices experiments that had cost him neither labour nor thought. I can see neither fraud nor injustice in Turner selling his later pictures. They were bought voluntarily by men with their eyes open. If they were slight, they were wonderful; they were what no one else could do; they were gorgeous ideals of colour and effect; they were efforts to carry Art beyond its hitherto known limits. Turner did not know that they were unworthy of him; his sight and brain were failing: but there was still the lifetime of a great man in each of them; they were what only such a man at the end of life could do: and after all, as even his enemies avow, the worst of them were of great interest; wonderful proofs of power, failing only because trying for impossibilities. They had a value as riddles, experiments, and prophecies.

'Turner's late peculiarities,' says Mr. Jones, 'in painting arose from the neglect of his earlier works by the public. If he had been encouraged at the time he painted the "Carthage," the "Tenth Plague," and the "Garden of the Hesperides," he would not have become eccentric in his art; his preference for the style of picture last named is proved by his leaving the pictures of the "Rise of Carthage" and the "Dutch Coast" to the National Gallery, on the condition of their being hung between the "Seaport" and the "Mill" by Claude Lorraine. His latter style, though possibly extravagant, was only an excess in representing the developments of Nature. He exaggerated all he saw, but the foundation was truth. The vivid and warm colouring of Nature he painted with the deepest reds and yellows; the greys he attempted to imitate with blues of too strong a tint; yet the whole was true in principle, both in general and in particular. Warm colour was never admitted where reason and experience denied its presence, and the same with cold colours; and, although such a gorgeous display of colour may not often be seen in Nature, yet it may be seen partially and in gradation.'

CHAPTER XXX.

THE BUSINESS MAN.

TURNER, who began life by painting sailors with pigtails in Dover Harbour, lived to see railways in full operation and to profit by them, having sold a small meadow of his at Twickenham for a very large sum to the South-Western Railway Company. The narrative of the negotiation, as related to me by Mr. Williams, who managed the matter for him, exhibits him to us in a new light. The sale happened after this wise:—

'In the autumn of 1848 the late Joseph Mallord William Turner, Esq., R.A., who was one of the copyholders of the Duke of Northumberland's manor of Isleworth Syon, in Middlesex, called on Thomas Williams, Esq., of Northumberland House, the steward of the manor; and after stating that he had received a notice from the South-Western Railway Company that they required, under the authority of Parliament, for their proposed line of railway from Richmond to Windsor, a few square yards of a small piece of copyhold meadow land in the parish of Twickenham and lying detached from his residence there, he asked Mr. Williams what he had better do in the matter, when the following conversation took place :—

'*Mr. Williams.* — As, no doubt, Mr. Turner, you have a solicitor, you should consult him, for there must be a negotiation to enter into with the Railway Company as to the price and costs of conveyance.

'*Mr. Turner.*—I have no solicitor, Mr. Williams; and, as I understand that the matter must come before you as steward of the manor, I request you to undertake the business for me; for, if I employ a solicitor, I shall incur double costs.

'*Mr. Williams.*—As you have no solicitor, I will act for you with pleasure ; and, as the land is so small in quantity and detached from your residence, I think the railway company should take the whole. If I am able to induce them to do so, what do you expect to get for it? Remember, it is only little more than half an acre.

'*Mr. Turner.*—As I shall be compelled to let them have the few yards they require, I shall be glad to sell the whole ; and I think I ought to get 300*l.* for it.

'Mr. Williams had the land, which had frontages to two roads, surveyed and valued as building-ground; and, after much discussion and many interviews with the surveyors, the price agreed upon for the whole of the half-acre of land was 550*l.* When Mr. Turner was told this by Mr. Williams, his eyes sparkled with delight, and he said, "A good price, indeed; more than I hoped for. Thank you very much. But I suppose I shall have some heavy costs and fees to pay out of it ? " Mr. Williams told him he thought he ought to give the surveyor he had employed a cheque for twenty guineas, for he had obtained a large price for him ; but he had stipulated that all the other costs for abstract of title, conveyance, and fees should be paid by the Railway Company. Mr. Turner readily gave Mr. Williams a cheque for the surveyor ; and, when the conveyance was ready for his signature, Mr. Williams accompanied Mr. Turner to the office of the solicitors of the Company (Messrs. Dalrymple and Drake, in Old Palace Yard), on December 28, 1848, when he executed the deed, and received a cheque for the purchase money, 550*l.*

'On getting into the street Mr. Turner observed, "Oh dear! This cheque is on Currie's, in Cornhill, and I must go there for the cash." Mr. Williams saved him that trouble by taking him to his bankers, Messrs. Drummond, Charing Cross, where he got the cheque cashed, and handed to him the bank-notes. Mr. Turner then shook Mr. Williams by the hand, thanked him again for his great success on his behalf, and took his way home. Mr. Williams saw Mr. Turner several times afterwards, but this transaction with the Railway Company was never alluded to.

'A few weeks afterwards Mr. Drake, the solicitor of the Railway Company, whom Mr. Turner saw when he executed the conveyance, requested Mr. Williams to ask Mr. Turner's permission to shew him a picture he had purchased as a Turner. When Mr. Williams mentioned this request to Mr. Turner, he replied, "No, Mr. Williams; certainly not. If Mr. Drake has purchased a Turner, he ought to know it as a Turner. I was once silly enough to look at a picture that I was told had been painted by me, and I found myself soon after stuck up in a witness box, giving evidence about it. I then said, I'll never be so silly again."'

The narrative, which is admirable for its business-like clearness, does not, it will be seen, fail to record how Turner's eyes sparkled when he heard of the large price that had been obtained for him; but, sordid as many represented him to be, we do not find him hesitating for a moment to pay the surveyor the handsome sum of twenty guineas, at Mr. Williams's suggestion. Whether he ought also to have given Mr. Williams more than mere barren thanks, depends entirely on the relative position of the two men. No doubt it gave him great pain so soon afterwards to have to refuse Mr. Williams a favour; but Turner was not the man to break through a principle on any mere impulse of courtesy.

The following letter of 1822 doubtless refers to a negotiation with Hurst and Robinson, upon which a celebrated anecdote is based. It is an answer to a proposition to engrave four of his pictures, which might be executed in rivalry of Wilson and Woollett's greatest efforts; and it reveals his ambition to excel Wilson, his early model. It will be noted how severe, business-like, and guarded he is in his arrangements (he had had many rude lessons, I have no doubt), and how he cautiously excepts the 'Carthage' picture from the list:—

'J. Robinson, Esq.,
'90 Cheapside,
'Corner of Ironmonger Lane.

'June 28, 1822, Friday morning.

'My dear Sir,—In the conversation of yesterday respecting prints, you said that if I would have engraved a plate worthy of any of my pictures, that you would take 500 impressions, provided none were sold to any other person for two years. If you really meant the said offer for me to think of, it appears to me that my scheme, which I mentioned to you in confidence, would hold—viz. four subjects to bear up with, the "Niobe," "Ceyx," "Cyledon," and "Phaeton" (in engraving as specimens of the power of the British school). Whether we can in the present day contend with such powerful antagonists as Wilson and Woollett would be at least tried by size, security against risk, and some remuneration for the time of painting. The pictures of ultimate sale I shall be content with; to succeed would perhaps form another epoch in the English school ; and, if we fall, we fall by contending with giant strength.

'If the "Hannibal," or the "Morning of the Chase," be taken, the first plate would stand thus:—

1. Plate, in two years.
2. Picture to be painted, three years.
3. Ditto and two years longer, fourth.
4. Ditto and ditto—five years the four plates.

Or if all the pictures are painted, if thought more desirable, then take the pictures now done, "Carthage" picture excepted ; one year more must be added, making six years, which allows one year for painting each picture, and two to engrave it, and put into the hands of different engravers immediately. Mr. Pye to engrave one or more if your arrangement with him would not be interrupted thereby, or the general arrangements of time broken in upon, for six years added to forty-five is not a trifle.

> 'Yours most truly,
> ' J. M. W. TURNER.

'P.S.—This is *private*; if not to be thought of, burn it immediately, and only mention on July 1 the receipt of the said note.'

Hurst and Robinson were the successors of the famous Alderman Boydell, the originator of the Shakespeare Gallery. Desirous of imitating their predecessor in the publication of works of importance, and making great ventures for large profit and wide fame, they waited on Turner to buy his two celebrated pictures of the 'Rise' and the 'Fall of Carthage.' His price was soon ascertained. 'One thousand guineas each; not a farthing less.' Mr. Robinson, parrying the thrust with the ordinary tradesman's skill of fence, without any notion of the demand being a serious one, blandly suggested, 'Say eight hundred guineas each, Mr. Turner.'

The painter turned round upon him like a hurt lion; his clear grey eyes flashed with fury; and his stature acquired increase from the indignation of his soul. Was he going to have his masterpieces, that surpassed Claude, higgled for by a printseller? 'No,' he cried; 'I'd rather keep them for my winding-sheet;' and he meant it, too; for the bitter heats and chills of life had tempered that soul of his into stuff harder than steel. But, say his malignant detractors what they may, could a man who was a mere sordid miser have found it in his heart to spurn a cheque for 1,600 guineas?

According to Mr. Alaric Watts, the larger plates from his works, albeit of unrivalled beauty as works of Art, were productive of small profit to their publishers. Indeed, the series of 'Views in England and Wales,' issued in conjunction with Mr. Charles Heath, yielded 'so Flemish a balance of profit' as to compel its discontinuance at the twenty-fourth part in 1838, when it became necessary to sell off the stock and copper plates in order to adjust the accounts. The whole property accordingly was submitted to Mr. Bohn for 3,000*l.*; but, his offer being 200*l.* below that sum, it was entrusted to Messrs. Southgate for sale by auction. On the day appointed for the sale, to the vexation of many who had come prepared to purchase portions of it, Turner stepped in and bought it privately, at the reserved price of 3,000*l.*; immediately after which he walked up to the well-known bibliopole and said, ' So, sir, you were going to buy my " England and Wales," to sell cheap, I suppose—make umbrella prints of them, eh? But I have taken care of that. No more of my plates shall be worn to shadows.' Upon Mr. Bohn representing that his object was the printed stock—which was very large— rather than the copper plates, ' Oh ! very well,' was the reply. ' I don't want the stock; I only want to keep the coppers out of your clutches. So, if you like to buy the stock, come and breakfast with me to-morrow, and we will see if we can deal.' When Mr. Bohn presented himself at nine o'clock the next morning, the artist, giving no thought to the breakfast to which he had invited, unceremoniously enquired, ' Well, sir, what have you to say?' ' I have come to treat with you for the stock of your " England and Wales," ' was the answer. ' Well, what will you give?' was the sternly definite demand. It was then explained that in the course of the previous negotiation the coppers and copyright had been valued at 500*l.*; so that 2,500*l.*, the balance remaining after deduction of that sum, would be the amount to be handed over to the painter. ' Pooh!' was the contemptuous reply; ' I must have 3,000*l.*, and keep my coppers; else good morning to you;' and thus the interview closed.

Mr. Alaric Watts tells several good stories to shew what a repugnance Turner had to part with money. Thus he gave a Margate boatman one of his best sea sketches rather than pay him in hard cash ; and the old hall-porter of Mr. Walter Fawkes, of Farnley Hall, who kept the village alehouse, was the recipient of a drawing of great value in liquidation of a trifling score of some four or five pounds. The mode in which discovery was made of the latter transaction was not a little curious. On retiring from Mr. Fawkes's service to take his father's post at the rural house of entertainment, the man was desirous of purchasing the old hall-chair in which he had been wont to sit for so many years ; and, being allowed to appraise it himself at four pounds, he offered, instead of cash, the capital drawing which his father had accepted from Turner in acquittance of his bill.

CHAPTER XXXI.

TURNER AND CHANTREY.

THE good-natured, jovial sculptor had a boundless admiration for Turner's genius ; no one at the time better appreciated the mental scope of the artist. His lance was ever in rest to tilt against his maligners ; hydras that seemed to sprout out fresh tongues the faster the club fell and the brand scarred. Yet he was of the old dark school of Art, and thought Turner a heretic for venturing out of the glorious twilight region in his 'Carthage,' 'The Tenth Plague,' and 'Crossing the Brook'— the first two epics in themselves, and the last worth all the pseudo-pastoral poetry written from the time of Theocritus to that of Shenstone. He would never, however, allow anyone in his hearing to disparage his friend's imagination ; he could not endure the sneers of those who, alive only to faults, were blind to merits. The gorgeous colours he admired, though he did not altogether approve them; the breadth of air he would allow no one to gainsay. Turner's wonderful appreciation of forms, his perfect chiaroscuro, and the learning and grace with which he varied the lines of his compositions ; his mountains, skies, water, trees, ships, and buildings ; all these commanded his warmest praise. In these respects he thought no one was more profound in the knowledge of Art than Turner. Chantrey estimated him as a poetic genius of the highest rank ; in depicting light and atmosphere, as the greatest of past or present painters; perhaps unsurpassable as a consummate arranger of lines in his landscape and architectural compositions. He was well assured that his effects were the result not merely of observation and selection, but of long thought and treasured learning.

Chantrey and Turner, who both of them liked Lord Egremont's rough, hearty manner and kind nature, often met at Petworth ; when Turner would rise early and get all his work done before the other guests were well about ; so that, like Sir Walter Scott, he could idle the rest of the afternoon as he chose, to the astonishment of those who did not know his mode. When Turner was executing a series of landscapes for the dining-room Chantrey was there. The painter, who, besides being reserved and loving quiet, had Art secrets of his own, worked always with his door locked, and no one but the master of the house was ever admitted. The sculptor, resenting this seclusion, with mischievous good-humour determined to play Turner a trick ; and accordingly one day, when all was still in the house, he paced down the corridor, imitating Lord Egremont's peculiar step and cough, and, arrived at the mysterious door, gave two distinct sharp raps, which were his Lordship's signal for admittance ; when Turner instantly shuffled up, the key turned, and Chantrey slipped in before the mistake could be discovered. This dexterous feat of Chantrey's became a standing joke at Petworth and at Academy meetings.

In the years 1828 and 1837 the two were on the same Royal Academy Council. There they were in their element, for, though one was jovial and the other reserved, they both had humour and enjoyed each other's jokes ; they understood and appreciated each other. Chantrey liked Turner's pictures, and Turner liked Chantrey's sculpture. Both were of humble origin, and neither was ashamed of the clay of which he was made ; not even a herald's imagination could invent pedigrees for the London barber or the small Hallamshire yeoman. Yet Chantrey did not spare his friend. He made free of his pictures, and joked about all their eccentricities, whether of form or of colour. It is not the joke, it is the manner that wounds ; it is not the jest of a friend that stings, it is the visible intention to give pain that barbs the word. Before Turner's face Chantrey waved the jester's harmless bladder of peas ; when his back was turned he drew the sword to guard his absent friend, and spoke in raptures of the pictures he had just been parodying.

The two friends must have had many subjects in common on which to talk. Chantrey was also a landscape artist; and both were enthusiastic disciples of Izaak Walton; and Turner no doubt derived considerable benefit from his friend's knowledge of geology.

Turner hated plagiarism. At one of the councils a drawing of 'The Falls of Terni' came under notice. Turner declared fiercely that it was a copy of his own drawing. 'Swear to it; sure of it; sure of it.' (No one could represent the dead, resistless fall of a great body of water like Turner. Harding, among others, imitated this very Terni : Mr. Munro, I think, has the drawing.) The secretary, benevolently anxious to excuse the imitator, suggested, 'Perhaps, Mr. Turner, the artist only selected the same spot as you did. This would account for a resemblance that may after all be mere chance.' 'No, no, Howard,' was Chantrey's observation; 'if the artist had really been there, then you might be sure his drawing would not be like Turner's.' He meant that Turner was not a mere copying-machine; but a selector, reviser, readjuster of Nature— elevating what was important, and depressing what was detrimental or insignificant; throwing in effect, yet never forgetting the prime value of truth and likeness.

On one of those pleasant varnishing-days of old the weather was very raw and cold, Chantrey, brimming over with fun as usual, went up with his beaming red face to a picture of Turner's which was specially luminous with orange chrome. Pretending to warm his hands at it, as at a fire, the sculptor said, 'Why, Turner, this is the only comfortable place in the room. By-the-bye, is it true, as I have heard, that you've got a commission at last to paint a picture for the Sun Fire Office?' Turner would have chewed the cud of this joke for many a long day after his old-fashioned, chuckling manner.

Chantrey's jokes with him on varnishing-days were innumerable. He was as full of tricks and mischief as when, as a boy, he had carried the milk cans to market. Once, when there was a report that the great artist was using some water-colour to tone his picture of 'Cologne,' Chantrey, either to test the fact, or probably disbelieving the story, went up to the picture, and, wetting his finger, drew a great school-boy cross on the sail of one of the vessels. To his horror, surprise, and bitter regret, he found that he had removed so many inches of glazing. Turner, however, was not even ruffled ; he laughed heartily at the sculptor's temerity, and at once repaired the mischief.

During Turner's generally solitary rambles on the Continent, Chantrey used to feel great anxiety for his absent friend's health and safety, as his intended route was seldom known to any-one, and no one knew the day he would return. To Jones, Shee, Chantrey, and other friends it was always a great relief when he got back.

On the morning of November 26, 1841, the day after Chantrey died very suddenly at his house, No. 13 Eccleston Street, Pimlico, Turner called, expecting to find his friend Jones in the chamber of death. He did find him there ; but he could not speak ; he only wrung his hand with affectionate, almost passionate vehemence, and rushed out of the house without uttering a word.

> The grief that will not speak
> Whispers the o'erfraught heart and bids it break.

Was this a man without heart and without affections, the mere money-grubber and sordid Harpagon ?

CHAPTER XXXII.

THIRST FOR KNOWLEDGE IN OLD AGE.

ONE of the most admirable points in Turner's mind was that it never grew old. Far from petrifying into unreceptive fixity, it maintained to the last its thirst for knowledge, and was ready to grow with the world's growth. Like Reynolds, Turner continued to experiment without cessation. A striking proof of this continuous mental development is supplied by the interest he took in the science of optics and in the science of photography. Mr. Mayall, of Regent Street, kindly furnishes me with an interesting account :—

'Turner's visits to my *atelier* were in 1847, '48, and '49. I took several admirable daguerreotype portraits of him, one in the act of reading ; a position rather favourable for him on account of his weak eyes and their being rather bloodshot. I recollect one of these portraits was presented to a lady who accompanied him. My first interviews with him were rather mysterious ; he either did state, or at least led me to believe, that he was a Master in Chancery, and his subsequent visits and conversation rather confirmed this idea. At first he was very desirous of trying curious effects of light let in on the figure from a high position, and he himself sat for the studies. He was very much pleased with a figure study I had just completed of " This Mortal must put on Immortality;" he wished to bring a lady to try something of the kind himself. This was in 1847 ; and I believe he did fix a day for that purpose. However, it happened to be a November fog, and I could not work. He stayed with me some three hours, talking about light and its curious effects on films of prepared silver. He expressed a wish to see the spectral image copied, and asked me if I had ever repeated Mrs. Somerville's experiment of magnetising a needle in the rays of the spectrum. I told him I had.

'I was not then aware that the inquisitive old man was Turner the painter. At the same time I was much impressed with his inquisitive disposition, and I carefully explained to him all I then knew of the operation of light on iodised silver plates. He came again and again, always with some new notion about light. He wished me to copy my views of Niagara—then a novelty in London—and enquired of me about the effect of the rainbow spanning the great falls. I was fortunate in having seized one of these fleeting shadows when I was there, and I showed it to him. He wished to buy the plate. At that time I was not very anxious to sell them. I told him I had made a copy for Sir John Herschel, and with that exception did not intend to part with a copy. He told me he should like to see Niagara, as it was the greatest wonder in Nature ; he was never tired of my descriptions of it. In short, he had come so often, and in such an unobtrusive manner, that he had come to be regarded by all my people as "our Mr. Turner."

'This went on through 1848, till one evening I met him at the soirée of the Royal Society ; I think it was early in May 1849. He shook me by the hand very cordially, and fell into his old topic of the spectrum. Some one came up to me and asked if I knew Mr. Turner ; I answered I had had that pleasure some time. "Yes," said my informant, rather significantly ; "but do you know that he is *the* Turner?" I was rather surprised, I must confess ; and later on in the evening I encountered him again, and fell into conversation on our old topic. I ventured to suggest to him the value of such studies for his own pursuits, and at once offered to conduct any experiments for him he might require, and, in fact, to give up some time to work out his ideas about the treatment of light and shade. I parted with him on the understanding that he would call on me ; however, he never did call again, nor did I ever see him again.

'I recollected putting aside a rather curious head of him in profile ; and, you may be sure, on the following morning after this interview I lost no time in looking up the portrait, which, I regret to say, one of my assistants had without my orders effaced. I am almost certain you will be able to trace some of the daguerreotypes of him, for I made at least four, for which he paid me ; and some I rubbed out where we had tried the effect of a sharp, narrow cross light, in which some parts of the face were left in strong shadow.

'I need not add that at that time I was a struggling artist, much devoted to improving my art, and had just bought a large lens in Paris, six inches in diameter. I let Turner look through it, and the expressions of surprise and admiration were such that I ought at once to have known him in his true character. However, he was very kind to me, and by some sort of innuendo he kept up his Mastership in Chancery so well that I did not. He sent me many patrons. I used to hear about him almost daily. When somewhat desponding of my success one day, I told him London was too large for a man with slender means to get along. He sharply turned round and said, " No, no ; you are sure to succeed ; only wait. You are a young man yet. I began life with little, and you see I am now very comfortable." " Yes," I replied ; " and if I were on the same side of Chancery you are, perhaps I might be comfortable also." I was at that time fighting the battle of the patent rights of the daguerreotype. He smiled and said, "You'll come out all right ; never fear." My recollection now is that he was very kind and affable to me, rather taciturn, but very observant and curious. He would never allow me to stop working when he came, but would loiter and watch me polish the plates and prepare them, and take much interest in the result of my labours.

' I recollect Mr. Spence, the naturalist, sitting to me, and was struck at the time with the resemblance of the two heads. I mentioned this to Turner, and I showed him the portrait of Mr. Spence. Mr. Spence was stouter. Turner stooped very much, and always looked down. He had a trick of putting his hand into his coat pocket, and of muttering to himself.

' Whatever others may have said of his parsimonious habits, I cannot recollect one act of his that would lead me to infer he was other than a liberal, kind-hearted old gentleman.'

When Mr. Mayall, whose photographic fame now is European, made his first start in a small shop in the Strand, the wonderful science was uncertain in its results, and few there were who could at that time foresee the influence it would exercise over Art. One day, however, during the moral epidemic of the railway mania, when Mr. Hudson ruled England, and all the world, from the countess to the costermonger, knelt down and laid their heads on the pavement of Capel Court in passionate idolatry of the golden calf, at Mr. Mayall's door hung photographs intended to satirise the national folly. On one side there was a Stock Exchange man, radiant at shares being at a premium ; on the other was the same man in maniacal despair at the Great Bubbleton Railway shares falling down to nothing. These pictures (almost the earliest attempts to make photography tell a story) attracted crowds; and among them Turner. So interested was he, indeed, that he came into the shop, and asked to see the gentleman who designed them. After this he came so often that an Abernethy chair was habitually placed for him, so that he might watch Mr. Mayall without interrupting him at work. He took great interest in all effects of light, and repeatedly sat for his portrait in all sorts of Rembrandtic positions.

Turner at this time painted in whichever room of his house suited the season of the year and the weather. The gallery was very cold ; and from want of warmth several of the valuable prints, which were rolled up in great brown paper bundles, were blotted and spoiled by the damp. The house looked as if it had been deserted for fifty years ; and the area was a sort of House of Parliament for all the cats in the neighbourhood.

Mr. Trimmer tells me that among Turner's sketches and drawings were many which he knew to be by other hands, for Turner was a great collector of topographical sketches ; and he well remembers a relation of his—a naval officer—giving Turner some sketches of Gibraltar.

I have heard people, friends of Turner, assert that Mr. Ruskin's book killed him, by increasing his fame, leading him more into society, and so altering his social habits. Thus the poet Clare was driven mad entirely by late London hours, and the wear and tear of incessant frivolous parties. Latterly Turner was always to be seen between ten and eleven at the Athenæum Club, discussing his half-pint of sherry. As his health failed he became most talkative after his wine, and rather dogmatic. In earlier days he was always shy, especially before ladies ; but if thoroughly at his ease and once roused, or in a vein of joking, he could be very social and amusing. He was somewhat anxious to obtain a repute for general knowledge, and was a reader of all the best books and reviews of the day. The ' Edinburgh,' then in the height of its fame, was one of his special favourites.

At one time the 'Yorkshire Stingo' was his nocturnal resort ; but he abandoned it on being recognised there by a friend. Little did the convivial frequenters of that hostelry suspect who was the old man that took up his station in the corner. A friend of mine remembers often seeing him rather the worse for grog at Offley's, in Henrietta Street, when Macready was bringing out the 'Tempest.' Turner, who at that time regularly attended the theatre, used to be most indistinctly voluble on the subject of Shakespeare and of Macready's scenic effects.

CHAPTER XXXIII.

THE ARTISTS' BENEVOLENT FUND.

MR. DAVID ROBERTS, one of Turner's oldest friends, writes—

'I think it must have been in the year 1823 or 1824 that, being called on to attend a meeting of the stewards of the Artists' General Benevolent Fund at the "Crown and Anchor" in the Strand, I first saw Turner ; and my first impression, thus obtained, was anything but what I had in my imagination formed of this great painter. I had come from the Theatre Royal, Edinburgh, to Drury Lane, and my friend Stanfield and myself, at that time young men, were trying our best to improve upon the great scene-painters, of whom we were the successors at Old Drury. De Loutherbourg and Greenwood we knew only by fame ; but the mighty painter of the day that all spoke of, and whose works were the all-in-all to every young artist, was TURNER, at Somerset House. The first works thought of by such as ourselves were Turner's. When Calcott exhibited his magnificent " Now for the Painter Rope," the following year brought out Turner's " *Now for the Painter.*" His works had been engraved by the greatest engravers of the day—George and William Cooke, John Pye, Edward Goodall, Miller of Edinburgh, and many others. As they were seated round a table covered with green baize—of course, with the exception of my friend whom I accompanied, John Wilson, all to me were strangers—a little square-built man came in, to whom all paid respect. The business having begun, he joined in the conversation, and made some weak attempts at wit—at least I thought so, for no one seemed to laugh at his jokes but himself ! So I asked who this very facetious little man was, and my astonishment on being told that it was "The Great Turner" (without meaning a pun) turned my head.'

Mr. Roberts has unconsciously anticipated by a year or two the celebrated picture 'Now for the Painter,' which was not exhibited till 1827. In 1824 Turner exhibited nothing at the Academy; and in the previous year appeared his 'Bay of Baiæ.'

It was in connection with the Artists' General Benevolent Institution, which he had himself helped to found, that Turner's tenderness shone out most conspicuously. But he was always for saving, for hoarding and scraping for future, even though they might be remote, emergencies. He was always for collecting and storing a treasure with which magnificent deeds of charity were to be done. He was a patient man, and looked forward to schemes of benevolence of wide scope. But meanwhile, complained some, there are the widows and orphans of poor artists starving. The necessities of the present are unprovided for, and postponed to the claims of the future. This saving for future charity, involving as it does present neglect, is too stoical for us; the groans of the poor reach our ears and rack our hearts; let us open the granary of our benevolence, and not keep heaping up corn against famines that may never arrive. Turner, however, was inflexible. With the increase of age waxed his wilfulness. He became proud, and expected submission and deference to his views, more especially since he was one of the founders. He could not help accumulating; it was in his blood. He had amassed when it was necessary; now he amassed because he did not know how to spend. He had for years saved for himself on principle; he saved now for others from habit.

The younger men were bent, with all respect to Turner, upon overthrowing this principle; they resolved to give their money nearly all away in contributions. But Turner was treasurer, and sternly refused to relax his hold. While he was at the door of the money room, no one could hope to effect an entrance save over his prostrate body. There was a growling conflict, but Turner was not to be moved. His opponents were equally obstinate, for they felt they combated for a principle. At length, with the dogged tenacity to his own views eminently characteristic of himself, he abandoned the Society for ever. In vain did Mr. Cockerell, one of the opposition, go to Queen Anne Street to discuss the matter with him. He would hardly see him; he growled; he would not relent even when he was warned 'that he would one day have to answer to the widows and orphans to whom he had refused bread.' As far as I can understand, Turner all but showed his expostulator the door; so sore and indignant was he at what I dare say he denounced as the ingratitude of the Society to himself personally. The Society then, leaving the implacable Achilles, proceeded on their own way, and that way prospered; Mr. Hardwicke, one of the leaders of the opposition, becoming treasurer under Mr. Mann. The subscriptions thereupon increased rapidly, insomuch that from 300*l.* given away in 1830, the Society advanced until in 1861 they distributed 1,050*l.* Even their opponents acknowledged its progress, and their rivals of the Literary Fund compared it most favourably, both as to economy and as to the general result of its management, with their own association.

Upon this subject of Turner's angry secession from a charity he had helped to found Mr. Roberts represents—

'To Turner we owe the founding and carrying out of this admirable charity, the Artists' General Benevolent Fund. Unfortunately, his views respecting its management differed from those of other directors, particularly from those of one of them, who afterwards became its leader, Mr. Andrew Robertson, the miniature painter. Turner was for hoarding its funds, and distributing but a small part yearly to its charity; the other directors wished to relieve the applicants as they required. That they were right is proved by the interest taken in its prosperity at the present day. Turner thought otherwise, and seceded from it; still he deserves the honour of having originated it. The other fund, only granting relief to those who subscribed and were members, was in reality but a benefit fund for its own members. What Turner's views may have been, had his wish been complied with by his co-directors, it is difficult now to say; but it is just possible that, instead of the *muddle*

A A 2

made at last with his large means, he might have left all to the benevolent purpose of providing for his less fortunate brethren.'

If Turner really entertained this generous project, it would serve to excuse his somewhat haughty efforts to control the wishes of the majority.

In 1809 the melancholy poverty of Mr. Tagg, a once well-known etcher, was the occasion for a meeting of artists at the Gray's Inn Coffee House; and in 1810 was founded the Artists' Joint Stock Fund, Mr. Mulready being a prominent worker in the charitable cause. Two separate funds were raised; the Benevolent and the Joint Stock; with the object of granting annuities to members who became superannuated, or were unable to work from protracted illness. A small annual payment secured membership, and was supplemented by a voluntary subscription made by some.

In 1812, on the death of Mr. Pether, several of the Joint Stock Society members tried to alienate the money of the Benevolent Fund by devoting it to purposes of general charity, instead of confining it to the relief of members only; and in 1827 a Charter of Incorporation was obtained, by which the Annuity Fund and the Benevolent Fund were united.

In 1825 was entertained a proposal made by Mr. John Pye to publish engravings for the benefit of the Artists' Fund; and accordingly, Mr. Mulready having obtained the King's permission to have his celebrated picture of the 'Wolf and Lamb' engraved, the task was entrusted to Mr. J. W. Robinson, and the result was a profit of about 903*l.*

In 1814 the disaffected members, who desired to devote the funds to purposes of general charity without any regard to encouraging self-respect and prudence, started the Artists' General Benevolent Institution.

CHAPTER XXXIV.

TWILIGHT.

TURNER was not an exhibiter at the Royal Academy Exhibition of 1851. This was a sign of declining health which his friends did not fail to notice with alarm. He came, however, to the private view, when those who saw him thought him breaking up fast. It was evident that he could not live the year out. He was shaky; he was feeble; no longer the sturdy, dogged, strange being of old, he was now the broken, decrepit old man.

Many of the Academicians knew that Turner latterly had another home besides the murky house in Queen Anne Street; but they did not dare openly to express their curiosity. He was evidently taken more care of; he was better dressed; he was more cleanly and tidy than in former years; he even ventured on a red velvet waistcoat, and his linen had more daylight whiteness about it than it had had for years.

His prolonged absence from the Academy meetings, at which he had hitherto been so regular an attendant, alarming his friends, one of them, Mr. David Roberts, wrote to Queen Anne Street, expressing the great regret of his brethren thereat, and begging him, if he was ill and could not attend, to let him know, in order that he might come and see him; adding the assurance that he might rely with confidence on the secret of his place of residence being unrevealed, if he desired it not to be known. To this communication Turner did not reply; but some two weeks after he appeared at Mr. Roberts's studio in Fitzroy Square, sadly broken and ailing. Evidently he was deeply moved by the letter his friend had written, for he said, 'You must not ask me; but, whenever I come to town, I will always come to see you.' 'I tried to cheer him up,' says Mr. Roberts, 'but he laid his hand upon his heart and replied, " No, no; there is something here which is all wrong." As he stood by the table in my painting-room, I could not help looking attentively at him, peering in his face, for the small eye was as brilliant as that of a child, and unlike the glazed and "lack-lustre eye" of age. This was my last look. The rest is soon told. None of his friends had seen him for months ; indeed, I believe I was the last, together with my friend George Jones, who I afterwards learnt had that day also called on him.'

Once only after this did he visit his friend. It was some two months before his death, which occurred in December of the same year.

There was one, however, who mourned and wondered at Turner's absence from Queen Anne Street far more than any of his other friends could have deplored and speculated upon his withdrawal from their circle ; and that was poor Mrs. Danby—the guardian of his murky house, the servant who had for so many long years of rain and sunshine been faithful to his interests. She was deeply troubled by Turner's mysterious disappearance; she was sure he was ill, but yet knew not how to find him amid the labyrinths of London. At last, one day, as she was brushing an old coat of his, in turning out a pocket she found and pounced upon a letter addressed to him by a friend who lived at Chelsea. There, then, she felt sure he must be ; and it was her duty to sally forth and discover him.

Attended by a companion as aged and infirm as herself, the poor old lady, whose uneasiness now was unfortunately aggravated by the addition of jealousy, braced herself up to the execution of her troublesome mission. Whatever might have been the difficulties attending their progress thither, they contrived to reach the cottage by the river-side. The adjoining cottage they found to be devoted to the sale of light refreshments, one of which was the conventional ginger-beer ; and the outlay of twopence enabled them to hold a gossip with the proprietor, in the course of which a little judicious interrogation soon satisfied them that the lady and the old gentleman next door must be the great painter and his landlady. They were grieved, however, to learn that the gentleman had been very unwell, and that he had seldom been out for the last two months. Hereupon they made all possible haste home, and Mrs. Danby lost

ROOM IN WHICH TURNER DIED, AT CHELSEA.

no time in communicating her information to a relative and to
Mr. Harpur, who subsequently was one of the executors. This
gentleman hastened to find out the cottage at Chelsea, but he
was only in time to see Turner fast sinking. On the next day
he was no more.

Some time before this, feeling himself to be dangerously ill,
Turner had sent for a well-known doctor from Margate whom
he had previously employed, and in whose skill he reposed
implicit confidence. The sick man, who had once declared
that he would give all his money if he could but be twenty once
again, watched the physician's face with eager anxiety. When
he was told that death was near, 'Go down-stairs,' he exclaimed ;
'take a glass of sherry, and then look at me again.' The doctor
did as he was bidden ; but he could not alter his judgment.
Turner, however, would not believe that the awful change was
so nigh. He had no religious hope, I am afraid, to cheer him
at that hour. He must then have realised the miserable insuf-
ficiency of all his fame and wealth ; and the dark dread of anni-
hilation must have overpowered the heart of one who had done
so much to make men love God's beautiful world.

On that final day—I believe within an hour of his death—
his landlady wheeled his chair to the window, to enable him
to look upon the sunshine in which he delighted so much,
mantling the river and illuminating the sails of the passing boats.

Of Turner's reasons for thus secreting himself at Chelsea
like a runaway bankrupt numerous explanations have been
advanced ; but the most popular version of the matter is as
follows :—

Requiring change of air for his health, Turner went to Chelsea in search of lodgings. These he found at a moderate cost
at a little cottage not far from the present Cremorne pier, which
looked on the river, and had a railed-in roof, from which he
could observe sky effects. The landlady, seeing a little, thick-
set, shabby man, asked him for 'reference ;' which demand
provoked the angry retort, 'My good woman, I'll buy the house
outright.' Next she proposed to draw up an agreement ;
which he parried by exhibiting a roll of bank-notes, and
offering to pay in advance. This was most satisfactory

to his mystery-loving nature. Another difficulty, however, awaited him. The landlady wanted her proposed lodger's name; 'in case, sir, any gentleman should call, you know.' The requisition was a searching one. 'Name?' was the puzzled exclamation, repeated by way of obtaining relief; 'what is *your* name?' 'My name is Mrs. Booth.' 'Then, I'm Mr. Booth;' and by that name Turner was known there. But, unfortunately for the story, he did not carry about rolls of bank-notes which he could flourish. All that was found in his pockets after his death was a solitary half-crown—black from its long seclusion in a grimy, unvisited pocket.

In the streets of Chelsea, and all along the shore of the Thames, Turner was known to the street boys as 'Puggy Booth,' and by the small tradesmen he was designated 'Admiral Booth;' for the popular notion was that he was an old admiral in reduced circumstances. I am told that up to the period of his very last illness he would often rise at daybreak, and with blanket or dressing-gown carelessly thrown over him go out upon the railed-in roof to see the sun rise and to observe the colour flow, flushing back into the pale morning sky. In this tenacity of the dying man to his old love there is to me something very touching, almost sublime. Him Nature could never weary. With the true humility of genius he felt how much he had to learn, and how inimitable was the beauty of the world he had tried to depict.

He died with the winter-morning sun shining upon his face as he lay in bed. The attendant drew up the window-blind, and the luminary shed its beams upon the dying artist—the sun he had been wont to regard with such love and veneration. The sun of the 'Building of Carthage' and of the 'Frosty Morning' still shone on with unfading brightness; but the painter who had so often essayed to render its globe of living flame lay lifeless in an upper room of the river-side cottage— not far from the spot where he first floated out in a boat to study Nature, or from that Lambeth Palace which was the subject of his first water-colour drawing; and within easy reach of that Battersea which had been the subject of his first effort in oil—no longer the bright-eyed, ambitious boy, full of living genius and young hope, but the wrinkled, faded, worn-out old man, rich and famous, now only cumbering the earth till the vault can be opened for him to repose, in his regal mausoleum, between Reynolds and Barry.

For many months his old friend at Heston had seen nothing of him ; but when Mr. Trimmer was apprised of his death, and of the fact that he had himself been appointed one of the executors to the will, the reverend gentleman forthwith set out to town. When he knocked at the familiar door in Queen Anne Street, it was opened by Hannah Danby, who started at his recognition. She had, it would seem, heard he was dead, and was at first disposed to set him down as a ghost. There he learned that Turner had left him, in common with his co-executors, the choice of any one of his pictures with the exception of the ' Téméraire,' priority of selection to be determined by seniority ; but the codicil embodying this bequest was cancelled. Indeed, seeing that it did not except the ' Building of Carthage,' we are compelled to adopt the conclusion that this codicil must have been the product of an unduly weakened mind, and never could have been intended to hold good.

For some time before his death Turner had been very mysterious about his residence. One evening, during a sharp shower, he took shelter in a public-house, where he sat in the farthest corner with his glass before him, when an artist who knew him came in and began with, ' I didn't know you used the house ; I shall often drop in now I've found out where you quarter.' Turner looked at him, knit his brows, emptied his glass, and, as he rose to go out, said, ' Will you ? I don't think you will.' While at Chelsea a gentleman who knew him well chanced to be out on business in that neighbourhood, and found him in the same steamboat with himself, going towards the City. Seeing him in tidy condition, with his face clean shaved and his shoes blacked, and altogether looking as if he had just left home, he dropped some remark about his living in the district, wondering to see him abroad at that early hour. ' Is that your boy ? ' was all the response to be had from Turner, pointing to the gentleman's son.

To my kind friend Mr. Trimmer I am indebted for the

following interesting account of the appearance of Turner's
house after his death :—

'I had often visited Turner, partaken with my father of a
déjeuner à la fourchette, and had had my pockets crammed with
biscuits, after the olden fashion. Now, when I entered, all
was altered ; the master mind was gone ; the mainspring had
snapped. The same aged attendant let us in, but all was the
silence of death. I will describe the interior. First, the entrance hall. Here were several casts, from the antique, of
Centaurs in conflict with the Lapithæ, and a picture of Sir
Joshua, all very trite and depressing. Turning to the right
was the dining-room ; over the fire-place a small model of a
female figure, and a small Wilson obscured by smoke, quite in
keeping with the sombre walls. In Turner's time there was
also a picture of Tassi, Claude's master. Backwards stretched
a large unfurnished room filled with unfinished pictures ; then
a larger and drearier room yet ; lastly, a back room, against
the walls of which stood his unfinished productions, large full-
length canvasses placed carelessly against the wall, the damp
of which had taken off the colours altogether, or had damaged
them. Some canvasses had a coat of white run over the ground,
doubtless the work of Turner senior ; the next stage was
putting in large masses of black and white, apparently with the
spatula ; at least, the brush seemed used but sparingly. Turner
is said to have laid in his dead-colouring with body colour ;
but, so far as my inspection extended, I saw no traces of it ;
it rather seemed fat oil. In common with the great masters,
the colours were well loaded, both lights and darks, but of a
darker tint than when finished. Among them was an extraordinary picture of the "Carnival," red and black predominating.
Here Turner revelled in all his luxury. A little before his
death (I think Mr. Griffiths is my authority, and he was one of
Turner's oldest friends and associates) Turner used to go to
the top of the house he lodged in to see the fireworks at Vauxhall.

'There were many pictures there condemned by a discerning public. Several of Turner's admirers say that there are
parts of these no one could do but Turner. I must confess

that I can see no merit in them. Some of the figures, with all the defects of Rembrandt immensely exaggerated, showed an absence of all drawing, and effects of light and shade unrealised by Nature and outraging all analogies.

'Then we went into Turner's sleeping apartment. It is surprising how a person of his means could have lived in such a room; certainly he prized modern luxuries at a very modest rate.

' I reserved his studio as the finale of my inspection. This, during his lifetime, had been enshrined in mystery, and the object of profound speculation. What would his brother-artists have given some thirty years before to have forced an entrance when Turner was at the height of his fame! Often when shown into his gallery had I seen him emerge from that hidden recess. The august retreat was now thrown open; I entered. His gloves and neckhandkerchief lay on a circular table, which had in the middle a raised box (with a circle in the centre) with side compartments; a good contrivance for an artist, though I had never seen one of the kind before. In the centre were his colours, the great object of my attraction. I remember, on my father's observing to Turner that nothing was to be done without ultramarine, his saying that cobalt was good enough for him; and cobalt to be sure there was, but also several bottles of ultramarine of various depths; and smalts of various intensities, of which I think he made great use. There was also some verditer. The next object of interest was the white; there was a large bottle of blanc d'argent, and another of flake white. Before making this inspection I had observed that Turner used silver white. His yellow pigments consisted of a large bottle of chrome. There was also a bottle of tincture of rhubarb and some iodine, but whether for artistical or medicinal use I cannot say. Subsequently I was told by his housekeeper that ultramarine was employed by him very sparingly, and that smalt and cobalt were his usual blues. She was in the habit of setting Turner's palette. The palette—at least that in use, for he possessed two large splendid ones—was a homely piece of square wood, with a hole for the thumb. Grinding colours on a slab was not his practice, and his dry colours were rubbed on the palette with cold-drawn oil. The colours were mixed daily, and he was very particular as to the operation. If they were not to his mind, he would say to Mrs. Danby, " Can't you set a palette better than this ?" Like Wilson, Turner used gamboge ; simply pounded and mixed with linseed cold-drawn oil.

' His brushes were of the humblest description, mostly large round hog's tools, and some flat. He was said to use very short handles, which might have been the case with his water colours ; but I observed one very long-handled brush, with which I have no doubt he put in the effective touches in his late pictures. According to his housekeeper, he used the long brush exclusively for the rigging of ships, &c. However, there were a great many long-haired sables, which could not have been all employed for rigging. She also said that he used camel's hair for his oil pictures ; and formerly he showed my father some Chinese brushes he was in the habit of using. When he had nearly finished a picture, she said, he took it to the end of his long gallery, and there put in the last touches.

' I next inspected his travelling-box. Had I been asked to guess his travelling library, I should have said Young's " Night Thoughts " and Izaak Walton ; and there they were, together with some inferior translation of Horace. His library was select, but it showed the man. A red morocco pocket-book, from the wear and tear it exhibited, one might have imagined to have been his companion through life. There were cakes of water-colour fastened on a leaf, the centres of which were worn away ; the commonest colours, and one being a cake of verditer ; one or two sable brushes and lead pencils, not in wood, with which he seemed to have drawn outlines in his sketch-book. These consisted of a few lines which he used to say no one could make out but himself. I have some doubts if he could have made them out himself without the assistance of other drawings ; and he seems to have purchased detail views of foreign scenery, of which there was a large assortment well thumbed ; the drudgery of the art, of which master minds avail themselves.

' There is no doubt that in his early pictures he used wax,

from their having turned yellow ; there was a jar of wax melted with rose madder and also with blue, which must have been used very recently, though it might have been for water colours. There was also a bureau of old colours and oils, which I looked over very carefully ; a bottle of spirit varnish and a preparation of tar, tubes of magilp, old bladders of raw umber and other dark earths, all Newman's, from whom might be learned what colours he used.

' The above, with numerous unframed pictures around the apartment, were the contents of his painting-room, which had no skylight. It had been originally the drawing-room, and had a good north light, with two windows.

' I must confess that a deep melancholy pervaded me as I made this inspection. Till of late years I had been in the habit of entering the house from my childhood ; the owner was no more ; he stood alone in the world, and his race was extinct.

' There was a small deal box on a side table, the lid of which my father raised to show me its contents. It was covered with a glass, and under it was the cast of the great Turner. Dear old Turner ! There he lay with his eyes sunk and his lips fallen in. He reminded me strongly of his old father, whom long years before I had seen trudging to Brentford market from Sandicomb Lodge, to lay in his weekly supplies. Alas for humanity ! This was the man whom in my childhood I had attended with my father, and been driven by on the banks of the Thames ; whom I had seen sketching with such glee on the river's banks, as I gathered wild flowers in my earliest years ; who had stuffed my pockets with sweetmeats, had loaded me with fish, and made me feel as happy as a prince.

' On his calm face were written the marks of age and wreck, of dissolution and reblending with the dust. This was the man whose worst productions contained more poetry and genius than the most laboured efforts of his brother-artists ; who was the envy of his rivals, and the admiration of all whose admiration was worth having ; nor was it without emotion or with a dry eye that I gazed on so sad a sight.

'During the Great Exhibition in 1851 he came to Queen Anne Street, and gave Mrs. Danby strict orders to admit no one ; and accordingly none of the visitors saw his pictures. At this time his gallery was in a most dilapidated state ; the wet was running down some of his best pictures, through the leaks I had noted twenty years before and pointed out to him. Had the pictures been seen, it would have been at a great disadvantage.'

Mr. David Roberts recognised the undertaker at Turner's grand funeral as being the man who had managed the interment of poor Patrick Nasmyth, at Lambeth, fourteen years before. The functionary had thriven since then ; and he who had helped to bury the poor worn-out pauper artist at Lambeth now followed the great rich man to his grand mausoleum in St. Paul's.

The ' Times ' gave the following account of the funeral :—

'The mortal remains of the great artist who has just been removed from us, full of years and honours, were received within the walls of St. Paul's, and borne to their final resting-place in the catacombs. Whatever hesitation might have been felt by the mass of those who gazed on the later efforts of his brush in believing that he was entitled to the highest rank in his profession, none of his brethren seemed to have any doubt of his decided excellence, and the best of them all have ever readily admitted his superiority in poetry, feeling, fancy, and genius. Long ere his death he had the felicity of knowing that his name and his works were regarded with that reverential respect and estimation which is given to other artists by posterity alone, and his earlier productions have been placed among the classical ornaments of our choicest collections and galleries for many years. Even those who could only sneer and smile at the erratic blaze of his colour, shifting and flickering as the light of the aurora, lingered minute after minute before the last incomprehensible " Turner " that gleamed on the walls of the Academy, and the first name sought for upon the catalogue by the critic, artist, and amateur, as well as by those who could not understand him when they found him, was his also. Many of the most distinguished of our painters, and many private friends, paid the last tribute of respect to his remains, and followed his hearse yesterday, and a long procession of mourning coaches and private carriages preceded it to the Cathedral. Among those who attended the sad ceremonial were Mr. Harpur, the chief mourner, with crape hatband and scarf, Mr. Jones, Mr. P. Hardwicke, Mr. Munro, Mr Griffiths, Sir Charles Eastlake, Mr. Mulready, Mr. Chalon, Mr. Cooper, Mr. Bailey, Mr. Leslie, Mr. Pickersgill, Mr. C. Stanfield, Mr. Maclise, Mr. Witherington, Mr. Roberts, Mr. Barry, Mr. Knight, Mr. Landseer, Mr. Webster, Mr. Herbert, Mr. Cope, Mr. Westmacott, Mr. Grant, Mr. Creswick, Mr. Redgrave, Dr. Mayo, Mr. Hart, Mr. Cockerell, Mr. Copley Fielding, Mr. Haghe, Colonel Thwaites, Mr. Windus, Mr. Hardwicke, the Rev. Mr. Kingsley, Mr. Stokes, Mr. Marsh, Dr. Price, Mr. Bartlett, Mr. Drake, and Mr. Pound. His housekeeper—for the deceased was a bachelor—was also in the funeral procession, with Mrs. F. Danby. When the hearse arrived at the entrance to the Cathedral the coffin was received by the clergy, and the procession slowly stepped up the aisle—the singing boys, vicars choral, vergers, minor canons, the Dean (Milman), the Archdeacon, the Ven. Hale Hale, the Canon Residentiary, and the Rev. Mr. Champneys being in attendance, and forming in front of the pall-bearers and mutes. The choristers chanted the Dead March in Saul, and the organ pealed through the aisle as the coffin was borne into the chapel, where it was laid down while the Dean read the commencement of the service for the dead, after which it was raised ; and while it was being carried towards the catacombs the rest of the service was performed according to the rubric, and at the conclusion the coffin was deposited in one of the vaults. It bore the simple inscription, "Joseph Mallord Turner, Esq., R.A., died Dec. 19, 1851, aged 79 years."[1] A considerable crowd was attracted outside by the ceremonial, and about five hundred persons were present in the aisles and the chapel.'

From the estimate of his genius supplied by the 'Times' of December 23, 1851, I take a few passages :—

'The Fine Arts in this country have not produced a more

---

[1] He was really only seventy-six, having been born in April 1775.

remarkable man than Joseph Mallord William Turner, whose death it was yesterday our duty to record ; and, although it would here be out of place to revive the discussions occasioned by the peculiarities of Mr. Turner's style in his later years, he has left behind him sufficient proofs of the variety and fertility of his genius to establish an undoubted claim to a prominent rank among the painters of England. So great is the value of his drawings that 120 guineas have not unfrequently been paid for a small sketch in water colours ; and a sketch-book, containing chalk drawings of one of Turner's river tours on the Continent, has lately fetched the enormous sum of 600 guineas. The prices of his more finished oil paintings have ranged in the last few years from 700 to 1,200 or 1,400 guineas. All his works may now be said to have acquired triple or quadruple the value originally paid for them. Mr. Turner undoubtedly realised a very large fortune, and great curiosity will be felt to ascertain the posthumous use he has made of it. His personal habits were peculiar, and even penurious, but in all that related to his art he was generous to munificence, and we are not without hope that his last intentions were for the benefit of the nation and the preservation of his own fame. . . .

' Mr. Turner seldom took much part in society, and only displayed in the closest intimacy the shrewdness of his observation and the playfulness of his wit. Everywhere he kept back much of what was in him ; and while the keenest intelligence, mingled with a strong tinge of satire, animated his brisk countenance, it seemed to amuse him to be but half understood. His nearest social ties were those formed in the Royal Academy, of which he was by far the oldest member, and to whose interests he was most warmly attached. He filled at one time the chair of Professor of Perspective, but without conspicuous success, and that science has since been taught in the Academy by means better suited to promote it than a course of lectures. In the composition and execution of his works Mr. Turner was jealously sensitive of all interference or supervision. He loved to deal in the secrets and mysteries of his art, and many of his peculiar effects are produced by means which it would not be easy to discover or to imitate. . . . For nearly sixty years Mr. Turner contributed largely to the arts of this country. He lived long enough to see his greatest productions rise to uncontested supremacy, however imperfectly they were understood when they first appeared in the earlier years of this century ; and, though in his later works and in advanced age force and precision of execution have not accompanied his vivacity of conception, public opinion has gradually and steadily advanced to a more just appreciation of his power. He is the Shelley of English painting—the poet and the painter both alike veiling their own creations in the dazzling splendour of the imagery with which they are surrounded, mastering every mode of expression, combining scientific labour with an air of negligent profusion, and producing in the end works in which colour and language are but the vestments of poetry.'

Turner's will, copied from the Registry of the Prerogative Court of Canterbury, will be found in full in my Appendix ; but here, in view of biographical facts, I insert a condensed version of its various clauses. First he leaves to his executors and trustees all his freehold, leasehold, and personal estates, which, after payment of his just debts, he enjoins them immediately after his death to sell, and directs that the sums obtained by such sale be united to the money already invested by him in the Three per Cents. Then come the bequests—To Price Turner and Jonathan Turner, his two uncles, 5*l.* each ; and to his nephews, John, Joshua, and Jonathan (the sons of Price Turner), 25*l.* each. To Hannah Danby, his old housekeeper, niece of John Danby, musician, 50*l.* a year for her natural life ; to the housekeeper's aunt, Sarah Danby, 10*l.* a year ; and to Evelina and Georgiana Danby, daughters of Sarah Danby, 50*l.* a year each ; the first quarterly payment to be due at the expiration of six months from his decease.

To the National Gallery he left ' Dido Building Carthage' and the picture formerly in the Tabley Collection ; but upon the express condition that they be hung between the two pictures painted by Claude, entitled ' The Sea Port' and ' The Mill,' and be from time to time properly cleaned, framed, repaired, and protected ; and, if these conditions were not accepted within twelve months of his decease, they were to

be taken to form part of the charitable funds hereinafter mentioned.

With the residue of his funded property he designed to found
a charity for decayed artists of the male sex, born in England
and of English parents only, and of lawful issue. A suitable
building was to be provided in an eligible place, and the institution to be under the control of five trustees ; these being
represented by his executors, and future trustees being elected,
three from the Royal Academicians and two from non-members.
The institution was to be called ' Turner's Gift,' and to be
governed by the ordinary rules of charitable institutions devoted
to a similar purpose ; and the trustees were directed to reimburse themselves for all reasonable expenses that they might be
put to in attending to such functions. This will, which is dated
June 10, 1831, and attested by George Cobb, Clement's
Inn ; John Saxon, Bruton, Somersetshire ; and Charles Tull,
Winchester Street, London, is written in various legal hands
—all except the first codicil, the whole of which is in Turner's
own handwriting. A further codicil requires that the gallery
devoted to his pictures should be respectable, and worthy of
the object, and that it should be viewed gratuitously. If the
money should prove to be inadequate, and the charity could
not be founded within five years of his death, then that part of
his will was to be null and void, and his estate was to be disposed of in the following manner :—The pictures were to be kept
entire and unsold in 47 Queen Anne Street, West, and to be
called the ' Turner Gallery,' Hannah Danby being the custodian
at 100*l.* a year, with 50*l.* for an assistant ; and Georgiana Danby
and Evelina Danby, or Dupree, each having 100*l.* a year.
The residue was left to the Royal Academy on condition of
their annually giving, on his birthday, the 23rd of April, a
dinner of the cost of 50*l.* Sixty pounds a year were assigned
to a Professorship of Landscape at the Royal Academy, and a
gold medal worth 20*l.* for the best landscape every second year.
In the event of the Royal Academy refusing this residue, it was
bequeathed to Georgiana Danby and her heirs absolutely, after
the erection of a monument in immediate proximity to his
remains.

In another codicil Turner, revoking all the legacies to his uncles and nephews, and to Georgiana and the other Danbys, leaves his finished pictures to the National Gallery, provided a room or rooms were built for their reception, with the distinct title of ' Turner's Gallery.' The pictures were not to be removed from Queen Anne Street till such rooms were built; but if all fell through, and the lease could not be renewed, then the pictures were to be sold. In this codicil he names Thomas Griffiths, Esq., of Norwood, Surrey; John Ruskin, Esq., the younger, of Denmark Hill; Philip Hardwicke, Esq., of Russell Square; and Henry Harpur, of Kennington Cross, Lambeth, gentleman, to act in conjunction with the trustees and executors already named in the will; and to each of them is left the sum of nineteen guineas for the purchase of a memorial ring. The codicil is dated August 2, 1848, and is attested by Joseph Tibbs and Thomas Schroeder.

The next codicil annuls the gifts to the National Gallery, if the ' Turner Gallery' be not built within ten years after his decease. In failure of this, a gratuitous exhibition was to take place at the house in Queen Anne Street, and the pictures finally sold. The sum of a thousand pounds was reserved for the erection of a monument to himself in St. Paul's, where he desired to be buried among his brothers in Art; and to his housekeeper in Queen Anne Street, and Sophia Caroline Booth, of Chelsea, he left severally an annuity of 150*l.*; out of the sale of the finished pictures, 1,000*l.* to the Pension Fund of the Academy, the gold medal for Landscape Art to be paid out of it; 500*l.* to the Artists' General Benevolent Fund; 500*l.* to the Foundling; 500*l.* to the London Orphan Fund; and to Mrs. Wheeler and her two sisters 100*l.* each, free from legacy duty. Mr. Munro's name is added to the previous list of his executors and trustees. This last codicil bears the date of February 1, 1845, and is attested by Mr. Joseph Tibbs and Mr. Thomas Schroeder, clerks to Mr. Harpur.

The only land at Twickenham which, at his death, stood in the name of Turner was about three-quarters of an acre on the fourth roadside of the common, which he bought at the time the Richmond and Twickenham Railroad was forming.

The will in the Appendix, as I have before intimated, is extracted from the Registry of the Prerogative Court of Canterbury. The first part, together with the second, third, and fourth codicils, is written in a legal hand, but not by one and the same person ; and the first codicil is entirely in Turner's own handwriting.

Unfortunately for the poor artists of England, the will being a most cloudy document, full of confusions and interpolations, it was disputed by the next of kin, who endeavoured to establish that the testator was of unsound mind. But this effort to annihilate its validity failed, the testator being held to be of sound mind, and capable of making a legal disposition of his estate. The trustees and executors thereupon filed a Bill in Chancery on the 25th of April, 1852, praying the Court to construe the will and to enable them to administer the estate. The next of kin, by their answer, contended that, since it was impossible to place any construction upon the will at all, it was necessarily void ; and further that, even if the will could be carried out according to the intention of the testator, it was still void, as the bequests came within the Statute of Mortmain.

The next proceedings were in the Vice-Chancellor's Court, before Vice-Chancellor Sir R. T. Kindersley ; and the following report of a day's proceeding in the suit Trimmer *v.* Danby is a sample of many such days :—

'This suit relates to the will of the late Mr. Turner, the celebrated artist, who left a great number of testamentary papers in all stages of alteration, erasure, and cancellation, and some in duplicate, but so mutilated as to be virtually destroyed, but generally executed. The executors applied for probate upon all, and five—namely, one will and four codicils—were ultimately proved ; and conflicting claims arising under the will, this suit was instituted, and Mr. Hardwicke appointed receiver. The testator left pictures of a very great value at his house, 47 Queen Anne Street, and after bequeathing them to the trustees and directors for the time being of the National Gallery, with certain directions, declared that in case such pictures should not be accepted within one year from his decease, his executors and trustees should found a charitable institution for decayed

artists, to be called " Turner's Gift ;" but in case such institution could not be legally founded, then he appointed Hannah
Danby the custodian and keeper of his pictures, with 100*l.* a
year for so doing, and to keep them entire and unsold at his
residence, to be viewed gratuitously by the public, and called
" Turner's Gallery." The testator's property was sworn under
140,000*l.*, and the next of kin and heir-at-law having made claims
the cause now came on upon minutes and for a reference to
chambers, and the chief question was, whether the pictures
should remain in their present position, which it was alleged
was calculated to damage them by reason of damp, &c., until
their final destination could be determined upon.

'The Solicitor-General and Mr. Wickens appeared for the
Crown ; Mr. Follett and Mr. W. Morris for the next of kin ;
Mr. J. U. Terrell for the executors and trustees ; Mr. Swanston
and Mr. Stevens for Hannah Danby ; Mr. Walker and Mr.
Roxburgh for the heir-at-law ; and Mr. Willcock and Mr. Ellis
for other parties.

'The Vice-Chancellor said that if his own opinion were to
prevail, or he was entitled to have any leaning upon the subject, he should favour the idea of those valuable works of Art
becoming national property ; but as it was most important,
whatever might be the event of the suit, that they should meantime be protected from injury, the best way would be to refer
the question to three gentlemen to be chosen, and he (the Vice-
Chancellor) would, if all parties concurred, himself see them on
the subject.

'Mr. Hardwicke, Sir C. Eastlake, and Mr. Clarkson Stanfield were then chosen.

'Solicitor for the plaintiff, Mr. Drake ; for the Crown, Mr.
Raven ; for the next of kin and heir-at-law, Mr. Tepper.'

On Wednesday, the 19th of March, 1856, the following decision was given by Vice-Chancellor Kindersley :—

'Between Henry Scott *Trimmer* George Jones Charles
Turner Philip Hardwicke Henry Harpur and Hugh Andrew
Johnston Munro Plaintiffs Hugh *Danby* (since deceased) Mary
Tepper (since deceased) William Turner (since deceased)
Thomas Price Turner Mary Matthews John Widgery and

Mary Ann Turner his wife John Turner Sophia Caroline
Booth and Her Majesty's Attorney-General Defendants And
Between Henry Harpur Plaintiff Henry Trimmer Samuel
Rogers George Jones Charles Turner John Ruskin the younger
when he shall come within the Jurisdiction of the Court Philip
Hardwicke and Hugh Andrew Johnston Munro Defendants
And Between the said Henry Scott Trimmer George Jones
Charles Turner Philip Hardwicke Henry Harpur and Hugh
Andrew Johnston Munro Plaintiffs Grace Coham Turner John
Thome Turner Mary Eliza Turner William Coham Turner
Marcella Danby Caroline Malissa Nixon and Theresa Danby
Symondson Defendants And Between the said Henry Scott
Trimmer George Jones Charles Turner Philip Hardwicke
Henry Harpur and Hugh Andrew Johnston Munro Plaintiffs
Jabez Tepper Defendant

' By original Bill and supplemental orders

' *Extract*

' This Court doth Declare by consent of all parties by their
Counsel (except the Plaintiffs who by their Counsel submit to
act as this Court shall direct and except the Attorney-General
who does not oppose the same) that all the Pictures Drawings
and Sketches by the Testator's hand without any distinction of
finished or unfinished are to be deemed as well given for the benefit of the public and Doth order that the same when selected
and ascertained in manner hereafter mentioned be retained
by the Trustees for the time being of the National Gallery accordingly and it is ordered that Sir Charles Locke Eastlake
Knight President of the Royal Academy and John Prescott
Knight Royal Academician and in case they disagree an umpire to be named by them by writing under their hands to be at
liberty to select from the said Pictures Drawings and Sketches
now in the National Gallery pursuant to the order made in
these Causes dated the 4th day of August 1854 such of the
Pictures Drawings and Sketches as shall in their opinion have
been painted drawn or sketched by the Testator's hand without any distinction of finished or unfinished such selection to

be verified by affidavit and all parties (except the plaintiffs who by their Counsel submit to act as this Court shall direct and except the Attorney-General who does not oppose the same) by their Counsel consenting to abide by the selection of the said Sir Charles Locke Eastlake and John Prescott Knight or in case they disagree then by the selection of such umpire as aforesaid and upon the additional probate duty (if any) and the legacy duty payable in respect of such Pictures Drawings and Sketches being paid or effectually released and the sum of one hundred and eighty-one pounds ten shillings being one moiety of the expenses of removing the Testator's works of art to the place where they are now deposited being repaid to the said Executors to be by them accounted for as part of the Testator's General Estate. It is ordered that the Pictures Drawings and Sketches so to be selected be retained by the Trustees for the time being of the said National Gallery and this Court doth declare that the Trustees for the time being of the said National Gallery are entitled to hold the two Pictures that is to say Dido Building Carthage and the Picture formerly in the De Tabley Collection now in their possession under the order of the 26th day of July 1852 discharged from the agreement of the 12th day of November 1852 in the pleadings of these Causes mentioned But this order is to be without prejudice to the claim (if any) of the persons in respect of the Legacies bequeathed by the 4th Codicil to the said Testator's Will to the Artists' General Benevolent Fund to the Foundling Hospital and to the London Orphan Fund and by the like consent and submission and the Attorney-General not opposing and the Trustees of the Royal Academy of Arts in London by their Counsel waiving all claim to the Legacy of one thousand pounds by the said Will bequeathed to the Pension Fund of the Royal Academy and all other benefit under the said Will and Codicils This Court doth declare that the Trustees for the time being of the Royal Academy of Arts in London are entitled to the sum of twenty thousand pounds sterling free from Legacy duty and it is ordered that the legacy duty payable in respect thereof be raised by the said Plaintiffs Henry Scott Trimmer George Jones Charles Turner Philip

Hardwicke and Henry Harpur by a sale of a sufficient part of the said Bank 3*l.* per Cent. Annuities or of the said reduced 3*l.* per Cent. Annuities respectively forming part of the said Testator's Estate and It is ordered that the said last named Plaintiffs do on or before the 10th day of October next transfer to the Trustees for the time being of the said Royal Academy so much of the said 3*l.* per Cent. Consolidated Bank Annuities or of the said 3*l.* per Cent. Reduced Annuities as will according to the market price of the said Consolidated Bank Annuities or Reduced Annuities on the day of such transfer be equal in amount to the said sum of twenty thousand pounds sterling And it is ordered that the said last named Plaintiffs do pay to the said Trustees of the said Royal Academy interest on the said Twenty thousand pounds after the rate of 4*l.* per Cent. per annum from the 30th day of June 1856 to the time of such transfer out of any Cash which may be in their hands or by sale of a sufficient part of the said 3*l.* per Cent. Consolidated Bank Annuities or Reduced Annuities and by the like consent and submission and the said Attorney-General not opposing this Court doth declare that subject to legacy duty (if any) the legacy of one thousand pounds by the Testator directed to be expended in erecting a monument in St. Paul's Cathedral was a good and valid legacy and it is ordered that the plaintiffs Henry Scott Trimmer George Jones Charles Turner Philip Hardwicke and Henry Harpur do on or before the 14th day of November next transfer into the name and with the privity of the Accountant-General of this Court in trust in the 1st 3rd and 4th above mentioned Causes to an account to be entitled "The monument account" of the plaintiffs subject to legacy duty (if any) so much of the said 3*l.* per Cent. Consolidated Bank Annuities now standing in the name of the said Testator and forming part of his Estate as will at the market price of such Bank Annuities on the day preceding the day of bespeaking such transfer be equal to the sum of one thousand pounds and interest thereon at 4*l.* per Cent. after deducting income tax thereon from the end of one year after the said Testator's death to the day preceding the day of bespeaking such transfer the amount thereof and the said market price to be verified by

affidavit and the said Accountant-General is to declare the
trust thereof accordingly subject to the further order of this
Court.

'J. A. MURRAY.
'C. R. & W.'

The documents in this Chancery suit, which extended to
four years, are of several tons' weight. The bills of costs alone
would fill a butcher's cart. How Turner would have groaned
to see the lawyers fattening themselves on his hard-earned
savings !

A compromise was eventually effected between all the
parties to the suit ; and on March 19, 1856, a decree was pronounced, with their consent, to the following effect :—

1. The real estate to go to the heir-at-law.
2. The pictures, &c., to the National Gallery.
3. 1,000*l.* for the erection of a monument in St. Paul's
Cathedral.
4. 20,000*l.* to the Royal Academy, free of legacy duty.
5. Remainder to be divided amongst next of kin.

The interest and accumulations were to stand as an in-
demnity to the said plaintiffs in respect of their contingent
liabilities for rent and costs of the leasehold estates of testator
or devisee, and of any claims upon them in respect of any
undertaking on the part of the testator ; but all *engraved plates*
were to be destroyed or cancelled.

The *engravings* (mentioned in Order made on August 4,
1854), and the pictures, drawings, and sketches, not selected by
Eastlake and Prescott, were assigned to the defendants ; and
the trustees of the National Gallery were to deliver up the same
to Jabez Tepper, on behalf of them.

In relation to the discussions in Parliament about the
Turner bequest the 'Art Journal' wrote—

'On June 27, in the House of Lords, Lord St. Leonards
asked the President of the Council whether any steps had been
taken to provide a separate gallery for Turner's pictures,
according to the conditions under which they were bequeathed
to the nation. "The trustees of the National Gallery took

324 pictures, besides a vast quantity of water-colour drawings, and the Royal Academy 20,000*l.* in money, and both the nation and the Royal Academy believed they held the property as their own, not subject to any conditions." Lord St. Leonards read the codicils of the will of Mr. Turner, to prove that the pictures were left in trust to the National Gallery, on the condition that a separate room should be built for them, to be called the Turner Gallery. He then proceeded to comment on the exhibition of these works by gaslight, observing that, if even every precaution were taken to secure them against injury from gas vapour, they were yet exposed to great risk.

' The rooms containing the Turner pictures were erected two or three years ago for the reception of the collection on its removal from Marlborough House ; the money voted for the building containing these apartments was 10,000*l.*, and the erections were spoken of as " temporary." For the purposes for which they were intended, these rooms are well suited ; they are not lighted according to the best principle, yet Turner's pictures were never seen until they were placed there. In Marlborough House they were—as their Lordships described Turner's will—" ambiguous ;" and it is not, therefore, matter of wonder that the " Avalanche" should have been criticised hanging upside down. Turner painted for light, and admitted into his works the smallest proportion of dark—a rule of Art which, to be apprehended, demands the fullest measure of daylight. As we see " Crossing the Brook " in that gallery, it is the grandest landscape of this or any other time ; but in a lower light its beauties would be obscured. Lord St. Leonards is resolved that its present abiding-place shall not be the permanent home of the collection, for he concluded his speech with the expression of a hope that the Government, in moving the Civil Service estimates, would propose a vote of credit for the immediate commencement of a Turner Gallery.

' It was a principal condition of the bequest that a room for the reception of the pictures should be completed in ten years from the death of the testator ; but Lord Granville's reply does not indicate on the part of the Government any immediate intention of fulfilling the conditions of the bequest. Though many plans have been proposed, they have not yet been considered. Lord Overstone said he could easily understand that the trustees of the National Gallery found themselves in an embarrassing position in consequence of the serious " ambiguities " which attached to the Turner trust. It is a slur upon the memory of the man that the trustees should shrink from dealing with the provisions of the will. He was not unfrequently mysterious with his brush ; he seems to have been more so with his pen, for his will is even more difficult of interpretation than his " Fallacies of Hope." But yet he must be had in charitable and grateful remembrance, for the history of Art records no similar act of munificence. We must, however, look at things as they present themselves, and in doing so we discover in the gold a large alloy of baser metal than usual. Even the most rabid of the Turnerini will not presume to deny that the great painter hampered his presentation of the " Carthage " with the condition that it should be placed between the " Claudes ;" they will not deny that he left money to glorify himself in a statue ; nor can they deny that the condition of his great bequest is absolute in respect of the separate room to be called the " Turner ; " and of his minor bequest to the Royal Academy, with the medal equally to be called the " Turner." These things are public property ; they may be separated from an estimate of the worth of the public presentation, but they cannot be sifted out as mere *caput mortuum* in an estimate of the man. While Turner was a living myth in that miserable house in Queen Anne Street—which, from its superior dirtiness and preferable dilapidation, was by the population of the neighbouring areas reputed as the den of a mysterious man who was seen only in the morning and evening twilight—while he lived in Queen Anne Street he was misunderstood and universally adored. With the artistic section of society he was great by common acclamation ; with the rest of the world he was great by the grace of public benevolence. He was continually before the world in black and white—that is, in engraving ; and in clear-obscure Turner was greater than any man that has ever lived. He had his periodical paroxysms of colour ; but still his lights

and darks were always right, and every engraved subject was a
precious lucid interval.   Then indeed

> ' Fata canit, foliisque notas et nomina mandat.

And further, like the Sibyl, he cared not to revert to multitudes
of his inditings, as is shown by the thousands of sketches that
are still in the possession of the trustees.   At the bidding of
the hierarchy of the art, whole populations have bowed before
the " Napoleon," and the " Ulysses and Polyphemus," and the
" Gardens of the Hesperides ;" and, because they do not understand them, would canonise the man who painted them, did
they consider a niche in the calendar a condition sufficiently
respectable for him.   It was by no means necessary that
Turner should expose himself in his will, by raising his patro-
nymic into an historical institution.   But for that we might
have all believed that he was totally pictorial ; that all vulgar
essences had been driven off in the passage of a longer course
of years than falls to the lot of many men.   To having lived
so long under a veil it is a bad consummation that he should
at last have placed himself under a microscope.   The comparisons between the " Liber Studiorum " and the " Liber Veritatis," and between the " Carthage" and the " Claudes," are in
favour of Turner ; but the proclaimed challenge of the comparisons is against him.   These comparisons would infallibly
have been drawn ; but, in forcing them, Turner was less just
to himself than his friends have been.   It is ungrateful to look
at Turner through himself.   Through his works he assumes
proportions attained not even by the genii of the Eastern tales
—in this view he is more worthy of a pyramid than Cheops,
and his pyramid is a more pleasing erection.

' Lord St. Leonards and Lord Overstone are unwilling to
consider the portion of the Kensington galleries allotted to the
Turners as fulfilling the conditions of the will.   The pictures
are most perfectly exhibited where they now are ; but, if the
legal authorities on whom Lord Granville relies for the interpretation of the terms of the bequest determine that another room
shall be built, it is high time that the money were voted and
the work begun.

' Thanks to an order of the House of Lords, on a motion of Lord St. Leonards, Turner's Will and the various codicils attached to it have been printed *in extenso*. The immediate occasion of this publication was the official representation of the Trustees of the National Gallery to her Majesty's Treasury respecting the care and custody of the pictures. The period within which provision was to be made, under the will, for the gallery to be named after the testator was limited to ten years after his decease. This will shortly expire ; and, although the decree of Vice-Chancellor Kindersley delivered the pictures to the Trustees without express reference to this condition of time, there are, say the Trustees, grave doubts, supported by high legal authority, whether that condition does not still bind them to erect the gallery on pain of forfeiture. It is added that, whatever be the legal effect of this decree, there is no doubt of the moral obligation under which the Trustees lie. They think Turner intended that his pictures should be exhibited in immediate proximity to the other pictures forming the National Gallery, and, in order that they may be enabled to carry out this intention, they appeal to their Lordships of the Treasury, adding that, whether they hold the pictures under the will or the decree, or both, there is no doubt of their being under a moral as well as legal obligation to see the undoubted wishes of the testator fulfilled. It is urged that it is not fitting to impair the completeness of the general collection of national pictures by the severance from it of such surpassing examples of the British school. To this is added a reminder that on repeated occasions the temporary character of the present location of the Turner pictures has been made the subject of express acknowledgment and assurance. The representation concludes by calling attention to the report of the late Mr. Braidwood on the increased danger of lighting public buildings with gas, under the influence of which the British Museum Trustees decided against lighting that building. The Trustees state that they would not consider their responsibility met were they not to draw the attention of their Lordships to the questionable nature of the present location of the Turner pictures, and the arrangements under which they are now ex hibited by gaslight.'

'The Select Committee appointed to consider in what manner the conditions annexed by the will of the late Mr. Turner, R.A., to the bequest of his pictures to the Trustees of the National Gallery can best be carried out ; and, having completed such enquiry, then to consider and report the measures proper to be taken with respect to the Vernon Gallery, and the prospective measures proper to be taken with respect to any future gifts of the same kind ; and to whom were referred copies of the will and codicils of the late Mr. Turner, R.A., and of the decree of the Vice-Chancellor Kindersley, establishing the right of the nation to the pictures of Mr. Turner, given by him to the public, and also of the representations lately made by the Trustees of the National Gallery to the Treasury upon the subject of Mr. Turner's gift of his pictures to the nation, and to report thereon to the House, have reported—

'" That the Committee have met and considered the subject-matter referred to them, and have come to the following resolutions, viz.—

'" That the late Mr. Turner, R.A., by his will gave to the Trustees of the National Gallery his picture of ' Dido Building Carthage,' and his picture formerly in the De Tabley Collection, for ever, subject to the direction that they should be kept and placed always between the two pictures painted by Claude, the ' Seaport ' and the ' Mill ;' and the right of the Trustees to these pictures was declared by the decree after mentioned ; and the two pictures have ever since been, and now are, placed in the National Gallery between the two Claudes, according to Turner's will.

'" That Mr. Turner made several codicils to his will. By the first codicil, which was superseded by the later ones, he desired a gallery to be erected for his pictures (except the two given by his will), and that they should be maintained and ex-hibited as a separate collection, to be called ' Turner's Gallery.' By the second codicil he gave his finished pictures (except the ' Dido ' and the De Tabley pictures) to the Trustees of the National Gallery, provided that a room or rooms were added to the National Gallery, to be entitled ' Turner's Gallery ;' in the meantime they were not to be removed until rooms were built ; the Trustees of the National Gallery were not to have any power over the pictures unless his wish was fully carried out by them ; it was his will that such pictures should either remain and be called 'Turner's Gallery,' and be the property of the nation, or remain at his house as one entire gallery, to be viewed gratuitously ; if the lease could not be renewed, the pictures were to be sold. By the third codicil, if the National Gallery should not carry out the provisions in the second codicil within five years, on or before the expiration of the lease of his present gallery, then he declared his bequest to the National Gallery to be void, and in that case his gallery to be continued upon the terms mentioned in his last codicil. By the fourth and last codicil he limited ten years for offering his finished pictures to the National Gallery ; if rooms were not built, the pictures were to be exhibited gratuitously during the existence of the lease of his Queen Anne Street house, except the last two years, and then the pictures were to be sold. By the decree of the Court of Chancery, made in March 1856, the Court declared that all the pictures, drawings, and sketches, wholly or partially by the testator's hand, without any distinction of finished or unfinished, were to be deemed as well given for the benefit of the public, and were to be retained by the trustees for the time being of the National Gallery.

' " That under the above testamentary dispositions and the decree of the Court of Chancery, the nation is now in possession of 362 pictures painted by Turner, and of a very large number of water-colour drawings of the highest excellence ; and the nation ought, in the opinion of this House, to carry out the conditions annexed to the gift in like manner as the conditions annexed to the gift of the two pictures now between the two Claudes have been complied with.

' " That, for want of a room to receive them at the National Gallery, the pictures are now at Kensington, but the power of the trustees of the National Gallery has been preserved over them ; and it was publicly announced that they were removed to Kensington only as a temporary measure.

' "That Turner died in December 1851, and, in the opinion of this House, no further delay should take place in providing a room or rooms for the reception and exhibition of his pictures and drawings, now the property of the nation, in connexion with the National Gallery, to be called 'Turner's Gallery.'

' "That it is expedient that the finished pictures by Turner should be forthwith deposited and properly hung in one of the rooms of the present National Gallery, according to the plan which Mr. Wornum, the keeper, has stated in his evidence that he is prepared to carry out.

' "But this arrangement, as it will necessarily involve considerable inconvenience in the exhibition of the pictures now in the National Gallery, must be considered as of a strictly temporary character, pending the execution of some more enlarged and comprehensive plan.

' "That, with a view to provide such accommodation, Mr. Pennethorne, the architect, has stated in his evidence that he can undertake to erect rooms fully sufficient for the reception of the Turner pictures at the back of the present National Gallery, within a period of time not exceeding twelve months, and at a cost not to exceed 25,000*l.*

' "That unless there be some reasonable prospect of seeing a noble gallery worthy of the fine collection of pictures by the ancient masters and British artists which the country now possesses, and which is, year by year, receiving additions of great importance, erected upon a comprehensive plan on the present or any other site, it appears desirable that steps should be forthwith taken for making the limited addition to the present gallery suggested by Mr. Pennethorne.

' "That with regard to the second portion of the order of reference—viz. 'And having completed such enquiry, then to consider and report the measures proper to be taken with respect to the Vernon Gallery, and the prospective measures proper to be taken with respect to any future gifts of the same kind,' the late period of the Session making it impossible for the Committee fully to consider the important questions involved, the Committee beg to recommend to the House that the subject be again referred early in the ensuing Session.

' " And the Committee have directed the Minutes of Evidence taken before them, together with an Appendix, to be laid before your Lordships.

' " July 30th." '

In a letter which appeared in the 'Times' soon after Turner's death Mr. Ruskin undertook to select, sift, and arrange the drawings that Turner left to the nation. He divided them into three classes : first, finished water-colour drawings ; secondly, studies from Nature, or first thoughts for pictures, in colour ; and thirdly, sketches in pencil or pen and ink ; the drawings belonging to the two latter classes being in various stages of completion.

In the first class are 45 drawings of the 'Rivers of France,' 57 illustrating Rogers's poems, 23 of the 'River Scenery' and 'Harbours of England,' 4 marine vignettes, 5 middle-sized drawings (including the beautiful 'Ivy Bridge'), and a drawing, some 3 feet by 2, finished with exquisite care, of a scene in the Val d'Aosta ; numbering 135 in all.

The larger number of studies forming the second class are light sketches, valuable only to artists or to those interested in the processes of Turner's mind and hand. The total number of those catalogued by Mr. Ruskin as important is 1,757.

The sketches of the third class usually are more elaborate than the coloured ones. They consist of studies from Nature or for compositions, in firm outlines, usually on grey paper, heightened with white. Among other subjects more or less complete they embrace 50 of the original drawings for the 'Liber Studiorum,' and many of the rest are of large folio size.

Mr. Ruskin prefaced his letter with the explanation that his active executorship to the Turner estate confined itself to the cataloguing of these drawings, and that, finding his stewardship involved some legal difficulties, he threw it up ; and he concluded by assuring the trustees of the National Collections and the country at large that no one was so eminently fitted to arrange and provide for the exhibition of the Turner drawings as himself, but that he would undertake the task only on condition of the entire management of the drawings, in every particular, being entrusted to him. He expressed his desire to apply himself to the work, and undertook to begin it immediately upon receiving the appointment, and further, in order to prove the working of the system proposed, to furnish 100 of the frames, with their cases, at his own cost. Within six weeks of the day on which he might be permitted to begin work (illness or accident not interfering) he engaged to have the 100 drawings arranged, framed, accompanied by a printed explanatory catalogue, and ready for public inspection.

Mr. Ruskin was in Scotland, visiting Dumblane, Jedburgh, and other favourite sites of Turner, when he received a letter informing him that the trustees of the National Gallery had granted him permission to arrange the Turner drawings for the nation. From the autumn of 1857 to May 1858, accordingly, he laboured assiduously ; and I can bear witness to this labour of love. Mr. Ruskin's account of the condition in which he found the drawings is full of interest, and not without pathos. He says—

' In seventeen boxes in the lower room of the National Gallery I found upwards of 19,000 pieces of paper, drawn upon by Turner in one way or another. Many on both sides. Some with four, five, or six subjects on each side (the pencil point digging spiritedly through from the foregrounds of the front into the tender pieces of sky on the back). Some in chalk, which the touch of the finger would sweep away. The best book of studies for his great shipwrecks contained about a quarter of a pound of chalk débris, black and white, broken off the crayons with which Turner had drawn furiously on both sides of the leaves ; every leaf, with peculiar foresight and consideration of difficulties to be met by future mounters, containing half of one subject on the front of it, and half of another on the back. Others in ink, rotted into holes. Others (some splendid-coloured drawings among them) long eaten away by damp and mildew, and falling into dust at the edges, in various states of fragile decay. Others worm-eaten ; some mouse-eaten ; many torn half-way through ; numbers doubled (quadrupled, I should say) into four, being Turner's favourite mode of packing for travelling ; nearly all rudely flattened out from the bundles in which Turner had finally rolled them up and squeezed them into the drawers in Queen Anne Street. Dust, of thirty years' accumulation, black, dense, and sooty, lay in the rents of the crushed and crumpled edges of these flattened bundles, looking like a jagged black frame, and producing altogether unexpected effects in brilliant portions of skies, whence an accidental or experimental finger-mark of the first bundle unfolder had swept it away.

'About half, or rather more, of the entire number consisted of pencil sketches in flat oblong pocket-books, dropping to pieces at the back, tearing laterally whenever opened, and every drawing rubbing itself into the one opposite. These first I paged with my own hand, then unbound, and laid every leaf separately on a clean sheet of perfectly smooth writing-paper, so that it might receive no further injury. Then enclosing the contents and boards of each book (usually ninety-two leaves, more or less drawn on both sides, with two sketches on the boards at the beginning and end) in a separate sealed packet, I returned it to its tin box. The loose sketches needed more trouble. The dust had first to be got off them (from the chalk ones it could only be blown off), then they had to be variously flattened; the torn ones to be laid down, the loveliest guarded so as to prevent all future friction, and four hundred of the most characteristic framed and glazed, and cabinets constructed for them, which would admit of their free use by the public.'

How sad is the record! These sketches were the drift and débris of a moraine, the lumber of an unhappy man's life, the half-fulfilled purposes of a confused, entangled life. What despair there was in that dread of looking over the records of the past; despair of working his destiny into one harmonious whole! Who is there, looking at his own lumber, that does not say to himself, there are so many more unfulfilled intentions, so many dwarfed expectations, so many stunted hopes, so many disappointments added to the old store?

CHAPTER XXXV.

THE TURNER PORTRAITS.

THERE was at one time a notion current to the effect that no portrait of Turner existed, whereas no great artist perhaps was oftener sketched.   From behind pictures, and from the ambush of dark corners of exhibition rooms, the busy pencil was perpetually recording him.   Mulready drew him ; Count d'Orsay drew him ; Gilbert drew him ; Linnel drew him ; Dance drew him ; Mr. Munro drew him ; Mr. Fawkes drew him ; and, according to Peter Cunningham, so did Maclise and Mr. Charles Turner.   Yet the secretive painter never sat willingly but once. He had a settled idea that, if the public saw his portrait, they would think less of his pictures.

It is certain that Turner sat to Dance for the portrait published in 1800, when he was R.A., and twenty-five years old.   This portrait, which is one of a series of Academician portraits published by George Dance, represents a handsome young man, with rather large features, a full, prominent nose, a fine, strong-willed chin, and a rather sensual mouth, the lower lip of which is fleshy, and the upper lip beautifully curved. The eyebrow is arched, and the eyelids are long, presenting a great depth between the eye and the eyebrow.   The forehead is full, but rather receding, and is covered with a stray wisp of hair, as Turner always kept it.   The hair, close, thick, and somewhat stubborn-looking, is long behind, and tied with a black ribbon ; and he wears a white cravat, the ends of which bulge out in front of his waistcoat.   The cape of his coat is of immense width, and the lapels are thrown back in a careless yet somewhat cavalier way.   Indeed, unless Dance's pencil has flattered, Turner here looks a frank, handsome-hearted young man of genius.   The portrait might stand for that of a young general or a young statesman, for the expression is at once winning and commanding.

In 1851, the year of Turner's death, a clever caricature of him was published by that feeble dilettante Count d'Orsay, which Landseer is said to have retouched. It must have been drawn from memory not many months before, at some soirée at which Turner and the Count were both present—perhaps at Mr. Windus's. The Count evidently drew him, not from any admiration of his genius, of which he probably understood nothing, but as being a character, and old-fashioned in dress and manner. Some of Turner's friends hold it to be a base caricature, while others esteem it as being, after all, the best likeness extant. For myself, I regard it as at least an admirable record of his costume and attitude. The enormous, loose, large-buttoned dress coat, with the square wide tails and the outside pockets, is very characteristic; so are his white cravat and frilled shirt; and so are the meagre dancing-shoes and the rudely-made trousers. I like, too, the grim listening air with which, as he stands near the piano, he stirs round his cup of tea. Whether he ever wore that wobegone aspect, however, I cannot say, though the amateur artist has certainly given the face a look of declining health and vitality. The nose sharpens, the cheeks sink, the mouth falls in, the eye is feeble, even the hair is lean and sickly. Death is very near at hand with the great artist, and is watching him even now in that room echoing with music and sparkling with lights.

At a dinner party given on a varnishing-day at Mr. Wells's Landseer exhibited a little portrait of Turner that he had painted on his palette at the Academy that morning. It was very clever; everyone liked it; many even thought it perfect. Unluckily an artist present induced Sir Edwin (who knew not how to refuse) to give it him; and, in order to carry it home, the gratified recipient of the gift put it into his hat. The colours were wet; and, when the artist took off his hat on reaching home, he found that the picture had stuck to his hair. It was entirely blurred and spoiled, and the likeness effaced.

Mr. White, the well-known picture dealer of Maddox Street, has in his possession the precious portrait of Turner painted surreptitiously by Linnel, from sittings unconsciously given him at Mr. Daniel's dinner parties. Mr. White naturally enough attaches great value to this relic, and keeps it enclosed in a sort of altar case, as if it were a Leonardo or a Raphael ; yet many of the best judges do not estimate it for its accuracy as a likeness. It was arranged by Mr. Daniel that at these premeditated dinners Linnel should sit opposite Turner, so as to carry off a vivid memory of his face ; but few men, and those only born portrait painters, can remember faces with perfect accuracy ; and even then merely as sketches, and not in detail of outline and colour. With all its defects, however, especially that of being rather smaller than life, it is an interesting picture, and worthy of record. The portrait with this strange history represents him in almost the prime of life, and in the fantastic full-dress of the George IV. period—red velvet waistcoat, dandy coat with velvet collar, and a high wall of stiff black satin stock, the ends cascading down over his shirt front, and fastened with a red coral breast-pin. It is not the barber's son we see, but the great Mr. Turner, R.A., who proposed an Irish tour to Mr. Thomas Moore—the Turner who was kind to poor Campbell, and who climbed up Arthur's Seat with Sir Walter.

Mr. Ruskin is one of those who do not think this portrait like him. On the other hand, Mr. Griffith, who knew Turner at the time when it was taken, considers it 'a very good likeness.' My application to Mr. Linnel for his version of the circumstances attending it produced the following letter :—

'The history of my portrait of Turner the Great is a very short one. I painted it from recollection, at the request of a friend of his, at whose table we frequently met. I made no memorandum at the time of meeting, but painted from memory entirely, the first opportunity. I believe the portrait was painted about 1837, and as the friend for whom it was intended died, it remained with me until I sold it to Mr. D. T. White, the picture dealer in Maddox Street, Hanover Square. I have also a very careful outline of Turner's father, taken when attending his son's lecture at the Royal Academy, about 1810, and a sketch of his eyes and brow looking down at the lecturer. The picture was intended for Mr. Birch, of Birmingham, and was, I believe, valued at 200 guineas ; it is now worth triple that sum.

It is a vivacious likeness, and highly interesting to those who knew the great painter twenty years ago.'

Yet another portrait is recorded by Mr. Lovell Reeve. Mr. Charles Turner, A.R.A., the mezzotint engraver of his ' Liber Studiorum,' and his oldest and most constant friend, was so desirous of securing a likeness of him at all hazards that he availed himself, from time to time, of every opportunity of collecting memoranda for the purpose. At length he obtained a most characteristic portrait in oil (small half-size) of Turner in the act of sketching. The singularity of his dress and figure is scrupulously attended to, and it has been pronounced an admirable and faithful likeness. Mr. C. Turner engraved this portrait twenty years before his death.

' He at length,' says another account, ' obtained a portrait of his friend, which has been pronounced by Sir Charles Eastlake, Mr. George Jones, Mr. Alfred Chalon, Mr. David Roberts, Mr. Willmore, and other friends of the great deceased who have seen it to be an admirable and faithful likeness.'

Turner distinctly told one of his friends that he sat for Dance's portrait of him. His less enthusiastic friends describe him as having a red Jewish face with staring bluish-grey eyes, and the smallest and dirtiest hands on record. His complexion was very coarse and weather-beaten; his cuticle that of a stage-coachman or an old man-of-war boatswain. It was as tough as the skin of a rhinoceros, and red as the shell of a boiled lobster. That complexion told of rough days, when the rain had driven in his eyes as he sat on diligence roofs, or in boats lifting over enormous waves. The sea wind had buffeted him; the hot Italian sun had parched and browned him. His dress was always careless and often dirty ; and his sleeves were long, so as to hide his small, pliable hands. Latterly he improved in his costume, thanks to the care of his Chelsea housekeeper, and even was resplendent at Academy meetings in a red velvet waistcoat. On one occasion he was particularly struck by his friend Jones's blue waistcoat, and its contrast with a red scarf worn underneath. ' I like that, Joney,' said Turner ; ' good bit of colour, Joney ; ' and soon after he appeared in the same effective dress. A hat with the nap carefully brushed the wrong way was also one of his characteristics.

'Turner had fine intelligent eyes, dark blue or mazarine,' says Mr. Trimmer; 'but, as it is said of Swift's, they were heavy rather than animated. He had a pleasing but melancholy expression. His conversation was always sensible, and in all matters connected with his profession invaluable. He dressed in black, with short black gaiters, and, though neat, was not smart. He was retired in his habits, and sensitive in his feelings; he was an excessively kind-hearted person, and fond of children, says one who knew him. His domestic life was founded on the models of the old masters, his conversation was most correct, and no one more upheld the decencies of society.[1]

'He had been accused of miserly habits; but, as it was known full thirty years before his death that he was accumulating his property for decayed artists and their families, he cannot be charged with selfishness. If he exacted from publishers the market value of his great talents, do such persons as a class act differently with inferior talents? I believe he was hard in his dealings with engravers; in fact, he was averse to any but first-rate hands engraving his pictures.'

Turner's own portrait, as painted by himself, is rather brown in colour, but fine in expression. The forehead is high, and the rather too large nose is cleverly concealed by being taken full-face. The lip is full, but not unduly so, and the chin strong and Napoleonic. The young artist wears a huge cape to his coat, the fashionable double waistcoat, and a full white handkerchief, with pendent ends, round his neck. The colour is wanting in tenderness, and in trying for breadth the greys have been sacrificed.

Turner's iron-grey eyes (they were really blue), says Mr. Goodall, seemed to strike through you; they revealed a great consciousness of power. When animated, they were quite handsome, testifies an old friend; they were blue as enamel, and were round, staring, and bull-like as those of Frederick the Great's.

---

[1] It is remarkable that in his will he restricts his charities to persons born in lawful wedlock.

Leslie, who derided D'Orsay's libel, erred in saying that Turner neither sat to anyone, nor ever would sit; but it is true he thought himself coarse, ugly, unpoetical-looking. He describes him as short and stout, and with a sturdy, sailor-like walk. 'There was, in fact, nothing elegant in his appearance,' writes he, 'full of elegance as he was in Art. He might have been taken for the captain of a river steamer at first sight, but a second would find far more in his face than belongs to any ordinary mind. There was that peculiar keenness of expression in his eye that is only seen in men of constant habits of observation. His voice was deep and musical.'

John Gilbert, one of the first of modern draughtsmen on wood, took a sketch of him on one of the varnishing-days of the last Exhibition at the British Institution (1841) to which he contributed. Turner's picture was not completed, for latterly he always finished on the walls. Mounted on a box, the little squab man was 'scumbling' (driving opaque paint in a transparent coat) over the rays of the sun, which, in the exact centre of the picture, projected like the boss on an ancient shield. Gilbert watched him as he worked thus, and took a sketch, which he afterwards from memory elaborated. This sketch (which appeared long ago in one of Cassell's publications) represents, very humorously and vigorously, the awkward, untidy dress of the painter; and the swab of a handkerchief hanging from the side pocket of his tail-coat, the large, almost Jewish nose, the loose, slovenly trousers, and the eagle eyes, are not easily forgotten.

One of Turner's detractors, the late Mr. Rippingille, gives the following hostile view of his manner, face, and bearing :—

'Personally, Turner was as much a character as his house, and as cold and forbidding in aspect. I have witnessed meetings between him and those who considered themselves in the light of friends. I have seen a "friend" seize his arm in a public room, and attempt to walk and to speak with him; and have seen him receive much the same treatment as a butcher would meet with who attempted to put his arm under the fore-leg of an unsocial and impracticable pig. It is said he could talk, and that he had a good deal of sedate fun, seasoned with a spice of sarcasm : I have heard casual remarks from him, which betrayed neither of these qualities — except, perhaps, a little of the last, which I observed was accompanied with a certain self-complacent grunt. He professed to know me personally, and once or twice I have put this knowledge to the direct test by asking him who I was, and by his reply have ascertained that his recollection was about as good as his word, or his acquaintance. I know a gentleman who sat next him at a dinner table, one, too, of such a stock of resources and acquirements as would move a Stoic ; but not more than a few words could be obtained from Turner. It was clear that Turner was at home, from the familiar way in which he addressed one of the ladies of the family ; and his silence or sulkiness was afterwards accounted for by the master of the house calling him aside, and pointedly asking him what was the matter, when it was ascertained that, upon handing him his cheque for a seven-hundred-pound picture, he had forgotten to pay the hire of the coach in which Turner had come and brought the picture with him. There is but little dependence to be placed upon the numerous stories extant, and by no means to his credit ; I therefore speak only of what I know and saw. Turner was a short, vulgar-looking man, with an ordinary head, and a coarse, red, " pimply " face, utterly devoid of any degree of refinement or intelligence. I cannot recollect any other clever man I ever saw who did not carry evidence of the fact in his face ; Turner was the exception. It was impossible to make anything of such a head, such a face, look, and impression. So far from its bearing the impress of anything like thought, there was a vulgar, half-suppressed giggle, that seemed imprisoned in features too rigid or obstinate to let it escape ; while in the twinkle of his eye there was a kind of triumph and self-satisfaction, as much as to say, you might look, but you could not make him out ; but with this he showed no disposition to face, but to escape from, observation.'

This description is little better than an effusion of pure spite. From such men as its author too often come our satirists, our epigrammatists, and our critics ; and the world, leaning ever to the worst side, takes their bitterness for honesty. Yet the representation that Turner was a stumpy, ill-dressed man, with a red face and something of a satyr's mouth, is accurate ; but this was towards the close of his life.

I have seen an admirable picture of Turner by that clever caricaturist in colour Mr. Chalon, which gives him with rather a Jewish look, little staring grey eyes, arched, astonished eyebrows, and very scarlet face.   Mulready also once showed me an inimitable little sketch of Turner *furens*, taken by stealth at a sitting of the Academy Council whereat the artist was thwarted. He looks ready for a spring ; Achilles chafing in his tent could not have appeared more grandly furious. Mulready had caught the true, though momentary, expression.

Mr. Rippingille, who viewed Turner with the jaundiced eye of envy, further pronounces him to have been 'short, stumpy, and vulgar, without one redeeming personal qualification, slovenly in dress, not over cleanly, and devoid of all signs of the habits of a gentleman, or a man moving in good society.'

CHAPTER XXXVI.

TURNER'S ENEMIES.

MR. RUSKIN has laid about him, among Turner's detractors, with the club of a veritable Alcides ; but Hydra has many heads, and it takes a long time to brain and brand each particular head. Unable myself to wield the matchless weapons of that truly great writer, I shall dismiss these critics very briefly. Those who find Turner's works repulsively monotonous, or see nothing in them but central splashes of light, with surrounding groups of dark, I care not to answer. Those who find his figures more slovenly than Claude's, and evincing ' a coarse, unscrupulous mind and hand,' I can only refer to the admirable figures scattered through his engraved works, and to the fine picture of the ' Departure of Adonis,' at Mr. Munro's, painted in direct rivalry of Titian.

Fuseli was an early admirer of Turner, and so was Calcott. Hazlitt, too, in his essay on ' Imitation and Pedantry,' while condemning the vagueness of his later pictures, thus praises the general breadth of his genius :—

'We here allude particularly to Turner, the ablest land-scape painter now living, whose pictures are, however, too much abstractions of aërial perspective, and representations not so properly of the objects of Nature as of the medium through which they are seen.   They are the triumph of the knowledge of the artist, and of the power of the pencil over the barrenness of the subject.   They are pictures of the elements of air, earth, and water.   The artist delights to go back to the first chaos of the world, and to that state of things when the waters were separated from the dry land, and light from darkness, but as yet no living thing, nor tree bearing fruit, was seen upon the face of the earth. All is " without form and void." Some one said of his landscapes that they were " pictures of nothing and very like ." '

Among the German critics Dr. Waagen stands pre-eminent for pompous blundering.   He has one of those routine minds, unoriginal, bound by precedent and convention, and holding to the old and the safe.   Here is his dictum, which is evidently founded on a very scanty knowledge of Turner's works, especi-ally of his divine water-colour drawings, without which no one can judge of his greatness.   Dr. Waagen is no Solomon in his utterances, as the following will show :—

' Of all the English painters at the period of my first visit to England I knew least of Turner, having seen very few of his works, and those almost entirely of his later time.   In my two last visits (1850 and 1851) I endeavoured to repair this omission ; and, having succeeded in examining a number of his pictures and drawings of the most various periods, I feel myself qualified to give my deliberate opinion upon them.   It appears to me that Turner was a man of marvellous genius, occupying some such place among the English landscape painters of our day as Lord Byron among the modern English poets.   In point of fact, no landscape painter has yet appeared with such versa-tility of talent.   His historical landscapes exhibit the most ex-quisite feeling for beauty of lines and effect of lighting ; at the same time he has the power of making them express the most varied moods of Nature—a lofty grandeur, a deep and gloomy melancholy, a sunny cheerfulness and peace, or an uproar of all the elements.   Buildings he also treats with peculiar felicity ;

while the sea, in its most varied aspect, is equally subservient to his magic brush. His views of certain cities and localities inspire the spectator with poetic feelings such as no other painter ever excited in the same degree, and which is chiefly attributable to the exceeding picturesqueness of the point of view chosen, and to the beauty of the lighting. Finally, he treats the most common little subjects, such as a group of trees, a meadow, a shaded stream, with such art as to impart to them the most picturesque charm. I should therefore not hesitate to recognise Turner as the greatest landscape painter of all times, but for his deficiency in one indispensable element in every perfect work of Art—namely, a sound technical basis. It is true that the pictures and drawings of his earlier and middle period overflow with an abundance of versatile and beautiful thoughts, rendered with great truth of Nature ; but at the same time his historical landscapes never possess the delicacy of gradation and the magical atmosphere of Claude, nor his re-alistic works the juicy transparency and freshness of a Ruys-dael ; while many of his best pictures have lost their keeping by subsequent darkening, and with it a great portion of their value. In his later time, however, he may be said to have aimed gradually rather at a mere indication than a representa-tion of his thoughts, which in the last twenty years of his life be-came so superficial and arbitrary that it is sometimes difficult to say what he really did intend. Not that I overlook even in these pictures the frequent extraordinary beauty of composition and lighting, which renders them what I should rather call the beautiful souls of pictures. The raptures, therefore, of many of Turner's countrymen, who prefer these pictures to those of his early period, I am not able to share, but must adhere to the sober conviction that a work of Art executed in this material world of ours must, in order to be quite satisfactory, have a complete and natural body, as well as a beautiful soul. Of the earlier period of this great master the Gallery has no specimen. To his later time belongs " Lake Avernus, the Sibyl, and the Golden Bough " (No. 7), an historical composition ; while the two views of " Venice " (Nos. 51 and 57, the last of which, though somewhat glassy, is most attractive for effect of light) show his realistic tendency. In the picture "The Prince of Orange Landing at Torbay" (No. 75) he appears as a very spirited marine painter, though he is somewhat superficial in detail.'

About 1844 the wits (they are ever cruel) began to be most severe on the poor old painter, of whose greatness they were ignorant, and whose nobler works had pleased a previous generation. Turner keenly felt their cruelty and ingratitude. I append some of the smartest of these attacks on the dying lion, to show how clever and how cruel they were at once :—

'Trundler, R.A., treats us with some magnificent pieces.

'34. A Typhoon bursting in a Simoom over the Whirlpool of Maelstrom, Norway ; with a ship on fire, an eclipse, and the effect of a lunar rainbow.

> ' O Art, how vast thy mighty wonders are
>   To those who roam upon the extraordinary deep ;
>   Maelstrom, thy hand is here.
>   *From an unpublished poem.*

'4. (Great Room.)   Hippopotamuses at play in the River Scamander.

'1311. The Duke of Wellington and the Shrimp. (Seringa-patam, early morning.)

> ' And can it be, thou hideous imp,
>   That life is, ah ! how brief, and glory but a shrimp !
>   *From an unpublished poem.*

' We must protest against the Duke's likeness here ; for though his Grace is short, his face is not of an emerald green colour ; and it is his coat, not his boots, which are vermilion ; nor is it fair to make the shrimp (a blue one) taller than the conqueror of Assaye. With this trifling difference of opinion, we are bound to express our highest admiration of the work. It is the greatest that the English school of quiet landscape has produced. The comet just rising above the cataract in the foreground, and the conflagration of Tippoo's widow in the banyan forest by the sea-shore, are in the great artist's happiest manner.'[1]

'No. 77 is called "Whalers," by J. M. W. Turner, R.A., and embodies one of those singular effects which are only met with in lobster salads and in this artist's pictures. Whether he calls his picture "Whalers," or "Venice," or "Morning," or "Noon," or "Night," it is all the same; for it is quite as easy to fancy it one thing as another.'

'We had almost forgotten Mr. J. M. W. Turner, R.A., and his celebrated MS. poem, the "Fallacies of Hope," to which he constantly refers us, as "in former years;" but on this occasion he has obliged us by simply mentioning the title of the poem, without troubling us with an extract. We will, however, supply a motto to his "Morning: Returning from the Ball," which really seems to need a little explanation; and, as he is too modest to quote the "Fallacies of Hope," we will quote for him :—

> 'Oh, what a scene! Can this be Venice? No.
> And yet methinks it is—because I see,
> Amid the lumps of yellow, red, and blue,
> Something which looks like a Venetian spire.
> That dash of orange in the background there
> Bespeaks 'tis morning. And that little boat
> (Almost the colour of tomata sauce)
> Proclaims them now returning from the ball :
> This in my picture I would fain convey.
> I hope I do. Alas! *what* FALLACY!'[2]

Gilbert à Beckett, who laughed at everything, sacred or profane, laughed at Turner in his 'Almanac of the Month' (1846). Thackeray had laughed in 'Ainsworth's Magazine' at 'The Napoleon and Rock Limpet;' A Beckett laughed at the 'Undine and Masaniello,' calling it a 'lobster salad,' and saying the artist mixed his colours on the canvas, or pelted it with eggs. According to him, it was a 'fair specimen of this slap-dash school;' and the drawing represents him running along a wall, painting with a mop and a bucket.

---

[1] *Punch*, vol. vi. p. 200. 1844.
[2] *Ibid.*, vol. viii. pp. 233, 236. 1845.

The fact was that these sorry jokes were chiefly written by young men, who were totally ignorant of Art in general, and, living in the present, forgot the past, and Turner's antecedents in particular. It was as if an ape at St. Helena had sat down to write a Life of Napoleon, judging him only from daily observations of him on the island.

I am afraid the tradition is too true that Thackeray, that mighty and bitter satirist of poor humanity's weaknesses, had no small share in thus lashing the dotage of a great man's genius. Long after, however, I have heard he was shown some of Turner's finest water-colour drawings, upon which he exclaimed, 'I will never run down Turner again.' But the blows had already gone to the old man's heart, and it did no good to lament them then.

Of Turner's sensitiveness to criticism Mr. Ruskin writes with deep feeling: 'To censure Turner was acutely sensitive; owing to his natural kindness, he felt it for himself or for others, not as criticism, but as cruelty. He knew that, however little his higher power could be seen, he had at least done as much as ought to have saved him from wanton insult; and the attacks upon him in his later years were to him not merely contemptible in their ignorance, but amazing in their ingratitude. "*A man may be weak in his age,*" he said to me once, at the time when he felt he was dying ; "*but you should not tell him so.*" What Turner might have done for us, had he received help and love instead of disdain, I can hardly trust myself to imagine.'

By way of contrast to the (so-called) criticisms given on a preceding page, I here condense a few of the excellent remarks made by Burnet, Wilkie's engraver, on Turner's genius. They are as remarkable for their severe common sense as for the study, learning, and insight they display :—

'Objects with distinct outline have a tendency to advance. Wilson's idea was that no foreground ought to be painted nearer than thirty feet ; for this reason the plants in his foreground are broad and blunt. Where Turner makes foreground objects sharp and clear they are generally too small to interfere with the general breadth of his light and shade.

'A multiplicity of objects prevents repose and breadth of shadow. The later works of Turner were treated in a lighter key to avoid spottiness. In the composition of skies he is more original than any other painter. If the scene is bald, he breaks his skies into beautiful forms. If the piece is multitudinous, he uses the sky for repose ; he uses the skies too for contrast of cool or warm colour. Objectionable lines he loses in the darks of his clouds ; agreeable or characteristic lines he brings into notice by opposition of light.

'The skies are admirable, too, for perspective ; the clouds duly diminish in size towards the horizon.

'Turner's figures are not as true as Raphael's, or as correct as Paul Potter's, but they have " a broad, general look of Nature." We must not overlook the truth of character and bluff forms of Turner's fishermen and English sailors ; they are true transcripts of the men they represent—they are portraits. Keeping the foreground light and warm makes the distance retire. Turner (unlike Wilson) does this.

'Turner's earlier pictures are heavy ; these he gradually relieved by scumbling ; nor even in his later works did he adopt rich glazings, but perfected his effects by washes of delicate opaque colours, that counteracted heaviness, but likewise destroyed richness and depth. This habit grew upon him till his lighter tints at last acquired a milky whiteness. The pictures of Claude, put beside those of Turner, look dirty and dingy. He never seems to have imitated Hobbima and Ruysdael, but to have extracted the essence of their pictures. The landscapes of Rubens and Rembrandt contain many of his principles.

'Space seems to have been the guiding principle with Turner. While the pictures of many artists stretch merely from left to right of the canvas, his works lead the eye from the foreground to the distance. The light key of colour of the modern school owes its origin to Turner. Wilson, Gainsborough, and the dark Dutch school were henceforward laid on the shelf.

'His light tints, the result of pearly scumblings, make his light pictures as luminous as his water-colour drawings. No one but Turner has represented the tremulous, dewy mist stealing along the ground in fading sunset shadows.

'The American and French war left the country too much excited for any encouragement to painting. Hence the Academicians painted too many pictures, and in too slight a manner. The early works of Turner have a look of slightness in the execution.

'Turner's style influenced Calcott, Etty, and Wilkie. Lawrence, except in his lighter pictures, seldom relinquished his cool shadows. Owen's backgrounds have an affinity with Turner.

'The theory is false that would make objects less visible as they recede from the centre to the sides of a picture. We certainly see this treatment in Rembrandt, but then these pictures were placed in broad black frames that gave greater force to the contiguous light. Now that we have gold ornamented frames, Lawrence and Turner carry out light and colour to the borders of their gorgeous works.

'Turner cannot be said to have fallen on evil days. The British Institution and the Academy Exhibitions gave an impetus to British Art, and still more so did the formation of the National Gallery. He lived in a time of great poets, whose works he illustrated; he influenced the style of theatrical scenery and of panoramic exhibitions. He was born, too, in a time of much chemical change in the manufacture of pigments, and all new colours he daringly used, whether chrome yellow, emerald green, or cobalt blue.

'In other respects he was before his age; his large engravings did not succeed. They had to compete with Landseer's figure subjects and Wilkie's *genre* pictures. Steel engraving did justice to the latter, while landscape requires a slower and more expensive process. The innumerable small prints after his designs satisfied curiosity and sated the public.

'Turner used white grounds. His later pictures are too ethereal, prismatic, and poetic for the million; and thirst for novelty led Turner to the dreamy grandeur which he attained by light, and Rembrandt by dark. He was amazed by the later imitations of him, and by the want of encouragement of his early style. Water colours led him partly to this manner. The most evanescent of Turner's pictures will acquire a greater solidity as they grow older.

'Latterly his chief aim was breadth of light and strong contrast of hot and cold colour. His unfinished pictures are all cold blue sky, and warm orange-brown foreground.'

In his 'Handbook for Young Painters' Leslie, with great coolness of temper and no little severity of reasoning, vindicates Canaletti from some of Mr. Ruskin's attacks, and points out, but not invidiously, how open Turner himself occasionally was to censure. The extract is long, but I do not grudge the space :—

'Turner began with water colours, a mode of painting which he practised at later periods of his life with wonderful power. In his earliest works a resemblance may be noticed to Cozens (to whom he always acknowledged great obligations), and still more to Girtin, but with inferior power to either. Contemporary with both, and of about the same age with Girtin, had Turner died as young, his name would only have survived as that of a second-rate painter. His genius was of later development, and first appeared in those grand classic and marine subjects which he painted in the early part of the century. The sea pieces were his own ; the others were made up from various sources in Art ; and, though noble works, yet not generally those on which his fame will ultimately rest. His "Snow-Storm in the Alps," however, with " Hannibal and his Army," would alone justify the highest praises of his friends ; and his " Ulysses," painted at a much later period, is a poem of matchless splendour and beauty. Among the great multitude of his conceptions there may be doubtless other classical subjects equal to those direct from Nature, but they are exceptions to the rule by which he will be judged.

'I was equally delighted and surprised when I heard that a very young man had come forward, with extraordinary ability, knowledge and love of Nature, as the champion of Turner, at a time when (excepting by painters) his transcendent powers were little felt or understood. But I own I was disappointed, when I read Mr. Ruskin's " Modern Painters," at one of the modes he adopted in the vindication of the great artist's just claim to admiration.

'There is little enough of excellence in the world, and its appreciation is always in danger from the obtrusion of clever mediocrity, and that direction of criticism, with whatever ability it is conducted, is unfortunate that tends to obscure any of the true lights in Art, in order that one great luminary may shine the more brilliantly. I think, therefore, it was equally unnecessary and unsafe to the reputation of Turner to assume that he had fewer faults than other great painters, and to contrast his beauties with the faults, often indeed imaginary, of Claude, the Poussins, Cuyp, or Canaletti; unnecessary, because his excellences are of so high an order that his greatest admirers may fearlessly acknowledge all the defects with which he may be charged; and unsafe, because such a system of comparison might be more easily turned against him than against any painter that ever lived, for there never lived one in whose works greater absurdities or a larger number of impossible effects might be pointed out. Then, again, the assumption that other great painters are inferior to him, because they have not done the same beautiful things, is unfair. Mr. Ruskin describes in his own vivid manner four or five skies by Turner, and at the close of every such eloquent passage asks triumphantly, " Has Claude given this?" Now, it would be quite as easy to select from the works either of Claude, the Poussins, of Wilson, of Cuyp, of Ruysdael, and even of Canaletti, passages of peculiar beauty, and to ask, with as little chance of an affirmative reply, " Has Turner given this?"

'I have said that the faults Mr. Ruskin finds in the old masters are often imaginary; and, in proof of this, let us examine his remarks on the picture in the National Gallery, by Nicolas Poussin, called " Phocian." Mr. Ruskin says: "The first idea we receive from this picture is that it is evening, and all the light coming from the horizon; not so, it is full noon, the light coming steep from the left, as is shown by the shadow of the stick on the right-hand pedestal, for if the sun were not very high, that shadow could not lose itself half-way down, and if it were not lateral, the shadow would slope, instead of being vertical." Now the fact is that, if the sun were very high, the shadow of the stick would be continued instead of losing itself, and the effect in the picture is in reality in accordance with the more softened light of the sun when near the horizon, while the shadow of the man's head near the stick is placed exactly where an evening sun would cast it. It is true these shadows are thrown laterally into the picture, but this is quite consistent with as much of warm light as Poussin has shown in the horizon, and the contradiction of effects imagined by Mr. Ruskin has no existence ; while, were it worth while to look for blunders in Turner, we might notice that palpable one in the " Dido Building Carthage " of a shadow from a beam of wood projecting from the brick wall on the extreme left of the spectator, in a direction which can only come from a sun much higher than that in the picture. Another instance of the detection of a supposed falsehood by Mr. Ruskin in a great painter, but which in fact is a truth, occurs in his description of Canaletti's manner of treating water. After describing, with much severity, the ripples in the open part of a canal, he says (and in the way of censure) that " three hundred yards away all the houses are reflected as clear and as sharp as in a quiet lake." And most assuredly they are, because Canaletti painted what he saw, and the water as it approached the houses, being sheltered by them from the breeze that occasions the ripple in the middle of the canal, was there as calm as "a quiet lake." The reader will see a fine example of such treatment in the large Canaletti in the National Gallery. Mr. Ruskin is right in his censure of the manner, as too mechanical, in which the ripples are painted by Canaletti—a censure that applies to his execution generally. Still, the effect in Nature he meant to express is given, and his colour is always relatively true and well selected, though in a subdued scale ; and, however below Turner, Canaletti cannot be spared from the list of great painters ; and, in proof that Turner is at least as vulnerable, I would notice that, among the impossibilities in his pictures, we often find reflections on the uneven surfaces of large waves exactly perpendicular to the object reflected, and as they could only be seen on calm water.

'Mr. Ruskin, I know, will agree with me in considering it unfortunate for Turner that his picture of "Dido Building Carthage" is placed in the National Gallery beside Claude's "Embarkation of the Queen of Sheba;" for his notice of the two pictures of Carthage is among the few instances in which he admits a fault in Turner. "The foreground," he says, "of the 'Building of Carthage,' and the greater part of the architecture of the 'Fall,' are equally heavy, and evidently paint, if we compare them with genuine passages of Claude's sunshine." For my own part, when I look at the "Building of Carthage," I feel as if I were in a theatre decorated with the most splendid of drop scenes; but when I stand before Claude's "Embarkation," I am in the open air enjoying the sea breeze, and listening to the plash of the waves on the beach. Yet this does not convince me that Claude was a greater man than Turner, because it is a comparison of one of the most artificial pictures of the English painter with one of the most natural works of the Frenchman; and I only make the comparison to show that Claude is not to be deposed, to place on his throne one who wants it not, because he has raised himself to a throne unoccupied before, and from which his sway is extended over a wider dominion, though, for that very reason, with less absolute power in every corner of it. Claude could not paint a storm; Turner's sea storms are the finest ever painted; and, though Claude is best seen in tranquil sunshine, yet there are many beautiful and brilliant midday appearances, of perfect stillness, that were never seen on canvas till Turner gave them with a power precluding all imitation; and I can well believe, with Mr. Ruskin, in the truth of his Venetian scenes, those splendid palaces and churches under the brightest skies and reflected in the clearest waters. Others may have painted with more truth many of the lesser facts; but he alone has given the great facts that are the prevailing associations with Venice. I have never seen Switzerland; but I have known those who have gone there sceptics with respect to Turner's excellence, and returned worshippers; and I know enough of lake scenery to feel how great a painter he is of mountains and lakes, with all their changes of sunshine, cloud, and mist. Such are the things which are the real praise of this wonderful painter of light, and space, and air.

'I have read with attention Mr. Ruskin's remarks on Turner's trees and foliage, but without being convinced that he was so great a painter of these as of other features of Nature. With the exception of here and there a willow, and in his Italian views the frequent pine and cypress, I look in vain for a specific discrimination in his trees, or in the vegetation of his foregrounds, in which there is little that is English. I cannot remember an oak, an elm, an ash, or a beech, in any picture by him (only a fine decayed oak in one of his vignettes) ; nor do I remember anything much like the beauty of an English hedge. Neither has he expressed the deep fresh verdure of his own country ; and hence he is the most unfaithful (among great painters) to the essential and most beautiful characteristics of English midland scenery. Constable said to me, " Did you ever see a picture by Turner, and not wish to possess it ? " I forget the reply, but I might have named his " View from the Terrace at Richmond ; " from which, with the exception of the general composition, every beauty of that noble landscape is left out. I remember, in a summer of unusual drought, when the trees became embrowned and the grass was burnt up, that the colour of the woods and meadows seen from Richmond approached to that of Turner's picture ; but I never remember to have met with trees of such forms as those which he has placed in its foreground, in any part of the world ; nor am I acquainted, in Nature, with those trees often to be seen in his middle distances, which Mr. Ruskin accurately describes as shaped like pears with the stem downwards.'

Except one by Turner we have no recollection of any other picture by an artist of reputation in which snow is represented 'in action.' His 'Snow-Storm' was painted, and exhibited at the Academy, in 1842. In the catalogue it bore the title of 'Snow-Storm : Steamboat off a Harbour's Mouth making Signals, in Shallow Water, and going by the Lead ;' and we also learn, from the same authority, that the painter 'was in the storm the night the "Ariel"'—the name of the steamer—'left Harwich.'

Critics of all kinds, learned and unlearned, were furious when it was exhibited ; some of them described it as a mass of 'soapsuds and whitewash.' 'Turner,' says Mr. Ruskin, 'was passing the evening at my father's house on the day this criticism came out ; and after dinner, sitting in his arm-chair by the fire, I heard him muttering low to himself, at intervals, "Soapsuds and whitewash ! " again, and again, and again. At last I went to him, asking why he minded what they said. Then he burst out, 'Soapsuds and whitewash ! What would they have? I wonder what they think the sea's like ? I wish they'd been in it." It is thus, too often, that ignorance sits in judgment on the works of genius.'

One of the severest of his critics, Mr. Rippingille, writes of his works—

'Many of the pictures in the gallery appropriated to him in Marlborough House are lamentable examples of want of care, as well as conscience ; and, critically speaking, the collection, as a whole, somewhat impeaches the talent and powers of the artist, and to a very great extent impairs the influence exercised to swell his reputation as a grand imposition. None question Turner's merits and powers as a painter ; but these qualities are not found evidenced in *all* his works. The man of true taste and honesty will not fail to see a repulsive monotony of treatment pervading every subject, and a total absence, in most, of that freshness of feeling which is as often exhibited by himself as by any artist living or dead, and which ever attends an earnest yearning after excellence. In a great number of these productions there is no proof of the true motive ; such pictures appear to be made by a recipe, and to order. They are same, and mannered to excess. Each contains a large splash of light in the centre, with certain masses of *darks* grouped round. Nor is there often any variety, novelty, or ingenuity comprised in these ; so that the treatment, in a few examples, becomes vapid and commonplace. This continual trick, often much marred in the process by slovenly treatment, has the less to recommend it since it has no claim to originality in Art ; and, as regards Nature, it is partial, insulting, and injurious to the boundless and eternal variety of effects in which she presents herself to our notice and admiration. Take, as a test of the truth of this observation, the three or four pictures by Claude, hung in conjunction with about the same number of Turners in the National Gallery. In the first, as you enter, Claude gives you this effect of the sun in the centre of his picture, better executed and more effective than anything of the sort of which Turner is the imitator. But in Claude you do not find this effect repeated; in each of the other specimens are those varied effects by which Nature is ever characterised. Return to Turner, and in each example you find this effect repeated. Claude was a sloven in his figures; but what shall be said of Turner? Perhaps that he was a landscape and not a figure painter. Then he should not have put them into his pictures, but have done as sometimes Claude did, get another painter to do them. No man can look upon these works without perceiving the coarse, unscrupulous mind and hand from which they came, and which, in spite of all false criticism and sordid interests can do, will not save them from the condemnation of a wiser and more honest generation.'

The greatest impetus to Turner's fame was the publication in 1843 of Mr. Ruskin's first volume of the 'Modern Painters.' The painter whose reputation lay chiefly among his professional brethren, and who had somewhat tired the public with his later riddles, fantasies, and experiments, was now clearly proved to be the greatest landscape painter the world had ever known. With great genius, eloquence, and technical learning, and with a logic almost too subtle, Claude was lowered, Salvator crushed, Raphael criticised, and Turner's works reviewed, eulogised, explained, and elevated.

Such wonderful books on Art had never before been published. They exasperated some, electrified others, and delighted the majority. Works of Turner forgotten by the ordinary public were recalled; the painter's genius was focussed; and its lustre gained by the focussing. His timid admirers now grew bolder; his enemies were gradually silenced; then came the generous and magnificent bequest to awaken fresh interest; lastly, with deeper convictions, arose an almost universal thrill of proud satisfaction that England had at last produced a truly great painter. Those who at first affected to think the praise extravagant and paradoxical, gradually became converts ; and with each volume Turner's votaries increased in number.

Latterly there have been gainsayers, with whom I have no sympathy, treasonable enough to think that, though equally eloquent, industrious, acute, and original, Mr. Ruskin has become almost too voluminous and episodical, interlarding his commentaries on Turner with too much of Scriptural quotation, and growing almost too subtle in reasoning, and too technically and laboriously scientific. There are even heretics daring enough to doubt whether Turner ever plunged so deeply into geological theories, mythological mysteries, abstruse spiritualisms, and Biblical allegories as is made out. For myself, I do not think he went much further than Lempriere for his 'Polyphemus,' and some poor translation of Ovid for his 'Liber' subjects. He had meaning in all he did ; but it needed no Swedenborgian interpretation to discover it.

For myself, if there be such faults in the great Art critic, I forget them all when I read those splendid rhapsodies that swell on the ear with an almost Miltonic diapason, those exquisite passages of almost Athenian subtlety in reasoning, those elaborate and oratorical comparisons of the genius of different painters, those fervid outbursts, those eloquent and glowing comments on ancient and modern poets, those keen guesses that seem to lay bare before us the very soul of Titian, Angelico, Velasquez, or Veronese. When I read these, I grow regardless of all faults, and readily pardon them to an imagination as intense as that of Dante, if not so inventive ; to a soul as devout as that of Angelico, if not so simple ; to a colourist as gorgeous as Giorgione, if not of such depth ; to a genius as versatile as Turner, if his shaping power be less and his sense of composition weaker.

About this time appeared a race of young painters anxious for sounder and more finished painting, and less manufacture from old cracked conventional moulds. Need I say that Messrs. Millais, Holman Hunt, and Rossetti were the giants among them? A small magazine with an affected name, 'The Germ,' first organised the sect ; and slowly, through much anger and laughter, their works began to emerge in the Exhibitions. Mr. Millais's 'Ophelia' and 'Huguenot' were among the early pictures ; wonderful works for colour and finish, though not without certain drawbacks. Mr. Holman Hunt's 'Hireling Shepherd,' and 'Claudio and Isabella,' revealed both the power and the defects of the new school, its daring ambition, its indifference to beauty, and its determination to be unusual. Crimson flesh, rainbow sheep, ill-drawn horses, ugly, ascetic faces, and exaggerated trivialities were among its peculiarities ; and yet its admirers increased, especially when Mr. Ruskin advanced to the front, lance in hand, to prove that these men were painting on true Turner principles, that they were painting faithfully what they saw, with all truth and love, and that their finish was not minuter than that of the old masters. Their full daylight effects gratified those who were tired of the old brown studio gloom. Then came the great success of Mr. Millais's 'Order of Release,' a noble picture, almost without a fault ; and, still later, the even greater triumph of Mr. Holman Hunt's 'Christ in the Temple.'

The progress of photography doubtless led to much of this desire for finish and detail. Our school of Art had grown sadly slovenly ; it wanted a drastic and a tonic. Reynolds had done more harm by the sham idealism he taught than he had done good by the excellence of his example. But the new school still has much to learn. They disregard composition too much ; and they weaken their memories by the habit of drawing and painting everything, even to a straw, direct from Nature. Now, Turner might have taught them that Nature must be selected from, even must at times be slightly re-dressed and re-arranged, and that Nature is not always at her best, nor ripe for the painter.

In his celebrated pamphlet on 'Pre-Raphaelitism' Mr. Ruskin showed the true descent of the new sect's creed from the Turnerian principle of truth and finish. The following is the celebrated comparison between Millais and Turner, the short-sighted and the long-sighted man, in which the great writer elaborates his argument. He says—

'Suppose, for instance, two men equally honest, equally

industrious, equally impressed with a humble desire to render
some part of what they saw in Nature faithfully, and otherwise
trained in convictions such as I have above endeavoured to induce ; but one of them is quiet in temperament, has a memory
which nothing escapes, an invention which never rests, and
is comparatively near-sighted. Set them both free in the
same field, in a mountain valley. One sees everything, small
and large, with almost the same clearness—mountains and
grasshoppers alike, the leaves on the branches, the veins in the
pebbles, the bubbles in the stream ; but he can remember
nothing and invent nothing. Patiently he sets himself to his
mighty task ; abandoning at once all thoughts of seizing tran-
sient effects, or giving general impressions of that which his
eyes present to him in microscopical dissection, he chooses some
small portion out of the infinite scene, and calculates with
courage the number of weeks which must elapse before he can
do justice to the intensity of his perceptions, or the fulness of
matter in his subject. Meantime the other has been watching
the change of the clouds, and the march of the light along the
mountain-sides ; he beholds the entire scene in broad, soft
masses of true gradation, and the very feebleness of his sight is
in some sort an advantage to him in making him more sensible
of the aërial mystery of distance, and hiding from him the multitudes of circumstances which it would have been impossible for
him to represent. But there is not one change in the casting
of the jagged shadows along the hollows of the hills, but it is
fixed on his mind for ever ; not a flake of spray has broken
from the sea of cloud about their bases, but he has watched it
as it melts away, and could recall it to its lost place in heaven
by the slightest effort of his thoughts. Not only so, but
thousands and thousands of such images, of older scenes, remain congregated in his mind, each mingling in new associations with those now visibly passing before him, and these again
confused with other images of his own ceaseless, sleepless imagination, flashing by in sudden troops. Fancy how his paper
will be covered with stray symbols and blots, and undecipher-
able short-hand. As for his sitting down to " draw from Nature,"
there was not one of the things which he wished to represent

that stayed for so much as five seconds together ; but none of them escaped for all that—they are sealed up in that strange storehouse of his. He may take one of them out, perhaps, this day twenty years, and paint it in his dark room, far away.'

Remarkable is the strain in which Mr. Ruskin addresses the periodical writers of the day. His exhortation of them felicitously conveys at the same time a bit of kind advice to Turner :—

'Our periodical writers, therefore, may save themselves the trouble either of blaming or praising. Their duty is not to pronounce opinions upon the work of a man who has walked with Nature threescore years, but to impress upon the public the respect with which they are to be received, and to make request to him, on the part of the people of England, that he would now touch no unimportant work, that he would not spend time on slight or small pictures, but give to the nation a series of grand, consistent, systematic, and completed poems. We desire that he should follow out his own thoughts and intents of heart, without reference to any human authority. But we request in all humility that those thoughts may be seriously and loftily given ; and that the whole power of his unequalled intellect may be exerted in the production of such works as may remain for ever for the teaching of the nations. In all that he says we believe ; in all that he does we trust. It is therefore that we pray him to utter nothing lightly, to do nothing regardlessly. He stands upon an eminence, from which he looks back over the universe of God, and forward over the generations of men. Let every work of his hand be a history of the one, and a lesson to the other. Let each exertion of his mighty mind be both hymn and prophecy ; adoration to the Deity, and revelation to mankind.'

A friend of Turner's assured me that he once told him 'that he had never read a line of Ruskin.' At the same time there is a vague tradition of his being vexed at the panegyrics, and saying that Mr. Ruskin put ideas into his head he had never conceived. The two stories are mutually contradictory. It is impossible that both can be true, and it is unlikely that either is true.

Turner's Style.

In discussing Turner's finish, Mr. Ruskin praises the curves in his tree drawings, which, when you look long, ' seem to be all tremulous and wavering along every edge into endless melody of change ; ' and, in defending Turner from the charge of being unable to represent the higher snow-fields of the Alps, he writes with great truth—

'For rocks of this kind, being found only in the midst of the higher snow-fields, are not only out of the general track of the landscape painter, but are for the most part quite beyond his power—even beyond Turner's. The waves of snow, when it becomes a principal element in mountain form, are at once so subtle in tone and so complicated in colour and fold, that no skill will express them so as to keep the whole luminous mass in anything like a true relation to the rock darkness. For the distant rocks of the upper peaks are themselves when in light paler than white paper, and their true size and relation to near objects cannot be exhibited unless they are painted in the palest tones. Yet, as compared with their snow, they are so dark that a daguerreotype taken for the proper number of seconds to draw the snow-shadows rightly will always represent the rocks as coal-black. In order, therefore, to paint a snowy mountain properly we should need a light as much brighter than white paper as white paper is lighter than charcoal. So that, although it is possible with deep blue sky and purple rocks and blue shadows to obtain a very interesting resemblance of snow effect, and a true one up to a certain point (as in the best examples of body-colour drawing sold so extensively in Switzerland), it is not possible to obtain any of those refinements of form and gradation which a great artist's eye requires. Turner felt that, among these highest hills, no serious or perfect work could be done ; and although in one or two of his vignettes he showed his knowledge of them, his practice, in larger works, was always to treat the snowy mountains merely as a fading white cloud, concentrating the interest of his picture on nearer and more tractable objects.'

CHAPTER XXXVII.

TURNER'S ART LIFE.

TURNER'S first drawing exhibited at the Royal Academy was suspended in the humble room set apart for sculpture and drawings, miniatures and models in wax. The 'Rising Squall, Hot Wells' (1793) was one of the earliest pictures that made critics think a new poet had arisen. In the same year he went to make a drawing for Walker at Rochester, and soon after began his first oil picture. In 1794 he contributed drawings to several works; and in 1796 a picture of his obtained loud praise from the critics; including, I believe, the bitter, but generally just, Art satirist, (Pasquin) Williams.

Up to the year of his Associateship he had exhibited sixty-two pictures; of which forty were architectural, the remaining ones relating to British topography and landscape. His first subject picture was 'Fishermen Becalmed' (1799). Of his thirteen exhibited religious pictures, the 'Plague of Egypt' (1800) was the first; while of the thirty-seven mythological, 'Jason' led the way.

One of his earliest drawings was of the Pantheon after the fire (1792). The Pantheon had been used for masquerades, and also as a theatre and an opera house. The drawing represents the ruins of the front wall and portico. It is coloured in a dry manner, and the holes, once windows, are hung with icicles.

Turner's diploma picture was 'Dolbadern,' which, though imitative of Wilson's breadth, yet is full of the grand solemnity of evening; and 'the run-in of the dancing water' bright with the sunrise in 'Dunstanborough Castle' (1798) discloses an originality that no mere imitator could give.

Before we proceed further, however, let us review Turner's Art life; and for this purpose it will be best to adopt the division into three periods proposed by Mr. Ruskin.

Turner's first period Mr. Ruskin determines between 1800 and 1820 ; when he laboured as a student, imitating various old masters.

The second period is fixed between 1820 and 1835 ; when he
worked on the principles of Art he had discovered as a student,
doing what the theories of Art then required, and aiming at
beautiful ideal compositions rather than mere transcripts of
Nature.

The third period lies from 1835 to 1845 ; when, abandoning
the ideal, he reproduced his own simple impressions of Nature,
and associated them with his own deepest feelings. In 1845,
however, his health gave way, and his mind and sight began to
fail; insomuch that the artistic fruits of the last five years of
his life (he died in 1851) are of wholly inferior value.

The productions of his first period, thus defined, are notable
for a grey or brown colour, and sometimes for a heavy touch.
Turner now is more anxious for form than colour ; and the
colours, which are simple and few, are laid on unskilfully.
His colour was sober because he was studying sober-coloured
landscapes ; and, even as the touch of them was heavy, so
was his touch: but his imitation did not degenerate into copying.
He did not copy Vandervelde, but went to the sea and painted
it in the Vandervelde way; so that by degrees he learnt to
paint truer than Vandervelde himself.

In 1823 came his ' Bay of Baiæ ; ' revealing transition to
his second period. The chief characteristics of this period are
colour instead of grey, refinement instead of force, and quantity instead of mass. His light now is as near the brightness
of real light as possible; and his shadow is not of one colour,
but of various colours. He tries now for delicacy and tenderness of contrast instead of violence; and he also finds that
no one had yet given the quantity of Nature. The drawings of
this period, when not designed simply for display, are ' faultless
and magnificent.' The splendour and gladness of the world,
not its humiliation and pain, are now his chief objects.

His third period is marked by less mechanical effort, less
pride in new discoveries, and less ambitious accumulation,
together with increased depth of imaginative delight and a
quiet love of Nature. Occasionally, conscious of power, and
in defiance of critics, he paints only to astonish. The figures
are chalky in the face, and scarlet in the reflected lights. After

1840 foliage is ill painted, and it rarely occurs in any prominent mass.

Of this third period Mr. Ruskin instructs—

'Another notable characteristic of this third period is that, though his mind was in a state of comparative repose, and capable of play at idle moments, it was in its depth infinitely more serious than heretofore; nearly all the subjects on which it dwelt having now some pathetic meaning. Formerly he painted the "Victory" in her triumph, but now the "Old Téméraire" in her decay; formerly Napoleon at Marengo, now Napoleon at St. Helena; formerly the Ducal Palace at Venice, now the Cemetery at Murano; formerly the Life of Vandervelde, now the Burial of Wilkie.

'Lastly, though in most respects this is the crowning period of Turner's genius, in a few there are evidences in it of approaching decline. As we have seen, in each former phase of his efforts, that the full character was not developed till about its central year, so in this last the full character was not developed till the year 1840; and that character involved, in the very fulness of its imaginative beauty, some loss of distinctness, some absence of deliberation in arrangement, and, as we approach nearer and nearer the period of decline, considerable feebleness of hand. These several deficiencies, when they happen to be united in one of the fantasies struck out during retouching-days at the Academy, produce results which, at the time they appeared, might have justified a regretful criticism.'

Pictures of his First Period—1800 to 1820.

This summary of Turner's Art career contains comments on the National Collection chiefly, as being most typical.

One of the earliest pictures in the Turner Gallery is 'Moonlight: a Study at Millbank;' a view of the Thames looking east; a low-toned lamplight effect, formed on Dutch theories, but painted from the 'orbed maiden' herself. It is singular that a little west of the spot whence the view is taken, near Cremorne Pier, stands the cottage in which the painter died fifty-five years afterwards. Little could the hopeful young genius then anticipate the close of his career as a worn-out old man in the adjacent cottage!

In 1797 Turner probably was at the Lakes, for in the following year he exhibited 'Buttermere Lake, with part of Cromach Water;' in which a rainbow, breaking through a shower, is arching over the golden mist. Even at this date the painter was ambitious of daring atmospheric effects. Wordsworth's 'Lyrical Ballads' (to which Coleridge contributed the 'Ancient Mariner,' heralding the arrival of a new school of poetry) appeared this year (1798), when Turner was twenty-three years old.

About 1800 (probably a year or so earlier) he painted his mountain scene; with a castle on a hill in the middle distance, and a man angling in a stream in the foreground; taken perhaps in Wales, where he painted so many 'castle and mountain scenes.'

To this period, as well as to any other, we may assign the painting of 'Rizpah, the Daughter of Aiah, Watching the Dead Bodies of her Sons' at harvest time; guarding them by day from the vulture, and by night from the wolf. Turner was fond of this touching story, and it was engraved with some alterations in the 'Liber Studiorum.'

'The Sandpit,' with two cows on a bank and two men by a fire, to parallel the quietness, is of I know not what date; nor can I affix a certain date to the unexhibited 'Squally Weather,' representing a vessel stranded near a jetty, and boats in the foreground.

Mr. White, of Brownlow Street, possesses a picture exhibited by Turner in 1801, when he was working hard, with all the ardour and sensitive ambition of the man, to rival Vandervelde, and to become a great marine painter. It is called 'Dutch Boat in a Gale: Fishermen Putting Fish on Board.' Turner's greatest works at this time were all marine. The Duke of Bridgewater had just bought a large Vandervelde, the 'Rising of a Storm;' and the praise of this picture roused Turner, as the cackle about Claude led him afterwards to begin the 'Liber,' and to paint Carthaginian pictures. The Dutch picture contains a packet, three boats, three ships, a hard, flat,

SKIDDAW FROM DERWENTWATER

inky sky, and sails in sunshine to contrast. Turner, resolved to be larger, more boisterous and more real, gives us a misty sky, heavy, louring clouds, a real muddy sea, one enormous line of wave, and a beam of light pointing out a distant vessel. The ships are the heavy one-masted Dutch galliots formerly common on the Thames ; and the three Dutch men-of-war signal with their colours to the distant coast.

When Turner wandered into classic territory in 1800 to break a lance with Claude, the first subject he handled was that of Æneas meeting the Cumæan Sibyl near her cave at Lake Avernus, before he enters Hell to pluck the mystic golden bough, in order that, armed with that talisman, he may consult his dead father, Anchises. Turner could have no special interest in the legends of the ' Æneid;' but he painted from them because the old masters had done so, and he was still in the chrysalis state of imitation.

' The Slaying of the First-born ' (1802) has a strong element of grandeur, and the figures are by no means bad; but the subject, after all, was not adapted for the painter's genius. The same year he exhibited another Poussin subject, far grander in imagination, ' Jason in Search of the Golden Fleece.' Medea has drugged the monster dragon, of whom one gigantic coil alone is visible among the rocks, bushes, and shattered tree-trunks above the cavern ; which, by-the-bye, too closely resembles the Cloaca Maxima at Rome. This is one of Turner's most imaginative works. There is a fine sense of terror and danger and adventure in Jason's stealthy creep, and in the mystery thrown about the dragon and St. George, or Jason, whichever it is.

The Turner Gallery contains no picture that is with certainty known to have been painted in 1801, but 1802 yielded a full harvest. In that year he painted the portrait of himself in evening dress; a life-size bust portrait, showing traces of his Reynolds experiences. To the same date may be assigned the painting, which was exhibited then, of ' Morning on the Coniston Fells, Lancashire.' It is to be observed that he now quotes Milton in place of Thomson. This is a hilly landscape, with a mountain torrent and grey and mellow golden mists. Escaping

from the city life, he had been revelling in the fells and mountain lakes of more northern England.

In 1803 he exhibited his ' Holy Family' (the Virgin and
Child, with Joseph reposing in the open air); a bad imitation of
Reynolds ; an uninteresting picture, except as showing the extraordinary daring and versatility of the painter's mind, and his
uncertainty as yet in what road to direct his genius.

The same year he exhibited his celebrated picture of 'Calais
Pier;' the English packet arriving, and French fishermen
preparing to put to sea.   This effect of black and stormy
sky, with one glimpse only of blue, was the result of Turner's
first Continental tour.   He may have seen such an effect as he
arrived in the daily cutter from Dover after a passage of six
hours' duration over a chopping sea.   It was before the time of
the erection of the column in commemoration of the landing of
Louis XVIII.; and, as steamers were not as yet, only a little
wooden jetty conducted to Hogarth's Gate, whence the herring
and mackerel boats are putting off.

The blue peep of sky is too hard and bright, say the critics;
there is too much wave for a harbour sea, and there are too many
drenched touters to the right.   Nevertheless, the picture is a splendid one, and there is a fine purposeless anger and restlessness
about the foreground waves.   The figures, too, are good and full
of thought; especially that of the complaining fisherman, who
holds up deprecatingly to his wife the only half-filled bottle of
brandy ; and in the distance is a brig at anchor, with one sail
white in the sunshine.   Turner was always fond of Calais, from
grateful recollection, I suppose, of his traveller's joy at first
landing in the new world.   This picture was engraved by
Lupton; but the painter altered and altered it till it was spoiled;
hence it was never published.

The ' Vintage at Macon ' is a direct challenge to Claude,
as an admiring critic indicates; and it succeeds by carrying the
principles of the ' old master' to a far higher pitch, with
greater power and immeasurably greater technical skill; above
all, with a higher poetry ; the result being a perfect *quasi*-
classic idyl of the most lovely sort, illustrating joyfulness in a
way in which few can fail to recognise somewhat of solemnity.

'We look,' says a writer in the 'Athenæum,' 'from a terraced hill-side over a wide champaign, with a smooth river swerving towards our left from the distance in the centre of the picture; in the mid-distance is a bridge of round arches connecting the town, which occupies both sides of the stream at that part. Beyond the water to the utmost horizon, where are lines of dim blue and white mountains, the land is in wide undulations. On the immediate foreground, or terrace, is a mass of tall Claude-like trees, the dark foliage of which rises against the sky, and is of a somewhat conventional kind. Near the foot of this group of trees are male and female vintagers dancing with admirable grace and spirit of action. The wonderful point about the picture is its richness in every respect, whether we look at the deep, intense, yet glowing sky, the colour and contour of the landscape, the reflections in the calm water, or the banks there repeated. The last-named parts are admirable in their modelling, and, as examples of amazing skill in that way, may compete with anything of the kind that Turner produced. It is one of the most pathetic of pictures.'

In Turner's own handwriting, at the back of the 'Vintage at Macon,' we read, 'This picture not to be taken off the canvas.' Seguier told Burnet that the artist had the greatest horror of the picture being lined, having commenced it with sized colours on an unprimed cloth. 'It is now of a deep rich tone,' says Burnet, 'although when first painted it was coloured with the most vivid greens and yellows.'

This, the earliest fruit of his first Continental tour, was an evident imitation of Claude, but it lacks Claude's purity, serenity, and calm. With the lapse of time it is now black and cold in colour; learned, laboured, and imposing in its masses, and in the general effect of its composition. It was exhibited in 1803 (the tour was in 1802), and was painted for the first Lord Yarborough, grandfather of the present lord, who allowed it to be engraved for the benefit of the Artists' Benevolent Fund.

For the same noble patron he painted 'The Wreck of the "Minotaur" on the Haak Sands,' in 1810.

'The ship that is wrecked,' says a writer in the 'Art Journal,'
'lies almost broadside to the spectator on the right, and is
apparently a large Indiaman.

> 'A gorgeous freight that broad-sailed vessel bore—
> The blazing diamond and the blushing ore ;
> Spices that sighed their incense, till the sails
> Were fanned along on aromatic gales
> From Orient lands.

'She has struck on a rock somewhere on the British coast,
as is evidenced by the fishing-boats proceeding to assist in
rescuing the crew and passengers, some of whom, with their
luggage, are already in a large row-boat, and being borne
through the "yeast of waves," with small chance, as it would
seem, of ultimate escape. The two boats on each side are proceeding to the wreck; one lifted high on the crest of a huge
wave, the other scarcely visible as she sinks down in the
trough of the sea. Other vessels are seen standing off the immense hull, from the bowsprit of which figures are dropping into
a smaller boat below. In the immediate foreground is the
rudder of the Indiaman, tossed like a twig on the wild wilderness of waters. But all these are comparatively insignificant
portions of the picture. It is the wonderful "seascape" which
must strike every beholder with astonishment—the waves
tumbling, and boiling, and rushing madly over each other, now
forming lofty, impenetrable walls, now sinking into deep gulfs,
here white with foam and spray, there almost of inky blackness;
and, above all, the storm clouds driving in fierce anger, the
ministers of terror and destruction. The marvel is that, amid
such a hurricane of the elements above and below, seamen,
even with all the daring and hardihood which seems to be
theirs naturally, could be found tempting the death that appears
inevitable in the yawning chasms of water.

> 'The vessel now tossed
> Through the low-trailing track of the tempest is lost
> In the skirts of the thunder-cloud: now down the sweep
> Of the wind-cloven wave to the chasm of the deep

It sinks, and the walls of the watery vale,
Whose depths of dread calm are unmoved by the gale,
Dim mirrors of ruin, hang gleaming about;
While the surf-like chaos of stars, like a rout
Of death flames, like whirlpools of fire-flowing iron,
With splendour and terror the black ship environ.

'The picture has in it but little colour; it is painted almost throughout in a grey, leaden tone, which time has rendered darker and more opaque. The light falls chiefly on the foreground, the tan-coloured sail of the boat on the right being the "point;" it is repeated, however, on the crests of the distant waves ere they are lost amid the falling ruin. The whole scene vividly recalls to mind Shakespeare's lines in the "Tempest:"—

'O, I have suffered
With those I saw suffer; a brave vessel
Which had, no doubt, some noble creatures in her,
Dashed all to pieces. O, the cry did knock
Against my very heart!'

About 1805 Turner painted the 'Destruction of Sodom.' Lot and his family leave the burning City of the Plain at the moment the guilty curiosity of Lot's wife is punished by her conversion into a pillar of salt. The subject being unsuited to the painter's genius, one can only wonder it is so respectable in execution. The same year produced 'Fishing-Boats,' which was bought in 1853 for 1,250 guineas by Mr. F. T. Rufford, of Stourbridge. There is a beautiful repose about this scene, with its smooth shore, anchor on the sands, wooden jetties, and roll of majestic breakers.

In 1805 he also painted for Lord de Tabley, at that time Sir John Fleming Leicester, his more celebrated picture (never exhibited) of the 'The Shipwreck,' which C. Turner, J. Burnet, and F. Fielding afterwards engraved. Lady Leicester having lost a favourite nephew at sea, and being unable to endure the painful associations evoked by the scene emphasised by the artist, this great picture was exchanged by Sir John for the 'Sun Rising in a Mist,' now in the National Gallery. It represents a large Indiaman becoming a wreck, while fishing-boats endeavour to rescue the crew. The wreck labours in a terrific sea; and in the foreground are three boats, not by any means secure, crowded with frightened, huddled groups of men and women. Some of the passengers are dropping from the bow-sprit into the boat, which, to denote danger, is partly hidden by a wave. The broken rudder floats by on the dark and dirty water, which is opaque and cordy, and of a uniform grey, as if seen from a distance through rain and mist. The figures are admirably composed; and the objection of nobody looking wet is of no great weight, since coarse woollen sea-cloths have not a refractive surface, whether they be wet or dry. No marine painter ever painted with so sailor-like a mind as Turner. When Admiral Bowles saw the ' Wreck of the " Minotaur "' at the British Institution, he said, ' No ship or boat could live in such a sea.' That was just the sea Turner intended to paint.

Turner went down to Portsmouth in 1805 to witness the return of the Trafalgar fleet. He was always half a sailor at heart, and his eye must have expanded at the noble sight that for the time erased the memory of petty cares and purged all men's hearts of selfish fear.

In 1806[1] Turner returned to the classics, and exhibited his ' Goddess of Discord Showing the Apple of Discord in the Garden of the Hesperides.' Mr. Wornum pronounces this to be 'the best classical picture of the English school.' To me it seems full of knowledge and art, but most purposeless and uninteresting, besides being very dark. The figures, too, are rather sketchy, and hardly bear the prominence that is given them.

The story is hardly worth remembering how the three daughters of Hesperus dwelt in a garden in North Africa, keeping charge of the tree of golden apples (oranges ?), the gift of Earth and Juno. Discord, not being invited to the marriage of Thetis, obtained, by the aid of the dragon Ladon, one of these apples, for the purpose of spreading dissension among

---

[1] This year the British Institution opened in the Boydell Gallery, Pall Mall, an exhibition room built on the site of Dodsley's house. The sculpture over the door is by Banks.

the gods. The decision of Paris and the destruction of Troy were the results of this visit to the somewhat brown and dingy garden. The dragon lying along the summit of the rock Mr. Ruskin thinks a wonderful creation of the imagination. The creature's jaws to me appear thin, brittle, and powerless—not nearly so terrible as those of the alligator. It is said that Turner drew this monster from a stuffed dragon constructed for a London Christmas pantomime.

In 1806 Turner exhibited the 'Falls of Schaffhausen,' still grey in colour, with a rainbow half formed hanging over the tremendous rushing cataract that the rocks sever in two. In the foreground are introduced a backing waggon with kicking horses, a few bales and boxes, and some cattle being driven to the ferry boat. This picture was bought by the late Lord de Tabley, one of Turner's earliest friends. The present owner of the title, writing to me, says : 'I remember Turner speaking to me himself highly of this picture.' He probably visited Tabley Park, in Cheshire, in 1808, and Lowther Castle in 1810.

CHAPTER XXXVIII.

TURNER'S ART LIFE—(continued).

IN 1807 Turner exhibited at the Royal Academy his 'Blacksmith's Shop,' a picture painted in rivalry of Wilkie's 'Village Politicians,' which was exhibited the previous year. It was repurchased by the painter, at Lord de Tabley's sale in 1827, for 147l. Turner called it a 'Butcher Disputing with a Country Blacksmith on the Price of Iron and the Charge made for Shoeing his Pony.' In an unfinished sketch entitled the 'Harvest Home,' years after, he again attempted to rival Wilkie's 'Village Festival.' The figures in the 'Shop' are very good, and the fowls, shovel, butcher's tray, &c., are painted with admirable Dutch fidelity. It has often been said that Turner made this picture a mass of flame colour to destroy the effect of Wilkie's 'Blind Fiddler,' exhibited at the same time and hung between the ' Forge' and the ' Sun Rising through Vapour ;' but the fact is that the ' Forge' was No. 135, the ' Blind Fiddler' 147, and Turner's other picture No. 162. The scene is a sunshine interior, and there is now scarcely any red visible in it. The ' Sun Rising through Vapour' was one of the pictures he left to the National Gallery on condition of its being hung between two of Claude's.

After 1810 Turner painted the ' Wreck of the " Minotaur." ' That admirable writer on Art Mr. Tom Taylor praises the run of the vast waves, the helpless welter of the raft, the cork-like tossing of the boat on the crest of the breaker, the blinding fall of rain and spray and sea, and the storm cloud through which the wrecked hull looms desolately. But in this painting —Turner was still thinking of Vandervelde—it is all grey, where years later there would have been green blackness and creamy foam. There are few reflections, and nobody seems wet.

' The might of the sea and the nothingness of human strength and skill against its fury,' writes Mr. Taylor, ' have never been so represented on canvas as in this picture, which may be profitably compared with the "Shipwreck" in the National Gallery, an earlier picture by some five years. Attention should be called to the carefulness and intelligibility of Turner's composition. Amid all the apparent confusion of the over-crowded boats and the clash of drifting spars, masts, and rigging in the wild war of waters, the lines of the composition and the arrangement of light and shadow guide the eye and maintain a perfect balance of effect. Some Dutch galliots, the only craft which would have any chance of living in such a sea, with the ship's boats, are saving all they can under the lee of the huge hull, which lies on her beam ends on the sand. Nothing can exceed the drawing, action, and expression of the figures ; we are made to feel at once the contrast between the energy of those who are rescuing the drowning men and the exhaustion of those who have been dragged into the boat. Here, as in the "Shipwreck," Turner shows himself even a masterly figure painter. A remark, true of both pictures, has been made by Mr. Ruskin—that, with all the power shown in expressing the force and weight of waves, the painter nowhere expresses their wetness, nor the blinding effect of the spray on the edge of a sand. In truth, such a subject could not be represented truthfully, except as a mass of soapsuds and whitewash, to borrow the words depreciatingly applied by one of the critics to a picture of Turner's in 1842—a "Snow-Storm off Harwich, with a Steam-Boat off the Harbour Mouth making Signals."

'When he painted the "Wreck of the 'Minotaur,'" Turner, in his sea-painting, was still under the influence of Vandervelde. But, as Mr. Ruskin has properly pointed out, his way of using the old master's work was not to copy his pictures, but to go to the sea and paint that in Vandervelde's way. We may see this in the colour of the waves in this picture, though the canvas is so dirty that it is hard to discover from its present aspect what the original colour really was.'

' Altogether,' a critic in the 'Athenæum' writes, ' the "Wreck of the ' Minotaur '" is one of Turner's masterpieces, and in its way was probably never surpassed by him or any other artist. The present condition of this picture is, to say the least, anomalous. It appears as if, at some time now long past, it had undergone successive additions of what are called " warm tones." The surface is divided by brown tones of three different degrees ; sharp and dark lines divide these spaces from one another ; and to such a degree do these dark lines or boundaries prevail that the one on our left actually interferes with the composition by depriving some parts of the wreck of their proper force and expression. The finest part of the picture is the middle, where the " brown tone," although it is by no means inoffensive, still fails to hide the impressive way in which the painter has dealt with the wreckage of spars and sails where they are rolling in the hollow of tremendous billows.'

Even at this period Turner was most varied in his treatment of seas—in their character and colour, according to the weather, wind, and depth of water.

The 'Saltash' is a painting of this period—perhaps 1806 or 1807 ; judging from the half-effaced inscription on the brick wall to the right, ' England expects every man to do his duty.' It is merely a landing-place and shed, a quiet river margin, some lounging soldiers, sailors, fishwomen, and porters, and a passage for carts ; but all steeped in a Cuyp-like afternoon sunshine. The word ' Beer' is conspicuous on a signboard.

The ' Highland Bridge' and ' Old Margate Pier' are of this period. The Margate picture represents fishing-boats arriving and unloading at a seaport, and fishermen cleaning and selling fish. The tide is low, and there is a guardship, a two-decker, in the distance. This scene is pervaded by all the repose of middle life. It is a sultry day, with a gentle swell and a sunny ripple on the water. The fishing-boats are high and dry ; the fish on the beach are very beautiful and pearly in colour. The painter repurchased it at the Tabley sale for 519*l.*, being just 15*l.* more than he had sold it for.

In 1808 Turner exhibited the ' Death of Nelson' at the British Institution. The battle of October 21, 1805, is represented with sailor-like knowledge as acquired from the mizen starboard shrouds of the ' Victory.' To the right is the ' Redoubtable,' and beyond are the ' Téméraire,' the ' Bucentaur,' and the ' San Trinidada.' Nelson, just fallen, having been struck by a bullet from a rifleman in the mizen fore-jib of the ' Redoubtable,' is being carried down from the quarterdeck; and the midshipman who afterwards shot the rifleman is preparing to fire. The ' portrait' figures are rather shaky. The ' Victory' is discharging her starboard guns into the hull of the ' Redoubtable.' The painter has represented her mainmast as still sound, whereas it was partly shot away at the commencement of the action.

Turner most likely was at Margate on the 22nd of December, when the ' Victory' arrived there with the body of Nelson. Eventually she became the guardship at Portsmouth, and is now the flag-ship of the port admiral. The painter took a deep interest in all naval matters, and a victory like Trafalgar must have stirred him to the very heart.

Probably about the same year (1808) Turner executed another view of the great battle, which George IV., for whom it was painted, presented in 1829 to Greenwich Hospital, where it still adorns the Painted Hall. It was never exhibited. It is a broadside view, and represents the ' Redoubtable' as sinking, though really she did not sink till the next night. In fact,

Turner has, with epical grandeur, aggregated the events of several different hours. For instance, he assigns the glorious signal which went up at 11.40 A.M. to the same period of the action as that in which the mizen-mast fell, which snapped about 1 P.M.; and he represents the 'Achilles' as then burning, which did not catch fire till half-past four. The picture is a bad composition in point of Art, and is much disliked by naval critics. Nelson's favourite captain, Sir Thomas Hardy, pronounced it to be 'more like a street scene than a battle, and the ships more like houses than men-of-war;' and the emphatic comment of an old Greenwich pensioner was, 'I can't make English of it, sir; I can't make English of it. It wants altering altogether;' while another tar, vexed at seeing a visitor pore over it, erupted, 'What a Trafalgar ! It is a d—— deal more like a brickfield. We ought to have had a Huggins !' Now, of course these rude minds could have no true judgment about Art, which is a science, and not an instinct; but still the unanimity of their condemnation proves, I think, that the picture contains fatal errors. In short, Turner's ambition to paint a typically comprehensive picture involved the sacrifice of fidelity to the historic sequence of events.

In 1809 was exhibited his 'Spithead, with Boat's Crew Recovering Anchor.' A fresh breeze is blowing, we observe; various men-of-war lie anchored in the roadstead, and others are bearing up for anchorage. A distant view of the fortifications of Portsmouth is revealed through a cloudy sky; and a few boats and a buoy make up a picture of forcible colour and good distance: but exception has reasonably been taken to the negligence of depicting the sails of the ships bellying to the wind as though it were blowing at the same moment from various points of the compass. Turner, whose naval proclivities were strong, must have delighted to paint this view of the great station of our navy, where Cromwell first established a dry dock, and where the 'Royal George' sank.

'London from Greenwich' was painted in the same year. It has the Hospital and Park in the foreground. The picture was bought by Mr. Fawkes, but subsequently exchanged by the painter. 1809 also produced his half-Hogarthian, half-Wilkiean picture of the 'Garreteer's Petition;' which represents a lean poet at work by night in his Grub Street attic, the wall of which is wittily adorned with a plan of Parnassus and a Table of Fasts. To the same date belongs the painting of 'St. Mawes, Falmouth Harbour,' with a view of Pendennis Castle in the distance, engraved by W. Kernor.

About 1810 was painted his beautiful picture, unexhibited, of 'Abingdon, Berkshire,' with a morning view of the Thames and the outskirts of the town. The tall spire of the tower is visible, and in the foreground are the banks of the Berks and Wilts Canal, on which are a timber-waggon and cows. Of Burford Bridge, which is only a few miles to the south of Oxford, we also have a glimpse. The style is after Calcott, and the glowing tone has been taken by some to indicate evening, for the bearings are west.

In 1811 was exhibited his 'Apollo Killing the Python,' with a motto taken from Callimachus. The hidden meaning of the legend may be that the Python was a pestiferous marsh which was drained by an early benefactor of mankind; but the popular version has it that it was a dragon whose abode was in a valley beneath Mount Parnassus, and whose temerity in attacking Latona provoked the wrath of her son. In the picture Apollo, kneeling in the foreground, has just discharged his arrow, and the monster is in the act of dropping dead, a gory mass, from an eminence. A serious defect is that, from inadequacy of drawing, the glorious sun god looks puny and petty, and the monster's claws have but a feeble hold upon the rocks.

In the same year he painted the 'Quiet Ruin—Cattle in Water—Evening.'

In 1813, still classical and epical, and not yet immersed in landscape and colour, he exhibited 'Hannibal and his Army Crossing the Alps.' In painting the passage of the Carthaginian general and his vast army of 59,000 men over St. Bernard, 219 B.C., on the way to his fifteen years' conquest of Italy, Turner probably had no other wish than to give an epical effect to his Aosta sketches and remembrance of Alpine snow-storms. The picture is now dark, and heavy with dirt; but its gloom is grand, and the niveous darkness is charged with a monition of danger that no one knew how to convey better than Turner. He has further given a lively sense of the resistance of the Allobroges to the transit of the Carthaginian army. Turner's mind seems always to have had a dim notion of some analogy between Carthage and England.

In 1813 he painted a tranquil picture of the 'Thames at Kingston Bank,' as if by way of mental relief after his last epic presentment of war and danger; and he exhibited his 'Frosty Morning : Sunrise.' A striking reference to this fine picture occurs in a letter written by Archdeacon Fisher to Constable about one of his best landscapes:—' I have heard your great picture spoken of here by no inferior judge as one of the best in the Exhibition. It is a great thing for one person to say this. It is by units that popularity is gained. I only like one better, and that is a picture of pictures—the " Frost " by Turner. But then you need not repine at this decision of mine. You are a great man, and, like Bonaparte, are only to be beaten by a frost.' A gamekeeper, attended by a girl with a hare, men with a two-horse cart by the roadside, a muffled boy sliding, and a stage coach approaching from the distance, fill up the Yorkshire scene. The ground sparkles with frost, and the tall, spindly, bare tree conveys a sense of cold. The tone of this picture is beautifully soft, mellow, and subdued. The yellow cloudless sky, the crushed crisp grass, and the dead weeds are all perfectly painted.

In 1813 he also exhibited his Poussinesque picture of the 'Deluge ;' which was engraved by J. Quilley.

The first published work that introduced Turner's name to world-wide fame, however, was the 'Southern Coast,' begun in 1814, and got up with great difficulty and labour by the distinguished engraver of many of its beautiful plates, W. B. Cooke. The first of these drawings were made for 7*l.* 10*s.* each. Some of them have since been sold for 100 guineas, and, I believe, even for 200 guineas.

About the year 1814 he painted a picture of 'Coalbrook-dale ; which has since been called the 'Limekiln.' It is an excellent representation of twilight struggling with the artificial light from the kiln; and in texture and size it much resembles

the small picture by him at Kensington—a moonlight scene.
It was engraved by Lewis.

In 1814 he exhibited his 'Dido and Æneas Leaving Carthage on the Morning of the Chase;' engraved by W. R. Smith.
This is one of his twenty Carthaginian pictures, and one of the
first of his works in which he has introduced his favourite flat-topped stone-pines. Some critics rate it as one of the best of
his Claudesque pictures. The rather ambiguous ruined bridge,
and the gay figures with Dido and Æneas to the right, show
felicity of invention; but of course the city is no more African
than it is Esquimaux. As a dream, however, it has a certain
congruity.

The same year, more classical than ever, he exhibited at the
British Institution 'Apuleia in Search of Apuleius.' For the
incident he gave a reference to Ovid; but no mention of it
occurs in either Ovid, or Lucian, or the author of the Golden
Ass himself. It was a jocular affectation of the grave accuracy
of quotation. This picture was painted for the Earl of Egremont, as a companion to the celebrated Claude there; and was
engraved by Woollett. It is a hilly landscape, with a large
seven-arched bridge spanning a river with wooded banks; a
windmill and town on the right; and in the foreground Apuleia
and her companions questioning some peasants who are resting
in the shade of a tree. After a device of Poussin, one of the
rustics points to the name Apuleius, which is carved on a tree.

Wilson's popularity, it may be useful to remark here, dates
from an exhibition of his works at the British Institution in this
year.

In 1815 Turner exhibited ' Bligh Sand, near Sheerness, with
Fishing-Boats Trawling; Cloudy Sky '—the picture that he had
the proud pleasure of refusing to sell to his old enemy Sir John
Beaumont. The scene is at the mouth of the Thames, off
Candy Island, and near Cowling Marsh. The waves are dark,
but one sail is touched with sunlight. An artist who professionally examined the picture for me tells me that the sky was
painted with perishable sugar of lead, and has quite altered.

The same year Turner exhibited his wonderful picture of
' Crossing the Brook ;' engraved by A. Brandard. This vast

landscape is a view on the river Tamar, that divides Devonshire from Cornwall; the spectator looking towards Plymouth,
with Calstock Bridge in the middle distance. The locality is
near Morwell, Poulson Bridge; the woods of Cothele are
visible; and in the far distance is the estuary of the Tamar,
with the Hamoaze, where one hundred war ships are often
lying in ordinary. It was before the time of the breakwater,
the dockyard, and Brunel's bridge at Saltash; but the scene is
topographically incorrect. In colour the picture is rather blue
and cold. In the foreground are two pines and a couple of
children, with a dog carrying a bundle in its mouth across the
brook. The distance is truly wonderful, displaying the utmost
reach of the painter's knowledge and the very climax of his Art
magic. The eye can travel some twenty miles across bridge,
over dale and over meadow, through all degrees of blue haze and
melting sunshine vapour till it reaches the goal of the far
horizon. The soul does not feel cramped in view of this
picture. Its spatiosity exhilarates the spectator. 'Crossing
the Brook' was a great favourite with Turner. Such indeed
was his attachment to it that, when the engraver mentioned
that he should require to have it for two years in his possession
for the purpose of engraving, the painter hesitated, mumbled
something about the blank space in his gallery, and said that
two years was a long period at his time of life. 'When the
plate was nearly completed, he called upon me,' says Mr.
Brandard, the engraver, 'to go over the proof from the picture.
In the course of conversation he observed, "This picture was a
commission; but the gentleman was not satisfied. I was to
have had 500*l*. for it." Subsequently he refused 1,600*l*.'

Indeed, 1815 was a wonderful year with Turner, for in that
year he exhibited, besides 'Crossing the Brook,' 'Dido Building
Carthage;' the aim of the latter picture being to show the rise
of a maritime empire which he considered typical of England ;
France and Rome also no doubt being analogous in his mind.
With his habitual indifference to accuracy, he has fixed the site
of the city on a river, and has placed a bridge in front, with a
vast alps of Claudesque architecture, porticoes, and vestibules
half completed on either side. Surrounded by her people,

Dido stands on the left, watching the work; and the luminous sun in the centre fuses all objects to one golden focus of brightness. The inevitable stone pines are not absent. Fine, however, is the poetic instinct (to which Mr. Ruskin has done justice) with which the future naval greatness of Carthage is adumbrated by the figures of the dark, sinewy, long-limbed Carthaginian lads launching boats. The whole is a splendid dream. Turner was justly proud of the pictorial triumph when he determined to bequeath it to the nation on condition of its being hung yard-arm and yard-arm with Claude. It is to be regretted that the atmosphere, through rapid decay, is becoming hot and turbid, so that the purity of Claude now injures it by contrast.

Besides vigour and grasp, it displays some learning, neither Sichæus's tomb nor the Byrsa being forgotten. The treatment of the architecture of Carthage, which necessarily must have been Oriental, is full of pardonable anachronism, after the usual mode of the painter.

Turner seems to have considered the fate of Carthage as a moral example to England; ascribable as it was to the decline of agriculture, the increase of luxury, and besotted blindness, too prolonged, to the insatiable ambition of Rome.

When he found that it did not obtain a purchaser at the Academy, the pride which the painter took in this picture was seriously wounded; and in angry resentment of the neglect he thereafter sternly refused to part with it. Chantrey once or twice essayed to secure it for himself, but was startled by the discovery that the figures mounted with each successive application. From 500*l.* the advance was to 1,000*l.* and from 1,000*l.* it went to 2,000*l.* The baffled sculptor protested in vain. 'Why, what in the world, Turner, are you going to do with the picture?' he enquired. 'Be buried in it, to be sure,' was the surly reply.

In 1816 he exhibited 'Temple of Jupiter Panhellenius at Ægina,' with figures in the foreground dancing the Romaika, and Athens in the distance, eighteen miles away. The picture was painted from a sketch taken by Mr. H. Gally Knight in 1810. The ruin itself is a mere cluster of Doric pillars, but the painter's restoration of it assimilates it to the Parthenon.

In 1817 he returned full charge against Claude, and exhibited his 'Decline of the Carthaginian Empire: Hostages Leaving Carthage for Rome.' The perspective is bad; the sky, once fine, is now foxy; and the temples are somewhat leathery. The critics were severe against this picture, and even Mr. Ruskin condemns it; but Turner declared that he preferred it to its predecessor. When he wished to impress one with a sense of foreboding danger, grief, or terror, he generally introduced a sunset. The motto affixed to this adumbrates his meaning :—

> While o'er the western wave th' ensanguined sun
> In gathering haze a stormy signal spread,
> And set portentous.

In 1818 he exhibited his confused and unequal picture of the 'Field of Waterloo' (engraved by C. Lewis). It is a muddle of sublimity, a perfect fricassee of ill-drawn lumps of figures, yet loftily lurid in general effect. The quotation from Byron conveys the painter's design :—

> The thunder-clouds close o'er it, which when rent,
> The earth is covered thick with other clay,
> Which her own clay shall cover, heaped and pent,
> Rider and horse—friend, foe, in one red burial blent !

The picture is a striking proof of the inadequacy in Art of genius without the power of expression. In the foreground are witches of women searching for plunder by torchlight ; to the right is Hougoumont still burning ; in the distance are rising blue rocket-signals, sent up to guide the Prussian pursuit of the routed French army. Three years had elapsed after the battle before Turner painted Trafalgar ; and after the same period of time he painted Waterloo.

In 1819 he exhibited the 'Meuse : Orange Merchantman going to Pieces on the Bar ;' Brill church bearing south-east by south, and Maas-Sluis east by south. There is a sunny drift of rain, and a fresh breeze is blowing ; the weather continuing to be squally, and the boats on the broad estuary being still glossy. Boats are unloading the wreck, and fishermen picking up the oranges that bob here and there, while a boy is slyly pocketing some of the salvage on his own account.

The 'Tabley Lake and Tower,' also exhibited this year, is notable for its slaty-blue shallow water rippling in the wind.

To this year belongs the exhibition of his unpleasantly heavy picture of ' Richmond Hill on the Prince Regent's Birthday.' The figures dancing in the foreground are hideously drawn ; one lady has a neck like a giraffe. The distance, with wood and river, is of course pleasing.

Turner's visit to Rome took place this year.

I do not know to what date to refer the ' Cologne Evening,' in the Windus Collection ; a drawing originally made for Mr. Tomkinson. The view is from the descent of the Rhine, with Deutz and the bridge of boats.

CHAPTER XXXIX.

TURNER'S ART LIFE.
Second Period—1820 *to* 1835.

DEFYING all precedent, in this period Turner sought chiefly for brilliant colour, revealed a tendency to idealise, and maintained a delicate and deliberate handling and a cheerful manner. His sketch-books embrace notes of deer and park subjects, perhaps from Petworth, and sketches of Egremont and Cockermouth Castles. Careless as he usually was about notes taken for subsequent use and amplification, yet there is in this series a beautiful moonlight on a fine sea actually painted on the paper wrapper of an old parcel. This piece was one which he afterwards engraved himself.

Among the drawings of this period are the ' Dover ' and ' North Shields,' used in the ' Harbours of England ;' the beautiful ' Rochester' to be found in the ' Rivers of England ;' several studies for Calais pictures ; four sketches for the ' Rivers of France ;' and several of Evreux and Louviers. Among the Calais sketches are 'Fishing-Boats going out : Calais Harbour,'

'Fort Rouge,' a 'Calais Schooner out in a Breeze,' and a
'French Fisherman on Calais Sands collecting Bait.'

In 1820, after his return from Rome, Turner exhibited his
'Rome from the Vatican ; Raphael and the Fornarina in the
Corridor of the Loggia.' This is rather a hot picture, the fore-
ground of which is a pure fiction. In front are the Piazza of
St. Peter's, the Castle and Bridge of St. Angelo, and the
Colosseum ; and in the distance are the snow-topped Apen-
nines.

Probably in the same year he painted 'Rome, the Arch of
Titus, and the Campo Vaccino, as seen from the Colosseum.'
A religious procession is visible in the middle ; the Arch of
Titus is much exaggerated in size, and the foreground is un-
finished. This picture was never exhibited.

In 1823 Turner, still Claudesque, but in his own majestic
way, exhibited the 'Bay of Baiæ ; with Apollo and the Sibyl ;'
which Mr. Wornum designates a great masterpiece, and the
painter's first thoroughly original work. To the right is the
castle of the bay, and on the opposite side is Pozzuoli ; the
two figures under the tall pines being Apollo and the Sibyl,
whom he loved, and to whom he granted years of life as
numerous as the grains of sand she held in her hands ; but
who, upon soliciting the gift of perpetual youth, wasted away
to an echo. This is the Baiæ that Horace said was the fairest
bay in the whole world. It is close to Avernus, where Æneas
consulted the Sibyl, and whence Ulysses descended into hell.

Turner's secret resolve to bequeath his pictures to the
nation must have been greatly strengthened by the events
of 1824. In this year the British National Gallery of Pictures was founded during the administration of the Earl of
Liverpool, by the purchase of the collection of John Julius
Angerstein, Esq., consisting of thirty-eight pictures, and comprising nine specimens of the British school. This collection,
which thus formed the nucleus of the present National Gallery,
was secured to the nation by a grant of Parliament voted on
April 2, 1824 ; and on May 10 it was opened to the public
in the house of Mr. Angerstein in Pall Mall. In 1826 the
collection was increased by the liberal donation of sixteen

pictures from Sir George Beaumont, including five works of the British school ; and in 1831 it was enriched by the valuable bequest of the Rev. William Holwell Carr ; which comprised, however, only one English picture.

Up to the year 1847, nearly a quarter of a century after its foundation, the National Gallery contained only forty-one British pictures ; but its deficiency in that respect was well supplied by Mr. Robert Vernon's munificent donation of one hundred and fifty-seven pictures, all, with only two exceptions, by painters of the British school. That school is represented now in the National Gallery by three hundred and seventeen pictures by eighty-one masters, all, with the exception of those purchased with the Angerstein collection, either presented or bequeathed to the trustees ; yet the representation is most inadequate, embracing as it does barely half the painters of England.

In 1827 Turner exhibited his ' Pas de Calais ; Fishing-Boats off Calais ;'—' Now for the Painter,' as he entitled it, with a jocular reference to Calcott's ' Letting go the Painter.' It was engraved by Davison in 1830. This pleasant sunny picture, lighted up by numerous reflections, which represents passengers being put on board the packet, is the property of Mr. J. Naylor, of Liverpool.

He also exhibited ' Mortlake Terrace, Seat of William Moffatt, Esq. : Summer Evening ;' of which place he painted in the following year an early summer morning view. A broad light lies on the river ; the lime trees cast long shadows on the golden sward, where a garden chair and a portfolio tell of the artist ; and on the river are gilded barges and the glancing wherries of holiday-makers, to bark at which a dog has just leaped up on the parapet. Mr. Tom Taylor adduces the dog as a proof of Turner's reckless readiness of resource when an effect in Art was wanted. Suddenly conceiving that a dark object here would throw back the distance and increase the aerial effect, Turner instantly cut a dog out of black paper and stuck him on the wall ; where he still remains, for, either satisfied or forgetful, he never replaced him by a painted one.

' Walton Bridge ' also is a summer scene. The barges are

drawn up alongside the bank at the men's dinner hour, and the cows crowd down to the grassy margin to drink the cool water.

To this period also belongs the ' Cologne,' with the ' Treck-schuyt ' arriving. There is a 'rosy, twilight calm,' windless and soundless, about this picture.

In 1828, memorable for the painting of the ' Polyphemus,' Turner painted ' Petworth Park, Sussex,' for Lord Leconfield, the third earl. It was to decorate the Carved Chamber, sixty feet by twenty-four, of the old house of the Percys, and to fill the beautiful frames carved by Grinling Gibbons. In the foreground of the picture is the lake, and in the distance the tower of Tillington Church.

For Petworth he also painted the ' Chain Pier of Brighton ;' at that time the landing-place for London and Dieppe steamers, and one of the wonders of Lord Egremont's county, which was commenced in 1822 and opened in 1828. The sketch represents it at sunset, with the breakers coming in, and the management of the perspective is ingenious.

This year was exhibited a careless, sketchy, and unpleasing picture in imitation of Stothard, called the ' Birdcage Scene from Boccaccio.' The trees of the glen are pleasantly grouped, but the figures are bad, and the distant white castle is very crude and glaring. ' No such story as the " Birdcage " is in the " Decameron,"' says Mr. Wornum ; but I perfectly remember the story to which Turner alludes reservedly in his title.

1828 also witnessed the exhibition of his ' Carthage : Dido directing the Equipment of the Fleet,' painted for Mr. Broadhurst ; a river scene, with piled masses of Claudesque architecture. The subject, as representing the rise of the maritime empire and of Rome's rival, was merely an inferior repetition of the ' Building of Carthage.'

In 1829, the year of the ' Polyphemus,' Turner exhibited an Italian landscape to which he was pleased to attach the name of the ' Loretto Necklace.' To the right is a view of the town of Loretto (where the miraculous house is) on the summit of a hill, the slopes of which are bushy with olive trees ; and in the distance stretches the Adriatic. The picture derives its title from the necklace which a strangely-formed peasant, who is seated under some trees to the left, has placed on the neck of a girl.

The same year he painted at Rome a view of Orvieto, which he exhibited in 1830 at the Royal Academy. Orvieto is a town situated on the Lake of Bolsena between Rome and Florence, and famous for its Fra Angelico pictures. The sun is on the distant hill, and in the foreground are Italian women washing at a fountain. The picture was never sold.

CHAPTER XL.

THE 'POLYPHEMUS.'—1829.

WHEN Turner was long past the meridian of life, he was one day on a visit to his old friend the Rev. Mr. Trimmer, of Heston, near Brentford. Whether, the day being wet, neither sketching nor fishing was possible, and a sense of his classical deficiencies intruded itself in the enforced leisure, or whether the project had long been seriously entertained and only awaited the favourable moment for execution, we have no means of precisely determining. But it is certain that on the occasion of this visit to Mr. Trimmer a mutual bargain was concluded between the two friends; neither more nor less than that the clergyman should teach the artist Greek, and the artist instruct the clergyman in painting. Examples are not wanting in literary history of similar devotion at an advanced age to the acquirement of Greek. Cato, it is recorded, applied himself to it at seventy; and why should not Turner undertake the task at fifty? At any rate, the compact was made; the old Greek books were brought forth from their dusty corner, and master and pupil duly took up their stations. We can picture to ourselves the laborious energy expended by the artist in his novel sphere; but it was only for a brief season. He found that he made slender progress in the language, while the ardent enthusiast for Art profited largely by his instruction. 'I fear I

must give it up, Trimmer,' was the despairing exclamation ;
' you get on better with your painting than I do with my
Greek.' Thus ended Turner's dream of familiarising himself
with Homer in the original, and thence deriving inspiration for
many a soul-stirring subject.

Pope's version, however, gave access to the glorious poetry
of ' the blind old man of Scio's rocky isle ;' and we can have
little difficulty in believing that Turner selected his subject of
' Polyphemus ' from the ninth book of the ' Odyssey ' as rendered
by Pope.

Why he should have selected this particular subject it is
difficult to say.   The picture may have been merely the framework for a magnificent sunrise ; possibly he desired to write his
name on Homer's tomb, to ' share his triumph and partake his
gale ;' or it may be that something in the story of Ulysses
interested one who was also a traveller—wily, silent when need
be, and vigilant.   But he felt that he was undertaking something that timid Claude would not have dared to do, that would
have half-blinded sombre Poussin, and to Vandervelde would
have been a sheer impossibility.   There was room here for imagination and for truth.   He would associate all the hope and
splendour and joy of the morning with thoughts of human
bravery and freedom ; and invest it all, according to honoured
precedent, with classic interest.   It was a virgin subject.   Let
us consider the antecedents of the Homeric story, and see what
happened before the event pictured by the artist.

At sunset Ulysses and his vassals, upon approaching the
land of the Cyclops, hear the bleating of goats and sheep,
and see smoke rising here and there upon the mountains.
At daybreak Ulysses addresses his fellows, and announces
his determination to explore the land, to see if the people
were a pious and hospitable race, or mere savages, hostile
to strangers.

Close to the shore the brave explorer discovers a cave half
hid by laurels, and surrounded by slumbering flocks, which are
fenced in by blocks of rough marble overgrown with shadowy
pine and oak.   Attended by twelve men who carry with them a
jar of wine and another jar of provisions, Ulysses enters the

cave of the giant shepherd. .The cavern-palace echoes with
the cries of kids and lambs eager to be fed ; the shelves bend
with pressed cheeses ; and all around lie bowls and huge
milking-pails. His companions urge Ulysses to drive a flock
of goats to the ships, and therewith put off at once to sea ; but,
curious to see the giant, he rejects the wise counsel.

Having lighted a fire and supped, they prepare for sacrifice
and prayer ; when the giant comes, and throws down with the
sound of thunder at the door half a forest of wood that he has
brought home for fuel. Then Ulysses and his men hide themselves in fear, as the big-uddered flocks, driven before him,
pour into the cave. The giant first closes the entrance with a
rock that scarcely twenty four-wheeled cars could move, and
then proceeds to make his cheese and milk his flocks—putting
by the curd for his nightly feast.

The blaze of the fire that the giant kindles lights up all the
cave, and discovers the hiding Greeks. He asks their names ;
whereupon Ulysses tells him they are errant Greeks, and im-
plores hospitality in the name of the gods who protect and
avenge the wrongs of the poor. In a storm of rage the giant
declares that the Cyclops are a race superior to Jove the goat-
nursed ; and failing, through the lying craft of Ulysses, to discover where his ship is moored, he dashes out the brains of two
Greeks, and devours them, flesh and bone ; after which he drains
a hundred gallons or so of milk, and falls asleep amid his flock,
careless of his prisoners. Ulysses is almost tempted to slay
the monster in his sleep, but is restrained by remembering that
no mortal force could remove the rock that bars their flight.

On the morrow the giant arises, lights his fire, milks his
goats, and feeds his lambs ; after which he devours two more
of his prisoners in the coolest manner possible, and goes off
whistling to the mountains, driving his flocks before him, and
leaving the unhappy Greeks secure in the re-closed cave. All
that dreadful day of suspense the Greeks hold counsel, and at
last they decide to shape a tree (large as any mast) that is in
the cave into a huge spear or auger, and therewith to bore out
the monster's eye as he sleeps. Not long after they complete
their task and hide the fire-sharpened tree in the dust of the

cave, the giant returns ; when he again milks his flocks, makes his cheese with anxious care, and devours two more of the cowering Greeks. At this point of the proceedings Ulysses advances and, praying for release, offers the gluttonous cannibal some of the celebrated wine that the priests of Apollo had given him. The Cyclops drains three bowls of it and graciously promises to devour No-man (*outis*) last. Overcome by the copious draughts, the giant falls asleep. Now is the moment for vengeance. The men chosen by lot set the spear-tree on fire, and drive it into the wretch's eye, as shipwrights work a wimble to bore some vast beam. As the poet has it, Ulysses stands above on higher ground, and directs their efforts. The roars of Polyphemus bring the Cyclops crowding to the mouth of the barred-up cave, to ask what ails their kinsman ; when, remembering the name Ulysses had given him, he exclaims that ' No-man ' hurts him. ' If it is only a visitation from Jove, bear it, O Polyphemus ! ' say his selfish kinsfolk ; and away they go to their teams and to their merchandise.

Now the monster rolls back the rock from the cave's mouth, and sits there with extended arms, handling each sheep and goat as it passes, lest it should be an escaping Greek. But Ulysses is too much for him. For the Cyclops, like our mediæval giant, is, after all, rather a fool ; as the old Greek poet indeed confesses with more than his usual frankness in narrating the story. With osiers taken from the giant's bed the hero binds together the largest rams in threes ; and under the middle ram of each triplet he fastens one of his men, while he himself clings beneath the king of the flock, who comes out last. Cursing No-man, Polyphemus reluctantly dismisses the last of the flock, while he wonders at the leader lagging behind. Upon their release the Greeks joyously drive down throngs of sheep and goats to the vessels, and rejoin their comrades. In haste they drag aboard the sheep, and, seizing their oars, push off to sea. Once out at sea, though still in the shallows and within ear-shot, Ulysses shouts his taunt to the enraged and moaning monster, who hurls rocks at the departing vessel that all but sink it, and surge it back again towards the shore.

The painter has chosen not the moment of hurling the rocks,

but the moment when Ulysses, the destroyer of Troy, vociferates his real name, and the Cyclops with speaking-trumpet voice answers that such a man has indeed been prophesied as his destroyer; and when Polyphemus, in answer to the somewhat cruel exultation of Ulysses, with hands uplifted to heaven prays to his father Neptune to overwhelm Ulysses with misfortunes.

This is the moment of the picture. How it proves that genius is better than learning! Turner, as we know, was no deep student of Homer; he knew him only through the inadequate medium of Pope's translation; yet he paints the scene better than mere learning could have enabled him to paint it, and he commits no anachronism in its treatment. What is most remarkable is that a sure instinct for the truth seems to have guided him even where he had to invent, for those pierced rocks are said to be characteristic of the island of Corcyra, where the scene of the story is laid. Yet Turner was probably thinking of the Calf of Man or the Needles. Not that I am fond of the arched rock; we have had too much of it in theatrical scenery. The galley of Ulysses, be it observed, though perhaps an impossibility, is a grand impossibility, rather unwieldy and top-heavy into the bargain; a sort of cross, in fact, between a Venetian fishing-boat and the Lord Mayor's barge, made apparently of gold snuff-boxes, with gold pencil-cases for masts; but that is neither here nor there.

What vigour there is in the sun, that cometh forth like a bridegroom out of its chamber and rejoiceth like a strong man to run its course! What Orient splendour of colour fans out far beyond towards Ithaca and home! How determinately, too, the painter tells his story. See the Greek sailors flocking up the masts to unfurl sail. Observe Ulysses waving the blazing olive tree in defiance at the cursing giant; and also his men kneeling to entreat him to draw no more flying mountains upon them. Mark the oars thrusting forth and beginning to force the galley forward. There yonder, by a pardonable and even necessary anachronism, is the rest of the fleet with their prows dark against the growing light; while a figure in the middle vessel, with outstretched arms, announces the return of their chief, and their oars also are thrusting forth, ready to join in the flight. That driving smoulder of fire low to the left indicates the mouth of the fatal cave that still lies glowing ; and in shadow above, high on the cliff, the giant—a creature of mists, yet vast and terrible, even though a phantom of air—claws at his wound, and raises his supplicating hand to Neptune. Above him, through half-illuminated gloom and cloud, may be caught faint glimpses of sunny heights, daybreak striking out across the scene ; which may be summed up thus :—First the fact of sunrise, then the exulting vessel, radiant with boastful flags, and Ulysses flying like a deer before the hounds ; lastly, the cursing and defeated giant : such is the sequence of the picture. We know it is the vessel of Ulysses, because one flag bears his name, and another depicts the siege of Troy.

So lavish is Turner's genius that he must introduce at once and into the same picture both day and night, both joy and grief. Through the slant rays of the sun I descry Phœbus and his chariot horses (or rather I see the horses; for, thanks to sugar of lead, Phœbus has vanished). Next the painter desires to express the favour of the gods to the hero, Pallas having aided him in the cave, and Jove hating the old scalers of heaven's walls. This he does by giving us a shoal of sea nymphs urging on the vessel, and in a phosphorescent twilight driving before them the scaly flocks of Proteus. He embodies what he might have observed as he leant dreaming over the bulwarks of vessels cleaving by night Italian seas. The gleams of their track blend with the frothy ripples of the oars, and lead us on to the column of light with which the sun bisects the foreground. There is hardly a touch of pure, unbroken, or raw colour in all this picture ; yet not a touch but serves as a note in the great chromatic diapason. The great puffing cream-coloured sails, the red prows, the striped masts, the violet haze on the distant sea-rocks, the yellow glow of expanding sunlight, the horizon's bar of dense blue, the great ripple of red and golden cloudlets, the gleams on the upper cliff of the Cyclopean land—all these combine harmoniously to form the imperial picture.

For colour, for life and shade, for composition, this seems

to me to be the most wonderful and admirable of Turner's idealisms. This is a creation and a poem. The 'Téméraire,' though equally exquisite in its way, is only a natural incident poetically heightened—it is truth and poetry; whereas this is imagination and poetry. Yet Turner apparently valued the 'Téméraire' most, for he peculiarly reserved it in his will.

There can be, of course, no doubt that Turner selected this subject from the ninth book of the 'Odyssey.' Yet, with his usual secretive sort of fun, he loved to mystify busybodies and dilettanti about it. His friend the Rev. Mr. Judkin, who was neither a busybody nor a dilettante, but a friend of Constable's, and himself a very clever landscape artist, was one day dining with Turner at a large party. A lady sitting next to the clerical artist, with the curiosity traditionally supposed to be peculiar to her sex, was full of the glories of the 'Polyphemus,' the wonder of the last Exhibition. It formed the subject of one prolonged whispering. 'What do you think of Mr. Turner's great picture?' 'Is it not a lovely picture?'

Glum and shy, Turner is not unobservant of all this enthusiasm from his post across the table. He sees where the lady's glances fall after she addresses her whispers to Mr. Judkin, and his little beads of eyes roll and twinkle with fun and slyness. 'I know what you two are talking about, Judkin,' he gruffly exclaims; 'it is about my picture.' With a deferential wave of his glass Mr. Judkin acknowledges that that is the topic, and the lady smiles benignantly at the painter, who now is stimulated to indulgence in jocosity. 'And I bet you don't know where I took the subject from; come now—bet you don't.' 'Oh! from the old poet, of course, Turner; from the " Odyssey," of course,' was the confident reply. 'No,' grunted Turner, bursting into a chuckle. 'Odyssey!' Not a bit of it. I took it from Tom Dibdin. Don't you know the lines—

'He ate his mutton, drank his wine,
And then he poked his eye out?'

This is an excellent example of the joyous spirit of mystifi-cation which was so habitual to him, and apparently yielded him such intense gratification.

Turner was not superior to the temptation of occasionally appropriating the conceptions of others; and I have sometimes inclined to the suspicion that he derived his idea of treating the subject of 'Polyphemus' from Michael Angelo's grand Titanic sketch of 'Morning.'

CHAPTER XLI.

TURNER'S ART LIFE—(*continued*).

IN 1831 was exhibited his 'Caligula's Palace and Bridge; Bay of Baiæ.' Baiæ seems to have impressed him as the chief site of the ruins of some of old Rome's most stupendous works of luxury and power. Mistaking his text as usual, he has turned the bridge of boats that the mad Caligula built to frustrate a prophecy of the mathematician Thrasyllus into a substantial structure of stone, such as the thirteen arches of the Mole of Puteoli which Antoninus Pius restored. On the left of the picture are the ruins of the palace, and on the extreme right, in the distance, is Baiæ. The sun rises behind the ruin, and children are playing with goats in the foreground. The latter were, I believe, introduced (by consent of Turner) by Mr. E. Goodall, the engraver. Turner had a great sympathy with the ruins of Roman greatness, and was never tired of trying to express that sympathy with increased intensity.

Becoming more and more classic, he next exhibited 'The Vision of Medea :' not a great success. Medea is performing an incantation in the company of the Fates. Above her is the dragon chariot, with her twins ; and behind her is Medea again, throwing her murdered children into the burning palace. 'Watteau Painting,' a study on Du Fresnoy's principle to show that white may be used either to advance an object or to make it recede, was also a picture of this year, as was that uninteresting one 'Lord Percy under Attainder, 1606 ;' Lord Percy, when under attainder for the Gunpowder Plot, being visited by his two daughters—a subject offering poor scope for the painter.

In the same prolific year was exhibited 'Stranded Vessels off Yarmouth making Signals of Distress;' painted for Mr. J. Nash, and subsequently purchased by Mr. Sheepshanks. This fine picture represents the use of the apparatus invented by Mr. Manby, barrack-master of Yarmouth, and by which nearly a thousand lives were at various times saved.

In 1832 Turner exhibited his finest and most epical Italian picture, ' Childe Harold's Pilgrimage ; Italy :' one of the finest poems Italy has ever suggested to the artist, beside which the scenes of Poussin, Claude, and Wilson are mere grand scraps— single pages against an ample volume. It is an epitome of ancient and modern Italy ; and in it the painter has expressed all the rapture and regret embodied in the lines from Byron which he adopts for his motto :—

> Even in thy desert what is like to thee ?
> Thy very weeds are beautiful; thy waste
> More rich than other climes' fertility ;
> Thy wreck a glory ; and thy ruin graced
> With an immaculate charm which cannot be defaced.

The picture consists of a mountainous landscape with a winding river, to the right a broken bridge, and on the left a pile of ruins, while in the foreground is a solitary flat-topped dark-green pine, and a party of pleasure seated on a river brink. All the typical features of Italy—the ruins, the convents, the walled towns—are here ; and the evening sun going down behind the mountains tinges the dance and feast with a tone of mournfulness. The indefiniteness of the ruined bridge to the right is generally considered almost the only fault of this picture.

This was also the year of exhibition of his 'Landing of William of Orange,' and of ' Shadrach, Meshach, and Abednego coming forth from the Burning Fiery Furnace.' In the latter the painter gives the earliest intimation of his desire to experiment simply in wonderful effects of colour. There is a smirched blackness and sweeping flame about this small picture that is very grand, obscure as all else in it is. In the background is the image of Nebuchadnezzar.

Let me note here that Wilkie's 'Knox Preaching before Queen Mary and the Lords of the Congregation' was introduced to the public in this year, and found a purchaser in Sir Robert Peel for the liberal sum of 1,200 guineas. In violent contrast to that success, Turner had the bitter mortification of exhibiting three pictures and selling only one.

His first picture of Venice—'Venice: the Dogana, the Campanile of San Marco, the Ducal Palace, and Bridge of Sighs, with Canaletti Painting'—was exhibited in 1833. From this date he painted several pictures of Venetian scenery; never tiring apparently of the enchantment of that sea Cybele, though never rightly appreciating the poetry of its Oriental Gothic palaces, and always seeming inclined to whiten the buildings, in accordance with the conventional notions of classical architecture acquired in the office of the architectural draughtsman.

'Lake Avernus, the Fates, and the Golden Bough' was exhibited in 1834. Avernus, supposed to be the overflowing of Acheron, was fabled to be one of the entrances to Hell; and the golden bough, when plucked from the tree of Proserpine, enabled mortals to enter the dominions of Pluto with impunity. In the distance of this beautiful but mystic dream the painter has introduced the familiar Bay of Baiæ and Mount Vesuvius. This year he exhibited another Venetian picture, representing the 'Canal of the Giudecca, San Giorgio Maggiore, the Dogana,' and other objects, which, with its predecessor, was bought by Mr. Vernon. To this must be added a quiet home scene— 'St. Michael's Mount,' in the Sheepshanks Collection; not an objective, but a light and aërial picture, obviously designed to work out some theory of light and colour. The Mount is too light; and Turner's favourite subject, the fish market on the beach, is not wanting.

Sketches of the Third Period, from 1835 to 1844.

In this period Turner acquired dexterity of handling; his colour became tender and pensive; and, in quest of Nature alone, he now disdained both precedent and ideals, and sometimes, I fear, even truth. The sketches of chalk rocks on the

Meuse, of Rouen, Quillebœuf, and St. Germains, often grand, flowing, and full of brilliancy, tenderness and depth though they be, not seldom betray hasty execution from the painter's desire to make perpetual coloured sketches. To this division of his Art life belong a drawing of a vast unnamed fortress, which seems to provoke Mr. Ruskin's curiosity so much; Scenes on the Loire; the Theatre at Dijon; Honfleur; Ville-neuve, looking from Chillon towards Vevay; a Gallery of the Splügen; the Coblentz Bridge; and the Vignette of the Apparition at sunrise, for Rogers's poem of 'Columbus.' Twilights, moon-rises, and river scenes are plentiful, and they are all marked by a simple tenderness of colour.

Swiss and Venetian sketches are very numerous. He drew Lausanne, bathed in a rosy sunset; a morning view, looking from Brennen; Fluelen on the Lake of Lucerne, looking from Kussnach towards the Bernese Alps; and Mons Pilatus, dark against the sunset. Then comes his last visit to Venice; and for the hundredth time he sits down to make notes of San Giorgio, Santa Maria della Salute, the Bridge of the Riva del Schiavoni, and the lagoon between San Giorgio and the Cantieri.

Under the head of 'Supplementary Sketches' (including some of the three periods) we may mention the following, which serve to record at least the places he visited, and the special spots' and objects that arrested his attention and excited his interest.

Among his treasured sketch-books (for he never seems to have destroyed anything) was found a long series of notes taken during a visit to Rome in 1819, in which a fine sense of the Eternal City's fallen estate is conveyed by the poet-painter. He sketches the bridge and castle of St. Angelo, the city from Monte Mario and from the Barberini Villa, a fine but careless view of the Nymphæum of Severus, the Colosseum, and the Claudian Aqueduct—the latter passing effect painted perhaps at the moment, contrary to Turner's usual habit. He sketches also the Basilica of Constantine, the arches of Constantine and of Titus, the church of San Giovanni and Paolo, the Loggie (probably for his Raphael picture), and real acanthus growing among Corinthian pillars.

To these succeed the sketch-books numbered 247 and 507, full of memoranda of George IV.'s visit to Scotland, in which the form and the colour of the clouds are noted down for future use ; and these again are followed by records of visits to Huy Dinant (Rhine and Meuse), the junction of the Rhone and Arve, and Geneva, from various points of view.

Nor must we forget additional Venetian jottings, the fruits of infinite and untiring industry—the Custom House, St. Mark's Place, Casa Grimani, the Rialto, St. George, the Great Canal from the Casa Foscari to the Rialto, St. Mark's and St. Zachary's, the Doge's Palace and Mint, the Fruit and Coal Market, the Doge's Palace, and the Rialto again, on the east and on the west side. We have, besides, Naples, with its Claude-like shores, fish-wives from Dieppe, a sculptured tomb from Dresden, the sketch of the 'Arch of Titus' picture, long leaves of inscriptions and architectural drawings, the Borromean Islands, and seven studies of the Rhine at Andernach, with fine stormy sunset and drifts of cloud. Yet the best of these sketches are only an inch and a half long and three-quarters of an inch deep.

From these treasure chests, moreover, we are enabled to judge how conscientious and anxious Turner was about his perspective lectures ; for here is a mighty portfolio full of careful diagrams, massed-out shadows and reflected lights, huge perspective elevations of the dome of St. Peter's, the interchanged reflections of two glass balls, measured moonlight falling on the pillar of Trajan, the chiaroscuro of a jailer's lantern moving through the dark passages of Newgate, and studies of light and shade on hollow glass balls first empty and then half-filled. Most conspicuous are the exquisite knowledge and care disclosed by these diagrams.

The versatility and the elasticity of the painter's mind are copiously attested by these sketch-books. From rooms whose domesticity is signified by a cat, and from familiar objects like mackerel, turbot, and mutton, he passes on to Buckingham Gate in the Strand. Thence he flits to Orleans, Saumur, Havre, Harfleur, or Caudebec. Again he is on the Loire or the Carrara mountains ; anon he studies a burning ship at sunset (an unfinished oil picture), or takes up his post on a glacier near the source of the Arveron.   Most frequently he reverts to his favourite subject of the sea ; sketching masts and rigging, and boats labouring in a heavy sea, or swamped in the surf.   In this list must be included 'Carew Castle' (not later than 1800), published in 1834; 'Lancaster' (in the 'England'), 'Caernarvon Castle,' 'Wells Cathedral,' and sketches at and near York (of the second period); and, among the miscellaneous foreign sketches, 'Bellinzona,' studies of the Rhine on brown paper, and notes of his last tour in 1845, when he visited Fribourg, and made some fruitless pen and pencil sketches of the roofs, towers, and walls of that curious city.

About 1835 was painted his 'Heidelberg Castle in the Olden Time;' the palace of the German Emperor and the Counts of Baden, which the French partly destroyed in 1689, being restored by the artist according to his own fancy; and in this year he exhibited 'Line-Fishing off Hastings,' one of the Sheepshanks Collection.   A collier brig is wearing off shore, some boats are out fishing, and to the left is the castle.   The squally spray, the sunny haze, and the cliffs yellow against a dark, cool sea, are beautiful, but not without exaggeration.   Another Venetian picture, 'The Grand Canal, Venice, from the Madonna della Salute Church, looking towards the Riva degli Schiavoni,' in which the Campanile and the two famous pillars are introduced, also appeared in 1835, together with 'Ehrenbreitstein and the Tomb of Moreau,' subsequently the property of Mr. E. Bicknell.   This picture was a subject chosen expressly by Mr. J. Pye to engrave, and to it he devoted ten years off and on; Turner consenting to its being engraved on condition of receiving twelve proofs for the copyright.

In 1835 Scarlett Davis, a well-known artist of that day, addressing his friend Ince, a favourite pupil of David Cox, though now comparatively forgotten, who realised a considerable fortune by his profession, writes—

'I have no artistical chat for you, further than that Turner has painted a large picture of the "Burning of the Two Houses of Parliament;" but I have heard it spoken of as a failure—a devil of a lot of chrome.   He finished it on the walls the last two days before the Gallery opened to the public.   I am told it was good fun to see the great man whacking away with about fifty stupid apes standing round him, and I understand he was cursedly annoyed—the fools kept peeping into his colour box and examining all his brushes and colours.'

In the same letter occurs the following passage:—

' In my last I told you of the drawing I was making for Mr. Windus. I know it will give you great pleasure to hear that Turner has seen it and spoken in the highest terms of it, and that it now hangs in company with fifty of his best works.'

The previous communication mentions Davis's engagement upon 'a very difficult subject, the Interior of the Library of Mr. Windus, who has it filled with about fifty Turners. When you come to town we will go down to him (he lives at Tottenham), and I can assure you a *treat*. There are parts of some of them *wonderful*, and by G—d all other drawings look heavy and vulgar, even Calcott and Stanfield (even the immortal Vicars, Harding, and Pyne[1]).'

A few words of the writer of this letter.

Scarlett Davis was the son of a humble shoemaker at Hereford, whose juvenile evidence of a taste for drawing secured the generous patronage of a local clergyman. One of his earliest efforts (he was about seven years old) was to make a drawing of a cart and etch it all at one sitting, before retiring to rest. As a mere boy, he carried off the prize at the Society of Arts; and, when the judges looked round for the victor, his patron held him up on his hand and exclaimed, with a laugh, ' Here is the artist!' As he advanced in years Scarlett Davis became remarkable for a most fatal facility; he was able to make five sketches for the engraver in an hour. After two days of surreptitious drawing at Scarborough he returned with no less than one hundred and sixteen sketches. By the help of Lord Zetland, who became his patron, he went to Paris, where he painted a picture of the interior of the Louvre, at that time full of Napoleon's magnificent thievings. This picture was much ridiculed; but Etty, who was kind to him, liked it, and Lawrence valued it at 800*l.* After this he affected interiors. He always lacked finish, but his facility knew no decrease. Tradition has it that at the British Institution he once cleverly copied a

[1] Satirical, of course.—ED.

Rembrandt, for which he subsequently obtained ten guineas, in the brief space of six hours. In his opening days, during his residence at York, he made drawings for Robinson's 'Cottage Architecture,' and executed a mezzotint of Bolton Abbey.

Hitherto respectable, Davis at an early age married the sister of a girl to whom he had been engaged, and who had been seduced. After this he became drunken and debauched, and, being got out of prison by Dr. Simpson, died miserably before he had attained thirty. He seems to have been a reckless, eccentric, shifty man of talent; and there is a story of him one day running furiously into the house of a friend for the purpose of borrowing a pistol to shoot a 'vulgarian' who had dared to accuse him of charging three pounds too much for a portrait. His paintings of galleries were altered to suit his own ideas of grouping, colour, and effect, so that the historical value of them is slight. 'Davis,' writes the biographer of Etty and Blake, was 'one of those men of genius utterly devoid of honesty or moral sense. Lord Farnborough was his first great patron.'

In 1836 Turner exhibited 'Mercury and Argus;' a sunny Italian picture, with a villa, rivulet, lake, and the cow that gives the name to the composition. It was purchased by Mr. J. Naylor, of Liverpool. This was the year of Turner's tour in France and Switzerland in the company of Mr. Munro.

In 1837 was exhibited his 'Apollo and Daphne in the Vale of Tempe,' with the emblematical greyhound and hare in the foreground of the picture. The legend of Ovid which the painter illustrates is, that Cupid, angry at Apollo's coldness, wounded him with a golden arrow, and at the same time shot into Daphne's heart the leaden shaft of dislike and distrust. The wooded valley of Thessaly between Ossa and Olympus, I need scarcely say, Turner has idealised into a beautiful 'no man's land.'

Reverting once more to Carthage, that favourite halting-place of his imagination, he exhibited at the British Institution 'Regulus Leaving Rome to Return to Carthage.' This picture, a grand vision of Imperial Rome, was painted at Rome in 1829. It would have been in vain, I am sure, to have told Turner that

Regulus, after all, probably was not put to a cruel death by the Carthaginians.

The same year he painted that wild piece of imagination 'The Parting of Hero and Leander,' with a motto from Musæus. It is a dark and heavy picture, sadly wanting in concentration and clearness, and broken into many diffusive and conflicting lights. The temple at Lesbos is converted into a vast palace, crowded with endless terraces; there are two moons and a red sun above them ; and the halo foretells the storm which Leander is about to face in his hour and ten minutes' swim. Love and Hymen (I am afraid Hymen had not much to do with these meetings) are holding the guiding lamps. The figures are terribly misshapen.

In the following year he exhibited those two great pictures which he painted for his friend Mr. Munro, 'Ancient Italy' and ' Modern Italy;' two grand imaginative flights, in many respects worthy of his best days, but compositions rather than honest topographical realities. The first represents the banishment of Ovid from Rome, and consists primarily of a view of the Tiber looking south-west, as seen from the left bank. The bridge is the Pons Sublicius, the gallant defence of which by Horatius survives in Macaulay's famous lay. The Temple of Vesta and the Castle of St. Angelo are also introduced. A sarcophagus, moreover, intimates that Ovid died in exile, and against it leans a mysterious jack-screw, typical of we know not what. The modern picture represents a view of the Campagna combined with Tivoli ; a town on a hill, a woman confessing, a religious procession, and some Pifferari, those mountain pipers who visit Rome at Christmas to worship the Madonna.

In 1838 he also exhibited 'Phryne going to the Public Baths as Venus ;' into which, after his accumulative mode, he crowds Demosthenes being taunted by Æschines, his great rival in oratory. The baths are in the distance; and among others in the foreground, to the extreme right, is Phryne riding in a chariot as Venus. The two dogs playing with glass globes adumbrate, I suppose, the pursuit of pleasure. The figures are detestable, and the shadows all scarlet.

In 1839, the year of the exhibition of the 'Fighting Téméraire,' he sent to the Academy 'Agrippina Landing with the Ashes of her Husband, Germanicus.' The classic story merely serves as an excuse for vast, dreamy mountain piles of Greek temples and palaces ; and, as it happens, Agrippina really landed with her pious freight not at Rome, but at Brundusium, on the Adriatic. Exercising his royal prerogative to the full, as usual, the painter has moved the palace of the Cæsars from the left to the right bank of the Tiber, to suit his composition. As usual also in the later pictures, the colour is gorgeous, but the form is defective, and the bridge inaccurately placed.

And now we come to what the painter himself prized most highly—'The Old Téméraire.'

CHAPTER XLII.

'THE OLD TÉMÉRAIRE.'

From the early time when, as a boy, he first boated up and down the Thames, to that final day at Chelsea when he turned his dying eyes on the river he loved, Turner had all an Englishman's love for the water. He had been born on the banks of a great river ; his first school was situated in proximity to the Thames ; he lived much on the ocean ; he beat about year after year in all sorts of smuggler's boats ; he cruised largely by sea, round our own coast and many others ; and he breathed his last close to the very spot whither he had repaired as a boy to make his first sketches. All his life he retained a passion for the Thames and its 'black barges, patched red sails, and every possible condition of blue and white fog ;' and the secret of his attachment was that the scenes of his childhood were never obliterated from his memory. His early visit to his uncle the fishmonger and glue-boiler at Bristol perhaps originated his maritime tastes.

Mr. Ruskin opines that much of Turner's youth was spent in 'that mysterious forest' of masts below London Bridge, in cheap 'poor Jack' trips among seafaring people at Chelsea, or, in the other direction, at Greenwich and Deptford. This course of discipline could not have improved either his manners or his

morals. As a fact, hence he derived a certain nautical standard
of morality by which his subsequent life was regulated ; and the
coarseness observable in his rendering of the female form may
surely be traced to this early familiarity with the fish-wives of
Billingsgate. The training, however, was not without its advantages. It gave him exact knowledge of a ship's anatomy
and motion ; he learned thus early how vessels would balance
in any weather. Such, indeed, was the ardour of his nautical
bent that after his death a whole press was found full of such
naval sketches. One can conceive him as a boy anxiously
saving up shillings to spend upon boats, in order that he might
go and watch the floating castles.

It was this early love for ships and sailors that led him to
paint so many storms and shipwrecks, and so many salvage
boats ; to give us the ' Battle of Trafalgar' and the ' " Old
Téméraire " being Towed to her Last Moorings.' Let me here
insert an admirable anecdote furnished to Mr. Ruskin by the
Rev. Charles Kingsley. ' I had taken my mother and a cousin
to see Turner's pictures,' he writes ; ' and, as my mother knows
nothing about Art, I was taking her down the gallery to look at
the large " Richmond Park ; " but, as we were passing the
" Snow-Storm," she stopped before it, and I could harly get
her to look at any other picture ; and she told me a great deal
more about it than I had any notion of, though I have seen
many snow-storms. She had been in such a scene on the
coast of Holland during the war. When, some time afterwards,
I thanked Turner for his permission for her to see the pictures,
I told him that he would not guess what had [most] caught my
mother's fancy, and then named the picture ; but he said—

' " I did not paint it to be understood, but I wished to show
what such a scene was like. I got the sailors to lash me to the
mast to observe it. I was lashed for four hours, and I did not
expect to escape ; but I felt bound to record it if I did. But
no one had any business to like the picture."

' " But," said I, " my mother once went through just such a
scene, and it brought it all back to her."

' " Is your mother a painter ? "

' " No."

'"Then she ought to have been thinking of something else."

'These were nearly his words. I observed at the time he used "record" and "painter," as the title "author" had struck me before.'

This anecdote shows us Turner in his most heroic mood, forgetful of all danger in the pursuit of his art; and it is in this position that I should have liked to see him represented by the sculptor in his monument in St. Paul's.

The 'Téméraire' picture was exhibited at the Royal Academy in 1839. The subject was suggested to the painter by Stanfield. In 1838 Turner was with Stanfield and a party of brother-artists on one of those holiday excursions in which he so delighted, probably to end with whitebait and champagne at Greenwich. It was at these times that Turner talked and joked his best, snatching now and then a moment to print on his quick brain some tone of sky, some gleam of water, some sprinkling light of oar, some glancing sunshine cross-barring a sail. Suddenly there moved down upon the artists' boat the grand old vessel that had been taken prisoner at the Nile, and that led the van at Trafalgar. She loomed through the evening haze pale and ghostly, as she was being towed to her last moorings at Deptford by a little fiery, puny steam-tug. 'There's a fine subject, Turner,' said Stanfield. Accordingly Turner adopted it; and, as we all know, it proved to be one of his most poetical pictures.

Of the name of the picture the following anecdote is related :—

'In consequence of the prominent part the "Téméraire" took in the battle of Trafalgar, she was called among the sailors "the fighting 'Téméraire,'" *although she had never before or after the battle of Trafalgar a claim to the popular epithet* ; but Turner had so often heard her called "the fighting 'Téméraire'" that the name became to him a household word, and as such he entitled his poetical and beautiful picture when it was exhibited. But when the plate was engraved for the Royal Gallery of British Art, and it became necessary to give a brief but authentic history of the ship, and the truth was stated to Turner, he seemed almost in tears when he gave up his pet title, and said, " Call her, then, the ' Old Téméraire.'"'

The assertion that the 'Fighting Téméraire' had no claim to the title but for its doings at Trafalgar is, however, a mere bit of malice, designed to detract from Turner's sensibility. The 'Téméraire' had doubtless had her rubs as a French battle-ship ; we cannot trace her history before the too-daring vessel fell into our hands in the engagement of the Nile ; but she fought tremendously in that battle of giants at Trafalgar. She was the second ship in Collingwood's division, and was com-manded by Captain Hervey. The ' Victory ' bore down on the ' Redoubtable,' and was received with a broadside, the French instantly closing their lower-deck port for fear of the boarders, and firing no more great guns during the whole action. There-upon the 'Téméraire,' like a staunch comrade, fell on board the 'Redoubtable' on the other side, and the French ship 'Fougueux' was in like manner on board the ' Téméraire ;' so that the four vessels lay as if moored in dock, their heads all pointing the same way. Observing this, the lieutenants of the 'Victory' depressed their middle- and lower-deck guns, and fired with a diminished charge, lest the shot should pass through the ' Redoubtable' and pierce the ' Téméraire.'

Mr. Ruskin considers this achievement of 1839 the last picture Turner executed with his entire and perfect power. The 'Polyphemus,' painted in 1829, he claims as marking the beginning of Turner's central and best period of ten years. Singularly enough, while the picture of 1829 is a sunrise, the picture of 1839 is a sunset.

I submit a criticism, contributed by myself to the pages of the ' Athenæum ' of 1859, upon this picture, regarded mainly as a matchless tableau of colour :—

' The crown and paragon of the collection is the " ' Fighting Téméraire' Tugged to her Last Berth," which stands out from amongst them as a great flame-coloured Mexican cactus, the very emperor of flowers, would do in a nosegay of simple prim-roses. We place it first of all his works, because it excels in colour all landscapes, we might almost say, in the world ;—we place it first, because it excels in *colour*, and it was as a colourist that Turner excelled almost all painters. It is wonderful for all the qualities of colour, for brilliancy, contrast, breadth, tone, transparency, and light. And these fantasies are lavished on one of the simplest of heroic themes ;—an old man-of-war being towed to her last moorings—her grave—where, after a well-spent life, she will return to those primitive elements from whence her oaks first sprang. She is towed by a steamer, late in the sunset, which is smouldering fiercely out of the sky ; beyond the whirlpool of crimson and yellow, and flame-streaks of vermilion, a blue haze is creeping up the river to meet the night. Grand and warrior-like, stern, like an unconquered veteran, proud of trophy and scar, the "Téméraire" moves on, with its lance-like masts erect, its broad, pale, spectral hull looming stupendous and threatening over a water red as with the blood of past battles. A grand and touching sight is the old ship, so vast and thunderous in its sleeping and now well-nigh exhausted might—so staunch, so true, and indomitable it is. The tug seems to convoy it gently and lovingly, as the enormous bulk whitens and troubles the water. To the right we see dim through the blue vapoury twilight a factory, and masts and chimneys, all hinted with a divine art which astonishes and delights us. To the left of the sunset that still dominates and sways its dying torches rises the moon, cooling the picture with delicious semitones of grey and purple, fading away into pearl. Just below the sunset, the chief focus of light in the picture, rolls and wallows a huge black buoy, forming a mass which leads the eye to the strange shadows of the steamer's bows, brightening from dark brown to a yellow and more luminous duskiness. From the broad horizontal vermilion splash that is the core of the sunset to the palest blue and pearl of the moon region of the picture, is a grand compass for any painter's brush, and needed a hundred-fingered man and a ten-horse power of brain to attain it.

' In no picture we have ever seen can you pass through so far, and yet come to no wall that forces back the impatient and forth-flying imagination. Through a thousand semitones and half-notes of grey and neutral tint we reach the sovereign colours that rule the picture. The very relaxations and freedoms of the drawing seem true to the aërial witchery and beguilement of such an hour and such an evening. The winged trails of scattered sunset fire—the red reflections of the vessel—the yellow tinge on the sail—the brown shadows—the light trail of smoke in the distance—the rich-coloured vapours of the steamer's funnel—the junction of red and blue in the distance, where the sunset dips and fuses its edge into the blue river fog—are all so many points of chromatic harmony. As a picture it is the most glorious consummation of colouring ever painted by English fingers, or seen by English eyes. In exquisite transparency it surpasses water colours ; in strength and purity it transcends oil. It is the noblest English poem, founded on English scenery and English events, ever thrown on canvas. He who painted this deserves indeed a central seat in our wide Pantheon.'

Hearty as this encomium is, it does little justice to the chief merit of the picture, which is its matchless poetry and sentiment. Turner, no doubt, had often heard sailors' yarns of the 'Fighting Téméraire ;' and the Nelson men at Greenwich Hospital had, perhaps, talked of it till it stood in his mind as a thing with not merely a body but a soul. He might have heard that, when she left Plymouth for her last cruise, the officers and men in the dockyards gave her three cheers at parting— cheers of gratitude and regret. At Deptford she was to cease to be a ship, and to become a hospital hulk for the sailors of all nations. Turner, however, looked at her not as an old friend going to the grave, but as an old warrior going to his rest ; and, to celebrate its grand apotheosis, he turned the sky and earth into a gory battle-field ; and so in gorgeous sunset she moves in pomp to her burial. In the painter's eyes she then was no longer the pale ghost of her former self, but a war ship moving through the sulphurous flame at Trafalgar, with the blood oozing through her planks as the wine pours from the wine-press at vintage time. He knew, when he painted this picture, that he should touch the heart of England, because his own heart was touched as he painted it.

Had I not so often come unexpectedly upon subtle and underlying thoughts in Turner's works, I should have been inclined to doubt that the painter, in introducing the tug, meant to symbolise the rise of steam power and the downfall of wooden ships. Yet, though I think he merely painted what he saw, I am not sure that he had not this occult meaning also. His mind was quick and deep ; he generally saw all the sides of a thought, and all that could be done with it. Besides, we know from several of his pictures that he had a sublime idea of the power of steam.

Burnet, the excellent engraver of Wilkie's ' Blind Fiddler,' and an admirable writer on Art, is the author of some fine condensed remarks on the beauties of colour and composition in this picture. Unlike most engravers, who care for nothing but black and white, Burnet had a fine taste for colour ; and, moreover, he was always judicious in his views. The picture, he pointed out to me, is divided into hot and cold colours—a favourite arrangement of the painter's. To the left is the pale, huge man-of-war, towed by the dark tug ; and to the right is the setting sun ; the warm colour is on the sunny side, the cold and shadow around and above the ship. The bulk of the composition is on the ship's side, and to balance that comes the solitary dark buoy below the sun (repeating its shape), to the right. The sky, from a burning vermilion over the sun, passes through yellow to warm blue on the opposite side, while the cold blues melt into pearly greys around the new-risen moon. The steam tug is painted cool green ; her reflections are brown, warm, and neutral. Mr. J. T. Willmore, A.R.A., engraved this picture ; but no engraving, of course, can render the purity and richness of colour. It has also been coarsely chromo-lithographed.

Touching the price of this Koh-i-noor of a picture, a correspondent writes—

' Upon going into the Gallery soon after it opened, I was, as a purchaser of modern works at that time, so struck with the poetry and beauty of this most charming picture that I *instantly* went off to Queen Anne Street, where I was favoured with a long and interesting interview with the artist. Although he stated that the "Téméraire" was his " 200 guineas size," only, I urged him *again and again* to accept my cheque for *three* hundred ; and at length begged of him only to "*put a price* upon it." I would have given him *five* hundred guineas rather than have left it ; for I had set my heart upon the gem ! But although he offered to take a commission of the same size *at* 200 *guineas*, stating that " I might choose my own subject " likewise, I could not possibly induce him either to accept my offer or to put *any price* upon the " Téméraire." '

There was a story current to the effect that this great picture might have been bought at the Academy for 150*l.*, and that even at that sum it could not obtain a purchaser ; but its inaccuracy is demonstrated by the preceding communication.

Some years after the Exhibition, Leslie tried to buy it for Mr. James Lenox, of New York ; but Turner would not part with it. It had already been mentally placed by him among the pictures he would bequeath to the nation; and sacks of gold would not have diverted him from his resolve. In one of the codicils to his will, after his death set aside, Turner left each of his executors a picture. They were to choose for themselves (I believe), according to seniority ; but his pet, the ' Téméraire,' was specially excepted from the range of choice.

An early writer on Turner says—

' It has often been asked where, when, and how Turner acquired such knowledge of the sea and of ships ; and the question may be answered by stating that in his travels he always mingled with humble and practical men ; for, whether journeying by sea or land, he never parted with a penny without looking at it twice, and was in the habit of travelling by the most economical conveyance, as well as putting up at the most cheap houses ; and a good deal of his knowledge of seamanship was picked up during his trips to the North, to which he always went by a collier. Once he spent a whole summer in drifting about the Thames, for he was fond of the water ; and at the time of his death " Mr. Booth's " boat was moored off Battersea Bridge. Lord Egremont used to assert that Turner had a yacht; but we cannot ascertain this to be the case.'

' In the year 1839,' says Mr. Lupton, ' J. M. W. Turner presented the public with the sight of that highly-esteemed picture the " ' Téméraire ' being Towed to her Last Berth," the beauty and splendour of which were perhaps somewhat heightened by an occurrence which not unfrequently happens to pictures that are placed in juxtaposition during the arranging or hanging of pictures for public exhibition.

'The picture of the "Téméraire" was placed satisfactorily to Mr. Turner, and immediately over it was a picture by Geddes, A.R.A. — "A Lady and Children." Geddes was delighted with the splendour and brilliancy of Turner's picture ; but at the same time he saw at a glance that its splendour and brilliancy would entirely distract the spectator's attention from his own picture above, and that he must do something to make his picture more attractive, and share in the vividness or brilliancy of colour with Turner's picture beneath. So he resolved to repaint the floor of his picture, which was a plain, quiet colour, and make it more attractive to the spectator's eye ; accordingly he resolved to paint in a showy Turkey carpet. To accomplish this, he first painted the whole ground of his picture with a *flat, bright tint* of *vermilion*, as a ground-work for the pattern of the carpet to be painted, and then returned to an adjoining room to complete another picture he was painting on before the opening of the Exhibition. Turner was also in an adjoining room, touching up or varnishing another of his pictures. After a while he returned to look at his "Téméraire," when, in an instant, his eyes were attracted up to this *new mass* of bright vermilion of Geddes's picture. He was overheard to exclaim, "Oh, oh, Mr. Geddes ! " and immediately ran for his palette and brushes from the adjacent apartment. Immediately he cast a sly look first at Mr. Geddes's picture, and then at his own ; after which, taking his palette knife charged full of vermilion, he passed it right across his picture ; then stepping back, with another sly look at both pictures, another palette knife was charged with orange colour, then another charged with yellow, and so on, until he was satisfied that he had brought his picture up to the necessary brilliancy to contend with the bright vermilion ground above him in Geddes's picture.

' Returning the next day to look at his picture, Turner was

somewhat surprised to fine that the bright vermilion ground of Geddes's picture above his "Téméraire," and which he had taken so much pains to paint down, had been turned into a rich, quiet, comparatively speaking, sober-coloured Turkey carpet.'

CHAPTER XLIII.

TURNER'S ART LIFE—*(concluded)*.

IN 1840 Turner painted 'Bacchus and Ariadne;' a variation of the grand old Titian theme. In it he omits the sail of the vessel of Theseus, who, having slain the Minotaur, deserts Ariadne at Naxos. There is a city on a height, and a river below.

In this year he also produced 'Venice—the Bridge of Sighs;' the celebrated bridge connecting the Doge's palace with the State prison, which was built in 1589; besides 'Venice from the Giudecca;' a light and sunny picture; and the 'New Moon;' a seaport at sunset, with sands at low water, and a steamer in the distance.

In 1842 was painted 'Peace—the Burial of the Body of Sir David Wilkie.' This excellent painter, who came to England from Fifeshire in 1805, had died the June previous off Gibraltar, as he was returning from the East in the Oriental steamer. The old rivalry was now forgotten in regret at his death. In the distance of the picture are the rocket-signals rising from the signal-peak at Gibraltar.

This was the year in which he exhibited 'War—the Exile and the Rock Limpet;' a picture representing Napoleon on the shore of St. Helena at sunset, watching a solitary shell. The strange motto disclosed the eccentric and super-subtle meaning of the painter :—

> Ah! thy tent-formed shell is like
> A soldier's nightly bivouac alone,
> Amidst a sea of blood !
>   But you can join your comrades.

Owing to the wilfully eccentric reflections, Napoleon looks as if he was standing on stilts.

This was the year, too, of the 'Snow Storm—Steamboat off a Harbour's Mouth making Signals ; Shallow Water ; going by the Lead.' This is the picture that riveted the attention of Mrs. Kingsley, as has been narrated on a previous page, and the severe criticism upon which the painter, who encountered such a storm in the 'Ariel' steamer off Harwich, felt so acutely.

Tired now of plain sober truth, or determined to puzzle and astonish by prismatic experiments a public that would not buy his pictures and did not comprehend his genius, Turner in 1843 launched out into some of his wildest dreams. He exhibited 'Shade and Darkness, or the Evening of the Deluge ;' 'Light and Colour, or the Morning of the Deluge' (he was very fond of this parallelism of subjects) ; and the 'Opening of the Walhalla, 1842' (honour to King Ludwig of Bavaria !). The Walhalla, a Doric temple situate on a hill on the left bank of the Danube, near Regensburg, and containing two hundred marble busts of eminent Germans, was built by Leo von Klenze, and opened in October 1842. The topography of the picture is full of errors. The probability is that it was painted, with alterations, from a bad engraving. Delighted with the evidence of Bavarian love of Art and the blessings of peace supplied by the grand erection, Turner sent the picture as a present to King Ludwig ; but the monarch, unable to make anything of it, and perhaps ignorant of the artist's existence, lost no time in packing it up again and returning the gift, much, I should think, to the artist's wrath and indignation.

Venice still fascinating him, the same year gave birth to the 'Approach to Venice, looking towards Fusina,' painted from a sketch made in 1839–40 ; a noble picture, marking the advent of sunset ; and to 'The "Sun of Venice" going to Sea,' a pretty fantasy of a gaily-decked fishing-boat setting out heedless of the storm that will soon ruffle its gay plumage.

In 1844 Turner painted 'Fishing-boats bringing a disabled Ship into Port Ruysdael.' The port never existed save in the painter's mind ; but the name was intended as a tribute to the memory of Ruysdael, the Dutch landscape-painter. Two

Venetian pictures, the 'Venice, (the canal of the Giudecca, with the Dogana and the Church of Santa Maria della Salute), and 'Venice Quay,' with the Ducal Palace, the Riva degli Schiavoni and the Church of San Zaccaria, were also exhibited.

In 1845 was painted the 'Lake of Lucerne' for Mr. Windus. It now belongs to Mrs. De Patron, of Rodwell Rectory, Sussex. It is a view of the south-west from the hill above Brunnen ; the little lake steamer from Fluelan is approaching ; the Righi is not forgotten, nor the Brisen, with châlets, and other garnishing ; but the topography is in many respects untrue, says Mr. Wornum.

To 1845 also belong 'Venice—Noon—from the Canal of St. Mark ;' 'Venice—Sunset—a fisher ;' and his first picture of 'Whalers,' suggested by Beale's 'Natural History of the Sperm Whale.'

1846 produced more Venetian fantasies, such as 'Venice—Evening : going to the Ball ;' 'Venice—Morning : returning from the Ball ;' 'Whalers, entangled in Ice, boiling Blubber ;' and 'Whalers—Hurrah for the Whaler "Erebus !" Another Fish ! !' Beale, from whose book he took the subject of this last picture, does not mention any ship named the 'Erebus.' The same year he exhibited at the British Institution a riddle in paint called 'Queen Mab's Grotto ;' and some extraordinary works called 'Undine giving the Ring to Masaniello, Fisherman of Naples ;' 'The Angel standing in the Sun ; and 'The Hero of a Hundred Fights '—a scene in a casting-furnace.

In 1850 he grew calmer and returned for the last time to his old classical scenes ; but, alas ! with sadly impaired sight, and less mechanical as well as mental power. ' Æneas relating his Story to Dido ;' 'Mercury sent to admonish Æneas ;' 'The Departure of the Trojan Fleet ;' and the 'Visit to the Tomb '—an ominous title, were exhibited. Even to the last we see that the 'Story of Carthage,' as it is found either in fiction or in history, had peculiar charms for Turner.

Of a few of the later pictures the 'Athenæum' spoke thus : '"Phryne going to the Bath as Venus." Was ever such a heap of rag dolls ever brought together and called men and women.

Venuses, indeed !—say rather limp-lanknesses seen through a burnt-sienna fog in a classical dream after falling asleep over one of Racine's tragedies. The strongest imagination can hardly allow these longitudes to be women ; as for Phryne— bah ! In all the picture the trees are scraggy and ultra-man- nered both in drawing, composition, and colour. The distance, too, is the beautiful dream of a painter's strong memory, but still a dream. It is a world panorama, such a vision as Satan showed from the mount. A white brightness irradiates it all, and leaves unfixed the junction of earth and air.

'The "Bridge of Sighs." This is the dotage of a great mind. There is much straining, much weak and irresolute piling of paint, till it stands in ragged buttons all over the canvas. The mind's eye is dimmed and the hand grows feeble. The taste has grown morbid, and "lusts" for impossible and useless effects. The two extremes of the mind stand still firm. The sky-colour is still admirable, and the drawing worse than ever ; altogether, we must own with sorrow, shaky, foggy, blurred, and even non-existing. The figures, too, are now mere shapeless clothes-bags. The man who can praise such works as these is not a critic, but a partisan. True, the walls are of a pleasant pink, and the sky a tender blue. The bridge springs grandly, and the water is a sea of wonders, and shines like an ocean of melted jewels; but the affectations and excesses of the artist's mind are obvious. There is a wilful and obstinate exaggeration in everything—all the spiritual accidents are painted stronger than the tangible realities. The shadows are heavier than the boats—the sky than the buildings. It is, in fact, a beautiful dotage, and nothing else. It is interesting only as a decline and fall, as the end of a lifetime, as a comparison —*as a warning*.

'"The 'Sun of Venice' setting sail." This is a wonderful bit of a rainbow, rather surprising than pleasing and calming. It looks like a *tour de force*—a sort of slap in the face to an incredulous and dullard public. It is a phantasmagoria. The sails of the vessels are all blue, and red, and yellow, and there is a fly-about, vagaryish character about the whole that is not very rational or of this or any other world. The beauty of it is, that we do not see the eternal Englishman in it as we do in almost all past and existing landscapes—nor the thick, horny mist and suffused blueness of our mountain and lake exhalations. This is a poem founded on Italian experiences, but dreamy and ideal, and of the seventh heaven as much as if it were a scene from Shelley's "Alastor." Still, if the spectator is a thorough Turnerian, and chooses to take the seventh heaven for granted, he may rejoice in the trembling distance that is creating itself and growing from the air, and in the broad-winged, free, joyous flight of the flamingo-like vessel—which certainly has never been registered at Lloyd's.'

Among the pictures left unfinished by Turner were 'Richmond Bridge;' two Petworth subjects, 'Petworth Park' and 'Chichester Canal;' two mountain glens (the latter with Diana and Actæon sketched in)—the 'Sketch for the Harvest Home;' and the 'Sketch for the Greenwich Trafalgar.'

CHAPTER XLIV.

TURNER'S NOTE-BOOKS AND SKETCHES.

First style from 1800 *to* 1820; *or between the age of twenty-five and forty-five.*

IN 1802 Turner set forth upon his first Continental tour, and his sketch-books show that he took careful, formal and complete notes, near Grenoble, at Calais, and in Savoy. Many of these sketches he sold; afterwards, when they had been mounted in a folio, he rebought them; and finally he left them to the nation. He invested the Lake of Brienz with the gloom of a horizontal line of mist. The Lake of Geneva he took from Vevay; and Mont Blanc, Aosta, and his first glance of Italy filled him with delight. The Roman gate at Aosta, as being the first example he had presented to his vision of the classical school in which he had been brought up, was especially stimulating. This he utilised in after time for a design to Rogers's 'Italy.' From association of ideas with his first sight of a

Swiss lake, most likely, thereafter he invariably affected the vapour on his lakes, and this effect was one of the last he tried to reproduce on his final tour. His earliest trees had been Wilsonian in structure; his earliest studies of the Alps were Wilsonianly lumpy, and feebly drawn. In this first period his oil paintings were bold and dark, but his water-colours were delicate even to timidity.

In his first tour Turner seems to have had an eye for glaciers and fallen trees; but Mont Blanc and Grenoble were his favourite resting-places. He has a grand version of the Chartreuse, of the Ascent to Courmayeur, and of the valley of the Isère. Grenoble he assails from every side with special predilection, determining, as it were, to engrave it in his mind; and the thought of one of the 'Liber' drawings originated here; but the sketch is finer, says Mr. Ruskin. He draws the road to Grenoble from Voreppe, with the daylit Alps seen through a mountain-gap; and the Alps and Grenoble again, with a grand rolling sky. He sketches Grenoble, with finely outlined hills and clouds, marvelling much at the walls and fortified towers running up hill; and he draws Mont Blanc as seen from the Fort St. Louis.

An oil study of a mountain stream, still preserved, is dark and broad, the stones being outlined with great truth. In this period of his life, he also drew 'Edinburgh, from the Calton Hill.' Next—in sketch-books in the National Collection—we turn to a note of Rouen for the 'Rivers of France;' the view taken from St. Catherine's Hill, whence he observes sheep and a sawpit on the banks of the Seine, and Norman women in their enormous caps—always special points of interest to a new traveller. Then follow some colour notes on Claude and Titian, for, though he had not yet liberated himself from the fetters of imitation, he was beginning to give increased attention to the subject.

His old love for animals, too, now began to find vent in studies which were useful for future pictures. Thus we have teal flying, drawn in colour; mules' skeletons, human skeletons (used in the 'Liber'); studies of swans, where the water is rippled to express the agitation and anger of the birds; poultry-yards (the first thing he ever studied from Nature) ; market ware (from a sketch made at Rotterdam) ; and pigs and donkeys—the latter wonderful, a foal being drawn with scarcely more than one touch. Already Turner is a hoarder and miser in Art, covetous of everything he can turn to future use. He has a most retentive memory ; yet he crams his sketch-books with notes of the beautiful and the true. The composition of his later period is more easy and natural than are the earlier studies. Sometimes pen and pencil are united in the same sketch ; the pen stroke, however, never repeating the pencil stroke, but inserting some addition, some further thought, for Turner was not a man to waste time.

As for sea and sky, he never tired of them. We find a cathedral, with evening mist seething from the meadows ; a storm (in grey, subsequently engraved) ; notes of cross tides at twilight ; running waves ; distant sea ; sunshine on stormy evening sea ; sunset scenes ; breakers rolling in on the beach (in grey) ; and clear green waves, semi-transparent, darkening at their thin edges before the foam breaks out. He would, in fact, catalogue the ocean, after carefully taking an inventory of its numerous effects.

Mr. Ruskin also discovered in the sketch-books of a later time four studies of the rivers of France—four severe and noble studies of evening effects ; sketches of rooms at Petworth (in colour on grey paper) ; of the Priory and Castle of the Fair Gabrielle (used for the ' Keepsake ') ; of the Bridge of Boats at Rouen ; of St. Germain (looking up and down the Seine) ; and of Ambleteuse, Dieppe, Boulogne, and Vimaraux.

Later books contain a weak sketch from memory of Sir Thomas Lawrence's funeral ; but the painter soon returns to Nature, to draw in body-colours the severe lines of some castle-gate, or to make well-designed minor studies for his picture of the ' Deluge ;' to draw his favourite Folkestone, or to plunge again into Swiss scenery. He visits Contamines in Savoy, and sketches the Chamouni (of Fernely), which was engraved for the ' Liber ' by himself, and garnished with pines. One batch moreover contains an overworked sketch, poor in colour, of the battle of Fort Rock ; now at Farnley.

In these sketches he shows himself to have been as doggedly patient as he was accumulative and versatile. To-day he is drawing four pages of docks, water-sorrel, and foreshortened laurel-leaves (for the farmyard in the ' Liber') ; to-morrow he is painting an armchair in oil, and outlining slabs and vases for future use ; or he is down on the coast again, studying the shipping, drawing a cutter in chalk, and a pilot-boat in sepia—often, with habitual economy, using both sides of the leaf of his sketch-book, and sometimes with one and the same touch expressing many gradations and depths of colour.

In reviewing Turner's career, it should not be forgotten that the nobility of England were insufficiently advanced in the knowledge of Art to be able to understand and to appreciate Turner's genius. Only a few magnates—Lord de Tabley, Lord Egremont, Lord Yarborough, Lord Harewood, and a few others—ever patronised him ; and even their patronage was illiberal. From exhibition after exhibition his pictures came back to him unsold. It is a well attested fact that, while tenth-rate Caraccis and sordid Dutch pictures were being purchased in hundreds to fill the galleries of the nobility, Turner's Venetian pictures found recognition of merit among the merchants of Manchester. Cottonopolis cannot be deprived of that credit. Turning away, therefore, from the limited circle of the aristocracy, he made his appeal to the mighty middle-class with his engravings. These, and not his pictures, were the source of his fortune.

CHAPTER XLV.

TURNER'S SKETCH-BOOKS FROM 1790 TO 1800.

THERE are few drawings extant by Turner before 1790, when he was fifteen years old, and no oil-paintings before 1795, when he was twenty.

His first sketches [1] are characterised by a hard mechanical

[1] All the sketches here mentioned, save those bracketed otherwise, are in the National Collection.

fidelity, with an occasional evidence of tender carefulness that is promising, revealing, as it does, not merely a love of the work, but an anxiety to be, at any expense of time, exact.

About 1791 he begins a sketch of Malmesbury Abbey, always a specially favourite place with him; yet even then he makes a note of a shadow playing on the tree-trunks; and about the same period he makes two sketches of the River Avon, at Clifton. Looking up at the Hot Wells from Cook's Folly, he is careful in composition, and duplicates the vessels so as to lead the eye up and down the river; his trees are graceful and Wilson-like; the rigging and sail-shadows of his vessels are accurate; and for the first time he here notes an effect, afterwards a favourite one with him, that of representing a ship as apparently emerging from a bank. At Bristol he does not forget the Tower of St. Mary's, Redcliffe, where Chatterton wrote his early poems. The colour is well laid in his sketch of the Mewstone.

Visiting York about 1800, he sketches the transept and tower; presently we find him at Boston, making three or four pencil drawings. In these the architectural ornament is not all drawn, but bits are given with delicate precision, stenographic indications of what the complete performance would be like. Everything is pale, refined, cautious, almost feminine in its timid neatness,[1] 'useful to steady and refine his touch,' says Mr. Ruskin. It marks the acquisitive and hoarding nature of his mind; for here is a 'Kirkstall Abbey,' which he did not use till 1802; a 'Holy Island,' which he did not publish till 1808; and a 'Bolton Abbey' of about 1800, which was not given to the world till 1827. The 'Kirkstall,' with its hot and cold colours melting one into the other, appeared in the 'Liber.' To the same Yorkshire tour pertains a 'Leeds,' in minute pencil work, subsequently used for a large drawing. The artist's genius is here impressed by the picturesque of manufacturing industry. He sketches steam-engines ('fire-engines,' as they were called then) at Coalbrook Dale, Swansea copper works, and iron foundries at Madley Wood, and some fifty other

---

[1] Some four or five sketch-books, of a hundred leaves each, full of pencil notes of this kind, were found in Turner's chests.

places. Then he is back again to London, sketching the Savoy Chapel in grey ; perhaps with Girtin, working for Dr. Munro's half-a-crown a day and supper, or drawing sham Tivolis and exaggerated porticoes of St. Peter's, with fine, rich curves re-calling the memory of Cousins.

Even thus early his love of tender iris-gradations of colour begins to disclose itself in studies of cottages and cottage roofs ; and his tints acquire greater firmness, variety, and brilliancy. 'Carisbrook Castle' is finished, inch by inch, on white paper ; a system which renders him at once careful and certain, for he is anxious to learn to put the right colour at once quickly upon the paper, without blotting out or patching. Various and wide-reaching is his grasp also. To-day he sketches a cottage in-terior, paying special attention to the warm light a copper pan casts upon a blue jug, and to-morrow he makes dark notes of some dead ducks.

In the sketch-books of this period are found, moreover, memoranda of coast scenery, such as women sorting dry fish, and studies for the future 'Ivy Bridge,' a picture disclosing knowledge and precision of touch. Most numerous are indi-cations of the study of boats. There are foreshortened studies of rowing and sailing boats, whether coursing gaily along or stranded, and broken up into mere bundles of staves. With an eye to piercing the secret of Vandervelde, he collects analy-tical diagrams of Dutch boats. He is evidently bent on marine-painting and on coast scenery, as the event proved him to have been. Trees also are drawn—oaks sparingly, elms seldom, Scotch fir and willows occasionally. He seems to have been in Scotland about 1800, but his leafage is still cramped, and his foregrounds are laboured and stiff.

These early years of Turner's work are summed up by Mr. Ruskin as comprising so many volumes of architectural detail in pencil, so many years' work of grey tinting, and so many years of pencil-shading, without as yet much thought of anything but the most timid and neutral colour. During his arrangement of the drawings, he kindly allowed me to examine with him the principal sketch-books of the great artist. They were of all ages, from the books of his earliest boyhood to those of his latest tours ; and here are some of my notes upon them.

In a little red book with a clasp, marked June, 1813, I found various scraps of notes about chemistry, and several studies for pictures in rivalry of Claude—as usual, very slight. Some of the leaves are smeared by rubbing ; the lines are blunt, soft pencil lines ; the trees often loop, and some of the boughs are mere lank fingers and dark zigzags. Yet even these imply his striking qualities of multitude and distance. To secure variety of expression, however, the coarsest lines in the book seem to be modified here and there. Then come some obscure verses about 'Anna's kiss,' 'a look back—a toilsome dream,' and 'human joy, ecstasy, and hope,' and the like ; and in proximity thereto is the record of an order of Sir W. Pilkington's for some copies of the 'Harbours of the Coast' and of the 'Liber Studiorum.' To these succeed dancing nymphs and a Claude-like bridge ; more chemical details—notes of copal and other varnishes ; memoranda of anatto, turmeric, dragon's bood, and blues ; and finally nine pages are devoted to the topic of yellows, including orange oxide, Naples yellow, and paper-maker's yellow ; the closing passage being a scrap, I think, from Beckmann :— 'Potash added to a solution of iron, a brown precipitate falls, carbonate of potash separates, and yellow oxide, which soon becomes a beautiful yellow oxide.'

Occasionally the pictorial matter is diversified by useful receipts, such as an experienced traveller would be likely to treasure. Thus I found a receipt for making waterproof with linseed oil and gum elastic, and a prescription for the Maltese plague ; which last looks as though Turner's mind were tending eastward. The symptoms, he writes, are sickness, debility, shivering, headache, heat and thirst, followed by delirium, dark spots and ulcers. The remedies are emetics and purges, lemonade, and spongings with vinegar every two hours.

The next note-book I examined was a long one covered with parchment, and full of beautiful studies of skies stored up for future use ; skies of an orange purple, skies webbed with grey showers, skies veined with cross-currents of interwoven azure, skies of gorgeous red and yellow, and skies of transparent grey ;

together with blue fogs irradiated by red suns, moons going down, red horizons, and blood-red treble meteors, and, lastly, a glimpse of London with St. Clement's Church indicated by a pencil note.

A third book, bound in the cover of a Bible, was full of pencil sketches from Coutancey. In one leaf a plot is inscribed ' sunshine ; ' and in another ' yellowish grey.' The distance in one case is marked with dotted lines ; and there are notes of leaves, docks, and rush-flowers, with their curves and central ribs defined. The poetical element asserts itself here also. The verses in this volume turn chiefly on Content, and are either vague or pathetic, as thus on Scotch independence :—

A personal estate,
Far beyond purchase or the grasp of state.

Thou givest the humble roof content, devoid of fear.

And blissful joy
To its perhaps lone inmate.

Another book contained coloured studies for the ' Northern Coasts and the Harbours of England,' and compositions in the manner of Claude. The run of the waves and their sweeping leaps are beautifully given in these sketches ; but occasionally the shore is left weak, whereas the sky is finished, as being, I suppose, more difficult for the artist to remember. At intervals hard, dark ridges of colour are left to mark the crest of the waves ; and the seas are of all colours, from dull grey-green to soft blue and almost indigo-dark. In one instance a sail in the foreground has the yellow jewel-depth of the finest Cairngorm pebble. Dover and Portsmouth are among the places sketched. Often the artist seems lazy, hurried, or self-reliant, for there are merely red blots, or criss-crosses of grey. In one example there is more foam than wave visible; and I remember a beautiful one of the yellow ghost of a fishing-boat, with a little red man in it. In other sketches the sea rages in the foreground, rolling and leaping, while in the blue distance may be descried the faint outlines of white chalk cliffs.

In the next book, breaking away from English seas, we are

off sketching in imitation and in rivalry of Claude—Turner's great opponent with noblemen and art-collectors. Recumbent nymphs, receding arcades vanishing in perspective, and long flights of temple-steps intermingle with forests of masts forming classical St. Katherine's Docks, fêtes-champêtres after Watteau and Stothard, arches of Constantine, and Acropolises crowning imaginary hills.

One volume, dated 1809, contains notes on the Passage of the Simplon ; the wonderful Gorge of Gondo ; the Isola Bella ; and hints of the Lago Maggiore. They are on tinted paper, which is often used on both sides with an economy worthy of Pope. White chalk, that still lingers in dust between the leaves, marks avalanches and snow effects ; and Gondo, specially studied, is outlined with all a map-maker's care and fidelity. Endless Italian campaniles await future use, as well as gaps between rocks opening out from sunshine into dim whiteness. In mere portions of a page are minute drawings of the Simplon bridges, such as he may have utilised for Scott's ' Life of Napoleon.' Scraps of bad French obtrude themselves, and in one place ' two English ' assails us.

In a green book with red back I found memoranda of sea-side houses at Brighton, and of embattled towers and Tudor windows ; besides miscellaneous marine effects, at once most subtle and beautiful for their care and truth ; a camp on a cliff, and boys and boats innumerable. Among the more subtle effects were noted—foam, grey in shadow ; the reflection of a bright-coloured boat on a wet, shiny wall ; the reflection of a fisherman boy's form on a dun sail ; and the interchange of reflections between white and umbery sails.

Another sketch-book is valuable as containing studies of the nude figure made in the Academy Life School, apparently in his middle life, and probably for special objects. Some of these alone suffice to destroy the slanderous imputation that Turner, when he chose, and before his mind began to weaken, could not draw ; yet several of them certainly have an appearance of labour, though they are all rather painted than drawn. In one case the mouth is left unfinished, and in several others the faces are spoiled. Among these studies I found a female figure drawing a sword, the whole in yellow and black chalk ; and a figure seated on a rock, cleverly and sharply delineated, the high light especially being powerfully touched. Besides these are numerous studies of a female figure as Andromeda, with her head hanging down and her arms up ; a side view, a front view, and a back view. Some of the leaves of this book are purposely reddened.

In a book containing a sketch of Caernarvon Castle I found a pen outline and many boat effects, smoke rising against sails, and sails cutting against white, yellow, chalk suns.

Of all Turner's sketch books that came under my inspection, I think none interested me more than one full of sketches made at Rome, and chiefly in the Vatican galleries. They show the intense delight the artist must have felt in the classic city where he found on every hand ample materials for the contest he was ever maintaining with Claude. What had so long been the subject of his dreams he now realised. The visions of his schooldays, of those hours spent in academic and architectural study, stood embodied before him. And now his note-books are replete with classical detail, with drawings of statues, bas-reliefs, and inscriptions, to be used hereafter in the foregrounds of classical pictures. The same spirit of greedy acquisitiveness by which he was impelled to amass money operated to the ac-cumulation of facts pictorial. He exerted himself to the utmost in increasing his stores. Even in London he could not refrain from taking ten or a dozen views of so familiar a subject as London Bridge.

Under the head of 'My locanda, the Speranzellastrada, Speranzella,' with a reference to 'the Corona di Ferro,' as being an inn whereat an English waiter attended to the relief of those not 'up' in Italian, I find the addresses of friends, as 'Captain Graham, Via Gregoriana ;' and then we have a careful trans-cript of the Italian forms of enquiry to be addressed to the keepers of picture-galleries as to their contents. Next comes a caricature of himself, and thus we are conducted to his studies of the Campagna, the Aqueducts, and the Alban hills.

In addition to these I came upon a legion of classic orna-ments from the Vatican drawn hastily in pencil ; generally only a part finished from want of time, but the part finished always sufficient for the painter's use, and usually numbered for facility of reference. Among the objects selected for record are Priapi, satyrs, vases, griffins, Bacchantes, cippi, tombs, masks, leafage, Apollo, Psyche, female heads, and many inscriptions copied carefully in printed letters. I also found a few notes on pictures and statues, with occasional remarks on colours. In one instance Turner's mind seems to have directed itself to architectural reflections. Of St. Peter's he says sensibly :—

'The part by Bernini is good in the arrangement of the columns ; but, being very large, they convey the idea of greatness away from the façade of the building . . . . while in the upper corner, the most favourable view, the columns are cut by it, and the cupola has no base ; so that the dome, when approaching the steps, becomes secondary to the horizontal parts.'

The next note-book I turned over contained notes of a sea-journey between Marseilles and Genoa ; embracing Isle Margarite, Antibes, and Nice ; boats with lateen sails, and sketches of Genoa. After this I came upon drawings of London Bridge, interesting Indian-ink skies, notes of scenes on the banks of the Thames, studies of sails, and memoranda of a fête-champêtre and of ladies' dress—'caps, sleeves, black bow, black boddice, grey body, and yellow band.' This book is full of details of form and colour ; water-carts, haymakers, boys wading round boats, fishermen making love, travelling gypsies in red cloaks, green lanes, and sunlit poplars that shed radiance like lighted tapers. Here and there are bursts of wood-nymphs and other classical furniture ; but the most important and laborious efforts in the book are views of London Bridge, with St. Paul's and the Monument showing at various experimental distances. Now he tries the dome over the widest arch—now he crowds the balustrades with people, and introduces a hulk, barges, and the boats at the Tower Stairs—now he brings in bales for composition, and detains passing sails to break the lines of the arches or to vary their outline. Then he comes nearer, and tries a wharf, a tower, some additional roofs, or a dark steeple striping the light. Still he seems unsatisfied ; either his acquisitiveness never could have enough views of a

bridge that publishers and engravers often want plates of, or else
he cannot get the bridge to look quite as beautiful as he could
desire.   He changes the boats; he lifts St. Paul's, to try it in
all sorts of combinations; he moves the wharfs, and the shot-
tower; yet nothing seems to satisfy him, so greedy is he of all
its possible variations.

The next book contains jottings of expenses, and sketches
of classical subjects—Glaucus and Scylla, Dido and Æneas,
Ulysses and Nereus, and a sketch of the ' Polyphemus,' with the
giant hurling the stone.   Sometimes in these books we come
upon a flood of sea sketches and shore studies; fish being
packed or sold, steamers, notes of the moon's colours, slight
sketches in colour (the tones sometimes touched in with
coloured chalk), lightning, dismantled vessels, vermilion suns
and indigo seas, waves spitting round piles or combing upon
the shore, life-boats—in fact, all that could indicate a passionate
observer and lover of the sea.   These perhaps are succeeded
by Roman details, and a list of Lord Egremont's pictures; and
the variety of contents is further increased by warm, cold, grey
skies, and Naples-yellow suns.

In a book containing notes of Gothic ornaments from York
Minster, the internal anatomy of a boat, and some pencil skies,
marked ' W. Turner, 64 Harley Street,' I found a few verses
on love, which show that the heartache of earlier youth had not
yet quite gone.   They run :—

> Man, like the easy bark which sailing
>   On the treacherous sea, seeking the bubble pleasure.

And again :—

> Cares like waves in fell succession
> Frown destruction o'er his day ;

which I take to be very incoherent utterances of a great heart-
sorrow.

A parchment-covered book, with loops for a pencil, contains
views of Marne, St. Maure, Mons, Rouen Cathedral, Père-la-
Chaise, Notre Dame, and St. Gervais.

One volume I dived into was full of pen-and-ink sketches of
ladies conversing; and the next I stumbled on contained his

own plans for the villa at Twickenham, with computations of the expense for eleven doors, seven windows, and 2,200 feet of brick ; the cost of purchase being estimated at 4,000*l.*, and the cost of building at the same sum.

Just after a book containing the sketch for the Dryden tomb at Westminster, and views of (I think) Tilbury Fort, I found a volume of interesting easy studies of Edinburgh, dun-coloured, exact and timid ; the skies pale yellow and pale blue. One has the ruined chapel on the right, in the distance the Castle, and St. Giles's open diadem ; others have the blue Pent-lands, the Firth, Arthur's Seat, the Calton Hill, and the Castle in all aspects.

In a book dated 1808, and containing entries of the date of a cheque, is a sketch of Kirkstall Abbey ; and in another are early studies of deer, sheep, London Bridge, Children playing, and the Lord Mayor's Barge.

The original sketches of the Calais Pier picture show how bright Turner's colour was when his mind was made up ; and how sharp, firm, and confident his touch could be. The figures therein are more prominent than in the picture. The painter also makes a note of Sterne's Hotel ; and in another page sketches several spires, a coach, and some gable-ended houses.

One note-book is devoted to the record of numerous care-ful memoranda respecting the old masters, especially their flesh colours. He particularises the 'St. Jerome,' and more especi-ally the 'Dead Christ' by Titian, the under colours of the ground of which he pronounces to be Indian red and asphalt, the second colour being cold.

In another store I discovered sketches of the coast traversed on his way to and from Edinburgh, in the year of George the Fourth's visit. Bamborough, Scarborough, the Cheviots, and Fern Island are singled out for special emphasis of annotation. He makes notes of the passing sky colours, observes that smoke is colder when broken by warmth, and arrives at Edinburgh to watch with evident delight the gaiety and clamour, the firing of guns, the floating of flags, the processions of boats, the bonnets and kilts, the files of Highlanders and Scotch Greys, and the universal excitement of a national holiday. The admiral's barge and the men-of-war appeal to the painter; and he stops even to sketch a porter reading a newspaper.

One book containing views of Scarborough, Torbay, the gorges of the Alps, and a list of the Italian names for the days of the week, is bound somewhat irreverently, as the shoes of the miser in Hogarth's picture were mended, with a piece of the New Testament.

In a book of no value otherwise I found sketches of a great ship surrounded by small boats full of finely-dressed women and children; studies perhaps for Napoleon in the ' Bellerophon,' at Plymouth. Another, which has quite an exhaustive chart of all the features of Scarborough—cliffs, sands, pier, and castle, contains an immature attempt at satire on I know not what public monument, erected I know not where. It seems as if some ignoble Howard had somewhere usurped the place intended for a Nelson statue. But let the halting lines speak if they can.

> ' Can Howard ask in vain, and view the block
> Graced with the gift of Nelson, Bronté's rock,
> Still in the centre, and . . . . night
> Stands the first Earl's memento bolt upright,
> While modern Charles, now all so modest grown,
> Thrust from the corner Nelson mounts the throne.
> Served thus the castle yields the doubtful strife,
> And sparés the past . . . and clings to life.'

Most honest indignation, I have no doubt; but spoken with somewhat a stammering tongue !

A book of Oxford sketches, on tinted paper, contains studies of St. John's, Wadham, and New College Gardens; but the drawings of High Street are feeble, and the Gothic details careless and uncared for. He makes notes of the College arms, and marks the coach-office, Dr. Barnes's door, and one of the saints whose image I suppose he wanted to remember.

In a sketch-book containing a view of Borthwick I found many outbursts of colour; trials with the brush of small regions of purple and salmon colour; and notes of peculiarities of the building, which are not to be forgotten—broken freckles of blue and yellow, and brown washes deepening to red-purple distances of the iris-flower hue. Mixed up with these are perspective diagrams, showing Turner's solicitude about his lectures. And then recurs St. Paul's, with the sails of barges radiating in every possible way across the arches, and clouds blocked in to try effects of composition; with the dome and its reflections—the light and shade essayed in various balances— and masts spreading like clumps of lances. Masses of experimental colour—fawn, grey, yellow, and red, follow thereupon.

A book of the date of about 1810, containing a sort of itinerary of Devonshire and Dorsetshire, testifies to his eagerness for facts and truth. He takes notes like a spy or a pilot, and of matters even that seem quite out of his province. Berry Pomeroy Castle, he sets down, ' came into the possession of the Seymours 1551.' At Torbay, he records that it is twelve miles from Hope's Nose to Berry Head. At Brixham, the landing place of William III., he notes that a well there ebbs and flows, and adds the philosophic lament ' O humanum rerum vicissitudo !' With the present town of Fowey he is 'well pleased.' Near Place House reside the Le Foy family. Lulworth Cove has water for eighty tons burthen. Portland is four miles from Weymouth. Chesel-bank extends from —— to Abbotsbury, nine miles. Pebbles get smaller as we recede from Portland. The lighthouse at Portland is sixty-three feet high ; Torbay visible twenty-five leagues distant, near Caves Holes. Then we learn of the inhabitants of Portland, the ancient Belares ; Saxon mode of keeping accounts in law ; traces of Roman encampment behind the Portland Arms ; Abbotsbury, founded by Canute's steward ; the chapel ; sea-mark ; Dorchester ; half a mile to the right, amphitheatre, called Mambury, near Monckton ; Mardon Castle, most perfect oval encampment, treble ditch ; Lulworth Castle, built in 1600 ; first machine in 1760 ; Tuesday, market day ; spring at Nottington ; fixed air ; digestive salt, which resembles Moffat water ; barn-door ; Durdle Rock on north shore ; Lyme Regis ; Duke of Monmouth; Teignmouth; Danes and French ; Shilstone Cromlech ; logan stone ; Hallcombe, smallest parish ; Carews, four horseshoes remaining over door ; horse saved Carew ; man great distance at sea ; Tor Abbey; King John; Kent Hole, in which a naval officer ventured and was nearly suffocated ; Compton Castle ; and Haye Farm, near Exmouth, the birth-place of Raleigh. This book contains sketches of peaceful Devonshire rivers ; water-mills among hills ; champaign dotted with trees ; and cows feeding on quiet river banks.

It is not often we come upon Turner's very earliest works, though it is probable he hardly ever parted with his sketch-books, which to him were as cheque-books ; yet there is one, a large royal two-clasp volume, with large sketches drawn with a needle-pointed pencil. It contains a view of Harlech Castle (the date probably about 1798), seas and islands, stunted mountains, ruined churches, and valleys nestling among rocks.

Then comes the Bolton Book, with sketches of the Abbey and of Wharfdale. He has drawn people riding and pic-nicking ; he has even made, for greater completeness, a ground plan of the Abbey. The sketches of Launceston Castle and a Tudor house, in the same volume, are carefully picked out in pencil.

Among several sketches on the river are many admirably drawn studies of cattle and of figures at the plough. Turner has been careful to represent the ploughman as turning before his horses turn, and to write over the plough that the left stilt was the highest. In one of the river scenes occurs a subtle observation by him, worthy of one who took such pains to master every artifice of composition. He writes :—' Bargemen hanging clothes on the shrouds—to avoid long lines.' The meaning of which is that the clothes the bargemen hang upon the shrouds serve to break the perpendicular and unpleasantly straight lines, and that they therefore were not to be forgotten.

In his efforts to compose a motto for his Garden of the Hesperides picture, Turner rushed into a slough of poetry ; and perhaps even Turner, who, it must frankly be allowed, had a great alacrity for sinking, never achieved so deep a dive of bathos. I give it as completely as I am able to decipher it :—

> ' Discord, dire sister of ethereal Jove,
>   Coeval hostile even to heavenly love,
>   Rankling with rage, unasked the sport to share
>   At Psyche's marriage,

Rushed like a noxious blast of wintry skies
. . . . . Hesperian gardens rise.
The guardian dragon, in himself a host,
Awed by her presence slumbered at his post,
. . . . . . the golden apple took,
Love felt the wound, and Troy's foundation shook.'

From the book containing the above I transcribe the following passage, which I believe to be from one of his lectures
on perspective, and which therefore is invaluable :—

'Reflections not only appear darker, but larger than the
object which occasions them ; and if the ripple or hollow of
the wave is long enough to make an angle with the eye, it is on
these undulating lines that the object reflects, and transmits all
perpendicular objects lower towards the spectator ; but in receding lines, as well as objects, rules seem to lose their power,
and those guides that enable us to find some cause for near
objects, lose their power or become enfeebled by contraction
in remote ones. It has been asserted that all appear equal
from the base line of the water ; but these axioms I dissent
from. It is true that, by placing the eye equal to the water,
it comes up to the rules laid down ; but when the water is
ruffled on which all things are to be reflected, it is no longer in
right angles, but, according to the elevation of the spectator,
becomes more or less an angle of incidence. If the undulating surface of the liquid did not, by current or motion,
congregate forms, there would be no difficulty in simplifying
the rules.'

By way of variety we next have a page of accounts (his
mind ever painfully exact in money matters) ; and this is followed by sketches of horses feeding, and cows chewing grass.
The stolid side stare they deign to give to man, after which
they resume their suspended labour with a sottish contempt
and dull epicureanism, has been most happily conveyed.

All of a sudden the painter dashes off into a strain of reflection of more than oracular darkness :—

'They wrong virtue, enduring difficulties or worth in the
bare imitation of nature, all offers received in the same brain ;
but where these attempts arise above mediocrity, it would

surely not be a little sacrifice to those who perceive the value of the success to foster it by terms as cordial that cannot look so easy a way as those spoken of convey doubts to the expecting individual. For as the line that unites the beautiful to grace, and these offerings forming a new style, not that souls can guess as ethics. Teach them of both, but many serve as the body and the soul, and but presume more as the beacon to the headland which would be a warning to the danger of mannerism and the disgustful.'

The book wherein these tenebrose thoughts occur is dated November 3, 1820. Another startling scrap on the same subject runs thus :—

'' Tis a small space, by considering it and treating them as reflecting upon polished bodies, frequently the reflection appears so true, but are most fallacious to the great book of Nature.'

'The painting art toils after truth in vain.'

After this follow some historical notes touching the early history of England, in the course of which Suetonius is quoted to show that in the reign of Claudius our land was first called Britannia. The writer reasons awkwardly that, from the fact of several legions perishing and the country not being abandoned up to the last extremity, some support may be derived for the '*elucidation*' that Britain was considered mistress of the seas, 'her statue wearing a *naval coronet*.' All through life the painter was pursued by the same difficulty in finding the exact word he required.

Incoherences still more puzzling ensue about 'forty-four, the first Christian Church built, Glastonbury, Giraldus Cambrensis, Joseph of Arimathea, and Andati, English god of victory.'

These scraps, it may be, are notes from some Somersetshire guide-book read at an inn.

London Bridge meets us again in different views in the same volume, and there are plans for the picture gallery in Queen Anne Street—arrangements for back parlour and kitchen and for ventilation. The gallery is to have no blinds, only 'a moulding' to keep out the sun's rays. Then come more views of the river, with Bow Church and Somerset Stairs, and piers and warehouses, Truelove and his ironworks conspicuously marked, and, above all, the Church of St. Michael's, Cornhill. With an interval of a page or two these views are succeeded by the transcript of a gamut for the flute ; and it is curious that the very instrument for which the gamut is written was found in Turner's house after his death. He was a man of many aspirations ; and music clearly had its attractions for him, though he could not apply himself to its cultivation.

A Yorkshire sketch-book reveals his taste for social relaxation. It contains a patriotic song, which he might have heard on some festal occasion at Mr. Fawkes'. The pencilling is almost obliterated ; yet a few verses are to be picked out :—

Song—JOHN BULL.

' Here's a health to honest John Bull.
    When he's gone, will you find such another ?
So with hearts, as with bumpers, quite full,
    Here's a health to Old England his mother.

She gave him a good education,
    Taught him that cowards should swing,
To be true to the fame of the nation ;
    To be true to his church and his king.

Now John is a good-natured creature ;
    He's noble, and generous, and brave ;
He in conflict's a terrible fellow:
    He will fight, he will conquer, he'll save.

Some swear court and city are equal,
    " Rights of man " make a very fine sound—

.   .   .   .

Then the loom in the . . . would stand still,
    Equality's mantle be small,
We then must fight and . . . .
    For the pulpit, the town, and the hall.

He's happy as long as he's good—'

One page, bearing the date of December 31, 1825, has a sketch of a wooded river and a waterfall among trees.

An early Scotch volume shows that on one tour the painter set out from Edinburgh on July 18, and that he finished his book on August 1, at Gretna Green. In this volume are sketches of Queensferry, Linlithgow, Glasgow, Dumbarton, Douglas Castle, Ben*lowmon* (Benlomond), Inverary, and Loch Lomond (black shadows and green-brown rocks). The writings of Scott at this period had, I suppose, impressed Turner, and directed his attention towards antiquarian topics, for several notes like these are interspersed—' Linlithgow Church;' ' James saw apparition of old man ;' 'Built by Robert II.'

Next we have Loch Awe, Ben More, Castle Dochart, Loch Tay, Breadalbane (with rows of windows like gun-ports in the side of a frigate), Kenmore, Auchentyre, Tummel Brig, Blair-Athol, Dunkeld, Dumblane (in all the sketches, however rude, there is some gradation of colour given, and the skies are massed out), Bothwell Castle, Moffat, Regent Murray's Castle, Solway Frith and Moor, and, last of all, the celebrated Blacksmith's Shop on Gretna Green. No bad foray this into Scotland.

Turner's earliest book, the cover now half cut off, seems to have been filled by him with sketches when he was about fifteen years old. There is a back view of the Hotwells, from the Gloucestershire side, I think, pencil-washed ; and there are notes of gates, towers, and trees (with little pen-touches) at Sir W. Lippincote's ; women and barrows, bell-turrets and yew-trees, cliffs, boats, and, finally, hasty views of rocks, boats, and Welsh hills from the Old Passage. It also contains a profile sketch of St. Vincent Rocks ; a craft stranded on an island in the Severn (' sea' written large on one place) ; pages of experimental purple blots ; a bend of the Avon ; the tower of Thornbury church ; the Welsh coast from Cook's Folly ; trees and hills and ships. The study of Malmesbury Abbey from the meadows, over the roofs of houses, is a south-east view, and is dated 1791. The foliage is bad ; the trees are left a rank green with yellow tips. An orange walk is depicted ; grey and rusty stains are on the stones of the wall ; and the sky, low-toned, is seen through an arch. Sharp touches occur occasionally, but

INVERNESS

the whole composition is weak, plain, and timid, though exceedingly careful. Not a touch of unnecessary work, however, discloses itself; and, where there is detail, only a bit is finished to show how the rest is to be done.

Some of the sketches have the names written punctiliously over the shops—as 'Heath, Ormond, and Bradford, Milliners;' 'Grove Coffee House;' and 'G. Nappel, Dealer in Liquors.'

Last of all, we come to a Roman note-book, which contains memoranda of the following facts, and observations of Italian travel :—

Venus seated; Parma, two stages from Reggio; St. Prospero; Modena, palace and pictures; Bologna, wax models, very curious; John of Bologna, fountains; Forli (Tabernacle of Michael Angelo); Rubicon; St. Marino; Rimini; Arch of Augustus; Bridge over Foglia; Ancona; Loretto; Adriatic ramparts; Gate to Rome; River Clitumnus; Spoleto inscription; Terni; Cascade; Caduta della Marmora; Fall of Narni; Mount Viterbo; View of the Tiber; View of Rome above Baceano; Pons Milvius; Baths of Diocletian; Alban Mountains, to the south, bearing west to Antium; Tyrrhene Sea; Mount Soracte, thirty miles; Capitol; Colosseum; Square, obelisks; Fountain; Spada; Pompey's statue; Villas; Tivoli, suspended over precipice; Arno; Villa by San Antonio; Horace disputed; Tomb of Clodius near Gate Albano; Naples; Jews will not solicit alms; Tomb at foot of Mount Vesuvius; Annibal; Puteoli; Pompeii, female skeleton; Street of the Tombs; Salve Inn; Siren's Island; Guido; Aretino; Invented gamut; Pavia; Augustus viewed ashes of Drusus; Caffagiolo; Maraschino; delightful; Last Supper gone; Lugano; Vallambrosa; Turin; Mount Cenis; Campanile; Gate of Paradise; Lazzaroni.'

Little pen-and-ink views are interspersed, and we have further Italian notes :—

'Ponte Vacchino; Cortona; Villa Adrian; Colosseum; Tivoli; Arch of Severus; Villa Novale; Frascati; Fondi; Tomb of Cicero; Gaeta; Altar; Velletri; Terracina; Capua; Avernus; Posilipo; Naples: Agnano; Crater of Vesuvius

Cuma; Clitumnus; Pæstum; Loretto; Capri; Amalfi; Scylla; Salerno.'

On the fly-leaf of one sketch-book I discovered the subjoined inn-bill, which is eloquent of economy :—

	£	s.	d.
Egham—B. B. U. 1s. 3d.—2			
Hosby	0	5	0
Blackwater	0	3	6
Turnpike	0	1	0
July 13th	£2	14	6

This book contained sketches of Plymouth, Lyme-Regis, Land's End, Clovelly, and Fowey, dated May 1811 (?). There are also notes of figures ; one is that of a butcher leaning on his meat-tray.

CHAPTER XLVI.

THE 'LIBER STUDIORUM.'

IT was well known to men living in the early and in the middle period of Turner's professional career, that he did not often sell his larger oil-pictures. They were not sought after or appreciated by the aristocracy or fashionable picture-buyers, with few exceptions, such as Lord Egremont of Petworth, Lord Yarborough, Sir John Leicester, and Lord Ellesmere ; and this neglect may be traced and attributed mainly to the influence of Sir George Beaumont, an amateur artist, who accorded an absorbing preference to the works of Claude. To Sir George the fashionable patrons of art looked up as to an oracle of taste ; and to such an extent was his devotion to Claude carried that upon Sir George becoming the possessor of the 'Annunciation,' the little picture by Claude now in the National Gallery, he considered it so infinitely precious that he neither could nor did think it safe out of his sight. Indeed it is said that, when he drove out in his carriage, he always took it with him.

Whether there was anything personal or not in this advocacy

of Claude to the suppression of Turner, I know not ; but it is certain that Turner was well aware of the fact, and that he deeply felt the injustice of Sir George Beaumont's prejudice. We are enabled to estimate his abiding sense of the injury which he rightly conceived he had sustained in this connection, from the circumstance that he bequeathed to the nation two of his best pictures, on the special condition that they should be placed side by side with two of Claude's best pictures. Turner was anxious that posterity should render to his memory the tribute which had been withheld from him by his contemporaries. In the same spirit of artistic self-defence, he commenced his wonderful, beautiful, and highly esteemed 'Liber Studiorum,' as a companion to the 'Liber Veritatis' of Claude, first published by the Duke of Devonshire after his return from Italy.

The first 'Liber Studiorum' sketch was made at the house of his old friend Mr. Wells, the drawing-master at Addiscombe. Turner had not much business at the time, and thought that he could profitably employ his leisure by rivalling Claude. He had intended to publish one hundred numbers ; but the series did not extend beyond seventy, for in the long interval of publication he had become more successful ; and he did not then care to spend his time in speculation.

'Turner's celebrated publication, the "Liber Studiorum," says Miss Wells, ' entirely owes its existence to my father's persuasion, and the drawings for the first number were made in our cottage at Knockholt. He had for a long time urged upon Turner the expediency of making a selection from his own works for publication, telling him that it would surely be done after his death, and perhaps in a way that might not do him that justice which he could ensure for himself. After long and continued persuasion, Turner at length gave way ; and one day, when he was staying with us in Kent (he always spent a part of the autumn at our cottage) he said, "Well, Gaffer, I see there will be no peace till I comply ; so give me a piece of paper. There, now ! Rule the size for me, and tell me what I am to do." My father said, "Well, divide your subject into classes—say, Pastoral, Marine, Elegant Pastoral, and so forth ;" which was accordingly done. The first drawings were then and there made, and arranged for publication. This was in the autumn of 1806.'

For an early number he employed C. G. Lewis, the engraver, whose remuneration was six guineas for aquatinting an etching. Turner now wanted two more drawings etched and aquatinted for the same sum ; which being totally inadequate for the time and labour expended thereon, the drawings and plates were at once returned by Lewis. This led to a quarrel that lasted several years. Eventually, however, he had to pay Charles Turner eight guineas, and finally, I believe, the terms of other engravers rose to twelve. Yet even Turner could not have anticipated that a copy of the 'Liber' would one day sell for 3,000*l.*, nor could the engraver believe that proofs which he had actually used to light the fire with would fetch between eight and ten guineas apiece, and that he would be offered twenty-five guineas for any residue he could find of them.

There can be no question that Turner's 'Liber' utterly weighs down Claude's 'Liber ;' but we must not forget that it is unfair to institute a comparison between the two. Claude's was not a show-book, and never intended for publication. It was only a volume of slight sketches of pictures he had sold, preserved as memorials of them ; whereas Turner's was a book to the production of which several years were devoted. It was elaborated with extreme care, engraved for the most part with his own hands, and watched in all its processes with the most jealous and sagacious care. It was intended to exemplify his command of the whole compass of landscape art, and the boundless and matchless richness of his stores both of fact and of invention. These, indeed, showed his fearlessness of plagiarism, and were so many bold challenges to all his contemporaries.

The drawings for the 'Liber' mezzotints were of the same size as the plates, and were carefully finished in sepia. The proofs also were sometimes touched all over with the brush in sepia.

Turner's knowledge of engravers' effects was so marvellous that he has been known, when dissatisfied with a plate, to sit down and change a sunrise into a moonrise. It was no unusual thing for him, when a plate of the ' Liber' began to wear, to take it and reverse its whole effect, making all that was before light now dark, and all that was before dark now light. Indeed, concentrativeness of mind, and knowledge of light and shade, were Turner's greatest characteristics. To reverse the scale of chiaroscuro in a plate at five minutes' notice is as difficult as it would be for a musician to change the key of a sonata of Beethoven, and to play it off correctly at sight after the alteration. He covered the margins of proofs wtth advice and directions to his engravers.

In 1807 began the issue of the ' Liber Studiorum,' which was not completed until 1816. This wonderful work was published in dark-blue covered numbers, each containing five engravings. The subjects, embracing the whole domain of landscape-art, were divided into six heads, agreeably with the suggestion of his friend Wells :—First, Historical ; second, Pastoral ; third, Elegant Pastoral ; fourth, Mountain ; fifth, Marine ; sixth, Architectural. The width of the design and the thoroughness with which it is executed attest the power of his comprehensive mind. Of fragmentary effort he was always ashamed ; and no man more bitterly regretted mental trifling.

The publication of the ' Liber' stopped at the fourteenth number, thereby making in all (including the frontispiece, which Turner somewhat ostentatiously gave to his subscribers) seventy-one plates. Strange to say, this splendid work did not prove to be a remunerative speculation. It was therefore stopped as soon as he began the ' England and Wales,' and obtained other more profitable engagements. The ten plates intended for the fifteenth and sixteenth numbers of the work were more or less prepared for publication, and other plates were in various stages of progress. There can be no doubt that, had Turner been encouraged, the result of his challenge to Claude would have been a complete epitome of all possible classes of landscape art, varied by minutest particulars of the changeful effects of season and climate.

One of the first engravers chosen for the task was Charles Turner ; and the hard terms of his engagement were that he should engrave fifty drawings, and attend to the printing, publishing, and delivery of the numbers (for Turner was going to be his own publisher) at the miserable rate of eight guineas per plate. The painter was severe, exacting, and sensitively careful in his corrections and additions. The engraver toiled through the first twenty plates (forming Nos. 1, 2, 3, and 4) patiently. He then frankly complained of the terms, and asked two guineas more for each plate. One plate, which occasioned no little difficulty, was that of 'Windsor Castle,' with a view of Montem Hill and some Eton boys on it to the left. A few additional trees to the right, and angry demands to have the steps leading up Montem clearer, exhausted the endurance of the engraver. The painter, who had never had quarter given to him when he was struggling, now, in his turn, I grieve to say, gave no quarter. Such, unhappily, is the illiberal effect of early trial and difficulty.

Inflexibly exacting as he was, Turner could not understand how an engraver who had contracted to do fifty engravings should try to get off his bargain at the twenty-first. He flew into an inarticulate whirlwind of rage, the result of which was that painter and engraver never spoke for nineteen years. Reynolds, Dunkerton, Lupton, Say, Dawe, and others, were then employed ; the painter himself engraving some of his own drawings and etchings, while Lahee for twenty years superintended the printing. Meanwhile, the printsellers, who could not get sufficient percentage allowed them by Turner, would have nothing to do with the work. They little thought the day would come when a complete set would be worth 3,000l. or more, and a single unpublished plate would sell for 20l.

The manner in which the 'Liber' was got up and the engravings printed was unbusinesslike, fitful, and peculiar. He employed one of his female domestics to stitch the numbers, and it is hardly surprising to learn that she stole many of the plates and sold them privately. His superintendence of the printing and publication was most minute and yet most capricious. The alterations of effects were as numerous as the additions, as is evident from the artist's proofs (the touched proofs) still preserved by Mr. Pye, Mr. J. Dillon, and other collectors. To put in or take out a tree was nothing. Turner would sometimes change a sun into a moon, and the alteration was not always for the better. Sometimes, but rarely, the result would be a patchwork of incongruous intentions. Sometimes the design was so perfect and grand that it could not be changed or injured ; sometimes the result did not please the artist, and the hint of what it might have been set him thinking. Generally speaking, the alterations were made with consummate art merely to hide the wear and tear of the copper, the faintness, the blur, or the pallor of the plate's old age. But for the vigour of his inventive genius, all this would have verged on sharp practice ; but the fact is that out of these very defects he devised new beauties. These crafty tradesmanlike alterations, which, when studied, are the strongest proofs I know of his genius and of his thriftiness, were made under his own eye, if not by his own hand.

' These variations,' says Mr. Dillon, who possesses a superb collection of the etchings, ' render it extremely difficult to form a complete set of the first impressions of the " Liber." It appears that no set at the time when it was issued contained all the plates in the first state, or indeed in any one similar state. On the contrary, in the original numbers a very early and fine impression of one plate will be found in company with very late and bad impressions of another plate, as if one had been given with a rude sense of justice as a sort of compensation for the others.'

I am sorry to add that there can be no doubt, after the searching investigation of Mr. Stokes and other collectors, that Turner often took out the thickened letters of the plates in the bad third state, and engraved open letters higher up. In fact, he sold sham proofs, on which he made private marks and scratches to indicate to himself the various states.[1]

I forbear to press this charge as heavily as perhaps I should, because Turner is dead, and no one survives to defend him. The only defence I can conceive for him is, that possibly he might have considered that the entire change of the effect

[1] To illustrate this, Mr. Dillon's first copy of the ' Liber' did not contain a single engraving in the first state except the ' Palm,' which is of considerable rarity.

in the later states—the harmony being still as perfect as before —really made them new works. The new idea, and the strain on a new portion of the copper, he, perhaps, with his entangled logic, thought equivalent to a new thought, which he had no idea of selling for the ordinary price.

I now propose to go through the series of the ' Liber ' with short comments here and there.

Title-page.—The centre, the story of Europa, was engraved by Turner ; the rest cost him much trouble, with its classic and Gothic pillars, its sails, mast, and graceful peacock perched on a fragment of Greek ruin. This peacock is used also in another plate. As an overture contains hints of all there will be in the opera, so does this title-page foretell much that follows.

H. History.

' Æsacus and Hesperia.' As are several others, this is engraved by Turner, by whom all the ' Liber ' plates but two are etched. It is the finest and scarcest of the series. Mr. Ruskin lauds it as ' a consummate example of the arrangement of boughs. In the first state there are few or no rays of light in the face of Hesperia, which is turned to the front, and does not heed Æsacus. The print is called among enthusiasts " The White Face." '

' Jason.' In the first state the open letter H is close to the top line ; in the third state the darkened letter is turned to an open one higher up in the margin. That terrible coil of the monster no longer has glints of light on its bosses, but is hid in a soft brown twilight. This is a fine instance of the genius with which Turner altered his worn-out coppers. Jason is very expectant, and in most palpable earnest. The agile, armed figure is admirably hinted ; indeed, all through the ' Liber ' the figures are admirable, except the larger ones in the home pastoral scenes, which are rather weak, sketchy, and scarecrowy.

' Procris and Cephaius.' The story is well told, and the landscape beautiful.

' From Spenser's " Fairy Queen." ' No one has yet discovered the passage on which this fine imaginative picture of the resting warrior is founded.

'The Fifth Plague of Egypt' (Turner's first scriptural subject). The picture belonged to W. Beckford, Esq. In proofs the size of the picture is not given.

'Tenth Plague of Egypt.' The second states are marked S.

'Christ and the Woman of Samaria.' Very difficult to meet with in the first state.

'Rizpah' (2 Samuel, chap. xxi.). Turner afterwards painted this scene, but far less powerfully. It seems to me to be almost one of the finest and most imaginative scenes he ever conceived. The skeleton bodies are well drawn, and the mourning figure is worthy of a sculptor's attention. The moon, too, shines on the beginning of the barley-harvest, as the Bible tells us it did at the time Rizpah performed her ghastly watch.

E. P. Elegant Pastoral.

'Raglan Castle.' A reminiscence of an early tour.—'Cheptow, Junction of the Severn.' Drawn, etched, and engraved by Turner.

'The Clyde' (Falls). This was much altered by Turner, but not for the better. The bathing figures are full of grace. The early impressions have simply the inscription, '"Clyde," in the possession of John W. Turner;' the words 'drawing of the,' and the size of the picture being subsequently added.

'Castle.' To the right is a man playing a flute. Turner at one time learned the flute, as we have already seen.

'Bridge,' in middle distance. A tree in the foreground is remarkable for the fact that it casts three clearly distinct shadows. The other two stems were taken out in some alterations, I suppose, and the attendant shadows forgotten. Turner, like other great men, knew how to blunder.

'Woman playing Cymbals.'

'Stone Bridge, with Goats.'

'St. Catherine's Hill, near Guildford.'

'River Wye.'

'Alcove.'

'Isis.'

'Hindoo Devotions.' The later states have a mark to the left, and an H faintly scratched to the right. They have also a 'tabbied' or 'mackerel' sky.

'Hindoo Ablutions.' The later states are worked in a redder ink.

The 'Magdalen in Solitude.' The later states are known by two cross twigs in the trees to the right.

P. Pastoral.

'Norham Castle.' Turner was passionately fond of this spot, as I have shown elsewhere. The first published state has rays of light behind the castle ; afterwards the castle is darker, and made shapeless against the sun.

'Solway Moss.'

'Farmyard with Pigs.'

'Pembury Mill, Kent.' The figures are dull and laboured ; the whole uninteresting.

'Winchelsea, Sussex.'

'East Gate, Winchelsea.'

'Water-mill.' Artist's proofs have dog unfinished, and no white marks on the steps.

'Windmill and Lock.'

'Juvenile Tricks.' Poor.

'Young Anglers.'

'Bridge and Cows.'

'Farmyard and Cart.'

'Hedging and Ditching.' A fine drawing of a half-dead tree.

'Water-cress Gatherers.' Scene near Twickenham.

M. Marine and Mountains.

'Entrance of Calais Harbour.' Rare in the first states.

'Calm.' Extremely rare in the first state.

'Shipping.' In the possession of the Earl of Egremont. E scratched on the artist's proof.

Original sketch of a picture for W. Leader, Esq.

Picture in the possession of Sir John Mildmay, Bart. Remarkable for the effect of light and motion in the boat and figures.

'Smugglers.' By some called ' Flint Castle.'

'Coast of Yorkshire, near Whitby.' Fine rough sea and wreck. The shrieking and praying woman reminds me of some of the elder Vernet's figures.

'Marine Dabblers.'

'The Source of the Arveron, in the Valley of Chamouni, Savoy, Mer-de-Glace.' The ice is very boldly treated, but its spiky ridges are, I think, too hard and rigid. In the first published state a solitary bird is introduced to the left. The triangular peak near the top is supposed to be intended for Mont Blanc.

'Inverary Pier, Loch Fyne.' In the early impressions the effect of morning is wonderfully conveyed.

'Inverary Town and Castle, Scotland.' The drawing is in the possession of the Duke of Argyle.

'The Devil's Bridge.' The artist's proofs are most powerful before the rays of light were introduced behind the bridge, and the arch itself was lightened. The mule's skeleton is finely introduced. Turner was never tired of this wild Manfred scene.

'Mont St. Gothard.' The surprise of the hollow way is finely dwelt upon.

'Lac de Thun.' The early artist's proofs have no birds, no light on the sails, no fire in the distance, but a harsh straight line across the clouds, afterwards softened down.

This plate cost both artist and engraver much trouble. Mr. Dillon has the artist's proof of it, the margin of which is covered with Turner's pencilled directions to the engraver. 'Everything,' he annotates, ' conspires against the work.'

'Bonneville, Savoy,' was etched by Dawe.

'Chain of the Alps from Grenoble, Chambery.' In the later impressions the rays of the sun are scarcely visible. In the etching there is a marvellous mass of flat vine-growing country, with every field, hedge-row, and church-tower indicated in the shaded plate. The whole is afterwards softened and fused together. These etchings show with what extraordinary and severe truth Turner used to draw both with sketching-pencil and graver's needle.

'Mill near the Grande Chartreuse, Dauphiny,' etched by H. Dawe. The firs here are nobly drawn with vigorous brown lines of ink that quite rib the paper. The trees, indeed, all through the 'Liber' are varied and fine, particularly the willows and firs ; the elms are sometimes heavy and coarse.

'Ben Arthur, Scotland.'

'Peat Bog, Scotland.'

'Near Blair-Athol.'

'Hind Head Hill' (near Portsmouth). There is a double gibbet on the hill, with two highwaymen swinging. The mail-coach they once, perhaps, stopped and plundered is most suggestively sweeping round the dark right-hand road.

'Martello Tower, near Bexhill, Sussex.'

A. *Architectural.*

'Crypt—Castle.' Original drawing in the possession of John Soane, Esq.

'Interior of a Church.' I think it is that of his old friend, Mr. Trimmer, at Heston, near Brentford.

'Basle, Moonlight.' Two steeples to the right, vague in outline in the first published states, were afterwards thrown into sunshine, and made clear and sharp.

'Holy Island Cathedral.'

'Dunstanborough Castle,' from a picture in the possession of W. Penn, Esq. The size of picture, five by four, was added in later impressions. This plate is a great favourite of Mr. Ruskin's. One of Turner's earliest exhibited drawings was from this castle.

'Rivaulx Abbey, Yorkshire.'

'Dumblane Abbey, Scotland.'

'Ville de Thun, Switzerland.'

'Morpeth, Northumberland.' A fine instance of Turner's power of making a dull subject interesting.

'London from Greenwich.' A fine architectural drawing of

the Hospital, with deer (well-drawn) in the foreground, and forests of masts in the distance.

'Lauffenbourg, on the Rhine.'

In treating of the 'Liber,' Mr. Ruskin remarks that it is curious how few foreign subjects there are in it, although in the numbers dated 1808 and 1809 he gave views of Mont St. Gothard and the Little Devil's Bridge, and later of the Chartreuse. The English subjects are to the foreign subjects as two to one ; and these too are of the simplest and most everyday kind, such as the 'Farmyard,' the 'White Horse,' 'Watercress Gatherers,' and 'Hedging and Ditching.' The architectural subjects are not large, continental masses of buildings, but small, obscure ruins, as 'Rivaulx' and 'Dunstanborough.' To match with a crowd of English places, there are only three ill-considered and unsatisfactory foreign subjects, 'Basle,' 'Lauffenbourg,' and a 'Swiss Valley.' The home subjects are more complex, and treated with more knowledge and affection. Compare, for instance, the figures and sheep in the 'Hedging and Ditching,' and the 'East Gate, Winchelsea,' with the puzzled foreground and inappropriate figures in the 'Lake of Thun ;' or the cattle and road of the 'St. Catherine's Tree' with the foreground of the 'Bonneville ;' or the exquisite figure with the sheaf of corn in the 'Windmill' with the vintage of the Grenoble subject.

The same thing is observable in the 'Liber' foliage. There are reminiscences of English willows and English forest-glades in the heroic foliage of the 'Æsacus and Hesperia,' and the 'Cephalus;' the pines of Switzerland and Italy he failed in. In the 'Vale of Chamouni' they are in good masses; but he leaves them out where he can. His chestnuts are poor; olives he never learned to like; and the vines in the Grenoble foreground are wrong, weak, and bad.

The effect of Italy on Turner's mind, says Mr. Ruskin, is very puzzling. It gave him in the 'Liber' power and solemnity, as evidenced in the 'Rizpah,' the 'Fairy Queen,' 'Cephalus,' and 'Æsacus;' but he never seems to have entered thoroughly into the spirit of Italy ; and he generally introduced his Italian materials awkwardly into his large compositions.

'None but the Italian "Liber" subjects are thoroughly great;' but then he used the spirit rather than the actual details. The ' Rizpah ' is not Eastern ; the ' Jason ' rocks are mere Warwickshire sandstone ; ' Jason ' himself is not a Greek. In local character he utterly failed. The ' Tenth Plague ' reminds us of Belzoni; the ' Fifth,' of brick-kilns rather than of pyramids ; and the fire running along the ground is like the burning of manure.

' Of the large compositions which have much of Italy in them,' says Mr. Ruskin, ' the greater part are overwhelmed with quantity and deficient in emotion.' Adverting to the drawing of rocks, Mr. Ruskin praises the ' Mont St. Gothard ' of the ' Liber,' and compares it to the vulgarities of Salvator Rosa. No one but Turner seems ever to have attained the power of expressing the inward structure of rock through the outer curves.

Of the tree subjects in the ' Liber ' Mr. Ruskin praises most the ' Cephalus,' the ' Grande Chartreuse,' the ' Blair-Athol,' ' Juvenile Tricks,' and ' Hedging and Ditching.' For the management of the upper boughs, as I have already noted, the ' Æsacus ' is a consummate example of truth, simplicity, and exquisite management of lines.

Of Turner's power of conveying a sense of horror, Mr. Ruskin writes respecting the ' Jason:'—' No paths, nor cloven hills; nothing but a gleam of pale horizontal sky, that broods over pleasant places far away, and sends in, through the wild overgrowth of the thicket, a ray of broken daylight into the hopeless pit. No flaunting plumes nor brandished lances, but stern purpose in the turn of the crestless helmet, visible victory in the drawing-back of the prepared right arm behind the steady point. No more claws, nor teeth, nor manes, nor stinging tails. We have the dragon, like everything else, by the middle. We need see no more of him. All his horror is in that fearful, slow, grinding upheaval of the single coil. Spark after spark of it, ring after ring is sliding into the light ; the slow glitter steals along him step by step, broader and broader ; a lighting of funeral lamps one by one, quicker and quicker; a moment more, and he is out upon us, all crash and blaze, among those broken trunks; but he will be nothing then to what he is now. . . . .

'Now observe in this work of Turner that the whole value of it depends on the character of curve assumed by the serpent's body; for had it been a mere semicircle, or gone down in a series of smaller coils, it would have been, in the first case, ridiculous, as unlike a serpent, or, in the second, disgusting, nothing more than an exaggerated viper; but it is that *coming straight* at the right hand which suggests the drawing forth of an enormous weight, and gives the bent part its springing look, that frightens us. Again, remove the light trunk on the left, and observe how useless all the gloom of the picture would have been if this trunk had not given it depth and hollowness. Finally, and chiefly, observe that the painter is not satisfied, even with all the suggestiveness thus obtained; but to make sure of us, and force us, whether we will or not, to walk his way, and not ours, the trunks of the trees on the right are all cloven into yawning and writhing heads and bodies, and alive with dragon energy all about us. Note especially the nearest with its gaping jaws and claw-like branch at the seeming shoulder; a kind of suggestion which in itself is not imaginative, but merely fanciful (using the term fancy in that third sense not yet explained corresponding to the third office of imagination); but it is imaginative in its present use and application, for the painter addresses thereby that morbid and fearful condition of mind which he has endeavoured to excite in the spectator, and which in reality would have seen in every trunk and bough, as it penetrated into the deeper thicket, the object of its terror.'

The subscription price of the 'Liber Studiorum' was 17*l*. 10*s*. Before Turner's death a copy sold for thirty-one guineas; and since that event fine copies have realised 3,000*l*. Unsuccessful as it was in a business point of view, the prices obtained now for sets seem almost fabulous. Engraved by Charles Turner and others, at a cost varying from five to seven guineas only per plate, proof impressions of single plates have recently sold for upwards of 10*l*., and proofs touched by the artist himself for more than double that amount.

Some time before Mr. Charles Turner's death Messrs. Colnaghi bought all his 'Liber' proofs and trials of effect for a large sum. When the money (1,500*l.* I believe) was paid, the old engraver wrung his hands, and, with tears in his eyes, exclaimed, 'Why, good God, I have been burning banknotes all my life.' Many of these proofs, worth large prices, had been used to light the fire.

Mr. Ruskin, whose comments on the hopelessness and sadness of Turner's mind are both copious and just, says that sunset and twilight, and on ruins too, were his favourite effects. His later drawings were chiefly made to record the triumph of human power; ruined fortresses and mountain-roads were always his special delight. Of the 'Liber' he shows that a feeling of decay and humiliation gives solemnity to all its simplest subjects, even to his view of daily labour. In the pastoral by the brook-side the child is in rags and lame. In the 'Hedging and Ditching' the labourer is mean and sickly, and the woman slatternly. The water-mill is a ruin; and the peat-bog is dreary.

'Of human pride,' says this wonderful writer, 'see what records: Morpeth tower, roofless and black. Gate of Old Winchelsea wall, the flock of sheep driven round it, not through it; and Rivaulx choir; and Kirkstall crypt; and Dunstanborough, far above the sea; and Chepstow, with arrowy light through traceried windows; and Lindisfarne, with failing height of wasted shaft and wall; and, last and sweetest, Raglan, in utter solitude, amid the wild wood.'

Mr. Wornum testifies of the 'Liber:'—'No proof set of the plates was ever issued; but at the completion of the series Turner arranged them in sets and sold them, in 1820, for fourteen guineas. In a set so purchased by Mr. John Pye, the engraver, the earlier plates were invariably bad; the middle ones tolerably good; but towards the end several were proof impressions, and in an excellent state. Since Turner's death a single good proof has sold for as much as Turner charged for the entire series.'

The inference is that the first plates sold best, and that Turner, either from slovenliness or from fraud, shuffled together the different states, so that no one could get a perfect copy without buying several copies.

Turner had an awful sense of the sorrow of life and of the omnipresence of Death. 'There is no form of violent death,' writes Mr. Ruskin, 'which he has not painted; and the noblest of all the plates of the "Liber Studiorum," except the "Via Mala," is one engraved with his own hand, of a single sailor, yet living, dashed in the night against a granite coast, his body and outstretched hands just seen in the trough of a mountain wave, between it and the overhanging wall of rock, hollow, polished, and pale with dreadful cloud and grasping foam.'

This is indeed one of the most imaginative of all Turner's figures; and the extremity of its despair and its touching hopelessness always strongly remind me of Cowper's sad but beautiful poem 'The Castaway.'

CHAPTER XLVII.

MR. RUSKIN'S NOTES ON THE TURNER SKETCHES.

THE notes which Mr. Ruskin gave to the world in 1858, upon the sketches and drawings bequeathed by Turner to the Nation and exhibited in that year in Marlborough House, are invested with so permanent a value that I am tempted to introduce here some of the choicest of the criticisms made by that illustrious exponent of the genius of the painter. It was he, my readers will remember, who assiduously applied himself to the arrangement of the accumulated materials, and who for that purpose passed in review every individual fragment, chest being explored by chest, and book after book.

Once understand this character of great work, and of Turner's most of all great work ; namely, that, just like good writing or good speaking, its value depends primarily on its matter, and on its manner only so far as it best sets forth and impresses the matter ; and you will see at once how you may really hope to follow and rival Turner. You have nothing to do but to give up all other thoughts and pursuits, and set yourself to gather and remember facts from Nature day by day. You must not let an hour pass without ascertaining something ; and you must never forget anything you have ascertained. You must persevere in this work all your life ; filling score after score, hundred after hundred, of note-books with your accumulated memoranda ; having no other thought, care, nor ambition than how to know more, and know it better ; and using every drawing you make to live by, merely as a piece of practice in setting down what you have learned. And by the time you are between fifty and sixty, supposing you also to have a natural capacity for art, such as occurs about once in Europe in two centuries, you will be able to make such a little grey paper sketch as that in No. 74.

The series of drawings now exhibited will be more useful than any others that could have been selected in convincing the public of the extent of Turner's study ; but they will be useful no less in showing the method of this study, in the distinct separation of records of form from records of colour, and in the enormous importance attributed to form, and to skill in what is properly termed 'drawing.' For there were current universally during Turner's lifetime, and there are still current very commonly, two great errors concerning him ; errors which not merely lose sight of the facts, but which are point blank contradictory of the facts :—It was thought that he painted chiefly from imagination, when his peculiar character, as distinguished from all other artists, was in always drawing from memories of seen fact, as we shall ascertain in the course of our examination of the drawings here catalogued. And it was commonly thought that he was great only in colouring, and could not draw ; whereas his eminent distinction above other artists, so far as regards execution, was in his marvellous precision of touch, disciplined by practice of engraving, and by perpetual work with the hard lead pencil point on white paper.

As far as I know the existing examples of painters' drawings, the galleries of Europe may be challenged to produce one sketch that shall equal the chalk study No. 45, or the feeblest of the pen and ink memoranda in the 71st and following frames. This was not merely the result of a peculiar gift for art ; it was, as the public will now see, the result of never-ceasing discipline. Hundreds of sketch-books of various sizes exist in the national collection, filled by Turner in his youth with pencil drawings. Having first gone through this labour with the hard pencil point, he proceeds to use the softer pencil for shading.

Soon afterwards he made himself a master in etching and mezzotint engraving ; the plate of the 'Source of the Arveron' is only an average specimen of his engraving ; and from that time forward to his death he used the hard-point—pen, pencil, or chalk —for at least two out of three of all his drawings : and at the very time—between 1840 and 1845—when all the world was crying out against him for his want of drawing, even his coloured sketches from nature were distinguished from all coloured sketches that had

ever been made before, by the continual use of the pen outline to
secure form.

One point only remains to be generally noticed,—that the
command of means which Turner acquired by this perpetual
practice, and the decision of purpose resulting from his vast
power at once of memory and of design, enabled him nearly
always to work straightforward upon his drawings, neither altering them, nor using any of the mechanical expedients for softening tints so frequently employed by inferior water-colour painters.
Many traditions indeed are afloat in the world of art respecting
extraordinary processes through which he carried his work in
its earliest stages; and I think it probable that in some of his
elaborately completed drawings, textures were prepared, by
various mechanical means, over the general surface of the paper
before the drawing of detail was begun. Also, in the large drawings of early date, the usual expedients of sponging and taking
out colour by friction have certainly been employed by him;
but it appears only experimentally, and that the final rejection of
all such expedients was the result of their trial experiment; for in
all the rest of the national collection the evidence is as clear as it
is copious, that he went straight to his mark; in early days finishing piece by piece on the white paper, and, as he advanced in skill,
laying the main masses in broad tints, and working the details
over these, never effacing or sponging, but taking every advantage
of the wetness of the colour, when first laid, to bring out soft lights
with the point of the brush, or scratch out bright ones with the end
of the stick, so driving the wet colour in a dark line to the edge of
the light; a very favourite mode of execution with him, for three
reasons: that it at once gave a dark edge, and therefore full relief, to
the piece of light; secondly, that it admitted of firm and angular
drawing of forms; and, lastly, that as little colour was removed
from the whole mass (the quantity taken from the light being only
driven into the dark), the quantity of hue in the mass itself, as
broadly laid, in its first membership with other masses, was not
much affected by the detailing process.

When these primary modifications of the wet colour had been
obtained, the drawing was proceeded with exactly in the manner
of William Hunt, of the old Watercolour Society (if worked in
transparent hues), or of John Lewis, if in opaque; that is to say,
with clear, firm, and unalterable touches one over another, or one
into the interstices of another; NEVER disturbing them by any
general wash; using friction only where roughness of surface was
locally required to produce effects of granulated stone, mossy
ground, and such like; and rarely even taking out minute lights;
but leaving them from the first, and working round and up to
them, and very frequently drawing thin, dark outlines merely by
putting a little more water into the wet touches, so as to drive the
colour to the edge as it dried; the only difference between his
manipulation and William Hunt's being in his inconceivably varied

and dexterous use of expedients of this kind,—such, for instance, as drawing the broken edge of a cloud merely by a modulated dash of the brush, defining the perfect forms with a quiver of his hand; rounding them by laying a little more colour into one part of the dash before it dried, and laying the warm touches of the light, *after* it had dried, outside of the edges. In many cases the instantaneous manipulation is quite inexplicable; for instance, I cannot conceive by what treatment of the colour he obtained the dark and exquisitely broken edge of wave in the first drawing in the frame No. 65.

It is quite possible, however, that, even in the most advanced stages of some of the finished drawings, they may have been damped, or even fairly put under water and wetted through, so as to admit of more work with the wooden end of the brush; nay, they may even have been exposed to strong currents of water, so as to remove superfluous colour, without defiling the tints anywhere; only most assuredly they never received any friction such as would confuse or destroy the edges and purity of separate tints. And all I can *assert* is that in the national collection there is no evidence of any such processes. In the plurality of the drawings the evidence is, on the contrary, absolute, that nothing of the kind has taken place; the greater number being executed on leaves of books, neither stretched nor moistened in any way whatever; or else on little bits of grey paper, often folded in four, and sometimes with the coloured drawings made on *both* sides of a leaf. The coarser vignettes are painted on sheets of thin drawing paper; the finer ones on smooth cardboard, of course without washing or disturbing the edges, of which the perfect purity is essential to the effect of the vignette.

I insist on this point at greater length, because, so far as the direct copying of Turner's drawings can be useful to the student (working from nature with Turner's faithfulness being the *essential* part of his business), it will be so chiefly as compelling him to a decisive and straightforward execution.

The best practice, and the most rapid appreciation of Turner, will be obtained by accurately copying those in body colour on grey paper; and when once the method is understood, and the resolution made to hold by it, the student will soon find that the advantage gained is in more directions than one. Turner's decision came chiefly of his truthfulness; it was because he meant always to be true that he was able always to be bold. And you will find that you may gain his courage if you will maintain his fidelity.

From the Catalogue I make the subjoined excerpts :—

NOTE.—Numbers are written on the frames only, because it seemed desirable that no dark points, such as would be formed by numerals large enough to be serviceable, should be set near the more delicate of the drawings; and it was necessary, of course, to observe the same system, even in cases where the numerals would have done no harm. The numbers of the frames are printed in this catalogue in larger type, and those of the drawings in small type, and when two or more drawings are put in one frame, their numbers are first put in the relative positions of the drawings, thus :—

19 Number of frame.

34,   35,   36,   37,   Numbers of drawings in their relative
38,   39,   40,   41,   position in the frame.

The reader thus sees without difficulty that No. 35 is the second drawing in the upper row, No. 40 the third in the second row, and so on ; he will then find the drawings catalogued and described in numerical order.

Period of Development.

I.

1. VIEW ON THE RIVER AVON. A sketch from nature, about the year 1791.

It should be kept in mind that Turner's work is separated by differences of style into five groups, corresponding to five periods of his life. He was born in 1775, and died in 1851. His time of real work extends over sixty years, from 1790 to 1850, and is properly to be divided thus:—

Period of Development	1790—1800.
,, The First Style	1800—1820.
,, The Second Style.	1820—1835.
,, The Third Style	1835—1845.
,, Decline	1845—1850.

In order to aid the memory (and the matter is worth remembering), it may be as well to include the fifteen years of childhood and boyhood in the period of development ; which will give a singular order of diminution in length to the five periods, thus:—

Development . . .	1775—1800 .	Twenty-five years.
First Style	1800—1820 .	Twenty years.
Second Style . . .	1820—1835 .	Fifteen years.
Third Style . . .	1835—1845 .	Ten years.
Decline	1845—1850 .	Five years.

It may also be generally observed that the period of development is distinguished by its hard and mechanical work ; that of the first style by boldness of handling, generally gloomy tendency of mind, subdued colour, and perpetual reference to precedent in composition ; that of the second style by delicate deliberation of handling, cheerful moods of mind, brilliant colour, defiance of precedent, and effort at ideal composition ; that of the third period by swiftness of handling, tenderness and pensiveness of mind, exquisite harmony of colour, and perpetual reference to nature only, issuing in the rejection alike of precedents and idealisms.

The period of decline is distinguished by impurity of colour, and uncertainty of purpose and of handling. The drawings belonging to it may be known at once by their surface being much rubbed and disturbed, and by the colours not having sharp edges.

I have not as yet found any drawings in the collection prior to 1790; nor any important examples of the period of decline. The exhibited series ranges only from 1790 to 1845.

This view on the Avon is as juvenile in character as a drawing well can be. It is not, however, as far as I can judge by the laying in of the sky, earlier than the two coloured pieces beside it, which are on leaves out of the same book.

2. NORTH-WEST VIEW OF MALMESBURY ABBEY. 1791. So described on the back in Turner's early writing.

It was a favourite subject with him in after-life ; and it has here had the boy's best work on it, besides being well looked at as he worked. Note the playing of the shadows on the trunks of the trees on the left.

3. VIEW FROM COOK'S FOLLY (so described on the back), 'looking up the river Avon, with Wallis Wall and the Hot Wells.'

In all these drawings, feeble as they are, the power of composition already manifests itself. His love of continuity leads him to duplicate his vessel in each river sketch, in order to lead us down or up the river ; and the trees with tablefork boughs, in the manner of Wilson, already meet with a graceful and Homeric interchanging of branches.[1] How accurate, for a boy, the drawing of the rigging of the large ship, with the shadows of the sails on each other ! This emergence of a ship in full sail from beneath a bank was a favourite idea with him, even to his latest time.

2.

4. THE MEWSTONE. Showing some progress in laying colour, and interesting as the first thought of one of his best known works.

3.

5. TOWER OF ST. MARY REDCLIFFE, BRISTOL.
6. TRANSEPT AND TOWERS OF YORK CATHEDRAL.
7. TOWER OF BOSTON, LINCOLNSHIRE.

These three drawings are fair examples of his pencil studies of architecture. Four or five sketch-books, containing not fewer than a hundred leaves each, are filled with drawings of this kind; and I believe the work to have been of the greatest service in steadying and refining his touch.

It will be observed that, throughout, the sketches are made not for effect but for *information* ; a little bit of each portion of the building being completely drawn, the rest indicated. All Turner's sketches from nature are made on this great principle ; though the kind of information sought, and the shorthand by which it is stated, vary with the subject and the period.

[1] See 'Modern Painters,' vol. iii. p. 190.

The total absence of any apparent feeling for bold or gloomy effect, and the delight in delicacy and precision of form, are very singular, when regarded as the first manifestations of the mind which was to conceive the 'Death of the Python.'

4.

8. MALMESBURY ABBEY. Sketch in pencil, of the same date as the three preceding ones, but showing in the trees the power of composition he had already reached, as well as his landscape 'touch' at this period.

5.

9. First sketch from nature of the subject in the 'Liber Studiorum.' 'KIRKSTALL ABBEY.'

10. First sketch from nature of the subject in the 'Liber Studiorum.' 'HOLY ISLAND.'

Those who are familiar with the compositions of the 'Liber' will be surprised to see how they were founded on the sketches of his boyhood. The 'Holy Island' was published in 1808, the 'Kirkstall' in 1812; while both of these sketches have been made about 1795.

20.

41, 42. TWO MEMORANDA OF COAST SCENERY. I hope the reader observes the steady perseverance of the painter in always sketching for information, and not for the sketches' sake. The inscriptions on these outlines do not improve their effect, but they preserve the important facts. Some words I must leave to the deciphering of the ingenious reader; but thus much is legible:— 'Sky darkish purple; rolling clouds, warm; * * a warm lighter orange green; rocks, warm ochre; purple shadow: * * * brilliant orpiment sails, excepting the (hieroglyphic for upright sail) white, beautifully reflected in the sand, with the sky and white figures streaming down. * * * Straw and Fish. Boy with Dog-fish. Women sorting.'

Note the intense resolve to have the facts, not only of the place, but of the moment: the boy with his dog-fish to be in his own place; nobody else instead of him; and he not to be moved anywhere else.

21.

43. SKETCH FROM NATURE OF THE SUBJECT OF THE OIL PICTURE OF 'IVY BRIDGE.' As interesting as No. 12, being in like manner the first idea of one of his most important works, a grand oil picture now in the possession of E. Bicknell, Esq., of Herne Hill. The study for the drawing in this gallery is in frame No. 16.

44. BED OF A STREAM. One of the most instructive pieces of evidence I could find of the local finishing of his drawings; and as remarkable for precision of touch as for predetermination of design. Note especially the dark greyish-brown dash of shadow from the right, diagonally cast to the top of the white stones, at once defining them in light, and with true outlines; and look how transparent the pool of the stream is becoming, and how bright its fall, by help only of a few well-placed touches of brown and grey.

This sketch should be copied again and again by all students who wish to understand Turner; limiting themselves to precisely his number of touches to bring out the result, as they would be limited in a problem at chess to mate in so many moves.

22.

45. STUDY OF SCOTCH FIR.

46. STUDY OF WILLOW. Two examples of an extensive series of drawings made in Scotland; as far as I can judge, about the year 1800. It has already been stated that several volumes are filled with pencil drawings of this kind, completely worked out in light and shade. This enormous quantity of pencil shading gave him perfect evenness of execution, besides exercising him thoroughly in the virtue of all others most necessary to a painter,— Patience.

We see, gradually, how we are to proceed in order to become good painters. First, five or six volumes full of pencil drawings of architectural detail. Next, a year or so of grey tinting at half-a-crown a day. Next, a year or two of pencil shading, carrying our work well up to the paper's edge; and chess problems in colour going on all the while. The action of his hand is, however, cramped a good deal in this foliage, and throughout the foregrounds of the drawings belonging to this Scottish series. It is not till this stiffness of hand is conquered that we can consider the period of Development as past, and that of the First Style begun.

First Style.

25.

51. CITY OF AOSTA. Turner has been especially struck by the levelness of the plain in which Aosta is built, in the midst of the Alps. He has taken unusual pains to mark this character, and its classicalness as opposed to the wild Swiss peaks above. Remember, this was the first sight he ever had of Italy.

26.

52. ROMAN GATE AT AOSTA, WITH STREET OF THE TOWN. Turner has been rather puzzled by the Swiss cottages, which were not reconcilable with academical laws of architecture. He sits down to his triumphal arch with great zeal, and a satisfied conscience.

53. ROMAN GATE AT AOSTA, WITH THE ALPS. ('Le Arc de Triumph (sic), Ville de Aoust.') These studies are the materials used in the vignette of Aosta, Rogers's Italy.

27.

54. CASTLE OF AOSTA.

55. CASTLE OF AOSTA. This drawing, which I found in another parcel, is placed with the pencil study of which it is the amplification, that it may be seen how much the painter was yet hampered by old rules and formal precedents. He is still trying to tame the Alps into submission to Richard Wilson; but finds the result unsatisfactory, and leaves it unfinished.

But I am much puzzled by the feebleness of the drawing, and could almost imagine it a pupil's copy from one of Turner's. The laying in of the clouds, however, cannot but be his; and it is to be noted in general that while, during his first period, his handling was bold both in pencil and oil-colour, his water colours were frequently delicate, and even, as in the present instance, timid, in the extreme.

28.

56. GLACIERS OF GRINDELWALD.

57. FALLEN TREES. The glaciers are out of their place in our tour; but it is well that we should see them, and the shattered trunks beneath, just after the meek classicalism of No. 55. No hope of taming the Alps, or softening them, in these.

I cannot make out, in the sketch of Grindelwald, where he has got to in the valley, or whether he means the upper white peaks for Alp or glacier. If he intends them for Alp, they are exaggerated; if for ice, I do not understand how he has got pines to come between the two masses.

The other sketch is marked by him simply 'G. C.' (meaning Grande Chartreuse.) It is very noble.

29.

58. THE ASCENT TO CORMAYEUR.[1] ('Ville de Salle, Valley de Aust.¹ La Côte Sud de Mont Blanc.') Perfectly true to the spot, as indeed most of these drawings are.

59. VALLEY OF THE ISÈRE. ('Valley de Iser.') Coming down from the Alps, the road through the valley appears to us disagreeably long and straight. We resolve to have a steady look at it; on which it occurs to us that, nevertheless, it will draw.

---

[1] It is amusingly characteristic of Turner that all his mistakes in spelling are economical. Many bad spellers waste their letters, but Turner never. 'Engin' for engine; 'Aust' for Aoste, or Aouste; 'sumit' for summit, or sommite; 'Iser' for Isère; 'Le Alps' for les Alpes; 'Chatruse' for Chartruse, &c.

44.

77. FOLKESTONE. Finished drawing of a favourite subject. He painted it afterwards still more elaborately. This second drawing is in the possession of Sir John Hippisley, Bart.

45.

78. STUDY OF A CUTTER. I have never seen any chalk sketch which for a moment could be compared with this for soul and power. Note, among other wonderfulnesses of it, the way the two sails are gradated, each with one zigzag touch; one of deepening grey, the other of fading white.

46.

79. STUDY OF A PILOT BOAT. What its companion is among chalk sketches, this is, as far as I know, among sepia ones ; having no rival in its kind. The figure of the old sailor throwing the coil of cable is, without exception, the most wonderful piece of energetic action I have ever seen rendered by means so simple, even Tintoret's work not excepted.

These drawings were on leaves of a folio book, which, for the most part, is dashed over with such things on both sides of its thin grey leaves ; the peculiar ingenuity of the arrangement being that each leaf has half of *one* sketch on its front, and half of *another* on its back, so that mounting one whole sketch must generally hide the halves of two. The further advantage of the plan is that the white chalk touches, on which everything depends, rub partly off every time the leaves are turned ; besides that a quantity of the said chalk, shattered by Turner's energetic thrusts with it, is accumulated in a kind of Alpine débris in the joints, shaking out, and lodging in unexpected knots of chalk indigestion whenever the volume is shut ; and, to make the whole thing perfect, the paper is so thin and old that it will hardly bear even the most loving handling, much less the rack and wear of turning backwards and forwards on a mount, if attached by one edge.

The best that can be done with it is to mount—as all the drawings of this series are mounted—by the extreme edges merely, the most important drawings ; hiding, without injury to them, the least important ; and cataloguing them carefully for reference if required. The two leaves here shown have only two or three sea pieces at the backs of them ; but half the stern of the pilot boat is unfortunately left on the opposite leaf—sacrificed to the unities. It would have spoiled a whole harbour full of ships on the other side if it had been taken away.

47.

80. MARINE.   81. MARINE.

48.

82. MARINE.   83. MARINE.

Four studies of pictures of about the same date, 1803 or 1804, as the preceding folio drawing. Very fine.

49.

84. STUDY OF AN ARM CHAIR. In oils. He painted a great deal of furniture, as well as vases, seals, parchments, and anything else that came in his way, or that his patrons liked to have drawn when he was staying at their houses.

50.

85—88. STUDIES FROM FOUR DIFFERENT POINTS OF THE SAME GROUP OF DOCK LEAVES. I think meant for the farmyard, with cart, in the ' Liber Studiorum.'

51.

89—92. VARIOUS STUDIES OF VEGETATION. Note the foreshortened leaf of laurel, and the memorandum, ' Water sorrel, &c. *June.*'

53.

94. STUDY OF PIGS.
95. STUDY OF DONKEYS. Both wonderful, quite beyond telling. There is an etching of Rembrandt's which approaches the upper study, but by no means equals it. Examine it for a quarter of an hour through a magnifying-glass, and you will see something of what it is. Compare also the drawings in frame No. 16 in the next window. The expression of the head of the donkey-foal with one modulated touch of brown is another chess problem which may be earnestly recommended to students.

54.

96, 97. STUDIES OF MARKET-WARE. Two leaves from a pocket-book filled at Rotterdam.

55.

98. VIEWS IN ROUEN.
99. STUDY OF NORMAN CAPS. Two leaves from a pocket-book filled at Normandy. The No. 98 is interesting because it contains, at the lower right-hand corner, the first sketch from Nature of the lovely subject, painted in the ' Rivers of France,' ' Rouen from St. Catherine's Hill,' of which the engraving is placed beneath it. The posts of the gateway on the left, the diligence in the road, the village and poplars, will all be found indicated in the little pencil drawing.

59.

105. STUDY OF TEAL, FLYING. It is well to have these two drawings side by side, because they are entirely characteristic of the manners of the first and second periods. The darkness and breadth of No. 104 belong to the first, and the brightness, refinement, and active energy in the drawing of the living bird to the second. No words are strong enough to express the admirableness of the sketch No. 105. There is only one other equal to it in the National Collection, and I believe only one in the world superior to it—of a ringdove at Farnley. There are, however, many studies of game by Turner, besides this ringdove, at Farnley. The peculiar execution by which the spotted brown plumage is expressed, and the wonderful drawing and colour reached at one touch, as far as they are consistently possible, render these bird drawings of Turner more utterly inimitable than, so far as I know, anything else he has done.

But he loved birds, and was kind to them, as he was to all living creatures.

Opposite to these studies of birds are now placed some supplementary sketches of the same kind, in the frames Nos. 122, and 123. The uppermost contains examples of his rapid memoranda of groups that pleased him, caught as he stood looking into his poultry yard; the central one, two studies of swans, fine beyond all expression. Observe especially the grand respect of Turner for local colour—the swan's black beak being to him, as it would be to every simple and honest observer, one of the main points in the creature. Observe in the lower of Turner's two sketches how grandly he has indicated the agitation of the water, as partly the means of expressing the anger of the bird.

Second Style.

These sketches are very interesting in the way the original pencilling on the spot is partly employed, and partly crossed out, by the pen work. Thus, in 128, the pencil is left to indicate the timbers which support Fort Rouge, but the square sail is drawn right over the zigzag which indicates the pier on the left; and in 129 a square sail indicated in pencil in the same place is given up; and never touched with the pen. Though, however, more shown in this drawing than usual, the principle is one of those which Turner held most fixedly and constantly. Whatever material a touch may have been made with—colour, pencil, or chalk—he will either use it or contradict it, but he will never repeat it. He will either leave his pencil mark to stand alone for timbers, or draw right across it, and let it stand for nothing; but he never will draw a pen line above it, and let it stand for half and half with ink. So in colour. He will either leave a colour as it is, or strike another

over it to change it ; but never lay two touches over each other of
the same tint. The principle is well known as essential to good
colouring ; but it is not so generally known as essential to the good
penning in of a pencil sketch that the pen should never go over a
pencil line. The shake of the sails in the wind, in either of these
Calais Harbour sketches, is, I should think, enough to cool the
gallery on hot days. But in all respects these four sketches are
inestimable : not the least precious drawing being the No. 131, in
which, as an indication of the pace at which they were all done,
observe the two dark lines of curving wave on the left, struck from
beneath, both drawn into loops, as with one dash of the pen. Then
note the attention of mind as this dashing was done. The first
wave on the left breaks slightly, and has only a few white dots at
its edge ; the second completely, and has a great many. After
this has broken there are only low waves on the sand, and all the
curved waves are therefore drawn lightly !

72.

132. EVREUX.   133. MARKET PLACE, LOUVIERS.
134. VERNON.
135. VERNON; and some place beside, topsy-turvy.

All magnificent. Note in the Evreux, respecting the matters we
have just now been speaking of, how carefully the white is laid on
the cathedral so as to leave the pencil touches to stand for buttress
shadows. The running flock of sheep to the right are intended to
get rid of the vertical stability of the cathedral, which Turner had
rather more of than he liked. It is quite wonderful also how the
dots of white in these sheep increase the look of space in the city
which he had rather less of than he liked. He never throughout his
life was pleased with things that stood quite straight up; and though
contented enough with a village or a cottage, when he drew a city,
he liked a large one. Usually he sets all his cathedral and church
towers from three to six feet off the perpendicular, being provoked
with them for not behaving gracefully, like ships in a breeze. But
the flock of sheep is here a more prudential expedient to obtain
his beloved obliquity.

MARKET-PLACE AND CHURCH OF LOUVIERS. Not good; an
instructive example of his want of feeling for Gothic architecture
when seen near.

VERNON. Two studies on one sheet. The lowermost one is
the bridge in the distance of the upper one, seen the other way.
The massive look of the rectangular houses on the bridge is purposely increased by the opposition of the sharp points of the boats ;
it is a favourite artifice of Turner's. The three round packages, on
the contrary, repeat and increase the look of multitudinousness in
the bridge arches.

These buildings on the bridge are mills ; the wheels are indicated in the arches below, and more plainly in the next sketch.

This is very characteristic of France ; the water power of the

French rivers, irrespective of tide, being much greater than of ours.

VERNON ; from farther below the bridge. Observe, in the last sketch, the way the oval packages, with the figure above them, point up through the bridge; and compare the use of the great crest-shaped rudders of boats in this one. These groups of radiating lines are to give connection between the foreground and bridge in each case ; without them they would run in two painfully separate and parallel lines. The figures in No. 128 are arranged in similar lines, to help in sending the boat well out of the harbour.

73.

136. MARLY. Realised for the Keepsake.
137. NEAR ST. GERMAIN, LOOKING UP THE SEINE.
138. CASTLE OF THE FAIR GABRIELLE. Also realised for the Keepsake.
139. NEAR ST. GERMAIN, LOOKING DOWN THE SEINE.

The plan of composition in 137 is very curious. A double group of trees, with *one* circle beneath it, carrying the eye out to the left ; a treble group of trees, with *two* circles beneath it (wheels of diligence), carrying the eye out to the right ; a man in the middle, with a couple of circles, one on each arm, to join the groups ; the windows of the diligence to repeat and multiply the arches of the building on the hill ; the galloping horses to oppose vertical stability, as the sheep in No. 132. 138 is more careless in work than the rest, but most careful in composition, and highly interesting as an example of Turner's favourite scheme of carrying his main masses by figure foundations, like the rich sculptured bases to Lombardic pillars. Two figures to the two trees on left ; many figures to many trees in centre; two figures to two trees on right ; two black figures bowing to each other from opposite sides of the avenue, to increase its symmetry of shade. In each case the figures extend below to nearly the breadth to which the trees branch above. We have first an upright lover to an upright tree ; a graceful lady, with flowing train, to graceful tree with bending top ; a completely recumbent group in centre to completely independent foliage of centre ; sloping lines converging below on the right, for sloping boughs converging above on the right. The artifice is concealed and relieved by one bold diagonal line begun by the child in the centre, and carried by a straight tree-trunk to the top of the picture. 139 is also rather careless, but marvellous in expression of the course of stream by the gradated laying on of white. The postillion straddling up the hill is essential to sustain the group of tall trees. The black figure in the centre, by its excessive darkness, balances postillion and trees together ; then the dark island leads the dark masses out of the picture.

74.

140. AMBLETEUSE ?   141. DIEPPE.

142. MEMORANDA OF BOULOGNE, AMBLETEUSE, AND VI-
MARAUX.

143. BRIDGE OF BOATS AND UPPER BRIDGE AT ROUEN.

141 is the most delicate pen and ink sketch among this series of
drawings, exquisitely beautiful in action of sails. 140 is one of the
most laconic in line, and the other two among the most economic in
paper.

75.

144—146. SKETCHES OF ROOMS AT PETWORTH. I am not
sure of the date of these, or of the drawings in the next frame, but
I believe them to be considerably earlier in the central period than
the French sketches we have been examining. But as we are now
coming to a series of coloured drawings on grey paper, these may
be fitly considered together with the others ; and it is well to close
our examples of the second period with some thoroughly characteristic drawings, rather than with those which approximate to the
third : and the brilliancy, not without slight harshness, of these
studies is quite peculiar to the second time ; the colour of the
third period, however pure, being always soft.

The study of curtains is very like a bit of Tintoret's work in oil,
quite Venetian in the enrichment of colour in the shadows. The
Pisani Veronese, together with the grand Turner studies of local
colour, of which these three are so singular examples, will, I hope,
establish on a firmer basis the practice of colour in England.
There is a curious illustration, by the way, in the Veronese, of the
statement I gave of his general principle of local colour in ' Modern
Painters ;'[1] the black tresses in the ermine being reinforced in
blackness towards the *light*, so that the last touch comes with an
edge blacker than ink against the full white, while the delicate
violets of the princess's robe are reinforced in the *shadow*. Observe
also how straightforward Veronese is, like Turner, in all his work
—the unfinished and forgotten figures in the distance on the left
showing his method, and the absolute decision as to what he was
going to do before a touch was laid.

76.

147—150. FOUR EVENING STUDIES AT PETWORTH. The
first and last so severe in tone as almost to take the character of
the first period, but all noble.

77.

151—154. FOUR SUBJECTS SKETCHED FOR THE ' RIVERS OF
FRANCE.' These four drawings, belonging to the third period, are
placed with those from Petworth in order to mark the peculiar use
of the pen characteristic of Turner's most advanced work. He was
about to enter on the pursuit of effects of colour more soft and illu-
sive than any that he had yet attempted; and precisely in proportion to this softness of general effect was the firm retention of form

[1] Vol. iv. chap. iii. §§ 14, 16.

by the pen drawing in all his careful memoranda. Multitudes of slighter sketches occur without it, but nearly all the best drawings of the period have it definitely; and its presence instantly marks a work of the advanced time, though the work may be of the advanced time without having it, as 154 in this frame. 153 is a beautiful and characteristic example of the treatment. See note on 177.

Third Style.
78.

155—158. FOUR FRENCH SUBJECTS, I believe, on the Meuse, 157 being certainly Dinant. These, with those placed below on the same screen, form a perfectly typical illustration of the great work of the early third period—glowing in colour, deep in tenderness and repose. The upper and lower frames give examples of the slighter drawings, and the central frame of perfect ones.

79.

159. HAVRE (?)   16c. ROUEN.
161. ST. GERMAIN (?)   162. QUILLEBŒUF.

Four of the very highest quality. It is impossible to have a drawing containing more of the essence of all that is best in Turner than the Havre. The subtlety of gradation of grey light from behind the fort to the left; of shadow at the edge of the fort itself; of rosy colour from the dark edge of the lightest cloud; of green in the water, caused not by reflection, but by the striking of the rainy sunshine on its local colour, and the placing of the boat's flag, and the radiating lines of the rain, to express the drift of breeze which is coming out of the light of the sky, are all in his noblest manner.

160. It is raining in the *distance* of No. 159; but here, between us and the lights, making the forms indistinct, expressed only by outline. In the St. Germain we have an effect of misty morning; and in the Quillebœuf of a grey and colourless day.

81.

167—170. FOUR FRENCH SUBJECTS. Except the first, Tancarville, I do not as yet know the subjects. They are examples of the inferior work of the period. Turner wasted much time because he could not resist the impulse to make a coloured sketch of everything he saw; and it was only occasionally, when he was undisturbed by new ideas or visions, that he finished his work rightly. But all are equally instructive respecting modes of execution; observe especially that, however great his hurry, he prepares his under colour rightly, and then throws another tint over it to *leave* in perfect purity even such a little light as the wake of the dabchick in 170, which anybody else would have taken out afterwards.

83.

177. THE GREAT FORTRESS. I have seen, at different times, at least twenty drawings by Turner of this wonderful place, and

have never been able to find out where it is. If any traveller can tell me, I should be grateful. I think No. 153 is the same place; at all events No. 153 is the place I want to find the name of.

92.

201. VILLENEUVE, LOOKING FROM CHILLON TOWARDS VEVAY.

202. GALLERY ON THE SPLUGEN.

203. VEVAY, LOOKING ACROSS THE LAKE TO MEILLERIE.

Examples of pencil memoranda of finest late time; taken in three degrees of haste. The first, tolerably careful, with the future position of clouds entirely arranged; 203, sketched in angry haste, because the tower of the church had been first drawn too big, and too far to the right, its ghost still appearing on the right; and 202, an instance of the slightest notes he thought it worth while to take.

93.

204. FORTRESS, EVENING.

205. LAUSANNE, IN ROSY SUNSET.

I do not know the subject of the first sketch, but both are intensely characteristic of Turner's modes of thought in his last period; simplicity of effect, and tenderness with depth of colour prevailing over all detail. The green-blue waters of the Lake of Geneva delighted him always, and the sketch 205 has been made for the sake of their contrast with the rosy light.

94.

207. COBLENTZ, WITH THE BRIDGE OF BOATS OVER THE RHINE.

This last was a favourite sketch of Turner's.

95.

208. FLUELEN (HEAD OF LAKE LUCERNE).

209. LAKE LUCERNE, LOOKING FROM KUSSNACHT TOWARDS THE BERNESE ALPS; MONT PILATE ON THE RIGHT, DARK AGAINST SUNSET.

Two examples of his most rapid memoranda in colour of conceptions that pleased and interested him at his most powerful time. It is worth while pausing to analyse the first. The little darker spot on the middle of the cliff on the left is a chapel with a small belfry, and it will be noticed that the yellow colour leaves a white light at the belfry and on the flat shore below. The sun was to be just above the chapel, and to show a stream of white light down from behind it. Then just above the chapel to the right the pencil markings form a loop; the touch being struck upwards first, and then zigzagged down to the right. This is because that touch goes right round the edge of a ravine, cut into the hill beyond the chapel. It follows it round, and indicates a piny slope by the zigzag. Both touches would have been drawn from the top downwards, if there had been two hills, one in front of the other, instead of a ravine cut into the single mass.

Then one running touch draws the outline of the great cliff, and another within it the edge of its precipice; afterwards followed with the violet colour, leaving light on the summit. The blue lake horizon, with a clump of trees, is indicated by one dash of the brush, with more water added afterwards to thin it. But I never could understand how this is done—and he does it constantly—without disturbing the white spots of broken light.

97.

212. SAN GIORGIO MAGGIORE. Venice.

213. SANTA MARIA DELLA SALUTE. Venice. His thoughts, towards the close of his life, were continually hovering between Venice and the Lake of Lucerne.

Supplemental Series.

III.

232. A FOREGROUND AT ROME.

The motive of this last study has been the occurrence of the real living acanthus among the fallen Corinthian capitals. It is very characteristic of Turner to be interested in such an accident as this.

112.

FOUR LEAVES FROM A SKETCH-BOOK FILLED ON THE WAY TO AND FROM SCOTLAND, BY SEA, ON THE OCCASION OF GEORGE THE FOURTH'S VISIT TO EDINBURGH.

These are the first examples given in this series from Turner's smaller note-books, on which, however despised they may be by persons who look only for the attractive qualities of drawing, his peculiar eminence as a painter chiefly depended. It was in these that his observations of nature were accumulated, day by day, and moment by moment, until his mind became an inexhaustible treasury of natural facts, which imagination might afterwards arrange and combine at her pleasure.

There are two hundred and forty-seven of these books in the National Collection containing from fifty to ninety leaves each, nearly always drawn upon on both sides.

The leaves 233 and 235 in this frame are good examples of his mode of studying skies. He rarely, as already stated, sketched from them in colour, perceiving that the colours changed much too fast to be set down with fidelity; and considering all imperfect and untruthful colour memoranda as simply deceptive and harmful.

His method was to outline as fast as possible the forms, and write down the colours of the clouds, in any sky effect which interested him; afterwards, if he thought it desirable, he appears deliberately to have made a study of the sky in colour, as he remembered it; but he never tried to pursue at the instant the changes of coloured clouds.

The leaf 235 is a note of changes of effect at sunrise.

116.

The book from which 265 and 266 are taken contains 270 leaves, all drawn on both sides; but there are only about ninety as full of subject as these examples. These leaves measure four and a half inches by three; one of them contains seven subjects on one side, and four on the reverse; and the other has ten subjects on one side, and five on the reverse. Taking the lowest average of ten subjects for each leaf, there are, therefore, at least 900 subjects in the third part of the book.

265 has seven subjects from Andernach on the Rhine, showing stormy sunsets and drifts of clouds, all completely designed; the best, that on the left in the second row from the bottom, only measures one inch and a half in length by three quarters of an inch in height.

The leaf 266 has also Rhine subjects.

267 shows a most interesting outline sketch near the Borromean Islands on Lago Maggiore. The effects, names of towns, &c., are written on it: thus (in the sky), 'Light,' 'Blue Clouds,' 'Rays,' 'Cloudy, yet none below the mountains,' 'Gueriano?' on left, 'Laveno' on right (names of villages). (On the lake): 'Sea green with dark waves.' 'Boats have the (hieroglyphic for awning) over the edge, close seat behind for the tiller, which is changed, the Maggiore one had the tiller (another hieroglyphic), the steersman sat on the spare oar.'

Observe in the hieroglyphic for the awning Turner's intensity of habitual accuracy, in marking by the two dots *a*, *b*, the thicker timbers at the sides of the boat in which the bent laths which carry the awning are inserted. This side of the leaf contains four subjects, its reverse four slighter ones. He has written the words 'Rosa,' 'Gothard,' over what he supposed to be the respective mountains: neither of them is however visible from this part of Lago Maggiore; he has mistaken lower peaks for them.

118.

270. STUDIES FROM CLAUDE AND IN FRANCE.

The uppermost subject is a beautiful little view of Dieppe. The second from the top, a scene on Dieppe beach, with two fish-wives quarrelling; during the course of the discussion Mr. Turner has noted their costume, thus:—

Fish-wife on the left	*Fish-wife on the right.*
' W.' (white) cap.	' W.' (white) cap.
' W.' (white) shoulder-kerchief.	* * * (illegible) 'with red sparks.'
' G.' (green) bodice.	
' R.' (red) gown.	' White garters.'
' W. P.' white petticoat.	' Each, a fish-knife.'
(To the right of her feet) ' B.' (black) stockings.	

134.

296. ORLEANS: THE THEATRE AND CATHEDRAL.
297. NANTES: PROMENADE NEAR THE CHATEAU.

These are both variations of subjects designed for the ' Rivers of France,' and engraved in that series. They are not to be considered as studies for them, but as examples of Turner's way of turning a subject this way and that in his mind. He makes a sketch of Orleans Cathedral from a given corner of a street, and at a given hour of the afternoon. A year or two afterwards, perhaps, he looks at the sketch, and thinks he would like to try it about twenty yards more to the left, and half an hour later, or an hour earlier; in which cases he is nearly sure to put in the same figures in some different position. This study of Orleans is about an hour earlier in the afternoon than the engraved one, and a hundred yards farther down the street. It is by no means so beautiful as the engraved one; but the Nantes is far prettier, being an idea of a finer day. The engraved drawing is of a bleak grey afternoon, and taken from the end of the walk, where the colossal statues become principal objects, and they are not interesting ones.

152.

337. FRIBOURG. (Canton Fribourg.) Sketched on, I believe, his last Swiss journey (1845).

153.

338. FRIBOURG. Companion to the foregoing. Out of a book containing fourteen sketches of this city; all more or less elaborate; and showing the way in which he used the pencil and pen together, up to the latest hour of his artist's life. The lesson ought surely not to be lost upon us when we consider that from Turner, least of all men, such indefatigable delineation was to have been expected; since his own special gift was that of expressing mystery, and the obscurities rather than the definitions of form. If a single title were to be given, to separate him from others, it ought to be ' the painter of clouds.' This he was in earliest life; and this he was, in heart and purpose, even when he was passing days in drawing the house roofs of Fribourg; for the sketches which at that period he liked to be asked to complete were such as those in

the hundredth frame, of soft cloud wreathing above the deep Swiss waters.

All other features of natural scenery had been in some sort rendered before;—mountains and trees by Titian, sun and moon by Cuyp and Rubens, air and sea by Claude. But the burning clouds in their courses, and the frail vapours in their changes, had never been so much as attempted by any man before him. The first words which he ever wrote, as significative of his aim in painting, were Milton's, beginning 'Ye mists and exhalations.' And the last drawing in which there remained a reflection of his expiring power, he made in striving to realise, for me, one of these faint and fair visions of the morning mist, fading from the Lake Lucerne.

'There ariseth a little cloud out of the sea, like a man's hand.'
'For what is your life?'

CHAPTER XLVIII.

TURNER'S GENIUS.

A Résumé of Mr Ruskin's Criticisms on the Chief Features of his Styles.

WITH all the delights of a perpetual study of Nature in her loveliest haunts, Turner's life was an unhappy one. Born in a sordid house, his mother insane, the dwarfed mind of his father unable to comprehend his aspirations, unfortunate in love, struggling on as a small drawing-master and painter of backgrounds ; then battling with the engravers and publishers, and the work he illustrated selling badly ; with no wife to share his cares and console him in his disappointments ; surrounded by jealous rivals, neglected by the rich cognoscenti of the day, unable to sell the most favourite works of his genius, he arrived at middle life before he could be said to have attained any certainty of fame. In a room that resembled the miserable Barry's, he lived his enthusiast life, with no companion but his old housekeeper—the somewhat more than housekeeper though other than wife—finally retiring to a fresh haunt at Chelsea to die, untended but by the mercenary love of a low mistress, with no hope for the next world, as there had been none in this. Who can wonder at the melancholy result of such an entangled and ill-arranged existence—blunders growing from blunders, and culminating in a confused and half-cancelled will? Relations, disregarded or disliked, dispute the legacies. The noble charity that had been his central thought for forty years falls to the ground (surely Turner must have moved in his coffin if he heard the decision); and a poor 20,000*l.* goes to the Royal Academy—a body already groaning with useless wealth.

Unhappy result of a confused life! While the grand design of charity is defeated, the inferior part of Turner's ambition is gratified by the erection of a 1000*l.* statue in St. Paul's, where he lies tranquilly between Sir Joshua and Barry; a Turner gallery is devoted to his best and his worst works; and a Turner gold medal is given away at stated periods; but the ample scheme of beneficence planned by himself is not achieved.

To Mrs. Radcliffe and Thomson Mr. Ruskin assigns the credit of having effected an escape from the Queen Anne formalism of literature. In both these writers we find expressions of attachment to wild nature. Cowper, Thomson, and Bishop Percy did much to revive a love of the simple and the natural. Then came Scott and the Lake poets to develope it further, and to teach us to sympathise with Gothic architecture, all agreeing in their passion for natural scenery. To supply the same want in Art, Turner and his brother landscape-painters arose.

Turner never imitated Salvator Rosa, because he had rocks and torrents of his own to go and copy and recompose from. He imitated Morland, Wilson, Reynolds, and Loutherbourg, because they were the fashion, but never West or Fuseli. Tintoret and Paul Veronese were of service to him, says Mr. Ruskin. With Titian Turner competed in his 'Venus and Adonis.' He has been heard to rebuke a young man at a party for foolishly running down Titian; and the putting in of the beech-leaves in the upper right-hand corner of 'Peter Martyr' he has been known to mention with 'singular delight.' One day, at the British Institution, as he was looking with admiration at a glowing Cuyp, he said to a friend, 'They would have called that too warm if I had done it.'

For the Earl of Essex he painted several views of Cashiobury, of the highest quality. One of these, once in the collection of Mr. Windus, in which the light falls on the floor of a vaulted apartment through a stained glass window, stands unequalled. In it he has introduced a rich Persian table-cover, which for careful finish is as elaborate as anything of the Dutch masters.

On the subject of his treatment of trees Mr. Ruskin writes : 'These two characters, the woody stiffness hinted through muscular line, and the inventive grace of the upper boughs, have never been rendered except by Turner ; he does not merely draw them better than others, but he is the only man who has ever drawn them at all. Of the woody character, the tree subjects of the " Liber Studiorum" afford marked examples ; the "Cephalus and Procris," "Scenes near the Grand Chartreuse," and " Blair-Athol," " Juvenile Tricks," and " Hedging and Ditching," may be particularised ; in the England series, the " Bolton Abbey " is perhaps a more characteristic and thoroughly Turner-esque example than any. . . . In the group of trees on the left in Turner's " Marley," we have there perfect and ceaseless intricacy to oppose to Poussin, perfect and unbroken repose to oppose to Hobbima, and in the unity of these the perfection of truth. This group may be taken as a fair standard of Turner's tree-painting. We have in it the admirably-drawn stems, instead of the claws or the serpents ; full, transparent, boundless intricacy, instead of the shell pattern ; and misty depth of inter-mingled light and leafage, instead of perpetual repetition of one mechanical touch.'

The reproach of gaudiness of colour will not now be advanced against Turner except by those who have not studied the burning crimsons and purple of a summer sunset or the luminous folds of a white cloud with the sun on it. Turner used pure colour only in minute touches, knowing that all paint was clay compared with light and flame. Once, to give verdure with sunshine on it, he used pure yellow in this way, in his determination to express its relative intensity of light.

He never expends detail on near objects in cold sky blue ; he uses it only where Nature uses it, and brings in his warm colour directly detail and surface become visible by light. His works are distinguished by the intensity of light he sheds through every hue, as he never lowers his middle tint to give greater value to his high light, as the old masters did. It is this unusual brilliancy that makes his pictures sometimes appear to ignorant critics glaring and dazzling. No one is more cautious and sparing in the use of pure colour than Turner. He attains his brilliancy by his variety and subtlety of semi-tones. He stipples his grounds, not his shadows, with one broad yet sharp touch.

Mr. Ruskin says that there is no instance in the works of Turner of anything so faithful and imitative of sunshine as the best parts of Cuyp; but at the same time there is not such solecism in them. Cuyp gives us only a narrow view of Nature, and is too intent on the truth of his omnipresent sunshine to think of any other truth. Cuyp is trying for tone, not colour; he is giving us a monochrome in gold colour. But Turner wants colour, and he must give us both cold and warm colour. He must have his contrast and his balance, his forte and his piano. When he shows us the sunset in the west, he shows us the colour dying off cold to the east. As instances of this sacrifice of tone to colour, Mr. Ruskin adduces the blue and white stripes on the drifting flag in the 'Slave Ship,' and the white part of the dress of the 'Napoleon,' which, though valuable for colour, are discordant in tone.

The best proof of the grammatical accuracy of the tones of Turner is the perfect and unchanging influence of all his pictures at any distance. Some of them seem to me too artificially balanced with hot and cold colour; yet Turner did what no one had attempted before. He gave us reverse tones in one picture.

Adverting to this, Mr. Ruskin comments:—

'Colour without form is less frequently obtainable; and it may be doubted whether it be desirable; yet I think that to the full enjoyment of it a certain sacrifice of form is necessary; sometimes by reducing it to the shapeless glitter of the gem, as often Tintoret and Bassano; sometimes by loss of outline and blending of parts, as Turner; sometimes by flatness of mass, as often Giorgione and Titian.

' Now, in Turner's power of associating cold with warm light no one has ever approached, or even ventured into the same field with him. The old masters, content with one simple tone, sacrificed to its unity all the exquisite gradations and varied touches of relief and change by which Nature unites her hours with each other. They gave the warmth of the sinking sun, overwhelming all things in its gold; but they did not give those grey passages about the horizon, where, seen through its dying light, the cold and the gloom of night gather themselves for their victory. Whether it was in them impotence or judgment it is not for me to decide. I have only to point to the daring of Turner in this respect as something to which Art affords no matter of comparison, as that in which the mere attempt is, in itself, superiority.'

In the ' Rivers of France ' you see very small quantities of excessive light or excessive shade. Always sharp, decisive, and conspicuous, the mass of the picture is infinitely graduated middle tint. In later works Turner surrounds light with shade.

In criticising Turner's skies, Mr. Ruskin says:—

' Take up one of Turner's skies, and see whether he is as narrow in his conception, or as niggardly in his space. It does not matter which we take; his sublime " Babylon " is a fair example for our present purpose. Ten miles away down the Euphrates, where it gleams last along the plain, he gives us a drift of dark elongated vapour, melting beneath into a dim haze which embraces the hills on the horizon. It is exhausted with its own motion, and broken up by the wind in its own mass into numberless groups of billowy and tossing fragments, which, beaten by the weight of storm down to the earth, are just lifting themselves again on wearied wings, and perishing in the effort. Above these, and far beyond them, the eye goes back to a broad sea of white illuminated mist, or rather cloud melted into rain, and absorbed again before that rain has fallen, but penetrated throughout, whether it be vapour or whether it be dew with soft sunshine, turning it as white as snow. Gradually, as it rises, the rainy fusion ceases. Now, this is Nature ! It is the exhaustless living energy with which the universe is filled; and what will you set beside it of the works of other men ?'

Mr. Ruskin speaks nobly of Turner's pathetic interest in the sea, and of his inexhaustible knowledge of shipping. It is hardly necessary to remark upon the depth of his attachment to the Thames. I believe he kept a boat on the river; it is certain that he once spent a whole season sailing up and down to the Nore and back. His first oil picture was 'Moonlight at Millbank;' indeed, four several pictures, typical of four different periods in his career, were devoted to the imperial river—'Mill-bank,' 'Greenwich,' 'Kingston,' and 'Richmond.'

Mr. Dillon, one of the great Turner collectors, discourses beautifully of his genius:—

'The premature discontinuance of that work (the "Liber") would appear to have left incomplete the plan he had formed of formally arranging and expressly illustrating the varied objects of art under these or other heads; but the intellect which suggested the division, and the grasp of mind which sought to unite or combine them into a system, continued to direct all his after-labours, and to connect them into one harmonious whole. His mind was a generalising mind. Whatever his subject, there is always in him a "touch of nature," or a word of truth, which, recalling the past or revealing the future, connects the part with the whole, leads us from Art to Nature, and conducts us from the individual landscape to the universe. Thus, for example, it is not "Coniston Fells" only which we see; it is *morning* amongst the Fells. It is not "Calais Sands," but the far-stretched shores of the ocean. It is not "Rome," ancient or modern, or the "Fighting 'Téméraire' tugged to her last berth to be broken up;" it is not of these only we are reminded, but of the fate and fall of nations. There lie the ghastly, grisly skeletons, protected from the birds of the air and the beasts of the field by Rizpah ! The darkness of night has fallen on them; but the moonlight, beaming on the distant sheaves, reveals to us, or reminds us, that when the sons of Saul were slain it was "in the days of harvest—in the first days, in the beginning of the barley harvest." What appear, on first sight, to be Turner's wildest visions had an eye to order and reality, as well as to beauty; and even his experiments on colour were founded on a theory, and tended to a system. He illustrates "Shade and Darkness," "Light and Colour," by the evening before and the morning after the Deluge, and conveys "Goethe's Theory" by the destruction and renovation of a world.'

One of Turner's favourite subtleties was to introduce scarlet into his skies when he wished to indicate death or ruin. He did so in the 'Téméraire,' the 'Fall of Carthage,' the 'Slaver,' the 'Ulyssses,' the 'Napoleon,' and the 'Goldau,' and even in a little sad and tender sketch of dawn made by him in his last years; of which Mr. Ruskin gives us this wonderful verbal picture:—

'It is a small space of level shore; beyond it a fair soft light in the east, the last storm-clouds melting away oblique into the morning air; some little vessel—a collier, probably—has gone down in the night, all hands lost; a single dog has come ashore utterly exhausted, its limbs failing under it; sinking into the sand, it stands howling and shivering. The dawn-clouds have the first scarlet upon them, a feeble tinge only, reflected with the same feeble blood-stain on the sand.'[1]

Mr. Ruskin directs attention to the fact that, in a drawing designed as a companion to the 'Goldau,' Turner represents the sun rising above Morgarten, and gilding the two peaks that protect the village that gives its name to Switzerland. In all his Carthaginian, Venetian, and Roman pictures, says the same admirable critic, Turner dwelt on three morals. Carthage he selected to illustrate the dangers attending the pursuit of wealth; Rome to show the fate of ambition; and Venice to prove the vanity of pleasure and luxury.

For Turner his powerful advocate justly claims pre-eminent superiority in the representation of the various forms and phenomena of the cloudy sky, and in the drawing of mountains

[1] There was also a depth in Turner's imagination not always visible to the hasty.

and stones, with a thorough knowledge of their spirit and organisation. Turner was the first to accommodate the foreground to the distance, and to show that it was possible to express foreground proximity without detaining the eye by madeout forms. These he deliberately leaves imperfect, and so leads you on to the distance that he takes most delight to express, and in the expression of which his great power lay. He shows us just as much as the eye sees of forms to which its focus is not directed. He makes his figures vague lest they should detain the eye from the magical blue fold on fold of the distance. Had he put in better-drawn figures, the landscape would at once have been destroyed.

Turner gives us all varieties of clouds crowded together; wind-compelled, as in the 'Shylock;' blended with the sky itself, as in the 'Mercury and Argus;' in equal-rounded flakes, to express repose, as in the 'Acro-Corinth;' in fiery-flying fragments, as in the 'Téméraire;' woven together with fine threads of intermediate darkness, as in the 'Napoleon;' and in fleecy lines, as in the 'Alps at Daybreak,' in Rogers' poems. The form, depth, and perspective of each cloud, as well as its individuality, are rendered by him. 'Rouen' (in the 'Rivers of France') is adduced by Mr. Ruskin as a special example of the quality of infinity imparted by the painter to his horizon. Equally remarkable is he for mists, mountain melting into cloud, and the horizon into the twilight; for dew rising from hill pastures, and storms gathering over cliffs. I must add that Turner's storms, deep without blackness, and sharp in outline, as in his 'Pæstum,' 'Stonehenge' and 'Winchelsea Castle,' are inadequately rendered by the engravers, who blacken the shadows and blunt the sharp edges of the colour.

Generally speaking, I have abstained from quoting any passages from Mr. Ruskin, merely for their poetry, unless they really contained some exposition of Turner's style and mind ; but the following I cannot pass by, especially as I have not myself seen the picture referred to :—

'But I think the noblest sea that Turner has ever painted, and, if so, the noblest certainly ever painted by man, is that of the 'Slave Ship,' the chief Academy picture of the Exhibition of 1840. It is a sunset on the Atlantic, after prolonged storm ; but the storm is partially lulled, and the torn and streaming rain clouds are moving in scarlet lines to lose themselves in the hollow of the night. The whole surface of sea included in the picture is divided into two ridges of enormous swell, not high nor local, but a low, broad heaving of the whole ocean, like the lifting of its bosom by deep-drawn breath after the torture of the storm. Between these two ridges the fire of the sunset falls along the trough of the sea, dyeing it with an awful but glorious light, the intense and lurid splendour which burns like gold, and bathes like blood.'

In the ' Pas de Calais' there is a buoy poised on the ridge of a sea wave, that casts its reflection vertically down the flank of the wave that slopes steeply. It is a mistake. But the vertical line is wanted, and Turner trusted to few of his public spending much time in observing the reflection of buoys on waves.[1]

For examples of the sea as viewed at the distance of twenty or thirty yards from the shore, where Turner generally places the spectator, beyond the first line of breakers, see the ' Land's End,' 'Fowey,' 'Dunbar' and 'Langbourne.' The latter is remarkable for the fine dark furrows of tremendous swell. The tossing of the individual lines expresses the sea's fitfulness and fury, its ' unwearied reckless incoherency.' The waves are notable for their expression of weight, and intensity is secured by the sense of breadth, not of mere height. Reserving his chief strength for coast sea, Turner too closely followed the Dutch painters in their treatment of the open sea.

For still water, the 'Château of Prince Albert' deserves study. It expresses great width ; the eye is kept moving over the surface. With the endless reflections of sun, sky, and foliage, not one is traceable to its exact source. Everything is given correctly, yet nothing is given too definitely, because the painter knows what to show, and what to conceal. It has not been revealed how Turner obtained some of the surface he

---

[1] In the above sentence, as in many other places, I have to thank Mr. Ruskin for criticisms which I have condensed, but left unaltered in essentials.

gives as water, but it looks like a modification of body colour ; as in the distance of the ' Devonport, with the Dockyard.' For extended surface of water, see the 'Loch Katrine' and ' Derwentwater' in Scott's poems, and the 'Loch Lomond' vignette to Rogers' poems ; of which the first shows distant breeze on the water ; the second, slight motion prolonging the reflection of the waves ; and the third, full ripple over the whole surface. For distant rivers, with exquisite perspective, let us turn to the coursing stream in ' Dryburgh and Melrose' and 'Rouen, from St. Catherine's Hill ; ' and for indicating the height of the observer above the river, and the loss of reflections, we may consult ' Caudebec.'

Of his exquisite finish Mr. Ruskin writes :—

' Every quarter of an inch of Turner's drawings will bear magnifying ; and much of the finer work in them can hardly be traced, except by the keenest sight, until it is magnified. In his painting of " Ivy Bridge" the veins are drawn on the wings of a butterfly not above three lines in diameter ; and I have one of his smaller drawings of "Scarborough " in my own possession, in which the mussel shells on the beach are rounded, and some shown as shut, some as open, though none are as large as the letters of this type ; and yet this is the man who was thought to belong to the " dashing" school, literally because most people had not patience or delicacy of sight enough to trace his endless details.'

Turner was always on the alert, says Mr. Reeve, for any remarkable effect. In 1792, when he was eighteen years of age, the Pantheon, in Oxford Street, was burnt down. It happened to be a hard frost at the time, and large icicles were seen the next morning depending from the different parts of the ruins. The young artist quickly repaired to the spot ; and his picture, the ' Pantheon on the Morning after the Fire,' exhibited in the Royal Academy in the following May, witnessed the force with which the scene was impressed upon him. In like manner, the 'Burning of the Houses of Parliament,' forty years afterwards, was an event that could not escape the pencil of Turner. He repaired to the spot to make sketches of the fire at different points, and produced two pictures ; one for the

Academy, another for the British Institution. Here was a glowing subject for his palette. Lord Hill, on looking closely to the latter picture, exclaimed, 'What's this? Call this painting? Nothing but dabs.' But upon retiring, and catching its magical effects, he added, 'Painting! God bless me! So it is!' The picture of 'Hail, Rain, and Speed,' with its wonderful interpretation of a night railway train, produced at a still later period of Turner's life, was another instance in which the great artist's attention had been caught by the hissing, and puffing, and glowing fire of the locomotive.

Turner's wide sympathy is indicated by Mr. Ruskin in the following passage :—

'Look at the girl putting her bonnet on the dog, in the foreground of the "Richmond, Yorkshire;" the juvenile tricks of the "Marine Dabblers," of the "Liber Studiorum;" the boys scrambling after their kites in the "Woods of the Greta and Buckfastleigh;" and the notable and most pathetic drawing of the "Kirby Lonsdale Churchyard," with the schoolboys making a fortress of their larger books on the tombstone, to bombard with the more projectile volumes. And, passing from these to the intense horror and dismay of the "Rizpah," consider for yourself whether there was ever any other painter who could strike such an octave. Whether there has been or not, in other walks of art, this power of sympathy is unquestionably in landscape unrivalled. . . . . As few, in looking at the "Cephalus and Procris" of Turner, note the sympathy of those faint rays that are just drawing back and dying between the trunks of the far-off forest, with the ebbing life of the nymph, unless, indeed, they happen to recollect the same sympathy marked by Shelley in the "Alastor :" but the imagination is not shown in any such modifications. However, in some cases they may be valuable, and I note them merely in consequence of their peculiar use in religious art, presently to be examined.'

Turner seldom drew a place as it really was. He gave not the place itself, but the impression it produced upon him. He would reduce a whole day's journey into a sketch, in order to focus all the features of a region into one impression, and to set that before the spectator's mind. This habit arose from the conventional compositions to which Turner had been accustomed from a boy ; in the days of Wilson, Nature being held to be unfit to be seen till the artist had improved her. This reprehensible untruthfulness Mr. Ruskin thus ingeniously defends :—

'But if a painter has inventive power, he is to treat his subject in a totally different way ; giving not the actual facts of it, but the impression it made on his mind.

'And now, once for all, let it be clearly understood that an "impression on the mind" does not mean a piece of manufacture. The way in which most artists proceed to invent, as they call it, is this : they choose their subject, for the most part well, with a sufficient quantity of towns. mountains, ruined cottages, and other materials, to be generally interesting ; they then fix on some object for a principal light ; behind this put a dark cloud, or, in front of it, a dark piece of foreground ; then they repeat this light somewhere else in a less degree, and connect the two lights together by some intermediate ones. If they find any part of the foreground uninteresting, they put a group of figures into it ; if any part of the distance, they put something there from some other sketch ; and proceed to inferior detail in the same manner, taking care always to put white stones near black ones, and purple colours near yellow ones, and angular forms near round ones. All this being as simply a matter of recipe and practice as cookery ; like that, not by any means a thing easily done well, but still having no reference whatever to "impressions on the mind."

'But the artist who has real invention sets to work in a totally different way. First, he receives a true impression from the place itself, and takes care to keep hold of that as his chief good ; indeed, he needs no care in the matter, for the distinction of his mind from that of others consists in his instantly receiving such sensations strongly, and being unable to lose them ; and then he sets himself as free as possible to reproduce that impression on the mind of the spectator of his picture.

'Now, observe, this impression on the mind never results from the mere piece of scenery which can be included within the limits of the picture. It depends on the temper into which the mind has been brought, both by all the landscape round and by what has been seen previously in the course of the day ; so that no particular spot upon which the painter's glance may at any moment fall is then to him what, if seen by itself, it will be to the spectator far away ; nor is it what it would be even to that spectator if he had come to the reality through the steps which Nature has appointed to be the preparation for it, instead of seeing it isolated on an exhibition wall. For instance, on the descent of the St. Gothard, towards Italy, just after passing through the narrow gorge above Faido, the road emerges into a little breadth of valley, which is entirely filled by fallen stones and debris, partly disgorged by the Ticino as it leaps out of the narrower chasm, and partly brought down by winter avalanches from a loose and decomposing mass of mountain on the left. Beyond this first promontory is seen a considerably higher range, but not an imposing one, which rises above the village of Faido. The etching is a topographical outline of the scene, with the actual blocks of rock which happened to be lying in the bed of the Ticino at the spot from which I chose to draw it. The masses of loose debris (which, for any permanent purpose, I had no need to draw, as their arrangement changes at every flood) I have not drawn, but only those features of the landscape which happen to be of some continual importance : of which, note, first, that the little three-windowed building on the left is the remnant of a gallery built to protect the road, which once went on that side, from the avalanches and stones that come down the *couloir* in the rock above. It is only a ruin, the greater part having been, by said avalanches, swept away, and the old road, of which a remnant is also seen on the extreme left, abandoned, and carried now along the hill-side on the right, partly sustained on rough stone arches, and winding down, as seen in the sketch, to a weak wooden bridge, which enables it to recover its old track past the gallery. It seems formerly (but since the destruction of the gallery) to have gone about a mile farther down the river on the right bank, and then to have been carried across by a longer wooden bridge, of which only the two abutments are seen in the sketch, the rest having been swept away by the Ticino, and the new bridge erected near the spectator.

'There is nothing in this scene, taken in itself, particularly interesting or impressive. The mountains are not elevated or particularly fine in form, and the heaps of stones which encumber the Ticino present nothing notable to the ordinary eye ; but, in reality, the place is approached through one of the narrowest and most sublime ravines in the Alps, and after the traveller, during the early part of the day, has been familiarised with the aspect of the highest peaks of the Mount St. Gothard. Hence, it speaks quite another language to him from that in which it would address itself to an unprepared spectator ; the confused stones, which by themselves would be almost without any claim upon his thoughts, become exponents of the fury of the river by which he journeyed all day long ; the defile beyond, not in itself narrow or terrible, is regarded, nevertheless, with awe, because it is imagined to resemble the gorge that has just been traversed above, and, although no very elevated mountains immediately overhang it, the scene is felt to belong to, and arise in its essential characters out of, the strength of those mightier mountains in the unseen north.

'Any topographical delineation of the facts, therefore, must be wholly incapable of arousing in the mind of the beholder those sensations which would be caused by the facts themselves, seen in their natural relations to others ; and the aim of the great inventive landscape painter must be to give the far higher and deeper truth of mental vision, rather than that of the physical facts, and to reach a representation which, though it may be totally useless to engineers or geographers, and, when tried by rule and measure, totally unlike the place, shall yet be capable of producing on the far-away beholder's mind precisely the impression which the reality would have produced, and putting his heart into the same state in which it would have been had he verily descended into the valley of Airlo.

Now, observe, if in his attempt to do this the artist does not understand the sacredness of the truth of *impression*, and supposes that, once quitting hold of his first thought, he may, by philosophy, compose something prettier than he saw, and mightier than he felt, it is all over with him. Every such attempt at composition will be utterly abortive, and end in something neither true nor fanciful—something geographically useless and intellectually absurd. But if, holding fast his first thought, he finds other ideas insensibly gathering to it, and, whether he will or not, modifying it into something which is not so much the image of the place itself as the spirit of the place, let him yield to such fancies and follow them wherever they lead. For, though error on this side is very rare among us in these days, it is possible to check these finer thoughts by mathematical accuracies, so as materially to impair the imaginative faculty. I shall be able to explain this better after we have traced the actual operation of Turner's mind on the scene under discussion.

'Turner was always, from his youth, fond of stones (we shall see presently why). Whether large or small, loose or imbedded, hewn into cubes or moulded into boulders, he loved them as much as William Hunt loved pine-apples and plums ; so that this great litter of fallen stones, which to anyone else would have been simply disagreeable, was to Turner much the same as if the whole valley had been filled with plums and pine-apples, aud delighted him exceedingly, much more than even the gorge of Dazio Grande just above. But that gorge had its effect upon him also, and was still not well out of his head when the diligence stopped at the bottom of the hill, just at that turn of the road on the right of the bridge, which favourable opportunity Turner seized to make what he called a ' memorandum' of the place, composed of a few pencil scratches on a bit of thin paper, that would roll up with others of the sort and go into his pocket afterwards. These pencil scratches he put a few blots of colour upon (I suppose at Bellinzona the same evening, certainly not upon the spot) and showed me this blotted sketch when he came home. I asked him to make me a drawing of it, which he did, and casually told me afterwards (a rare thing for him to do) that he liked the drawing he had made. Of this drawing I have etched a reduced outline, in which the whole place is altered in scale, and brought up to the general majesty of the higher forms of the Alps. In my topographical

sketch there are a few trees rooted in the rock on this side of
the gallery, showing by comparison that it is not above four or
five hundred feet high. These trees Turner cuts away, and
gives the rock a height of about a thousand feet, so as to imply
more power and danger in the avalanche coming down the
couloir.

'Next, he raises, in a still greater degree, all the mountains
beyond, putting three or four ranges instead of one, but uniting
them into a single mossy bank at their base, which he makes
overhang the valley, and thus reduces it nearly to such a chasm
as that which he had just passed through above, so as to unite
the expression of this ravine with that of the stony valley.
The few trees in the hollow of the glen he feels to be contrary
in spirit to the stones, and fells them as he did the others; so
also he feels the bridge in the foreground by its slenderness to
contradict the aspect of violence in the torrent. He thinks the
torrent and avalanches should have it all their own way here-
abouts ; so he strikes down the nearer bridge, and restores the
one further off, where the force of the stream may be supposed
less. Next, the bit of road on the right, above the bank, is not
built on a wall, nor on arches high enough to give the idea of
an Alpine road in general; so he makes the arches taller, and
the bank steeper, introducing, as we shall see presently, a
reminiscence from the upper part of the pass.

'I say he *thinks* this, and *introduces* that; but, strictly speaking, he does not think at all. If he thought, he would instantly go wrong; it is only the clumsy and uninventive artist
who thinks. All these changes come into his head involuntarily—an entirely imperative dream, crying, "Thus it must
be."'

Of Turner's distance we read:—

'To so singular an extent will the form of things come out
gradually through the mist, as you look long at Turner's effects
of this kind, that many of his admirers have thought that he
painted the whole scene first, with all its details, and then
threw the mist over it: but it is not so, and it cannot be done
so. All efforts to copy Turner on such a plan will end in total
discomfiture. The misty effect is, indeed, partly given by

breathing one colour over another; but the forms of objects are not thus rendered indistinct; if they were, the picture would look as if it had been rubbed over with blue paint, accidentally, after it was finished, and every spectator would wish to clear off the upper colour and see what was underneath. The misty appearance is given by resolvedly confusing, altering, or denying the form at the moment of painting it; and the virtue of the work is in the painter's having perfectly clear and sharp conception of all that he chooses to confuse, alter, or deny; so that his very confusion becomes suggestive, his alteration decorative, and his denial affirmative. And it is because there is an idea with, and in—not under—every touch, that we find the objects rising into existence as we gaze.'

On the subject of Turner's 'Mystery,' the designed indistinctness of detail, Mr. Ruskin says:—

'He shows you the spots on trout on a rock in a foreground, but you cannot count them ; the painter never intended you should. Try to draw a piece of patterned muslin or lace (of which you do not know the pattern) a little way off, and rather in the shade; and be sure you get all the grace and *look* of the pattern without going a step nearer to see what it is. Then try to draw a bank of grass with all its blades, or a bush with all its leaves, and you will soon begin to understand under what a universal law of obscurity we live, and perceive that all *distinct* drawing must be *bad* drawing, and that nothing can be right till it is unintelligible.'

Mr. Ruskin does not, I am now convinced, in the least exaggerate the subtleties of Turner's imagination. In the picture of the 'Mewstone' there were some strange weird clouds introduced, which had a demoniacal air about them; insomuch that Mr. Stokes was struck by them, and asked Turner if he did not mean them for the demons and angels of the storm. Turner confessed the intention. 'In the same way,' writes Mr. Ruskin, 'the blasted trunk on the left, in Turner's drawing of the spot where Harold fell at the battle of Hastings, takes, where its boughs first separate, the shape of the head of an arrow. This, which is mere fancy in itself, is imagination, as it supposes in the spectator an excited condition of feeling dependent on the history of the spot.'

Of Turner's torrents we are thus instructed :—

'We see, therefore, why Turner seizes on these curved lines of the torrent, not only as being among the most beautiful forms of nature, but because they are an instant expression of the utmost power and velocity, and tell us how the torrent has been flowing before we see it. For the leap and splash might be seen in the sudden freakishness of a quiet stream, or the fall of a rivulet over a mill-dam ; but the undulating line is the attribute of the mountain-torrent, whose fall and fury have made the valleys echo for miles ; and thus, the moment we see one of its curves over a stone in the foreground, we know it has come far and fiercely. And in the drawing we have been speaking of, the "Lower Fall of the Tees," in the foreground of the "Killiecrankie," and "Rhymer's Glen," and of the "St. Maurice" in Rogers' "Italy," we shall find the most exquisite instances of the use of such lines; but the most perfect of all is the "Llanthony Abbey," which may be considered as the standard of torrent drawing.'

Turner's Alps are eminently true in structure, and might have been drawn by a geologist—the sharp aiguille, the plank-like slab, the fissures, the ridges, he knew them all. For hills, the 'Caudebec,' in the 'Rivers of France,' is a fine example. Honfleur, and the scene between Clairmont and Mauves, are also fine examples of grand and simple treatment. The latter shows the furrowing of hills by descending water. You can traverse them mile after mile, such endless detail is there, and yet such breadth ; never an inch of unmeaning surface, be they the wooded hills and undulating moors of North England, the rolling surges of Southern England park and forest, the soft vine-clad ranges of the French côteaux, casting shadows on silver leagues of glancing rivers, or the olive-whitened promontories of Alp and Apennine.

Of Turner's mountains Mr. Ruskin observes :—

'But look at the mass of mountain on the right in Turner's "Daphne hunting with Leucippus." It is simple, broad, and united as one surge of a swelling sea; it rises in an unbroken line along the valley, and lifts its promontories with an equal slope. But it contains in its body ten thousand hills. There is not a quarter of an inch of its surface without its suggestion of increasing distance and individual form. First, on the right, you have a range of tower-like precipices, the clinging wood climbing along their ledges and cresting their summits, white waterfalls gleaming through its leaves; not, as in Claude's scientific ideals, poured in vast torrents over the top, and carefully keeping all the way down on the most projecting parts of the sides; but stealing down, traced from point to point, through shadow after shadow, by their evanescent foam and flashing light—here a wreath and there a ray—through the deep chasms and hollow ravines, out of which rise the soft, rounded slopes of mightier mountain, surge beyond surge, immense and numberless, of delicate and gradual curve, accumulating in the sky until their garment of forest is exchanged for the shadowy fold of slumberous morning cloud, above which the utmost silver peak shines islanded and alone. Put what mountain painting you will beside this of any other artist, and its heights will look like molehills in comparison, because it will not have the unity and the multiplicity which are in Nature, and, with Turner, the signs of size.'

Again let us attend to Mr. Ruskin's beautiful illustration of Turner's 'Mystery' :—

'There is yet not one atom in its whole extent and mass which does not suggest more than it represents; nor does it suggest vaguely, but in such a manner as to prove that the conception of each individual inch of that distance is absolutely clear and complete in the master's mind, a separate picture fully worked out; but yet, clearly and fully as the idea is formed, just so much of it is given and no more, as Nature would have allowed us to feel or see; just so much as would enable a spectator of experience and knowledge to understand almost every minute fragment of separate detail, but appears to the unpractised and careless eye just what a distance of Nature's own would appear, an unintelligible mass. Perhaps the truth of this system of drawing is better to be understood by observing the distant character of rich architecture than of any other object. Go to the top of Highgate Hill on a clear summer morning at five o'clock, and look at Westminster Abbey; you

will receive an impression of a building enriched with multitudi‑
nous vertical lines. Try to distinguish one of these lines all the
way down from the one next to it ; you cannot. Try to count
them ; you cannot. Try to make out the beginning or end of
any one of them ; you cannot. Look at it generally, and it is
all symmetry and arrangement ; look at it in its parts, and it is
all inextricable confusion. Am I not at this moment describing
a piece of Turner's drawing with the same words by which I
describe Nature ? '

Turner used to say that he found moonlights very difficult.
Petter, Barrett, and Louthenbourgh had tired the public of
them. The finest I know in his works is the ' Villa Madonna'
in Rogers' ' Italy.' His early picture of moonlight at Millbank
is very opaque, and is more like lamplight. It is imitative of a
Dutch effect.

All Turner's works betray a truly Wordsworthian recognition
of detail and a love of common things. His sympathy is with
the life he sees and shares in. Under the ruined Northumbrian
castle he shows you the steamer ; and in the foreground of the
scene, where the avalanche falls and the inundation rises, he
places the homely red bundle and the gridiron. He was too
great a man to affect archaisms. ' The utmost that Turner
ever allows in his foregrounds, ' says Mr. Ruskin, ' is a water-lily
or two, a cluster of heath or foxglove, a thistle sometimes, a
violet or daisy, or a bindweed bell, just enough to lead the eye
into the understanding of the rich mystery of his more distant
leafage.' But, while thus expressing my profound admiration
of the genius of Turner, I should not be a lover of truth were
I to conceal my opinion of his faults. In many respects he
was born at an unfortunate period. At first he was compelled
to be imitative in order to sell. He was now trying to see
Nature like Vandervelde—now to turn English hills into Pous‑
sin's mountains—now to lap his canvas in Cuyp's sunshine ;
sometimes because the manner of these painters was more like
Nature than he could yet reach, but more often because buyers
would not look at any picture that was not in the Vandervelde
or Claude manner. Later he was possessed of a baser spirit,
that of rivalry ; not the wish to paint like Claude, because
Claude's manner sold, or because Claude often obtained a

serenity of air that was pure and exquisite, but because he was determined to show that he could paint better than Claude, with more grandeur and more thought.

Turner, born in a Claude atmosphere, nursed at the foot of a Vandervelde, and nurtured on the poetical food of Thomson and Akenside, lived long enough to see a new and daring, sect of reformers arise in Art—men whose creed emerged from the Gothic reaction, and was the advancement of the old Wordsworthian lines into new regions of convention. Indirectly they were disciples of Tennyson and assailants of all academic and eclectic precedent. They arose to renovate Art by a series of great experiments not altogether untinged with rashness, obstinacy, arrogance, pedantry, affectation, and absurdity. They talked of Dante and the thirteenth century, of Giotto, Cimabue, and Fra Angelico; they resolved to paint no more effete subjects, but to read and think for themselves. They were all young men, of course; and they laughed bitterly at the old conservatives, at the Don Quixote painters and the conventional landscape-painters, at the sham idealists and the inflated historical painters. They were religionists, these young men, and really in earnest; but quaint, well read, and fond of chivalry and the Italian poets.

Nor can I (as I am making a clean breast of it) conceal the fact that, whether from carelessness, or fatigue, or experiment, Turner's colour was often weak, and sometimes downright bad. In his Yorkshire drawings his blue distances (perhaps faded often have a disagreeable green tinge about them. In some of the England series there is a violent foxy tone, very hot and oppressive; and the Roman oil pictures not seldom betray an excess of mustardy yellow, which might have seemed beautiful at the time, but is now quite out of tone. Vermilion shadows in flesh I have not a word to say for; nor do I like the opacity of his Vandervelde period more than I do the crude staring whites of the architecture in some of his later Venetian pictures.

'Turner is exceedingly unequal,' says Mr. Ruskin; 'most frequently in elaborate compositions from redundant quantity. Sometimes from over-care, as very signally in a large and most laboured drawing of "Bamborough Castle." Sometimes his eye for colour seems to fail, as in " Rome from the Forum," "Cicero's Villa," and " Building of Carthage." Sometimes criminally, from taking licences, or indulging in conventionalities. His dry sea that does not wet the boat in one of his storms is specially reprehensible, and so is the occasional foxy colour, as in his drawing of "Oxford" in Mr. Munro's collection. His "Blenheim" is an almost unique instance of failure in composition, as the Duke's house is the last thing the eye observes. There is sometimes, too, a livid purple about his colour which is far from pleasing.'

Mr. Ruskin observes, when we come to treat of the sublime :—

' I shall only point to an unfortunate instance of inexcusable and effectless exaggeration in the distance of Turner's vignette to Milton, " The Temptation on the Mountain," and desire the reader to compare it with legitimate exaggeration in his vignette to the second part of " Jacqueline," in Rogers' poems.'

Too much, I incline to believe, is made by Mr. Ruskin of Turner's dragon in the ' Garden of the Hesperides.' The jaws are thin and weak, and would break off when they took a bite at a stone ; and the flabby claws do not hold on with any tenacity.

Of the faultiness in Turner's second period Mr. Ruskin affirms :—

' He saw there were more clouds in any sky than ever had been painted, more trees in every forest, more crags on every hill-side ; and he set himself with all his strength to proclaim this great fact of quantity in the universe.

' Now, so long as he introduced all these three changes in an instructive and unintruding way, his work was noble ; but the moment he tried to idealise, and introduce his principles for the sake of display, they led him into depths of error proportioned exactly to the extent of effort. His painting, at this period, of an English town or a Welsh hill was magnificent and faultless ; but all his idealism, mythology, romance, and composition in general were more or less wrong. He erred through all, and by reason of all, his great discoveries. He erred in colour, because, not content with discerning the brilliancy of Nature, he tried to enhance that brilliancy by every species of colour accessory, until colour was killed by colour, and the blue skies and snowy mountains, which would have been lovely by themselves, were confused and vulgarised by the blue dresses and white complexions of the foreground figures. He erred in refinement, because, not content with the natural tenderness of tender things, he strove to idealise even strong things into tenderness, until his architecture became transparent and his ground ghostly ; and he erred finally and chiefly in quantity.'

I have tried carefully, yet without malice, to show that Turner was not immaculate; that his genius was not exhaustive of all the capacities of Art; and that, with all his knowledge and industry, a genius may still arise to combine great truth and quantity with better drawing of the figure, less classic convention, and a more exact delineation of Nature. His faults in linear perspective were not unfrequent, although he had made that science his special study ; his colour was subject to aberrations; and in oil painting his work too often was experimental and perishable. Through his too frequent use of dangerous vegetable colours and uncertain vehicles, his skies darken and crack, and his distemper pictures wash out. Indeed, I sometimes fear that in time we shall have, after all, to turn to the wonderful ' Liber ' as the great monument of his genius.

It must not be thought that Turner always drew such distorted doll-figures as those in the ' Phryne,' the ' Exile,' and others. In the drawings of his best period the figures, though often mere specks, generally are firmly, expressively, and intelligently drawn ; not seldom with admirable grace and truth. In the ' Liber ' they are generally beautiful in respect of line and composition ; and the life-studies in his sketch-books are not unworthy of a professional figure-painter. The ' Venus and Adonis ' in Mr. Munro's gallery is ostentatiously well drawn. In his best moments no one knew better than Turner how to express momentary action in a figure. The illustrations to Scott contain figures worthy of any landscape painter, and infinitely superior to the puerile inanities of Claude, which are so feeble and so unreal. In his later pictures Turner's sense of form became utterly weakened, partly, perhaps, through decrease of mental power, but in a larger degree by his sensuous sacrifice of every other quality to that of colour.

The fatal conventionalisms of an artificial and past age had too deep a hold on Turner's mind. The dreams of a false and obscene mythology which he could not understand, and with which the great world never did and never again will sympathise, excited his imagination. He could not really appreciate our national architecture; and the Gothic ruins which he spent half his life in drawing never touched his heart as they did Scott's and Wordsworth's. Moreover, he had a fatal belief in the necessity of rearranging Nature. Few of his later works are faithful representations of the places they pretend to describe. He was always remaking the world according to some ideal theory of his own.

On the whole, I think Turner was better at water-colour painting than at oil. He never acquired the built-up solidity of Titian's handling, or the vigour and dash of Velasquez. To the last he was rather a 'niggler' in oil; often brown and heavy, and, oftener still, flimsy and fantastic in execution, confounding the shadow and the substance, heightening the colour, and exaggerating the reflections and subtleties of Nature. I am sure that, with the exception of the 'Polyphemus' and the 'Téméraire,' his water-colour drawings are more unapproachable than his oil; more aërial, more tender, more magical. I am not sure indeed if his 'Liber Studiorum,' for variety, grasp, versatility, and handling, is not, both in the etchings and in the unfinished states, more wonderful than anything else he did.

Of his later works I am no defender. They are dreams, challenges, theories, experiments, and absurdities. The figures are generally contemptible, and the pyrotechnic colour rises sometimes almost to insanity, and occasionally sinks into imbecility. With the eye dim and the sense of form lost, the outlines are gone, and the sentiment only remains. Certainly they are what no one else could achieve, but then no one wishes to achieve them. As a German writer has clearly shown, Turner latterly became colour-blind.

Were I asked to try to describe in as few words as possible the special characteristics of Turner's genius, I should eulogise neither the versatility that led him from poor English hedgers and ditchers to Jason on the war-trail and Ulysses triumphing at the sunrise, nor the industry that produced twenty thousand sketches, but rather the wide sympathy that made him take as great an interest in a plain Scottish peatbog as in the most gorgeous visions of modern Italy, or in the wildest depths of the Alps, in the aërial perspective of which he revels in the ' Modern Italy,' the ' Bay of Baiæ,' and the ' Crossing of the Brook;' and the extraordinary ' multitude ' and quantity observable in his ' Grenoble ' in the ' Liber,' and other such efforts. Turner was the first who ventured to p!ace twenty miles of landscape within the four walls of a frame. He was the first to attempt all natural phenomena, the first to give us storm and sunshine; in fact, to widen on all sides the hitherto narrow bounds of landscape painting.

All through my book I have felt great difficulty in deciding how to make use of Mr. Ruskin's beautiful, profound, and generally true criticisms of Turner's genius. I felt that, if I were too heedlessly to call him in as an auxiliary, I should certainly be overwhelmed by my ally, as the Britons were by the Saxons they rashly summoned to their support; and yet how could I reject the assistance of one whose name has become indissolubly bound up with that of Turner ? It was not possible for me to dispense with his aid. I have therefore used his books throughout, but only when I was obliged. I have quoted him with all due brevity, and, where I could, have even condensed his words. I have also gathered together into one chapter as many as possible of his more valuable generalisations. The chief subject upon which I regret to differ from him is that of Turner's constant and, as I hope, indefensible habit of altering the places he drew, so that they are seldom topographically correct; and yet the ingenious defence of his advocate, I must own, makes one pause in his censure.

In writing this biography, I have felt the sensations that must be experienced by the restorer of a fine old Gothic church when he is peeling the moss from the marred face of some calm stone figure. I have concealed no faults, because I love truth. I have detracted from no virtues, because I respect the memory of Turner. I know that I shall offend his fanatic eulogists by declaring that I do not like the theoretical, obscure, and sketchy pictures of his old age; and his more discriminating admirers by confessing that I estimate him more highly as a water-colour painter than as an oil-painter, and by showing that he too often exaggerated and revised Nature. His enemies will be annoyed that I have not shown him pure soot; his older friends that I have not clothed him in shining silver. I have neither coloured his virtues nor concealed his vices. Miserably insufficient as I know my book to be, I can boldly affirm that it is entirely truthful ; and therefore it may live.

LINES ON THE TURNER STATUE FOR ST. PAUL'S.

BY R. J. LANE, ESQ., A.E.R.A.

'In habit as he lived' and wrought,
And listened as sweet Nature taught,
Turner in simple guise
Upon a rock observant stands;
He pauses as the scene expands
In splendour to his eyes;
Then glancing o'er the land, the sea,
Sets his creative fancy free.

And as the sculptor's lofty reach
Aspires in metaphor to teach,
Thus, in immortal stone,
MacDowell's ready wit suggests
The rock on which great Turner rests
Unshackled and alone.

APPENDIX.

A COMPLETE CATALOGUE OF ALL TURNER'S ENGRAVED WORKS,

FROM THE PAPERS OF THE LATE MR. STOKES, OF GRAY'S INN, WHO DEVOTED MANY YEARS TO ITS COMPILATION; KINDLY COMMUNICATED TO ME BY MR. GRIFFITH, OF NORWOOD, ONE OF TURNER'S EXECUTORS.

Summary of Mr. Stokes's Catalogue.

<table>
<tr><td>9 Almanacs, Oxford.</td><td>40 Illustrations to Scott's Prose, Cadell.</td></tr>
<tr><td>1 Anniversary.</td><td>3 Illustrations, Tilt, Poems. •</td></tr>
<tr><td>61 Annual Tour, 1833, 4, 5.</td><td>15 Itinerant (see Copper-plate Mag.).</td></tr>
<tr><td>7 Britannia Depicta.</td><td>18 Italy, Hakewell.</td></tr>
<tr><td>3 Cassiobury.</td><td>15 Keepsake.</td></tr>
<tr><td>15 Copper-plate Mag. Itinerant.</td><td>5 Leodis and Elmete.</td></tr>
<tr><td>1 Craven, Antiquities of.</td><td>2 Lincoln, Select Views in.</td></tr>
<tr><td>3 Durham, Surtees'.</td><td>3 Mawman's Tour.</td></tr>
<tr><td>2 Dunster Castle.</td><td>6 Poets of England.</td></tr>
<tr><td>96 England and Wales.</td><td>Pocket Books.</td></tr>
<tr><td>5 Holloway, published by.</td><td>17 Rivers of England.</td></tr>
<tr><td>7 Gallery of British Engravers.</td><td>61 Rivers of France, Annual Tour, 1833, 4, 5.</td></tr>
<tr><td>7 Himalaya, Views in the.</td><td>20 Richmondshire.</td></tr>
<tr><td>26 Illustrations to the Bible.</td><td>13 Scotland, Provincial Antiquities.</td></tr>
<tr><td>9 ,, Finden, Lord Byron.</td><td>40 Southern Coast of England.</td></tr>
<tr><td>17 ,, Murray.</td><td>5 Sussex.</td></tr>
<tr><td>20 ,, Campbell.</td><td>8 Whalley, Parish of.</td></tr>
<tr><td>4 ,, Epicurean.</td><td>3 Wight, Isle of.</td></tr>
<tr><td>7 ,, Milton.</td><td>22 Yorkshire in Richmondshire.</td></tr>
<tr><td>75 ,, Rogers' Italy.</td><td>1 Faith of Perrin, Welch Pil. Prog.</td></tr>
<tr><td>23 ,, Poems.</td><td>Mezzotintos.</td></tr>
<tr><td>24 ,, Cadell, 1834, Scott's Poems.</td><td>Subscription Plates.</td></tr>
<tr><td>21 Plates of Liber Studiorum.</td><td>&c. &c.</td></tr>
<tr><td>20 Unpublished do.</td><td></td></tr>
</table>

1794.

Rochester.........Walker and Storer	*Itinerant, Walker's Cop.-pl. Mag.*, May 1..............	6½	4¼
Chepstow ....,,Storer	Do. Nov. 1	6¼	4¼

1795.

Nottingham.*	J. Walker	*Itinerant*, Feb. 28	$6\frac{1}{2}$	$4\frac{1}{4}$
Bridgenorth	Do.	Do. Aug. 1	$6\frac{5}{8}$	$4\frac{1}{4}$
Matlock	J. Widnell	Do. Oct. 1	$6\frac{1}{2}$	$4\frac{1}{4}$
Birmingham	Storer	Do. Nov. 2	$6\frac{1}{2}$	$4\frac{1}{4}$
The Tower of London	T. Tagg	*Pocket Magazine*, Jan. 1	$4\frac{5}{8}$	$2\frac{5}{8}$
Cambridge	Do.	Do. June 1	$4\frac{5}{8}$	$2\frac{5}{8}$
Worcester	Rothwell	(?) Do. (Harrison&Co.)Aug. 1	$4\frac{5}{8}$	$2\frac{5}{8}$
Guildford	Do.	(?) Do. Oct. 1	$4\frac{5}{8}$	$2\frac{5}{8}$

1796.

Chester	J. Walker	*Itinerant*, Jan. 1	$6\frac{5}{8}$	$4\frac{3}{4}$
Peterborough	Do.	Do. May 1	$6\frac{5}{8}$	$4\frac{3}{4}$
Neath, 1796 or 5	G. Murray	*Lady's Pocket Magazine*, Oct. 1	$4\frac{5}{8}$	$2\frac{5}{8}$
Tunbridge (?)		Do.		

Bath.	Bristol.	Wallingford.
Staines.	Northampton.	Windsor.

1797.

Westminster Bridge	J. Walker	*Itinerant*, Aug. 1	$6\frac{5}{8}$	$4\frac{3}{8}$
Ely	Do.	Do. March 1	$6\frac{3}{4}$	$4\frac{1}{4}$
Flint, from Park Gate	Do.	Do. Aug. 1	$6\frac{1}{2}$	$4\frac{1}{4}$
Hampton Court, Herefordsh.	Do.	Do. Sept. 1	$6\frac{5}{8}$	$4\frac{1}{4}$
Grantham Church, Lincolnshire (from a sketch by Schnebbelie) B. Howlett		*Views in the Co. of Lincoln*,† March 1	7	$5\frac{1}{4}$

1798.

Sheffield	J. Walker	*Itinerant*, Aug. 1	$6\frac{1}{2}$	$4\frac{3}{4}$
Wakefield	Do.	Do. Oct. 1		

1799

Christ Church, from the Meadows J. Basire	*Oxford Almanac*	$17\frac{1}{2}$	$12\frac{1}{2}$
Durham (?)			

1800.

Fonthill House, Wilts	W. Angus	*Angus' Seats*	$7\frac{3}{8}$	$5\frac{1}{4}$
Ancient Crosses at Whalley.	J. Basire	*Whitaker's 'Parish of Whalley.'*		
Farnley	Do.	Do. Plate 5.		
Remains of Whalley Abbey.	Do.	Do. Plate 6.		
Cloisters of do	Do.	Do. Plate 7.		
Remains of do	Do.	Do. Plate 8.		
Clitheroe, fr. EadsfordBridge.	Do.	Do. Plate 11.		
Browsholme	Do.	Do. Plate 12.	$10\frac{1}{8}$	$6\frac{9}{5}$
Stonyhurst	Do.			
The Sherbourne Chapel in Milton Church	J. Basire			
Dunster Castle, Somersetshire, North-east View	S. Rawle	May 1	$14\frac{5}{8}$	$9\frac{1}{4}$
Do. South-east View	Do.	May 1	$14\frac{1}{2}$	$9\frac{1}{4}$

* Republished from the same copper retouched (*see* Bust in front), in 'Gentleman's Magazine,' 1821.

† Published by W. Miller, Old Bond Street; came out in Nos., 1797-1801.

1801.

Hampton Court, Herefordshire. J. Storer	*Beauties of England and Wales**	6	3⅞
Sleaford Church, Lincolnshire. B. Howlett	*Select Views in the Co. of Lincoln.*		
Chapel and Hall of Oriel College. J. Basire	*Oxford Almanac*	17½	12½

1802.

Inside View of the East End of Merton College .... J. Basire	*Oxford Almanac*	17½	12½

1803.

Wickham, from the Marlow Road. W. Byrne	*Britannia Depicta*............	8½	5⅞
Eton, from the Slough Road. Do.	Do.............................	8½	6

1804.

Worcester College &c.......J. Basire	*Oxford Almanac*	17½	12⅝
Windsor, from the Forest, Berks. J. Greig	*Views of London and its Environs*....................	7¼	5½

1805.

Inverary. ....J. Heath	*Mawman's Tour.*		
Loch Lomond................... Do.	Do.		
Patterdale	Do.		
Abingdon, from the Thames. W. Byrne	*Britannia Depicta.*		
Newbury, from Speen Hill. Do.	Do.		
Donnington Castle...W. & L. Byrne	Do.		
Inside of Brasenose College, Quadrangle .... J. Basire	*Oxford Almanac*	17¾	12½

1806.

Exeter College, All Saints' Church, from the Turl .... J. Basire	*Oxford Almanac*	17¾	12¾

1807.

Inside View of the Hall of Christ Church....................J. Basire	*Oxford Almanac*	17¼	13
Liber Studiorum, No 1...C. Turner			

1808.

Oxford, from the South side of Heddington Hill...............J. Basire	*Oxford Almanac*	17⅝	12⅝
Liber Studiorum, Nos. 2 and 3.			

1809.

Liber Studiorum, No. 4.

1810.

Part of Chester Castle ...W. Byrne	*Britannia Depicta*............	8½	6
Distant View of Chester ... Do.	Do......................	8½	6

1811.

View of the Cathedral of Christ Church ....J. Basire	*Oxford Almanac*	17¾	12¼
Liber Studiorum, Nos. 5, 6, and 7.			

* The only plate from Turner in the work.

1812.

South Transept of Fountains Abbey. *Whitaker's History and Antiquities*
J. Basire   *of Craven in the County of York.*
Liber Studiorum, Nos. 8, 9, and 10.

Oxford Almanacs.

1799	Christ Church, from the Meadows	J. Basire.
1801	Chapel and Hall of Oriel College.........................	Do.
1802	Inside View of the East End of Merton College Chapel	Do.
1804	Worcester College &c.	Do.
1805	Inside of Brasenose College, Quadrangle...............	Do.
1806	Exeter College, All Saints' Church from the Turl ...	Do.
1807	Inside View of the Hall of Christ Church	Do.
1808	Oxford from the South Side of Heddington Hill ...	Do.
1811	Cathedral of Christ Church, and part of Corpus Christi College	Do.

Isle of Wight, by J. Landseer.

Orchard Bay	J. Landseer.
Shanklin Bay...	Do.
Freshwater Bay...	Do.

1	Cassiobury, Herts—Seat of the Earl of Essex	Howell & Son.
1	The Great Cloister at Cassiobury, Herts	Aquatint, Hill
2	The West Front of Cassiobury	Do.
3	View from the N.W.	Do.

Engravings from Leodis and Elmete.

Leodis and Elmete; or an Attempt to Illustrate the Districts described
in those works by Bede, and supposed to embrace the lower portions
of the Airedale and Wharfdale, together with the entire Vale of Calder,
in the County of York. By Thomas Durham Whitaker, LL.D.,
Vicar of Whalley, and Rector of Heysham, in Lancashire. Printed
by T. Davison, London, for Robinson, Son, and Holdsworth, Leeds.

View of Gledhow......................................	G. Cooke, p. 131.
View of Harewood House	J. Scott, p. 168.
Flower Garden Porch at Farnley	Vig. p. 192.
Gateway to the Flower Garden at Farnley.	
Bay Window in the Flower Garden at Farnley.	

Engravings from Drawings by Turner in Whitaker's 'History of Richmondshire.' *2 vols. folio. Longman.* 1823.

Vol.				
I. p.	83	Richmond	Mar. 3, 1819	W. R. Smith.
,,	94	Richmond Castle and Town	June 6, 1820	J. Archer.
,,	113	St. Agatha's Abbey	Feb. 14, 1822	J. Le Keux.
,,	115	Aste Hall	Aug. 28, 1821	J. Scott.
,,	142	High Tore......................	Sept. 12, 1821	J. Landseer.
,,	152	Eggleston Abbey	Dec. 1822	T. Higham.
,,	184	Junction of the Greta and the Tees...................	Aug. 2, 1819	John Pye.
,,	194	Brignols Church	Oct. 25, 1821	S. Rawle.
,,	197	Wycliffe	Mar. 1, 1823	John Pye.
,,	222	Marrick Abbey, Swaledale	Dec. 1822	J. C. Varrall.

Vol. I. p. 393 Aysgarth Force .... June 1, 1820   J. Scott.
  ,,   412 Simmer Lake .... Oct. 25, 1822   H. Le Keux.
  ,,   413 Moss Dale Fall .... Aug. 22, 1822   G. Middiman.
  ,,   Hardraw Fall .... Oct. 1, 1818   John Pye.
Vol. II. p. 204 Crook of Lune .... Aug. 10, 1821   J. Archer.
  ,,   250 Ingleborough................. Jan. 2, 1822   C. Heath.
  ,,   263 Hornby Castle .... June, 1822   W. Radclyffe.
  ,,   277 Kirby Lonsdale Churchyard Jan. 25, 1821   C. Heath.
  ,,   317 Heysham and Cumberland } Aug. 22, 1822   W. R. Smith
            Mounts .... }
  ,,   343 Weathercote Cave............ Oct. 30, 1821   G. Middiman.

Additional in Yorkshire.

Wentworth House............ ——, 1816,   G. Cooke.
Gillside .... —— ——   S. Rawle.

Engravings from Turner in Cooke's ' Southern Coast.' Published in Nos., 4to, 12s. 6d. per No. ; Imperial 4to, Proofs, 18s.

	No.			
1814	1	St. Michael's Mount ....Date on plate	Jan. 1	1814
		Poole		
	2	Land's End	Mar. 1	1814
		Weymouth		
	3	Lulworth Cave..................................	June 1	
	4	Corfe Castle	Nov. 1	
1815	5	Lyme Regis	Do.	
		Dartmouth	June 1	1815
		Teignmouth	Do.	do.
1816	6	Falmouth	Mar.	1816
		Mewstone	Feb. 1	Do.
	7	Plymouth Dock, from Mount Edgecumbe	Oct. 1	Do.
1817	8	Plymouth, with Mount Batten	May 1	1817
		Pendennis Castle................................	Do.	do.
		Bow-and-Arrow Castle, Portland..................		
		Bexhill, Martello Tower (Lib. Stud.)		
1818	9	East and West Looe	July 1	1818
		Ilfracombe	Do.	do.
		Tintagel	Do.	do.
1820	10	Watchet	April 1	1820
		Bridport	Do.	do.
		Fowey ....Date on plate	April 1	1820
1821	11	Lulworth Castle	Jan. 1	1821
		Torbay from Brixham.............................	Do.	do.
		Minehead	Do.	do.
1824	12	Margate	Feb.	1824
		Rye	March	
		Clovelly	Do.	do.
	13	Hythe	Dec.	
		Ramsgate.......................................		
		St. Mawes	Sept.	
1825	14	Brighton	Sept. 1	1825
		Bocastle	Mar. 10	
		Combe Martin...................................	Jan. 1	

	No.			
1826	15	Portsmouth	Feb. 15	
		Folkestone	Feb. 24	1826
		Deal	April 1	
		Dover, from Shakspeare's Cliff	May 6	
		Whitstable	May 8	Do.
		Mount Edgecumbe	April 13	

Turner's 'England and Wales,' 1827–1838.

No.
3 Aldborough ...... E. Goodall.
9 Alnwick .... J. Willmore.
18 Arundel Castle and Town
            T. Jeavons.
14 Ashby de la Zouche
            W. Radclyffe.
3 Barnard Castle ...... R. Wallis.
21 Beaumaris ...... W. R. Smith.
12 Bedford......... J. T. Willmore.
16 Blenheim House W. Radclyffe.
1 Bolton Priory......... R. Wallis.
19 Boston .... T. Jeavons.
15 Brentburn Priory J. C. Varrall.
4 Buckfastleigh Abbey R. Wallis.
19 Caernarvon Castle W. Radclyffe.
17 Carew Castle......... W. Miller.
8 Carisbrook Castle C. Westwood.
18 Christ Church College, Oxford
            J. Redway.
14 Chatham .... W. Miller.
2 Colchester .... R. Wallis.
17 Coventry .... S. Fisher.
23 Crickheith Castle ... S. Fisher.
8 Cowes.................. R. Wallis.
1 Dartmouth Cove W. R. Smith.
8 Devonport Dockyard T. Jeavons.
4 Dover Straits......... W. Miller.
19 Dudley ....R. Wallis.
23 Durham Cathedral ...W. Miller.
8 Dunstanboro' Castle
            R. Brandard.
16 Ely Cathedral ...... T. Higham.
12 Eton College ... W. Radclyffe.
6 Exeter .... T. Jeavons.
21 Flint Castle...... J. H. Heenor.
11 Folkestone ...... J. Horsburgh.
5 Entrance to Fowey Harbour
            W. R. Smith.
11 Gosport .... R. Brandard.
21 Harlech Castle... W. R. Smith.
7 Hampton Court Palace.
            C. Westwood.
9 Holy Island ... W. Tombleson.
15 Kenilworth Castle... T. Jeavons.

No.
22 Keswick Lake ... W. Radclyffe.
22 Kidwelby Castle ... T. Jeavons.
6 Kilgarren Castle J. T. Wilmore.
5 Knaresborough...... T. Jeavons.
1 Lancaster .... R. Wallis.
16 Langhorne Castle
            J. Horsburgh.
2 Launceston ...... J. C. Varrall.
18 Llanberris Lake J. T. Wilmore.
22 Llangollen...... Do.
20 Llanthony Abbey Do.
20 Longship's Lighthouse
            W. R. Smith.
7 Louth .... W. Radclyffe.
22 Lowestoffe ......W. R. Smith.
11 Ludlow Castle ...... R. Wallis.
21 Lyme Regis .... T. Jeavons.
6 Malmesbury Abbey
            J. C. Varrall.
13 Malvern Abbey...J. Horsburgh.
14 Margate .... R. Wallis.
17 Nottingham ...... W. J. Cooke.
5 Okehampton ... J. T. Willmore.
3 Oxford .... W. Brandard.
12 Pembroke Castle... T. Jeavons.
17 Penmaen Mawr J. T. Willmore.
13 Plymouth .... W. J. Cooke.
20 Powis Castle ... J. T Willmore.
4 Prudhoe Castle ... E. Goodall.
13 Richmond Hill... W. R. Smith.
24 Richmond Terrace
            J. T. Willmore.
2 Richmond, Yorkshire
            W. R. Smith.
6   ,,   ,, J. T. Willmore.
1 Rivaulx Abbey ... E. Goodall.
24 Rochester, Strood, Chatham
            J. C. Varrall.
14 St. Catherine's Hill, Guildford
            J. H. Kernot.
10 St. Mawes   Do.
24 St. Michael's Mount   S. Fisher.
13 Salisbury .... W. Radclyffe.
3 Saltash .... W. R. Smith,

No.
9 Stamford .... W. Miller.
7 Stonehenge............ R. Wallis.
9 Stonyhurst .... J. B. Allen.
15 Tamworth Castle J. T. Willmore.
24 Tees, Chain Bridge over the
                  W. R. Smith.
2 Do. Fall of the ... E. Goodall.
10 Trematon Castle ... R. Wallis.
11 Tynemouth ...... W. R. Smith.
16 Upnor Castle ...... J. B. Allen.
19 Ulleswater ...... J. T. Willmore.

No.
4 Valle Crucis Abbey J.C. Varrall.
10 Walton Bridge ...   Do.
15 Warwick Castle ...... R. Wallis.
23 Whitehaven Castle
                  W. R. Smith.
23 Winandermere J. T. Willmore.
10 Winchelsea .... J. Henshall.
12 Windsor Castle ...... W. Miller.
20 Worcester............ T Jeavons.
7 Yarmouth .... W. Miller.

Published by Holloway for the 'England and Wales.'

Harborough Sands (vign.)... Allen.
Lowestoffe Lighthouse (vign.) Do.
Lowestoffe (vign.)............... Do.

Aldborough (vign.) ....Allen.
Dymchurch (do.)
Orfordness....................... Do.

Two other plates unfinished.

Engravings from Turner in 'The Rivers of England.' Mezzotinto. Published by W. B. Cooke, 1824.

Totnes, on the Dart.
Dartmouth.................. Reynolds.
Dartmouth Castle.........T. Lupton.
Stangate Creek, on the Medway
                  T. Lupton.
Rochester, on the Medway Do.
Wirkworth Castle, on the Coquet
                  T. Lupton.
KirkstallAbbey,on theAire, Bromley.
Kirkstall Lock, on the Aire ... Jay.

Norham Castle, on the Tweed
                  C. Turner.
Newcastle, on the Tyne T. Lupton.
Shields, on the Tyne ... C. Turner.
BroughamCastle,on the Eamont, Jay.
Arundel Castle,on the Arun, Phillips.
More Park, on the Colne.
Mouth of the Humber ... Phillips.
Okehampton, on the Okement
                  C. Turner.

Engravings from Turner in 'The Ports of England.' Mezzotinto.

Whitby .... T. Lupton.
Scarborough .... Do.
Sheerness .... Do.

Dover .... T. Lupton.
Ramsgate .... Do.
Portsmouth .... Do.

Views in Sussex, from Turner. W. Cooke.

Vale of Ashburnham.
Battle Abbey.
Brightling Observatory.

Crowhurst.
Heathfield. (?)
Pevensey Bay. (?)

Bodiam Castle   ⎫
Hurstmonceux Castle   ⎬
             Unpublished.

Hakewell's 'Picturesque Tour of Italy.' J. Murray, 1820. From Hakewell's Sketches, made in 1816–17.

The Rialto, Venice .... J. Pye.
Cascade of Torni ...... J. Landseer.
Bridge at Narni ...... J. Middiman.
Rome—Bridge and Castle of St.
   Angelo .... G. Hollis.
Do. The Forum from the Capi-
   tol .... G. Cooke.
Do. From the Farnese Gardens.
   Figures by Mitan ... G. Hollis.

Rome—The Forum Romanum
                  J. Le Keux.
Do. From the Monte Testaccio
                  J. Byrne.
Do. From the Monte Marco Do.
The Tomb of Cecilia Metella Do.
La Riccia .... J. Pye.
The Lake of Narni
              Middiman and Pye.

Naples from the Mole... G. Cooke.
Florence from the Ponte alla Carraia .... S. Rawle.
Florence from the Chiesa al Monte
                              G. Cooke.

Florence from Fiesoli. W. R. Smith.
Isola Bella, Lago Maggiore
                              J. Fitler.
Turin from the Superza... J. Mitau.

Provincial Antiquities and Picturesque Scenery of Scotland, with Descriptive Illustrations by Sir Walter Scott. 2 *vols.* 1826.

The Vignette, Stirling Castle
The Title Vignette.   [G. Cooke
Crichton Castle .... G. Cooke.
Dunbar .... J. B. Allen.
Dunbar Castle .... E. Goodall.
Roslin Castle .... W. R. Smith
Edinburgh from the Calton Hill
                              G. Cooke.

Heriot's Hospital.   Figures by G.
    Cooke.................. Le Keux.
Edinburgh High Street...   Do.
Borthwick Castle ....   Do.
Tantallon Castle ...... E. Goodall.
Linlithgow Palace ...... R. Wallis.
The Bass Rock .... W. Miller.

Lord Byron's Works. *Murray's Edition,* 11 *vols.* 8*vo.* 1825.

Vol. 1 Temple of Minerva, Cape
        Colonna. Sketch by Allison.
  ,,   2 Tomb of Cecilia Metella.
        Childe Harold.
  ,, 11 Negropont. Bride of Abydos. Sketch by Allison.

Vol. 3 Acropolis of Athens. Siege
        of Corinth.
  ,,   9 Malta.   Adieu to Malta.
        MS. Poem.
  ,, 10 Rhodes.   Don Juan, from
        the Sea looking on Pharos
        and Town.
  ,, 11 The Drachenfels.

Finden's Landscape and Portrait Illustrations to the Life and Works of Lord Byron. *Murray and Till.* 1833.

Vol. 1 Gibraltar, from a sketch by
        Reinagle. 1833.
  ,,   1 Malta.
  ,,   1 Acropolis of Athens. Sketch
        by Allison. 1832.
  ,,   1 Temple of Minerva. Sketch
        by Allison. 1832.

Vol. 2 Tomb of Cecilia Metella.
  ,,   2 Rhodes.
  ,,   2 Drachenfels.
  ,,   3 Cephalonia.   Sketch by W.
        Page.
  ,,   3 Negropont. Sketch by Allison.

Works of Lord Byron and Life by Moore. 17 *vols.* *Murray.* 1834.

Vol. 1 Sta. Maria della Spina Pera,
        after Page.
  ,,   5 The Gate of Theseus, at
        Athens.
  ,,   7 The Plain of Troy, after
        Page.
  ,,   8 Bacharach.
  ,,   8 The Castle of St. Angelo.
  ,, 10 Corinth, after Page.
  ,, 11 The Bridge of Sighs, after
        T. Little.
  ,, 11 The Bernese Alps.

Vol. 13 The Walls of Rome. Tomb
        of Caius Sextus.
  ,, 14 Parnassus, after Page (Gally
        Knight ?)
  ,, 14 The Field of Waterloo.
  ,, 15 Scio, after Page.
  ,, 15 Genoa.
  ,, 16 Cologne.
  ,, 16 St. Sophia, after T. Barry.
  ,, 17 The School of Homer, after
        Page.
  ,, 17 Castellated Rhine.

From ' The Keepsake.' 1828 to 1837.

1828	Florence .... E. Goodall.		1833	Ehrenbreitstein ....Wallis.
1829	Lake of Albano ...... Wallis.		,,	Falls of the Rhine . J.B. Allen.
,,	Lago Maggiore.. W. R. Smith.		1834	Havre .... Wallis.
1830	Virginia Water........ Wallis.		,,	La Belle Gabrielle ... Miller.
,,	Do. .... Do.		1835	———
1831	Saumur .... Do.		1836	Fire at Sea ...... Williamson.
	Nantes...............Willenden.		,,	The Wreck.........H. Griffith.
1832	———		1837	The Sea! the Sea! Willmore.

From ' The Anniversary.' 1829.

1829 Fonthill, Burn and Trees, Tower in the distance .... T. Crostick.

From Heath's ' Gallery of British Engravings.' Longman. 1836.

Lake Albano (from ' Keepsake ')		Virginia Water .... Wallis.
	Wallis.	Ehrenbreitstein .... Do.
Florence .... Goodall.		Palace of La Belle Gabrielle Miller.
Virginia Water .... Wallis.		Marly .... Do.

Engravings from Turner, in Finden's ' Illustrations of the Bible.'

Mount Moriah	After	Barry	E. Finden.
Red Sea and Suez	Do.	J. G. Wilkinson......	
Valley of Sinai..................	Do.	Gally Knight	Allen.
Wilderness of Sinai............	Do.	Major Felix	E. Finden.
Jericho	Do.	Rev. R. Masters ...	W. Finden.
The Dead Sea		....	E. Finden.
Engedi and Convent of St. Saba	Do.	Barry	Allen.
Ramah and Rachel's Tomb...	Do.	Sir A. Edmonstone...	
Solomon's Pools	Do.	Barry	J. Stephenson.
Jerusalem from Mount of Olives	Do.	Barry	Allen.
Jerusalem, N.W. View	Do.	Barry	W. Finden.
Jerusalem, Pool of Bethesda	Do.	Barry	E. Finden.
Jerusalem, from the Latin Convent.			
Valley of the Brook Kedron..	Do.	Barry	E. Finden.
Bethlehem	Do.	Barry and R. Masters	Do.
Nazareth	Do.	Barry	Do.
Joppa	Do.	Sir A. Edmonstone..	Do.
Sidon	Do.	Barry	W. Finden.
Assos		....	Do.
Rhodes............................		....	S. Fisher.
Corinth, Cenchrea	Do.	R. Cockrell	E. Finden.
Mount Lebanon, Convent of St. Antonio	Do.	Barry	W. Finden.
Lebanon from Tripoli........		....	E. Finden.
Babylon	Do.	Sir R. Kerr Porter..	J. Cousen.
Nineveh	Do.	C. J. Rich	W. Radclyffe.
Egypt, near the Pyramids ...	Do.	Barry	E. Finden.

From 'Italy,' a Poem by Samuel Rogers. London, T. Cadell. 1830.

From Rogers' Poems. London, T. Cadell. 1834.

From the Prose Works of Sir Walter Scott. Cadell, Edinburgh. 1834.

Vol. 24 Dunstaffnage... W. Miller.
        Linlithgow ... Do.
,, 25 Glencoe......... Do.
        Killicrankie ... Do.
,, 26 Inverness ...... Do.
        Fort Augustus Do.

Vol. 27 Rouen ... W. Richardson.
        Calais......... J. Horsbury.
,, 28 Château d'Arc, near Dieppe
               W. Forrest.
     Abbeville ... J. Horsbury.

From the Poetical Works of Sir Walter Scott. 12 *vols.* Cadell, Edinburgh. 1834.

Vol. 1 Carlisle............ Goodall.
       Smailholme Tower Do.
,, 2 Jedburgh Abbey. Brandard.
       Johnny Armstrong's Tower
               Goodall.
,, 3 Kelso .... Wallis.
       Lochmaben Castle
               Willmore.
,, 4 Caerlaverock Castle
               Goodall.
       Hermitage Castle...Wallis.
,, 5 Dryburgh Abbey... Miller.
       Bemerside Tower
               Horsbury.
,, 6 Melrose .... Miller.

Vol. 6 Newark Castle, W.J. Cooke.
,, 7 Edinburgh .... Miller.
       Ashestiel ...... Horsbury.
,, 8 Loch Katrine ...... Miller.
       Loch Achray ...... Do.
,, 9 Junction of the Greta and
       Tees............... J. Pye.
       Bowes Tower... E. Webb.
,, 10 Loch Corriskin...Le Keux.
       Staffa .... Goodall.
,, 11 Skiddaw .... Miller.
       Mayburg ...... Horsbury.
,, 12 Berwick-upon-Tweed
               Miller.
       Abbotsford...... Le Keux.

From Illustrations (Landscapes, Historical, and Antiquarian) to the Poetical Works of Sir Walter Scott, Bart. C. Tilt, London. 1834.

Roslin and Hawthornden
     W. R. Smith.

Crichtoun Castle
     W. B. Cooke.

Tantallon
     W. B. Cooke.

The Rivers of France, by J. M. W. Turner. 'The Annual Tour,' 1833, 4, 5.

Château Gaillard (vign.)... Cousen.
Orléans .... Higham.
Blois .... Brandard.
Palace at Blois .... Wallis.
Beaugency .... Brandard.
Amboise...................... Smith.
Château d'Amboise .... Allen.
St. Julien Tours .... Radclyffe.
Tours........................... Wallis.
Canal of the Loire & Cher...Jeavons.
Tours (looking back) ... Brandard.
Saumur...................... Willmore.
Rietz, near Saumur...... Brandard.
Montjean .... Willmore.
St. Horent .... Brandard.
Between Clairmont and Mauves
               Miller.
Château Hamelin ...... Brandard.
Clairmont................... Willmore.
Scene on the Loire .... Wallis.

Côteaux de Mauves .... Wallis.
Nantes, Château de .... Miller.
Nantes (vign.) .... Allen.
Havre .... Do.
Havre, Tower of Francis I... Wallis.
Graville...................... Brandard.
Harfleur .... Cousen.
Château de Tancarville...Brandard.
Lillebonne Château ...... Jeavons.
Do. and Tower... Willmore.
Caudebec...................... Allen.
Junièges .... Armytage.
La Chaise de Gargantua Brandard.
Rouen........................... Miller.
Do. looking up the River. Brandard.
Rouen Cathedral .... Higham.
Do. looking down the River. Miller.
Quillebœuf .... Brandard.
Between Quillebœuf and Villequier
               Brandard.

Château de la Maillerie... Brandard.
Honfleur .... Cousen.
Light-towers of Heve (vign.) Do.
Château de Gaillard fr. the E. Smith.
Pont de l'Arche .... Willmore.
Vernon .... Do.
Between Nantes and Vernon
Brandard.
Nantes .... Radclyffe.
Bridge of Meulan............ Cousen.
From the Terrace of St. Germain
Allen.
St. Denis .... Fisher.
Bridges of St. Cloud and Sèvres
Radclyffe.

The Lanterne at St. Cloud
Willmore.
Bridge of St. Cloud from Sèvres
Fisher.
Paris from the Barrière de Passy
Willmore.
Pont Neuf .... Miller.
Marché aux Fleurs ...... Radclyffe.
Hôtel de Ville .... Jeavons.
Boulevard .... Higham.
Confluence of the Seine and Marne
Armytage.
Meben .... Miller.
Troyes .... Armytage.

From the Works of Milton, 7 vols. John Macrone. 1835.
The Poetical Works, 1 vol. Tegg. 1841.

Expulsion from Paradise.
Mustering of the Warrior Angels.
Fall of the Rebel Angels.
The Temptation on the Pinnacle.

The Temptation on the Mountain.
St. Michael's Mount—Shipwreck of
Lycidas.
Ludlow Castle.

From Campbell's Poetical Works. Moxon. 1837.

Summer Eve—Rainbow.. Goodall.
Andes Coast .... Do.
Prague .... Do.
Sinai .... Wallis.
Swiss Valley .... Goodall.
O'Connor's Child .... Do.
Lochiel's Warning......... Do.
Battle of the Baltic ...... Do.
Hohenlinden................. Wallis.
Lochgyle .... Do.

The Soldier's Dream...... Goodall.
The Last Man.............. Do.
Wyoming .... Do.
Do.   the Waterfall... Do.
Rolandseck.................. Do.
The Beech-tree's Petition Do.
Camp Hill, Hastings...... Do.
Death Boat of Heligoland Do.
Ehrenbreitstein .... Do.
Oran .... Miller.

From 'The Epicurean,' with Vignette Illustrations by J. M. W.
Turner, Esq., R.A. London, John Macrone. 1839.

On the Nile.
The Trial of the Ring.

The Garden.
The Chaplet.

From Views in India, chiefly among the Himalaya Mountains.
Drawn by Lieut. G. F. White, 31st Regt. Fisher, Son, &
Co. 1836–37.

Vol. 1 Part of the Ghaut during the Fair at Hurdwar .... Higham.
,,   1 Mussores from Landour .... Allen.
,,   1 Snowy Range from Tyne or Marma...................... Goodall.
,,   1 View near Jubberah .... Cousen.
,,   2 Falls near the Source of the Jumna .... Cousen.
,,   2 Valley of the Dhoon from the Landour Ridge............ Floyd.
,,   2 Rocks at Colgony on the Ganges .... Goodall,

From 'Faith of Perrin' (Pilgrim's Progress). Fisher. 1847.

Frontispiece Vignette.

Subscription Plates from Turner.

Dido and Æneas—Morning of the Chase	Smith	24	16
Caligula's Bridge	Goodall	24	16
Juliet after the Masquerade	Hollis	$22\frac{3}{4}$	$16\frac{1}{2}$
Mercury and Herse (upright)	Cousins	$18\frac{1}{4}$	15
Crossing the Brook (upright)	Brandard	$18\frac{1}{4}$	15
Heidelberg	T. A. Prior.		
Zurich	Do.		
The Lake of Lucerne	Wallis.		
Hastings	Do.		
The Grand Canal, Venice	W. Miller.		
The Rhine, Osterprey, and Feltzen	Do.		
The Rhine, Neuwied, and Weissenhurn	R. Brand.		
Ancient Italy	Willmore.		
Modern Italy	Do.		
Venice	Do.		
Dover Castle	Do.		
The Departure of Regulus	D. Wilson.		
Tivoli	E. Goodall.		
Cologne	Do.		
Old London Bridge	Do.		
Oxford	Do.		
Ehrenbreitstein	J. Pye.		
The Golden Bough	Prior.		
The Lake of Nerni			

Single Plates Engraved from Turner.

The Mausoleum at Brocklesby, begun 1787, completed by James Wyatt	F. C. Lewis.
Hylton Castle	S. Rawle.
Dunster Castle, from the S.W. 1800	Do.
Do. Do. from the N.W.	Do.
Raby Castle	Do.
Hampton Court, Herefordshire, in 'The Beauties of England and Wales.' 1801	S. Storer.
Fonthill House, Wilts. 1800. 'Angus' Seats' (?)	W. Angus
Windsor, from the Forest. 1804. Select Views of London and its Environs	J. Greig.
Pope's Villa. Figures by C. Heath. April 1, 1811	J. Pye.
Fishing Boats. December 19, 1811	Fittler.
Autumn, Sowing Grain. June 1, 1813	Hassel & Co., London.
Redclyffe Church, Bristol. From 'The Lady and Gentleman's Annual Pocket Ledger.' 1814	J. Pye.
Kirkstall Abbey Crypt. Britton's 'Architectural Antiquities.' 1814	Scott.
Antiquities of Pola. Vignette to Title-page. Allison. 1813	G. Cooke.
Colebrook Dale	F. C. Lewis.

New Weir on the Wye .... F. C. Lewis.
Arundel Castle. 1820 .... G. Cooke.
View near Plynlimmon. Coloured Print. T.
  Clay, Ludgate Hill, July 1, 1820 .... T. H. Fielding.
Calais Pier. Mezzotinto. (Never finished) ...... Lupton.
The Eddystone Lighthouse. Mezzotinto. 1824 Do.
Ehrenbreitstein during the Demolition of the For-
  tress in 1819, from the Quay at Coblentz. 1824 J. C. Allen.
Sunrise. Whiting Fishing at Margate. Mezzo-
  tinto. June 1, 1825 .... T. Lupton.
Wilton House. Published by Sir R. Colt Hoare.
  January 1, 1825 .... T. Higham.
Bolton Abbey. 1826 .... E. Finden.
Richmond Hill. 1826 .... E. Goodall.
Norham Castle. 1827 .... Percy Heath.
Ivy Bridge, Devonshire .... Allen.
Source of the Tamar .... W. B. Cooke.
Plymouth........... .... Do.
Rivaulx Abbey, Yorkshire .... J. C. Bentley.
The Tower of London. 1831 .... W. Miller.
The Shepherd. 1840 .... Do.
The Thames at Mortlake .... W. J. Cooke.
Damon and Pythias .... Bacon.
Fish Market, Rotterdam .... W. Floyd.
The Bell Rock Lighthouse .... J. Horsbury.
Llangollen .... Willmore.
Barnard Castle .... Do.
Fetcham Park... Do.
Holy Island. (Only 15 published on India paper,
  and 10 plain) .... Do.
Burning of the Houses of Parliament .... Do.
St. Germain en Laye .... R. Wallis.
Whitby............. .... Do.
The Ship on Fire .... Willmore.
Abbey Pool. 1846 .... J. Cousen.
Whitby.. Do.
St. Agatha's Abbey .... Do.
Mount Vesuvius .... T. Jeavons.
A View of Oxford, etched by L. Pye, engraved by C. Heath.
High Street, Oxford .... Do.
Frontispiece Vignette. 'Faith of Perrin.' (Pil-
  grim's Progress.) S. Fisher. 1847 .... E. Goodall.
Raglan Castle and the Mill. Coloured Lithograph
Grouse Shooting. Chromo-Lithograph. 1854...
Snipe Shooting ....
The Blue Lights... R. Carrick.
The Bridge at Tours. 1856.......................

Mezzotintos from Turner.

The Garden of Boccaccio. Unpublished .... J. B. Luilley.
The Deluge. Unpublished .... F. C Lewis.
The Field of Waterloo. Unpublished .... Do.

Fishing Boats off Calais. Unpublished............ Davison.
Calais Pier. Unpublished .... T. Lupton.
Whiting Fishing off Margate........................... Do.
The Eddystone Lighthouse .... Do.
The Wreck of the Minotaur .... Cousins and Barlow.
The Wreck .... C. Turner.
A Shipwreck, from the same Picture .... F. Fielding.
The Burning Mountain. Engraved in Colours ... C. Turner.

Plates of the ' Liber Studiorum,' by J. M. W. Turner, R.A., P.P.

No. 1. Jan. 20, 1807	Cows in Brook...................	P.	C. Turner.
	Woman with Tambourine ...	E.P.	Do.
	Vessels aground. Flint	M.	Do.
	Basle	A.	Do.
	Jason.................................	H.	Do.
No. 2. Feb. 20, 1808	Barn and Straw-yard	P.	Do.
	Boy Piping (Castle in mid. dis.)	E.P.	Do.
	Mount St. Gothard	M.	Do.
	Ships ; Gale of Wind	M.	Do.
	Holy Island Cathedral	A.	Do.
No. 3. June 10, 1808	Pembury Mill	P.	Do.
	Bridge in Mid. Dis..............	E.P.	Do.
	Dunstanborough Castle	A.	Do.
	Lake of Thun	M.	Do.
	The Fifth Plague of Egypt...	H.	Do.
No. 4. May 29, 1809	Farm-yard, with Cock	P.	Do.
	The Clyde.........................	E.P.	Do.
	Little Devils' Bridge	M.	Do.
	Ships.................................	M.	Do.
	Morpeth	A.	
No. 5. Jan. 1, 1811	Juvenile Tricks..................	P.	W. Say.
	Hindoo Worshipping	E.P.	R. Dunkarton.
	Coast of Yorkshire	M.	W. Say.
	Hind Head Hill	M.	I. W. T.
	Greenwich Hospital............	A.	C. Turner.
No. 6. June 1, 1811	Lock and Mill	P.	W. Say.
	Junction of the Wye and Severn	E.P.	I. W. T.
	Marine Dabblers	N.	W. Say.
	Near Blair-Athol	M.	Do.
	Lauffenbury	A.	T. Hodgetts.
No. 7. June 1, 1811	Young Anglers....................	P.	R. Dunkarton.
	St. Catherine's Hill............	E.P.	J. C. Easling.
	Martello Towers, Bexhill ...	M.	W. Say.
	Inverary Pier	M.	I. W. T.
	From Spenser's 'Fairie Queene'	H.	J. Hodgetts.
No. 8. Feb. 1, 1812	Water Mill	P.	R. Dunkarton.
	Woman at a Well	E.P.	W. Say.
	Crypt of Kirkstall Abbey ...	A.	J. M. W. T.
	Coast Scene, Sunset	M.	{ W. Annis and J. C. Easling.
	Cephalis and Procris	H.	G. Clint.

No. 9. April 23, 1812   Winchelsea ....   P.   J. C. Easling.
                        Goats on a Bridge ....   E.P.   T. C. Lewis.
                        Calm ....   N.   I. W. T.
                        Peat Bog ....   M.   G. Clint.
                        Rizpah ....   H.   R. Dunkarton.
No. 10. May 23, 1812   Hedging and Ditching ......   P.   J. C. Easling.
                        The River Wye ....   E.P.   W. Annis.
                        Chain of Alps, Chamberi ...   M.   W. Say.
                        Mer de Glace ....   M.   I. W. T.
                        Rivaulx Abbey..................   A.   H. Dawe.

The Frontispiece was given in this No.   I. W. T.; J. C. Easling.

No. 11. Jan. 1, 1816   Solway Moss....................   P.   T. Lupton.
                        Magdalen Ruding..............   E.P.   W. Say.
                        Mill near the Grand Chartreuse   M.   H. Dawe.
                        Entrance to Calais Harbour..   M.   I. W. T.
                        Dunblane Abbey ....   A.   T. Lupton.
No. 12. Jan. 1, 1816   Norham Castle..................   P.   C. Turner.
                        River, with Woods. Goodrich   E.P.   I. W. T.
                        Ville de Thun ....   A.   T. Hodgetts.
                        Source of the Avernon ......   M.   I. W. T.
                        Tenth Plague of Egypt ......   H.   W. Say.
No. 13. Jan. 1, 1819   Water-cress Gatherers.........   P.   T. Lupton.
                        Water, with Round Temple..   E.P.   H. Dawe.
                        Bonneville......................   M.   Do.
                        Inverary Castle..................   M.   C. Turner.
                        Hesperia ....   H.   I. W. T.
No. 14. Jan. 1, 1819   East Gate, Winchelsea ......   P.   S. W. Reynolds.
                        Isis................................   E.P.   W. Say.
                        Ben Arthur ....   M.   T. Lupton.
                        Interior of a Church............   A.   I. W. T.
                        Woman of Samaria ....   H.   S. W. Reynolds.

Unpublished Plates of the ' Liber Studiorum.'

Premium Landscape.........W. Say.
Glaucus and Scylla ....   Do.
Sheep-washing; Windsor Castle
                            C. Turner.
Dumbarton ....T. Lupton.
Crowhurst..................H. Dawe.
Temple of Jupiter, Ægina.
Swiss Bridge, Mount St. Gothard.
Ploughing, Eton ....T. Lupton.
Pan and Syrinx.
Stonehenge at Daybreak.

The Felucca.
Aqueduct over Mountain Torrent.
Storm over the Lizard.
Moonlight at Sea.   The Needles.
Moonlight on River, with Barges.
The Thames near Kingston.
The Deluge.
Flounder-fishing near Battersea.
Narcissus and Echo.
Cows on a Bank.

CATALOGUE OF ALL THE PICTURES EXHIBITED BY TURNER IN THE ROYAL ACADEMY AND BRITISH INSTITUTION BETWEEN THE YEARS 1787 AND 1850, WITH THE QUOTATIONS APPENDED.

EXHIBITION XXII. 1790.

J. W. TURNER, *Maiden Lane, Covent Garden.*

1 View of the Archbishop's Palace, Lambeth.

EXHIBITION XXIII. 1791.

W. TURNER, 26 *Maiden Lane, Covent Garden.*

2 King John's Palace, Eltham.
3 Sweakley, near Uxbridge, the seat of the Rev. Mr. Clarke.

EXHIBITION XXIV. 1792.

W. TURNER, 26 *Maiden Lane, Covent Garden.*

4 Malmesbury Abbey.
5 The Pantheon, the morning after the fire.

EXHIBITION XXV. 1793.

W. TURNER, *Hand Court, Maiden Lane, Covent Garden.*

6 View on the River Avon, near St. Vincent's Rock, Bristol.
7 Canterbury: Gate of St. Augustine's Monastery.
8 The Rising Squall, Hot Wells, from St. Vincent's Rock, Bristol.

EXHIBITION XXVI. 1794.

W. TURNER, *Hand Court, Maiden Lane, Covent Garden.*

9 Second Fall of the River Monach, Devil's Bridge, Cardiganshire.
10 Great Malvern Abbey, Porch of, Worcestershire.
11 Canterbury, Christ Church Gate.
12 Tintern Abbey, Monmouthshire, Inside of.
13 Canterbury Cathedral, St. Anselm's Chapel, with part of St. Thomas à Becket's crown.

EXHIBITION XXVII. 1795.

W. TURNER, 26 *Maiden Lane, Covent Garden.*

14 Lincoln Cathedral, St. Hugh, the Burgundian's Porch at.
15 Marford Mill, Wrexham, Denbighshire.
16 Peterborough Cathedral; West Entrance.
17 Tintern Abbey, Monmouthshire, Transept of.
18 Shrewsbury: Welsh Bridge.
19 View near the Devil's Bridge, Cardiganshire; with the River Ryddol.
20 Choir in King's College Chapel, Cambridge.
21 Cathedral Church at Lincoln.

EXHIBITION XXVIII. 1796.

W. TURNER, *Hand Court, Maiden Lane, Covent Garden.*

22 Fishermen at Sea.
23 Salisbury Close Gate.
24 St. Erasmus, in Bishop Islip's Chapel, Westminster Abbey.
25 Wolverhampton, Staffordshire.
26 Llandilo Bridge, and Dynevor Castle.

27 Interior of a Cottage: a study at Ely.
28 Chale Farm, Isle of Wight.
29 Llandaff Cathedral, South Wales.
30 Waltham Abbey, Essex, Remains of.
31 Ely Minster, Transept and Choir of.
32 Bath Abbey, West Front of.

EXHIBITION XXIX. 1797.
W. TURNER, *Hand Court, Maiden Lane.*

33 Moonlight: a study at Millbank.
34 Fishermen coming Ashore, at sunset, previous to a Gale.
35 Glamorganshire, Ewenny Priory, Transept of.
36 Salisbury Cathedral, Choir of.
37 Ely Cathedral, South Transept.
38 Salisbury Cathedral, North Porch of.

EXHIBITION XXX. 1798.
W. TURNER, *Hand Court, Maiden Lane.*

39 Winesdale, Yorkshire—an Autumnal Morning.
40 Morning amongst the Coniston Fells, Cumberland.

> ' Ye mists and exhalations that now rise
> From hill or streaming lake, dusky or gray,
> Till the sun paints your fleecy skirts with gold
> In honour to the world's Great Author rise.'
> Milton, *Paradise Lost,* book v.

41 Dunstanburgh Castle, N.E. Coast of Northumberland—Sunrise after a squally night.

> ' The precipice abrupt,
> Breaking horror on the blacken'd flood,
> Softens at thy return.—The desert joys,
> Wildly through all his melancholy bounds.
> Rude ruins glitter ; and the briny deep,
> Seen from some pointed promontory's top
> Far to the blue horizon's utmost verge,
> Restless, reflects a floating gleam.'
> Thomson's *Seasons.*

42 Refectory of Kirkstall Abbey, Yorkshire.
43 Norham Castle, on the Tweed—Summer's Morn.

> ' But yonder comes the powerful King of Day,
> Rejoicing in the East ; the lessening cloud,
> The kindling azure, and the mountain's brow
> Illumined,—his near approach betoken glad.'
> Thomson's *Seasons.*

44 Holy Island Cathedral, Northumberland.
45 Ambleside Mill, Westmoreland.
46 Dormitory and Transept of Fountains Abbey—Evening.

> ' All ether soft'ning, sober evening takes
> Her wonted station on the middle air ;
> A thousand shadows at her beck—
> In circle following circle, gather round,
> To close the face of things.'
> Thomson's *Seasons.*

47 Buttermere Lake, with part of Cromack Water, Cumberland—a Shower.

> ' Till in the western sky the downward sun
> Looks out effulgent—the rapid radiance instantaneous strikes
> Th' illumined mountains—in a yellow mist
> Bestriding earth—the grand ethereal bow
> Shoots up immense, and every hue unfolds.'
> Thomson's *Seasons.*

48 A Study in September of the Fern House, Mr. Lock's Park, Mickleham, Surrey.

EXHIBITION XXXI. 1799.

W. TURNER, *Hand Court, Maiden Lane, Covent Garden.*

49 Fishermen Becalmed previous to a Storm—Twilight.

50 Harlech Castle, from Trwgwyn Ferry—Summer's Evening, Twilight.

> ' Now came still evening on, and twilight grey
> Had in her sober livery all things clad.
> .   .   .   .   .   .   Hesperus that led
> The starry host rode brightest till the moon,
> Rising in clouded majesty, unveil'd her peerless light.'
>
> Milton's *Paradise Lost*, book iv.

51 Battle of the Nile, at ten o'clock, when the L'Orient blew up, from the Station of the Gun-boats between the Battery and Castle of Aboukir.

> ' Immediate in a flame
> But soon obscured with smoke, all heaven appear'd
> From these deep-throated engines belch'd, whose roar
> Imbowell'd with outrageous noise the air,
> And all her entrails tore, disgorging foul
> Their devilish glut, chain'd thunderbolts and hail
> Of iron globes.'—Milton's *Paradise Lost*, book vi.

52 Kilgerran Castle, on the Twyvey—hazy Sunrise, previous to a sultry day.

53 Sunny Morning ; the cattle by *S. Gilpin, R.A.*

54 Abergavenny Bridge, Monmouthshire—clearing up after a showery day.

55 Salisbury Cathedral, Inside of the Chapter House of.

56 Salisbury Cathedral, West Front of.

57 Caernarvon Castle.

> ' Now rose
> Sweet evening, solemn hour ; the sun, declined,
> Hung golden o'er this nether firmament,
> Whose broad cerulean mirror, calmly bright,
> Gave back his beamy visage to the sky
> With splendour undiminish'd.'—Mallet.

58 Morning, from Dr. Langhorne's ' Visions of Fancy.'

> ' Life's morning landscape gilt with Orient light,
> Where Hope, and Joy, and Fancy hold their reign,
> The grove's green wave, the blue stream sparkling bright,
> The blithe hours dancing round Hyperion's wain.
> In radiant colours youth's free hand portrays,
> Then holds the flattering tablet to his eye.
> Nor thinks how soon the vernal grove decays,
> Nor sees the dark cloud gathering o'er the sky.
> Mirror of life, thy glories thus depart.'

59 Warkworth Castle, Northumberland—thunderstorm approaching at sunset.

> ' Behold, slow settling o'er the lurid grove,
> Unusual darkness broods ; and, growing, gains
> The full possession of the sky ; and on yon baleful cloud
> A redd'ning gloom, a magazine of fate,
> Ferments.'—Thomson's *Seasons*.

60 Dolbadern Castle, North Wales.

> ' How awful is the silence of the waste
> Where Nature lifts her mountains to the sky ;
> Majestic solitude, behold the tower,
> Where hopeless Owen, long imprison'd, pined
> And wrung his hands for liberty in vain.'

EXHIBITION XXXII. 1800.

W. TURNER, A., 64 *Harley Street.*

61   The Fifth Plague of Egypt.

> ' And Moses stretched forth his hands towards heaven, and the Lord sent thunder and hail, and the fire ran along the ground.'—*Exodus* ix. 23.

62   View of the Gothic Abbey (Afternoon) now building at Fonthill, the seat of William Beckford, Esq.

63   South-west View of the Gothic Abbey (Morning) now building at Fonthill, the seat of W. Beckford, Esq.

64   Caernarvon Castle, North Wales.

> ' And now on Arvon's haughty towers
>   The bard the song of pity pours,
>   For oft on Mona's distant hills he sighs,
>   Where, jealous of the minstrel band,
>   The tyrant drench'd with blood the land,
>   And, charm'd with horror, triumph'd in their cries.
>   The swains of Arvon round him throng
>   And join the sorrows of his song.'

65   South View of the Gothic Abbey (Evening) now building at Fonthill, the seat of W. Beckford, Esq.

66   East View of the Gothic Abbey (Noon) now building at Fonthill, the seat of W. Beckford, Esq.

67   North-east View of the Gothic Abbey (Sunset) now building at Fonthill, the seat of W. Beckford, Esq.

EXHIBITION XXXIII. 1801.

W. TURNER, A., 75 *Norton Street, Portland Road.*

68   Dutch Boats in a Gale ; fishermen endeavouring to put their fish on board.

69   The Army of the Medes destroyed in the Desert by a Whirlwind—foretold by Jeremiah xv. ver. 32, 33.

70   London—Autumnal Morning.

71   Pembroke Castle, South Wales—thunderstorm approaching.

72   St. Donat's Castle, South Wales—Summer Evening.

73   Chapter House, Salisbury.

EXHIBITION XXXIV. 1802.

* JOSEPH MALLORD WILLIAM TURNER, R.A., 75 *Norton Street, Portland Road.*

74   Fishermen upon a Lee Shore in Squally Weather.

75   The Tenth Plague of Egypt.

> Ver. 29. ' And it came to pass, that at midnight the Lord smote all the firstborn in the land.'
> Ver. 30. ' And Pharaoh rose, he and all the Egyptians ; and there was a great cry in Egypt ; for there was not a house where there was not one dead.'

76   Ships bearing up for Anchorage.

77   The Falls of the Clyde, Lanarkshire—Noon.

> *Vide* Akenside's *Hymn to the Naiades.*

78   Kilchern Castle, with the Cruchan-Ben Mountains, Scotland—Noon.

79   Edinburgh, New Town, Castle, &c., from the Water of Leith.

80   Jason.

81   Ben Lomond Mountain, Scotland—the Traveller.

> *Vide* Ossian's *War of Caros.*

* Turner signed his name in full after 1802.

EXHIBITION XXXV. 1803.

J. M. W. TURNER, R.A., 75 *Norton Street, Portland Road.*

82 Bonneville, Savoy, with Mont Blanc.
83 The Festival upon the Opening of the Vintage of Maçon.
84 Calais Pier, with French Poissards preparing for Sea, an English Packet arriving.
85 Holy Family.
86 Château de St. Michael, Bonneville, Savoy.
87 St. Hughes denouncing Vengeance on the Shepherd of Cormayeur, in the Valley of d'Aoust.
88 Glacier and Source of the Arveron going up to the Mer de Glace, in the Valley of Chamouni.

EXHIBITION XXXVI. 1804.

J. M. W. TURNER, 64 *Harley Street.*

89 Boats carrying out Anchors and Cables to Dutch Men-of-War, 1665.
90 Narcissus and Echo.

> ' So melts the youth, and languishes away,
> His beauty withers, and his limbs decay ;
> And none of those attractive charms remain,
> To which the slighted Echo sued in vain.
> She saw him in his present misery,
> Whom, spite of all her wrongs, she grieved to see :
> She answer'd sadly to the lover's moan,
> Sigh'd back his sighs, and groan'd to every groan :
> "Ah ! youth, beloved in vain !" Narcissus cries ;
> "Ah ! youth, beloved in vain !" the nymph replies.
> " Farewell !" says he. The parting sound scarce fell
> From his faint lips, but she replied, " Farewell !" '

91 Edinburgh, from Calton Hill.

EXHIBITION XXXVIII. 1806.

J. M. W. TURNER, R.A., 64 *Harley Street.*

92 Fall of the Rhine at Schaffhausen.
93 Pembroke Castle—clearing up of a thunderstorm.

EXHIBITION XXXIX. 1807.

J. M. W. TURNER, R.A., 64 *Harley Street.*

94 A Country Blacksmith disputing upon the price of Iron, and the price charged to the Butcher for Shoeing his Pony.
95 Sun Rising through Vapour—Fishermen cleaning and selling fish.

EXHIBITION XL. 1808.

J. M. W. TURNER, R.A., Professor of Perspective, 64 *Harley Street and West End, Upper Mall, Hammersmith.*

96 The Unpaid Bill, or the Dentist reproving his Son's prodigality.

EXHIBITION XLI. 1809.

J. M. W. TURNER, R.A., Professor of Perspective, 64 *Harley Street and West End, Upper Mall, Hammersmith.*

97 Spithead ; Boat's crew recovering an anchor.
98 Tabley, the seat of Sir J. F. Leicester, Bart.—Windy day.
99 Tabley, Cheshire, the seat of Sir J. F. Leicester, Bart.—Calm Morning.
100 The Garreteer's Petition.

> 'Aid me, ye powers ! Oh, bid my thoughts to roll
> In quick succession, animate my soul ;
> Descend, my muse, and every thought refine,
> And finish well my long, my *long-sought* line.'

EXHIBITION XLII. 1810.

J. M. W. TURNER, R.A., Professor of Perspective, 64 *Harley Street, and West End, Upper Mall, Hammersmith.*

101 Lowther Castle, Westmoreland, the seat of the Earl of Lonsdale ; North-west view from Ulleswater Lane—Evening.
102 Lowther Castle, Westmoreland, the seat of the Earl of Lonsdale (the north front), with the river Lowther—Midday.
103 Petworth, Sussex, the seat of the Earl of Egremont—Dewy morning.

EXHIBITION XLIII. 1811.

J. M. W. TURNER, *West End, Upper Mall, Hammersmith.*

104 Mercury and Hersé.

> ' Close by the sacred walls in wide Munichio's plain,
> The God well pleased beheld the virgin train !'
> Ovid's *Metamorphoses.*

105 Apollo and Python.

> ' Envenom'd by thy darts, the monster coil'd,
> Portentous, horrible, and vast his snake-like form :
> Rent the huge portal of the rocky den,
> And in the throes of death he tore
> His many wounds in one, while earth,
> Absorbing, blacken'd with his gore.'
> *Hymn of Callimachus.*

106 Somer Hill, near Tunbridge, the seat of W. F. Woodgate, Esq.
107 Whalley Bridge, and Abbey, Lancashire ; Dyers washing and drying cloth.
108 Windsor Park, with horses by the late Sawry Gilpin, Esq., R.A.
109 November: Flounder-fishing.
110 Chryses.

> 'The trembling priest along the shore returned,
> And in the anguish of a father mourned ;
> Disconsolate, not daring to complain,
> Silent he wander'd by the sounding main,
> Till safe at distance to his God he prays,
> The God who darts around the world his rays.'
> Pope's Homer's *Iliad*, book i.

111 May : Chickens.
112 Scarborough, Town and Castle—Morning—Boys collecting crabs.

EXHIBITION XLIV. 1812.

J. M. W. TURNER, Esq., R.A., *Queen Anne Street West.*

113 View of the Castle of St. Michael, near Bonneville, Savoy.
114 View of the High Street, Oxford.
115 Oxford, a View of, from the Abingdon Road.
116 Snow Storm: Hannibal and his army crossing the Alps.

> 'Craft, treachery, and fraud—Salassian force,
> Hung on the fainting rear ! then Plunder seized
> The victor and the captive—Saguntum's spoil,
> Alike became their prey ; still the chief advanced,
> Looked on the sun with hope ; low, broad and wan.
> While the fierce archer of the downward year
> Stains Italy's blanch'd barrier with storms.
> In vain each pass, ensanguined deep with dead,
> Or rocky fragments, wide destruction roll'd.
> Still on Campania's fertile plains—he thought,
> But the loud breeze sobbed, Capua's joys beware.
> *MS. P. Fallacies of Hope.*

EXHIBITION XLV. 1813.

J. M. W. TURNER, Esq., R.A., *Queen Anne Street West.*

117 Frosty Morning.

> ' The rigid hoar frost melts before his beam.'
> Thomson's *Seasons.*

118 The Deluge.

> ' Meanwhile the south wind rose, and, with black wings
> Wide hovering, all the clouds together drove
> From under heaven. . . . . . .
> . . . . . . The thicken'd sky
> Like a dark ceiling stood, down rush'd the rain
> Impetuous, and continued till the earth
> No more was seen.'—Milton's *Paradise Lost.*

EXHIBITION XLVI. 1814.

J. M. W. TURNER, R.A., *Queen Anne Street West, and at Solus Lodge, Twickenham.*

119 Dido and Æneas.

> ' When next the sun his rising light displays,
> And gilds the world below with purple rays,
> The Queen, Æneas, and the Tyrian Court
> Shall to the shady woods for sylvan games resort.'
> Dryden's *Æneis*, book iv.

EXHIBITION XLVII. 1815.

J. M. W. TURNER, R.A., Professor of Perspective, *Sandycombe Lodge, Twickenham, and Queen Anne Street West.*

120 Bligh Sand, near Sheerness—Fishing-boats trawling.
121 Crossing the Brook.
122 Dido Building Carthage : or the Rise of the Carthaginian Empire.
123 The Battle of Fort Rock, Val d'Aouste, Piedmont, 1796.

> ' The snow-capt mountain, and huge towers of ice,
> Thrust forth their dreary barriers in vain ;
> Onward the van progressive forced its way,
> Propelled ; as the wild Reuss, by native glaciers fed,
> Rolls on impetuous, with ev'ry check gains force
> By the constraint upraised ; till, to its gathering powers
> All yielding, down the pass wide Devastation pours
> Her own destructive course. Thus rapine stalk'd
> Triumphant ; and plundering hordes, exulting, strew'd,
> Fair Italy, thy plains with woe.'—*Fallacies of Hope, MS.*

124 The Eruption of the Souffrier Mountains, in the Island of St. Vincent, at midnight, on the 30th of April 1812 ; from a sketch taken at the time by Hugh P. Keane, Esq.

> ' Then in stupendous horror grew
> The red volcano to the view,
> And shook in thunders of its own,
> While the blaz'd hill in lightnings shone,
>   Scatt'ring thin arrows round.
> As down its sides of liquid flame
> The devastating cataract came,
> With melting rocks, and crackling woods,
> And mingled roar of boiling floods,
>   And roll'd along the ground !'

125 The Passage of Mount St. Gothard, taken from the centre of the Teufels-Brück (Devil's Bridge), Switzerland.
126 The Great Fall of the Riechenbach, in the Valley of Hasle, Switzerland.
127 Lake of Lucerne, from the Landing-place at Fluelen, looking towards Bauen and Tell's Chapel, Switzerland.

J. M. W. TURNER, R.A., Professor of Perspective, *Sandycombe Lodge*
Twickenham, and Queen Anne Street West.

128   The Temple of Jupiter Panhellenius restored.

> "'Twas now the earliest morning ; soon the sun,
> Rising above *Ægina*, poured his light
> Amid the forest, and, with ray aslant
> Entering its depth, illumed the branching pines,
> Brighten'd their bark, tinged with a redder hue
> Its rusty stains, and cast along the ground
> Long lines of shadow, where they rose erect
> Like pillars of the temple.'

129   View of the Temple of Jupiter Panhellenius, in the Island of Ægina,
with the Greek National Dance of the Romaika ; the Acropolis
of Athens in the distance.   Painted from a sketch taken by
H. Gally Knight, Esq., in 1810.

J. M. W. TURNER, R.A., Professor of Perspective, *Sandycombe Lodge,*
Twickenham, and Queen Anne Street West.

130   The Decline of the Carthaginian Empire.—Rome, being determined
on the overthrow of her hated rival, demanded from her such
terms as might either force her into war, or ruin her by compliance.   The enervated Carthaginians, in their anxiety for peace,
consented to give up even their arms and their children.

> ' At Hope's delusive smile,
> The chieftain's safety and the mother's pride
> Were to the insidious conqueror's grasp resign'd ;
> While o'er the western wave th' ensanguined sun,
> In gathering haze, a stormy signal spread,
> And set portentous.'

J. M. W. TURNER, R.A., Professor of Perspective, *Sandycombe Lodge*
Twickenham, and Queen Anne Street West.

131   Raby Castle, the seat of the Earl of Darlington.
132   Dort, or Dordrecht—the Dort Packet-boat, from Rotterdam,
becalmed.
133   The Field of Waterloo.

> ' Last noon beheld them full of lusty life,
> Last eve in Beauty's circle proudly gay ;
> The midnight brought the signal sound of strife,
> The morn, the marshalling in arms—the day,
> Battle's magnificently stern array !
> The thunder-clouds close o'er it, which when rent,
> The earth is covered thick with other clay
> Which her own clay shall cover, heaped and pent,
> Rider and horse—friend, foe, in one red burial blent.

134   Landscape—Composition of Tivoli.

J. M. W. TURNER, R.A., Professor of Perspective, *Sandycombe Lodge,*
Twickenham, and Queen Anne Street West.

135   Entrance of the Meuse—Orange Merchantman on the bar going to
pieces; Brill Church bearing S.E. by S., Marensluys E. by S.
136   England—Richmond Hill, on the Prince Regent's Birthday.

> ' Which way, Amanda, shall we bend our course ?
> The choice perplexes.   Wherefore should we choose?
> All is the same with thee.   Say, shall we wind
> Along the streams? or walk the smiling mead?

> Or court the forest glades? or wander wild
> Among the waving harvests? or ascend,
> While radiant summer opens all its pride,
> Thy hill, delightful Sheen?'—Thomson.

EXHIBITION LII. 1820.

J. M. W. TURNER, R.A., Professor of Perspective, Member of the Roman Academy of St. Luke, *Sandycombe Lodge, Twickenham, and Queen Anne Street West.*

137   Rome from the Vatican—Raffaelle, accompanied by La Fornarina, preparing his pictures for the decoration of the Loggia.

EXHIBITION LIV. 1822.

J. M. W. TURNER, R.A., Professor of Perspective, *Sandycombe Lodge, Twickenham, and Queen Anne Street West.*

138   What you will !

EXHIBITION LV. 1823.

J. M. W. TURNER, R.A., Professor of Perspective, *Queen Anne Street West, and Sandycombe Lodge, Twickenham.*

139   The Bay of Baiæ, with Apollo and the Sibyl.
       'Waft me to sunny Baiæ's shore.'

EXHIBITION LVII. 1825.

J. M. W. TURNER, R.A., Professor of Perspective, *Queen Anne Street West, and Sandycombe Lodge, Twickenham.*

140   Harbour of Dieppe (Changement de Domicile).

EXHIBITION LVIII. 1826.

J. M. W. TURNER, R.A., Professor of Perspective, *Queen Anne Street West, and Sandycombe Lodge, Twickenham.*

141   Cologne—the Arrival of a Packet-boat—Evening.
142   Forum Romanum ; for Mr. Soane's Museum.
143   The Seat of William Moffatt, Esq., Mortlake—Early (summer) morning.

EXHIBITION LIX. 1827.

J. M. W. TURNER, Esq., R.A., Professor of Perspective, *Queen Anne Street West.*

144   'Now for the Painter' (rope)—Passengers going on board.
145   Port Ruysdael.
146   Rembrandt's Daughter.
147   Mortlake Terrace, seat of William Moffatt, Esq.—Summer's evening.
148   Scene in Derbyshire.
       'When first the sun with beacon red.'

EXHIBITION LX. 1828.

J. M. W. TURNER, R.A., *Queen Anne Street West.*

149   Dido directing the Equipment of the Fleet, or the Morning of the Carthaginian Empire.
150   East Cowes Castle, the seat of J. Nash, Esq.—the Regatta beating to windward.
151   East Cowes Castle, the seat of J. Nash, Esq.—the Regatta startin for their moorings.
152   Boccaccio Relating the Tale of the Bird-cage.

EXHIBITION LXI. 1829.

J. M. W. TURNER, R.A., Professor of Perspective, *Queen Anne Street West*

153   The Banks of the Loire.
154   Ulysses Deriding Polyphemus : Homer's Odyssey.

155 The Loretto Necklace.
156 Messieurs les Voyageurs on their return from Italy (par la Diligence)
    in a Snow-drift upon Mount Tarra, 22nd of January 1829.

EXHIBITION LXII. 1830.

J. M. W. TURNER, R.A., Professor of Perspective, *Queen Anne Street West.*
157 Pilate Washing his Hands.

> 'When Pilate saw that he could prevail nothing, but that rather a
> tumult was made, he took water, and washed his hands before the multi-
> tude, saying, I am innocent of the blood of this just person : see ye to it.'—
> *St. Matthew* xxvii. 24.

158 View of Orvieto ; painted in Rome.
159 Palestrina : composition.

> ' Or from yon mural rock, high-crown'd Præneste,
>   Where, misdeeming of his strength, the Carthaginian stood,
>   And marked, with eagle eye, Rome as his victim.'
>   *MS. Fallacies of Hope.*

160 Jessica.

> *Shylock.*—' Jessica, shut the window, I say.'
>   *Merchant of Venice.*

161 Calais Sands, low water—Poissards collecting bait.
162 Fish-market on the Sands—the Sun rising through a vapour.
163 Funeral of Sir Thomas Lawrence ; a sketch from memory.

EXHIBITION LXIII. 1831.

J. M. W. TURNER, R.A., Professor of Perspective, *Queen Anne Street West.*
164 Life-Boat and Manby Apparatus going off to a stranded Vessel
    making signals (blue lights) of distress.
165 Caligula's Palace and Bridge.

> ' What now remains of all the mighty bridge
> Which made the Lucrine Lake an inner pool,
> Caligula, but massive fragments, left
> As monuments of doubt and ruined hopes
> Yet gleaming in the morning's ray, that tell
> How Baiæ's shore was loved in times gone by ?'
>   *MS. Fallacies of Hope.*

166 Vision of Medea.

> ' Or Medea, who in the full tide of witchery
> Had lured the dragon, gained her Jason's love,
> Had filled the spell-bound bowl with Æson's life,
> Yet dashed it to the ground, and raised the poisonous snake
> High in the jaundiced sky to writhe its murderous coil,
> Infuriate in the wreck of hope, withdrew,
> And in the fired palace her twin offspring threw.'
>   *MS. Fallacies of Hope.*

167 Lucy, Countess of Carlisle, and Dorothy Percy's Visit to their
    father, Lord Percy, when under attainder upon the supposition
    of his being concerned in the Gunpowder Plot.
168 Admiral Van Tromp's Barge at the entrance of the Texel, 1645.
169 Watteau Study by Fresnoy's Rules.

> ' White, when it shines with unstained lustre clear,
> May bear an object back, or bring it near.'
>   Fresnoy's *Art of Painting*, p. 496.

170

> ' In this arduous service (of reconnaissance) on the French coast, 1805,
> one of our cruisers took the ground, and had to sustain the attack of the
> flying artillery along shore, the batteries, and the fort of Vimieux, which
> fired heated shot, until she could warp off at the rising tide, which set in
> with all the appearance of a stormy night.'—*Naval Anecdotes.*

Exhibition LXIV. 1832.

J. M. W. TURNER, R.A., *Queen Anne Street West.*

171   Childe Harold's Pilgrimage.—Italy.

> 'And now, fair Italy !
> Thou art the garden of the world.
> Even in thy desert what is like to thee?
> Thy very weeds are beautiful, thy waste
> More rich than other climes' fertility :
> Thy wreck a glory, and thy ruin graced
> With an immaculate charm which cannot be defaced.'
>
> Lord Byron, canto iv.

172   The Prince of Orange, William III., embarked from Holland and landed at Torbay, November 4th, 1688, after a stormy passage.— *History of England.*

> 'The yacht in which His Majesty sailed was, after many changes and services, finally wrecked on Hamburg Sands, while employed in the Hull trade.'

173   Van Tromp's Shallop, at the Entrance of the Scheldt.

174   Helvoetsluys ; the City of Utrecht, 64, going to sea.

175

> 'Then Nebuchadnezzar came near to the mouth of the burning fiery furnace, and spake, and said, Shadrach, Meshach, and Abed-nego, ye servants of the most high God, come forth, and come hither. Then Shadrach, Meshach, and Abed-nego came forth of the midst of the fire.'— *Daniel* iii. 26.

176   Staffa, Fingal's Cave.

> 'Nor of a theme less solemn tells
> That mighty surge that ebbs and swells,
> And still, between each awful pause,
> From the high vault an answer draws.'
>
> Sir Walter Scott's *Lord of the Isles*, canto iv.

Exhibition LXV. 1833.

J. M. W. TURNER, R.A., Professor of Perspective, *Queen Anne Street West.*

177   Rotterdam Ferry-boat.

178   Bridge of Sighs, Ducal Palace, and Custom House, Venice ; Canaletti painting.

179   Van Goyen, looking out for a subject.

180   Van Tromp, returning after the battle off the Dogger Bank.

181   Ducal Palace, Venice.

182   Mouth of the Seine, Quillebœuf.

> This estuary is so dangerous from its quicksands, that any vessel taking the ground is liable to be stranded and overwhelmed by the rising tide, which rushes in in one wave.

Exhibition LXVI. 1834.

J. M. W. TURNER, R.A., Professor of Perspective, *Queen Anne Street West.*

183   The Fountain of Indolence.

184   The Golden Bough (*MS. Fallacies of Hope*).

185   Venice.

186   Wreckers.—Coast of Northumberland, with a steamboat assisting a ship off shore.

187   St. Michael's Mount, Cornwall.

Exhibition LXVII. 1835.

J. M. W. TURNER, R.A., *Queen Anne Street West.*

188   Keelmen heaving in coals by night.

189   The Broad Stone of Honour (Ehrenbreitstein), and Tomb of Marceau; from Byron's *Childe Harold.* ·

> ' By Coblentz, on a rise of gentle ground,
> There is a small and simple pyramid
> Crowning the summit of the verdant mound
> Beneath its base are hero's ashes hid,
> Our enemy's—but let not that forbid
> Honour to Marceau . . . . .
> . . . . . . He was Freedom's champion !
> Here Ehrenbreitstein, with her shattered wall,
> Yet shows of what she was.'

190   Venice, from the Porch of Madonna della Salute.

191   Line-fishing, off Hastings.

192   The Burning of the Houses of Lords and Commons, October 16th, 1834.

EXHIBITION LXVIII. 1836.

J. M. W. TURNER, R.A., Professor of Perspective, *Queen Anne Street West.*

193   Juliet and her Nurse.

194   Rome, from Mount Aventine.

195   Mercury and Argus.

EXHIBITION LXIX. 1837.

J. M. W. TURNER, R.A., Professor of Perspective, *Queen Anne Street West.*

196   Scene.—A Street in Venice.

> ' *Antonio.*—Hear me yet, good Shylock.
> *Shylock.*—I'll have my bond.'
> *Merchant of Venice*, Act iii. Sc. 3.

197   Story of Apollo and Daphne.—Ovid's *Metamorphoses.*

> ' Sure is my bow, unerring is my dart ;
> But, ah ! more deadly his who pierced my heart.
>   *   *   *   *
> As when th' impatient greyhound, slipt from far,
> Bounds o'er the glebe to course the fearful hare,
> She in her speed does all her safety lay ;
> And he with double speed pursues the prey.'

198   The Parting of Hero and Leander—from the Greek of Musæus.

> ' The morning came too soon, with crimsoned blush,
> Chiding the tardy night and Cynthia's warning beam ;
> But Love yet lingered on the terraced steep,
> Upheld young Hymen's torch and failing lamp,
> The token of departure, never to return.
> Wild dashed the Hellespont its straitened surge,
> And on the raised spray appeared Leander's fall.'

199   Snow Storm, Avalanche, and Inundation; a Scene in the upper part of Val d'Aouste, Piedmont.

EXHIBITION LXX. 1838.

J. M. W. TURNER, R.A., Professor of Perspective, *Queen Anne Street West.*

200   Phryne going to the Public Bath as Venus—Demosthenes taunted by Æschines.

201   Modern Italy—the Pifferari.

202   Ancient Italy—Ovid banished from Rome.

EXHIBITION LXXI. 1839.

J. M. W. TURNER, R.A., *Queen Anne Street West.*

203   The Fighting Téméraire tugged to her last Berth to be broken up, 1838.

> ' The flag which braved the battle and the breeze
> No longer owns her.'

204 Ancient Rome—Agrippina landing with the Ashes of Germanicus. The Triumphal Bridge and Palace of the Cæsars restored.

> ‘ The clear stream,
> Aye,—the yellow Tiber glimmers to her beam,
> Even while the sun is setting.’

205 Modern Rome—Campo Vaccino.

> ‘The moon is up, and yet it is not night ;
> The sun as yet divides the day with her.’—Lord Byron.

206 Pluto carrying off Proserpine.—Ovid’s *Metamorphoses.*

207 Cicero at his Villa.

Exhibition LXXII. 1840.

J. M. W. TURNER, R.A., *Queen Anne Street West.*

208 Bacchus and Ariadne.

209 Venice, the Bridge of Sighs.

> ‘ I stood upon a bridge, a palace and
> A prison on each hand.’—Byron.

210 Venice, from the Canale della Giudecca, Chiesa di S. Maria della Salute, &c.

211 Slavers throwing overboard the Dead and Dying. Typhoon coming on.

> ‘ Aloft all hands, strike the topmasts and belay ;
> Yon angry setting sun and fierce-edged clouds
> Declare the Typhoon’s coming.
> Before it sweeps your decks, throw overboard
> The dead and dying—ne’er heed their chains.
> Hope, Hope, fallacious Hope !
> Where is thy market now ?’—*MS. Fallacies of Hope.*

212 The New Moon ; or ‘I’ve lost my Boat, you shan’t have your Hoop.’

213 Rockets and Blue Lights (close at hand) to warn Steamboats off Shoal-water.

214 Neapolitan Fisher-Girls surprised Bathing by Moonlight.

Exhibition LXXIII. 1841.

J. M. W. TURNER, R.A., *Queen Anne Street West.*

215 Ducal Palace, Dogana, with part of San Giorgio, Venice.

216 Giudecca, la Donna della Salute and San Giorgio.

217 Rosenau, seat of H.R.H. Prince Albert of Coburg, near Coburg, Germany.

218 Depositing of John Bellini’s Three Pictures in La Chiesa Redentore, Venice.

219 Dawn of Christianity (Flight into Egypt).

> ‘That star has risen.’—Rev. T. Gisborne’s *Walks in a Forest.*

220 Glaucus and Scylla.—Ovid’s *Metamorphoses.*

Exhibition LXXIV. 1842.

J. M. W. TURNER, R.A. *Queen Anne Street West.*

221 The Dogana, San Giorgio, Citella, from the steps of the Europa.

222 Campo Santo, Venice.

223 Snow Storm ; Steamboat off a harbour’s mouth making signals in shallow water, and going by the lead. The author was in that storm on the night the Ariel left Harwich.

224 Peace—Burial at Sea.

> ‘The midnight torch gleam’d o’er the steamer’s side
> And Merit’s corse was yielded to the tide.’
> *MS. Fallacies of Hope.*

225 War. The exile and the rock limpet.

> 'Ah ! thy tent-formed shell is like
> A soldier's nightly bivouac, alone
> Amidst a sea of blood . . . .
> . . . but can you join your comrades?'
>   *MS. Fallacies of Hope.*

EXHIBITION LXXV. 1843.
J. M. W. TURNER, R.A., *Queen Anne Street West.*

226 The Opening of the Walhalla, 1842.

> 'L'honneur au Roi de Baviere.'
> 'Who rode on thy relentless car, fallacious Hope?
> He, though scathed at Ratisbon, poured on
> The tide of war o'er all thy plain, Bavare,
> Like the swollen Danube to the gates of Wien ;
>   But peace returns—the morning ray
> Beams on the Walhalla, reared to science and the arts,
> And men renowned, of German fatherland.'
>   *MS. Fallacies of Hope.*

227 The 'Sun of Venice' going to Sea.

> 'Fair shines the morn, and soft the zephyrs blow a gale,
> Venicia's fisher spreads his painted sail,
> Nor heeds the demon that in grim repose
> Expects his evening prey.'

228 Dogana, and Madonna della Salute, Venice.
229 Shade and Darkness.—The Evening of the Deluge.

> 'The moon puts forth her sign of woe unheeded ;
> But disobedience slept ; the darkening Deluge
>   Closed around,
> And the last token came : the giant frame-work floated,
> The scared birds forsook their nightly shelter screaming,
> And the beasts waded to the Ark.'—*Fallacies of Hope.*

230 Light and Colour (Goethe's Theory)—The Morning after the Deluge
     —Moses writing the Book of Genesis.

> 'The Ark stood firm on Ararat ; th' returning sun
> Exhaled earth's humid bubbles, and, emulous of light,
> Reflected her lost forms, each in prismatic guise
> Hope's harbinger, ephemeral as the summer fly
> Which rises, flits, expands, and dies.'—*Fallacies of Hope.*

231 St. Benedetto, looking towards Fusina.

EXHIBITION LXXVI. 1844.
J. M. W. TURNER, R.A., *Queen Anne Street West.*

232 Ostend.
233 Fishing Boats bringing a disabled ship into Port Ruysdael.
234 Rain, Steam, and Speed.—The Great Western Railway.
235 Van Tromp, going about to please his masters, ships a sea, getting a
     good wetting.—*Vide Lives of Dutch Painters.*
236 Venice—Maria della Salute.
237 Approach to Venice.

> 'The path lies o'er the sea, invisible ;
> And from the land we went
> As to a floating city, steering in,
> And gliding up her streets as in a dream,
> So smoothly, silently.'—Rogers's *Italy.*
> 'The moon is up, and yet it is not night;
> The sun as yet disputes the day with her.'—Byron.

Venice Quay—Ducal Palace.

Exhibition LXXVII. 1845.

J. M. W. TURNER, R.A., *Queen Anne Street West.*

239 Whalers.—*Vide* Beale's *Voyage*, p. 163.
240 Whalers.—*Vide* Beale's *Voyage*, p. 175.
241 Venice—Evening ; Going to the Ball.—*MS. Fallacies of Hope.*
242 Morning ; Returning from the Ball, St. Martino.—*MS. Fallacies of Hope.*
243 Venice—Noon.—*MS. Fallacies of Hope.*
244 Venice—Sunset ; a Fisher.—*MS. Fallacies of Hope.*

Exhibition LXXVIII. 1846.

J. M. W. TURNER, R.A., *Queen Anne Street West.*

245 Returning from the Ball (St. Martha).
246 Going to the Ball (San Martino).
247 'Hurrah for the Whaler Erebus ! another fish !'—Beale's *Voyage.*
248 Undine giving the Ring to Massaniello ; Fishermen of Naples.
249 The Angel standing in the Sun.

> 'And I saw an angel standing in the sun ; and he cried with a loud voice, saying to all the fowls that fly in the midst of heaven, Come and gather yourselves together unto the supper of the great God ;
> 'That ye may eat the flesh of kings, and the flesh of captains, and the flesh of mighty men, and the flesh of horses, and of them that sit on them, and the flesh of all men, both free and bond, both small and great.'
> *Revelation* xix. 17, 18.

> 'The march of arms, which, glittering in the sun,
> The feast of vultures ere the day was done.'—Rogers.

250 Whalers (boiling blubber) entangled in floe ice, endeavouring to extricate themselves.

Exhibition LXXIX. 1847.

J. M. W. TURNER, R.A., *Queen Anne Street West.*

251 The Hero of a Hundred Fights.

> An idea suggested by the German invocation upon casting the bell in England called tapping the furnace.—*MS. Fallacies of Hope.*

Exhibition LXXXI. 1849.

J. M. W. TURNER, R.A., *Queen Anne Street West.*

252 The Wreck Buoy.
253 Venus and Adonis.

Exhibition LXXXII. 1850.

J. M. W. TURNER, R.A., *Queen Anne Street West.*

254 Mercury sent to admonish Æneas.

> 'Beneath the morning mist,
> Mercury waited to tell him of his neglected fleet.'
> *MS. Fallacies of Hope.*

255 Æneas relating his Story to Dido.

> 'Fallacious Hope beneath the moon's pale crescent shone;
> Dido listened to Troy being lost and won.'
> *MS. Fallacies of Hope.*

256 The Visit to the Tomb.

> 'The sun went down in wrath at such deceit.'
> *MS. Fallacies of Hope.*

257 The Departure of the Fleet.

> 'The orient moon shone on the departing fleet,
> Nemesis invoked, the priest held the poisoned cup.'
> *MS. Fallacies of Hope.*

BRITISH INSTITUTION.

EXHIBITION 1806.
J. M. W. TURNER, R.A., 64 *Harley Street.*

258   Narcissus and Echo.

From Ovid's *Metamorphoses.*

259   The Goddess of Discord choosing the Apple of Contention in the Garden of the Hesperides.

EXHIBITION 1808.
J. M. W. TURNER, R.A., *West End, Upper Mall, Hammersmith, and Harley Street.*

260   The Battle of Trafalgar, as seen from the mizen starboard shrouds of the Victory.

261   Jason ;—from Ovid's *Metamorphoses.*

EXHIBITION 1809.

262   Sun rising through Vapour, with Fishermen Landing and cleaning their Fish.

EXHIBITION 1814.
J. M. W. TURNER, R.A., *Harley Street, Cavendish Square.*

263   Apuleia in search of Apuleius.

Vide Ovid's *Metamorphoses.*

EXHIBITION 1817.
J. M. W. TURNER, R.A., *Queen Anne Street, Cavendish Square.*

264   View of the Temple of Jupiter Panhellenius, in the Island of Ægina, with the Greek National Dance of the Romaika : the Acropolis of Athens in the distance ; painted from a sketch taken by H. Gally Knight, Esq., in 1810.

EXHIBITION 1835.
J. M. W. TURNER, R.A., *Queen Anne Street.*

265   The Burning of the House of Lords and Commons, 16th October 1834.

EXHIBITION 1836.

266   Wreckers on the North Shore.
267   Fire of the House of Lords.

EXHIBITION 1837.

268   Regulus.

EXHIBITION 1838.

269   Fishing Boats, with Hucksters bargaining for Fish.

EXHIBITION 1839.

270   Fountain of Fallacy.

> ' Its Rainbow dew diffused fell on each anxious lip,
> Working wild fantasy, imagining ;
> First, Science, in the immeasurable
>   Abyss of thought,
> Measured her orbit slumbering.'—*MS. Fallacies of Hope.*

EXHIBITION 1840.

271   Mercury and Argus.

EXHIBITION 1841.

272   Snow Storm, Avalanche, and Inundation in the Alps.
273   Blue Lights (close at hand) to warn Steamboats off Shoal-water.

EXHIBITION 1846.

274   Queen Mab's Cave.

> 'Frisk it, frisk it, by the moonlight beam.'
>   *Midsummer Night's Dream.*
> 'Thy orgies, Mab, are manifold.'
>   *MS. Fallacies of Hope.*

CATALOGUE OF PICTURES GIVEN BY TURNER TO THE NATION, NOW IN THE NATIONAL GALLERY.

The Sun rising in Mist.
Dido building Carthage.
Portrait of himself.
Moonlight.
Buttermere Lake.
Coniston Fells.
Cattle in Water.
Æneas with the Sibyl.
Rizpah.
Castle.
View in Wales, Castle.
Sandpit.
Clapham Common.
Sea Piece.
The Tenth Plague.
Jason.
Calais Pier.
The Holy Family.
Destruction of Sodom.
View of a Town.
The Shipwreck.
The Garden of the Hesperides.
Blacksmith's Shop.
Death of Nelson.
Spithead.
The Garreteer's Petition.
Greenwich Hospital.
St. Mawes, Cornwall.
Abingdon, Berkshire.
Windsor.
Ruin, with Cattle.
Apollo and the Python.
Avalanche.

Hannibal crossing the Alps.
Kingston Bank.
Frosty Morning.
The Deluge.
Dido and Æneas.
Apuleia in search of Apuleius.
Bligh Sand.
Crossing the Brook.
The Decline of Carthage.
The Field of Waterloo.
Orange Merchantman going to Pieces.
Richmond Hill.
Rome, from the Vatican.
Rome, the Arch of Titus.
The Bay of Baiæ.
Carthage.
Scene from Boccaccio.
Ulysses deriding Polyphemus.
The Loretto Necklace.
Pilate washing his Hands.
View of Orvieto.
Caligula's Palace and Bridge.
The Vision of Medea.
Watteau Painting.
Lord Percy under Attainder.
Childe Harold's Pilgrimage.
The Fiery Furnace.

Heidelberg Castle.
Regulus leaving Rome.
Apollo and Daphne.
Hero and Leander.
Phryne going to the Bath.
Agrippina.
The Téméraire.
Bacchus and Ariadne.
The New Moon.
Venice, Bridge of Sighs.
Burial of Wilkie.
The Exile and the Rock Limpet.
Steamer in a Snowstorm.
The Evening of the Deluge.
The Morning after the Deluge.
The Opening of the Walhalla.
Approach to Venice.
The 'Sun of Venice' going to Sea.
Port Ruysdael.
Van Tromp.
Rain, Steam, and Speed.
Venice, the Giudecca.
Venice, the Quay.
Venice, Noon.
Venice, Sunset.
Venice. Going to the Ball.
Venice. Returning from the Ball.
Whalers.

Whalers.	Æneas relating his Story to Dido.	The Battle of Trafalgar.
Whalers boiling Blubber.	Mercury sent to admonish Æneas.	Richmond Bridge.
Queen Mab's Grotto.		Fire at Sea.
Massaniello.		Petworth Park.
The Angel in the Sun.	The Departure of the Trojan Fleet.	Chichester Canal.
Tapping the Furnace.		Mountain Glen.
	The Visit to the Tomb.	Harvest Home.

List of the Turner Drawings and Sketches, exhibited with the Turner Collection of Pictures.

THE LIBER STUDIORUM.

Fifty-one Water-colour Drawings in brown, being the greater portion of the original Drawings made for the so-called *Liber Studiorum*, or 'Book of Studies,' in imitation of Claude's *Liber Veritatis*, or 'Book of Truth.' The prints, in brown ink, from these drawings were published in numbers, from the year 1808 until 1819. Many of the plates were etched, and some engraved, by Turner himself.

Compositions.
No.
1 Jason.
2 Solitude.
3 Bridge with Goats.
4 Bridge in middle distance.
5 Cephalus and Procris.
6 Pastoral.
7 Pastoral with Castle.
8 Woman playing Tambourine.
9 The Tenth Plague of Egypt.
10 Hindoo Devotions.
11 Hindoo Ablutions.
12 Christ and the Woman of Samaria.

Foreign Views.
13 Laufenburg on the Rhine.
14 The Lake of Thun, Switzerland.
15 Thun, Switzerland.
16 The Little Devil's Bridge, Altdorf.

No.
17 Mount St. Gothard.
18 Bonneville, Savoy.
19 The Alps from Grenoble to Chamberi.

British Views.
20 Norham Castle, on the Tweed.
21 Holy Island Cathedral.
22 Morpeth.
23 Rivaulx Abbey, Yorkshire.
24 Crypt, Kirkstall Abbey.
25 Dunstanburgh Castle.
26 Coast of Yorkshire.
27 Winchelsea.
28 East Gate, Winchelsea.
29 Hind Head Hill.
30 Martello Towers, Bexhill.
31 St. Catherine's Hill, near Guildford.
32 Pembury Mill, Kent.

No.
33 Greenwich Hospital.
34 Chepstow Castle, River Wye.
35 The Wye and the Severn.
36 Flint Castle : Smugglers.
37 Dumblane Abbey.
38 Peat Bog, Scotland.
39 View near Blair-Athol.
40 The Clyde.
41 Inverary Castle.

Various.
42 Sketch for Sea Piece.
43   Do.
44 Bridge and Cows.
45 Watermill.
46 Stackyard.
47 Farmyard with Pigs.
48 Hedging & Ditching.
49 Marine Dabblers.
50 Young Anglers.
51 Juvenile Tricks.

Sketches and Drawings extending over a period of nearly Sixty Years, arranged as nearly as practicable in Chronological Order.

FIRST PERIOD: EARLY SKETCHES.

No.	Subject.	Method.
1	North-west View of Malmesbury Abbey— View on the River Avon, 'from Wallace's Wall'—'View of Cook's Folly,' looking up the Avon, 'with Wallace's Wall and the Hot Wells'	In Water Colour.
2	The Mewstone	Do.
3	Tower of St. Mary Redcliffe, Bristol— Transept and Towers of York Cathedral—Tower of Boston, Lincolnshire	Pencil Outline.
4	Malmesbury Abbey	Do.
5	Kirkstall Abbey—Holy Island Cathedral	Do.
6	Leeds—Bolton Abbey	Do.
7	Fire (Steam) Engine, Coalbrook Dale— Copper Works, Swansea—Fire Engine, Coalbrook Dale—Iron Foundry, Maidley Wood—Fire Engine, Coalbrook Dale—Fire Engine near Glasmount (So named at the backs)	Pen and Ink.
8	View of the Interior of the Savoy Chapel	Light and Shade.
9	View of Tivoli	Do.
10	Study of Shipping	Do.
11	Portico of St. Peter's, Rome	Do.
12	Study of a Cottage	Water Colour.
13	A Cottage Roof	Do.
14	Carisbrook Castle	Do.
15	An Interior	Do.
16	Landscape	Do.
17	Three Studies of Boats	Do.
18	Do. Do.	{ Body Colour on Brown and on Blue.
19	Seven Studies of a Shipwreck—Sketch of a Boat	Pen and Ink.
20	Two Coast Scenes	Do.
21	Sketch for Picture of Ivy Bridge, Devon —Study of a Stream	Pencil and Water Colour.
22	Two Studies of Fir and Willow	Pencil on Brown.

SECOND PERIOD, FROM ABOUT 1802.

No.	Subject.	Method.
23	Study near Grenoble	Pencil and Chalk on Brown.
24	The Lake of Brientz—Vevay	Do.
25	Convent of the Great St. Bernard—The Town of Aosta	Do.
26	Roman Gate, Aosta—Another View of the same	Do.
27	Castle of Aosta, two Views	{ Pencil and Chalk on Brown, and Water Colour.
28	Glaciers, Grindelwald—Fallen Trees	Pencil and Chalk on Brown.

No.	Subject.	Method.
29	The Ascent to Cormayeur—Valley of the Isere	Pencil and Chalk on Brown.
30	The Road from Voreppe to Grenoble—Mont Blanc from Fort St. Louis	Do.
31	The Alps, looking towards Grenoble—Grenoble with Mont Blanc	Do.
32	Two Views of Grenoble	Do.
33	View of an English Country Seat	Do.
34	Study of a Mountain Stream	Oil Colours.
35	Edinburgh from Calton Hill	Drawing in Water Colour.
36	Building, with Cattle	Body Colour on Blue.
37	Funeral of Sir Thomas Lawrence	Water Colour.
38	Contamines, Savoy	Body Colour on Brown.
39	Source of the Arveron	Chalk on Brown.
40	Valley of Chamouni	Do. and Body Colour.
41	Battle of Fort Bard, Val d'Aosta, 1800; exhibited in 1815	Drawing in Water Colour.
42	Ivy Bridge, Devon	Do.
43	Two Studies of a Figure, for Picture of Deluge	Chalk on Blue.
44	Sketch of a Group of Figures, for Picture of Hannibal	Do.
45	Study of a Cutter	Do.
46	Study of a Pilot Boat	Pen and Ink on Blue.
47	Two Marine Sketches	Pen and Chalk on Blue.
48	Do.　　Do.	Do.
49	Study of an Arm Chair	Oil Colours.
50	Four Studies of Dock Leaves	Pen and Ink.
51	Do.　　Plants	{ Pen and Ink on White and Brown.
52	Study of Sheep	Pencil.
53	Study of Pigs and of Donkeys	{ Body Colour on Brown and on Blue.
54	Do.　Dutch Hardware &c.	Pencil and Pencil Outlines.
55	Views in Rouen—Norman Caps	Pencil.
56	Studies on the Seine—Sketches from Claude	Do.
57	Studies of a Skeleton	Chalk on Brown.
58	Dead Ducks	Colour and Chalk.
59	Study of a Teal flying	Water Colour.

Nine Views of Rome, 1819.　*Sketches in Body Colour.*

1 Rome from Monte Mario.
2 Rome from the Barberini Villa.
3 Bridge and Castle of Sant' Angelo from St. Peter's.
4 The Colosseum.
5 The Basilica of Constantine.

6 The Arches of Constantine and Titus.
8 The Church and Convent of the Quattro Coronati.
9 The Claudian Aqueduct.

THIRD PERIOD, FROM ABOUT 1820.

60	Two Landscapes	Pencil Outlines.
61	Do.	Do.
62	Do.	Do.

No.	Subject.	Method.
63	Landscape—Moonlight	Water Colour.
64	A Stormy Sky	Do.
65	Three Marine Sketches	Do.
66	Do. Do.	Body Colour on Blue.
67	Dover	Drawing in Water Colour.
68	North Shields	Do.
69	Rochester..	Do.
70	Four Sketches—Rivers of France.........	Body Colour on Blue.
71	Four Sketches—Calais	Pen and Ink on Blue.
72	Evreux Market-place — Louviers — and two Sketches of Vernon..................	Pen and Ink on Blue.
73	Marly, near St. Germain, looking up the River—Castle of the Fair Gabrielle—and near St. Germain, looking down the River	Pen and Ink.
74	Four Studies — Ambleteuse (?) Dieppe and Rouen	Do.
75	Three Sketches of Rooms at Petworth...	Body Colour on Blue.
76	Four Sunset Studies at Petworth	Do.
77	Four Sketches—Rivers of France.........	Do.
78	Do. Do.	Do.
79	Do. Do.	Do.
80	Do. Do.	Do.
81	Do. Do.	Do.
82	Do. Do.	Do.
83	Do. Do.	Do.
84	Do. Do.	Do.
85	Do. Do.	Do.
86	Do. Do.	Do.
87	Two Studies for Vignettes, Rogers's Columbus....................................	Water Colour.
88	Two Vignettes	Do.
89	Do.	Do.
90	Studies of Swiss Costume	Do.
91	French Dance in Sabots....................	Body Colour on Blue.
92	Villeneuve—Gallery on the Splügen—Vevay	Pencil on Brown.
93	Fortress—Lausanne, Sunset	Water Colour.
94	Moselle Bridge, Coblentz—Bridge over the Rhine, Coblentz	Do.
95	Two Views on Lake Lucerne	Do.
96	The Lake of Annecy	Water Colour.
97	San Giorgio Maggiore, and Santa Maria della Salute, Venice	Do.
98	The Riva degli Schiavoni, and Lagoon, Venice	Do.
99	Sunset, Lake Lucerne—Night, Zurich ...	Do.
100	Morning on Lake Lucerne, three Sketches	Do.

101 View of Rome. Date 1819. (Full of accurate detail.)
102 Rome—the Bridge and Castle of St. Angelo. (Lovely colour.)
103 Rome from Monte Mario. (Beautiful middle distance.)

104 Rome from the Barberini Villa.
105 Rome—Nymphæum of Alexander Severus. (Fine, but careless.)
106 The Claudian Aqueduct at Rome.
107 The Colosseum at Rome.
108 The Basilica of Constantine at Rome.
109 The Church of St. Giovanni e Paolo at Rome.
110 The Arches of Constantine and Titus at Rome.
111 Study for the Oil Pictures of the Loggie. (A foreground at Rome.)
112 Four leaves from a Sketch-book filled on the way to and from Scotland by Sea, on the occasion of George the Fourth's Visit to Edinburgh.
113 Ten leaves from a Book of Sketches on the Rhine and Meuse—Huy and Dinant.
114 Six leaves from a Sketch-book on the Lake of Geneva—Junction of the Rhone and Arve ; Studies of Boats ; Lausanne from the North ; Lausanne from the East ; Geneva from the West ; Geneva from the West at a greater distance.
115 Twelve leaves from a Sketch-book at Venice, comprising Santa Maria della Salute ; the Custom House ; St. Mark's Place ; Casa Grimani and the Rialto ; St. George's and St. Mary's of Health ; the Grand Canal from Casa Foscari to the Rialto ; Riva degli Schiavoni, with St. Mark's and St. Zachary's ; the Doge's Palace and Mint ; the Fruit Market ; the Coal Market ; the Rialto, with the West side of the Grand Canal ; the Rialto, with the East side of the Grand Canal.
116 Three leaves from Note-books—Seven Sunsets and Sketches of Clouds from Andernach on the Rhine ; the Borromean Islands on Lago Maggiore.
117 Two leaves of a Note-book filled at Naples.
118 Studies from Claude and in France—View near Dieppe ; Fishwives quarrelling on Dieppe Beach.
119 View of Dresden.
120 The Arch of Titus. Same from the side.
121 Studies of Light and Shade in and on hollow glass balls.
122 Angry Swans.
123 Studies of Poultry.
124 Buckingham Gate (?) Hungerford Bridge.
125 Source of the Arveron.
126 Study for the drawing of Grenoble.
127 Ditto.
128 A Mountain Stream. (In oil.)
129 Study of Masts and Rigging.
130 Boat in Heavy Sea. Boat Swamped in Surf.
131 Three Studies of a Ship on Fire.
132 Sunset over a Town. Twilight. (Same as at Petworth.)
133 Town on the Loire (Saumur ?) ; Huy on the Meuse from above the Château ; Dinant on the Meuse.
134 Orléans (Theatre and Cathedral). Nantes (Promenade near the Château).
135 Promenade at Nantes. Dressing for Tea. Firelight and Cat.
136 Havre (?). Harfleur. Caudebec. Saumur. (Mr. Ruskin thinks the Harfleur specially beautiful.)
137 Saumur. Montjean. (Study for a drawing [Saumur ?] made for the 'Keepsake.')

138 Studies on the Loire and Meuse. Huy. (Morning effect.)
139 Study of a Town on the Loire. The Carrara Mountains from Sarzana.
140 Vignette of Turbot and Mullet.
141 Vignette of Mackerel.
142 Swiss Fortress—Grenoble.
143 Calm. Fresh Breeze. (Pen Studies.)
144 Carew Castle about 1800 (published 1834). Lancaster. (First Sketches of England Series.)
145 Caernarvon Castle. Wells Cathedral.
146 Two Bridge subjects.
147 Cologne Cathedral—on the Rhine. ('Magnificent and of his finest time.'—*Ruskin.*)
148 Sketches at and near York. (Pencil—Middle time.)
149 Sequel to ditto.
150 On the Rhine. (Brown paper—Late.)
151 Bellinzona. (Very late.)
152 Fribourg. (Probably last Swiss journey, 1845.)
153 Fribourg, companion. (From a book with fourteen detailed sketches.)

MISCELLANEOUS COLLECTIONS.

(IN THEIR PRESENT STATE.)

Turner's Pictures and Drawings in the Gallery of F. H. Fawkes, Esq., Farnley Hall, near Leeds.

OIL PAINTINGS.

Lake of Geneva, from above Vevay, and looking towards the Valley of the Rhone.
Pilot with Red Cap hailing a Smack in stormy weather.
The Victory returning from Trafalgar, beating up Channel, in three positions ; fresh breeze.

Coast Scene—Sunset, with men-of-war at anchor ; fine weather.
Landscape.
(The last five were painted from 1808 to 1816.)
Dort—Holland. 1818.
Rembrandt's Daughter. 1827.

WATER-COLOUR DRAWINGS.

English.

Scarborough, Yorkshire.
Flounder-fishing, Putney Bridge.
Cottage Scene.
Fountains Abbey, Yorkshire.
Bolton Abbey, Yorkshire.
The Strid, Bolton Abbey.
High Force—Tees River.
Wharfedale, from Chevin Park.
Lancaster Sands.

Coast Scene.
Windermere, Westmoreland.
Loch Fine, Argyleshire.
View of Coniston, Westmoreland.
  „   „   and Old Man.
First-rate, taking in stores.
Old House, Farnley.
Party on the Moors, 12th August.

Swiss.

Valley of Chamouni, looking eastward.

Mont Blanc, from Val D'Aosta.

Lake of Lucerne, from Fluelen.

Teufels-Brück, St. Gothard.

Falls of the Reichenbach, Valley of Grindelwald.

Source of the Avernon, Chamouni.

Valley of Chamouni.

Montanvert and Mer de Glace.

Lac de Brientz—Moonlight.

Mont Cenis—Snow-storm.

Lausanne and Lake of Geneva.

Mont Blanc, from Chamouni.

Vevay and Lake of Geneva.

Sallenche.

Bonneville, Savoy.

Falls of Staubach, Lauterbrunnen.

Falls of Reichenbach.

Italian.

Venice, from Fusina.

The Rialto, Venice.

Rome, from Monte Mario.

„ „ Pincio.

The Colosseum, Rome.

Interior of St. Peter's, Rome.

Naples, and Bay.

Eruption of Mount Vesuvius.

Ships hailing a Pilot off the Tagus.

All these drawings were made between the years 1803 and 1820.

WATER-COLOUR DRAWINGS IN CASES,

Illustrative of Poems by Lord Byron and Sir W. Scott and Moore.

Frontispiece.

''Tis Greece, but living Greece no more.'—Byron's *Giaour*.

' Day sat on Norham's Castle steep.'—Scott's *Marmion*.

' If you would view fair Melrose aright,

You must view it by the pale moonlight.'

Scott's *Lay of the Last Minstrel*.

' Lone Glenartney's hazel shade.'—Scott's *Lady of the Lake*.

' Here, 'twixt rock and river, grew

A dismal grove of sable hue.'—Scott's *Rokeby*.

' Lalla Rookh.'—*Moore*.

DRAWINGS OF 1822.

Frontispieces to ' Chronology,' by Walter Fawkes, Esq.

Pyramids, for Ancient History. | Stonehenge, for Modern History.

Illustrative of Periods of English History.

The Reformation.

First Period of the Civil War.

Second do. do.

Third do. do.

Fourth do. do.

Swords of Oliver Cromwell, Sir Thomas Fairfax, and Lambert, as preserved at Farnley Hall.

Banners of the Royal side.

Banners of the Parliamentarians.

Revolution of 1688.

WATER-COLOUR DRAWINGS.

London, from windows of 45 Grosvenor Place, when in possession of Walter Fawkes, Esq.

Drawing-room of 45 Grosvenor Place.

Frontispiece to Catalogue of Water-colour Drawings in 45 Grosvenor Place.

Top of a Snuff-box—Grouse, Partridge, and Gun.

WATER-COLOUR DRAWINGS OF BIRDS.

From Nature.

Head of a Moor Buzzard.
Head of White Owl.
Jay, dead.
Head of Cuckoo.
Head of Green Woodpecker.
Goldfinch.
Robin Redbreast.
Ringdove, dead.
Head of Game-cock.
Head of Cock Pheasant.

Head of Hen Pheasant.
Head of Turkey-cock.
Head of Peacock.
Head of Grouse.
Grouse Hanging.
Head of Partridge.
Head of Woodcock.
Kingfisher, dead.
Head of Heron.
Head of Guinea-fowl.

SKETCHES ON THE RHINE (in a Case).

Mayence and Cassel.
Mayence. N.
Mayence. S.
Palace of Breberech.
Johannisberg.
Rudisheim, looking to Bingen Klopp. N.
Bingen Ehrenfels, looking out of Loch.
Abbey of Bingen, looking into Loch.
Bingen Loch and Mansethurn. N.
Bautsburg. S.
Sonneck on left—on right, Bacharach in the distance.
Fürstenberg.
Bacharach and Stableck.
Pfalz Caub and Outenfels.
Oberwesel and Schonberg Castle.
Lurleyberg. N.
Goerhausen and Hatz Castle.
Lurleyberg. S.
Lurleyberg and Goerhausen. N.
Lurleyberg. S.
Lurleyberg.
Goerhausen. N.
Lurleyberg. S.
Ditto.
Hatz Castle, with Rheinfels. W.
From Rheinfels, looking over St. Goar to Hatz.

Hirzenach. N.
Rheinfels, looking to Hatz and Goerhausen.
Castles of the Two Brothers, with Sternberg and Lieberstein.
Boppart.
Peterhoff.
Marksburg. S.
Oberlanstein. N. Chapel.
Entrance of the Lahn. S.
Abbey, near Coblentz. S.
Back of Ehrenbreitstein, from the Pfaffen.
From Ehrenbreitstein.
Quay of Coblentz.
Bridge over the Moselle, Coblentz.
Neuwied and Weissenthurm. N.
Weissenthurm and Hoché, Monument.
Andernach. N.
Roman Tower, Andernach. N.
Hamerstein. S.
Remagen (S.) and Lintz.
Rolandsworth Nunnery (N.), with Drachenfels.
Drachenfels and Nunnery.
Drachenfels.
Godesberg. S.
Rhein Gate, Cologne. S.
Cologne. N.

SKETCHES (IN CASES) OF THE FARNLEY PROPERTY.

Case 1.

Otley Lodges.
Approach to Farnley Hall from the West.
Dairy, Farnley.

Old Porch—Flower Garden.
Old Part of House and ditto.
Old Fairfax Gateway, and Firs.
West Lodge, (designed by Turner).

Wharfe and Chevin, from Park.
Glen to Loch Tiny.
Glen leading to Loch Tiny.
Loch Tiny and Summer-house.
,, and Almscliffe.
,, and Boat-house.

Loch Tiny and Lindley Hall.
Banks of Washburne. S.
Lindley Mill. S.
Lindley Bridge, Wood, and Hall.
Guy Barn, Bank, and Ford.

Case 2.

Caley Hall.
Rocks in Caley Park.
,, East.
West Entrance to ditto.
Newall Old Hall.
Lindley Old Hall.
Hawkworth Old Hall.
Fairfax Cabinet.

Oak Room at Farnley Hall.
Old Staircase.
Study.
Ditto.
Painted Window.
Modern Staircase.
Dining-room.
Drawing-room.

All these drawings made between 1806 and 1820.

SKETCHES FRAMED.

Washburne. N.
Junction of Wharfe and Washburne Rivers, with Farnley Hall in
the distance.

Turner's Drawings in the Collection of J. Ruskin, Esq.

PAINTINGS.

'Shylock.' The Rialto at Venice. | Slaver Throwing Overboard the
Dead.

DRAWINGS.

Richmond, Yorkshire—Town and
Castle, from the banks of the
River. E.
Richmond, Yorkshire, from the
Moors. E.
Richmond, Yorkshire—the Town
and Castle, from Footpath above
River. E.
Warwick. E.
Constance. S.
Salisbury. E.
Lucerne Town, from above. S.
,, ,, from Lake. S.
,, Lake, from Brunnen. S.
,, ,, from Fluelen. S.
,, ,, with Rigi. S.
Pass of St. Gothard, near Faido. S.
Lake of Lug, from Goldau.
Lake of Lug, near Aart. S.
Coblentz. S.
Winchelsea. E.
Gosport. E.
Richmond, Surrey. E.

Dudley. E.
Devonport. E.
Schaffhausen Town. S.
,, Falls. K.
Arona—Lago Maggiore. K.
Château de la Belle Gabrielle. K.
Llanthony Abbey. E.
Derwent Water. E.
Okehampton. E.
Rochester. E.
Buckfastleigh Abbey. E.
Bolton Abbey. E.
Nottingham. E.
Harlech. E.
Devonport. E.
Carisbrook Castle. E.
St. Catherine's Hill. E.
Flint Castle. E.
Scarborough (once at Farnley).
Farnley Hall (once at Farnley).
Grandville. (Unpublished drawing
on coast of France.)
Iso'a Bella. (Hakewell's 'Italy.')

Turin from Superga. (Hakewell.)

Yarmouth. (Unpublished. A body-colour drawing—Sailors illustrating Trafalgar by models of the ships.)

Lebanon. (For Finden's Bible.)

Pool of Solomon. Do.

Pool of Bethesda. Do.

Jericho. Do.

Corinth. Do.

Rhodes. Do.

Combe Martin. (Southern coast.)

Barcastle. Do.

Wolf's Hope. (Small.)

St. Cloud. Do.

Pisa. (Byron vignette.)

School of Homer. Do.

Gate of Theseus. (Byron vignette.)

Ashestiel. (Vignette to Scott's Poems.)

Linlithgow. Do.

Margate. (Harbours of England.)

Malta. (Life of Byron.)

Rouen, from St. Catherine's Hill. (Rivers of France.)

Seventeen Drawings of the Loire series. (Rivers of France.)

Namur, on the Meuse.

Dinant, on the Meuse.

On the Meuse. Do.

Sketches of Venice.

Early Sketches (various).

The letter E in above list means England series ; S, Swiss series, meaning a series executed for various private persons by Turner after the year 1842, of which two only, belonging to Mr. Windus of Tottenham, have been engraved. None of mine have. K means made for the 'Keepsake.'—J. RUSKIN.

Water-colour Drawings by Turner in possession of H. A. Munro, Esq., of Hamilton Place, Piccadilly.

Florence, with Michael Angelo's Fortifications.

Marly.

Lucerne from Brunnen.

Lucerne (or Zurich)—Moonlight.

Knömadt (Lucerne).

Zurich.

St. Gothard.

Ditto, Airolo in the distance.

The Splügen.

Criccieth Castle.

Dunstanboro' Castle.

Pembroke Castle.

Ullswater.

Lichfield. (Not engraved.)

Knaresborough.

Coventry. (Rainy effect.)

Lowestoffe—Stormy.

Chain Bridge on the Tees.

Worcester.

Christ Church, Oxford.

Kenilworth—Moonlight.

Blenheim. (Bad colour.)

Lancaster Sands.

Chatham from Fort Pitt.

Bedford.

Richmond Hill.

Val Crucis Abbey. (Girtin's yellow tone.)

Leicester Abbey.

Kidwelly.

Malmesbury Abbey.

Ashby-de-la-Zouche. (Badly engraved.)

St. Germain. (Faded.)

Louth—Horse Fair.

Caernarvon Castle—Boys Bathing.

The Temple of Ægina.

Northampton—Election-time.

Whitehaven.

Ludlow.

Venice. (Not engraved.) (?)

Bellinzona.

Sallenche. (Pencil sketch.)

Coloured sketches of same place.

Whalley Abbey.

Temple of Venus. (Early.)

Iffley Mill, near Oxford. (Early.)

Hindshead Hill, Surrey. (Early.)

Pencil Sketch of same.

An Abbey. (Hearne's manner.)

Dover. (Early.)

Cliffs, with Rainbow. (Early.)
Abbey Crypt. (Early.)
Ludlow Castle.

Nantwich &c.
Waterfall. (Early.)

A List of the Turner Pictures in the Petworth Gallery.

In his early Manner.

The Thames at Eton.
The Thames at Windsor.
The Thames near Windsor.
The Thames at Weybridge.
Tabley House and Lake, Cheshire.

Sea Piece—Indiaman and Man-of-War.
Evening — Landscape with Cattle &c.
Echo and Narcissus.

In his Later Manner.

Jessica, 'Merchant of Venice.'

In the Carved Room.

Chichester Canal—Sunset.
The Chain Pier at Brighton.

Petworth Park and Lake, with Cricketers &c.
The Lake in Petworth Park.

Turner Drawings in the Collection of Mr. Smith, of Southwick Street.

Harlech Castle. (Early blue drawing.)
Two small Drawings of St. Albans Abbey, *circa* 1790.
Ruins of Corfe Castle in 1792.
Tintern Abbey (interior), in 1793.
Tivoli, *circa* 1795.

Waterfall — dated 1795. (From Lord Essex's Collection.)
Plymouth, from Mount Battery. Engraved for W. S. Cooke for the 'Southern Coast,' published 1817.

Lord Yarborough's Collection.

The Wreck of the Minotaur.   On the Haak Sands in 1810.
The Opening of the Vintage of Maçon.

Collection of Mr. Henderson.

Early Drawing by Turner of Dover Castle from the Harbour.
Three other Views in the Harbour of Dover. (Later.)
Four Sketches after the late Mr. Henderson, made probably between 1790 and 1793.
A View of Edinburgh Castle, after Hearne. (The figure omitted.) Hearne's view was engraved 1780.
Two Drawings on the Seine, Paris. (I believe from Girtin's work.)
A Drawing of the Ouse Bridge, York.

A Drawing of Cowes, (?) in the Isle of Wight, after one by Hearne.
Magdalen Bridge and the Tower of Magdalen College (probably in 1794 or 1795).
Three larger drawings, the result of Turner's first tour ; one dated 1793.
The West Window of Shrewsbury Cathedra[1].
Tintern Abbey.
Christchurch, Oxford.

(These were executed on commission for Mr. Henderson.) [2]

Collection of Charles Borrett, Esq., in Queen Anne Street.

George the Fourth leaving Ireland and embarking at Kingstown on the 3rd of September 1821. (The setting sun in this picture can only be compared with the two finest sun-pictures which he left to the nation—I mean Collingwood's vessel tugged to her last berth, and the Ulysses and Polyphemus. The picture is full of golden colour.)

The Arch of Ancona.

A View in Venice.

Wreck off Margate.

Queen Adelaide Landing at Southampton on her return from Malta.

Coast View, with Afternoon Sun.

Battle Abbey.

Calais Pier—Boats going off to a Shipwreck.

The Earthquake at Lisbon.

Falls of the River Dove.

Conway Castle.

Swiss Cottage.

The Castle of Dieppe, with Turner among other figures in the foreground.

The Interior of the Alhambra.

Highgate Church from Hampstead.

The Wreckers.

The Thames at Gravesend, and many other pictures by Turner, almost all of which are signed with his name or initials.

Collection of J. E. Fordham, Esq., of Milbourn Bury, near Royston.

View of a Gateway at Gloucester, with the Cathedral Tower.   (Early.)

Fowey Harbour.   (Engraved in the 'Southern Coast.')

Vale of Llanrwst, N.B.

Shakspeare's Monument at Stratford-on-Avon.

Fort Augustus, N.B.

Loch Achray, N.B.

Meeting of the Greta and Tees at Rokeby.

Derwent Water and Skiddaw.   (These five highly finished drawings are engraved as illustrations to Scott.)

Whitby, Yorkshire.

Alnwick Castle by Moonlight.   (Engraved in the 'England and Wales.'

Lake of Nemi.   (A small but very highly finished drawing, of which there is a private plate.)

Margate, with the Sun rising on the Sea.   (Signed, and dated 1822.)

Lake of Narni.   (Engraved.)

Oberwesel.   (Engraved. Dated 1840.)

The last two drawings represent the afternoon of a cloudless day with heat.

Collection of John Hugh, Esq., Manchester.

'1st. "Outline drawings, in pen or pencil, thinly washed in Indian ink or Prussian blue." The drawings in question have, some of them, *more* colour than Mr. Taylor says, and do *not* seem to me of so very early a date, judging both from the abounding effect of atmosphere in them all, as well as the masterly drawing and the subjects. For instance, one is of the 'Bay of Naples.' I suspect that he made these careful drawings *at many* periods, for his own use, as notes to work from. Of this class I have thirty drawings, chiefly made on the South Coast, in the neighbourhood of Dover and Folkestone.

Then came an early period certainly, but with more colour; not at all *outline* drawings, but finished as much as he could at the time. I call this period No. 2, and date it from 1790 to 1795 of '96. Of this period I have four drawings, and also three drawings—'Interior of New College Chapel,' 'Malvern Abbey,' and a 'Gate at Durham Cathedral,' of the same period.

No. 3. period is that referred to by Mr. Taylor in speaking of 'Falls of Clyde' as 'wrought out within the limits of a narrow scale of colours, but masterly in the disposition of the masses,' &c. Of this period I have twelve drawings, some of them of importance for size and subject, viz. :—

Edinburgh, from Leith Water.	View in Yorkshire Highlands.
Falls of Clyde.	Inverary.
View in Yorkshire Highlands.	Plymouth Citadel.

Some of the smaller ones are not only carefully finished, but full of poetry. These were all probably produced between 1810 and 1814. The two largest measure about 3 feet 6 inches by 2 feet 4 inches.

No. 4 period—or periods, I ought to say; for I believe the works I have and range under No. 4 were made from about 1825 to 1833. Many of them are well known, and are all, or almost all, engraved. They are as follow :—

'England and Wales' Series :—

Malvern Abbey and Gate.	Cowes.
Dartmouth Cove.	Upnor Castle, on the Medway.
Land's End & Longship's Lighthouse.	

For other works:—

Hastings, from the Sea.	Plymouth Sound, looking up into
Rivaulx Abbey and Valley.	the Catwater.
	Mount St. Michael.

Bible Series :—

Dead Sea.	Moses showing the Tables of the Law to the People.

Vignettes :—

Frontispiece to 'Lay of Last Minstrel.'	Mayence.
	Bridge of Sighs, for Rogers's Poems.

Twelve drawings in sepia for the published and the unpublished 'Liber' views. These are of the same size as the plates in the 'Liber,' and are all carefully finished.

Oil Paintings :—
> The Grand Canal at Venice. (The well-known picture engraved by Miller.)
> The Mouth of the Maas. (An earlier picture, painted about 1815 for the Harcourt family.)
> A small Sea-piece. (Which Mr. Griffiths had about same time.)

'Liber' Engravings :—
> A complete book in the state of *proofs*, all either initialed by *Charles* Turner or J. Lupton, and also by Miss Mary Constance Clark or J. H. Hawkins, from whom I had the whole.
> A complete book of the etchings.
> Above thirty early proofs before letters, nearly all touched on by Turner, and sometimes with his written instructions for alterations; some are touched all over by him *with brush,* in sepia.

Unpublished Plates of the ʻLiberʼ:—
    Ten etchings, some touched and written upon,
    Twelve proofs before letters, all touched by him more or less; and
       some of these are unique.

Collection of B. G. Windus, Esq., of Tottenham Green.

Drawing of Tynemouth (for the Series for ʻEngland and Walesʼ).
Paintings:—
    The Dawn of Christianity—Flight into Egypt.   (Circular.)
    Glaucus and Scylla.

Collection of F. Dillon, Esq.—Water-colour Drawings.

Vesuvius in Calm.
Vesuvius in Eruption.
The Eddystone Lighthouse—part of a Wreck in the foreground.

Interior of Westminster Abbey.
Drawing for Hakewell's ʻItaly.ʼ
Two of the Yorkshire Series.

Collection of Mr. Bale.

Bridge in the Tees Valley. (Matchless.)
Ingleborough. (Unsurpassable.)
Lyme Regis.

Guildford.
Llanthony.
Welsh View.

    In the same collection, Snowdon, and Sunrise from St. Peter's, by Girtin; and Glaciers, and Gondolfo, by Cozens. The glaciers radiant with the most spiritual beauty.
    Destroyed by fire, Drawing of Brignal Church, near Rokeby (engraved for the Yorkshire Series).

Oil Pictures at Mr. Munro's.

Cicero's Villa.
Ancient Italy.
The Green Buoy.
Rotterdam.

The Forum.
The Avalanche.
Modern Italy.
Loch Katrine.

Venice — Moonlight and illuminations.
Venus and Adonis.

Collection of Sir John T. Hippisley.

Folkestone.
Scene on the Borders of Wales.

Byron Drawings:—
    Marathon.
    The Rhine.

Collection of John Naylor, Esq.

Cologne—the Arrival of a Packet-boat (Evening).

Dieppe.

    The above two were purchased at Mr. Wadmore's sale for about 4,000*l.*

Pas de Calais—Now for the Painter (rope). (Passengers going on board.)
Dutch Fishing-boats. (Purchased from Turner direct.)
Venice.

Moonlight Scene on the Tyne—Getting in Coals by Night.
Mercury and Argus. (The upright engraved picture.)
Rockets and Blue Lights. (The engraved picture.)

Miscellaneous.

The Fifth Plague of Egypt. (Formerly Mr. Beckford's; is now Mr. Young's.)

Fishermen endeavouring to put their Fish on board. (In the Bridgewater Gallery.)

Fishermen upon a Lee-shore in Squally Weather. (In the collection of Mr. White, of Brownlow Street.)

Van Tromp entering the Texel. (In the Soane Museum.)

Battle of Trafalgar. (Painted Hall, Greenwich.)

Mercury and Argus. (In the late Sir John Swinburne's collection.)

Temple of Jupiter. (Mr. Wynne Ellis.)

Cologne; Dieppe; Guard-ship at the Nore. (Mr. Wadmore, of Stamford Hill.)

Venice. (Mr. Lewis Pocock.)

Tivoli: Drawing. (Mr. Allnut.)

Dover: Drawing. (Mr. Dillon.)

Ivy Bridge: Oil-picture. (E. Bicknell, Esq., Herne Hill.)

Schaffhausen: Water-colour. (P. Hardwicke, Esq.)

On the Lake of Brientz. 'Bold, and very beautiful.'—RUSKIN. Water-colour. (Sir John Swinburne.)

Grenoble: Water-colour. (Mrs. Holford, Hampstead.)

Folkestone: Water-colour. (Sir John Hippisley, Bart.)

A large Picture in Oil—View of Raby Castle—is at Newton House, the seat of Her Grace the Duchess Dowager of Cleveland. Thus described : This view of Raby was painted for the late Duke when Earl of Darlington. It was one of the *few things* the Duchess took away, though I believe she had the power by will of *stripping* Raby of every article—furniture, plate, &c.; and this act was the means of reconciling the present Duke to her.

At Streatham Castle (Mr. Bowes') there are two beautiful water-colour drawings of Gillside; one or two of Hilton Castle. It is probable the above are all engraved in 'Surtees' History of the County of Durham.'

Two views of Gillside, by J. M. W. Turner. No. 1, on the right-hand side of the chimney-piece, represents Gillside in the distance, thus forming almost an accessory to, instead of the principal object in, the picture. This arrangement gives greater space to the landscape, and thus admits of the beautiful variety of tint so conspicuous in Nature and the works of this greatest of modern painters. The sky of the picture is more tranquil, or rather less striking, than is generally seen in Turner's paintings, and accords well with the air of perfect repose which characterises the scene, giving it that *pensive* effect so often observed in an English landscape at noonday. The hazy grey of the distant hills, the neutral tint of the middle distance, gradually *ripening* (if the term may be used) into the rich yet subdued colouring of the fore-ground, the winding of the river marking admirably the perspective, and giving distance to the scene; the graceful form and exquisite tint of the tree nearest the eye—all combine to form a composition at once true to Nature and perfect in Art. No. 2, on the left-hand side, is, like No. 1, remarkable for the admirable blending of colours of infinite variety with Nature's own richness of tint, but 'softened all and tempered into beauty.' Chastened, mellowed, and subdued, the tone of the sky, which is much wilder than in No. 1, is repeated in the fainter colouring of the river; a gentle mist arises, like breath, from the bosom of the water, mingling and contrasting with the warm tints of the foliage on its banks. The whole composition of this picture consists in a series of half-tones admirably varied and repeated in the hills, corn-fields, trees, and rivers, producing that effect, changeful yet consistent, so visible in the harmonious versatility Nature displays in all her works, and which it required the wonderful accuracy and unrivalled observation of Turner to seize and delineate.

Collection of E. Bicknell, Esq.

Oil-paintings.

Calder Bridge, Cumberland.
Campo Santo, Venice. Ex. R.A. 1842.
Venice–the Giudecca Canal &c. 1841.
Ehrenbreitstein. 1827.
Wreckers—Coast of Northumberland: Steamboat assisting ship off shore. 1834.

Van Goën looking for a Subject. Antwerp. 1833.
Palestrina. 1830.
Port Ruysdael. 1827.
Ivy Bridge, Devon.
Brielle, on the Maas, Holland.

Drawings.

The Rigi.
Lake of Lucerne.
Scarborough.

Mowberry Lodge, Ripon.
Woodcock Shooting.

Grouse Shooting.
Two Views in the Himalayas.

Vignettes.

Castle of Elz.
Rouen.
Château Gaillard.

Hâvre.
Lake of Geneva, from the Jura.

Lighthouse of the Hève.

PICTURES AND DRAWINGS BY J. M. W. TURNER, R.A., SOLD BY MESSRS. CHRISTIE, MANSON, & WOODS; WITH DATE OF SALE, DESCRIPTION IN CATALOGUE, PRICES, AND NAMES OF PURCHASERS.

Dr. Monro's Collection.

1833.

June 26. Views and ruins. (In colours, on cards.) 10*l.* 10*s.* Moon, Boydell, & Co. 10.

,, Do. 8*l.* 18*s.* 6*d.* Turner. 10.

,, Do. 8*l.* 18*s.* 6*d.* Do. 10.

,, Do. 9*l.* 9*s.* Dixon. 10.

,, View of London from the Temple Gardens. (Blue and Indian ink.) 4*l.* 4*s.* Wells. 4.

,, Porchester Castle; Carisbrook; and Wenlock, North Wales. 4*l.* 8*s.* Wells. 4.

,, Slate Quarries, North Wales. 2*l.* 2*s.* Moon, Boydell, & Co. 4.

,, Llanberis &c. 3*l.* 3*s.* Colnaghi. 5.

,, Llangollen, Lodore, Llanberis, &c. 3*l.* 13*s.* 6*d.* Wells. 6.

,, Colebrooke Dale, Windermere, and Keswick. 3*l.* 7*s.* Linden. 6.

,, Hadley Church, Wilsden, and Waltham. 5*l.* Wells. 4.

,, Kenilworth, Hadley, &c. In colours. 7*l.* 7*s.* Boys. 3.

,, Conway Castle. 3*l.* 5*s.* Molteno. 4.

,, Fetcham Park &c. 3*l.* 5*s.* Wells. 6.

1833.

June 26. Dover, Ashstead Park, Egham, &c. (Sketches, in blue and Indian ink.) 3*l.* 3*s.* Colnaghi. 4.

,, View in Norbury Park. 5*l.* 15*s.* 6*d.* Colnaghi. 14.

,, Southwell Minster, Sandwich Church, &c. 4*l.* 6*s.* Turner. 6.

,, Dorking, Mickleham, and Upminster Churches. 4*l.*4*s.* Molteno. 5.

,, The Ruins of the Savoy Palace. 3*l.* 3*s.* Turner. 4.

,, Kenilworth and Warwick Castles. 9*l.* 9*s.* Woodburn. 4.

,, Boxhill, Hadley, and Mickleham Churches, &c. 2*l.* 5*s.* Turner. 4.

,, Ragland and Tunbridge Castles &c. 4*l.* 4*s.* Wells. 5.

,, View near Dedham, Essex ; Tunbridge, &c 5*l.* 10*s.* Wells. 6.

,, Windsor Castle, Blackheath, &c. 4*l.* 14*s.* 6*d.* Molteno. 6.

,, Views in Wales. (In Indian ink and pencil.) 3*l.* 15*s.* Boys. 7.

,, Do. do. 4*l.* 12*s.* Turner. 6.

,, Sketches. 2*l.* 4*s.* Colnaghi. 3.

,, Views in Cumberland. (Colours.) 7*l.* 7*s.* Wells. 4.

,, Do. in Wales. (Blue and Indian ink.) 4*l.* 6*s.* Boys. 4.

,, Do. in Cumberland. (Do.) 5*l.* 10*s.* Hawley. 4.

,, Shipping in Dover Harbour. (In Indian ink.) 5*l.*5*s.* Turner. 9.

,, Llangollen, Glenton in Cumberland, &c. (Colours.) 12*l.* 1*s.* 6*d.* Boys. 4.

,, Views on the Lakes &c. (Indian ink.) 7*l.* 7*s.* Gordon. 12.

,, Do. Conway Castle &c. (Do.) 6*l.* 6*s.* Wells. 9.

,, Kenilworth Castle &c. (Do.) 7*l.* 7*s.* Boys. 12.

,, Views on the Lakes in Cumberland. 5*l.* 15*s.* 6*d.* Stanley. 10.

,, A View at Brighton, and two of cottages. (Colours.) 7*l.* Boys. 3.

,, Views at Dover &c. (Blue and grey.) 4*l.* 8*s.* Churchill. 9.

,, Chesterford Bridge, Marlow, &c. 5*l.* 5*s.* Boys. 4.

,, Views in Wales and on the Lakes. 6*l.* Gordon. 10.

,, Otterspool, Staffordshire; Bromley, &c. 2*l.* 2*s.* Green. 5.

,, St. Anselm's Chapel. (Upright, colours.) 12*l.* 12*s.* Turner.

,, Views in Norbury Park. (Colours.) 11*l.* 11*s.* Tiffin. 2.

,, Great Bookham Church, Surrey. 4*l.* 15*s.* Sargeant.

,, Farm Buildings, Studies from Nature (Colours.) 8*l.* 8*s.* Colnaghi. 2.

,, Views in North Wales. (Colours.) 10*l.* 10*s.* Boys. 3.

,, Magdalen College, Oxford, and Dover Church. (Colours.) 17*l.* 6*s.* 6*d.* Boys. 2.

,, Chepstow Castle. 20*l.* 9*s.* 6*d.* Boys.

VIEWS IN ITALY.

June 27. Astroni, Radicofani, and Gaeta. 8*l.* 8*s.* Hixon. 3.

,, Isola Borromeo, near Ambrogiana, &c. 5*l.* 10*s.* Moon, Boys, & Co. 3.

,, Santa Giustina at Padua, Inspruck, &c. 5*l.* 10*s.* Linden. 4.

,, Château de Baiæ, Sestii di Levante, &c. 7*l.* Thane. 3.

,, Near Portici &c. 7*l.* Griffiths. 3.

,, Rocca del Papa, Chartreuse, &c. 6*l.* 15*s.* Hixon. 3.

,, Isola Borromeo &c. 5*l.* 10*s.* Hixon. 3.

,, Vernazza, San Michele, Piedmont, and one near Lerici, 6*l.* 6*s.* Moon, Boydell, & Co. 3.

1833.
June 27. Lago di Guarda &c. 5*l*. Hixon. 3.
,, Near Agnibella, Naples, &c. 7*l*. Hixon. 3.
,, Portici ; near Florence, &c. 6*l*. 15*s*. Griffiths. 3.
,, Chiaveri, and St. Pietro d'Arena. 6*l*. 10*s*. Moon, Boydell, & Co. 2.
,, Porto Venereo &c. 6*l*. 10*s*. Moon, Boydell, & Co. 3.
,, Tivoli &c. 5*l*. Colnaghi. 3.
,, Monte Circio, Romiglione, and the Road to the Scuola di Virgilio. 6*l*. 6*s*. Clay.
,, Views of Rome and Tivoli. (Sketches in blue and Indian ink.) 3*l*. 10*s*. Colnaghi.
,, The Corsini and Albani Palaces, &c. (Do.) 12*l*. 12*s*. Molteno. 13.
,, The Coliseum, the gate, and amphitheatre at Capua, &c. (Do.) 6*l*. 10*s*. Moon & Co. 12.
,, In the Neighbourhood of Naples &c. (Do.) 7*l*. 7*s*. Turner. 9.
,, The Villa Negroni, Castle of St. Elmo, Naples, &c. (Do.) 8*l*. Moon, Boydell, & Co. 10.
,, The Lago Maggiore, Vatican, &c. (Do.) 6*l*. 6*s*. Turner. 10.
,, Views in Italy. (Do.) 7*l*. 10*s*. Turner. 8.
,, Do. 5*l*. 15*s*. Griffiths. 7.
,, Views in Switzerland. (Sketches in blue and Indian ink.) 7*l*. Turner.
,, The Castle of Chillon, Views in Savoy, &c. 5*l*. Moon, Boys, & Co. 8.
,, Tivoli and Naples, moonlight. (Colours.) 12*l*. 1*s*. 6*d*. Moon, Boys, & Co. 2.
,, Gandolfo and Tivoli, a pair. (Colours.) 15*l*. 17*s*. Thane. 2.
,, The Cascade at Tivoli. (Indian ink and blue, &c.) 3*l*. 3*s*. Boys. 4.
,, The Portico before St. Peter's &c. (Do.) 4*l*. 4*s*. Linden. 3.
,, The Sibyl's Temple at Tivoli &c. (Do.) 5*l*. 15*s*. Monro. 4.
,, Views at Tivoli &c. 5*l*. 10*s*. Moon, Boys, & Co. 4.
,, View of Rome &c. 7*l*. Molteno. 4.
,, The Bridge at Civignon. (In colours.) And three in Indian ink —Views in Rome. 8*l*. 8*s*. F. Moon. 4.
June 28. Views of Dover. (Indian ink and blue.) 3*l*. 3*s*. Moon. 6.
,, Architectural. (Do.) 5*l*. 10*s*. Rogers. 5.
,, Britton Ferry &c. (Do.) 5*l*. 15*s*. 6*d*. Boys. 7.
,, Views in Italy. (Do.) 5*l*. 5*s*. Molteno. 7.
,, Do. in Wales &c. (Do.) 4*l*. Boys. 7.
,, The Gateway at Exeter, Dover Priory, &c. (Do.) 3*l*. 15*s*. Boys. 6.
,, Sketches from Nature —one in the manner of Loutherbourg. (Colours.) 4*l*. 4*s*. Roberts. 3.
,, View of Malmesbury Abbey and a Water-mill. 8*l*. 18*s*. 6*d*. A. Monro. 2.
,, Sketches from Nature, Dover, &c. 5*l*. 5*s*. Colnaghi. 3.
,, Langdale, Bedkellert, &c., Wales. (In Indian ink.) 5*l*. 18*s*. Boys. 4.
,, Views in Cumberland &c. (Do.) 8*l*. 7*s*. 6*d*. Hixon. 4.
,, Do. on the Thames. 4*l*. 4*s*. Melville. 3.
,, Do of St. Albans Abbey. 2*l*. 15*s*. Boys. 2.

1833.

June 28. Richmond &c. (Indian ink.) 3*l.* 15*s.* Boys. 8.

,, Views in North Wales. (Do.) 4*l.* 4*s.* Boys. 9.

,, Vale Crucis Abbey, Dover Priory, &c. (Do.) 4*l.* 10*s.* Boys. 8.

,, Views of Dartmouth, Lancaster, &c. (Do.) 4*l.* 4*s.* Boys. 8.

,, Dover Harbour. (Do.) 4*l.* 14*s.* 6*d.* Boys. 9.

,, Views in Cumberland, &c. (Do.) 5*l.* 10*s.* Boys. 8.

VIEWS IN ITALY &c.

July   2. Views in Switzerland. 3*l.* Moon. 3.

,, The Convent at Camaldoli, Florence, Brescia,&c. 9*l.*9*s.* Rogers. 6.

,, In Switzerland, &c. 7*l.* Moon, Boys, & Graves. 4.

,, The Lake of Bolsena, &c. 8*l.* 8*s.* Hixon. 3.

,, Rimoggio, and near Florence. 5*l.* G. Morant. 3.

,, The Valley of Vaucleuse, Lago Maggiore, &c. 6*l.* 6*s.* Moon, Boys, & Graves. 3.

,, View near St. Michele, in Savoy, &c. 6*l.* Moon, Boys, & Graves. 4.

,, Blackfriars Bridge, and one other. 2*l.*18*s.* Moon, Boys, & Graves.

,, Ruined Monument on the Via Appia, Castle at the Granatello, Portici, &c. 5*l.* 7*s.* 6*d.* Shirley. 4.

,, The Sibyl's Temple at Tivoli &c. 6*l.* Hixon. 3.

,, Entrance of the Alps between Turin and Novalese, and a View near Salerno. 3*l.* 6*s.* Moon, Boys, & Graves. 2.

,, The Entrance to the Tyrol &c. 6*l.* Moon, Boys, & Graves. 3.

,, Portici, &c. 5*l.* Hixon. 3.

,, Naples, Lake on Mount Cenis, Lake of Como. 7*l.*10*s.* Moon, Boys, & Graves. 3.

,, Florence, The Campagna of Rome, &c. 7*l.* 7*s.* Moon, Boys, & Graves. 3.

,, The Castle of St. Elmo, Casino Samazzaro, and a View near Vietri. 4*l.*4*s.* Hixon. 3.

,, View near Valombrossa, and one near Bolsena. 2*l.*18*s.* Hixon. 2.

,, The Bridge of Augustus, Leghorn, &c. 7*l.* 10*s.* Shirley. 3.

,, Isola Borromeo, and Prince Doria's Palace. 3*l.* 3*s.* Shirley. 2.

,, Castle at Ferrara, Portici, and Titus's Baths. 5*l.*15*s.* Hixon. 3.

,, In the Apennines. 3*l.* 10*s.* Moon, Boys, & Graves. 2.

,, Isola Bella, Isola Borromeo, &c. 3*l.* 10*s.* Hixon. 3.

,, The Temple of Venus at Baiæ, and one at Grisone. 4*l.* 8*s.* Shirley. 2.

,, The Walls of Naples. 3*l.* Moon, Boys, & Graves. 2.

,, The Temple of Minerva Medica. 2*l.*6*s.* Moon, Boys, & Graves. 2.

,, The Villa Belvidere, Padua, &c. 4*l.*4*s.* Moon, Boys, & Graves. 3.

,, View at Terracina &c. 4*l.* 8*s.* Moon, Boys, & Graves. 3.

,, The Lake of Bolsena, Vietri, &c. 5*l.* 5*s.* Money. 3.

,, Salerno, one near Padua, &c. 4*l.* 12*s.* White. 3.

,, Bergamo, Salerno, &c. 5*l.* 5*s.* Moon, Boys, & Graves. 3.

,, The Porta Pinciana, and Aqueduct near Portra Maggiore. 5*l.* 5*s.* Moon, Boys, & Graves. 3.

,, The Minister's Villa at Portici, Cardinal Spinelli's Palace, &c. 4*l.* 8*s.* Hixon. 3.

,, The Villa Salviati &c. 4*l.* 8*s.* Rogers. 2.

1833.
July 2. Near Amalfi, Capo Miseno, &c. 4*l.* 12*s.* Rice. 3.
  ,,   Florence, Manasola, &c. 5*l.* 5*s.* Moon, Boys, & Graves. 3.
  ,,   The Lake of Albano, Narni, and Terni. 14*l.* 14*s.* Shirley. 3.
  ,,   Do.   Bolsena, Vicho, &c. 7*l.* 15*s.* Moon, Boys, &
           Graves. 3.

1851.
May   24 Summer Hill, Kent, with Cattle in Shallow Water. (Painted
           for Mr. Alexander.) 315*l.* Mr. Fletcher.
  ,,   The Sheer Hulk. Bought in at 185*l.*
June 13 The Whaler—'Hurrah for the whaler Erebus and the fish!'—
           Beale's *Voyage.* 299*l.* Gambart.
  ,,   Saltash Harbour. 330 guineas. Mr. Bicknell.
  ,,   The Lock. (Engraved in the 'Liber Studiorum.') Bought in
           at 360 guineas.

Mr. Granville Penn's Collection.

July 10 View of Corfe Castle, taken from the Sea. 483*l.* Mr. Gambart.

1852.   *Sigismund Rucher's Collection.*

March 26 Flint Castle. (In water-colours.) 152*l.* Mr. Agnew.
April 1 Dummil Bridge, Fifeshire. (Painted in 1812.) 105*l.* Mr. Gambart.

Collection of William Wells, of Redleaf.

May   20 A Harbour Scene—Sunset, Ships of War at Anchor : numerous
           Figures on the Sands near a Jetty. 672*l.* Mr. Graves of
           Pall Mall.

Mr. Ellis's Collection.

May   22 A View on the Teign. Bought in at 225*l.*
  ,,   A View on the Wye—Evening. Bought in at 315*l.*

Four Water-colour Drawings, sold by Order of the Court of Chancery.
(Evans v. *Heath.)*

May   22 Graville on the Seine. (Engraved in the 'Southern Tour.') 33*l.* 12*s.*
  ,,   The Confluence of the Seine and Marne. 42*l.*
  ,,   The Château de Maillerie. 46*l.* 4*s.*
  ,,   The Boulevard des Italiens at Paris, with numerous Figures.
           47*l.* 5*s.* (These four bought by Mr. Lambe, of Gracechurch
           Street.)
  ,,   A View of Edinburgh, from the Water of Leith. (A large
           drawing.) Bought in at 210*l.*
  ,,   The Brunnig Passage from Marengen to Grundewald. (Painted
           in the master's finest time.) Bought in at 120*l.*

1853.   *Collection of E. S. Ellis, Esq.*

April 6 A Seashore, with a Fishing-boat pushing off, a Lugger making
           for the mouth of a Harbour, a fine gleam of Sunshine breaking
           through the Clouds above. (Another example of the powers
           of the great master. Oils.) 1,312*l.* 10*s.* Mr. Gambart.
April 12 View of Edinburgh from the Calton Hill. (Small.) 31*l.* 10*s.*
           Mr. Cubitt.

1853.

April 12 Smugglers. (Said to have been painted for Mr. Smith, at the Sussex Hotel, in 1818.) Bought in at 210*l.*

,,   Limekilns—a Night Scene. Bought in at 65 guineas.

Collection of W. J. Broderip, Esq.

June 18 The Dogana and Church of San Giorgio at Venice. (Painted for Sir Francis Chantrey, at whose decease this picture passed direct into Mr. Broderip's possession. Exhibited at the Royal Academy in 1841 ; a pendant to the picture now in the Vernon Gallery. A work of the rarest beauty and excellence.) 1,155*l.* Mr. Egg.

Collection of B. G. Windus, Esq.

June 20 Venice—Going to the Ball. 'Fallacies of Hope' MS. (Exhibited in the R. A. 1846. No. 117.) 546*l.* Mr. Gambart.

,,   Morning—Returning from the Ball, St. Martino. (Exhibited in the R. A. 1846. No. 162.) 640*l.* Wallis.

,,   Dawn of Christianity—Flight into Egypt. 'That star has risen.' (Exhibited in the R. A. 1841. No. 532.) Bought in at 730*l.*

,,   Glaucus and Scylla. (Painted on panel. Exhibited in the R. A. 1841. No. 542.) Bought in at 735*l.*

,,   The Approach to Venice. 'The path lies o'er the sea.' (Described by Mr. Ruskin in 'Modern Painters' as 'one of the most beautiful bits of colour ever done by any man, by any means, at any time.') 850*l.* Mr. Gambart.

1854.   ### Collection of James Wadmore, Esq.

May   5 Cologne, with boats full of figures on the Rhine, the tower of St. Martin's Church seen above the city walls ; a glowing sunset diffusing a magical light over the whole composition. 2,100*l.* Mr. Grundy, for Mr. Naylor of Liverpool.

,,   The Harbour of Dieppe. (An elaborate composition of numerous vessels, buildings, and figures, seen under the full glare of an afternoon's sun.) 1,942*l.* 10*s.* The same purchaser.

,,   The Guardship at the Nore. 1,606*l.* Mr. Rought.

Collection of William Cave, Esq.

June 29 Kilganan Castle. (This important and scientific work was exhibited in 1799, and was in Lord De Tabley's collection.) 525*l.* Mr. Wallis.

1855.   ### Collection of Dr. Roupell.

Feb. 24 A Lake Scene, with buildings, fire, and moonlight. 47*l.* 5*s,* Mr. Wallis.

Collection of the Duke of Argyll.

March 17 A View of Inverary from the Sea, with boats in a breeze. (A drawing in water colours.) 88*l.* Mr. White.

Mr. M'Crachen's Collection, from Belfast.

March 31 St. Mawes. (The drawing engraved in the 'Southern Coast.') Bought in at 47*l,*

1855.
April 21 A Coast Scene—View of the Old Pier at Great Yarmouth at low water, with shipping and numerous figures. (Signed, and dated 1813.) 199*l.* Mr. George.

May 8 Prudhoe Castle. (Water colours.) 31*l.* 10*s.* Mr. Wallis.
,, Dilston Castle, Northumberland. (Water colours.) 22*l.* Mr. Wallis.
,, Bow-and-Arrow Castle, Isle of Portland. (Engraved in the 'Southern Coast.' Water colours.) 51*l.* Mr. Agnew.
,, Combe Martin. (Engraved in the 'Southern Coast.' Water colours.) 52*l.* 10*s.* Mr. Wallis.
,, Larne Castle, Caermarthenshire. (Engraved in the 'England and Wales.' Water colours.) 129*l.* Mr. Rought.
,, Conway Castle. (Water colours.) 110*l.* Mr. Bale.
,, Rivaulx Abbey. (Water colours.) 46*l.* Mr. Gambart.
,, The Tomb of Cecilia Metella. (Water colours.) Bought in at 25*l.*

Collection of C. Macdonald, Esq.

May 29 Newark Castle. (From Lord De Tabley's collection.) Bought in at 470*l.*

1856. ### Collection of Samuel Rogers, Esq.

May 8 Stonehenge. (Drawing in water colours, engraved in 'England and Wales.') 304*l.* Mr. Wallis.

The Property of Lord Delamere.

May 24 Carrying out an Anchor—a grand sea-piece, with a fleet of Dutch men-of-war lying-to in a strong breeze; fishermen in a boat carrying out an anchor.
,, A Dutch Coast Scene, with fishermen hauling up a boat in shallow water near the shore; vessels under sail; grand effect of approaching storm. [The two above-named pictures were sold by private contract for 3,000*l.* to Mr. White, of Brownlow Street.]

1857. ### Leopold Redpath's Sale.

May 23 The Lock. (Engraved in the 'Liber Studiorum,' and in the Royal Gallery of British Art.) 525*l.* Mr. Gambart.

Collection of W. Prior, Esq.

,, A View in the Alps, 1814. (In Indian ink.) 5*l.* 15*s.* Mr. Wallis.
,, St. Agatha's Abbey. (Water colours.) 127*l.* Mr. Rought.
,, Conway Castle, 1829. (Water colours.) 117*l.* Mr. Wallis.

1858. ### Collection of Drawings of the Earl of Harewood.

May 1 Interior of Westminster Abbey—a Chapel north of the Choir. (Water colours.) 109*l.* Col. Pennant.
,, Kirkstall Abbey, with a waterfall. (Water colours.) 65*l.* Mr. Townend.
,, Norham Castle, with cows watering—Evening. (Water colours.) 109*l.* Colnaghi.
,, Pembroke Castle, with grand stormy sky. (Water colours.) 210*l.* Mr. Miller, of Preston.

1858

May   1 A Lake Scene in the North of Italy, with cattle and figures—
            Warm afternoon's sun. 278*l.* Mr. White, of Brownlow Street.
  ,,   Harewood Castle. (Water colours.) 52*l.* 10*s.* Mr. Beaumont.

Collection of John Miller, Esq., of Liverpool.

May   20 Hythe Church. (A slight study. Water colours.) 5*l.* 5*s.* Mr.
            Gambart.
  ,,   An Old Watermill. (Water colours.) 24*l.* Mr. Gambart.
  ,,   Hatfield Castle. (Water colours.) 18*l.* 18*s.*   Do.
  ,,   Hampton Court, Hereford—the Seat of Mr. Arkwright. (Water
            colours.) 6*l.* 16*s.* 6*d.*
  ,,   The Bass Rock. (Water colours. Exhibited at Manchester.)
            125*l.* Mr. Farrer.
  ,,   Rokeby. (Water colours. Exhibited at Manchester.) 38*l.* 17*s.*
            Mr. Gambart.
  ,,   Hougoumont. (Water colours. Exhibited at Manchester.)
            33*l.* 12*s.* Mr. Gambart.
  ,,   Kelso. (Water colours. Exhibited at Manchester.) 42*l.*
            Mr. Gambart.
  ,,   Edinburgh. (Water colours.) 53*l.* 11*s.* Mr. Rought.
  ,,   The Cathedral of Milan. (Exhibited at Manchester. Water
            colours.) 47*l.* 5*s.* Mr. Gambart.
  ,,   The Amphitheatre at Verona. (Water colours.) 46*l.* 4*s.* Mr.
            Gambart.
  ,,   Bemerside Tower. (Water colours. The frontispiece vignette
            to ' Sir Tristram,' vol. i. Exhibited at Manchester.) 29*l.*
            Mr. Gambart.
  ,,   Quai de Carte at Paris. (Water colours.) 36*l.* 15*s.* Mr.
            Addington.
  ,,   Rye. (Water colours.) 73*l.* 10*s.* Mr. Farrer.
  ,,   St. Mawes. (Water colours.) 75*l.* 12*s.* Mr. Gambart.
  ,,   Plymouth. (Engraved in the ' Southern Coast.' Water colours.
            Exhibited at Manchester.) 115*l.* 10*s.* Mr. Gambart.
  ,,   Windsor Castle. (A very small work in water colours.) 7*l.* 7*s.*
  ,,   View of Henley House, on the Thames. (This picture was
            painted for Mr. Wright, of Upton.) 131*l.* Mr. Robertson.
  ,,   View of the Pummell Bridge. (Exhibited at Manchester.)
            126*l.* Mr. Gambart.
  ,,   The Whale-ship. 367*l.* 10*s.* Mr. Gambart.
  ,,   Van Tromp. 567*l.* 5*s.*   Do.
  ,,   Saltash, Devon. 430*l.*   Do.

Collection of Mr. Pilkington.

June 22. Bridport. (Water colours.) 73*l.* Mr. Gambart.

1859.   ### Collection of Mr. Green.

Feb. 12. A View of Blackheath. (A small early sketch, made for Mr.
            Green, of Blackheath.) 15*l.* 15*s.* Mr. Waters.

Collection of B. G. Windus, Esq.

March 26 The Bridge of Sighs, Venice. (The vignette drawing engraved
            in Byron's works.) 72*l.* Mr. Gambart.

1859.

March 26 The Lake of Zug. (A fine drawing in water colours, not engraved.) 210*l.* Mr. Gambart.

,, Bellinzona. (A beautiful drawing, not engraved.) 189*l.* Mr. Pritchard.

Collection of R. Chambers.

March 29 Pont Aberglaslynn. (A sketch.) 4*l.* 10*s.* Mr. White.

,, Westminster Bridge. (A slight drawing.) 5*l.* 5*s.* Mr. Gambart.

,, Flint, North Wales. (A slight drawing.) 6*l.* 10*s.* Mr. Gambart.

,, View of Northampton. (Sketch.) 3*l.* 13*s.* 6*d.* Mr. Chadwick.

,, Chepstow Castle and Bridge. (Slight sketch.) 15*l.* Mr. Gambart.

,, Llanthony Abbey. (In water colours.) 14*l.* 14*s.* Mr. Gregory.

,, Abergavenny Bridge—Clearing-up after a Shower. (This drawing was exhibited at Somerset House in 1799.) 25*l.* Mr. Gambart.

,, The Porch of Great Malvern Church. (In water colours.) 21*l.* Mr. Gambart.

,, Ely Cathedral. (An early drawing.) 11*l.* 11*s.* Mr. Warbury.

,, Chelsea Hospital. (An early drawing.) 4*l.* 5*s.* Mr. Chadwick.

,, Matlock Bridge. (An early drawing.) 9*l.* 19*s.* 6*d.* Mr. Warbury.

Collection of E. Rodgett, Esq., of Preston.

May 14 Warwick Castle. (In water colours; an early work.) Bought in at 49*l.*

,, Cashiobury Castle. (An early drawing.) Bought in at 25*l.*

,, Portsmouth. (The engraved drawing.) 107*l.* Mr. D. White.

,, Hampton Court. (The engraved drawing.) 168*l.* Mr. Dixon.

,, Dartmouth. (The drawing engraved in the 'Southern Coast.') 162*l.* Mr. Agnew.

July 9 Kidwelly Castle, the seat of the Bishop of St. David's. (An early drawing.) 9*l.* 19*s.* 6*d.* Mr. White.

1860. *Collection of the Rev. H. S. Trimmer.*

March 17 A small Landscape. (In pencil. A present from the artist.) 1*l.* 1*s.* Mr. Locke.

,, A Landscape. (In the manner of Gainsborough.) 1*l.* Mr. Waters.

,, A Sea-piece, with fishing-boats. (A small picture.) 46*l.* Mr. Hooper.

,, A View of a Town on a River. 7*l.* Mr. Delaine.

Collection of G. R. Burnett, Esq.

March 24 An Italian Scene, with an archway. (An early drawing.) 15*l.* 15*s.* Mr. Wallis.

,, Kilchern Castle, with a rainbow. (A grand drawing in water colours.) 367*l.* Mr. Flatow.

1860.

March 24 Autumnal Sunset at Sea. (Painted for Sir John Mildmay.) 590*l.* Mr. Shepherd.

,, The Grand Canal at Venice. (The celebrated work engraved by Miller; painted in 1834.) 2,520*l.* Mr. Gambart.

,, Ostend—a stormy effect at Sea. 1,732*l.*

,, Neapolitan Bathers Surprised. 225*l.* Mr. Flatow.

,, London, from Battersea Fields. (A drawing made in 1812.) Bought in at 300 guineas.

,, Bemerside Tower. (Vignette frontispiece to 'Sir Tristram.' In water colours.) 37*l.* 16*s.* Mr. Wallis.

Collection of J. Heugh, Esq., of Manchester.

April 28 Bamborough Castle. (Drawing in water colours.) 525*l.* Mr. Pennett.

,, Lyme Regis. (The drawing engraved in the 'England and Wales.') 190*l.* Mr. Gambart.

Collection of George Hibbert, Esq.

May 2 Plymouth Citadel. (The drawing engraved by Cooke; purchased by Mr. Hibbert from Turner.) 126*l.* Mr. Rought.

,, The Plains of Italy. (An early drawing.) 17*l.* Mr. Wallis.

,, The Custom House, London. (The engraved drawing.) 49*l.* Mr. Wallis.

,, Corinth. (The drawing engraved in the Bible Series.) 106*l.* Mr. Gambart.

,, The Children of Israel in the Valley of Horeb. (The engraved drawing.) 107*l.* Mr. Agnew.

Collection of W. Herring, Esq.

May 14 Rochester Castle. (An early drawing made for the Rev. P. Douglas, an early patron of Turner.) Bought in at 39*l.*

Collection of J. M. Thetford, Esq., of Singleton House.

May 28 The Desert of Sinai. (The drawing engraved in the Bible Series.) 85*l.* Mr. Gambart.

,, St. Ive's, Cornwall. (The engraved drawing.) 73*l.* 10*s.* Mr. Vokins.

Collection of H. Bradley, Esq.

May 28 An English Lake Scene, with a church, and cattle in a pool of water. (In water colours.) 80*l.* Mr. Rought.

,, A Scotch Lake Scene, with peasants. (The companion drawing.) 79*l.* Mr. Agnew.

,, Dover, from the Sea. (The celebrated engraved drawing.) 317*l.* Mr. White.

Collection of John Mitchell, Esq., of Bradford.

May 28 Milan Cathedral. (The engraved drawing.) 45*l.* Mr. Gambart.

,, The Colosseum. (The engraved drawing.) 46*l.* Mr. Agnew.

,, Cumberland Fells. (A drawing.) 12*l.* Do.

,, View of a Mansion in Essex. (A drawing.) 14*l.* Mr. Pocock.

,, Bow-and-Arrow Castle. (The engraved drawing in the 'Southern Coast.') 58*l.* Mr. Gambart.

1860. *Collection of Mr. Wallis.*

March 16 The Burning of the Houses of Parliament. (Exhibited at the British Institution in 1835.) 708*l.* Mr. White.

By Messrs. Sotheby & Wilkinson.

1861. *Collection of Prints of Mr. George Smith.*

March A Choice Proof Set of 'England and Wales.' 115*l.*
,, Turner's 'Southern Coast.' (Proofs and etchings.) 90*l.*

By Messrs. Christie & Manson.

Collection of Mr. Fairre, of Rosemount, Liverpool.

,, View of Stamford. (Made for 'England and Wales' Series.) 198*l.* Jones.
,, Lucerne. (One of the last drawings made by Turner. Engraved.) 210*l.* Jones.

Collection of Mr. Uzielli.

April The Bass Rock. (Painted at Abbotsford for Sir W. Scott.) 158*l.* 11*s.* Vokins.
June What You Will—a landscape, with many figures. 245 guineas. Agnew.
,, Loch Katrine. 750 guineas. D. J. White.

1862. *Collection of Mr. Plint.*

March Pegwell Bay. (Middle style.) 83 guineas.
,, Milan Cathedral. (Wonderfully airy and fine. Engraved.) 60 guineas. Croft.
,, Carlisle. (Engraved. The famous drawing.) 96 guineas. Agnew.
,, Hythe. (Engraved in 'The Southern Coast.') 96*l.* 12*s.* White.
,, The Wreck. (A vignette; a perfect work of its kind. Engraved in 'The Keepsake.') 84 guineas. Smith.
,, Smalliholme Tower. (Engraved.) 65 guineas. Smith.
,, An Illustration to 'The Black Dwarf.' (Engraved.) 48 guineas. Smith.
,, An Illustration to 'Guy Mannering.' (Engraved.) 58 guineas. Vokins.
,, Sidmouth. (Engraved.) 63 guineas. Vokins.
,, Cologne. (Engraved.) 76 guineas. Agnew.
,, Venice. (Engraved.) 73 guineas. Smith.
,, A Coast Scene, with boats and figures. 36*l.* 15*s.*

Collection of Mr. Langton, of Liverpool.

May Lancaster. ('England and Wales' Series.) 305 guineas. Follet.

Collection of Mr. B. G. Windus.

July Dawn of Christianity—'Flight into Egypt.' (R.A. 1841.) 335 gs.
,, Glaucus and Scylla. (R.A. 1841.) 280 gs.

1863. By Messrs. Foster & Co.

February Lochmaben Castle. (Vignette.) 50 guineas. Greatorex.

1863.   *Collection of Mr. Bicknell.*

May.   Antwerp—Van Goyen looking for a Subject. 2,510 guineas.

,,   Helvoetsluys—The 'City of Utrecht,' 64-gun ship, going to
        Sea. 1,600 guineas.

,,   Ivy Bridge, Devon. 880 guineas. Martineau.

,,   Wreckers, Coast of Northumberland. 1,890 guineas.

,,   Calder Bridge, Cumberland. 500 guineas. H. Bicknell.

,,   Venice—The Campo Santo. (A most glorious picture.) 2,000 gs.

,,   Do.   The Giudecca &c. (Equally good, but hardly so
        lovely.) 1,650 guineas.

,,   Ehrenbreitstein. 1,800 guineas.

,,   Port Ruysdael. (Probably the culmination of the painter's
        natural style.) 1,900 guineas.

,,   Palestrina. 1,900 guineas. H. Bicknell.*

BY MESSRS. CHRISTIE & MANSON.

,,   Four early works.—1. Winchester Cross. 2. Ruins in Italy.
        3. Bay of Naples. 4. Lake of Nemi. 95 guineas. Various.

,,   Count D'Orsay's Portrait of Turner. (Sketched at an evening
        party. Pen and ink. One of the most fortunate likenesses,
        though caricatured.) 50 guineas. Agnew.

,,   Himalaya Mountains, and the companion drawing. (Both
        engraved.) 330 guineas. Vokins.

,,   The Lighthouse at Havre—moonlight. 105 guineas. Moore.

,,   The Lake of Geneva, from the Jura; Mont Blanc in the
        distance. 141 guineas. Grindlay.

,,   Lighthouse of the Hève, mouth of the Seine. 103 guineas.
        Colnaghi.

,,   The Righi. 296 guineas. Agnew.

,,   Copley Fielding, Traeth Mawr, North Wales. 420 guineas Wells.

,,   Castle of Elsy on the Moselle, Rouen, and Château Gaillard.
        160, 200, and 170 guineas. Agnew.

,,   Lake of Lucerne. 180 guineas. Colnaghi.

,,   Plymouth Sound. (Engraved.) 122 guineas. Vokins.

        The Pilkington Collection of drawings by Turner was sold to
        Mr. Wells at the following prices :—†

,,   Scarborough Castle, Boys Crab-fishing. 250 guineas.

,,   Mowbray Lodge, Ripon, Yorkshire, Earl Ripon's Seat. 510 gs.

,,   Grouse Shooting—The Moor, with portrait of the Artist ; the
        dogs painted by Stubbs. 430 guineas.

---

* These pictures which brought such magnificent prices were got from the artist direct,
at prices varying from 250 to 350 guineas each.

† *Prices of Turner's original Bicknell's Sale.*

Antwerp—Van Goyen looking for a Subject, 1833 (£315), £2,635. 10s.
Helvoetsluys, 'The City of Utrecht' going to sea, 1832 (£283. 10s.), £1,680.
Ivy Bridge, Devon (£283. 10s.), £924.
Wreckers, Coast of Northumberland, 1834 (£288. 15s.), £1,984. 10s.
Calder Bridge, Cumberland (£288. 15s.), £525.
Venice—The Campo Santo, 1842 (£262. 10s.), £2,000.
Venice—The Giudecca, Sta. Maria della Salute, &c., 1841 (£262), £1,732. 10s.
Ehrenbreitstein (£401), £1,890.
Port Ruysdael, 1827 (£315), £1,995.
Palestrina, 1830 (£1,050), £1,995.
Himalaya Mountains, two (£36), £346. 10s.

1863.
May   Woodcock Shooting, Scene on the Chiver.   510 guineas.

Collection of Mr. Allnutt.

June   A River, crossed by a bridge, hills on either side, cows in shallow water—evening. (Stated to be the painter's work on admission as A.R.A., 1799, which can only mean that it was exhibited in that year ; and is probably that given in Rodd's List as 'Abergavenny Bridge, Monmouthshire—clearing up after a showery day,' No. 326 in Royal Academy Catalogue.) 385 guineas.   Lord Ashburton.
       This work was also at the Art Treasures Exhibition under the title of 'Bridge at Abergavenny.'

,,   Leeds. (Engraved in 'England and Wales.') 320gs. Vokins.

,,   Distant View of Fonthill Abbey, the lake below, wooded foreground—morning.   260 guineas.   Webb.

,,   The companion, the same, sheep feeding, stream in front—evening. 100 guineas.   Cox.

,,   Tivoli.   1,800 guineas.   Lord Ashburton.

,,   The engraving from the same, by Goodall, copper-plate, and 465 impressions, many of them proofs before letters, executed for Mr. Allnutt.   420*l*.   Agnew.
       The Drawing was No. 1033 at the International Exhibition. It appears to have been exhibited at the Royal Academy in 1818, No. 474 ; and was at the Art Treasures Exhibition, No. 309, then the property of W. Wilson, Esq.

,,   The Pass of the Simplon.   103*l*.   Webb.

July   Sidon.   197*l*. 8*s*.

,,   Suez.   200*l*. 11*s*.

December Hythe.   (Painted 1824 'Southern Coast' Series. Engraved.] 126*l*.   Graves.

,,   Mount Lebanon.   157*l*. 10*s*.   Graves.

1864.   *Collection of Mr. T. H. M'Connel.*

June   25 Lowestoft.   134*l*. 10*s*.   Agnew.

From Various Private Collections.

July   A Sea View.   656*l*.   Webster.

,,   Barnes Terrace, on the Thames, 1827.   1,102*l*. 10*s*.   Webster

,,   Fourteen Numbers 'Liber Studiorum,' chiefly with Turner'. initials in the corners.   63*l*.   Graves.

1865.   *Collection of John Davis and others.*

April   Exeter, from the River. (From the 'England and Wales.'] 514*l*.   Cox.

Lighthouse at Havre, moonlight ; The Lake of Geneva from the Jura ; and Lighthouse of the Hève, mouth of the Seine (131. 5*s*.), brought respectively £160. 5*s*., £148. 1*s*., and £108. 3*s*.

The Righi (£84), £310. 16*s*.

The Castle of Elsy, Rouen, and Château Gaillard (cost £131. 5*s*.), brought respectively £168, £210, and £178. 10*s*.

The Lake of Lucerne (£84), £714.

The Pilkington Drawings, by Turner, of Yorkshire Scenes :—Scarborough Castle, Mowbray Lodge, Grouse Shooting, and Woodcock Shooting (cost £600) brought respectively £546, £535. 10*s*., and £535. 10*s*. ; total, £2,068. 10*s*.

1865.   *Drawings by Turner.*

April.   A Town in the Tyrol. 483*l.* Agnew.
  ,,   River Scene in the Tyrol. 420*l.* Vokins.
  ,,   Lake Scene, with mountains on either side. 157*l.* Vokins.
  ,,   View in the Tyrol—'Going to Market.' 158*l.* Agnew.
  ,,   Pass of St. Bernard. 84*l.* Vokins.
  ,,   Town on a River in Savoy. 286*l.* Agnew.
  ,,   Do.   with Figures in a Boat. 304*l.* Agnew.
  ,,   Sunrise. 49*l.* Vokins.
  ,,   Sunset. 50*l.* Vokins.

                        Pictures by Turner.

  ,,   An Italian Landscape. 472*l.* Agnew.
  ,,   Landscape—'Woman with a Tambourine,' like the last.
            (Engraved in the 'Liber Studiorum.') 494*l.* Agnew.
  ,,   The Beacon on the Rock. 316*l.* Agnew.
  ,,   Off Margate Pier. 210*l.* Agnew.
  ,,   Morning after the Wreck. 157*l.* Sharpe.
  ,,   Kingsgate Bay, Margate—Emigrants Landing. 168*l.* E. F. White.
  ,,   Squally Weather. 69*l.* Bicknell.
  ,,   Wreckers—Early Morning. 52*l.* Vokins.
  ,,   Sunset. 132*l.* Agnew.
  ,,   Off Margate—A Hazy Morning. 136*l.* Bicknell.
  ,,   View off Margate—Evening. 162*l.* Agnew.
  ,,   Palestrina, from the Bicknell collection. 2,205*l.* Miller.

    Collection of Mr. John Knowles, of the Theatre, Manchester.

  ,,   Set of the 'England and Wales' Series. (Engraver's proofs on
            India paper.) 105*l.* Jones.
  ,,   The Amphitheatre at Verona. (Engraved, 3¼ in. by 5¾ in.) 74*l.*
            Agnew.
  ,,   Valetta Harbour. (6½ in. by 10½ in., engraved.) 241*l.* C. White.
  ,,   Saltash. (11 in. by 16 in., 'England and Wales' Series. En-
            graved.) 220*l.* Vokins.

                    Collection of Mr. David Cox.

  ,,   'Tintagel Castle.' 155 guineas. Agnew.

                    Collection of Mr. Dyce.

May   Portrait of Turner, on canvas. 21*l.* Agnew.

        Collection of Mr. T. Greenwood, of Sandfield Lodge.

  ,,   'Durham.' 35*l.* Colnaghi.
  ,,   'Malvern Church and Abbey.' 42*l.* Chester.
  ,,   'Sistron.' 63*l.* Greenwood.
  ,,   View near Geneva. 39*l.* Greenwood.
  ,,   'Ramsgate from the Sea.' 120*l.* Cox.
  ,,   'Plymouth Sound.' (Engraved.) 120*l.* Lloyd.
  ,,   'Mountain Fort, near Geneva.' 25*l.* Greenwood.
  ,,   'Sidmouth.' 74*l.* Lloyd.

        BY MESSRS. SOTHEBY, WILKINSON, & HODGE.

June   'Liber Studiorum.' 450*l.*

1865.   By Messrs. Christie & Manson.

Collection of Sir W. Call, Bart.

June   8   The Mouth of the Thames.   (Early.)   307*l.*   Colnaghi.

Collection of the Rev. C. H. Hartshorne and others.

,,   Lake Albano. 351*l.*   Grundy.

Collection of J. R. Williams, Esq.

June   Wolf's Hope, (*Vide* 'Guy Mannering.')   158*l.*   Gibbs.
,,   Lochmaben Castle. 68*l.*   Agnew.

1866.
March   A Welsh Bridge. (1795.)   27*l.*   Colnaghi.
,,   Conway Castle.   (Early.)   39*l.*   Bourne.
,,   St. Michael's Mount.   ('England and Wales.' One of the best
         as well as most famous works of the painter.) 299*l.*   Tooth.
June   Melrose Abbey. 44*l.*   Agnew.

Collection of Mr. Bishop, of Plymouth.

April   Group of Trees near Lowther Castle. 18 guineas.   Bourne.

Collection of Mr. Curling, of Maesmawr Hall, Welshpool.

May   'The Southern Coast of England,' 165 engravings and etchings.
       38*l.*   Bicknell.

By Messrs. Foster & Co.

,,   Geneva. 185 guineas.   Rowney.

By Messrs. Christie & Manson.

Collection of Mr. G. Young and others.

,,   The Seventh Plague of Egypt.   (Engraved in the 'Liber
        Studiorum' as 'The Fifth Plague of Egypt.' Beckford col-
        lection. International Exhibition.) 1,060*l.*   Earl Grosvenor.
,,   Orfordness. (Water colour. 'England and Wales.') 383*l.* Agnew.
,,   Passing the Cross. 199*l.*   Sergeant.

1867.   *Collection of Messrs. Colnaghi, Scott, & Co.*

March   View in the neighbourhood of Sisterton. 110*l.*   Marshall.
,,   Wreck Ashore. 840*l.*   Wilson.
,,   A Complete Copy of the 'Liber Studiorum.' 109*l.*   Tilly.

Collection of A. H. Campbell, Esq., M.P.

June   The Mouth of the Seine. 113*l.*   Agnew.
,,   Fowley Harbour. 155*l.*   Ames.

1868.   *Collection of the late Mr. B. G. Windus, of Tottenham.*

February. Tynemouth. (Engraved in the 'England' Series.) 304*l.* Vokins,
,,   A Ruined Abbey. 86*l.*   Agnew.
,,   The West Front of Wells Cathedral. 105*l.*   Haig.

1868.   *Collection of the late Mr. W. M. Bigg.*

March   Langharne Castle. 451*l.* Vokins.
April   Loch Maben. (Engraved.) 68*l.* Colnaghi.
,,   Penmaenmawr. 493*l.* Maclean.
,,   Lago di Garda. 210*l.* Agnew.
,,   Richmond, Yorkshire. 525*l.* Isaacs.
,,   Narni. 446*l.* Colnaghi.
,,   Oberwesel. 903*l.* Agnew.
,,   Rhodes. 180*l.* Cox.

     Collection of the late Mr. D. T. White, of Maddox Street.

,,   Portrait of Turner. 77*l.* 14*s.* Somes.
,,   Cassiobury. 50*l.* Tooth.
,,   Loch Achray. 18 guineas. Maclean.

     Collection of the late H. A. J. Munro, Esq.

May   Book of Prints, 'Liber Studiorum,' 14 numbers, with his auto-
       graph on the covers. 80*l.* Noseda.
,,   An Italian River Scene. 147*l.* Vokins.
,,   An Italian Valley. 141*l.*
,,   The Valley of Martigny. 105*l.* T. Woolner.
,,   The Valley of the Rhone. 84*l.* Colnaghi.
,,   Swiss Valley. 35*l.* E. White.
,,   Warwick Castle. ('England and Wales.') 420*l.* Baker.
,,   Turner's 'Liber Studiorum.' 85*l.* Rimell.

     Collection of the late C. J Palmer, Esq., and others.

,,   The Burning of the Houses of Parliament. 1,455*l.* Agnew.

By Messrs. Sotheby & Co.

     Collection of the late Sir John Hippisley.

,,   'Liber Studiorum.' (In fine early state, 78 subjects and 8
       etchings.) 336*l.* 16*s.* 6*d.*

1869.   *Collection of P. Allen, Esq. of Sedgly Park, Manchester.*

March   Inverary. 199*l.* Agnew.
,,   The Temple of Jupiter at Ægina. 220*l.* Gambart.

April   *Collection of Mr. Ruskin.*

,,   Battle Abbey. (Second period.) 101*l.* Gambart.
,,   Coast Scene. (Early.) 52*l.* Agnew.
,,   Sketch for—or more probably commencement of—a drawing of
       the Bass Rock. (Middle time.) 80*l.* Agnew.
,,   Dead Pheasant. (Finished.) 50*l.* Vokins.
,,   Margate Pier. (Finest period.) 73*l.* Colnaghi.
,,   Study of Storm and Sunshine. 67*l.* Vokins.
,,   Luxembourg. (Sketch, a little later than the 'Rivers of France.')
       60*l.* Vokins.
,,   On the Rhine. (Sketch.) 53*l.* Agnew.
,,   The Niessen. (Late.) 120*l.* Colnaghi.
,,   Mountains at the Head of the Lake Thun. (Late.) 136*l.* Agnew.

1869.

,,   Bellinzona. 107*l.* Vokins.
,,   The Desolate Bed of an Alpine Stream. 106*l.* Agnew.
,,   Alpine Torrent and Pass. (Late.) 124*l.* Agnew.
,,   Scene in the Tyrol. 161*l.* Agnew.
,,   The Glacier des Bossons. 64*l.* Colnaghi.
,,   The Lake of Brienz. (Early.) 327*l.* Agnew.

A DIFFERENT PROPERTY.—*Engravings.*

,,   A Copy of 'England and Wales.' 52*l.* Inman.
,,   The 'Liber Studiorum.' (Original subscriber's copy.) 31*l.* Martin.
,,   A Scene in Cumberland, with a Rainbow. 81*l.* Agnew.
,,   Whalley Abbey. 42*l.* Agnew.
,,   An Italian Convent. 35*l.* Agnew.
,,   Interior of Eveny Priory. 106*l.* Agnew.
,,   Beeston Castle, Cheshire. 133*l.* Agnew.
,,   The Rhone at Geneva. 147*l.* Agnew.
,,   A River Scene. 31*l.* Levy.
,,   The Val d'Aosta. 147*l.* Agnew.
,,   Aldborough, Suffolk. (Engraved for, but not published in, the 'England and Wales' Series.) 106*l.* Agnew.
,,   Whitby. (Same.) 210*l.* Agnew.
,,   A Harbour Scene. (Not engraved.) 210*l.* Agnew.
,,   Warkworth Castle. 110*l.* Agnew.
,,   A Landscape, with a Female Peasant and a Sheep on a Road. 740*l.* Agnew.

1870.   *Collection of the late T. S. Cafe, Esq.*

April   'England and Wales.' 68*l.* Sotheran.
,,   Do.   Another copy. (First state.) 73*l.* Martin.

Collection of the late Mr. E. Bullock, of Handsworth.

,,   Venice—the Dogana and Church Sta. Maria della Salute. (R. A. 1844.) 2,688*l.* Agnew.

Collection of the late G. Rennie, Esq.

,,   Pendennis Castle. (Engraved for 'The Southern Coast.') 142*l.* Vokins.

Collection of the late James Holland.

,,   Conway Castle. 55*l.* Maclean.
,,   Christchurch, Oxford, 1794. 46*l.* Vokins.

1871.   *Collection of the late Mr. T. Agnew and other owners.*

May   The Rape of Europa. 309*l.* Cassell.
,,   The Falls of the Clyde. 357*l.* Campbell.

Collection of Messrs. Wilkinson and E. Radley.

,,   A View near Plymouth. 47*l.*
,,   Study of a Sky, and an Alpine Valley. 21*l.*
,,   View on the Moselle. 12 guineas.

1871.

May   Study of Clouds—Moonlight. 5 guineas.

,,   A Lake Scene. 15 guineas.

,,   A River Scene, with a Church and Boat. 11*l.*

,,   The Falls of Terni. 15 guineas.

,,   Luxembourg. 50 guineas.

,,   Durham. 57*l.*

,,   A View on the Moselle. 7 guineas.

,,   Boats near a Pier. 26*l.*

,,   Walton Bridge. 17*l.*

,,   The Entrance to Battle Abbey. 94*l.*

,,   Brienne. 103*l.*

By Messrs. Sotheby, Wilkinson, & Co.

July   'Liber Studiorum'—Mill near the Grand Chartreuse, Dauphiny. 25*l.* Halstead.

,,   Lock and Windmill. 35*l.* Mrs. Noseda.

,,   Norham Castle. 29*l.* Colnaghi.

,,   Rizpah. 14*l.* Holloway.

,,   Another, touched upon by Turner. 52*l.* Colnaghi.

,,   Procris and Cephalus. 41*l.* Colnaghi.

,,   The Tenth Plague of Egypt. 19*l.* Agnew.

,,   Isis. 45*l.* Mrs. Noseda.

,,   Blair-Athol. 45*l.* Mrs. Noseda.

,,   Solway Moss. 35*l.* Mrs. Noseda.

By Messrs. Christie & Manson.

1872.   *Collection of Francis Broderip, Esq.*

February A Gothic Ruin. 15*l.*

,,   Magdalen College and Bridge. 81*l.*

,,   A View of a Gentleman's House, with Figures and Animals. 71*l.*

,,   Ludlow Castle and Bridge. 630*l.*

,,   Stonyhurst College. (Engraved.) 472*l.*

,,   Grenoble, on the Isère. 1,470*l.*

Collection of the late John Harris, Esq., and others.

March   Glaucus and Scylla. (R. A. 1841.) 530*l.*

,,   The Dawn of Christianity. (1841.) 966*l.*

Collection of T. R. Leyland, Esq.

,,   Llangollen.   ('England and Wales.') 735*l.*

,,   Saltash.   Do.   472*l.*

,,   Harlech.   Do.   472*l.*

,,   St. Michael's Mount.   Do.   577*l.*

,,   The Lake of Albano. ('Keepsake.') 525*l.*

,,   Deal. ('Harbours of England.') 252*l.*

,,   Le Havre. ('Keepsake.') 399*l.*

,,   Père la Chaise. (Illustrations to Scott.) 180*l.*

,,   Light-Towers of La Hève. 168*l.*

,,   A Swiss Pass—Effect of Storm. 651*l.*

,,   Old Buildings and Boats. (In Indian ink.) 6*l.*

,,   Fishing Boats. 2 guineas.

1872.

March Margate Harbour. 204*l.*

,, Emigrants Embarking at Margate. (A sketch.) 199*l.*

,, Sunset after a Storm. (A sketch.) 90*l.*

Collection of G. R. Burnett, Esq.

,, St. Agnes's Hill. ('England and Wales.') 367*l.*

,, Kelso Bridge. 141*l.*

,, Brienne. 153*l.*

,, Whitehaven. 86*l.*

,, On the Medway. (A sketch in oil.) 60*l.*

Collection of the late Mr. Gillott.*

April 'Going to the Ball'—S. Martino, Venice; and 'Returning from the Ball'—S. Martha, Venice. 3,200 guineas.

* THE GILLOTT SALE.

The prices obtained at the sale surpassed any hitherto given for pictures by English landscape painters, and the general interest felt in the splendid works of Gainsborough, Bonington, Crome, Constable, Turner, Collins, and Linnell was something quite extraordinary. The rooms of the auctioneers (Messrs. Christie, Manson, and Woods) were completely besieged, and hundreds of persons could not even get within sight of the auctioneer ; while, at the close of the sale, the street was blocked with carriages and the pavement crowded with gentlemen and ladies eager to hear what the Turners sold for. These pictures were the last in the day's sale, which, though a short affair, consisting of only about sixty lots, was the most exciting contest of two hours ever witnessed in the renowned arena of art and picture buyers. The first of the Turners was the small coast scene, a slight work of his earliest time, which sold for 300 guineas, however, to Mr. Betts. 'Early Morning on the Coast,' of similar quality, sold for 270 guineas to Mr. Conway. A sunny landscape, like Wilson, and another similar in treatment, sold to Mr. Cox for 75 and 115 guineas each. Next came the small 'Kilgarren Castle,' which was knocked down at 600 guineas, and the auctioneer announced that it was purchased for the National Museum of New York. For the larger picture of Kilgarren, one of the painter's grandest works, America was also a competitor, the Museum acquiring the noble example at the price of 2,700 guineas, which must now be considered a very moderate one. The sea piece, with an Indiaman and two fishing boats, sold for 800 guineas to Mr. Betts. The magnificent sea piece known as the 'Junction of the Thames and Medway,' said to be taken from the Nore, with the Isle of Sheppey and Sheerness seen in the distance, formerly in the collection of Mr. J. Newington Hughes, of Winchester, fell to Mr. Agnew's bid of 4,350 guineas. This picture may be remembered to have been sold from the same easel about 25 years ago, for 1,200 guineas, which was then an unheard-of price for any English painter's work. The enormous price realised for the last-named picture was, however, to be surpassed in the next offered, the 'Walton Bridges,' which, after starting at 1,000 guineas, ran up quickly to £4,850, when Mr. Agnew made one enthusiastic bid of 5,000 guineas, and thus distanced all his competitors, carrying off the great prize of the collection. The following were the prices of the most important pictures by other masters :—J. Linnell, 'Bayswater in 1813,' 300 guineas ; G. S. Newton, R.A., 'Norman Peasant Girl in Church,' 400 guineas ; Bonington, 'Landscape, with a Man on a White Horse,' 200 guineas ; 'View of the French Coast,' by the same painter, 125 guineas ; also a 'View on the Seine,' 300 guineas ; and landscape, with timber-waggon, 520 guineas. Constable, 'The Approach to London from Hampstead,' a small picture, 8½ by 11½ in. for 385 guineas. By the same painter, a rustic landscape, 350 guineas ; 'A View on the Stour,' 650 guineas ; and 'Weymouth Bay,' 700 guineas. Old Crome, upright landscape, 170 guineas ; a landscape, with ruins, 130 guineas ; a rocky river scene, 305 guineas ; 'Mousehold Heath, with Windmill,' 360 guineas ; a rich wooded scene, with pool, 700 guineas. The twelve Nasmyths sold for full prices, from 160 to 390 guineas, the 'View of the Firth of Forth,' however, bringing the large price of 1,070 guineas—Agnew.

The second day's sale was, if possible, a scene of greater interest and excitement amongst the picture buyers than that of the preceding day, and the prices of the pictures ranged quite as high in some unexpected instances, especially in that of Webster's (R.A.) picture called 'Roast Pig'—a family party welcoming the arrival of their Sunday dinner from the baker's, of that delicacy which Charles Lamb called the 'princeps orbsoniorum.' For this a very lively contest speedily arose as it made its appearance on the easel, the bids running rapidly up to 3,000 guineas, where there was a lull, when Mr. Agnew

1872.

April Calais Sands. 1,575 guineas.

  ,, Rosenau. 1,850 guineas.

advanced, and in the end it fell to him at the enormous price of 3,550 guineas, amidst the applause of the assembly. This picture was painted for Mr. Gillott, and exhibited at the Academy in 1862, when it was said to have been a commission for 700 guineas. The famous 'Chess-players,' by Müller, which had been the admiration and talk of the gallery during the week, was fairly rivalled by Webster's clever piece of domestic *genre* when it came to the hammer, for though it rose in four bids to 3,000 guineas, it was knocked down, after a spirited competition between Mr. Addington and Mr. Agnew, for £3,950 to the latter gentleman. The other pictures by Müller fetched full, though not extravagantly high, prices. 'The Port of Rhodes,' from the Bullock collection, sold for 350 guineas, to Mr. White; 'Landscape with a Rainbow,' for 160 guineas, to Mr. Holloway; 'Interior of a Cottage,' 200 guineas, to Mr. Agnew; 'The Turkish Burial-ground at Pera,' for 270 guineas, Agnew; 'The Dogana,' from the Bullock collection, 350 guineas, Agnew; a fruit piece (one of his last works), 90 guineas, White; 'Hagar and Ishmael,' painted 1842, for 280 guineas; 'The Memnons,' for 315 guineas; 'The Treasure-finders,' for 410 guineas; a large landscape after a shower, with figures, attributed to W. Collins, from Mr. Proudfoot's collection, for 770 guineas, to Mr. Agnew. 'The Slave Market,' from Mr. Birch's collection, for 1,510 guineas, Agnew; 'The Bay of Naples,' a fine sunny picture, painted with great delicacy, was put up at 1,000 guineas, and fell to Mr. Agnew for 2,000 guineas. The large gallery picture of 'Dolgarrog Mill, near Conway,' certainly one of the artist's best works, sold for the moderate sum of 1,250 guineas, to Mr. Agnew. Great interest was shown in the three fine landscapes by Linnell; of these, the 'Hampstead Heath,' painted for Mr. Gillott, after being put up at 1,000 guineas, fell to Mr. Agnew for 1,660 guineas; 'The Eve of the Deluge,' painted 1848, also a commission from Mr. Gillott, was put up at 900 guineas, and bought by Mr. Rhodes for 1,040 guineas; the 'Woodlands,' a smaller picture than either of the others, exhibited in 1851, and recently sold in the Bullock collection for 1,500 guineas, reached the large price of 2,500. The well-known picture by Stanfield, exhibited recently at the Old Masters' Exhibition of the Academy 1870, 'The Wooden Walls of Old England' (old men-of-war laid up in the Medway), sold for 2,700 guineas to Mr. Rhodes. The four Turners, which we have already described, did not realise the high prices generally expected, the very beautiful picture of 'Calais Sands' selling for 1,700 guineas, to Mr. Agnew, who was the purchaser also of the view of 'Rosenau,' the seat of the late Prince Consort, which was knocked down at 1,850 guineas. The companion pictures, views of Venice, with parties in gondolas, called 'Going to the Ball' and 'Returning from the Ball,' painted in 1846, were bought by Mr. Tayleur, the first at 1,700 guineas, the last at 1,500 guineas. Maclise's large gallery picture of 'The Bohemian Gipsies,' which was last year sold in the sale of the late Mr. Agnew's collection for 400 guineas, now advanced to double that sum, falling to Mr. Rhodes at the price of 890 guineas. The 'Author's Introduction to the Players' was knocked down to Mr. Cox for 750 guineas. Mr. Frith's 'Dolly Varden,' was put up at 500 guineas, and fell to Mr. Agnew for 700 guineas; Mr. Faed's (R.A.) very pleasing little picture of the old man and his wife bidding good-bye to a party of emigrants, called 'Seeing them off,' fetched the high price of 700 guineas, sold to Mr. Agnew; the well-remembered landscape by Mr. Peter Graham, of the 'Cattle Tryst,' exhibited 1869, fell to Mr. Cox for 1,480 guineas. Mr. Erskine Nicol's pictures realised very high prices, the 'Both Puzzled' selling for 715 guineas to Mr. Agnew, and the 'Railway Booking Office' for 1,100 guineas to Mr. Rhodes. Mr. Hook's 'Cowherd's Mischief' (1868) sold for 700 guineas to Mr. Agnew, who was the purchaser also of the 'Passing Cloud,' by the same artist, at 600 guineas. Two large works of Francis Danby, 'The Arrival' and 'The Departure of Æneas,' sold for 130 and 105 guineas; John Philips's full length of the Prince Consort sold for 350 guineas, and his sketch of 'Grace Darling' for 190 guineas, to Mr. Colnaghi. The 'Travelling Jeweller,' by T. Webster, R.A., sold for 530 guineas to Mr. Rhodes. There were about 30 other pictures in the sale of less importance, and the total of the day's sale amounted to the large sum of £44,443, making, with that of the previous day, £74,161. 7s.

It will be interesting in connection with this sale to mention the prices obtained for Turner's pictures at the sale of the Munro collection in 1860, and the Bicknell in 1863, by Messrs. Christie and Manson. The 'Loch Katrine' sold for 555 guineas, to Mr. White; the 'Cicero's Villa at Tusculum,' to Lord Powerscourt for 2,470 guineas; 'A River Scene,' to Mr. Heugh for 1,270 guineas; 'The Wreck Buoy' for 1,500 guineas, to Mr. Agnew; the 'Ostend' for 1,650 guineas, and the 'View on the Grand Canal, Venice,' for 2,400 guineas, to Mr. Gambart; the 'Modern Italy' for 3,300 guineas, to Mr. Fallows. The Bicknell Turners realised the following prices:—The 'Antwerp,' 2,510 guineas, sold to Mr. Agnew; 'Helvoetsluys,' 1,600 guineas, Agnew; 'Ivy Bridge,' 880 guineas, Masterman; 'The Wreckers,' 1,890 guineas, Agnew; 'Calder's Bridge,' 500 guineas, H. Bicknell; 'The Campo Santo, Venice,' 2,000 guineas, Agnew; 'The Giudecca and Sta.

1872.

April   Kilgarren Castle, 630*l.*; and the same, with Bathers in the
           River. 2,835*l.*

,,   A Rocky River Scene, with a Cascade—a woman on a road
           going towards a cottage. 147*l.*

,,   On the Thames, with Boats and richly wooded Banks. 472*l.*

,,   The Source of the Tamar—a moor scene, with laden ponies de-
           scending a hill and figures burning weeds on a hill beyond. 367*l.*

May   Patterdale. 850*l.*

,,   Powis Castle. 1,270*l.*

,,   Windermere. 2,047*l.*

,,   Brentburn Priory. 1,113*l.*

,,   Zurich. 745*l.*

,,   Hastings Beach—the Fish Market. 1,155*l.*

,,   Heidelberg. 2,782*l.*

,,   Ehrenbreitstein. 2,782*l.*

,,   Bamborough Castle. 3,309*l.*

       Collection of the late Mrs. Bury and Mr. A. Wood.

,,   The Lake of Lucerne. 278*l.*

,,   A Garden Scene, with a Monument. 10 guineas.

,,   A Lake Scene, with Towers, Boats, and Figures. 53*l.*

1873.   *Collection of Mr. J. Pender.*

February Two Sketches. 91 guineas.

       Collection of Mr. Thomas Gilbert.

April   Slavers Throwing Overboard the Dead and Dying—Typhoon
           coming on. 550 guineas.

May   The Second Portion of the Engravings from the Works of Turner,
           comprising the whole of the sets of the book-plates to the Bible,
           Byron's Poetical Works, Campbell's Poetical Works, Milton's
           Poetical Works, Moore's 'Epicurean,' 'The Keepsake,'
           'Views in India,' Rogers' 'Italy' and 'Poems,' Scott's
           Novels and Poetical and Prose Works, and 'The Annual
           Tours,' 1833, 1834, 1835. Also the remaining copies of
           'The Provincial Antiquities of Scotland,' 'The Southern
           Coast,' Hakewell's 'Italy,' Whittaker's 'Yorkshire,' 'Views
           of Sussex,' and all the remaining impressions of 'Ehren-
           breitstein,' 'Cologne,' 'Oberwesel,' 'Narni,' 'Eddystone
           Lighthouse,' 'The Old Téméraire,' 'Tivoli,' touched proofs,
           etchings, &c.

,,   Sets of the Bible Cuts. 21 impressions each. (Engraved by
           Allen, Cousen, Finden, and Radclyffe.) India proofs, 43 lots,
           none exceeding 14*s.*

Maria Salute,' 1,650 guineas, Agnew; the 'Ehrenbreitstein,' 1,800 guineas, Agnew;
the 'Port Ruysdael,' 1,900 guineas, Agnew; and the 'Palestrina,' 1,900 guineas, H.
Bicknell. The last picture, it will be remembered, was contributed by Mr. Bicknell to
the Royal Academy Old Masters' Exhibition of this year. The portraits by Reynolds of
Gaudon, Banks, and Paul Sandby, on one canvas, sold for 135 guineas to Mr. Woodcock.
That of 'Anne Stewart, Countess of Galloway,' daughter of Sir James Dashwood, who
lived to be 87, and saw grow up 16 children, 86 grandchildren, and 35 great grandchildren,
sold for 300 guineas to Colnaghi. The portrait of Mrs. Yates, née Anna Maria Graham,
1737, wife of Richard Yates and friend of Garrick, sold for 300 guineas to Mr. Palmer.
The amount of the last day's sale was £36,830. 12*s.*; making, with the sums previously
obtained, the total of £130,548.

Sale of the Pictures of Mr. A. Fairrie, of Liverpool.

Five Turners; one an Italian subject, an early drawing, and Lichfield and Rochester, both early works; also the view of Stamford, one of the very best of his water-colours, which was engraved by Miller for the 'England and Wales'; and Lucerne, a later drawing, which also has been engraved, but which is as different as possible from the Lucerne at Farnley Hall —one of the most tender and poetical of Turner's poetical works. There is more colour and greater feeling of atmosphere in this Lucerne, but there is more exquisite repose and positive beauty about that at Farnley Hall.

Sale of Sir John Swinburne's Pictures.

(FROM CHANTREY'S COLLECTION.)

What you will. (The first picture in the artist's last manner.) **245** guineas.
    Agnew.

At the same Sale, from another Collection.

Loch Katrine. **750** guineas. D. J. White.

Sale of Turner Pictures, 24th November 1860.

A highly important sale of water-colour drawings at Messrs. Foster's. These
                            are the principal lots :—
Outside Walls of Rome. (A delightful sketch.) 3½ guineas.
View of London from Battersea. (A large, fine, and early drawing.) **135**
    guineas.
One of the most perfect of Turner's drawings, the famous and admirable
    Mount Sinai, engraved in the Bible Series, went for **72** guineas.
The Bridge of Sighs, Venice. (Engraved in the Rogers Series.) **80** guineas.

In the Collection of — Allnutt, Esq., Clapham.

The St. Gothard. (Early oil.)	Italian Scene. (Engraved.)
Abergavenny Bridge. (Clearing up after shower.)	Two large Water-colour Drawings of Fonthill, Wiltshire.

NOTE TO PAGE 593.

Mr. Ruskin has lately given 2,000*l.* worth of his Turner Drawings to the University of Oxford. It is said he contemplates a similar gift to the University of Cambridge.

AUTHENTIC COPY OF TURNER'S WILL (WITH THE CANCELLED CODICIL).

IN the name of God Amen I JOSEPH MALLORD WILLIAM TURNER R.A. of Queen Ann Street Cavendish Square in the county of Middlesex Esquire do make publish and declare this to be and contain my last Will and Testament in manner and form following that is to say after payment of all my just debts funeral expenses and the costs and charges of proving this my Will I give and bequeath unto my Executors and Trustees hereinafter named or the survivor of them his Executors or Administrators All the Freehold and Copyhold Estates whatsoever and wheresoever situated And also all my Leasehold and Personal Estates and property of every kind and description whatsoever and wheresoever situate of which I shall or may be possessed or be entitled to or interested in at the time of my decease To have and to hold the said Freehold and Copyhold Estates unto my said Executors their heirs and assigns To the use of them their heirs and assigns for ever and To have hold receive and take all my said Personal Estate (except as hereafter mentioned as to my pictures) unto them my said Executors their Executors and Administrators nevertheless as to the said Freehold and Copyhold Estates and the said Personal Estates Upon Trust that they my said Executors or the survivors or survivor of them their Heirs Executors or Administrators do and shall as soon after my decease as may be sell and dispose of all my said Freehold and Copyhold Estates and such part of my said Real and Personal Estate and effects (except as aforesaid) as shall not consist of money vested in the Public Stock Funds called Three pounds per cent. Consolidated Annuities or other Funds transferable at the Bank of England for the most money that can be had or obtained for the same either by Public Auction or Private Sale as shall be deemed best for the advantage and interest of my Estate to such person or persons as they may think fit And I do hereby authorise and empower my said Executors or the survivors or survivor of them and the Heirs Executors or Administrators of such survivor to sign seal and deliver good and sufficient Conveyances Assignments and Assurances to the purchasers thereof And I declare that the receipt or receipts of my said Executors or the survivor of them his Heirs Executors or Administrators shall from time to time be to the purchaser or purchasers of my said Freehold Copyhold and Personal Estate and every part thereof good and sufficient releases and discharges for so much of the purchase money as shall in such receipt or receipts be expressed to be received and such purchaser or purchasers shall not be bound to see to the application of such purchase money or be liable or accountable for the loss mis-application or non-application thereof or of any part thereof And upon further Trust to lay out and invest the monies to arise from such sale or sales of my said Freehold and Copyhold and Personal Estates and Effects in the purchase of like Three per cent. Consolidated Annuities in his or their names so that the same may form one fund together with such sum as I shall be possessed of in the said Three pounds per cent. Consolidated Annuities or any other stocks or funds standing in my name at the time of my decease and I direct that my said Executors or the survivors or survivor of them his Executors and Administrators shall stand possessed thereof Upon the Trusts and purposes hereafter mentioned that is to say Upon Trust to pay the several Legacies Annuities and Payments to the respective person hereafter named that is to say to Price Turner Jonathan Turner the present surviving Brothers of my late Father William Turner Fifty pounds each to the eldest son of Price John Joshua Jonathan Turner Twenty-five pounds each to Hannah Danby Niece of John Danby Musician Fifty pounds a year for her natural life to Eveline and Georgiana T the Daughters of Sarah Danby Widow of John Danby Musician Fifty pounds a year each for their natural lives and aforesaid Sarah Danby Widow of John Danby Musician the sum of Ten pounds a year for her natural life all which Annuities and Legacies I direct my Executors or the survivor of them his Executors or Administrators to pay and discharge out of the Annual Interest or Dividends that shall become due and payable from time to time upon the Three per cent. Consolidated Annuities or any other stocks or funds which may be standing in my name at the Bank of England at my decease or which may be purchased with the produce of my said Freehold and Copyhold and Personal Estates so directed to be funded as aforesaid the first quarterly payments of the said several Annuities to commence and be paid at the expiration of 6 months from the date of my decease And I direct my said Executors or the survivors or survivor of them his Executors or Administrators to set apart so much of the said Three per cent. Consolidated Annuities or any other stocks or funds as will be sufficient to pay the said several Annuities And I declare that upon the respective deaths of the said several Annuitants the principal sum of stock from which their several Annuities shall arise be applied in the manner hereafter ordered with regard to the residue of the said funds And I direct my Executors or the survivor of them his Executors or Administrators to pay the Legacies within 6 months next after my decease Also I give and bequeath unto the Trustees and Directors for the time being of a certain Society or Institution called the 'National Gallery' or Society the following pictures or paintings by myself namely Dido building Carthage and the picture formerly in the Tabley Collection To hold the said pictures or paintings unto the said Trustees and Directors of the said Society for the time being In Trust for the said Institution or Society for ever subject nevertheless to for and upon the following reservations and restrictions only that is to say I direct that the said pictures or paintings shall be hung kept and placed that is to say Always between the two pictures painted by Claude the Seaport and Mill and shall be from time to time properly cleaned framed preserved repaired and protected by the said Society and in case the said Pictures or Paintings are not within Twelve months next after my decease accepted and taken by the said Society under and subject to the above regulations restrictions and directions and placed as directed that then I will and direct that they shall be taken to and form part of the [fixed] Property of the Charity hereafter named and to be formed for the Maintenance and Support of Male Decayed Artists and by the Governors Trustees Directors or other persons having the care and management thereof placed in proper situations in the building or house to form such Charitable Institution and who are to properly preserve and keep them in repair And as to all the rest residue and remainder of the said Three pounds per cent. Consolidated Annuities or any other Stocks or Funds as shall not be required to pay the said several Annuities And also as to such part thereof as shall be set apart to pay the said Annuities as and when the said Annuitant shall severally and respectively depart this life I give and bequeath the same and every part thereof unto my Executors or the survivors or survivor of them Upon Trust that my said Executors or the survivors or survivor of them his Executors or Administrators shall and do apply and dispose of the same Upon and for the following uses trusts intents and purposes following that is to say It is my Will and I direct that a Charitable Institution be founded for the Maintenance and support of Poor and Decayed Male Artists being born in England and of English Parents only and lawful issue And I direct that a proper and suitable Building or Residence be provided for that purpose in such a situation as may be deemed eligible and advantageous by my Executors and the Trustees to the said Charitable Institution And that the same be under the direction guidance and management of [Four] Trustees for the time being for life whereof my said Executors during their lives shall be   provided they prove my Will and act in the Trusts thereof but not otherwise And I declare that in case my said Executors and the said other Trustees hereinafter nominated to act with them as to the said Institution or any of them shall die or become incapable of acting in the execution of the Trusts hereby created as to the said [Charitable] Institution that it shall and may be lawful to and for and I direct that the survivors or survivor of my said Executors and the said Trustees or the Executors or Administrators of such survivor by any deed or writing under their hands and seals shall be bound with all convenient speed after any of my said Executors or Trustees shall die or become incapable of acting in the said Trusts hereby created as to the said Institution to be signed sealed and delivered by them or him in the presence of and attested by two or more credible persons to appoint one or more person or persons being a Member or Members of the Royal Academy and two other persons not being Members of the said Royal Academy to act as Trustee or Trustees or as to the said [Charitable] Institution in the stead and place of such of my said Executors or of the said Trustees who shall so die or become incapable of acting in the execution of the Trusts hereby created so that the number of Trustees shall always be 7 exclusive of my Executors during their lives who shall prove this my Will and act in the Trusts thereof And I direct that immediately upon such appointment the said Trust Funds and every part thereof shall be transferred into the names of the surviving or continuing Trustee or Trustees and the said new Trustee or Trustees jointly so that the same be effectually vested in each surviving and continuing new Trustees and that all and every such new Trustees or Trustee shall and may from time to time act in the management execution and carrying on of the said Trusts hereby created as to the said [Charitable] Institution jointly with the surviving or continuing Trustee or Trustees in as full and ample a manner to all intents and purposes as if such new Trustee or Trustees had been originally appointed a Trustee or Trustees herein as to the said [Charitable] Institution And I direct that the said [Charitable] Institution shall be governed guided managed and directed by such rules regulations directions restrictions and management generally as other Public Charitable Institutions resembling this my present one are governed managed and directed And I hereby appoint my Executors who shall act in the execution of the trusts hereof and the survivors or survivor of them together with William Fredrick Wells of Mitcham Surrey Revd Henry Trimmer of Heston Samuel Rogers of St. James Place George Jones R.A. Charles Turner A.R.A. Esquire to be Trustee or Trustees of the said [Charitable] Institution And I direct that the number of Trustees for the time being be Five at all times and that they shall be composed and formed of Artists being Members of the Royal Academy together with Two persons not being Members of the said Royal Academy (except my Executors during their lives) And I declare that they shall be at liberty and have power in case they shall think it necessary for the more effectually and better establishment of the [Charitable] Institution to sell only part of the principal of the said Stock for the purpose of building a proper and fit house for the reception of the objects of the said Institution or that the said Trustees shall or may rent a proper house and offices for that purpose as they shall think fit and as shall be allowed by law but so that there always remain a sufficient amount of Stock to produce dividends and interest equal to the full maintenance and support of the respective individuals and the houses or buildings and premises before mentioned and which [Charitable] Institution I desire shall be called or designated 'Turner's Gift' and shall at all times decidedly be an English Institution and the persons receiving the benefits thereof shall be English born subjects only and of no other Nation or Country whatever And I do authorise and empower the respective Trustees for the time being from time to time to deduct retain and reimburse themselves and himself all such reasonable expenses as they shall be put unto in the execution and maintenance of the said Institution and the support and government thereof And I do hereby nominate constitute and appoint William Fredrick Wells of Mitcham Surrey The Revd Henry Trimmer of Heston Middx Samuel Rogers of St. James Place George Jones R.A. Duke St. Portland Place Charles Turner A.R.A. Warren Street Executors and Trustees of this my last Will and Testament And I do hereby revoke annul and make void all former or other Will or Wills by me at any time heretofore made and executed and do declare this alone to be and contain my last Will and Testament written and contained on eight sheets of paper to the seven first sheets of which I have set my hand and to the eighth and last I have set and subscribed my hand and seal this tenth day of June in the year of our Lord One thousand eight hundred and thirty-one.

Signed Sealed Published and Declared by the within-named Joseph Mallord William Turner as and for his last Will and Testament in the presence of us who at his request in his presence and in the presence of each other have subscribed our names as Witnesses thereto

JOSEPH MALLORD WM. TURNER (L.S.)

GEO. COBB Clements Inn
JOHN SAXON Bruton Somerset
CHARLES TULL Winchester St. London.

August 20 1832

the first

I direct that this may be taken as a Codicil to my Will as regards a certain Charitable Institution therein named and called Turner's Gift which I mean to be carried into effect by giving my whatever sum or sums of money may be standing in my name in the Three per cent. Consols Bank of England for the erection of the Gallery to hold my Pictures and places houses or apartments for one two three or more persons according to circumstances or means which my Executors may find expedient keeping in view the first objects I direct namely is to keep my Pictures together so that they may be seen known or found at the direction as to the mode how they may be viewed gratuitously I leave to my Executors and that the building may for their reception be respectable and worthy of the object which is to keep and preserve my Pictures as a collection of my works and the monies vested in my name in the Reduced for the endowment of the same and charitable part for decay^d Artists as before mentioned provided the other vested sum or sums in Navy 5 per cent. be equal to pay all demands and bequests before mentioned or mentioned in any subsequent Codicil in case only of there being any legal objection to the Institution and carrying into effect my Will as to the said Institution Charity of Turners Gift But it is my express desire that the said Institution Charity or Gift be formed and kept up in case it can legally be done without risk of the funds to be employed therein going into any others hands than for those purposes but if it be found impossible to fully carry the same into effect within five years from my death and then and in that case I revoke annul and make void that part of my said Will which relates to the formation of the said Charitable Institution and the funds and property set apart or to form a part thereof shall then be taken as residue of my Estate and Effects and I thereby give and bequeath the said residue of my said Estate and Effects in manner and form following that is to say I direct my Executors or the survivors of them or his Executors or Administrators to keep all the Pictures and Property in Queen Ann St West N° 47 held under lease of the Duke of Portland Intire and unsold And I direct the rent for the said premises held terms of years together with all charges for repairs and covenants therein entered into be paid and all necessary charges for keeping and taking care insurance from fire preservation* cleansing and holding the same as Turner's Gallery out of the 3 per cent. Consols and likewise for renewing from time to time the said Lease after the present held term of years shall have expired and re-building the same if requisite or necessary I do direct my Executors Administrators or Assigns so to do out of the said Stock vested in the Bank of England and to consider and appoint Hannah Danby the Custodian and Keeper of the Pictures Houses and Premises 47 Queen Ann Street and One hundred a year for her service therein during her natural life and Fifty pounds for her assistance service which may be required to keep the said Gallery in a viewable state at all times concurring with the object of keeping my Works together and to be seen under certain restrictions which may be most reputable and advisable To Georgianna Danby One hundred a year for her natural life and to Evelina Danby or Dupree One hundred a year for her natural life the residue of my property in the funds after said bequests are provided for I give to the Trustees of the Royal Academy subject to their having every year on the 23rd of April (my birth day) a dinner to the sum of 50£ to all the Members of Academy and if 60 more will be left to be for a Professor in Landscape to be read in the Royal Academy elected from the Royal Academicians or a Medal called Turner's Medal equal to the Gold Medal now given by the Academy say 20£ for the best Landscape every 2 [3] years and if the Trustees and Members of the Royal Academy do not accept of this offer^d residue I give the same to Georgia Danby or her Heirs after causing a Monument to be placed near my remains as can be placed*

J. M. W. TURNER

Augt 1832   —————————————————

This is a Codicil to my Will dated the Tenth day of June One thousand eight hundred and thirty one and which I request to be taken as part of my Will together with a Codicil dated the Twentieth day of August One thousand eight hundred and thirty-two and a† Codicil dated the Twenty-ninth day of August One thousand eight hundred and forty six I revoke the following bequests made by my Will namely Fifty pounds and Fifty pounds to Price Turner and Jonathan Turner and also the bequest of Twenty-five pounds to the eldest sons of Price John Joshua and Jonathan Turner I revoke also the bequest of Fifty pounds to Hannah Danby for her natural life also the bequest to Evelina and Georgiana of Fifty pounds each for their natural lives And I also revoke the legacy of Ten pounds to Sarah Danby for her natural life And as to my finished Pictures except the Two mentioned in my Will I give and bequeath the same unto the Trustees of the National Gallery provided that a room or rooms are added

---

* This Codicil is not attested.
† The revoked Codicil ; for copy, *vide post.*

to the present National Gallery to be when erected called 'Turner's Gallery' in which such pictures are to be constantly kept deposited and preserved and it is my wish that until such room or rooms be so erected that my said Pictures remain in my present Gallery and House in Queen Ann Street under the sole controul and management of the Trustees and Executors appointed hereby and by my Will And I direct my Trustees to appoint Hannah Danby to reside in the said House and to be the custodium of the said pictures and to be paid One hundred and fifty pounds during her life but in case she shall be such custodium and receive the One hundred and fifty pounds per annum then the One hundred and fifty pounds per annum given to her by the* Codicil of the Twenty-ninth day of August One thousand eight hundred and forty-six shall cease And I also direct that the rent of the said House and the repairs shall be paid out of my estate Provided always and I do express my will and meaning to be that the said pictures shall not be removed from my present House and Gallery until and unless the said rooms are attached to the National Gallery in manner aforesaid nor shall the Trustees of the said National Gallery have any power whatever over the said Pictures unless my wish as before declared as to the said rooms is fully carried out by them it being my will and meaning that either such pictures shall remain and be and called 'Turner's Gallery' and be the property of the Nation or that they shall remain entire at my said House and Gallery during the existence of the present lease and if my wishes are not carried by the Trustees of the National Gallery during the existence of such lease then I direct my Trustees or the survivor of them or the Executors Administrators or Assigns of such survivor to renew the lease thereof from time to time at the expense of my estate to the intent and purpose that such pictures may always remain and be one entire Gallery and for the purpose of regulating such Gallery it is my wish that so many of the Pictures as may be necessary shall be seen by the public gratuitously so that from the number of them there may be a change of Pictures either every one or two years as my said Trustees shall think right and from and after the decease of the said Hannah Danby my Trustees shall have power to appoint any other custodium of the said Gallery at a Salary of Sixty pounds a year but in case my said Trustees shall not be able to renew the lease of my said Gallery then I direct the said Pictures to be sold I nominate and appoint Thomas Griffiths of Norwood in the county of Surrey esquire, John Ruskin the younger of Denmark Hill Camberwell in the county of Surrey esquire Philip Hardwicke of Russell Square in the county of Middlesex esquire and Henry Harpur of Kennington Cross Lambeth in the county of Surrey gentlemen to be Trustees and Executors of my Will jointly with William Frederick Wells Henry Trimmer Samuel Rogers George Jones and Charles Turner named in my Will as Trustees and Executors And I give unto each of them that shall act in the trusts of the execution of this my Will the sum of Nineteen pounds nineteen shillings each for a ring

And whereas in my said Will there are many interlineations marked in the margin by me with my initials And I do declare that all such interlineations were made in my said Will before I executed the same

In Witness whereof I the said Joseph Mallord William Turner have to this Codicil to my last Will and Testament contained in two sheets of paper set my hand to the first sheet hereof, and to this second and last

---

* The revoked Codicil.

sheet my hand and seal this Second day of August One thousand eight hundred and forty-eight.

Signed sealed published and declared by the said Joseph Mallord William Turner as and for a Codicil to his last Will and Testament in the presence of us who in his presence at his request and in the presence of each other have at the same time subscribed our names as Witnesses hereto } J. M. W. TURNER (L.S.)

> JOSEPH TIBBS } Clerks to Mr. Harpur
> THOMAS SCHROEDER } Kennington Cross Surrey

This is also a Codicil to my* within Will and my meaning is that in case the National Gallery shall not carry out the provisions contained in my within Codicil within the term of Five years on or before the expiration of the lease of my present Gallery then I do declare my bequest to the National Gallery is void And in that case I direct my Gallery to be continued upon the Terms mentioned in my within Codicil In Witness whereof I the said Joseph Mallord William Turner have to this Codicil to my last Will and Testament set my hand and seal this Second day of August One thousand eight hundred and forty-eight

Signed sealed published and declared by the said Joseph Mallord William Turner as and for a Codicil to his last Will and Testament in the presence of us who in his presence at his request and in the presence of each other have at the same time subscribed our names as Witnesses hereto } J. M. W. TURNER (L.S.)

> JOSEPH TIBBS
> THOˢ SCHROEDER

This is a Codicil to my Will Now I do hereby as to the disposition of my finished Pictures limit the time for offering the same as a gift to the Trustees of the National Gallery to the term of Ten years after my decease and if the said Trustees of the said National Gallery shall not within the said space of Ten years have provided and constructed a room or rooms to be added to the National Gallery that part thereof to be called Turners Gallery Then I declare the gift or offer of the said finished pictures to be null and void and of none effect and in that case I direct the said Pictures to be exhibited gratuitously by my Trustees and Executors during the existence of the lease of my present House and Gallery except the last Two years of the said term And then the said finished Pictures are to be sold by my Trustees and Executors I do give and bequeath unto my Trustees and Executors the sum of One thousand pounds and I direct them to lay out and expend the same in erecting a Monument in Saint Pauls Cathedral Church London where I desire to be buried among my Brothers in Art I give and bequeath unto Hannah Danby residing with me and Sophia Caroline Booth late of Margate one annuity of One hundred and fifty pounds

---

* This Codicil is indorsed on the second sheet of the preceding Codicil and not on the Testator's Will.

each And as to the produce of the said finished pictures when sold I give thereout the sum of One thousand pounds to the Pension Fund of the Royal Academy (provided they give a Medal for Landscape Painting and marked with my name upon it as Turners Medal silver or gold in their discretion) Five hundred pounds to the Artists General Benevolent Fund Five hundred pounds to the Foundling Hospital Lamb's Conduit Street Five hundred pounds to the London Orphan Fund and the residue of the produce to fall into the residue of my estate for the benefit of the intended Hospital in my Will mentioned I give and bequeath unto Mrs. Wheeler and her two sisters Emma and Laura One hundred pounds each free from Legacy Duty I hereby nominate and appoint Hugh Johnston Munro of North Britain to be a Trustee and Executor to act with the other Trustees and Executors appointed by my Will and Codicils And I hereby expressly declare that the Trustees and Executors appointed by my Codicils shall have equal powers and be clothed with the same authorities to all intents and purposes as if they had been appointed by my original Will instead of being appointed by any codicil thereto In Witness thereof I the said Joseph Mallord William Turner have to this my third Codicil (I having revoked my Codicil dated the Ninth day of August One thousand eight hundred and forty-six*) contained in two sheets of paper set my hand to the first sheet thereof and to this second and last sheet my hand and seal this First day of February One thousand eight hundred and forty-nine

Signed sealed published and declared by the said Joseph Mallord William Turner as and for a Codicil to his last Will and Testament in the presence of us who in his presence at his request and in the presence of each other have at the same time subscribed our Names as Witnesses hereto the word ' Will ' having been first interlined in the first sheet hereof } **J. M. W. TURNER** (L.S.)

JOSEPH TIBBS } Clerks to Mr. Harpur
THO⁵ SCHROEDER } Kennington Cross Surrey

The foregoing Will and Four Codicils were proved on the 6th day of September 1852 in the Prerogative Court of the Archbishop of Canterbury by the Reverend Henry Scott Trimmer Clerk (in the Will written ' The Rev^d. Henry Trimmer ') George Jones Esquire and Charles Turner Esquire three of the surviving Executors named in the will and Philip Hardwick (in the second Codicil written ' Hardwicke ') Esquire and Henry Harpur Esquire two of the Executors named in the second Codicil—power reserved of making the like grant to Hugh Andrew Johnston Munro—(Samuel Rogers Esquire and Thomas Griffith in the second Codicil written ' Griffiths' and John Ruskin the younger having first renounced)—Effects sworn under £140,000 and that Testator died on or about the 19th day of December 1851.

The following is a copy of the revoked Codicil of the 29th day of August 1846 so far as the same can be made out. Note that this Codicil was written and executed in duplicate. Both parts are cancelled, and they re not equally legible.

* The revoked Codicil is dated 29th August 1846.

This is a Codicil to be added to and taken as part of the last Will and Testament of me Joseph Mallord William Turner of Queen Ann Street Harley Street in the county of Middlesex Esquire Whereas the Residuary Legatee mentioned in my Will has died Now I hereby appoint

and Sophia Caroline Booth to be such Residuary Legatees And I do hereby give and bequeath to them all such Estate right and powers as if they had been appointed Residuary Legatees in and by my Will And inasmuch as it may take some time before the full provisions of my Will may be fully performed I do hereby give unto the said Hannah Danby and Sophia Caroline Booth one Annuity or clear yearly sum of One hundred and fifty pounds each And I do declare that they shall be joint Custodiers and Keepers of the Gallery or Foundation mentioned in my Will And I do give and bequeath unto my Executors the sum of One thousand pounds and I do direct them to lay out and expend the same in erecting a Monument for me and for my memory in Saint Pauls Cathedral Church London where I desire to be buried among my Brothers in Art In witness whereof I have hereunto set and subscribed my hand and seal the Twenty-ninth day of August One thousand eight hundred and forty-six

Signed sealed published and declared
by the said Joseph Mallord William Turner
as and for a Codicil to his last Will and
Testament in the presence of us who in   J. M. W. TURNER (L.S.)
his presence at his request and in the
presence of each other have hereunto at
the same time subscribed our Names as
Witnesses

Note—One part attested by { J. HUBBARD }   Clerks to Mr. Harpur
{ HY. WATTS }   Kennington Cross

The other part attested by { J. HUBBARD }   Clerks to Mr. Harpur
{ THO⁸ SCHROEDER }

Note that, the two parts not being equally cancelled, it is possible to make out a copy with the aid of both, and not otherwise.

The following condensation of the last report issued by the Government makes our readers acquainted with the latest aspect of this ill-managed business :—

' The Report of the Committee of the House of Lords upon the manner of fulfilling the conditions of Turner's Will contains so much matter interesting to artists, that we shall make running extracts from the evidence of the various witnesses examined, quoting briefly those subjects which are of current importance. With regard to the duty of fulfilling the conditions of Turner's will, the Director stated that it was the general wish, and more especially the wish of the Trustees of the National Gallery, to fulfil them. He considered the removal of the pictures from South Kensington a departure from the obligation to do so. He considered, and other witnesses fully agreed, that a selection of Turner's pictures would be indispensable ; that many were unfit for public exhibition, as being unfinished, and therefore only of interest to artists, to whom a reserve might be advantageously displayed. It was elicited that under the Act, 19th & 20th Vict. c. 29, s. 3, the Trustees were at liberty to accept portions of a bequest of pictures and return the remainder, in which case the last would fall into the residuary estate of the testator ; by this Act it would seem, says Sir Charles Eastlake, "that the Trustees would not have the option of setting aside the certain pictures for the purposes of study ; it would appear that such pictures ought to go to the nearest of kin." With Mr. Ruskin the witness thought that the Turner collection would enable six separate collections of a most instructive character to be made. The next matter which arose illustrated in no small degree the progress of public taste and the growth of a sound judgment in Art. Habitual visitors to the National Gallery remember how the pictures of West, which countryfolks loyally considered as the real gems of the collection, gradually disappeared, first going on to the stair-landing, then on the stairs, thence into the hall, and finally, how they took a dive and vanished altogether to the region below, only to re-appear upon the ample walls of South Kensington. Miss Angelica Kauffmann's works followed to fit obscurity, and were not missed. These weedings were, of course, desirable and right ; and the evident willingness of the Trustees to part with the two large Guidos shows how the people have learnt to prize the real above the meretricious art. Years ago the people crowded before these big pictures, were fascinated by the minaudering nudities, and thought far more of an ill-drawn and clay-cold "Christ crowned with thorns" than of the "Ariadne" or the Raphaels ; now the case is so much altered, that some sort of apology is thought needful for a proposition to send them to Dublin or Edinburgh, and "it would be a great relief to the Gallery" to do so. It is even said that the fact of transferring indifferent pictures to the above cities "might deter people from leaving inferior pictures, which might be rather an advantage." As to the disposal of the Turner pictures, the witness considered various courses were open, supposing it were absolutely necessary to house them in the National Gallery before the expiration of the decade after referred to. "One would be to place them in the National Gallery, removing an equivalent number of pictures to the South Kensington Museum. I should say not the Mediæval pictures, but the Dutch, Flemish, and Spanish pictures, because that would make room enough ; the Mediæval might be added, if necessary, but the removal of these alone would not make room enough in the Gallery. Another course would be to place the Turner pictures in the rooms below, where many of them once were, but where they were not exhibited ; the Vernon pictures were exhibited in those rooms : they were so badly placed as hardly to be visible, but still they occupied the walls of rooms in the National Gallery. If that were done, and if some were placed in such space as can be afforded in the upper rooms, the legal conditions would be complied with." In the event of immediate action not being imperative, the witness would prefer the pictures should remain where they are ; but he hoped this very inquiry would urge the Government to carry out what the public had been waiting for so long—namely, the erection of a New National Gallery, to contain the works of the old masters, the British school, and the best works of Turner. He is entirely opposed to gas in the neighbourhood of pictures, and, notwithstanding the high authorities asserting its harmlessness, he could not believe it to be so ; he thought the works should be examined, to decide the question, from decade to decade, as change would be exceedingly gradual. Photographs of the cracks in certain pictures have been taken, which could be compared with the originals from time to time ; not the slightest change has been observable hitherto. It would not be possible to provide a better temporary place than South Kensington for the reception of the pictures, but the more temporary it was the better. With regard to the Royal Academy vacating the National Gallery, Sir Charles did not know what arrangement is pending with the present Government, but under the last Government it was decided that the Royal Academy should be removed to Burlington House, and the members would, upon a site to be granted, erect an edifice for themselves. It would depend upon the terms offered whether the Academy would hold themselves ready to vacate on the requisition of the Government ; on those above named it would certainly do so. Mr. Redgrave was examined. If it was put to him he should not exhibit in the National Gallery many of Turner's pictures which are now at South Kensington ; he does not think they do Turner's fame any justice, being in such an unfinished state that they are caviare to the multitude ; there are some which would not even benefit students,—the works of one whose powers were failing. Mr. Redgrave regretted there is no exhibition of Turner's water-colour drawings. Turner was the father of water-colour art in this country, and, with a very few exceptions, there were no examples of his work in the Gallery. It would be desirable to change the works exhibited from time to time, so that they might pass successively under the public eye ; with proper arrangements as to light, a series of water-colour drawings might be as safely exhibited as oil-pictures. (Mr. Wornum expressed a very decided opinion in opposition to this.) The witness was not prepared to say that they will not gradually fade, any more than that oil-pictures will not deteriorate in time ; but he believed that, under due conditions, they may be preserved, and thought, taking into account Turner's fame and the impression he has made upon the world at large, it is better that one hundred thousand should see these drawings annually, than that ten thousand should see them in ten centuries. (It is well worth while for the public to give good heed to this opinion, for it is now acted upon, and may be still more so. It is opposed to all the feelings and experience of amateur collectors and the conservators of great galleries. Which party is in the right should de decided at once. We may, out of sheer heedlessness, be destroying the heritage of our children in Art.) With regard to the complete exhibition of Turner's works, and the manner in which he conceived that artist desired his will should be carried out, the witness thought he had two views— "One was that in our National Gallery there should be a tribune, or *salon carré*, in which the choice works of all schools should be gathered together ; and he desired to have some of his best works in that collection : he specially named two that should be put with the Claudes. In no arrangement that can be made (I speak with deference to Sir E. Eastlake) could you place these Turners by the Claudes in a sequence of schools ; they must be in a collection forming the cream of various schools." In the second place, Mr. Redgrave considered Turner wished his works to be kept together as far as possible, in order to form a part of a British School of Art in the National Gallery. The witness was of opinion that if the powers given by the above-named Act of Parliament for the disposal of bequests of works of Art, irrespective of conditions attached thereto by the testator, were known to the latter, there would be no difficulty in dispensing with those conditions, as the Act declares, beforehand, an intention so to deal with bequests.—In reply to a question, the witness said that most deceased British artists of eminence are represented in the National Gallery—that is, if the Collections at South Kensington are the National Gallery ; "but then Turner's will is carried out, because his pictures are in part of the National Gallery. Adopting this view, I consider that Turner's will is carried out ; but if he wished his pictures to be in Trafalgar Square, in connexion with the Old Masters, neither his pictures, nor the other British pictures, are in the National Gallery, since they are both at South Kensington." Mr. R. N. Wornum, Keeper and Secretary of the National Gallery, was examined. Presuming it were desirable to remove the pictures now in the Kensington Museum to Trafalgar Square, he would wish to build a wing over the east side of the barrack-yard, running from the new square room contiguous to the new large gallery, which would give the space of perhaps four such rooms as the new gallery. He would propose a wing on iron pillars, giving great headway to the barracks. These rooms would not only hold the Turner Collection, but those of Vernon, Bell, and the Old English pictures. Such a work might be constructed in a few months, and would be · permanent. A corresponding wing could be made hereafter, where the workhouse now stands, and the extremities of the two wings joined by a cross gallery. The gallery proposed would cover part of the barrack-yard, and be of great service to the soldiers when drilling in wet weather. By adding this wing the pictures would be better seen, as they would be more accessible to the public at Trafalgar Square than at South Kensington. The nation possesses 362 pictures, 105 of which are finished oil pictures ; the remainder contains many that are "mere botches." There are 19,000 and odd altogether, including pencil and water-colour sketches ; "the mass of them are of no value whatever." The witness's opinion is, that water-colour drawings generally fade on being exposed to the light, but that pencil, chalk, and sepia drawings do not fade. To exhibit all the water-colour drawings of Turner that might be exhibited would require a very large space. Turner, in one of the codicils to his will, directed the course of changing the drawings in succession to be pursued. The finest of them were exhibited for one year at Marlborough House, and withdrawn from fear of injuring them by a constant exposure to the light ; these are now framed, and may be seen on application ; probably twenty persons apply to do so in the course of a year ; but there is really no one to show them, except myself,—and I have not time. If we are to be liable to public applications to see these drawings, "I must have a curator for the purpose. 1800 are prepared for public exhibition, if we had a place and a servant who could watch them." 400 are in frames, and 1,400 mounted. If the Royal Academy were removed, there might be more accommodation for the pictures than in the proposed wing, "because we should have the sculpture-room, which would be a very good room for the exhibition of these framed and mounted drawings." If the wing were built, there would be room to display the water-colour drawings in frames, changing them from time to time. "I am sure they (water-colour drawings) fade, because I have often seen drawings which have faded. When a drawing has been taken out of a frame, where the frame has covered part of the drawing, the colours protected have been more intense than the part of the drawing which has been exposed to the light. You do not detect deterioration in oil pictures so readily as you do in water-colour drawings." Mr. J. Pennethorne was examined. He would not recommend a temporary building being added to the National Gallery, but a permanent enlargement, so as to comprise part of what would ultimately be a very fine building ; therefore, if anything is to be done for the temporary accommodation of the pictures, it ought to be done inside the present building. A permanent gallery might be completed in nine months. The witness had submitted a plan to the Chief Commissioner of Works for a further extension, and would undertake, if needful, to erect a complete and sufficient National Gallery in connexion with the present site in two years. In this plan there would be no alteration of the present building, except breaking through the two internal doorways. "There would be a great advantage in building at the back, because you need not go to so much outlay for architectural ornament ; but, besides that, we are, without difficulty, enabled to have recourse to all those means of lighting which a good deal interfere with the architecture of a building facing a public street. I propose to build an addition to the National Gallery, in such a manner that the ground-floor of it should be built upon columns, so that it should serve as a colonnade for the soldiers, thereby increasing their accommodation. The ground-floor of this building would not be necessary for the purpose of the Gallery, and would be valuable for the barracks. There are two passages through the building : one to the barracks, and the other to Castle Street. I propose not to encroach upon the last, but to let that be the boundary of the new buildings. In doing that, I have only to take from the workhouse half its site, leaving the other half on which to re-erect the schools and parish offices, &c. The witness would begin with a gallery, 136 feet long, over the barrack-yard, which would accommodate the Turner pictures. The cost of the entire building would be about 100,000*l.* ; it would cover an area of 30,000 feet : that of the present National Gallery and the Royal Academy taken together cover 20,000 feet superficial. The portion of the scheme which is considered pressing to be executed, would form a portion of the larger design, and be consistent with an alteration of the façade to the south. The witness would undertake to build that portion required for the Turner pictures for 25,000*l.* in nine months. It would cost about 100,000*l.* to erect a similar building in the rear of Burlington House to that proposed for the National

Gallery. If the Royal Academy were removed, there would be plenty of room in Trafalgar Square for all the pictures belonging to the nation ; but that would be turning the Academy into the streets ; they ought to be allowed two years to find a new home, even in Burlington House. The Turner Collection requires 3500 feet of wall for exhibition.

NOTE TO p. 176.

Account-books of Mr. W. B. Cooke.

W. B. Cooke, Dr. to J. M. W. Turner.			
1817.			
February 20	£	s.	d.
Drawing of Ilfracombe Coast	10	10	0
March 1.			
Loan of Drawing of the Eddystone for Rivers of Devon	5	5	0
Loan of Drawing of Junction of Tamar for Rivers of Devon ...	5	5	0
Loan of Drawing of Plymouth Sound for Rivers of Devon	5	5	0
June.			
Brixham, Coast	10	10	0
Fowey, Coast	10	10	0
Love	10	10	0
July.			
Tintagel, Coast	10	10	0
Bridport, Coast	10	10	0
Winchelsea	6	6	0
Arisbantony (?)	6	6	0
Two Drawings of Vesuvius for Pompeii ...	31	10	0
	£122	17	0

1817.			
		£ s.	d.
Paid August 4	40	0	0
1818.			
Paid Mr. Turner for one Drawing of Vesuvius (Pompeii)	15	15	0
August 21.			
Paid Mr. Turner for another Drawing of Vesuvius, for Pompeii..	15	15	0
August 21.			
Paid Mr. Turner	51	7	0
	£122	17	0

W. B. Cooke, Dr.			
1818.			
July.	£	s.	d.
Battle Abbey	6	6	0
August 31.			
Hastings from the Sea, for Mr. Fuller's Work	42	0	0
Watchet, Coast	10	10	0
Dunster	10	10	0
Mount Edgecombe ...	10	10	0
	£79	16	0

1818.	Cr.		
August 29.		£ s.	d.
Paid Mr. Turner in Bills as follows :—			
One at six months for	43	10	0
One at nine months for	30	0	0
Copper for ' Liber Studiorum'(three plates)	1	1	6
Recd. Gairdner's Views on the Rhine, charged in Arches Account...	1	4	0
	£75	15	6

W. B. Cooke, Dr.

	£	s.	d.
Three Drawings(Rhine)	85	1	0
Lulworth Castle.........	10	10	0
Margate	10	10	0
Dover.—Large Drawing for Exhibition 1823: Shipwreck at Margate, Sunrise	189	0	0
Touching Tomkinson's Cuyp	2	2	0
TouchingChelseaReach	2	2	0
Colne	8	8	0
Rochester	8	8	0
Norham	8	8	0
Coast, St. Mawes	10	10	0
Touching Cuyp's Horse	2	2	0
Do. Boat	2	2	0
Girtin's Kirkstone......	2	2	0
Dartmouth	8	8	0
Rivers, do	8	8	0
1824.			
Folkestone	68	0	0
	£96	12	0
Rye	10	10	0
Coville Bay	10	10	0
Hythe	10	10	0
Ramsgate	10	10	0
	£138	12	0

1822.

	£	s.	d.
September.			
Bill four months for three Drawings (Rhine) ...	85	1	0
Paid Mr. Turner for Lulworth Castle and Margate	21	0	0
1823.			
March 18.			
Bill at two months......	50	0	0
July 27.			
A Bill at two months for the loan of two Drawings, No. 1 Rivers, and touching Tomkinson's Cuyp and Girtin's Chelsea Reach...................	21	0	0
September 5th.			
Bill at four months ...	69	10	0
Do. at five months ...	69	10	0
October 1.			
Bill at two months for Loan of three Drawings for No. 2 Rivers	25	4	0
Liber Studiorum, Arches paid	31	10	0

W. B. Cooke, Dr. to J. M. W. Turner.

1822.

	£	s.	d.
Three Drawings of the Rhine	85	1	0
Lulworth Castle, Coast	10	10	0
Margate, Coast	10	10	0
Dover.—Large Drawing for the Exhibition 1823: Shipwreck and Margate, Sunrise ...	189	0	0
Touching Tomkinson's Cuyp	2	2	0
TouchingChelseaReach	2	2	0
Loan of More Park, Rivers	8	8	0
Do. Rochester, do.	8	8	0
Do. Norham, do.	8	8	0
St. Mawes, Coast......	10	10	0
Carried forward ...	£334	19	0

1822.   Cr.

	£	s.	d.
September.			
Bill at four months for three Drawings of the Rhine	85	1	0
Paid Mr. Turner for Lulworth Castle and Margate	21	0	0
1823.			
March 18.			
Bill at two months ...	50	0	0
July 27.			
Bill at two months for the Loan of two drawings (Rivers), and touching Tomkinson's Cuyp and Chelsea Reach	21	0	0
Carried forward ...	£177	1	0

	£	s.	d.
Brought forward ...	334	19	0

1822.

| Touching Traveller, Cuyp .... | 2 | 2 | 0 |

1824.

Large Drawing of Smugglers Fishing Gin ...	63	0	0
Rye, Coast...............	10	10	0
Clovelly Bay, do.	10	10	0
Ramsgate do.	10	10	0
'Liber Studiorum,' fourteen numbers at 1*l.* 1*s.* : twenty per cent. allowed.........	11	15	0

| | £474 | 16 | 0 |

	£	s.	d.
Brought forward ...	177	1	0

1822. Sept. 5.

| Bill at four months ... | 69 | 10 | 0 |
| Do. at five months ... | 69 | 10 | 0 |

October 1.

Bill at two months, paid at Oxford, for Loan of More Park, Rochester, and Norham Castle...................	25	4	0
Arch paid for Rye, Clovelly Bay, and Hythe Coast	31	10	0
Arch to pay Ramsgate	10	10	0

1824.

July 17.

| Two Bills as follows, for balance, one dated June 25th, at four months, another dated June 25, at five months, each for 45*l.* 15*s.* 6*d.* .... | 91 | 11 | 0 |

| | £474 | 16 | 0 |

1824. W. B. Cooke, Dr.

July 22

	£	s.	d.
Loan of three drawings for Rivers, as follows:			
Brougham Castle...	8	8	0
Totness	8	8	0
Okehampton Castle	8	8	0

| | £25 | 4 | 0 |

1824. Cr.

July 22.

	£	s.	d.
Bill at two months, for Broughton Castle, Totness, Okehampton ...	25	4	0

1825.

Jan. 14.

	£	s.	d.
Loan of two Drawings, as follows:			
Rainbow (Arundel Castle)	8	8	0
Bromleys (Kirkstall Abbey)	8	8	0

| | 16 | 16 | 0 |

1825.

Jan. 14.

	£	s.	d.
Bill at two months for Arundel Castle and Kirkstall Abbey	16	16	0

W. B. Cooke, Dr.	£	s.	d.	Cr.	£	s.	d.
Bill held by Mr. Turner, dated September 9th, and which remains unpaid	20	0	0	By Frame of Glass sent to Sir Anthony Carlisle from W. B. Cooke	4	10	0
Touching Vandervelde in No. 6 Gems	2	2	0				
Sandgate Creek Rivers, Loan of	8	8	0				
Two first Drawings of the continuation of the Coast (purchased by Mr. Tomkinson)	52	10	0				
	£91	8	0